MYSTERY INDEX

Subjects, Settings, and Sleuths
of 10,000 Titles

MYSTERY INDEX

Subjects, Settings, and Sleuths of 10,000 Titles

by
Steven Olderr

American Library Association
Chicago and London 1987

Designed by Marcia Lange

Composed by Mary Mills and Rob
    Carlson in Elite 12 on an
    IBM Personal Computer/NEC
    Spinwriter

Printed on 50-pound Glatfelter,
    a pH-neutral stock, and bound
    in B-grade Holliston linen cloth
    by Edwards Brothers, Inc.
    ∞

Library of Congress Cataloging-in-Publication Data

Olderr, Steven
    Mystery index.

    1. Detective and mystery stories, English--Indexes.
2. Detective and mystery stories, American--Indexes.
I. Title.
PR830.D4043 1987   016.823'0872   87-1294
ISBN 0-8389-0461-0   R
                      823.0872
                      Olde
                      886072

For
Marion Drummond O'Rand
who has brought the gift of reading to thousands.
Thanks, Mom!

Contents

Preface

I have the privilege of working at a public library with a
very large mystery collection and a corps of avid readers who
use it. This book is an attempt to provide for those patrons
access not only to our own collection but to the major body
of mystery and detective fiction.

A mystery, as defined by our patrons, has as its focus the
detection or solution of a crime. Often, but not always, there
is a murder involved. Mysteries are not suspense, not espionage, not gothics, and not romance, but they may have elements
of all of these.   The line of distinction frequently blurs.
When I couldn't be sure about the category, the title was included. I have generally included only twentieth-century titles
published in hardbound that the user has a reasonable expec-
tation of retrieving from a library or through interlibrary
loan. I have always been willing to make exceptions for the
benefit of the user.

Good bibliographic control of mystery literature is an
emerging discipline. When a book was not at hand and three
different sources listed three different versions of a title,
I went with the source considered to be the most reliable.

Mystery literature is written for the enjoyment of the reader.
I hope that this index helps you find the books you want to
read and that you spend many happy hours with them.

Acknowledgments

A project of this size is not easily accomplished alone. I have been particularly fortunate in receiving the assistance of a number of people. Bettina MacAyeal of the American Library Association was in at the beginning and freely gave encouragement and sound advice all the way through to the end. She was joined at various times by Marcie Lange, Helen Cline, and other staffers, who were uniformly helpful. It was a pleasure working with all of them.

Candy Smith, Elinor Hackett, and Rita Marsden of the Riverside Public Library served as an impromptu panel of mystery experts and helped determine what would be most useful for users. Joe Nowak not only kept manuscript production on schedule with his blindingly fast typing, but also was able to check for errors and offer suggestions for improvement along the way.

Patricia Olderr played an important part in most of the problem-thrashing sessions on the way to completion, and formed a mother and daughter team with Theresa Pingatore to double-check for omissions and typos. William Olderr assisted with the organization of the manuscript. Violet Rosier of the Eisenhower Public Library kept me supplied with the secondhand catalog cards on which this book was written.

If you find merit in this work, know that the road was paved by the talents and generosity of these people and others I may have inadvertently omitted. I am most grateful.

Directions for Use

Main Entry Section

All works are listed by author or editor. If there is a variation between British and American editions, the work is listed by the American title. If you're looking for a British title, you may find it easier to look in the Title Index.

Each main entry lists author, American and British titles, publishers, and the main characters. The number after a character's name (preceded by #) indicates the order of his or her appearance within an author's publications.

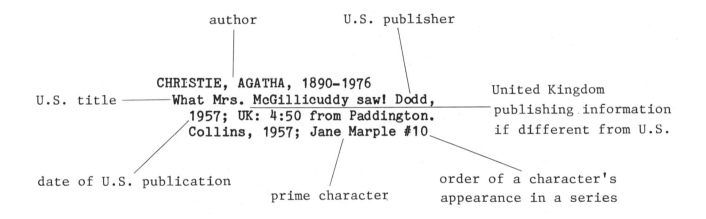

Title Index

All titles are listed. Initial articles (a, an, the) are ignored for filing purposes.

Subject Index

Time spent browsing in this section can be very rewarding. Examine in particular the listings under DETECTIVES. United

States locations list the state first; that is, "ILLINOIS--CHICAGO." Canadian settings are in this order: "CANADA--ONTARIO -- TORONTO." Other countries simply have country followed by the city or area, such as "FRANCE -- PARIS," "ENGLAND -- COASTAL."

Character Index

If most of an author's books feature a particular character, then only the author's name is given. If an author used many different main characters, then individual titles are given as well.

Main Entry Section

ABBOT, ANTHONY (pseud. of Fulton
  Oursler, 1893-1952)
  About the murder of a man afraid of
    women. Farrar, 1937; UK: Collins,
    1937; Thatcher Colt #6
  About the murder of a startled lady.
    Farrar, 1935; UK: The murder of a
    startled lady. Collins, 1936;
    Thatcher Colt #5
  About the murder of Geraldine
    Foster. Covici, 1930; UK: The
    murder of Geraldine Foster.
    Collins, 1931; Thatcher Colt #1
  About the murder of the circus
    queen. Covici, 1932; UK: The
    murder of the circus queen.
    Collins, 1933; Thatcher Colt #4
  About the murder of the clergyman's
    mistress. Covici, 1931; UK: The
    crime of the century. Collins,
    1931; Thatcher Colt #2
  About the murder of the night club
    lady. Covici, 1931; UK: The murder
    of the night club lady. Collins,
    1932; Thatcher Colt #3
  The creeps. Farrar, 1939; UK:
    Murder at Buzzard's Bay. Collins,
    1940; Thatcher Colt #7
  The shudders. Farrar, 1943; UK:
    Deadly secret. Collins, 1943;
    Thatcher Colt #8
ABELMAN, PAUL
  Shoestring. Parkwest, 1984; Eddie
    Shoestring
  Shoestring's finest hour. Parkwest,
    1985; Eddie Shoestring #2
ABERCROMBIE, BARBARA
  Good riddance. Harper, 1979; UK:
    Macdonald, 1979

  Run for your life. Morrow, 1984;
    Sarah Hoyt
ABRAHAMS, DORIS CAROLINE, see
  BRAHMS, CARYL (pseud.)
ABRAHAMS, PETER
  The fury of Rachel Monette.
    Macmillan, 1980; UK: Muller,
    1981; Rachel Monette
ADAMS, CLEVE F., 1895-1949. For other
  mysteries by this author, see
  SPAIN, JOHN
  And sudden death. Dutton, 1940; Rex
    McBride
  The black door. Dutton, 1941
  Contraband. Knopf, 1950; UK:
  Borderline cases. Cassell, 1952
  The crooking finger. Reynal, 1944;
    Rex McBride
  Decoy. Dutton, 1941; Rex McBride
  The private eye. Reynal, 1942; John
    J. Shannon
  Sabotage. Dutton, 1940; UK: Death
    at the damn. Cassell, 1946; Rex
    McBride
  Shady lady. Ace, 1955; Rex McBride
  Up jumped the devil. Reynal, 1943;
    Rex McBride
  What price murder. Dutton, 1942
ADAMS, HAROLD
  The naked liar. Mysterious Press,
    1985; Carl Wilcox
ADAMS, HERBERT
  The body in the bunker. Lippincott,
    1935; UK: Collins, 1935
  The golf house murder. Lippincott,
    1933; UK: John Brand's will.
    Methuen, 1935
  The strange murder of Hatton, K.C.
    Lippincott, 1933; UK: The knife.
    Collins, 1934; Mark Braddon

1

ADLER, WARREN, 1927 --
American quartet. Arbor House,
1982; Fiona Fitzgerald
American sextet. Arbor House, 1983
Trans-Siberian express. Putnam,
1977; UK: Macmillan, 1977
AIKEN, JOAN, 1924 --
The embroidered sunset. Doubleday,
1970; UK: Collancz, 1970; Lucy
Culpepper
AIRD, CATHERINE (pseud. of Kinn
Hamilton McIntosh, 1930 --)
Harm's way. Doubleday, 1984; C. D.
Sloan
Henrietta who? Doubleday, 1968; UK:
Macdonald, 1968; C. D. Sloan #3
His burial too. Doubleday, 1973;
UK: Collins, 1973; C. D. Sloan #6
Last respects. Doubleday, 1982;
C. D. Sloan #10
A late phoenix. Doubleday, 1971;
UK: Collins, 1970; C. D. Sloan #5
A most contagious crime. Doubleday,
1967; UK: Macdonald, 1967; C. D.
Sloan #2
Parting breath. Doubleday, 1978;
UK: Collins, 1977; C. D. Sloan #8
Passing strange. Doubleday, 1981;
UK: Collins, 1980; C. D. Sloan #10
The religious body. Doubleday, 1966;
UK: Macdonald, 1966; C. D. Sloan
#1
Slight mourning. Doubleday, 1975;
UK: Collins, 1975; C. D. Sloan #7
Some die eloquent. Doubleday, 1980;
UK: Collins, 1979; C. D. Sloan #9
The stately home murder. Doubleday,
1970; UK: The complete steel.
Macdonald, 1969; C. D. Sloan #4
ALBRAND, MARTHA (pseud. of Heidi
Huberta Freybe, 1914 --)
A call from Austria. Random House,
1963; UK: Hodder, 1963
A day in Monte Carlo. Random House,
1959; UK: Hodder, 1959; Mark
Travers
Manhattan North. Coward McCann,
1971; UK: Hodder, 1972
ALDING, PETER (pseud.). For other
stories by this author, see
JEFFRIES, RODERIC or ASHFORD,
JEFFREY (pseud.)
All leads negative. Harper, 1967;
UK: The CID room. Long, 1967

Betrayed by death. Walker, 1982;
Insp. Fusil
Call back to crime. UK: Long, 1972;
Insp. Fusil; Constable Kerr #6
Circle of danger. UK: Long, 1968;
Insp. Fusil; Constable Kerr #2
Despite the evidence. Saturday
Review Press, 1972; UK: Long,
1971; Insp. Fusil; Constable Kerr
#5
Field of fire. UK: Long, 1973;
Insp. Fusil; Constable Kerr #7
Guilt without proof. UK: Long,
1970; Insp. Fusil; Constable Kerr
#4
Murder among thieves. McCall, 1970;
UK: Long, 1969; Insp. Fusil;
Constable Kerr #3
Murder is suspected. Walker, 1978;
UK: Long, 1977; Insp. Fusil;
Constable Kerr #10
The murder line. UK: Long, 1974;
Insp. Fusil; Constable Kerr #8
Ransom town. Walker, 1979; UK:
Long, 1979; Insp. Fusil;
Constable Kerr #11
Six days to death. UK: Long, 1975;
Insp. Fusil; Constable Kerr #9
ALDYNE, NATHAN (pseud. of Dennis
Schultz and Michael MacDowell)
Cobalt. St. Martin's, 1982
Slate. Villard, 1984; Daniel
Valentine; Clarisse Lovelace
Vermilion. Avon, 1980; Daniel
Valentine; Clarisse Lovelace
ALEXANDER, COLIN JAMES see JAY,
SIMON (pseud.)
ALEXANDER, KARL
A private investigation. Delacorte,
1980; UK: Severn, 1981; Sara
Scott
Time after time. Delacorte, 1979;
UK: Panther, 1980; H. G. Wells;
Jack the Ripper
ALINGTON, ADRIAN RICHARD, 1895-1958
The amazing match test crime. UK:
Chatto, 1939
ALINGTON, CYRIL A., 1872-1955
Blackmail in Blankshire. UK: Faher,
1949; John Craggs; James
Castleton
Crime on the Kennet. UK: Collins,
1939
Mr. Evans. UK: Macmillan, 1922

ALLAN, STELLA
  A dead giveaway. St. Martin's,
    1981; UK: Collins, 1980
ALLEN, H. WARNER
  The uncounted hour. UK: Constable,
    1936
ALLEN, HENRY
  Fool's mercy. Houghton, 1982;
    Gordon Sault
ALLEN, MICHAEL, 1939 --
  Spence and the holiday murders.
    Walker, 1978; UK: Spence in Petal
    Park. Constable, 1977; Ben Spence
  Spence at Marlby Manor. Walker,
    1982; Ben Spence
  Spence at the blue bazaar. Walker,
    1979; UK: Constable, 1979; Ben
    Spence
ALLEN, STEVE
  The talk show murders. Delacorte,
    1982; Roger Dale
ALLINGHAM, MARGERY, 1904-1966. See
  also CARTER, YOUNGMAN
  The Allingham case book. Morrow,
    1969; UK: Chatto, 1969; Albert
    Campion
  The Allingham minibus. Morrow,
    1973; UK: Chatto, 1973; Albert
    Campion
  The Black Dudley murder. Doubleday,
    1940; UK: The crime at Black
    Dudley. Jarrolds, 1929; Albert
    Campion #1
  A cargo of eagles. Morrow, 1968;
    UK: Chatto, 1968; Albert Campion
    #2
  The case book of Mr. Campion.
    American Mercury, 1947; Albert
    Campion #13
  The case of the late pig.
    Doubleday, 1937; UK: Hodder, 1937;
    Albert Campion #8
  The China governess. Doubleday,
    1962; UK: Chatto, 1963; Albert
    Campion #18
  Dancers in mourning. Doubleday,
    1937; UK: Heinemann, 1937; Albert
    Campion #9
  Death of a ghost. Doubleday, 1934;
    UK: Heinemann, 1934; Albert
    Campion #6
  The estate of the beckoning lady.
    Doubleday, 1955; UK: The beckoning

lady. Chatto, 1955; Albert
    Campion #16
  The fashion in shrouds. Doubleday,
    1938; UK: Heinemann, 1938; Albert
    Campion #10
  Flowers for the judge. Doubleday,
    1953; UK: Heinemann, 1936; Albert
    Campion #7
  Gyrth chalice mystery. Doubleday,
    1931; UK: Look to the lady.
    Jarrolds, 1931; Albert Campion #3
  Kingdom of death. Doubleday, 1933;
    UK: Sweet danger. Heinemann,
    1933; Albert Campion #5
  The mind readers. Morrow, 1965;
    UK: 1965; Albert Campion #19
  Mr. Campion and others. UK:
    Heinemann, 1939; Albert Campion
    #8 [sic]
  Mr. Campion, criminologist.
    Doubleday, 1937; UK: Heinemann,
    1939; Albert Campion #8 [sic]
  More work for the undertaker.
    Doubleday, 1949; UK: Heinemann,
    1948; Albert Campion #14
  Mystery mile. Doubleday, 1930; UK:
    Jarrolds, 1930; Albert Campion #2
  Pearls before swine. Doubleday,
    1945; UK: Coroner's pidgin.
    Heinemann, 1945; Albert Campion
    #12
  Police at the funeral. Doubleday,
    1932; UK: Heinemann, 1931; Albert
    Campion #4
  Tether's end. Doubleday, 1958; UK:
    Hide my eyes. Chatto, 1958;
    Albert Campion #17
  The tiger in the smoke. Doubleday,
    UK: Chatto, 1952; Albert Campion
    #15
  Traitor's purse. Doubleday, 1941;
    UK: Heinemann, 1941; Albert
    Campion #11
ALLISON, E. M. A.
  Through the valley of death.
    Doubleday, 1983; Brother Barnabas
    #1
AMBERLEY, RICHARD (pseud. of
  Paul Henry James Bourquin,
  1916 --)
  Dead on the stone. UK: Hale, 1969;
    Insp. Martin
  Incitement to murder. UK: Hale,
    1968; Insp. Martin

AMBLER, ERIC, 1909 --
A coffin for Dimitrios. Knopf,
1939; UK: The Mask of Dimitrios.
Hodder, 1939; Charles Latimer
The intercom conspiracy. Atheneum,
1969; UK: Weidenfeld, 1970;
Charles Latimer #2
AMES, DELANO, 1906 --
Coffin for Christopher. Washburn,
1954; UK: Crime, gentlemen,
please. Hodder, 1954; Jane Brown;
Dagobert Brown
The Cornish Coast conspiracy. UK:
Amalgamated, 1942; Sexton Blake
Corpse diplomatique. Rinehart,
1951; UK: Hodder, 1950; Jane
Brown; Dagobert Brown
Crime out of mind. Washburn, 1956;
UK: Hodder, 1956; Jane Brown;
Dagobert Brown
For old crime's sake. Lippincott,
1959; UK: Lucky Jane. Hodder,
1959; Jane Brown; Dagobert Brown
Landscape with corpse. Washburn,
1955; UK: Hodder, 1955; Jane
Brown; Dagobert Brown
The man in the tricorn hat.
Regnery, 1966; UK: Methuen, 1960;
Juan Llorca
The man with three chins. Regnery,
1968; UK: Methuen, 1965; Juan
Llorca
The man with three Jaguars.
Regnery, 1967; UK: Methuen, 1961;
Juan Llorca
Murder begins at home. Rinehart,
1950; UK: Hodder, 1949; Jane
Brown; Dagobert Brown #2
Murder, Maestro please. Rinehart,
1952; UK: Hodder, 1952; Jane
Brown; Dagobert Brown
No mourning for the matador.
Washburn, 1953; UK: Hodder, 1953;
Jane Brown; Dagobert Brown
Nobody wore black. Rinehart, 1950;
UK: Death of a fellow traveler.
Hodder, 1950; Jane Brown; Dagobert
Brown
Not in utter nakedness. Dial, 1932;
UK: They journey by night. Hodder,
1932
She shall have murder. Rinehart,
1949; UK: Hodder, 1948; Jane
Brown; Dagobert Brown

She wouldn't say who. Washburn,
1958; UK: Hodder, 1957; Jane
Brown; Dagobert Brown
AMIS, KINGSLEY, 1922 --
The Riverside Villas murder.
Harcourt, 1973; UK: Cape, 1973;
Peter Furneaux
ANDERSON, FREDERICK IRVING,
1877-1947
The book of murder. Dutton, 1930;
Oliver Armiston
The notorious Sophie lady. UK:
Heinemann, 1925; Oliver Armiston
ANDERSON, J. R. L.
Death in a high latitude.
Scribner's, 1984; Peter Blair
Death in the Caribbean. Stein &
Day, 1978; UK: Gollancz, 1977;
Peter Blair
Death in the city. Scribner's,
1982; UK: Gollancz, 1977; Peter
Blair
Death in the greenhouse.
Scribner's, 1983; UK: Gollancz,
1978; Peter Blair
Death in the North Sea. Stein &
Day, 1978; UK: Gollancz, 1975;
Peter Blair
Festival. St. Martin's, 1980; Piet
Deventer
A sprig of sea lavender. St.
Martin's, 1979; UK: Gollancz,
1978; Piet Deventer
ANDERSON, JAMES, 1936 --
The affair of the bloodstained egg
cosy. McKay, 1977; UK: Constable,
1975
The alpha list. Walker, 1973; UK:
Constable, 1972
ANDERSON, JOHN, see ANDERSON,
J. R. L.
ANDERSON, POUL, 1926 --
Murder bound. Macmillan, 1962;
Trygre Yamamura
Murder in black letter. Macmillan,
1960; Trygre Yamamura
Perish by the sword. Macmillan,
1959; Trygre Yamamura
ANGUS, DOUGLAS ROSS, 1909 --
Death on Jerusalem Road. Random
House, 1963; Derek Crome
ANTHONY, DAVID (pseud. of William
Dale Smith, 1929 --)

Blood on a harvest moon. Coward
McCann, 1972; UK: Collins, 1972;
Morgan Butler
The midnight lady and the mourning
man. Bobbs, 1969; UK: Collins,
1970; Morgan Butler
ANTHONY, PETER (pseud. of Anthony
Joshua Shaeffer and Peter Levin
Shaeffer)
How doth the little crocodile?
Macmillan, 1957; UK: Evans, 1952;
Mr. Verity #2
The woman in the wardrobe. UK:
Evans, 1951; Mr. Verity #1
ARD, WILLIAM THOMAS, 1922-1960
A private party. Rinehart, 1953;
UK: Rogue's murder. Hammond, 1955;
Timothy Dane
ARDEN, WILLIAM (pseud.). For other
mysteries by this author, see
COLLINS, MICHAEL (pseud.) or SADLER,
MARK (pseud.)
A dark power. Dodd, 1968; UK: Hale,
1970; Kane Jackson #1
Deadly legacy. Dodd, 1973; UK:
Hale, 1974; Kane Jackson #5
Deal in violence. Dodd, 1969; UK:
Hale, 1971; Kane Jackson #2
Die to a distant drum. Dodd, 1972;
UK: Murder underground. Hale,
1974; Kane Jackson #4
The Goliath scheme. Dodd, 1971; UK:
Hale, 1973; Kane Jackson #3
ARMSTRONG, ANTHONY (pseud. of George
Anthony Armstrong Willis)
The trail of fear. McCrae Smith,
1929; UK: Jimmie Rezaire. Paul,
1927; Jimmie Rezaire
ARMSTRONG, CHARLOTTE, 1905-1969
The better to eat you. Coward
McCann, 1954; UK: Davies, 1954;
David Wakely
The case of the weird sisters.
Coward McCann, 1943; UK: Gifford,
1944; MacDougal Duff #2
A drain of poison. Coward McCann,
1956; UK: Davies, 1956
Dream of fair woman. Coward McCann,
1966; UK: Collins, 1966; Matt
Cunneen
The gift shop. Coward McCann, 1967;
UK: Collins, 1967; Harry
Fairchild; Jean Cunliffe

The innocent flower. Coward McCann,
1945; UK: Death filled with
glass. Cherry Tree, 1945;
MacDougal Duff #3
Lay on, MacDuff! Coward McCann,
1942; UK: Gifford, 1943;
MacDougal Duff #1
The protege. Coward McCann, 1970;
UK: Gifford, 1970
The turret room. Coward McCann,
1965; UK: Collins, 1965
The witch's house; Coward McCann,
1963; UK: Collins, 1964; Annabel
O'Shea
ARMSTRONG, GEORGE ANTHONY, see
ARMSTRONG, ANTHONY (pseud.)
ARNOLD, MARGOT (pseud. of Petronelle
Marguerite Mary Cook, 1925 --)
The Cape Cod caper. Playboy, 1980;
Penelope Spring; Toby Glendower
Death of a voodoo doll. Playboy,
1982; Penelope Spring; Toby
Glendower
Death on the Dragon's Tongue.
Playboy, 1981; Penelope Spring;
Toby Glendower
Exit actors, dying. Playboy, 1979;
Penelope Spring; Toby Glendower
Zadok's treasure. Playboy, 1980;
UK: Chivers, 1982; Penelope
Spring; Toby Glendower
ARRIGHI, MEL, 1933 --
Alter ego. St. Martin's, 1983;
Hank Mercer
ARTHUR, FRANK (pseud. of Frank
Arthur Ebert, 1902 --)
Another mystery in Suva. UK:
Heinemann, 1956; Insp. Spearpoint
#2
Confession to murder. UK: United
Writers, 1974
Murder in the tropic night.
UK: Jenkins, 1961; Insp.
Spearpoint #3
The throbbing dark. UK: Jenkins,
1963; Insp. Spearpoint #4
Who killed Netta Maull? UK:
Gollancz, 1940; Insp. Spearpoint
#1
ASHBY, R. C., 1899 --
Death on tiptoe. UK: Hodder, 1931
Out went the taper. Macmillan,
1934; UK: Hodder, 1934

ASHE, GORDON (pseud.). For other mysteries by this author, see CREASEY, JOHN; MARRIC, J. J. (pseud.); MORTON, ANTHONY (pseud.); YORK, JEREMY (pseud.)

The big call. Holt, 1975; UK: Long, 1964; Patrick Dawlish #40

A blast of trumpets. Holt, 1976; UK: Long, 1975; Patrick Dawlish #48

A clutch of coppers. Holt, 1969; UK: Long, 1967; Patrick Dawlish #42

The crime haters. Doubleday, 1960; UK: Long, 1961; Patrick Dawlish #35

The croaker. Holt, 1972; UK: The speaker. Long, 1939; Patrick Dawlish #2

The dark circle. UK: Evans, 1960; Patrick Dawlish #36

Dark mystery. UK: Long, 1948; Patrick Dawlish #18

Day of fear. Holt, 1978; UK: Long, 1956; Patrick Dawlish #31

Death from below. Holt, 1968; UK: Long, 1963; Patrick Dawlish #39

Death in a hurry. UK: Evans, 1952; Patrick Dawlish #25

Death in diamonds. UK: Evans, 1951; Patrick Dawlish #23

Death in flames. UK: Long, 1943; Patrick Dawlish #10

Death in high places. UK: Long, 1942; Patrick Dawlish #9

Death on demand. UK: Long, 1939; Patrick Dawlish #1

Death on the move. UK: Long, 1945; Patrick Dawlish #13

Double for death. Holt, 1969; UK: Long, 1954; Patrick Dawlish #28

Drop dead. Ace, 1954; UK: The long search. Long, 1953; Patrick Dawlish #26

Elope to death. Holt, 1977; UK: Long, 1959; Patrick Dawlish #34

Engagement with death. UK: Long, 1948; Patrick Dawlish #19

Give me murder. UK: Long, 1947; Patrick Dawlish #16

A herald of doom. Holt, 1975; UK: Long, 1974; Patrick Dawlish #47

Here is danger! UK: Long, 1946; Patrick Dawlish #15

Invitation to adventure. UK: Long, 1945; Patrick Dawlish #14

The kidnapped child. Holt, 1971; UK: The snatch. Long, 1955; Patrick Dawlish #30

Kill or be killed. UK: Evans, 1949; Patrick Dawlish #21

A life for a death. Holt, 1973; UK: Long, 1973; Patrick Dawlish #46

The man who laughed at murder. Doubleday, 1960; UK: Don't let him kill. Long, 1960; Patrick Dawlish #37

Missing or dead? UK: Evans, 1951; Patrick Dawlish #24

Murder most foul. UK: Long, 1942; Patrick Dawlish #7

Murder too late. UK: Long, 1947; Patrick Dawlish #17

Murder with mushrooms. Holt, 1974; UK: Evans, 1950; Patrick Dawlish #22

A nest of traitors. Holt, 1971; UK: Long, 1970; Patrick Dawlish #44

No need to die. Ace, 1957; UK: Death in the trees. Long, 1954; Patrick Dawlish #29

The pack of lies. Doubleday, 1959; UK: Come home to death. Long, 1958; Patrick Dawlish #33

A plague of demons. Holt, 1977; UK: Long, 1976; Patrick Dawlish #49

A promise of diamonds. Dodd, 1964; UK: Long, 1965; Patrick Dawlish #41

A puzzle in pearls. UK: Long, 1949; Patrick Dawlish #20

A rabble of rebels. Holt, 1972; UK: Long, 1971; Patrick Dawlish #45

Rogues rampant. UK: Long, 1944; Patrick Dawlish #12

Rogue's ransom. Doubleday, 1961; UK: Long, 1962; Patrick Dawlish #38

A scream of murder. Holt, 1970; UK: Long, 1969; Patrick Dawlish #43

Secret murder. UK: Long, 1940; Patrick Dawlish #5

A shadow of death. Holt, 1976; UK: Long, 1968; Patrick Dawlish #42

Sleepy death. UK: Long, 1953;
Patrick Dawlish #27

A taste of treasure. Holt, 1966;
UK: Long, 1966; Patrick Dawlish
#41

Terror by day. UK: Long, 1940;
Patrick Dawlish #4

There goes death. UK: Long, 1942;
Patrick Dawlish #8

Two men missing. UK: Long, 1943;
Patrick Dawlish #11

Wait for death. Holt, 1972; UK:
Long, 1957; Patrick Dawlish #32

'Ware danger! UK: Long, 1941;
Patrick Dawlish #6

Who was the jester? UK: Newnes,
1940; Patrick Dawlish #3

ASHE, ROSALIND
The hurricane wake. Holt, 1977; UK:
Hutchinson, 1977

Moths. Holt, 1976; UK: Hutchinson,
1976; Insp. Blunt

ASHENHURST, JOHN M.
The World's Fair murders. Houghton,
1933; Al Bennett

ASHFORD, JEFFREY (pseud.). For other
mysteries by this author, see
JEFFRIES, RODERIC; ALDING, PETER
(pseud.)
The anger of fear. Walker, 1979;
UK: Long, 1978; Det. Athana

The burden of proof. Harper, 1963;
UK: Long, 1962

Counsel for the defense. Harper,
1961; UK: Long, 1960

The D.I. Harper, 1962; UK:
Investigations are proceeding.
Long, 1961; Don Kerry #1

The double run. Walker, 1973; UK:
Long, 1973

Guilt with honor. Walker, 1982; Bob
Howe

The loss of the Culion. Walker,
1981; Bill Stenem

A man will be kidnapped. Walker,
1972; UK: Long, 1972; Supt. Abbott

A sense of loyalty. Walker, 1984;
Miba Sterling

The superintendent's room. Harper,
1965; UK: Enquiries are
continuing. Long, 1964; Don Kerry
#2

Three layers of guilt. Walker,
1976; UK: Long, 1975; Insp. Crane

ASHFORTH, ALBERT

Murder after the fact. St.
Martin's, 1984; Clinton Ball

ASHTON, WINIFRED, see DANE, CLEMENCE
(pseud.)

ASIMOV, ISAAC, 1920 --
Asimov's mysteries. Doubleday,
1968; UK: Rapp, 1968; Wendell
Orth

The caves of steel. Doubleday,
1954; UK: Boardman, 1954; Elijah
Baley #1

Murder at the ABA. Doubleday, 1976;
UK: Authorized murder. Gollancz,
1976; Darius Just

The naked sun. Doubleday, 1957;
UK: Joseph, 1958; Elijah Baley #2

Tantalizing locked room mysteries.
Walker, 1982

The 13 crimes of science fiction.
Doubleday, 1979

A whiff of death. Walker, 1968; UK:
Gollancz, 1968; Lou Brade

ASWAD, BETSY, 1939 --
Winds of the old day. Dial, 1980;
Rosalind Roth

ATKINS, MEG ELIZABETH
Palimpsest. St. Martin's, 1982;
Henry Beaumont

ATKINSON, ALEX, 1916-1962
Exit Charlie. Knopf, 1956; UK:
Davies, 1955

AUBREY, EDMUND (pseud. of Edmund S.
Ions)
Sherlock Holmes in Dallas. Dodd,
1980; Sherlock Holmes

AUBREY-FLETCHER, HENRY LANCELOT, see
WADE, HENRY (pseud.)

AUDEINARS, PIERRE, 1909 --
And one for the dead. Walker,
1981; UK: Long, 1975; Insp.
Pinaud #19

The better path of death. Walker,
1983; Insp. Pinaud

The confessions of Hercule. UK:
Low, 1947; Hercule Renard #4

The crown of night. Harper, 1962;
UK: Long, 1962; Insp. Pinaud #4

The delicate dust of death. UK:
Long, 1973; Insp. Pinaud #16

The dream and the dead. UK: Long,
1963; Insp. Pinaud #5

Fair maids missing. Doubleday,
1965; UK: Long, 1964; Insp.
Pinaud #7

The fire and the clay. UK: Long,

1959; Insp. Pinaud #2

The flame in the mist. Curtis, 1971; UK: Long, 1969; Insp. Pinaud #13

Hercule and the gods. Rinehart, 1946; UK: Pilot, 1944; Hercule Renard #1

A host for dying. Curtis, 1972; UK: Long, 1970; Insp. Pinaud #14

Nightmare in rust. UK: Long, 1975; Insp. Pinaud #18

No tears for the dead. UK: Long, 1974; Insp. Pinaud #17

Now dead is any man. Walker, 1980; UK: Long, 1978; Insp. Pinaud

The obligations of Hercule. UK: Low, 1947; Hercule Renard #3

Slay me a sinner. Walker, 1980; UK: Long, 1979; Insp. Pinaud

Stolen like magic away. UK: Long, 1971; Insp. Pinaud #15

The street of grass. Harper, 1963; UK: The wings of darkness. Long, 1963; Insp. Pinaud

The temptation of Hercule. UK: Pilot, 1945; Hercule Renard #2

A thorn in the dust. UK: Long, 1967; Insp. Pinaud #10

Time of temptation. Doubleday, 1966; UK: Long, 1966; Insp. Pinaud #9

The turns of time. Harper, 1962; UK: Long, 1961; Insp. Pinaud #3

The two imposters. UK: Long, 1958; Insp. Pinaud #1

The veins of compassion. UK: Long, 1967; Insp. Pinaud #11

The white leaves of death. UK: Long, 1968; Insp. Pinaud #12

A woven web. Doubleday, 1965; UK: Dead with sorrow. Long, 1965; Insp. Pinaud #8

BABSON, MARIAN

Bejewelled death. Walker, 1982; Sarah Orpington

Cover up story. UK: Collins, 1971; Douglas Perkins #1

Cruise of a deathtime. Walker, 1984

Dangerous to know. Walker, 1981; UK: Collins, 1980; Tom Paige

Death swap. Walker, 1985; Nancy Harper

Death warmed up. Walker, 1982

A fool for murder. Walker, 1984

The lord mayor of death. Walker, 1979; UK: Collins, 1977

Murder, murder, little star. Walker, 1980; UK: Collins, 1977; Frances Armitage

Murder on show. UK: Collins, 1972; Douglas Perkins #2

Murder sails at midnight. UK: Collins, 1975

A trail of ashes. Walker, 1985

The twelve deaths of Christmas. Walker, 1980; UK: Collins, 1979; Det. Knowles; Det. Preston

BACON PEGGY (pseud. of Margaret Frances Bacon Brook, 1895 --)

Inward eye. Scribner's, 1952

BAGBY, GEORGE (pseud. of Aaron Marc Stein, 1906 --). For other books by this author, see STEIN, AARON MARC or STONE, HAMPTON (pseud.)

Another day--another death. Doubleday, 1968; UK: Hale, 1968; Insp. Schmidt #36

Better dead. Doubleday, 1978; UK: Hale, 1979; Insp. Schmidt #43

Bird walking weather. Doubleday, 1939; UK: Cassell, 1940; Insp. Schmidt #5

Blood will tell. Doubleday, 1950; Insp. Schmidt #18

The body in the basket. Doubleday, 1954; UK: Macdonald, 1956; Insp. Schmidt #24

Coffin corner. Doubleday, 1949; Insp. Schmidt #17

Cop killer. Doubleday, 1956; UK: Boardman, 1957; Insp. Schmidt #27

Corpse candle. Doubleday, 1967; UK: Hale, 1968; George Bagby; Insp. Schmidt #35

The corpse with the purple thighs. Doubleday, 1939; Insp. Schmidt #6

The corpse with the sticky fingers. Doubleday, 1952; Insp. Schmidt #21

The corpse wore a wig. Doubleday, 1940; Insp. Schmidt #7

Dead drunk. Doubleday, 1953; UK: Macdonald, 1954; Insp. Schmidt #23

Dead on arrival. Doubleday, 1946; Insp. Schmidt #11

Dead storage. Doubleday, 1956; UK: Boardman, 1959; Insp. Schmidt #26

Dead wrong. Doubleday, 1957; UK:

Boardman, 1958; Insp. Schmidt #28

Death ain't commercial. Doubleday, 1951; Insp. Schmidt #19

Dirty pool. Doubleday, 1966; UK: Bait for a killer. Hammond, 1967; Insp. Schmidt #34

A dirty way to die. Doubleday, 1955; UK: Macdonald, 1956; Insp. Schmidt #25

Drop dead. Doubleday, 1949; Insp. Schmidt #16

Evil genius. Doubleday, 1961; UK: Hammond, 1964; Insp. Schmidt #31

Give the little corpse a great big hand. Doubleday, 1953; UK: Macdonald, 1954; Insp. Schmidt #22

Guaranteed to fade. Doubleday, 1978; UK: Hale, 1979; Insp. Schmidt #44

Here comes the corpse. Doubleday, 1941; Insp. Schmidt #8

Honest reliable corpse. Doubleday, 1969; UK: Hale, 1969; Insp. Schmidt #37

I could have died. Doubleday, 1979; UK: Hale, 1980; Insp. Schmidt #45

In cold blood. Doubleday, 1948; Insp. Schmidt #15

Innocent bystander. Doubleday, 1977; UK: Hale, 1978; Insp. Schmidt #40

Killer boy was here. Doubleday, 1970; UK: Hale, 1971; Insp. Schmidt #38

The most wanted. Doubleday, 1983; Insp. Schmidt

Mugger's day. Doubleday, 1979; UK: Hale, 1980; Insp. Schmidt #46

Murder at the piano. Covici, 1935; UK: Low, 1936; Insp. Schmidt #1

Murder calling "50." Doubleday, 1942; Insp. Schmidt #10

Murder half baked. Covici, 1937; UK: Cassell, 1938; Insp. Schmidt #3

Murder on the nose. Doubleday, 1938; UK: Cassell, 1939; Insp. Schmidt #4

Murder's little helper. Doubleday, 1963; UK: Hammond, 1964; Insp. Schmidt #32

My dead body. Doubleday, 1976; UK: Hale, 1978; Insp. Schmidt #41

Mysteriouser and mysteriouser.

Doubleday, 1965; UK: Murder in wonderland. Hammond, 1965; Insp. Schmidt #33

The original carcase. Doubleday, 1946; UK: Aldor, 1947; Insp. Schmidt #12

The real gone goose. Doubleday, 1959; UK: Boardman, 1960; Insp. Schmidt #30

Red is for killing. Doubleday, 1941; UK: Long, 1944; Insp. Schmidt #9

Ring around a murder. Covici, 1936; Insp. Schmidt #2

Scared to death. Doubleday, 1952; Insp. Schmidt #20

The starting gun. Doubleday, 1948; Insp. Schmidt #14

The three-time losers. Doubleday, 1958; UK: Boardman, 1958; Insp. Schmidt #29

The tough get going. Doubleday, 1977; UK: Hale, 1978; Insp. Schmidt #42

The twin killing. Doubleday, 1947; Insp. Schmidt #13

Two in the bush. Doubleday, 1976; UK: Hale, 1976; Insp. Schmidt #39

BAGLEY, DESMOND, 1923 --

Flyaway. Doubleday, 1979; UK: Collins, 1978; Max Stafford

BAILEY, H. C. 1878-1961

The apprehensive day. Doubleday, 1942; UK: No murder. Gollancz, 1942; Reggie Fortune #17

The best of Mr. Fortune. Pocket Books, 1943; Reggie Fortune #20

The bishop's crime. Doubleday, 1941; UK: Gollancz, 1940; Reggie Fortune #16

Black land, white land. Doubleday, 1937; UK: Gollancz, 1937; Reggie Fortune #13

Call Mr. Fortune. Dutton, 1920; UK: Methuen, 1920; Reggie Fortune #1

Case for Mr. Fortune. Doubleday, 1932; UK: Ward, 1932; Reggie Fortune #7

The cat's whisker. Doubleday, 1944; UK: Dead man's effects. Macdonald, 1945; Reggie Fortune #21

A clue for Mr. Fortune. Doubleday, 1936; UK: Gollancz, 1936; Reggie Fortune #11

The Garston murder case. Doubleday, 1930; UK: Garston's. Methuen, 1930; Joshua Clunk #1

The great game. Doubleday, 1939; UK: Gollancz, 1939; Joshua Clunk #5; Reggie Fortune #14

Honour among thieves. Doubleday, 1947; UK: Macdonald, 1947; Reggie Fortune #24

The life sentence. Doubleday, 1946; UK: Macdonald, 1946; Reggie Fortune #23

Meet Mr. Fortune. Doubleday, 1942; Reggie Fortune #18

Mr. Clunk's text. Doubleday, 1939; UK: Gollancz, 1939; Joshua Clunk #6

Mr. Fortune explains. Doubleday, 1931; UK: Ward, 1930; Reggie Fortune #6

Mr. Fortune finds a pig. Doubleday, 1943; UK: Gollancz, 1943; Reggie Fortune #19

Mr. Fortune here. Doubleday, 1940; UK: Gollancz, 1940; Reggie Fortune #15

Mr. Fortune objects. Doubleday, 1935; UK: Gollancz, 1935; Reggie Fortune #10

Mr. Fortune, please. Dutton, 1928; UK: Methuen, 1928; Reggie Fortune #4

Mr. Fortune speaking. Dutton, 1931; UK: Ward, 1930; Reggie Fortune #5

Mr. Fortune wonders. Doubleday, 1933; UK: Ward, 1933; Reggie Fortune #8

Mr. Fortune's case book. UK: Methuen, 1936; Reggie Fortune #12

Mr. Fortune's practice. UK: Methuen, 1923; Reggie Fortune #2

Mr. Fortune's trials. Dutton, 1926; UK: Methuen, 1925; Reggie Fortune #3

Nobody's vineyard. Doubleday, 1942; UK: Dead man's shoes. Gollancz, 1942; Joshua Clunk #8

Orphan Ann. Doubleday, 1941; UK: The little captain. Gollancz, 1941; Joshua Clunk #7

The queen of spades. Doubleday, 1944; UK: Slippery Ann. Gollancz, 1944; Joshua Clunk #9

The red castle mystery. Doubleday, 1932; UK: The red castle. Ward, 1932; Joshua Clunk #2

Save a rope. Doubleday, 1948; UK: Saving a rope. Macdonald, 1948; Reggie Fortune #25

Shadow on the wall. Doubleday, 1934; UK: Gollancz, 1934; Reggie Fortune #9

Shrouded death. UK: Macdonald, 1950; Joshua Clunk #11

The sullen sky mystery. Doubleday, 1935; UK: Gollancz, 1935; Joshua Clunk #3

The twittering bird mystery. Doubleday, 1937; UK: Clunk's claimant. Gollancz, 1947; Joshua Clunk #4

The wrong man. Doubleday, 1945; UK: Macdonald, 1946; Joshua Clunk #10; Reggie Fortune #22

BAILEY, HILEA (pseud. of Ruth Lenore Marting, 1907 --)

Breathe no more my lady. Doubleday, 1946; Hilea Bailey; Hilary Bailey

Give thanks to death. Doubleday, 1940; Hilea Bailey; Hilary Bailey

The smiling corpse. Doubleday, 1941; Hilea Bailey; Hilary Bailey

What night will bring. Doubleday, 1939; Hilea Bailey #1; Hilary Bailey #1

BAKER, CARLOS, 1908 --

The Gay Head conspiracy. Scribner's, 1973

BAKER, NORTH and BOLTON, WILLIAM

Dead to the world. Doubleday, 1944; Danny Michaels

BALL, DORIS BELL COLLIER, see BELL, JOSEPHINE (pseud.)

BALL, JOHN, 1911 --

Chief Tallon and the S.O.R. Dodd, 1984; Jack Tallon

The cool cottontail. Harper, 1966; UK: Joseph, 1967; Virgil Tibbs #2

The eyes of the Buddha. Little, 1976; UK: Joseph, 1976; Virgil Tibbs #5

Five pieces of jade. Little, 1972; UK: Joseph, 1972; Virgil Tibbs #4

In the heat of the night. Harper,
1965; UK: Joseph, 1966; Virgil
Tibbs #1

Johnny get your gun. Little, 1969;
UK: Joseph, 1970; Virgil Tibbs #3

The killing in the market.
Doubleday, 1978; Hamlyn, 1980;
John Harbizon

Police chief. Doubleday, 1977; UK:
Hale, 1982; Jack Tallon

Then came violence. Doubleday,
1980; UK: Joseph, 1981; Virgil
Tibbs #6

Trouble for Tallon. Doubleday,
1981; Jack Tallon

BALLARD, WILLIS TODHUNTER, 1903-1980
Dealing out death. McKay, 1948;
Bill Lennox #3

Lights, camera, murder. Belmont,
1960; Bill Lennox #4

Murder can't stop. McKay, 1946;
Bill Lennox #2

Murder Las Vegas style. Tower,
1967; Bill Lennox #5

Pretty Miss Murder. Permabooks,
1961; Max Hunter #1

Say yes to murder. Putnam, 1942;
Bill Lennox #1

The seven sisters. Permabooks,
1962; Max Hunter #2

Three for the money. Permabooks,
1963; Max Hunter #3

BALLINGER, BILL S. (pseud. of William
Sanborn Ballinger, 1912 --)
The body beautiful. Harper, 1949;
Barr Breed #2

The body in bed. Harper, 1948; Barr
Breed #1

Portrait in smoke. Harper, 1950;
UK: The deadlier sex. Dan April

The tooth and the nail. Harper,
1955; UK: Rinehart, 1955

BALLINGER, WILLIAM S., see BALLINGER,
BILL S.

BALMER, EDWIN, 1883-1959
Dragons drive you. Dodd, 1934
Keeban. Little, 1923; UK: Arnold,
1923
Resurrection Rock. Little, 1920
That Royle girl. Dodd, 1925; Joan
Daisy Royle

BALMER, EDWIN and MACHARG, WILLIAM.
See also MACHARG, WILLIAM and
BALMER, EDWIN

The achievements of Luther Trant.
Small, Maynard, 1910; Luther
Trant

BALMER, EDWIN and WYLIE, PHILIP
The shield of silence. Stokes,
1936. UK: Collins, 1937

BANKOFF, GEORGE ALEXIS, see BRADDON,
GEORGE (pseud.)

BANKS, CAROLYN, 1941 --
The darkroom. Viking, 1980; UK:
Corgi, 1981; Al Amatucci
Mr. Right. Viking, 1979; UK:
Corgi, 1981

BANKS, OLIVER
The Carravaggio obsession. Little,
1984; Amos Hatcher #2
The Rembrandt panel. Little, 1980

BARDIN, JOHN FRANKLIN, 1916 -- , see
TREE, GREGORY (pseud.)

BARKER, DUDLEY, see BLACK, LIONEL
(pseud.)

BARNARD, ALLAN, ed.
The harlot killer. Dodd, 1953; Jack
the Ripper

BARNARD, ROBERT, 1936 --
Blood brotherhood. Walker, 1978;
UK: Collins, 1977
The case of the missing Bronte.
Scribner's, 1983; Perry Trethowan
Corpse in a gilded cage.
Scribner's, 1984
Death and the princess. Scribner's,
1982; Perry Trethowan
Death by sheer torture. Scribner's,
1982
Death in a cold climate.
Scribner's, 1981; UK: Collins,
1980; Insp. Fagermo
Death of a literary widow.
Scribner's, 1980; UK: Posthumous
papers. Collins, 1979; Greg
Hocking
Death of a mystery writer.
Scribner's, 1978; UK: Unruly son.
Collins, 1978; Sgt. Meredith
Death of a perfect mother.
Scribner's, 1981
Death of an old goat. Walker, 1977;
UK: Collins, 1974; Insp. Royle
Death on the high C's. Walker,
1978; UK: Collins, 1977
Fete fatale. Scribner's, 1985;
Helen Kitterege

A little local murder. Scribner's,
1983; UK: Collins, 1976; Insp.
Parrish

School for murder. Scribner's,
1984; Insp. Pumfrey

BARNES, LINDA
Bitter finish. St. Martin's, 1983;
Michael Spraggue

Dead heat. St. Martin's, 1984;
Michael Spraggue #3

BARNETT, JAMES, 1920 --
The firing squad. Morrow, 1981;
Owen Smith

Marked for destruction. Secker &
Warburg, 1984; Owen Smith

BARRETT, MONTE, 1897?-1949
Murder at Belle Carmille. Bobbs,
1943; UK: Boardman, 1956

The Pelham murder case. White
House, 1930; Peter Cardigan

BARROLL, CLARE
A strange place for murder.
Scribner's, 1979; Lisa Thorne

BARRY, CHARLES
The corpse on the bridge. Dutton,
1928; UK: Methuen, 1927; Lawrence
Gilmartin

Death of a first mate. Dutton,
1935; UK: Hurst, 1935

The detective's holiday. Dutton,
1926; UK: Methuen, 1926; Lawrence
Gilmartin

Secrecy at Sandhurst. UK: Hurst,
1951

The witness at the window. Dutton,
1927; UK: Methuen, 1927; Lawrence
Gilmartin

BARRY, JOE
The clean-up. Arcadia House, 1947;
Rush Henry

The fall guy. Mystery House, 1945;
Rush Henry

The pay off. Mystery House, 1943;
Rush Henry

The third degree. Mystery House,
1943; Rush Henry

Three for the money. Handi-Books,
1950; Bill August

The triple cross. Mystery House,
1946; Rush Henry

BARTH, RICHARD
The Condo kill. Scribner's, 1985;
Margaret Binton

One dollar death. Dial, 1982;
Margaret Binton #3

The rag bag clan. Dial, 1978;
Margaret Binton

A ragged plot. Dial, 1981; Margaret
Binton

BASHFORD, H. H., 1880-1961
Behind the fog. Harper, 1927; UK:
Heinemann, 1926

BAWDEN, NINA (pseud. of Nina Mary
Mabey Kark, 1925 --)
Change her for Babylon. UK:
Collins, 1955; Insp. Walker

Eyes of green. Morrow, 1953; UK:
Who calls the tune. Collins, 1953

The odd flamingo. UK: Collins, 1954

BAX, ROGER (pseud.). For other books
by this author, see GARVE, ANDREW
(pseud.); SOMERS, PAUL (pseud.)
Death beneath Jerusalem. Nelson,
1938

A grave case of murder. Harper,
1951; UK: Hutchinson, 1951; Insp.
James

Two if by sea. Harper, 1949; UK:
Came the dawn. Hutchinson, 1949

BAXT, GEORGE, 1923 --
The Dorothy Parker murder case.
St. Martin's, 1984; Dorothy
Parker; Alexander Woolcott

"I!" said the demon. Random House,
1969; UK: Cape, 1969; Max Van
Larsen; Sylvia Plotkin

The neon graveyard. St. Martin's,
1979; Valentine Norton

A parade of cockeyed creatures.
Random House, 1967; UK: Cape,
1968; Max Van Larsen #1; Sylvia
Plotkin #1

Process of elimination. St.
Martin's, 1984; Laura Graymoor;
Harvey Graymoor

A queer brand of death. Simon &
Schuster, 1966; Cape, 1967;
Pharoah Love #1

Swing low, sweet Harriet. Simon &
Schuster, 1967; Pharoah Love #2

Topsy and evil. Simon & Schuster,
1968; Pharoah Love #3; Satan
Stagg

BAY, AUSTIN
The coyote cried twice. Arbor
House, 1985; Bill Buchanan

BAYER, WILLIAM, 1939 --
Switch. Simon & Schuster, 1984;
Frank Janek

Twice removed. Simon & Schuster, 1984; Frank Janek

BEATON, M. C.

Death of a gossip. St. Martin's, 1985; Insp. Blair; Hamish Macbeth

BECK, HENRY CHARLTON

Death by clue. Dutton, 1933

BECK, K. K.

Death in a deck chair. Walker, 1984

BEEDING, FRANCIS (pseud. of John Leslie Palmer and Hilary Adam St. George Saunders)

Death walks in Eastrepps. Mystery House, 1931; UK: Hodder, 1931; Insp. Wilkins

The hidden kingdom. Little, 1927; UK: Hodder, 1927; Prof. Kreutzemark #2

Murdered: one by one. Harper, 1937; UK: No fury. Hodder, 1937; George Martin #2

The Norwich victims. Harper, 1935; UK: Hodder, 1935; George Martin #1

The seven sleepers. Little, 1925; UK: Hutchinson, 1925; Prof. Kreutzemark #1

BELL, JOSEPHINE (pseud. of Doris Bell Ball, 1897 --)

All is vanity. UK: Longman, 1940; David Wintringham #6

Bones in the barrow. Macmillan, 1955; UK: Methuen, 1953; David Wintringham #11; Steven Mitchell #7

The catalyst. Macmillan, 1967; UK: Hodder, 1966

Curtain call for a corpse. Macmillan, 1965; UK: Death at half term. Longman, 1939; David Wintringham #4; Steven Mitchell #4

A deadly place to stay. Walker, 1983; George Cole; Amanda Drew

Death at the Medical Board. Ballantine, 1964; UK: Longman, 1944; David Wintringham #8

Death in clairvoyance. UK: Longman, 1949; David Wintringham #9; Steven Mitchell #5

Death in retirement. Macmillan, 1956; UK: Methuen, 1956; David Wintringham #13

Death of a con man. Lippincott, 1968; UK: Hodder, 1968; Insp. Rawlinson

Death on the bourough council. UK: Longman, 1937; David Wintringham #2

Death on the reserve. Macmillan, 1967; UK: Hodder, 1966; Henry Frost #2

Easy prey. Macmillan, 1959; UK: Hodder, 1959; Claude Warrington-Reeve #1; Steven Mitchell #9

Fall over cliff. Macmillan, 1956; UK: Longman, 1938; David Wintringham #3; Steven Mitchell #2

Fiasco in Fulhorn. Macmillan, 1963; UK: A flat tyre in Fulhorn. Hodder, 1963; Claude Warrington-Reeve #3; Steven Mitchell #11

Fires at Fairlawn. UK: Methuen, 1954; David Wintringham #12

From natural causes. UK: Longman, 1939; David Wintringham #5

Murder in hospital. UK: Longman, Green, 1937; David Wintringham #1; Steven Mitchell #1

Murder on the merry-go-round. Ballantine, 1965; UK: The China roundabout. Hodder, 1956; David Wintringham #14

No escape. Macmillan, 1966; UK: Hodder, 1965; Timothy Long

The Port of London murders. Macmillan, 1958; UK: Longman, 1938; Steven Mitchell #2

A question of inheritance. Walker, 1981; UK: Hodder, 1980; Amy Tupper; Philip Bennet

The seeing eye. UK: Hodder, 1963; David Wintringham #15; Steven Mitchell #8

A stroke of death. Walker, 1977; UK: Such a nice client. Hodder, 1977; Lucy Summers

The summer school mystery. UK: Methuen, 1950; David Wintringham #10; Steven Mitchell #6

Treachery in type. Walker, 1978; UK: A swan-song betrayal. Hodder, 1978

Trouble at Wrebcin Farm. UK: Longman, 1942; David Wintringham #7

The trouble in Hunter Wood. Walker, 1977; UK: Hodder, 1976

The upfold witch. Macmillan, 1964;
UK: Hodder, 1964; Henry Frost #1

A well-known face. Washburn, 1960;
UK: Hodder, 1960; Claude
Warrington-Reeve #2; Steven
Mitchell #10

The Wilberforce legacy. Walker,
1969; UK: Hodder, 1969

Wolf! Wolf! Walker, 1980; UK:
Hodder, 1979

BELL, VICARS, 1904 --
Death darkens council. Faber, 1952;
Dr. Baynes

BELLAIRS, GEORGE (pseud. of Harold
Blundell, 1902 --)

All roads to Sospel. Walker, 1981;
UK: Close all roads to Sospel.
Gifford, 1947; Thomas Littlejohn
#54

Bones in the wilderness. UK:
Gifford, 1958; Thomas Littlejohn
#30

Calamity at Harwood. Macmillan,
1945; UK: Gifford, 1943; Thomas
Littlejohn #6

The case of the demented Spiv.
Macmillan, 1950; UK: Gifford,
1950; Thomas Littlejohn #15

The case of the famished parson.
Macmillan, 1949; UK: Gifford,
1949; Thomas Littlejohn #13

The case of the scared rabbits. UK:
Gifford, 1947; Thomas Littlejohn
#10

The case of the seven whistlers.
Macmillan, 1948; UK: Gifford,
1948; Thomas Littlejohn #11

The corpse at the carnival. UK:
Gifford, 1958; Thomas Littlejohn
#28

Corpses at Enderby. UK: Gifford,
1954; Thomas Littlejohn #21

The crime at Halfpenny Bridge. UK:
Gifford, 1946; Thomas Littlejohn
#9

Crime in Leper's Hollow. UK:
Gifford, 1952; Thomas Littlejohn
#18

The cursing stones murder. UK:
Gifford, 1954; Thomas Littlejohn
#22

Dead march for Penelope Blow.
Macmillan, 1951; UK: Gifford,
1951; Thomas Littlejohn #16

Death before breakfast. British
Book Centre, 1962; UK: Gifford,
1962; Thomas Littlejohn #36

Death brings in the New Year.
Macmillan, 1951; UK: The case of
the headless Jesuit. Gifford,
1950; Thomas Littlejohn #16

Death drops the pilot. UK: Gifford,
1956; Thomas Littlejohn #25

Death in dark glasses. Macmillan,
1952; UK: Gifford, 1952; Thomas
Littlejohn #17

Death in desolation. UK: Gifford,
1967; Thomas Littlejohn #44

Death in despair. UK: Gifford,
1960; Thomas Littlejohn #33

Death in High Provence. UK:
Gifford, 1957; Thomas Littlejohn
#26

Death in Room Five. UK: Gifford,
1955; Thomas Littlejohn #23

Death in the fearful night. UK:
Gifford, 1960; Thomas Littlejohn
#32

Death in the night watches.
Macmillan, 1946; UK: Gifford,
1945; Thomas Littlejohn #8

Death in the wasteland. British
Book Centre, 1964; UK: Gifford,
1963; Thomas Littlejohn #38

Death of a busybody. Macmillan,
1945; UK: Gifford, 1942; Thomas
Littlejohn #3

Death of a shadow. UK: Gifford,
1964; Thomas Littlejohn #40

Death of a tin god. UK: Gifford,
1961; Thomas Littlejohn #34

Death on the last train. Macmillan,
1949; UK: Gifford, 1948; Thomas
Littlejohn #12

Death sends for the doctor. UK:
Gifford, 1957; Thomas Littlejohn
#27

Death spins the wheel. UK: Gifford,
1965; Thomas Littlejohn #41

Death treads softly. UK: Gifford,
1956; Thomas Littlejohn #24

Devious murder. Walker, 1980; UK:
Gifford, 1973; Thomas Littlejohn
#52

Fatal alibi. UK: Gifford, 1968;
Thomas Littlejohn #46

Fear round about. Walker, 1981; UK:
Gifford, 1975; Thomas Littlejohn
#53

The four unfaithful servants. UK: Gifford, 1942; Thomas Littlejohn #2

Half-mast for the deemster. UK: Gifford, 1953; Thomas Littlejohn #20

He'd rather be dead. UK: Gifford, 1945; Thomas Littlejohn #7

Intruder in the dark. UK: Gifford, 1966; Thomas Littlejohn #42

A knife for Harry Dodd. UK: Gifford, 1953; Thomas Littlejohn #19

Littlejohn on leave. UK: Gifford, 1941; Thomas Littlejohn #1

Murder adrift. UK: Gifford, 1972; Thomas Littlejohn #51

Murder gone mad. UK: Gifford, 1968; Thomas Littlejohn #47

Murder makes mistakes. UK: Gifford, 1958; Thomas Littlejohn #29

Murder masquerade. Tower, 1981; UK: The body in the dumb river. Gifford, 1961; Thomas Littlejohn #35

The murder of a quack. Macmillan, 1944; UK: Gifford, 1943; Thomas Littlejohn #5

Murder will speak. Macmillan, 1943; UK: The dead shall be raised. Gifford, 1942; Thomas Littlejohn #4

The night they killed Joss Varran. UK: Gifford, 1970; Thomas Littlejohn #49

Outrage on Gallows Hill. UK: Gifford, 1949; Thomas Littlejohn #14

Pomeroy, deceased. UK: Gifford, 1971; Thomas Littlejohn #50

Single ticket to death. UK: Gifford, 1967; Thomas Littlejohn #45

Strangers among the dead. UK: Gifford, 1966; Thomas Littlejohn #43

Surfeit of suspects. UK: Gifford, 1964; Thomas Littlejohn #39

Toll the bell for murder. UK: Gifford, 1959; Thomas Littlejohn #31

The tormentors. UK: Gifford, 1962; Thomas Littlejohn #37

Tycoon's death-bed. UK: Gifford, 1970; Thomas Littlejohn #48

BELLEM, ROBERT LESLIE, 1902-1968
Blue murder. Phoenix Press, 1938
Robert Leslie Bellem's Dan Turner, Hollywood detective. Popular Press, 1983; Dan Turner
The window under the sleeping nude. Handi-Books, 1950

BELLOC, HILAIRE, 1870-1953
The green overcoat. McBride, 1912; UK: Arrowsmith, 1912

BELSKY, DICK
One for the money. Academy Chicago, 1985; Lucy Shannon

BENNETT, ARNOLD
The loot of cities. Alston Rivers, 1905; Cecil Thorold
A tale of these days. Brent, 1908

BENNETT, JOLIN MCGREW
A local matter. Walker, 1985; Lord Tigranes

BENNETTS, PAMELA, see JAMES, MARGARET (pseud.)

BENSON, BEN, 1915-1959
The affair of the exotic dancer. Mill, 1958; Wade Paris #8
Alibi at dusk. Mill, 1951; UK: Corgi, 1952; Wade Paris #2
Beware the pale horse. Mill, 1951; UK: Muller, 1952; Wade Paris #1
The blonde in black. Mill, 1958; UK: Collins, 1959; Wade Paris #9
Broken shield. Mill, 1955; UK: Collins, 1957; Ralph Lindsay #3
The burning fuse. Mill, 1954; UK: Collins, 1956; Wade Paris #6
The end of violence. Mill, 1959; UK: Collins, 1959; Ralph Lindsay #6
The girl in the cage. Mill, 1954; UK: Collins, 1955; Ralph Lindsay #2
The huntress is dead. Mill, 1960; Wade Paris #10
Lily in her coffin. Mill, 1952; UK: Boardman, 1954; Wade Paris #3
The ninth hour. Mill, 1956; UK: Collins, 1957; Wade Paris #7
The running man. Mill, 1957; UK: Collins, 1958; Ralph Lindsay #5
Seven steps east. Mill, 1959; Ralph Lindsay #7
The silver cabinet. Mill, 1955; UK: Collins, 1956; Ralph Lindsay #4

Stamped for murder. Mill, 1952; UK:
Gannet, 1955; Wade Paris #4

Target in taffeta. Mill, 1953; UK:
Collins, 1955; Wade Paris #5

The Venus death. Mill, 1953; UK:
Muller, 1954. Ralph Lindsay #1

BENSON, E. F., 1867-1940

The blotting book. Doubleday, 1908;
UK: Heinemann, 1908

BENTLEY, E. C., 1875-1956

Trent intervenes. Knopf, 1938; UK:
Nelson, 1938; Philip Trent #3

Trent's last case. Knopf, 1929; UK:
Nelson, 1913; Philip Trent #1

Trent's own case. Knopf, 1936;
Constable, 1936; Philip Trent #2

BENTLEY, JOHN

Kill me again. Dodd, 1947; UK: Call
off the corpse. Hutchinson, 1947

The Landor case. UK: Chapman, 1937;
Richard Herrivell

BENTLEY, NICHOLAS, 1907-1978

The events of that week. St.
Martin's, 1972; UK: Collins, 1972

Inside information. Penguin, 1978;
UK: Duetsch, 1974

BERCKMAN, EVELYN, 1900-1978

The fourth man on the rope.
Doubleday, 1972; UK: Hamilton,
1972; Alison Pendrell

The hovering darkness. Dodd, 1957;
Denise Gilbert

No known grave. Dodd, 1958; UK:
Eyre, 1959; Kirk Halstead

She asked for it. Doubleday, 1969;
UK: Hamilton, 1970

A simple case of ill-will. Dodd,
1965; UK: Eyre, 1964

The strange bedfellow. Dodd, 1956;
UK: Eyre, 1957

The Victorian album. Doubleday,
1973; UK: Hamilton, 1973

BERESFORD, J. D., 1873-1947

The instrument of destiny. Bobbs,
1928; UK: Collins, 1928; Morgan
Fellows

BERESFORD, LESLIE, 1899 --

What's at the end? UK: Jenkins,
1937; Justin Marsh

BERGMAN, ANDREW

The big kiss-off of 1944. Hale,
1979; UK: Hutchinson, 1975; Jack
LeVine

Hollywood and LeVine. Holt, 1975;
UK: Hutchinson, 1976; Jack
LeVine; Humphrey Bogart

BERKELEY, ANTHONY (pseud. of Anthony
Berkeley Cox, 1893-1971). For other
works by this author, see ILES,
FRANCIS

Dead Mrs. Stratton. Doubleday,
1933; UK: Jumping Jenny. Hodder,
1933; Roger Sheringham #9

Death in the house. Doubleday,
1939; UK: Hodder, 1939

The Layton Court mystery.
Doubleday, 1929; UK: Jenkins,
1925; Roger Sheringham #1

Mr. Pidgeon's island. Doubleday,
1934; UK: Panic party. Hodder,
1934; Roger Sheringham #10

Murder in the basement. Doubleday,
1932; UK: Hodder, 1932; Roger
Sheringham #8; Insp. Moresby

The mystery at Lover's Cave. Simon
& Schuster, 1927; UK: Roger
Sheringham and the Vane mystery.
Collins, 1927; Roger Sheringham
#3; Insp. Moresby

Piccadilly murder. Doubleday,
1930; UK: Collins, 1929; Ambrose
Chitterwick; Insp. Moresby

The poisoned chocolates case.
Doubleday, 1929; UK: Collins,
1929; Roger Sheringham #5; Insp.
Moresby

A puzzle in poison. Doubleday,
1938; UK: Not to be taken.
Collins, 1938

The second shot. Doubleday, 1931;
UK: Hodder, 1930; Roger
Sheringham #6

The silk-stocking murders.
Doubleday, 1928; UK: Collins,
1928; Roger Sheringham #4; Insp.
Moresby

Top story murder. Doubleday, 1931;
UK: Top storey murder. Hodder,
1931; Roger Sheringham #7; Insp.
Moresby

Trial and error. Doubleday, 1937;
UK: Hodder, 1937; Ambrose
Chitterwick; Insp. Moresby

The Wychford poisoning case.
Doubleday, 1930; UK: Collins,
1926; Roger Sheringham #2

BERNARD, ROBERT. (pseud. of Robert
Bernard Martin, 1918 --)
Deadly meeting. Norton, 1970; Bill
Stratton
Death takes a sabbatical. Norton,
1967; UK: Death takes the last
train. Constable, 1967; Richard
Halsey
BEYNON, JANE
Cypress man. Bobbs, 1944
BIGGERS, EARL DERR, 1884-1933
Behind that curtain. Bobbs, 1928;
UK: Harrap, 1928; Charlie Chan #3
The black camel. Bobbs, 1929; UK:
Cassell, 1930; Charlie Chan #4
Charlie Chan carries on. Bobbs,
1930; UK: Cassell, 1931; Charlie
Chan #5
The Chinese parrot. Bobbs, 1926;
UK: Harrap, 1927; Charlie Chan #2
The house without a key. Bobbs,
1925; UK: Harrap, 1926; Charlie
Chan #1
Keeper of the keys. Bobbs, 1932;
UK: Cassell, 1932; Charlie Chan #6
Seven keys to Baldpate. Bobbs,
1913; UK: Mill, 1914
BINGHAM, JOHN, 1980 --
Brock and the defector. Doubleday,
1982; "Badger" Brock
Good old Charlie. Simon & Schuster,
1969; UK: I love, I kill.
Gollancz, 1968
Inspector Morgan's dilemma. Dodd,
1956; UK: The Paton Street case.
Gollancz, 1955; Insp. Morgan
The marriage bureau murders. UK:
Macmillan, 1977
Night's black agent. Dodd, 1961;
UK: Gollancz, 1961
The tender poisoner. Dodd, 1953;
UK: Five roundabouts to heaven.
Gollancz, 1953
BIRMINGHAM, GEORGE A. (pseud. of
James Owen Hannay, 1865-1950)
The hymn tune mystery. Bobbs,
1931; UK: Methuen, 1930; Insp.
Smallways
The lost lawyer. UK: Methuen, 1921
The search party. Doran, 1911; UK:
Methuen, 1909
Wild justice. Bobbs, 1930; UK:
Methuen, 1930

BISHOP, MORRIS GILBERT, see JOHNSON,
W. BOLINGBROKE (pseud.)
BLACK, LIONEL (pseud. of Dudley
Barker, 1910 --)
The bait. Paperback Library, 1968;
UK: Cassell, 1966; Emma Greaves
#2
Chance to die. UK: Cassell, 1965;
Emma Greaves #1
Death by hoax. Avon, 1978; UK:
Collins, 1974; Kate Theobald #3
Death has green fingers. Walker,
1971; UK: Collins, 1971; Kate
Theobald #2
Flood. Stein & Day, 1971; UK:
Breakaway. Collins, 1970
A healthy way to die. Avon, 1979;
UK: Collins, 1976; Kate Theobald
#4
The lady is a spy. Paperback
Library, 1969; UK: Two ladies in
Verona. Cassell, 1967; Emma
Greaves #3
Outbreak. Stein & Day, 1968; UK:
Cassell, 1968; David Greyson
The penny murders. Avon, 1979; UK:
Collins, 1979; Kate Theobald #5
Swinging murder. Walker, 1969; UK:
Cassell, 1969; Kate Theobald #1
BLACKBURN, JOHN, 1923 --
Bound to kill. Mill, 1963; UK:
Blue octavo. Cape, 1963
The broken boy. Mill, 1962; UK:
Secker, 1959
Deep among the dead men. UK: Cape,
1973
Murder at midnight. Mill, 1964;
UK: The winds of midnight. Cape,
1964
The young man from Lima. UK: Cape,
1968; Marcus Levin; Tania Levin
BLACKSTOCK, CHARITY (pseud. of Ursula
Torday, 1888 --). For other works
by this author, see BLACKSTOCK, LEE
All men are murderers. Doubleday,
1958; UK: The shadow of murder.
UK: Hodder, 1959
Dewey death. London House, 1958;
UK: Heinemann, 1956
BLACKSTOCK, LEE (pseud.). For other
works by this author, see
BLACKSTOCK, CHARITY
Woman in the woods. Doubleday,
1958; UK: Miss Fenny. Hodder, 1957

BLACKWOOD, ALGERNON, 1869-1951
Day and night stories. Dutton,
1917; UK: Cassell, 1917; John
Silence #2
John Silence, physician
extraordinary. Luce, 1909; UK:
Nash, 1908; John Silence #1
BLAISDELL, ANNE (British pseud. for
LIVINGTON, ELIZABETH)
BLAKE, ELEANOR A. (pseud. of Eleanor
Pratt, 1899 --)
The jade green cats. McBride, 1931;
John Kymmerly
BLAKE, NICHOLAS (pseud. of Cecil
Day-Lewis, 1904-1972)
The beast must die. Harper, 1938;
UK: Collins, 1938; Nigel
Strangeways #4; Insp. Blount
The corpse in the snowman. Harper,
1941; UK: Case of the abominable
snowman. Collins, 1941; Nigel
Strangeways #7
Dreadful hollow. Harper, 1953; UK:
Collins, 1953; Nigel Strangeways
#10
End of chapter. Harper, 1957; UK:
Collins, 1957; Nigel Strangeways
#12
Head of a traveler. Harper, 1949;
UK: Collins, 1949; Nigel
Strangeways #9; Insp. Blount
Minute for murder. Harper, 1948;
UK: Collins, 1947; Nigel
Strangeways #8
The morning after death. Harper,
1966; UK: Collins, 1966; Nigel
Strangeways #16
A penknife in my heart. Harper,
1959; UK: Collins, 1958
The private wound. Harper, 1968;
UK: Collins, 1968
A question of proof. Harper, 1935;
UK: Collins, 1935; Nigel
Strangeways #1
The sad variety. Harper, 1964; UK:
Collins, 1964; Nigel Strangeways
#15
The smiler with the knife. Harper,
1939; UK: Collins, 1939; Nigel
Strangeways #5; Georgia
Strangeways
The summer camp mystery. Harper,
1940; UK: Malice in wonderland.

Collins, 1940; Nigel Strangeways
#6
There's trouble brewing. Harper,
1937; UK: Collins, 1937; Nigel
Strangeways #3
Thou shell of death. Harper, 1936;
UK: Collins, 1936; Nigel
Strangeways #2
The whisper in the gloom. Harper,
1954; UK: Collins, 1954; Nigel
Strangeways #11
The widow's cruise. Harper, 1959;
UK: Collins, 1959; Nigel
Strangeways #13
The worm of death. Harper, 1961;
UK: Collins, 1961; Nigel
Strangeways #14
BLANC, SUZANNE
The green stone. Harper, 1961; UK:
Cassell, 1962; Miguel Menendes #1
The rose window. Doubleday, 1967;
UK: Cassell, 1968; Miguel
Menendes #3
The sea troll. Doubleday, 1969
The yellow villa. Doubleday, 1964;
UK: Cassell, 1965; Miguel
Menendes #2
BLEILER, EVERETT F., ed.
A treasury of Victorian detective
stories. Scribner's, 1979
BLOCH, ROBERT, 1917 --
The scarf. Dial, 1947; UK: Scarf
of passion. New English Library,
1972
Shooting star. Ace, 1958
BLOCHMAN, LAWRENCE G., 1900-1975
Bengal fire. Dell, 1947; UK:
Collins, 1937; Leonidas Prike
Bombay mail. Little, 1934; UK:
Collins, 1934; Leonidas Prike
Clues for Dr. Coffee. Lippincott,
1964; Dr. Coffee
Diagnosis: homicide. Lippincott,
1950; Dr. Coffee
Recipe for homicide. Lippincott,
1952; UK: Hammond, 1954; Dr.
Coffee
Red snow at Darjeeling. Saint
Mystery Library, 1960; UK:
Collins, 1938; Leonidas Prike
See you at the morgue. Duell, 1941;
UK: Cassell, 1946; Det. Kilkenny
Wives to burn. Harcourt, 1940; UK:
Collins, 1940

BLOCK, LAWRENCE, 1938 --
The burglar in the closet. Random
House, 1978; UK: Hale, 1980;
Bernie Rhodenbarr #2
The burglar who liked to quote
Kipling. Random House, 1979; UK:
Hale, 1981; Bernie Rhodenbarr;
Carolyn Kaiser
The burglar who painted like
Mondrian. Arbor House, 1983;
Bernie Rhodenbarr; Carolyn Kaiser
The burglar who studied Spinoza.
Random House, 1981; Bernie
Rhodenbarr; Carolyn Kaiser
Burglars can't be choosers. Random
House, 1977; UK: Hale, 1978;
Bernie Rhodenbarr #1
Eight million ways to die. Arbor
House, 1982; Matthew Scudder
In the midst of death. Dell, 1976;
Hale, 1979; Matthew Scudder
Like a lamb to slaughter. Arbor
House, 1984; Matthew Scudder; Chip
Harrison
Make out with murder. Fawcett,
1974; Leo Haig #1; Chip Harrison
#2
Sins of the father. Dell, 1977; UK:
Hale, 1979; Matthew Scudder #2
A stab in the dark. Arbor House,
1981; Matthew Scudder
The topless tulip murder. Fawcett,
1975; Leo Haig #2; Chip Harrison
#3
BLUNDELL, HAROLD, see BELLAIRS,
GEORGE (pseud.)
BODELSEN, ANDERS
One down. Harper, 1970; UK: Hit and
run, run, run. Joseph, 1970
Straus. Harper, 1974
Think of a number. Harper, 1969;
UK: Joseph, 1969
BODINGTON, NANCY HERMIONE, see
SMITH, SHELLEY (pseud.)
BODKIN, M. M'DONNELL, 1850-1933
The capture of Paul Beck. Little,
1911; UK: Unwin, 1911; Paul Beck
#3; Dora Myrl #2
Dora Myrl, the lady detective. UK:
Chatto, 1900; Dora Myrl #1
Paul Beck, detective. Dublin:
Talbot Press, 1929; Paul Beck #5
Paul Beck, The rule of thumb
detective. UK: Pearson, 1898; Paul
Beck #1

The quest of Paul Beck. Little,
1910; UK: Unwin, 1908; Paul Beck
#2
Young Beck: a chip off the old
block. Little, 1912; UK: Unwin,
1911; Paul Beck #4; Dora Myrl #3
BOILEAU, PIERRE and NARCEJAC, THOMAS
Who was Clare Jallu? UK: Barker,
1965
BOLAND, JOHN, 1913-1976
The Shakespeare curse. Walker,
1970; UK: Cassell, 1969
BOLES, PAUL DARCY
The limner. Crowell, 1975; Luke
Applegate
BOLTON, WILLIAM, see BAKER, NORTH
BOND, MICHAEL
Monsieur Pamplemousse. Beaufort,
1985; M. Pamplemousse
BOND, RAYMOND T., ed.
Famous stories of code and cipher.
Rinehart, 1947
Handbook for poisoners. Rinehart,
1951
BONETT, EMERY, see BONETT, JOHN and
EMERY
BONETT, JOHN and EMERY (pseud. of
John Hubert Arthur Coulson and
Felicity Winifred Carter [Coulson])
Better off dead. Doubleday, 1964;
UK: Better dead. Joseph, 1964;
Insp. Borges #1
Dead lion. Doubleday, 1947; UK:
Joseph, 1949; Prof. Mandrake #1
Murder on the Costa Brava. Walker,
1968; UK: This side murder.
Joseph, 1967; Insp. Borges #3
No grave for a lady. Doubleday,
1959; UK: Joseph, 1960; Prof.
Mandrake #3
No time to kill. Walker, 1972; UK:
Harrap, 1972; Insp. Borges #5
Not in the script. Doubleday, 1951;
UK: A banner for Pegasus. Joseph,
1951; Prof. Mandrake #2
The private force of murder.
Doubleday, 1966; UK: Joseph,
1966; Insp. Borges #2
The sound of murder. Walker, 1971;
UK: Harrap, 1971; Insp. Borges #4
BONNAMY, FRANCIS (pseud. of Audrey
Boyer Walz, 1960-1983)
Blood and thirsty. Duell, 1949; UK:
Murray, 1952; Peter Shane #7

Dead reckoning. Duell, 1943; Peter
Shane #3
Death by appointment. Doubleday,
1931; Peter Shane #1
Death on a dude ranch. Doubleday,
1937; Peter Shane #2
The king is dead on Queen Street.
Duell, 1945; Peter Shane #5
The man in the mist. Duell, 1951;
UK: Murray, 1952; Peter Shane #8
Portrait of the artist as a dead
man. Duell, 1947; UK:
Self-portrait in murder. Murray,
1952; Peter Shane #6
A rope of sand. Duell, 1944; Peter
Shane #4

BONNEY, JOSEPH L.
Death by dynamite. Carrick & Evans,
1940; Simon Rolfe
Look to the lady! Lippincott, 1947

BOORE, W. H., 1904
Cry on the wind. UK: Collins, 1967

BOOTH, CHARLES G., 1896-1949
Murder at high tide. Morrow, 1930;
UK: Hodder, 1930

BOOTON, KAGE, 1919 --
Andrew's wife. Doubleday, 1964
Quite by accident. Doubleday, 1972;
UK: Davies, 1974
Runaway home! Doubleday, 1967; UK:
Hale, 1968
Time running out. Doubleday, 1968;
UK: Hale, 1969
Who knows Julie Gordon? Doubleday,
1980; UK: Hale, 1981; Ida Pelham

BORGENICHT, MIRRIAM, 1915 --
A corpse in diplomacy. Mill, 1949;
UK: Panther, 1956
Extreme remedies. Doubleday, 1967;
UK: Hale, 1968
Fall from grace. St. Martin's,
1984; Nan Dunlap
True or false. St. Martin's, 1982;
Ada Weller

BORTHWECK, J. S.
The case of the hook-billed kites.
St. Martin's, 1982; Sara Deane

BORTNER, NORMAN STANLEY
Bond Grayson murdered! McCrae
Smith, 1936; Clifford Wells #1
Death of a merchant of death.
McCrae Smith, 1937; Clifford Wells
#2

BOSAK, STEVEN
Gammon. St. Martin's, 1985; Vernon
Bradlusky

BOSSE, M. J., 1926 --
The man who loved zoos. Putnam,
1974; UK: Gollancz, 1975;
Victoria Welch

BOSTON, CHARLES K. (pseud. for
GRUBER, FRANK)

BOUCHER, ANTHONY (pseud. for William
Anthony Parker White, 1911-1968).
For other mysteries by this author,
see HOLMES, H. H. (pseud.)
The case of the Baker Street
Irregulars. Simon & Schuster,
1940; Fergus O'Breen #2; Sherlock
Holmes
The case of the crumpled knave.
Simon & Schuster, 1939; UK:
Harrap, 1939; Lt. Jackson #1;
Fergus O'Breen #1
The case of the seven of Calvary.
Simon & Schuster, 1937; UK:
Hamilton, 1937; John Ashwin
The case of the seven sneezes.
Simon & Schuster, 1942; Fergus
O'Breen #4
The case of the solid key. Simon &
Schuster, 1941; Fergus O'Breen #3

BOURJAILY, VANCE
A game men play. Dial, 1980;
"Chink" Peters

BOURQUIN, PAUL HENRY JAMES, see
AMBERLEY, RICHARD (pseud.)

BOWEN-JUDD, SARA, see WOODS, SARA
(pseud.) or LEEK, MARGARET (pseud.)

BOWERING, GEORGE
Burning water. Beaufort, 1980;
George Vancouver

BOWERS, DOROTHY, 1904 --
The bells at Old Bailey. Doubleday,
1947; UK: The bells at Old
Bailey. Hodder, 1947; Insp.
Raikes
A deed without a name. Doubleday,
1940; UK: Hodder, 1940; Insp.
Pardoe; Sgt. Salt
Postscript to poison. UK: Hodder,
1939; Insp. Pardoe
Shadows before. Doubleday, 1940;
UK: Hodder, 1939; Insp. Pardoe;
Sgt. Salt

BOX, EDGAR (pseud. of Gore Vidal,
1925 --)

Death before bedtime. Dutton, 1953;
UK: Heinemann, 1954; Peter
Sargeant #2
Death in the fifth position.
Dutton, 1952; UK: Heinemann, 1954;
Peter Sargeant #1
Death likes it hot. Dutton, 1954;
UK: Heinemann, 1955; Peter
Sargeant #3

BOYD, JANE
Murder in the King's Road. British
Book Centre, 1954; UK: Harvill,
1953

BOYD, MARION (pseud. of Marion
Margaret Boyd Havighurst)
Murder in the stacks. Lothrop,
1934; Tom Allen

BOYER, RICHARD L., 1943 --
The giant rat of Sumatra. Warner,
1976; UK: Allen, 1977; Sherlock
Holmes

BOYER, RICK
Billingsgate Shoal. Houghton, 1982;
Charlie Adams
The penny ferry. Houghton, 1984;
Charlie Adams

BOYLE, JACK
Boston Blackie. H. K. Fly, 1919;
"Boston" Blackie

BOYLE, THOMAS
The cold stove league. Academy
Chicago, 1983
Only the dead know Brooklyn.
Godine, 1985; Francis DeSales

BRADBURY, RAY
Death is a lonely business. Knopf,
1985; Ray Bradbury

BRADDON, GEORGE
Judgment deferred. UK: Trelawny,
1948

BRADDON, M. E., 1837-1915
Lady Audley's secret. UK: Tinsley,
1862; Robert Audley

BRADLEY, MARY HASTINGS
Murder in the family. UK: Longman,
1931
Nice people murder. UK: Longman,
1952
Nice people poison. UK: Longman,
1952; Nicholas Parr

BRAHMS, CARYL (pseud. of Doris
Caroline Abrahams, 1901 --)

BRAHMS, CARYL and SIMON, S. J.
A bullet in the ballet. Doubleday,
1938; UK: Joseph, 1937; Adam
Quill #1; Troupe Stroganoff
Envoy on excursion. UK: Joseph,
1940; Adam Quill #3
Murder a la Stroganoff. Doubleday,
1938; UK: Casino for sale.
Joseph, 1938; Adam Quill #2;
Troupe Stroganoff
Six curtains for Natasha.
Lippincott, 1946; UK: Six
curtains for Stroganova. Joseph,
1945; Troupe Stroganoff
Stroganoff at the ballet. UK:
Joseph, 1975; Troupe Stroganoff

BRAMAH, ERNEST (pseud. of Ernest
Bramah Smith, 1868-1942)
Best Max Carrados detective
stories. Dover, 1972; Max
Carrados
The bravo of London. UK: Cassell,
1934; Max Carrados #5
The eyes of Max Carrados. Doran,
1924; UK: Richards, 1923; Max
Carrados #2
Max Carrados. Hyperion, 1975; UK:
Methuen, [1914]; Max Carrados #1
Max Carrados mysteries. Penguin,
1964; UK: Hodder, 1927; Max
Carrados #4
Short stories of today and
yesterday. UK: Harrap, 1929; Max
Carrados
The specimen case. Doran, 1925;
UK: Hodder, 1925; Max Carrados #3

BRAMLETTE, PAULA, see YATES, MARGARET
and BRAMLETTE, PAULA

BRAND, CHRISTIANA, 1909 --
Brand X. UK: Joseph, 1974; Insp.
Cockrill #9
Buffet for unwelcome guests.
Southern Illinois University
Press, 1983; Insp. Cockrill #10
Cat and mouse. Knopf, 1950; UK:
Lane, 1950; Insp. Chucky
The crooked wreath. Dodd, 1946;
UK: Suddenly at his residence.
Bodley Head, 1947; Insp. Cockrill
#3
Death in high heels. Scribner's,
1954; UK: Lane, 1941; Insp.
Charlesworth

Death of Jezebel. Dodd, 1948; UK:
Bodley Head, 1949; Insp. Cockrill
#4

Fog of doubt. Scribner's, 1953;
UK: London particular. Joseph,
1952; Insp. Cockrill #5

Green for danger. Dodd, 1944; UK:
Lane, 1945; Insp. Cockrill #2

Heads you lose. Dodd, 1942; UK:
Lane, 1941; Insp. Cockrill #1

The three-cornered halo. Scribner's,
1957; Insp. Cockrill #7; Henrietta
Cockrill

Tour de force. Scribner's, 1955;
UK: Joseph, 1955; Insp. Cockrill
#6

What dread hand? UK: Joseph,
1968; Insp. Cockrill #8

BRAND, MAX (pseud. of Frederic Austin,
1892-1944)

Big game. Paperback Library,
1974; Terrence Radway

BRANSON, H. C.

Beggar's choice. Simon & Schuster,
1953; John Bent #7

The case of the giant killer. Simon
& Schuster, 1944; UK: Bodley Head,
1949; John Bent #3

The fearful passage. Simon &
Schuster, 1945; UK: Bodley Head,
1950; John Bent #4

I'll eat you last. Simon & Schuster,
1941; UK: Lane, 1943; John Bent #1

Last year's blood. Simon &
Schuster, 1947; UK: Bodley Head,
1950; John Bent #5

The leaden bubble. Simon &
Schuster, 1949; UK: Bodley Head,
1951; John Bent #6

The pricking thumb. Simon &
Schuster, 1942; UK: Bodley Head,
1949; John Bent #2

BRAUN, LILLIAN JACKSON

The cat who ate Danish modern.
Dutton, 1967; UK: Collins, 1968;
Koko #2; Jim Qwilleran #2

The cat who could read backwards.
Dutton, 1965; UK: Collins, 1967;
Koko #1; Jim Qwilleran #1

The cat who turned on and off.
Dutton, 1968; UK: Collins, 1968;
Koko #3; Jim Qwilleran #3

BRAUTIGAN, RICHARD, 1935 --

Dreaming of Babylon. Delacorte,
1977; UK: Cape, 1978; C. Card

BRAWNER, H., see COFFIN, GEOFFREY and
BRAWNER, H.

BREAN, HERBERT, 1907-1973

The clock strikes thirteen. Morrow,
1952; UK: Heinemann, 1954;
Reynold Frame #3

The darker the night. Morrow, 1949;
UK: Heinemann, 1950; Reynold
Frame #2

Hardly a man is now alive. Morrow,
1950; UK: Murder now and then.
Heinemann, 1952; Reynold Frame #3

A matter of fact. Morrow, 1956; UK:
Collar for a killer. Heinemann,
1957

The traces of Brillhart. Harper,
1960; UK: Heinemann, 1961;
William Deacon #1

The traces of Merrilee. Harper,
1966; William Deacon #2

Wilders walk away. Morrow, 1948;
UK: Heinemann, 1949; Reynold
Frame #1

BREBNER, PERCY JAMES, 1864-1922

Christopher Quarles, college
professor and master detective.
Dutton, 1914; UK: Holden, 1921;
Christopher Quarles

The master detective. Dutton, 1916;
UK: Holden, 1922; Christopher
Quarles

BREEN, JON L.

The gathering place. Walker, 1984

Listen for the click. Walker, 1983;
Olivia Barchester

BREMNER, MARJORIE, 1916 --

Murder most familiar. Detective
Book Club, 1954; UK: Hodder, 1953

BRENNAN, JOHN NEEDHAM HUGGARD,
1914 -- , see WELCOME, JOHN
(pseud.)

BRETT, HY and BARBARA

Promises to keep. Harper & Row,
1981; Gil Ferguson #1; Connie
Ferguson #1

BRETT, JOHN

Who'd hire Brett? St. Martin's,
1981; John Brett

BRETT, SIMON, 1945 --

An amateur corpse. Scribner's,
1978; UK: Gollancz, 1978; Charles
Paris #4

Cast, in order of disappearance.
Scribner's, 1976; UK: Gollancz,
1975; Charles Paris #1

A comedian dies. Scribner's, 1979;
UK: Gollancz, 1979; Charles Paris
#5
The dead side of the mine.
Scribner's, 1980; UK: Gollancz,
1980; Charles Paris #6
Murder in the title. Scribner's,
1983; Charles Paris #9
Murder unprompted. Scribner's,
1982; Charles Paris #8
Not dead, only resting. Scribner's,
1984; Charles Paris
Situation tragedy. Scribner's,
1981; Charles Paris #7
So much blood. Scribner's, 1977;
UK: Gollancz, 1976; Charles Paris
#2
Star trap. Scribner's, 1978; UK:
Gollancz, 1977; Charles Paris #3

BREZ, E. M.
Those dark eyes. St. Martin's,
1984; Dave Axelrod

BRINTON, HENRY, 1901-1977
Drug on the market. Macmillan,
1957; UK: Hutchinson, 1956; John
Strang; Sally Strang

BRISTOW, GWEN and MANNING, BRUCE
The Guttenberg murders. Mystery
League, 1931
The invisible host. Mystery League,
1930

BROCK, LYNN (pseud. of Alister
McAlister, 1877-1943)
Colonel Gore's second case. Harper,
1926; UK: Collins, 1925; Col. Gore
#2
The deductions of Colonel Gore.
Harper, 1925; UK: The Barrington
mystery. Collins, 1924; Col. Gore
#1
The kink. Harper, 1927; UK:
Colonel Gore's third case.
Collins, 1925; Col. Gore #3
Murder at the inn. Harper, 1929;
UK: The Mendip mystery. Collins,
1929; Col. Gore #6
Murder on the bridge. Harper,
1930; UK: Q.E.D. Collins, 1930;
Col. Gore #7
The slip-carriage mystery. Harper,
1928; UK: Collins, 1928; Col. Gore
#4

BRODIE, JULIAN PAUL, see DENBIE,
ROGER (pseud.)

BRONSON, F. W., 1901-1966
The bulldog has the key. Farrar,
1949; Ed Brakely
The Uncas Island murders. Farrar,
1942

BROOK, MARGARET FRANCES BACON, see
BACON, PEGGY

BROOKS, VIVIAN COLLINS, see TRAVERS,
HUGH (pseud.)

BROOME, ADAM (pseud. of Godfrey
Warden James, 1888 --)
The Cambridge murders. UK: Bles,
1936; Insp. Bramley
The Oxford murders. UK: Bles, 1929;
Reggie Crofts; Barbara Playfair

BROUN, DANIEL
The subject of Harry Egypt. Holt,
1963

BROWN, FREDERIC, 1906-1972
The bloody moonlight. Dutton, 194 ;
UK: Murder in the moonlight.
Boardman, 1950; Ed Hunter #3;
Ambrose Hunter #3
Compliments of a fiend. Dutton,
1950; UK: Boardman, 1951; Ed
Hunter #4; Ambrose Hunter #4
The dead ringer. Dutton, 1948; UK:
Boardman, 1950; Ed Hunter #2;
Ambrose Hunter #2
Death has many doors. Dutton,
1951; UK: Boardman, 1952; Ed
Hunter #5; Ambrose Hunter #5
The deep end. Dutton, 1952; UK:
Boardman, 1953
The fabulous clipjoint. Dutton,
1947; UK: Boardman, 1949; Ed
Hunter #1; Ambrose Hunter #1
The far cry. Dutton, 1951; UK:
Boardman, 1952
The five day nightmare. Dutton,
1962; UK: Boardman, 1963
Here comes a candle. Dutton, 1950;
UK: Boardman, 1952
The late lamented. Dutton, 1959;
UK: Boardman, 1959; Ed Hunter #6;
Ambrose Hunter #6
The lenient beast. Dutton, 1956;
UK: Boardman, 1957; Frank Ramos
Mrs. Murphy's underpants. Dutton,
1963; UK: Boardman, 1965; Ed
Hunter #7; Ambrose Hunter #7
Night of the Jabberwock. Dutton,
1950; UK: Boardman, 1951; Doc
Stoeger

One for the road. Dutton, 1958; UK:
Boardman, 1959

The screaming mimi. Dutton, 1949;
UK: Boardman, 1950; Bill Sweeney

The wench is dead. Dutton, 1955;
Howard Perry

BROWN, MORNA DORIS, see FERRARS,
E. X. (pseud.)

BROWN, ROBERT CARLTON

The remarkable adventures of
Christopher Poe. Browne, 1913;
Christopher Poe

BROWN, ZENITH, see FORD, LESLIE
(pseud.) or FROME, DAVID (pseud.)

BROWNE, DOUGLAS G., 1884-1963

The Cotfold conundrums. UK: Methuen,
1933; H. H. Thew

The dead don't bite. UK: Methuen,
1933; Maurice Hemyock

Death in perpetuity. UK: Macdonald,
1950

Death in seven volumes. UK:
Macdonald, 1958; Insp. Dauncey;
Sgt. Hughjohn

Death wears a mask. Macmillan,
1954; UK: Hutchinson, 1940; Harvey
Tuke

The May-week murders. UK: Longman,
1937; Maurice Hemyock

Plan XVI. Doubleday, 1934; UK:
Methuen, 1934; H. H. Thew

Rustling end. UK: Macdonald, 1948;
Harvey Tuke

Too many cousins. Macmillan, 1953;
UK: Macdonald, 1946; Harvey Tuke

What beckoning ghost? UK:
Macdonald, 1947

BROWNE, HOWARD. For other works by
this author, see EVANS, JOHN
(pseud.)

BROWNE, HOWARD, 1908 --

The taste of ashes. Simon &
Schuster, 1957; UK: Gollancz,
1958; Paul Pine

BRUCE, LEO (pseud. of Rupert
Croft-Cooke, 1903-1979)

At death's door. UK: Hamilton,
1955; Carolus Deene #1

A bone and a hank of hair. British
Book Centre, 1961; UK: Davies,
1961; Carolus Deene #10

A case for Sergeant Beef. Academy
Chicago, 1980; UK: Nicholson,
1947; Sgt. Beef #6

A case for three detectives.
Stokes, 1937; UK: Bles, 1936;
Sgt. Beef #1; Peter Wimsey;
Hercule Poirot; Father Brown

Case with four clowns. Stokes,
1939; UK: Davies, 1939; Sgt. Beef
#3

The case with no solution. UK:
Bles, 1939; Sgt. Beef #4

The case with ropes & rings.
Academy Chicago, 1980; UK:
Nicholson, 1940; Sgt. Beef #5

Case without a corpse. Stokes,
1937; UK: Bles, 1937; Sgt. Beef
#2

Cold blood. Academy Chicago, 1980;
UK: Gollancz, 1952; Sgt. Beef #8

Dead for a ducat. UK: Davies,
1956; Carolus Deene #2

Dead man's shoes. UK: Davies,
1958; Carolus Deene #4

Death at Hallow's End. British
Book Centre, 1966; UK: Allen,
1965; Carolus Deene #14

Death at St. Asprey's School.
Academy Chicago, 1984; UK: Allen,
1967; Carolus Deene

Death by the lake. UK: Allen,
1971; Carolus Deene #21

Death in Albert Park. Scribner's,
1979; UK: Allen, 1964; Carolus
Deene #13

Death in the middle watch. UK:
Allen, 1974; Carolus Deene #22

Death of a Bovver boy. UK: Allen,
1974; Carolus Deene #23

Death of a commuter. UK: Allen,
1967; Carolus Deene #16

Death of cold. UK: Davies, 1956;
Carolus Deene #3

Death on Allhallowe'en. UK: Allen,
1970; Carolus Deene #20

Death on Romney Marsh. UK: Allen,
1968; Carolus Deene #18

Death on the black sandy. UK:
Allen, 1966; Carolus Deene #15

Death with blue ribbon. London
House, 1970; UK: Allen, 1969;
Carolus Deene #19

Die all, die merrily. British Book
Centre, 1961; UK: Davies, 1961;
Carolus Deene #9

Furious old women. UK: Davies,
1960; Carolus Deene #7

Jack on the gallows tree. Academy Chicago, 1983; UK: Davies, 1960; Carolus Deene #8

A louse for a hangman. UK: Davies, 1962; Carolus Deene #5

Neck and neck. Academy Chicago, 1980; UK: Gollancz, 1951; Sgt. Beef #7

Nothing like blood. UK: Davies, 1962; Carolus Deene #11

Our jubilee is death. UK: Davies, 1959; Carolus Deene #6

Such is death. London House, 1963; UK: Crack of doom. Davies, 1963; Carolus Deene #12

BRUTON, ERIC, 1915 --
Death in ten point bold. UK: Jenkins, 1957; Dr. Hook; Insp. Reynolds

The Finsburg mob. UK: Boardman, 1964; George Judd #2

The firebug. UK: Boardman, 1967; George Judd #5

The laughing policeman. UK: Boardman, 1963; George Judd #1

The Smithfield slayer. UK: Boardman, 1965; George Judd #3

The wicked saint. UK: Boardman, 1965; George Judd #4

BRYANT DOROTHY
Killing Wonder. A & A Books, 1981; Jessamyn Posey

BRYSON, CHARLES, see BARRY, CHARLES (pseud.)

BUCHANAN, EILEEN MARIE DUELL, see PETRIE, RHONA (pseud.)

BUCKINGHAM, BRUCE
Broiled alive. UK: Joseph, 1957; Don Pancho

Three bad nights. UK: Joseph, 1956

BUELL, JOHN, 1927 --
Four days. Farrar Straus, 1962; UK: Macmillan, 1962

The pyx. Farrar Straus, 1959; UK: Secker, 1960

BULLETT, GERALD, 1893-1958
Judgement in suspense. UK: Dent, 1946

The jury. Knopf, 1935; UK: Dent, 1935

BURGE, MILWARD RODON KENNEDY, see KENNEDY, MILWARD (pseud.)

BURGESS, GELETT (pseud. of Frank Gelett Burgess, 1866-1951)

Ladies in boxes. Alliance, 1942

The master of mysteries. Bobbs, 1912; Astrogon Kerby

A murder at the Dome. Book Club of California, 1937

Two o'clock courage. Bobbs, 1934; UK: Nicholson, 1934

BURKE, ALAN DENNIS
Getting away with murder. Atlantic-Little Brown, 1981; Bill Martell

BURKE, J. F., 1915
Kelly among the nightingales. Dutton, 1979; Sam Kelly

BURKE, JOHN, 1922 --
The black charade. Coward McCann, 1977; UK: Weidenfeld, 1977; Dr. Caspian #2

The devil's footsteps. Coward McCann, 1976; UK: Weidenfeld, 1976; Dr. Caspian #1

Ladygrove. Coward McCann, 1978; UK: Weidenfeld, 1978; Dr. Caspian #3

BURKE, THOMAS, 1886-1945
Murder at Elstree. UK: Longman, 1936

BURLEY, W. J., 1914 --
Death in a salubrious place. Walker, 1973; UK: Gollancz, 1973; Charles Wycliffe #4

Death in Stanley Street. Walker, 1974; UK: Gollancz, 1974; Charles Wycliffe #5

Death in willow pattern. Walker, 1970; UK: Gollancz, 1969; Henry Pym #2

Guilt edged. Walker, 1972; UK: Gollancz, 1971; Charles Wycliffe #3

The schoolmaster. Walker, 1977; UK: Gollancz, 1977

A taste of power. UK: Gollancz, 1966; Henry Pym #1

Three-toed pussy. UK: Gollancz, 1968; Charles Wycliffe #1

To kill a cat. Walker, 1970; UK: Gollancz, 1970; Charles Wycliffe #2

Wycliffe and the Beales. Doubleday, 1984; Charles Wycliffe

Wycliffe and the pea green boat. Walker, 1975; UK: Gollancz, 1975; Charles Wycliffe #6

Wycliffe and the scapegoat.
Doubleday, 1978; UK: Gollancz,
1978; Charles Wycliffe #8
Wycliffe and the schoolgirls.
Walker, 1976; UK: Gollancz, 1976;
Charles Wycliffe #7
Wycliffe in Paul's Court. Doubleday,
1980; UK: Gollancz, 1980; Charles
Wycliffe #9
Wycliffe's wild goose chase.
Doubleday, 1982; Charles Wycliffe

BURNHAM, DAVID, 1907 --
Last act in Bermuda. Scribner's,
1940; Insp. Hopkins

BURNS, REX, 1935 --
The Alvarez journal. Harper, 1975;
UK: Hale, 1976; Gabriel Wager #1
Angle of attack. Harper, 1979; UK:
Hale, 1980; Gabriel Wager #4
The avenging angel. Viking, 1983;
Gabriel Wager
The Farnsworth score. Harper, 1977;
UK: Hale, 1978; Gabriel Wager #2
Speak for the dead. Harper, 1978;
UK: Hale, 1980; Gabriel Wager #3
Strip search. Viking, 1984; Gabriel
Wager #6

BURTON, ANTHONY
Embrace of the butcher. Dodd, 1982;
Peter King

BURTON, MILES (pseud.). For other
works by this author, see RHODE,
JOHN (pseud.)
Accidents do happen. Doubleday,
1946; UK: Early morning murder.
Collins, 1945; Desmond Merrion #32
Beware your neighbor. UK: Collins,
1951; Desmond Merrion #44
Bones in the brickfield. UK:
Collins, 1958; Desmond Merrion #57
The cat jumps. UK: Collins, 1946;
Desmond Merrion #33
The Charabanc mystery. UK: Collins,
1934; Desmond Merrion #8
The Chinese puzzle. UK: Collins,
1957; Desmond Merrion #54
The clue of the fourteen keys.
Doubleday, 1937; UK: Death at the
club. Collins, 1937; Desmond
Merrion #15
The clue of the silver brush.
Doubleday, 1936; UK: The
milk-churn murder. Collins, 1935;
Desmond Merrion #11

The clue of the silver cellar.
Doubleday, 1937; UK: Where is
Barbara Prentice? Collins, 1936;
Desmond Merrion #14
A crime in time. UK: Collins,
1955; Desmond Merrion #51
Dark is the tunnel. Doubleday,
1936; UK: Death in the tunnel.
Collins, 1936; Desmond Merrion
#12
Dead stop. UK: Collins, 1943;
Desmond Merrion #28
Death at Ash House. Doubleday,
1942; UK: This undesirable
residence. Collins, 1942; Desmond
Merrion #26
Death at low tide. UK: Collins,
1938; Desmond Merrion #17
Death at the crossroads. UK:
Collins, 1933; Desmond Merrion #5
Death in a duffle coat. UK:
Collins, 1956; Desmond Merrion
#52
Death in shallow water. UK:
Collins, 1948; Desmond Merrion
#37
Death leaves no card. UK: Collins,
1939; Desmond Merrion #19
The death of Mr. Gantley. UK:
Collins, 1932; Desmond Merrion #4
Death of two brothers. UK: Collins,
1941; Desmond Merrion #24
Death paints a picture. UK:
Collins, 1960; Desmond Merrion
#61
Death takes a detour. UK: Collins,
1958; Desmond Merrion #56
Death visits Downspring. Doubleday,
1941; UK: Up the garden path.
Collins, 1941; Desmond Merrion
#25
The Devereux Court mystery. UK:
Collins, 1935; Desmond Merrion
#10
Devil's reckoning. Doubleday, 1949;
UK: Collins, 1948; Desmond
Merrion #38
The disappearing parson. Doubleday,
1949; UK: Death takes the living.
Collins, 1949; Desmond Merrion
#39
Fate at the fair. UK: Collins,
1933; Desmond Merrion #6

Found drowned. UK: Collins, 1956; Desmond Merrion #53

Ground for suspicion. UK: Collins, 1950; Desmond Merrion #41

The Hardaway diamonds mystery. Mystery League, 1930; UK: Collins, 1930

Heir to Lucifer. UK: Collins, 1947; Desmond Merrion #35

Heir to murder. UK: Collins, 1953; Desmond Merrion #46

Legacy of death. UK: Collins, 1960; Desmond Merrion #60

Look alive. Doubleday, 1950; UK: Collins, 1949; Desmond Merrion #40

The man with the tattooed face. Doubleday, 1937; UK: Murder in Crown Passage. Collins, 1937; Desmond Merrion #16

The menace on the downs. UK: Collins, 1931; Desmond Merrion #2

Mr. Babbacombe dies. UK: Collins, 1939; Desmond Merrion

Mr. Westerby missing. Doubleday, 1940; UK: Collins, 1940; Desmond Merrion #22

The moth-watch murder. UK: Collins, 1957; Desmond Merrion #55

Murder in absence. UK: Collins, 1954; Desmond Merrion #48

Murder of a chemist. UK: Collins, 1936; Desmond Merrion #13

Murder on duty. UK: Collins, 1952; Desmond Merrion #45

Murder out of school. UK: Collins, 1951; Desmond Merrion #43

Murder unrecognized. UK: Collins, 1955; Desmond Merrion #50

Not a leg to stand on. Doubleday, 1945; UK: Collins, 1945; Desmond Merrion #31

The platinum cat. Doubleday, 1938; UK: Collins, 1938; Desmond Merrion #18

Return from the dead. UK: Collins, 1959; Desmond Merrion #58

The secret of High Eldersham. Mystery League, 1931; UK: The mystery of High Eldersham. Collins, 1930; Desmond Merrion #1

The shadow on the cliff. Doubleday, 1944; UK: Four-ply yarn. Collins, 1944; Desmond Merrion #29

Situation vacant. UK: Collins, 1946; Desmond Merrion #34

A smell of smoke. UK: Collins, 1959; Desmond Merrion #59

Something to hide. UK: Collins, 1953; Desmond Merrion #47

The three corpse trick. UK: Collins, 1944; Desmond Merrion #30

The three crimes. UK: Collins, 1931; Desmond Merrion #3

To catch a thief. UK: Collins, 1934; Desmond Merrion #9

Tragedy at the thirteenth hole. UK: Collins, 1933; Desmond Merrion #7

Unwanted corpse. UK: Collins, 1954; Desmond Merrion #49

Vacancy with a corpse. Doubleday, 1941; UK: Death takes a flat. Collins, 1940; Desmond Merrion #21

A village afraid. UK: Collins, 1950; Desmond Merrion #42

Who killed the doctor? Doubleday, 1943; UK: Murder, M.D. Collins, 1943; Desmond Merrion #27

A will in the way. Doubleday, 1947; UK: Collins, 1947; Desmond Merrion #36

Written in dust. Doubleday, 1940; UK: Murder in the coalhole. Collins, 1940; Desmond Merrion #23

BUSH, CHRISTOPHER (pseud. of Charlie Christmas Bush, 1885-1973)

The body in the bonfire. Morrow, 1936; UK: The case of the bonfire body. Cassell, 1936; Ludovic Travers #14

The case of the amateur actor. Macmillan, 1956; UK: Macdonald, 1955; Ludovic Travers #46

The case of the April fools Morrow, 1933; UK: Cassell, 1933; Ludovic Travers #10

The case of the benevolent bookie. Macmillan, 1956; UK: Macdonald, 1955; Ludovic Travers #47

The case of the burnt Bohemian. Macmillan, 1954; UK: Macdonald, 1953; Ludovic Travers #42

The case of the careless thief. Macmillan, 1960; UK: Macdonald, 1959; Ludovic Travers #53

The case of the Chinese gong. Holt, 1935; UK: Cassell, 1935; Ludovic Travers #13

The case of the climbing rat. UK: Cassell, 1940; Ludovic Travers #22

The case of the corner cottage. Macmillan, 1952; UK: Macdonald, 1951; Ludovic Travers #39

The case of the corporal's leave. UK: Cassell, 1945; Ludovic Travers #29

The case of the counterfeit colonel. Macmillan, 1953; UK: Macdonald, 1952; Ludovic Travers #41

The case of the curious client. Macmillan, 1948; UK: Macdonald, 1947; Ludovic Travers #32

The case of the dead man gone. Macmillan, 1962; UK: Macdonald, 1961; Ludovic Travers #56

The case of the deadly diamonds. Macmillan, 1969; UK: Macdonald, 1967; Ludovic Travers #62

The case of the extra grave. Macmillan, 1962; UK: Macdonald, 1961; Ludovic Travers #55

The case of the extra man. Macmillan, 1957; UK: Macdonald, 1956; Ludovic Travers #48

The case of the fighting soldier. UK: Cassell, 1942; Ludovic Travers #24

The case of the flowery corpse. Macmillan, 1957; UK: Macdonald, 1956; Ludovic Travers #49

The case of the flying ass. UK: Cassell, 1939; Ludovic Travers #21

The case of the fourth detective. UK: Macdonald, 1951; Ludovic Travers #38

The case of the frightened mannequin. Macmillan, 1951; UK: The case of the happy warrior. Macdonald, 1950; Ludovic Travers #37

The case of the good employer. Macmillan, 1967; UK: Macdonald, 1966; Ludovic Travers #61

The case of the grand alliance. Macmillan, 1965; UK: Macdonald, 1964; Ludovic Travers #59

The case of the green felt hat. Holt, 1939; UK: Cassell, 1939; Ludovic Travers #20

The case of the happy medium. Macmillan, 1952; Ludovic Travers #40

The case of the Haven Hotel. UK: Macdonald, 1948; Ludovic Travers #33

The case of the heavenly twin. Macmillan, 1964; UK: Macdonald, 1963; Ludovic Travers #58

The case of the housekeeper's hair. Macmillan, 1949; UK: Macdonald, 1948; Ludovic Travers #34

The case of the jumbo sandwich. Macmillan, 1966; UK: Macdonald, 1965; Ludovic Travers #60

The case of the kidnapped colonel. UK: Cassell, 1942; Ludovic Travers #25

The case of the magic mirror. UK: Cassell, 1943; Ludovic Travers #26

The case of the missing men. Macmillan, 1947; UK: Macdonald, 1946; Ludovic Travers #31

The case of the murdered major. UK: Cassell, 1941; Ludovic Travers #23

The case of the platinum blonde. Macmillan, 1949; UK: Cassell, 1944; Ludovic Travers #28

The case of the prodigal daughter. Macmillan, 1969; UK: Macdonald, 1968; Ludovic Travers #63

The case of the purloined picture. Macmillan, 1951; UK: Macdonald, 1949; Ludovic Travers #36

The case of the red brunette. Macmillan, 1955; UK: Macdonald, 1954; Ludovic Travers #45

The case of the running man. Macmillan, 1959; UK: Macdonald, 1958; Ludovic Travers #52

The case of the running mouse. UK: Cassell, 1944; Ludovic Travers #27

The case of the Russian cross. Macmillan, 1958; UK: Macdonald, 1957; Ludovic Travers #50

The case of the sapphire brooch. Macmillan, 1961; UK: Macdonald, 1960; Ludovic Travers #54

The case of the second chance.
Macmillan, 1947; UK: Macdonald,
1946; Ludovic Travers #30

The case of the seven bells.
Macmillan, 1950; UK: Macdonald,
1949; Ludovic Travers #35

The case of the silken petticoat.
Macmillan, 1954; UK: Macdonald,
1953; Ludovic Travers #43

The case of the three lost letters.
Macmillan, 1955; UK: Macdonald,
1954; Ludovic Travers #44

The case of the three-ring puzzle.
Macmillan, 1963; UK: Macdonald,
1962; Ludovic Travers #57

The case of the triple twist.
Macmillan, 1958; UK: The case of
the treble twist. Macdonald, 1958;
Ludovic Travers #51

The case of the Tudor queen. Holt,
1938; UK: Cassell, 1938; Ludovic
Travers #18

The case of the unfortunate village.
UK: Cassell, 1932; Ludovic Travers
#8

The crank in the corner. Morrow,
1933; UK: The case of the three
strange faces. Cassell, 1933;
Ludovic Travers #9

Cut throat. Morrow, 1932; UK:
Heinemann, 1932; Ludovic Travers
#7

Dancing death. Doubleday, 1931; UK:
Heinemann, 1931; Ludovic Travers
#5

Dead man twice. Doubleday, 1930;
UK: Heinemann, 1930; Ludovic
Travers #4

Dead man's music. Doubleday, 1932;
UK: Heinemann, 1931; Ludovic
Travers #6

The death of Casino Revere.
Doubleday, 1930; UK: Murder at
Fenwold. Heinemann, 1930; Ludovic
Travers #3

Eight o'clock alibi. Holt, 1937;
UK: The case of the missing
minutes. Cassell, 1937; Ludovic
Travers #17

The kitchen cake murder. Morrow,
1934; UK: The case of the 100%
alibis. Cassell, 1934; Ludovic
Travers #12

The leaning man. Holt, 1938; UK:
The case of the leaning man.
Cassell, 1938; Ludovic Travers
#19

Murder on Monday. Holt, 1936; UK:
The case of the Monday murders.
Cassell, 1936; Ludovic Travers
#15

The perfect murder case. Doubleday,
1929; UK: Heinemann, 1929;
Ludovic Travers #2

The Plumely inheritance. UK:
Jarrolds, 1926; Ludovic Travers
#1

The tea-tray murders. Morrow,
1934; UK: The case of the dead
shepherd. Cassell, 1934; Ludovic
Travers #11

The wedding night murder. Holt,
1937; UK: The case of the hanging
rope. Cassell, 1937; Ludovic
Travers #16

BUTLER, GWENDOLINE. For other
mysteries by this author, see
MELVILLE, JENNIE (pseud.)

Coffin following. UK: Bles, 1968;
John Coffin #9

Coffin for baby. Walker, 1963; UK:
Bles, 1963; John Coffin #5

A coffin from the past. UK: Bles,
1970; John Coffin #11

Coffin in Malta. Walker, 1965; UK:
Bles, 1964; John Coffin #8

Coffin in Oxford. UK: Bles, 1962;
John Coffin #4

Coffin waiting. Walker, 1965; UK:
Bles, 1964; John Coffin #6

Coffin's dark number. UK: Bles,
1969; John Coffin #10

Dead in a row. UK: Bles, 1956;
John Coffin #1

Dine and be dead. Macmillan, 1960;
UK: Death lives next door. Bles,
1960; John Coffin #2

The dull dead. Walker, 1962; UK:
Bles, 1958; William Winter

Make me a murderer. UK: Bles,
1961; John Coffin #3

A nameless coffin. Walker, 1967;
UK: Bles, 1966; John Coffin #8

Olivia. Coward McCann, 1974; UK: A
coffin for the canary. Macmillan,
1974; John Coffin

Sarsen place. Coward McCann, 1974;
UK: A coffin for Pandora.
Macmillan, 1973; John Coffin #12

BUTTERWORTH, MICHAEL, 1924 -- , see
KEMP, SARAH (pseud.)

BYFIELD, BARBARA NINDE, 1930 --
Forever wilt thou die. Doubleday,
1976
A parcel of their fortunes.
Doubleday, 1979

BYFIELD, BARBARA NINDE and TEDESCHI,
FRANK L.
Solemn high murder. Doubleday,
1975; UK: Davies, 1976

BYRD, MAX
California thriller. Allison &
Busby, 1984; Mike Haller
Finders weepers. Allison & Busby,
1985; Mike Haller #3

BYROM, JAMES
Or be he dead. UK: Chatto, 1958
Take only as directed. UK: Chatto,
1959

CADELL, ELIZABETH (pseud. of Violet
Elizabeth Cadell, 1903 --)
The corner shop. Morrow, 1967; UK:
Hodder, 1966

CAIRD, JANET, 1913 --
In a glass darkly. Morrow, 1966;
UK: Murder reflected. Bles, 1965
The loch. Doubleday, 1969; UK:
Bles, 1968
Murder scholastic. Doubleday, 1968;
UK: Bles, 1967
Perturbing spirit. Doubleday, 1966;
UK: Bles, 1966
The shrouded way. Doubleday, 1973

CAIRNS, ALISON
Strained relations. St. Martin's,
1984; Toby Wilde

CAIRNS, CICELY
Murder goes to press. Macmillan,
1951; UK: Constable, 1950

CALVIN, HENRY
It's different abroad. Harper,
1963; UK: Hutchinson, 1963

CAMERON, OWEN, 1905 --
The butcher's wife. Simon &
Schuster, 1954; UK: Hammond, 1955
Catch a tiger. Simon & Schuster,
1952; UK: Hammond, 1954; Jake
Brown
The owl and the pussycat. Harper,
1949

CAMPBELL, D. FREDERICK, see
KEIRSTEAD, B. S.

CAMPBELL, GABRIELLE MARGARET VERE,
see SHEARING, JOSEPH (pseud.)

CAMPBELL, MARY ELIZABETH, 1903 --
Scandal has two faces. Doubleday,
1943; Matthew Craig

CAMPBELL, R. T. (pseud. of Ruthven
Todd, 1914 --)
Adventures with a goat. UK:
Westhouse, 1946; John Stubbs #2
Bodies in a bookshop. UK:
Westhouse, 1946; John Stubbs #3
The death cap. UK: Westhouse,
1946; John Stubbs #4
Death for madame. UK: Westhouse,
1946; John Stubbs #5
Swing low, sweet death. UK:
Westhouse, 1946; John Stubbs #6
Take thee a sharp knife. UK:
Westhouse, 1946; John Stubbs #7
Unholy dying. UK: Westhouse, 1945;
John Stubbs #1

CANADAY, JOHN, see HEAD, MATTHEW
(pseud.)

CANDY, EDWARD (pseud. of Barbara
Alison Neville [nee Boodson]
1925 --)
Bones of contention. Doubleday,
1983; UK: Gollancz, 1954; Insp.
Burnival #2
Which doctor? Rinehart, 1954; UK:
Gollancz, 1953; Insp. Burnival #1
Words for murder, perhaps.
Doubleday, 1984; UK: Gollancz,
1971; Insp. Burnival #3

CANNAN, JOANNA, 1898-1961
All is discovered. UK: Gollancz,
1962; Ronald Price #5
And be a villain. UK: Gollancz,
1958; Ronald Price #4
Body in the beck. UK: Gollancz,
1952; Ronald Price #2
Death at the Dog. Reynal, 1941;
UK: Gollancz, 1940; Guy Northeast
#2
Long shadows. UK: Gollancz, 1955;
Ronald Price #3
Poisonous relations. Morrow, 1950;
UK: Murder included. Gollancz,
1950; Ronald Price #1
They rang up the police. UK:
Gollancz, 1939; Guy Northeast #1

CANNELL, DOROTHY
The thin woman. St. Martin's, 1984;
Ellie Simmon
CANNING, VICTOR, 1911 --
Doubled in diamonds. Morrow, 1967;
UK: Heinemann, 1966
The finger of Saturn. Morrow, 1974;
UK: Heinemann, 1973; Robert Rolt
CAPON, PAUL, 1912-1969
Image of murder. UK: Boardman,
1949; Arnold Wragge
CAPUTI, ANTHONY
Storms and son. Atheneum, 1985;
Hugh Storm
CAREY, BERNICE, 1910 --
Their nearest and dearest.
Doubleday, 1953
CAREY, ELIZABETH, see MAGOON, CAREY
(pseud.)
CARGILL, LESLIE
Death goes by bus. UK: Jenkins,
1936; Morrison Sharpe
The lady was elusive. UK: Jenkins,
1952
Matrimony most dangerous. Roy,
1958; UK: Jenkins, 1949
CARKEET, DAVID, 1946 --
Double negative. Dial, 1980; Jeremy
Cook
CARLETON, MARJORIE, 1894-1964
Vanished. Morrow, 1955
CARMICHAEL, HARRY (pseud. of Leopold
Horace Ognall, 1908-1979)
Alibi. Macmillan, 1962; UK: Collins,
1961; John Piper #14; Quinn #11
Candles for the dead. Saturday
Review Press, 1976; UK: Collins,
1973; John Piper #27; Quinn #25
The dead of night. UK: Collins,
1956; John Piper #9; Quinn #6
The deadly night-cap. UK: Collins,
1953; John Piper #3; Quinn #2
Death leaves a diary. UK: Collins,
1952; John Piper #1; Quinn #1
Death trap. McCall, 1971; UK:
Collins, 1970; John Piper #22;
Quinn #20
Emergency exit. UK: Collins, 1957;
John Piper #10
Into thin air. Doubleday, 1958; UK:
Put out that star. Collins, 1957;
John Piper #11; Quinn #7
Justice enough. UK: Collins, 1956;
John Piper #8

The late unlamented. Doubleday,
1961; UK: Requiem for Charles.
Collins, 1960; Quinn #10
Marked man. Doubleday, 1959; UK:
Stranglehold. Collins, 1959; John
Piper #13; Quinn #9
Money for murder. UK: Collins,
1955; John Piper #7; Quinn #5
Most deadly hate. Saturday Review
Press, 1974; UK: Collins, 1971;
John Piper #23; Quinn #21
The motive. Dutton, 1977; UK:
Collins, 1974; John Piper #28;
Quinn #26
Murder by proxy. UK: Collins,
1967; John Piper #20; Quinn #17
Naked to the grave. Saturday
Review Press, 1973; UK: Collins,
1972; John Piper #25; Quinn #23
Noose for a lady. UK: Collins,
1955; John Piper #6; Quinn #4
Of unsound mind. Doubleday, 1962;
UK: Collins, 1962; John Piper
#15; Quinn #12
...or be he dead. Doubleday, 1958;
UK: Collins, 1959; John Piper
#12; Quinn #8
Post mortem. Doubleday, 1966; UK:
Collins, 1965; John Piper #18;
Quinn #15
The quiet women. Saturday Review
Press, 1972; UK: Collins, 1971;
John Piper #24; Quinn #22
Remote control. McCall, 1971; UK:
Collins, 1970; John Piper #21;
Quinn #19
Safe secret. Macmillan, 1965; UK:
Collins, 1964; John Piper #17;
Quinn #14
School for murder. UK: Collins,
1953; John Piper #4
The screaming rabbit. Simon &
Schuster, 1955; UK: Death counts
three. Collins, 1954; John Piper
#5
A slightly bitter taste. UK:
Collins, 1968; Quinn #18
Suicide clause. UK: Collins, 1966;
John Piper #19; Quinn #16
Too late for tears. Saturday
Review Press, 1975; UK: Collins,
1973; John Piper #26; Quinn #24
The vanishing trick. UK: Collins,
1952; John Piper #2

Vendetta. Macmillan, 1963; UK: Collins, 1963; John Piper #16; Quinn #13

Why kill Johnny? UK: Collins, 1954; John Piper #6; Quinn #3

CARNAC, CAROL (pseud. of Edith Caroline Rivett, 1894-1958)

Affair at Helen's Court. Doubleday, 1958; UK: Long shadows. Collins, 1958; Julian Rivers #14

The case of the first-class carriage. UK: Davies, 1939; Insp. Ryvet #3

Clue sinister. UK: Macdonald, 1947; Julian Rivers #3

Copy for crime. Doubleday, 1951; UK: Macdonald, 1950; Julian Rivers #6

Crossed skies. UK: Collins, 1952; Julian Rivers #8

Death in the diving pool. UK: Davies, 1940; Insp. Ryvet #7

A double for detection. UK: Macdonald, 1945; Julian Rivers #1

Impact of evidence. Doubleday, 1954; UK: Collins, 1954; Julian Rivers #11

It's her own funeral. Doubleday, 1952; UK: Collins, 1951; Julian Rivers #7

The missing rope. UK: Skeffington, 1937; Insp. Ryvet #1

Murder among members. UK: Collins, 1955; Julian Rivers #12

Murder as a fine art. UK: Collins, 1953; Julian Rivers #9

Over the garden wall. Doubleday, 1949; UK: Macdonald, 1948; Julian Rivers #4

A policeman at the door. Doubleday, 1954; UK: Collins, 1953; Julian Rivers #10

Rigging the evidence. UK: Collins, 1955; Julian Rivers #13

The striped suitcase. Doubleday, 1947; UK: Macdonald, 1946; Julian Rivers #2

Upstairs and downstairs. Doubleday, 1950; UK: Upstairs, downstairs. Macdonald, 1950; Julian Rivers #5

When the devil was sick. UK: Davies, 1939; Insp. Ryvet #2

CARNAHAN, WALTER, 1891 --

Hoffman's row. Bobbs, 1963; Abraham Lincoln

CARNEY, WILLIAM

The rose exterminator. Everest House, 1982

CARR, A. H. Z., 1902-1971

Finding Maubee. Putnam, 1970; UK: The Calypso murders. Hale, 1973; Xavier Brooke #1

CARR, GLYN (pseud. of Frank Showell Styles). For other mysteries by this author, see STYLES, SHOWELL

A corpse at Camp Two. UK: Bles, 1954; Abercrombie Lewker #8

The corpse in the crevasse. UK: Bles, 1952; Abercrombie Lewker #6

Death finds a foothold. UK: Bles, 1961; Abercrombie Lewker #13

Death of a weirdy. UK: Bles, 1965; Abercrombie Lewker #15

Death on Milestone Buttress. UK: Bles, 1951; Abercrombie Lewker #3

Death under Snowdon. UK: Bles, 1954; Abercrombie Lewker #7

Fat man's agony. UK: Bles, 1969; Abercrombie Lewker #17

Holiday with murder. UK: Bles, 1960; Abercrombie Lewker #12

The ice axe murders. UK: Bles, 1958; Abercrombie Lewker #10

Lewker in Norway. UK: Bles, 1963; Abercrombie Lewker #14

Lewker in Tirol. UK: Bles, 1967; Abercrombie Lewker #16

Murder of an owl. UK: Bles, 1956; Abercrombie Lewker #9

Murder on the Matterhorn. Dutton, 1953; UK: Bles, 1951; Abercrombie Lewker #4

Swing away, climber. Washburn, 1959; UK: Bles, 1956; Abercrombie Lewker #11

Traitor's Mountain. Macmillan, 1946; UK: Selwyn, 1945; Abercrombie Lewker #1

The youth hostel murders. Dutton, 1953; UK: Bles, 1952; Abercrombie Lewker #5

CARR, JESS

Murder on the Appalachian Trail. Commonwealth Press, 1985

CARR, JOHN DICKSON, 1906-1977. For other mysteries by this author, see DICKSON, CARTER (pseud.); DOYLE, ADRIAN CONAN

The Arabian Nights murder. Harper, 1936; UK: Hamilton, 1936; Gideon Fell #7

Below suspicion. Harper, 1949; UK: Hamilton, 1950; Gideon Fell #20; Patrick Butler #1

The blind barber. Harper, 1934; UK: Hamilton, 1934; Gideon Fell #3

The burning court. Harper, 1937; UK: Hamilton, 1937

The case of constant suicides. Harper, 1941; UK: Hamilton, 1941; Gideon Fell #13

Castle Skull. Harper, 1931; UK: Severn, 1976; Henri Bencolin #2; Jeff Marle

The corpse in the wax works. Harper, 1932; UK: The wax works murder. Hamilton, 1932; Henri Bencolin #4; Jeff Marle

The crooked hinge. Harper, 1938; UK: Hamilton, 1938; Gideon Fell #9

Dark of the moon. Harper, 1967; UK: Hamilton, 1968; Gideon Fell #24

The dead man's knock. Harper, 1948; UK: Hamilton, 1958; Gideon Fell #19

Death turns the tables. Harper, 1941; UK: Hamilton, 1942; Gideon Fell #14

Death-watch. Harper, 1935; UK: Hamilton, 1935; Gideon Fell #5

The devil in velvet. Harper, 1951; UK: Hamilton, 1951; Nicholas Fenton

Dr. Fell, detective, and other stories. Spivak, 1947; Gideon Fell #18

The eight of swords. Harper, 1934; UK: Hamilton, 1934; Gideon Fell #4

Fire, burn! Harper, 1957; UK: Hamilton, 1957

The four false weapons. Harper, 1937; UK: Hamilton, 1938; Henri Bencolin #5

The ghosts' high noon. Harper, 1969; UK: Hamilton, 1970; Jim Blake

Hag's nook. Harper, 1933; UK: Hamilton, 1933; Gideon Fell #1

He who whispers. Harper, 1946; UK: Hamilton, 1946; Gideon Fell #16

The house at Satan's Elbow. Harper, 1965; UK: Hamilton, 1965; Gideon Fell #22

The hungry goblin. Harper, 1972; UK: Hamilton, 1972; Wilkie Collins

In spite of thunder. Harper, 1960; UK: Hamilton, 1960; Gideon Fell #21

It walks by night. Harper, 1930; UK: Harper, 1930; Henri Bencolin #1

The lost gallows. Harper, 1931; UK: Harper, 1931; Henri Bencolin #3

The mad hatter mystery. Harper, 1933; UK: Hamilton, 1933; Gideon Fell #2

The man who could not shudder. Harper, 1940; UK: Hamilton, 1940; Gideon Fell #12

Panic in Box C. Harper, 1966; UK: Hamilton, 1966; Gideon Fell #23

Papa La-bas. Harper, 1968; UK: Hamilton, 1969

Patrick Butler for the defense. Harper, 1956; UK: Hamilton, 1956; Patrick Butler #2

The problem of the green capsule. Harper, 1939; UK: The black spectacles. Hamilton, 1939; Gideon Fell #10

The problem of the wire cage. Harper, 1939; UK: Hamilton, 1940; Gideon Fell #11

Scandal at High Chimneys. Harper, 1959; UK: Hamilton, 1959

The sleeping sphinx. Harper, 1947; UK: Hamilton, 1947; Gideon Fell #17

The three coffins. Harper, 1935; UK: The hollow man. Hamilton, 1935; Gideon Fell #6

Till death do us part. Harper, 1944; UK: Hamilton, 1944; Gideon Fell #15

To wake the dead. Harper, 1938; UK: Hamilton, 1938; Gideon Fell #8

CARROLL, JOY
Babykiller. Paperjacks, 1985

CARTER, YOUNGMAN, 1904-1969
Mr. Campion's farthing. Morrow, 1969; UK: Heinemann, 1969; Albert Campion #21

Mr. Campion's quarry. Morrow, 1971;
UK: Mr. Campion's falcon.
Heinemann, 1970; Albert Campion
#22

CARVIC, HERON
Miss Seeton draws the line. Harper,
1970; UK: Bles, 1969; Emily Seeton
#2
Miss Seeton sings. Harper, 1973;
UK: Davies, 1974; Emily Seeton #4
Odds on Miss Seeton. Harper, 1975;
UK: Davies, 1976; Emily Seeton #5
Picture Miss Seeton. Harper, 1968;
UK: Bles, 1968; Emily Seeton #1
Witch Miss Seeton. Harper, 1971;
UK: Miss Seeton bewitched. Bles,
1971; Emily Seeton #3

CASBERG, MELVIN A.
Dowry of death. Strawberry Hill,
1984; Prem Narayan

CASEY, ROBERT A.
The Jesus man. Evans, 1979

CASPARY, VERA, 1899 --
Evvie. Harper, 1960; UK: Allen, 1960
False face. UK: Allen, 1954
The man who loved his wife. Putnam,
1966; UK: Allen, 1966

CASTOIRE, MARIE and POSNER, RICHARD
Gold shield. Putnam, 1982; Vickie
Curran

CATALAN, HENRI (pseud. of Henri
Dupuy-Mazuel, 1885 --)
Soeur Angele and the bell ringer's
niece. UK: Sheed, 1957; Soeur
Angele
Soeur Angele and the embarrassed
ladies. UK: Sheed, 1955; Soeur
Angele
Soeur Angele and the ghost of
Chambord. UK: Sheed, 1956; Soeur
Angele

CAUDWELL, SARAH
The shortest way to Hades.
Scribner's, 1985
Thus was Adonis murdered.
Scribner's, 1981; Hilary Tamar

CAUNITZ, WILLIAM
One Police Plaza. Crown, 1984;
David Malone

CECIL, HENRY (pseud. of Henry Cecil
Leon, 1902-1976)
According to the evidence. Harper,
1954; UK: Chapman, 1954; Ambrose
Low #2; Col. Brain #3

Brothers in law. Harper, 1955; UK:
Joseph, 1955; Roger Thursby #1
Friends at court. Harper, 1956;
UK: Joseph, 1956; Roger Thursby
#2
The long arm. Harper, 1957; UK:
Much in evidence. Joseph, 1957;
Rosamond Clinch
Natural causes. UK: Chapman, 1953;
Col. Brain #2
No bail for the judge. UK: Chapman,
1952; Ambrose Low #1; Col. Brain
#1
Settled out of court. Harper,
1959; UK: Joseph, 1959
Sober as a judge. Harper, 1958;
UK: Joseph, 1958; Roger Thursby
#3
Unlawful occasions. British Book
Centre, 1974; UK: Joseph, 1962
A woman named Anne. Harper, 1967;
UK: Joseph, 1967

CHABER, M. E. (pseud.). For other
mysteries by this author, see
MONIG, CHRISTOPHER (pseud.) or
FOSTER, RICHARD (pseud.)
As old as Cain. Holt, 1954; Milo
March #3
The bonded dead. Holt, 1971; UK:
Hale, 1973; Milo March #20
Born to be hanged. Holt, 1973;
Milo March #21
The day it rained diamonds. Holt,
1966; UK: Macdonald, 1968; Milo
March #15
The flaming man. Holt, 1969; UK:
Hale, 1970; Milo March #18
The gallows garden. Holt, 1958;
UK: Boardman, 1958; Milo March #7
Green grow the graves. Holt, 1970;
UK: Hale, 1971; Milo March #19
Hangman's harvest. Holt, 1952;
Milo March #1
A hearse of a different color.
Holt, 1958; UK: Boardman, 1959;
Milo March #8
Jade for a lady. Holt, 1962; UK:
Boardman, 1962; Milo March #10
A lonely walk. Holt, 1956; UK:
Boardman, 1957; Milo March #6
A man in the middle. Holt, 1967;
Milo March #16
The man inside. Holt, 1954; UK:
Eyre, 1955; Milo March #4

No grave for March. Holt, 1953; UK:
  Eyre, 1954; Milo March #2
Six who ran. Holt, 1964; UK:
  Boardman, 1965; Milo March #12
So dead the rose. Holt, 1959; UK:
  Boardman, 1960; Milo March #9
Softly in the night. Holt, 1963;
  UK: Boardman, 1963; Milo March #11
The splintered man. Holt, 1955; UK:
  Boardman, 1957; Milo March #5
Uneasy lie the dead. Holt, 1964;
  UK: Boardman, 1964; Milo March #13
Wanted: dead men. Holt, 1965; UK:
  Boardman, 1966; Milo March #14
Wild midnight falls. Holt, 1968;
  Milo March #17
CHAIS, PAMELA
  Final cut. Simon & Schuster, 1981;
  Bud Bacola
CHALMERS, STEPHEN, 1880-1935
  The crime in Car 13. Doubleday,
  1930
CHALONER, JOHN
  Battorn line. St. Martin's, 1984
CHAMBERS, PETE (pseud. of Dennis
  Phillips, 1924 --)
  Murder is for keeps.
    Abelard-Schuman, 1962; UK: Hale,
    1961; Mark Peterson
CHANDLER, RAYMOND, 1888-1959
  The big sleep. Knopf, 1939; UK:
    Hamilton, 1939; Philip Marlowe #1
  Farewell, my lovely. Knopf, 1940;
    UK: Hamilton, 1940; Philip Marlowe
    #2
  The high window. Knopf, 1942; UK:
    Hamilton, 1943; Philip Marlowe #3
  The lady in the lake. Knopf, 1943;
    UK: Hamilton, 1944; Philip Marlowe
    #4
  Little sister. Houghton, 1949; UK:
    Hamilton, 1949; Philip Marlowe #5
  The long goodbye. Houghton, 1953;
    UK: Hamilton, 1953; Philip Marlowe
    #7
  Playback. Houghton, 1958; UK:
    Hamilton, 1958; Philip Marlowe #8
  Poodle Springs. Houghton, 1962;
    Philip Marlowe #9
  The simple art of murder. Houghton,
    1950; UK: Hamilton, 1950; Philip
    Marlowe #6

CHAPMAN, RAYMOND, see NASH, SIMON
  (pseud.)
CHASTAIN, THOMAS
  The diamond exchange. Doubleday,
    1981; Max Kauffman
  High voltage. Doubleday, 1979; UK:
    Hale, 1980; Max Kauffman
  Nightscape. Atheneum, 1982; Lilia
    Beddoes
  911. Mason/Charter, 1976; UK: The
    Christmas bomber. Cassell, 1976;
    Max Kauffman
  Pandora's box. Mason/Charter,
    1974; UK: Cassell, 1975; Max
    Kauffman
  Spanner. Mason/Charter, 1977; Max
    Kauffman; J. T. Spanner
  Vital statistics. Times Books,
    1977; J. T. Spanner
CHAZE, ELLIOTT
  Goodbye Goliath. Scribner's, 1983
  Little David. Scribner's, 1985;
    Kiel St. James
  Mr. Yesterday. Scribner's, 1984;
    Kiel St. James
CHERNYONOK, MIKHAIL
  Losing bet. Doubleday, 1984; Anton
    Birukov
CHESBRO, GEORGE C., 1940 --
  An affair of sorcerers. Simon &
    Schuster, 1979; UK: Severn, 1980;
    Robert "Mongo" Frederickson #3
  City of whispering stone. Simon &
    Schuster, 1978; UK: Severn, 1981;
    Robert "Mongo" Frederickson #2
  Shadow of a broken man. Simon &
    Schuster, 1977; UK: Severn, 1981;
    Robert "Mongo" Frederickson #1
CHESTERTON, G. K., 1874-1936
  Father Brown mystery stories.
    Dodd, 1962; Father Brown
  The Father Brown omnibus. Dodd,
    1935; Father Brown
  The incredulity of Father Brown.
    Dodd, 1926; UK: Cassell, 1926;
    Father Brown #3
  The innocence of Father Brown.
    Lane, 1911; UK: Cassell, 1911;
    Father Brown #1
  The poet and the lunatics. Dodd,
    1929; UK: Cassell, 1929; Gale
    Gabriel

The scandal of Father Brown. Dodd, 1935; UK: Cassell, 1935; Father Brown #5

The secret of Father Brown. Harper, 1922; UK: Cassell, 1927; Father Brown #4

The wisdom of Father Brown. Lane, 1915; UK: Cassell, 1914; Father Brown #2

CHEYNEY, PETER, 1896-1951

Callaghan. Belmont, 1973; UK: Dangerous curves. Collins, 1939; Slim Callaghan #2

Calling Mr. Callaghan. UK: Todd, 1953; Slim Callaghan #10

Can ladies kill? UK: Collins, 1938; Lemmy Caution #4

Dames don't care. Coward McCann, 1938; UK: Collins, 1937; Lemmy Caution #3

Don't get me wrong. UK: Collins, 1939; Lemmy Caution #5

Farewell to the admiral. Dodd, 1943; UK: Sorry you've been troubled. Collins, 1942; Slim Callaghan #6

I'll say she does! Dodd, 1946; UK: Collins, 1945; Lemmy Caution #11

It couldn't matter less. Arcadia House, 1943; UK: Collins, 1941; Slim Callaghan #4

Ladies won't wait. Dodd, 1951; UK: Collins, 1951; Michael Kells #2

Mr. Caution--Mr. Callaghan. UK: Collins, 1941; Slim Callaghan #5; Lemmy Caution #8

Never a dull moment. UK: Collins, 1942; Lemmy Caution #9

Poison ivy. UK: Collins, 1937; Lemmy Caution #2

Sinister errand. Dodd, 1945; UK: Collins, 1945; Michael Kells #1

They never say when. Dodd, 1945; UK: Collins, 1944; Slim Callaghan #8

This man is dangerous. Coward McCann, 1938; UK: Collins, 1936; Lemmy Caution #1

Time for Caution. Hounslow, Middlesex: Foster, 1946; Lemmy Caution #12

Uneasy terms. Dodd, 1947; UK: Collins, 1946; Slim Callaghan #9

The unscrupulous Mr. Callaghan. Handi-Books, 1943; Slim Callaghan #7

The urgent hangman. Coward McCann, 1939; UK: Collins, 1938; Slim Callaghan #1

You can always duck. UK: Collins, 1943; Lemmy Caution #10

You can't keep the change. Dodd, 1944; UK: Collins, 1940; Slim Callaghan #3

You'd be surprised. UK: Collins, 1940; Lemmy Caution #6

Your deal, my lovely. UK: Collins, 1941; Lemmy Caution #7

CHILDS, TIMOTHY, 1941 --

Cold turkey. Harper, 1979; UK: Hale, 1981; Peter Stokes

CHRISTIE, AGATHA, 1890-1976

The ABC murders. Dodd, 1936; UK: Collins, 1936; Hercule Poirot #12

The adventure of the Christmas pudding. UK: Collins, 1960; Hercule Poirot #36; Jane Marple #11

And then there were none. Dodd, 1940; UK: Ten little Niggers. UK: Collins, 1939

Appointment with death. Dodd, 1938; UK: Collins, 1938; Hercule Poirot #18

At Bertram's Hotel. Dodd, 1966; UK: Collins, 1965; Jane Marple #15

The big four. Dodd, 1927; UK: Collins, 1927; Hercule Poirot #5

The body in the library. Dodd, 1942; UK: Collins, 1942; Jane Marple #4

By the pricking of my thumbs. Dodd, 1968; UK: Collins, 1968; Tuppence Beresford #4; Tommy Beresford #4

Cards on the table. Dodd, 1936; UK: Collins, 1936; Hercule Poirot #14; Ariadne Oliver; Supt. Battle

A Caribbean mystery. Dodd, 1965; UK: Collins, 1964; Jane Marple #14

Cat among pigeons. Dodd, 1959; UK: Collins, 1959; Hercule Poirot #35

The clocks. Dodd, 1963; UK: Collins, 1963; Hercule Poirot #38

The crooked house. Dodd, 1949; UK:
Collins, 1949; Insp. Taverner

Curtain. Dodd, 1975; UK: Collins,
1975; Hercule Poirot #43

Dead man's folly. Dodd, 1956; UK:
Collins, 1956; Hercule Poirot #34;
Ariadne Oliver

Dead man's mirror. Dodd, 1937; UK:
Murder in the news. Collins, 1937;
Hercule Poirot #16

Death comes as the end. Dodd, 1944;
UK: Collins, 1945

Death in the air. Dodd, 1935; UK:
Death in the clouds. Collins,
1935; Hercule Poirot #11

Death on the Nile. Dodd, 1938; UK:
Collins, 1937; Hercule Poirot #17

Double sin. Dodd, 1961; Hercule
Poirot #37; Jane Marple #12

Easy to kill. Dodd, 1939; UK:
Murder is easy. Collins, 1939;
Luke Fitzwilliams; Supt. Battle #3

Elephants can remember. Dodd, 1972;
UK: Collins, 1972; Hercule Poirot
#41; Ariadne Oliver

Evil under the sun. Dodd, 1941; UK:
Collins, 1941; Hercule Poirot #23

Funerals are fatal. Dodd, 1953; UK:
After the funeral. Collins, 1953;
Hercule Poirot #32

Hallowe'en party. Dodd, 1969; UK:
Collins, 1969; Hercule Poirot #40;
Ariadne Oliver

Hercule Poirot's casebook. Dodd,
1984; Hercule Poirot

Hercule Poirot's early cases. Dodd,
1974; UK: Poirot's early cases.
Collins, 1974; Hercule Poirot #42

Hickory, dickory, death. Dodd,
1955; UK: Hickory Dickory Dock.
Collins, 1955; Hercule Poirot #33

The Hollow. Dodd, 1946; UK: Collins,
1946; Hercule Poirot #25

The Labours of Hercules. Dodd,
1947; UK: Collins, 1947; Hercule
Poirot #26

The man in the brown suit. Dodd,
1924; UK: Lane, 1924; Col. Race

The mirror crack'd. Dodd, 1963; UK:
The mirror crack'd from side to
side. Collins, 1962; Jane Marple
#13

Miss Marple: the complete short
stories. Dodd, 1985; Jane Marple

Miss Marple's final cases. UK:
Collins, 1979; Jane Marple

Mr. Parker Pyne, detective. Dodd,
1934; UK: Parker Pyne
investigates. Collins, 1934;
Ariadne Oliver; Parker Pyne

The moving finger. Dodd, 1942; UK:
Collins, 1943; Jane Marple #5

Mrs. McGinty's dead. Dodd, 1952;
UK: Collins, 1952; Hercule Poirot
#31; Ariadne Oliver

Murder at Hazelmoor. Dodd, 1931;
UK: The Sittaford mystery.
Collins, 1931; Insp. Warracott

The murder at the vicarage. Dodd,
1930; UK: Collins, 1930; Jane
Marple #1

Murder for Christmas. Dodd, 1938;
UK: Hercule Poirot's Christmas.
Collins, 1938; Hercule Poirot #19

Murder in Mesopotamia. Dodd, 1936;
UK: Collins, 1936; Hercule Poirot
#13

Murder in retrospect. Dodd, 1942;
UK: Five little pigs. Collins,
1943; Hercule Poirot #24

Murder in three acts. Dodd, 1934;
UK: Three act tragedy. Collins,
1935; Hercule Poirot #10

A murder is announced. Dodd, 1950;
UK: Collins, 1950; Jane Marple #7

The murder of Roger Ackroyd. Dodd,
1926; UK: Collins, 1926; Hercule
Poirot #4

Murder on the links. Dodd, 1923;
UK: Lane, 1923; Hercule Poirot #2

Murder on the Orient Express.
Dodd, 1934; UK: Collins, 1934;
Hercule Poirot #9

Murder with mirrors. Dodd, 1952;
UK: They do it with mirrors.
Collins, 1952; Jane Marple #8

The mysterious affair at Styles.
Grosset, 1920; UK: Lane, 1920;
Hercule Poirot #1

The mysterious Mr. Quin. Dodd,
1930; UK: Collins, 1930; Harley
Quin

The mystery of the blue train.
Dodd, 1928; UK: Collins, 1928;
Hercule Poirot #6

N or M? Dodd, 1944; UK: Collins,
1944; Tommy Beresford #3;
Tuppence Beresford #3

Nemesis. Dodd, 1971; UK: Collins, 1971; Jane Marple #16

Ordeal by innocence. Dodd, 1958; UK: Collins, 1958; Supt. Huish

The pale horse. Dodd, 1967; UK: Collins, 1961; Ariadne Oliver

Partners in crime. Dodd, 1929; UK: Collins, 1929; Tuppence Beresford #2; Tommy Beresford #2

The patriotic murders. Dodd, 1940; UK: One, two, buckle my shoe. Collins, 1940; Hercule Poirot #22

Peril at End House. Dodd, 1932; UK: Collins, 1932; Hercule Poirot #7

A pocket full of rye. Dodd, 1954; UK: Collins, 1953; Jane Marple #9

Poirot investigates. Dodd, 1925; UK: Lane, 1924; Hercule Poirot #3

Poirot loses a client. Dodd, 1937; UK: Dumb witness. Collins, 1937; Hercule Poirot #15

Postern of fate. Dodd, 1973; UK: Collins, 1973; Tuppence Beresford #5; Tommy Beresford #5

The regatta mystery. Dodd, 1939; Hercule Poirot #20; Jane Marple #3; Parker Pyne

Remembered death. Dodd, 1945; UK: Sparkling cyanide. Collins, 1945; Col. Race

Sad cypress. Dodd, 1940; UK: Collins, 1940; Hercule Poirot #21

The secret adversary. Dodd, 1922; UK: Lane, 1922; Tuppence Beresford; Tuppence Cowley #1; Tommy Beresford #1

The secret of Chimneys. Dodd, 1925; UK: Lane, 1925; Supt. Battle #1

The seven dials mystery. Dodd, 1929; UK: Collins, 1929; Supt. Battle

Sleeping murder. Dodd, 1976; UK: Collins, 1976; Jane Marple #17

So many steps to death. Dodd, 1955; UK: Destination unknown. Collins, 1954

There is a tide... Dodd, 1948; UK: Taken at the flood. Collins, 1948; Hercule Poirot #27

They came to Baghdad. Dodd, 1951; UK: Collins, 1951

Third girl. Dodd, 1967; UK: Collins, 1966; Hercule Poirot #39; Ariadne Oliver

Thirteen at dinner. Dodd, 1933; UK: Lord Edgeware dies. Collins, 1933; Hercule Poirot #8

Three blind mice. Dodd, 1950; Hercule Poirot #29; Jane Marple #6; Harley Quin

Towards zero. Dodd, 1944; UK: Collins, 1944; Supt. Battle #4

The Tuesday Club murders. Dodd, 1933; UK: Thirteen problems. Collins, 1932; Jane Marple #2

The under dog and other stories. Dodd, 1951; Hercule Poirot #30

What Mrs. McGillicuddy saw! Dodd, 1957; UK: 4:50 from Paddington. Collins, 1957; Jane Marple #10

Witness for the prosecution. Dodd, 1948; Hercule Poirot #28

CLARK, ALFRED ALEXANDER GORDON, see HARE, CYRIL (pseud.)

CLARK, DOUGLAS

Death after evensong. Stein & Day, 1970; UK: Cassell, 1969; Supt. Masters

Poacher's bag. UK: Gollancz, 1980; Supt. Masters; Insp. Green

Shelf life. Harper & Row, 1983; Supt. Masters; Insp. Green

CLARK, W. C., 1907 --

Murder goes to Bank Night. Hale, 1940; Chattin Whyte

CLARKE, ANNA

Game, set and danger. Doubleday, 1981; Helen Boyden

The lady in black. McKay, 1978; UK: Collins, 1977

Last judgement. Doubleday, 1985; Mary Morrison

The last voyage. St. Martin's, 1982; UK: Collins, 1976; Sally Livingstone

Letter from the dead. Doubleday, 1981; UK: Collins, 1977

One of us must die. Doubleday, 1980; UK: Collins, 1978

Plot counter-plot. Walker, 1975; UK: Collins, 1974

The poisoned web. St. Martin's, 1982; UK: Collins, 1979

Soon she must die. Doubleday, 1983

This downhill path. McKay, 1977; UK: The deathless and the dead. Collins, 1976

We the bereaved. Doubleday, 1983

CLARKE, T. E. B., 1907 --
  Murder at Buckingham Palace. St.
    Martin's, 1982; George V, King of
    England
CLASON, CLYDE B., 1903 --
  Blind drifts. Doubleday, 1937;
    Theocritus Lucius Westborough #3
  The death angel. Doubleday, 1936;
    UK: Heinemann, 1937; Theocritus
    Lucius Westborough #1
  Dragon's grave. Doubleday, 1939;
    UK: Heinemann, 1940; Theocritus
    Lucius Westborough #7
  The fifth tumbler. Doubleday, 1936;
    UK: Heinemann, 1937; Theocritus
    Lucius Westborough #2
  Green sliver. Doubleday, 1941; UK:
    Heinemann, 1948; Theocritus Lucius
    Westborough #10
  The man from Tibet. Doubleday,
    1938; UK: Heinemann, 1938;
    Theocritus Lucius Westborough
    #5
  Murder gone Minoan. Doubleday,
    1939; UK: Clue to the labyrinth.
    Heinemann, 1939; Theocritus Lucius
    Westborough #8
  Poison jasmine. Doubleday, 1940;
    Theocritus Lucius Westborough
    #9
  The purple parrot. Doubleday, 1937;
    UK: Heinemann, 1937; Theocritus
    Lucius Westborough #4
  The whispering ear. Doubleday,
    1938; UK: Heinemann, 1939;
    Theocritus Lucius Westborough
    #6
CLAYMORE, TOD (pseud. of Hugh
  Clevely)
  Appointment in New Orleans. UK:
    Cassell, 1950; Tod Claymore
  Dead men don't answer. UK: Cassell,
    1954; Tod Claymore
  Nest of vipers. UK: Cassell, 1948;
    Tod Claymore
  Rendezvous on an island. UK:
    Cassell, 1957; Tod Claymore
  Reunion in Florida. UK: Cassell,
    1952; Tod Claymore
  This is what happened. Simon &
    Schuster, 1939; UK: You remember
    the case. Nelson, 1939; Tod
    Claymore
CLAYTON, RICHARD HENRY MICHAEL, see
  HAGGARD, WILLIAM (pseud.)

CLEARY, JON, 1917 --
  Helga's web. Morrow, 1970; UK:
    Collins, 1970; Scobie Malone #2
  The high commissioner. Morrow,
    1966; UK: Collins, 1966; Scobie
    Malone #1
  Just let me be. UK: Laurie, 1950
  Justin Bayard. Morrow, 1956; UK:
    Collins, 1955
  The long pursuit. Morrow, 1967;
    UK: Collins, 1967
  Peter's pence. Morrow, 1974; UK:
    Collins, 1974
  Ransom. Morrow, 1973; UK: Collins,
    1973; Scobie Malone #3
  A sound of lightning. Morrow,
    1976; UK: Collins, 1976
  Vortex. Morrow, 1978; UK: Collins,
    1977; Jim McKechnie
CLEEVE, BRIAN, 1921 --
  Death of a painted lady. Random
    House, 1963; UK: Hammond, 1962
  Death of a wicked servant. Random
    House, 1964; UK: Hammond, 1963;
    Insp. O'Donovan
CLEMEAU, CARL
  The Ariadne clue. Scribner's, 1982
CLEMENTS, E. H., 1905 --
  The other island. UK: Hodder,
    1956; Allister Woodhead
  Perhaps a little danger. Dutton,
    1942; UK: Hodder, 1942
CLEVELY, HUGH, see CLAYMORE, TOD
  (pseud.)
CLINE, C. TERRY, JR., 1935 --
  Missing persons. Arbor House,
    1981; Joanne Fleming
CLINTON-BADDELEY, V. C., 1900-1970
  Death's bright dart. Morrow, 1970;
    UK: Gollancz, 1967; R. V. Davie
    #1
  My foe outstretch'd beneath the
    tree. Morrow, 1968; UK: Gollancz,
    1968; R. V. Davie #2
  No case for the police. Morrow,
    1970; UK: Gollancz, 1970; R. V.
    Davie #4
  Only a matter of time. Morrow,
    1970; UK: Gollancz, 1969; R. V.
    Davie #3
  To study a long silence. UK:
    Gollancz, 1972; R. V. Davie #5
CLOTHIER, PETER
  Chiaroscuro. St. Martin's, 1985;
    Jacob Molnar

CLOUSTON, J. STARER, 1870-1944
The lunatic at large. Appleton, 1900; UK: Blackwood, 1899; Francis Mandell-Essington

CLUTTON-BROCK, ALAN
Liberty Hall. Macmillan, 1941; UK: Lane, 1941

COBB, BELTON, see COBB, G. BELTON

COBB, G. BELTON, 1892-1971
Corpse at Casablanca. Abelard-Schuman, 1956; UK: Allen, 1956; Cheviot Burmann #17

COCHRAN, ALAN
Two plus two. Doubleday, 1980; Jason Price; Brooke Merit

CODY, LIZA
Bad company. Scribner's, 1983; Anna Lee
Dupe. Scribner's, 1981; UK: Collins, 1980; Anna Lee #1
Stalker. Scribner's, 1985; Anna Lee

COE, TUCKER (pseud. of Donald E. Westlake, 1933 --)
Don't lie to me. Random House, 1972; UK: Gollancz, 1974; Mitch Tobin #5
A jade in Aries. Random House, 1971; UK: Gollancz, 1973; Mitch Tobin #4
Kinds of love, kinds of death. Random House, 1966; UK: Souvenir, 1967; Mitch Tobin #1
Murder among children. Random House, 1968; UK: Souvenir, 1968; Mitch Tobin #2
Wax apple. Random House, 1970; UK: Gollancz, 1973; Mitch Tobin #3

COFFIN, GEOFFREY (pseud. of Mason F. VanWyck, 1901-1978) and BRAWNER, H.
The forgotten fleet mystery. Dodge, 1936; UK: Jarrolds, 1943; Scott Stuart #2
Murder in the Senate. Dodge, 1935; UK: Hurst, 1936; Scott Stuart #1

COHEN, ANTHEA
Angel without mercy. Doubleday, 1984

COHEN, OCTAVUS ROY, 1891-1959
The backstage mystery. Appleton, 1930; Jim Hanvey #3
Florian Slappey. Appleton, 1938; Florian Slappey #2
Florian Slappey goes abroad. Little, 1928; Florian Slappey #1

Gray dusk. Dodd, 1920; UK: Nash, 1920; David Carroll #1
Jim Hanvey, detective. Dodd, 1923; UK: Nash, 1924; Jim Hanvey #1
The May Day mystery. Appleton, 1929; Jim Hanvey #2
Midnight. Dodd, 1922; UK: Nash, 1922; David Carroll #3
Romance in crimson. Appleton, 1946
Six seconds of darkness. Dodd, 1921; UK: Nash, 1921; David Carroll #2

COHLER, DAVID KEITH, 1940 --
Freemartin. Little, 1981; Sam Knight
Gamemaker. Doubleday, 1980; Sam Knight

COKER, CAROLYN
The other David. Dodd, 1984; Andrea Perkins

COLE, G. D. H., 1889-1959
The Brooklyn murders. Seltzer, 1924; UK: Collins, 1923; Henry Wilson #1

COLE, G. D. H. and MARGARET
The Berkshire mystery. Brewer, 1930; UK: Burglars in bucks. Collins, 1930; Henry Wilson #7
Big business murder. Doubleday, 1935; UK: Collins, 1935; Henry Wilson #4
The Blatchington tangle. Macmillan, 1926; UK: Collins, 1926; Everard Blatchington #1; Henry Wilson #3
The brothers Sackville. Macmillan, 1937; UK: Collins, 1936; Henry Wilson #13; Insp. Fairford
Corpse in the constable's garden. Morrow, 1931; UK: Corpse in canonicals. Collins, 1930; Henry Wilson #8
Counterpoint murder. Macmillan, 1941; UK: Collins, 1940; Henry Wilson #19
Dead man's watch. Doubleday, 1932; UK: Collins, 1931
Death in the quarry. Doubleday, 1934; UK: Collins, 1934; Henry Wilson #12; Everard Blatchington #2
The death of a millionaire. Macmillan, 1925; UK: Collins, 1925; Henry Wilson #2

Dr. Tancred begins. Doubleday, 1935; UK: Collins, 1935; Dr. Tancred #1

Double blackmail. Macmillan, 1939; UK: Collins, 1939; Henry Wilson #15

End of an ancient mariner. Doubleday, 1934; UK: Collins, 1933; Henry Wilson #11

Greek tragedy. Macmillan, 1940; UK: Collins, 1939; Henry Wilson #16

A knife in the dark. Macmillan, 1942; UK: Collins, 1941; Elizabeth Warrender

Last will and testament. Doubleday, 1936; UK: Collins, 1936; Dr. Tancred #2

The man from the river. Macmillan, 1928; UK: Collins, 1928; Henry Wilson #4

The missing aunt. Macmillan, 1938; UK: Collins, 1937; Henry Wilson

Mrs. Warrender's profession. Macmillan, 1939; UK: Collins, 1938; Elizabeth Warrender; James Warrender

The murder at Crome House. Macmillan, 1927; UK: Collins, 1927; James Flint

The murder at the munition works. Macmillan, 1940; UK: Collins, 1940; Henry Wilson #17

Off with her head! Macmillan, 1939; UK: Collins, 1938; Insp. Fairford; Henry Wilson #14

Poison in a garden suburb. Payson and Clarke, 1929; UK: Poison in the garden suburb. Collins, 1929; Henry Wilson #6

The sleeping death. Doubleday, 1936; UK: Scandal at school. Collins, 1935; Everard Blatchington #3

Superintendent Wilson's cases. UK: Collins, 1933; Henry Wilson #10

Superintendent Wilson's holiday. Payson and Clarke, 1929; UK: Collins, 1928; Henry Wilson #5

Toper's end. Macmillan, 1942; UK: Collins, 1942; Henry Wilson #20

The walking corpse. Morrow, 1931; UK: The Great Southern mystery. Collins, 1931; Henry Wilson #9

Wilson and some others. UK: Collins, 1940; Henry Wilson #18

Wilson calling. UK: Vallencey, 1944; Henry Wilson #21

COLE, MARGARET, 1893-1980, see COLE, G. D. H. and MARGARET

COLIN, AUBREY
Death comes to dinner. UK: Hammond, 1965; Bill Burray
Hands of death. UK: Hammond, 1963; Bill Burray

COLIN, DEXTER
Service of all the dead. St. Martin's, 1979

COLLINS, MAX ALLEN, 1948 --
Bait money. Curtis, 1973; UK: New English Library, 1976; Frank Nolan
Blood money. Curtis, 1973; UK: New English Library, 1973; Frank Nolan
Kill your darlings. Walker, 1984; Mallory
No cure for death. Walker, 1983; Mallory
A shroud for Aquarius. Walker, 1985; Mallory
True crime. St. Martin's, 1985; Nathan Heller; John Dillinger
True detective. St. Martin's, 1983; Nathan Heller

COLLINS, MICHAEL (pseud. of Dennis Lynds, 1924 --). For other mysteries by this author, see ARDEN, WILLIAM (pseud.) or SADLER, MARK (pseud.)
Act of fear. Dodd, 1967; UK: Joseph, 1968; Dan Fortune #1
The blood-red dream. Dodd, 1976; UK: Hale, 1977; Dan Fortune #9
Blue death. Dodd, 1975; UK: Hale, 1976; Dan Fortune #8
The brass rainbow. Dodd, 1969; UK: Joseph, 1970; Dan Fortune #2
Freak. Dodd, 1983; Dan Fortune
Night of the toads. Dodd, 1970; UK: Hale, 1972; Dan Fortune #3
The night runners. Dodd, 1978; UK: Hale, 1979; Dan Fortune #10
Shadow of a tiger. Dodd, 1972; Dan Fortune #5
The silent scream. Dodd, 1973; UK: Hale, 1975; Dan Fortune #6
The slasher. Dodd, 1980; UK: Hale, 1981; Dan Fortune
Walk a black wind. Dodd, 1971; UK: Hale, 1973; Dan Fortune #4

Woman in marble. Bobbs, 1973; Dan
Fortune #7

COLLINS, RANDALL, 1941 --
The case of the philosopher's ring.
Crown, 1978; UK: Harvester, 1980;
Sherlock Holmes

COLLINS, WILKIE, 1824-1889
The moonstone. Harper, 1868; UK:
Tinsley, 1868; Sgt. Cuff
The queen of hearts. Harper, 1859;
UK: Hurst, 1859
The woman in white. Harper, 1860;
UK: Low, 1860

COMPTON, GUY, 1930 --
Disguise for a dead gentleman. UK:
Longman, 1964; Ben Anderson
Medium for murder. UK: Longman,
1963; Ben Anderson

CONNELL, RICHARD, 1893-1949
Murder at sea. Minton, 1929; UK:
Jarrolds, 1929

CONNINGTON, J. J. (pseud. of Alfred
Walter Stewart, 1880-1947)
The boat-house riddle. Little,
1931; UK: Gollancz, 1931; Clinton
Driffield #6
The Brandon case. Little, 1934; UK:
The ha-ha case. Hodder, 1934;
Clinton Driffield #9
The case with nine solutions.
Little, 1929; UK: Gollancz, 1928;
Clinton Driffield #3
The Castleford conundrum. Little,
1932; UK: Hodder, 1932; Clinton
Driffield #8
Common sense is all you need. UK:
Hodder, 1947; Clinton Driffield
#17
The counsellor. Little, 1939; UK:
Hodder, 1939; Mark Brand #1
The Dangerfield talisman. Little,
1927; UK: Benn, 1926; Conway
Westenhanger
The eye in the museum. Little,
1930; UK: Gollancz, 1929; Supt.
Ross #1
The four defenses. Little, 1940;
UK: The four defences. Hodder,
1940; Mark Brand #2
Gold brick island. Little, 1933;
UK: Tom Tiddler's island. Hodder,
1933
Grim vengeance. Little, 1929; UK:
Nemesis at Raynham Parva.

Gollancz, 1929; Clinton Driffield
#5
Jack-in-the-box. Little, 1944; UK:
Hodder, 1944; Clinton Driffield
#16
A minor operation. Little, 1937;
UK: Hodder, 1937; Clinton
Driffield #11
Murder in the maze. Little, 1927;
UK: Benn, 1927; Clinton Driffield
#1
Murder will speak. Little, 1938;
UK: For murder will speak.
Hodder, 1938; Clinton Driffield
#12
Mystery at Lynden Sands. Little,
1928; UK: Gollancz, 1928; Clinton
Driffield #4
No past is dead. Little, 1942; UK:
Hodder, 1942; Clinton Driffield
#15
The sweepstakes murders. Little,
1932; UK: Hodder, 1931; Clinton
Driffield #7
The tau cross mystery. Little,
1935; UK: In whose dim shadow.
Hodder, 1935; Clinton Driffield
#10
Tragedy at Ravensthorpe. Little,
1928; UK: Benn, 1927; Clinton
Driffield #2
Truth comes limping. Little, 1938;
UK: Hodder, 1938; Clinton
Driffield #13
The twenty-one clues. Little,
1941; UK: Hodder, 1941; Clinton
Driffield #14
The two-ticket puzzle. Little,
1930; UK: The two tickets puzzle.
Gollancz, 1930; Supt. Ross #2

CONSTANTINE, K. C.
Always a body to trade. Godine,
1983; Mario Balzac #6
The blank page. Saturday Review
Press, 1974; Mario Balzac #3
A fix like this. Saturday Review
Press, 1975; Mario Balzac #4
The man who liked slow tomatoes.
Godine, 1981; Mario Balzac #5
The man who liked to look at
himself. Saturday Review Press,
1973; Mario Balzac #2
The Rocksburg Railroad murders.
Saturday Review Press, 1972;
Mario Balzac #1

COOK, PETRONELLE MARGUERITE MARY, see
ARNOLD, MARGOT (pseud.)

COOK, THOMAS H.
Tabernacle. Houghton, 1983; Tom
Jackson

COOPER, BRIAN, 1919 --
Giselle. Vanguard, 1958; UK: A path
to the bridge. Heinemann, 1958;
Rod McKinnon
Monsoon murder. Vanguard, 1968; UK:
A mission for Betty Smith.
Heinemann, 1967; John Harrington
The murder of Mary Steers.
Vanguard, 1966; UK: Heinemann,
1965
A touch of thunder. Vanguard, 1962;
UK: Heinemann, 1961
The Van Langeren girl. Vanguard,
1960; UK: Heinemann, 1960

COPPER, BASIL
The dossier of Solar Pons.
Pinnacle, 1979; L. S. P. Books,
1980; Solar Pons #1
The further adventures of Solar
Pons. Pinnacle, 1979; L. S. P.
Books, 1980; Solar Pons #2
Necropolis. Arkham, 1980; UK:
Sphere, 1981; Clyde Beatty
The secret files of Solar Pons.
Pinnacle, 1979; Solar Pons
The uncollected cases of Solar
Pons. Pinnacle, 1980; Solar Pons

COPPLESTONE, BENNET (pseud. of
Frederick Harcourt Kitchin,
1867-1932)
The diversions of Dawson. Dutton,
1924; UK: Murray, 1923; William
Dawson
The lost naval papers. Dutton,
1917; UK: Murray, 1917; William
Dawson

CORBETT, ELIZABETH FRANCES
The house across the river. Reynal
& Hitchcock, 1934

CORBETT, JAMES
Murder minus motive. UK: Jenkins,
1943

CORES, LUCY, 1914 --
Corpse de ballet. Duell, 1944; UK:
Cassell, 1948; Andrew Torrent
Let's kill George. Duell, 1946; UK:
Cassell, 1950
Painted for the ball. Duell, 1943;
UK: Cassell, 1946; Andrew Torrent

CORY, DESMOND (pseud. of Shaun Lloyd
McCarthy, 1928 --)
Deadfall. Walker, 1965; UK:
Muller, 1965
The night hawk. Walker, 1969; UK:
Hodder, 1969

COTTRELL, DOROTHY
Silent reefs. Morrow, 1953

COUGHLIN, WILLIAM J., 1924 --
The stalking man. Delacorte, 1979;
UK: Magnum, 1981; Rony Russo

COULSON, JOHN HUBERT ARTHUR, see
BONETT, JOHN and EMERY

COX, ANTHONY BERKELEY, see BERKELEY,
ANTHONY (pseud.) or ILES, FRANCIS
(pseud.)

COXE, GEORGE HARMON, 1901 --
The Barotique mystery. Knopf,
1936; UK: Heinemann, 1937; Kent
Murdock #2
The big gamble. Knopf, 1958; UK:
Hammond, 1960; Kent Murdock #17
The camera clue. Knopf, 1937; UK:
Heinemann, 1938; Kent Murdock #3
The candid impostor. Knopf, 1967;
UK: Hale, 1969
The charred witness. Knopf, 1942;
UK: Swan, 1949; Kent Murdock #7
The crimson clue. Knopf, 1953; UK:
Hammond, 1955; Kent Murdock #14
Dangerous legacy. Knopf, 1946; UK:
Hammond, 1949; Spence Rankin
Deadly image. Knopf, 1964; UK:
Hammond, 1964; Flash Casey #6
Death at the Isthmus. Knopf, 1954;
UK: Hammond, 1956
Double identity. Knopf, 1970; UK:
Hale, 1971; Alan Carlisle
An easy way to go. Knopf, 1969;
UK: Hale, 1969; Kent Murdock #21
Error of judgement. Knopf, 1961;
UK: Hammond, 1962; Flash Casey #4
Eye witness. Knopf, 1950; UK:
Hammond, 1963; Kent Murdock #12
Fenner. Knopf, 1971; UK: Hale,
1973; Jack Fenner #2; Kent
Murdock #22
The fifth key. Knopf, 1947; UK:
Hammond, 1950; Kent Murdock #9
Flash Casey, photographer. Avon,
1946; Flash Casey #3
Focus on murder. Knopf, 1954; UK:
Hammond, 1956; Kent Murdock #15
Four frightened women.
Knopf, 1939; UK: The frightened

woman. Heinemann, 1939; Kent Murdock #4; Jack Fenner #1

The frightened fiancee. Knopf, 1950; UK: Hammond, 1953; Sam Crombie #1

The glass triangle. Knopf, 1940; Kent Murdock #5

The groom lay dead. Knopf, 1944; UK: Hammond, 1946

The hidden key. Knopf, 1963; UK: Hammond, 1964; Kent Murdock #19

The hollow needle. Knopf, 1948; UK: Hammond, 1951; Kent Murdock #10

The impetuous mistress. Knopf, 1958; UK: Hammond, 1959; Sam Crombie #2

Inland passage. Knopf, 1949; UK: Hammond, 1952

The inside man. Knopf, 1974; UK: Hale, 1975

The jade Venus. Knopf, 1945; UK: Hammond, 1947; Kent Murdock #8

The lady is afraid. Knopf, 1940; UK: Heinemann, 1940; Max Hale #2

Lady killer. Knopf, 1949; UK: Hammond, 1952; Kent Murdock #11

The last commandment. Knopf, 1960; UK: Hammond, 1961; Kent Murdock #18

Man on a rope. Knopf, 1956; UK: Hammond, 1958

The man who died too soon. Knopf, 1962; UK: Hammond, 1963; Flash Casey #5

The man who died twice. Knopf, 1951; UK: Hammond, 1954

Moment of violence. Knopf, 1961; UK: Hammond, 1962

Mrs. Murdock takes a case. Knopf, 1941; UK: Swan, 1949; Kent Murdock #6; Joyce Murdock

Murder for the asking. Knopf, 1939; UK: Hammond, 1940; Max Hale #1

Murder for two. Knopf, 1943; UK: Hammond, 1944; Flash Casey #2

Murder in Havana. Knopf, 1943; UK: Hammond, 1945

Murder on their minds. Knopf, 1957; UK: Hammond, 1958; Kent Murdock #16

Murder with pictures. Knopf, 1935; UK: Heinemann, 1937; Kent Murdock #1

Never bet your life. Knopf, 1952. UK: Hammond, 1955; Capt. Vaughn

No place for murder. Knopf, 1975; UK: Hale, 1976; Jack Fenner #4

One hour to kill. Knopf, 1963; UK: Hammond, 1964

One minute past eight. Knopf, 1957; UK: Hammond, 1959

One way out. Knopf, 1960; UK: Hammond, 1961

The reluctant heiress. Knopf, 1965; UK: Hammond, 1966; Kent Murdock #20

Silent are the dead. Knopf, 1942; Flash Casey #1

The silent witness. Knopf, 1973; UK: Hale, 1974; Jack Fenner #3

Uninvited guest. Knopf, 1953; UK: Hammond, 1956

The widow had a gun. Knopf, 1951; UK: Hammond, 1954; Kent Murdock #13

With intent to kill. Knopf, 1965; UK: Hammond, 1965

Woman at bay. Knopf, 1945; UK: Hammond, 1948

Woman with a gun. Knopf, 1972; UK: Hale, 1974

CRAIG, ALISA (pseud. of Charlotte MacLeod, 1922 --)

The grub and stakers move a mountain. Doubleday, 1981

A pint of murder. Doubleday, 1980; Modoc Rhys

The terrible tide. Doubleday, 1983; Holly Howe

CRAIG, JONATHAN (pseud. of Frank E. Smith, 1919 --)

The case of the beautiful body. Fawcett, 1957; UK: Fawcett, 1958; Pete Selby

CRAIG, M. S.

Gillean's chain. Dodd, 1983; Josh Walker

CRANE, CAROLINE, 1930 --

Coasts of fear. Dodd, 1980; UK: Hale, 1981; Jessica Hayden

The foretelling. Dodd, 1982

Trick or treat. Dodd, 1983; Brian Fresney

Woman vanishes. Dodd, 1984

CRANE, FRANCES, 1896 --

The amber eyes. Random House, 1962; UK: Hammond, 1962; Pat Abbott #25; Jean Abbott #25

The amethyst spectacles. Random
House, 1944; UK: Hammond, 1946;
Pat Abbott #6; Jean Abbott #6

The applegreen cat. Lippincott,
1943; UK: Hammond, 1945; Pat
Abbott #4; Jean Abbott #4

Black cypress. Random House, 1948;
UK: Hammond, 1950; Pat Abbott #11;
Jean Abbott #11

Body beneath a mandarin tree. UK:
Hammond, 1965; Pat Abbott #25;
Jean Abbott #26

The buttercup case. Random House,
1958; UK: Hammond, 1958; Pat
Abbott #22; Jean Abbott #22

The cinnamon murder. Random House,
1946; UK: Hammond, 1948; Pat
Abbott #8; Jean Abbott #8

The coral princess murders. Random
House, 1954; UK: Hammond, 1955;
Pat Abbott #18; Jean Abbott #18

The daffodil blonde. Random House,
1950; UK: Hammond, 1951; Pat
Abbott #13; Jean Abbott #13

Death in lilac time. Random House,
1955; UK: Hammond, 1955; Pat
Abbott #19; Jean Abbott #19

Death-wish green. Random House,
1960; UK: Hammond, 1960; Pat
Abbott #24; Jean Abbott #24

The flying red horse. Random House,
1949; UK: Hammond, 1949; Pat
Abbott #12; Jean Abbott #12

The golden box. Lippincott, 1942;
UK: Hammond, 1944; Pat Abbott #2;
Jean Abbott #2

Horror on the Ruby X. Random House,
1956; UK: Hammond, 1956; Pat
Abbott #20; Jean Abbott #20

The indigo necklace. Random House,
1945; UK: Hammond, 1947; Pat
Abbott #7; Jean Abbott #7

The man in gray. Random House,
1958; UK: The gray stranger.
Hammond, 1958; Pat Abbott #23;
Jean Abbott #23

Murder in Blue Street. Random
House, 1951; UK: Death in the blue
hour. Hammond, 1952; Pat Abbott
#14; Jean Abbott #14

Murder in bright red. Random House,
1953; UK: Hammond, 1954; Pat
Abbott #16; Jean Abbott #16

Murder on the purple water. Random
House, 1947; UK: Hammond, 1949;
Pat Abbott #10; Jean Abbott #10

The pink umbrella. Lippincott,
1943; UK: Hammond, 1944; Pat
Abbott #5; Jean Abbott #5

The polkadot murder. Random House,
1951; UK: Hammond, 1952; Pat
Abbott #15; Jean Abbott #15

The shocking pink hat. Random
House, 1946; UK: Hammond, 1948;
Pat Abbott #9; Jean Abbott #9

Thirteen white tulips. Random
House, 1953; UK: Hammond, 1953;
Pat Abbott #17; Jean Abbott #17

Three days in Hong Kong. UK:
Hammond, 1965

The turquoise shop. Lippincott,
1941; UK: Hammond, 1943; Pat
Abbott #1; Jean Abbott #1

The ultraviolet widow. Random
House, 1956; UK: Hammond, 1957;
Pat Abbott #21; Jean Abbott #21

The yellow violet. Lippincott,
1942; UK: Hammond, 1944; Pat
Abbott #3; Jean Abbott #3

CRAWFURD, OSWAL, 1834-1909
The revelations of Inspector
Morgan. Dodd, 1907; UK: Chapman,
1906; Insp. Morgan

CREASEY, JOHN, 1908-1973. For other
works by this author, see MARRIC,
J. J. (pseud.); ASHE, GORDON
(pseud.); MORTON, ANTHONY (pseud.);
YORK, JEREMY (pseud.)

Accuse the Toff. Walker, 1972; UK:
Long, 1943; Richard Rollison #11

Alibi. Scribner's, 1971; UK:
Hodder, 1971; Roger West #39

Battle for Inspector West. UK:
Paul, 1948; Roger West #6

The beauty queen killer. Harper,
1956; UK: A beauty for Inspector
West. Hodder, 1954; Roger West
#16

The blind spot. Harper, 1954; UK:
Inspector West at bay. Evans,
1952; Roger West #13

A bundle for the Toff. Walker,
1968; UK: Hodder, 1967; Richard
Rollison #51

Call the Toff. Walker, 1969; UK:
Hodder, 1953; Richard Rollison
#28

The case against Paul Raeburn. Harper, 1958; UK: Triumph for Inspector West. Paul, 1948; Roger West #7

The case of the innocent victims. Scribner's, 1966. UK: Hodder, 1960; Roger West #26

The creepers. Harper, 1952; UK: Inspector West cries wolf. Evans, 1950; Roger West #10

Death in cold print. Scribner's, 1962; UK: Hodder, 1961; Roger West #29

Death of a postman. Harper, 1957; UK: Parcels for Inspector West. Hodder, 1956; Roger West #19

Death of a racehorse. Scribner's, 1962; UK: Hodder, 1959; Roger West #25

Death of an assassin. Scribner's, 1960; UK: A prince for Inspector West. Hodder, 1956; Roger West #20

The dissemblers. Scribner's, 1967; UK: Puzzle for Inspector West. Evans, 1951; Roger West #12

A doll for the Toff. Walker, 1965; UK: Hodder, 1963; Richard Rollison #47

Double for the Toff. Walker, 1965; UK: Hodder, 1959; Richard Rollison #41

The executioners. Scribner's, 1967; UK: Hodder, 1967; Roger West #35

The extortioners. Scribner's, 1975; UK: Hodder, 1974; Roger West #42

Feathers for the Toff. Walker, 1970; UK: Hodder, 1964; UK: Long, 1945; Richard Rollison #15

The figure in the dust. Harper, 1952; UK: A case for Inspector West. Evans, 1951; Roger West #11

Follow the Toff. Walker, 1967; UK: Hodder, 1961; Richard Rollison #45

Fool the Toff. Walker, 1966; UK: Evans, 1950; Richard Rollison #23

The foothills of fear. UK: Hodder, 1961

Gelignite gang. Harper, 1956; UK: Inspector West makes haste. Hodder, 1955; Roger West #17

Getaway for Inspector West. Scribner's, 1972; UK: Inspector West leaves town. Paul, 1943; Roger West #2

Give a man a gun. Harper, 1954; UK: A gun for Inspector West. Hodder, 1953; Roger West #14

Hammer the Toff. UK: Long, 1947; Richard Rollison #18

Hang the little man. Scribner's, 1963; UK: Hodder, 1963; Roger West #31

Here comes the Toff. Walker, 1967; UK: Long, 1940; Richard Rollison #4

Hit and run. Scribner's, 1959; UK: Accident for Inspector West. Hodder, 1957; Roger West #21

Holiday for Inspector West. UK: Paul, 1946; Roger West #5

The hounds of vengeance. UK: Long, 1945

Hunt the Toff. Walker, 1969; UK: Evans, 1952; Richard Rollison #27

Inspector West alone. Scribner's, 1975; UK: Evans, 1950; Roger West #9

Inspector West at home. Scribner's, 1973; UK: Paul, 1944; Roger West #3

Inspector West regrets. Lancer, 1971; UK: Paul, 1945; UK: Hodder, 1965; Roger West #4

Inspector West takes charge. Scribner's, 1972; UK: Paul, 1942; Roger West #1

Introducing the Toff. UK: Long, 1938; UK: Long, 1954; Richard Rollison #1

Kill the Toff. Walker, 1966; UK: Evans, 1950; Richard Rollison #24

The killing strike. Scribner's, 1961; UK: Stike for death. Hodder, 1958; Roger West #24

A knife for the Toff. Pyramid Books, 1964; UK: Evans, 1951; Richard Rollison #25

Leave it to the Toff. Pyramid Books, 1965; UK: Hodder, 1962; Richard Rollison #48

Look three ways at murder. Scribner's, 1965; UK: Hodder, 1964; Roger West #32

Make-up for the Toff. Walker, 1967; UK: Hodder, 1956; Richard Rollison #35

A mask for the Toff. Walker, 1966;
UK: The Toff goes gay. Evans,
1951; Richard Rollison #26

Model for the Toff. Pyramid Books,
1965; UK: Hodder, 1957; Richard
Rollison #37

Murder, London--Australia.
Scribner's, 1965; UK: Hodder,
1965; Roger West #33

Murder, London--Miami. Scribner's,
1969; UK: Hodder, 1969; Roger West
#37

Murder, London--New York.
Scribner's, 1961; UK: Hodder,
1958; Roger West #23

Murder, London--South Africa.
Scribner's, 1966; UK: Hodder,
1966; Roger West #34

Murder on the line. Scribner's,
1963; UK: Hodder, 1960; Roger West
#27

Murder 1, 2, 3. Scribner's, 1960;
UK: Two for Inspector West.
Hodder, 1955; Roger West #18

Murder out of the past and
under-cover man. Leigh-on-Sea,
Essex: Barrington Gray, 1953;
Richard Rollison #29

A part for a policeman. Scribner's,
1970; UK: Hodder, 1970; Roger West
#38

Poison for the Toff. Pyramid Books,
1965; UK: The Toff on ice. Long,
1947; UK: Corgi, 1976; Richard
Rollison #17

Policeman's dread. Scribner's,
1964; UK: Hodder, 1962; Roger West
#30

A rocket for the Toff. Pyramid
Books, 1964; UK: Hodder, 1960;
Richard Rollison #43

Salute the Toff. Walker, 1971; UK:
Long, 1941; Richard Rollison #6

The scene of the crime. Scribner's,
1963; UK: Hodder, 1961; Roger West
#28

Send Superintendent West.
Scribner's, 1976; UK: Send
Inspector West. Hodder, 1953;
Roger West #15

A sharp rise in crime. Scribner's,
1979; UK: Hodder, 1978; Roger West
#43

A six for the Toff. Walker, 1969;
UK: Hodder, 1955; Richard
Rollison #33

So young to burn. Scribner's, 1968;
UK: Hodder, 1968; Roger West #36

A splinter of glass. Scribner's,
1972; UK: Hodder, 1972; Roger
West #40

Sport for Inspector West. Harper,
1958; UK: Inspector West kicks
off. Paul, 1949; Roger West #8

Stars for the Toff. Selwyn, 1968;
UK: Hodder, 1968; Richard
Rollison #52

The theft of Magna Carta.
Scribner's, 1973; UK: Hodder,
1973; Roger West #41

The Toff among the millions.
Walker, 1976; UK: Long, 1943;
Richard Rollison #10

The Toff and old Harry. Walker,
1970; UK: Long, 1948; Richard
Rollison #21

The Toff and the crooked Copper.
UK: Hodder, 1977; Richard
Rollison #59

The Toff and the curate. Walker,
1969; UK: Long, 1944; Richard
Rollison #13

The Toff and the dead man's
finger. UK: Hodder, 1978; Richard
Rollison #60

The Toff and the deep blue sea.
Selwyn, 1967; UK: Hodder, 1955;
Richard Rollison #34

The Toff and the fallen angels.
Walker, 1970; UK: Hodder, 1970;
Richard Rollison #54

The Toff and the golden boy.
Walker, 1969; UK: Hodder, 1969;
Richard Rollison #53

The Toff and the great illusion.
Walker, 1967; UK: Long, 1944;
Richard Rollison #14

The Toff and the kidnapped child.
Walker, 1965; UK: Hodder, 1960;
Richard Rollison #44

The Toff and the lady. Walker,
1975; UK: Long, 1946; Richard
Rollison #16

The Toff and the runaway bride.
Walker, 1964; UK: Hodder, 1959;
Richard Rollison #42

The Toff and the sleepy cowboy. Walker, 1975; UK: Hodder, 1974; Richard Rollison #58

The Toff and the spider. Walker, 1966; UK: Hodder, 1965; Richard Rollison #49

The Toff and the stolen tresses. Walker, 1965; UK: Hodder, 1958; Richard Rollison #39

The Toff and the terrified taxman. Walker, 1973; UK: Hodder, 1973; Richard Rollison #57

The Toff and the toughs. Walker, 1968; UK: The Toff and the teds. Hodder, 1961; Richard Rollison #46

The Toff and the trip-trip triplets. Walker, 1972; UK: Hodder, 1972; Richard Rollison #56

The Toff at Butlin's. Walker, 1976; UK: Hodder, 1954; Richard Rollison #31

The Toff at the fair. Walker, 1968; UK: Hodder, 1954; Richard Rollison #32

The Toff breaks in. UK: Long, 1940; UK: Long, 1955; Richard Rollison #5

The Toff down under. Walker, 1969; UK: Hodder, 1953; Richard Rollison #30

The Toff goes on. UK: Long, 1939; UK: Long, 1955; Richard Rollison #2

The Toff goes to market. Walker, 1967; UK: Long, 1942; Richard Rollison #8

The Toff in New York. Pyramid Books, 1964; UK: Hodder, 1956; Richard Rollison #36

The Toff in town. Walker, 1977; UK: Long, 1948; Richard Rollison #19

The Toff in wax. Walker, 1966; UK: Hodder, 1960; Richard Rollison #50

The Toff is back. Walker, 1974; UK: Long, 1942; Richard Rollison #9

The Toff on board. Walker, 1973; UK: Evans, 1949; Richard Rollison #22

The Toff on fire. Walker, 1966; UK: Hodder, 1957; Richard Rollison #38

The Toff on the farm. Walker, 1964; UK: Hodder, 1958; Richard Rollison #40

The Toff on the trail. UK: Everybody's Books, n.d. [1943?]; Richard Rollison #12

The Toff proceeds. Walker, 1968; UK: Long, 1941; Richard Rollison #7

The Toff steps out. UK: Long, 1939; UK: Long, 1955; Richard Rollison #3

The Toff takes a share. Walker, 1972; UK: The Toff takes shares. Long, 1948; Richard Rollison #20

The trouble at Saxby's. Harper, 1959; UK: Find Inspector West. Hodder, 1957; Roger West #22

Vote for the Toff. Walker, 1971; UK: Hodder, 1971; Richard Rollison #55

CRISPIN, EDMUND (pseud. of Robert Bruce Montgomery, 1921-1978)
Beware of the trains. Walker, 1962; UK: Gollancz, 1953; Gervase Fen #9

Buried for pleasure. UK: Gollancz, 1948; Gervase Fen #6

Dead and dumb. Lippincott, 1947; UK: Swan song. Gollancz, 1947; Gervase Fen #4

Fen country. Walker, 1980; UK: Gollancz, 1979; Gervase Fen #11

The glimpses of the moon. Walker, 1978; UK: Gollancz, 1977; Gervase Fen #10

Holy disorders. Lippincott, 1946; UK: Gollancz, 1946; Gervase Fen #2

The long divorce. Dodd, 1951; UK: Gollancz, 1951; Gervase Fen #8

Love lies bleeding. Lippincott, 1948; UK: Gollancz, 1948; Gervase Fen #5

The moving toyshop. Lippincott, 1946; UK: Gollancz, 1946; Gervase Fen #3

Obsequies at Oxford. Lippincott, 1945; UK: The case of the gilded fly. Gollancz, 1944; Gervase Fen #1

Sudden vengeance. Dodd, 1950; UK: Gollancz, 1950; Gervase Fen #7

CROFT-COOKE, RUPERT, see BRUCE, LEO (pseud.)

CROFTS, FREEMAN WILLS, 1879-1957
Antidote to venom. Dodd, 1939; UK: Hodder, 1938; Joseph French #18

Anything to declare? UK: Hodder, 1957; Joseph French #32

The cask. Seltzer, 1924; UK: Collins, 1920; Georges LaTouche; Insp. Burnley

The Cheyne mystery. Boni, 1920; UK: Inspector French and the Cheyne mystery. Collins, 1926; Joseph French #2

Circumstantial evidence. Dodd, 1941; UK: James Tarrant, adventurer. Hodder, 1941; Joseph French #21

Crime at Nornes. Dodd, 1935; UK: Crime at Guildford. Collins, 1935; Joseph French #13

Crime on the Solent. Dodd, 1934; UK: Mystery on Southampton water. Hodder, 1934. Joseph French #12

Dark journey. Dodd, 1951; UK: French strikes oil. Hodder, 1952; Joseph French #29

Death of a train. Dodd, 1947; UK: Hodder, 1946; Joseph French #26

Double death. Harper, 1932; UK: Death on the way. Collins, 1932; Joseph French #9

The double tragedy. Dodd, 1943; UK: The affair at Little Wokeham. Hodder, 1943; Joseph French #24

Enemy unseen. Dodd, 1945; UK: Hodder, 1945; Joseph French #25

Fear comes to Chalfont. Dodd, 1942; UK: Hodder, 1942; Joseph French #23

Found floating. Dodd, 1937; UK: Hodder, 1937; Joseph French #16

The futile alibi. Dodd, 1938; UK: The end of Andrew Harrison. Hodder, 1938; Joseph French #17

Golden ashes. Dodd, 1940; UK: Hodder, 1940; Joseph French #20

The Groote Park murder. Seltzer, 1925; UK: Collins, 1924; Insp. Ross

Inspector French's greatest case. Seltzer, 1925; UK: Collins, 1924; Joseph French #1

A losing game. Dodd, 1941; UK: The losing game. Hodder, 1941; Joseph French #22

The loss of the "Jane Vosper." Dodd, 1936; UK: Collins, 1936; Joseph French #14

Man overboard! Dodd, 1936; UK: Collins, 1936; Joseph French #15

Many a ship. UK: Hodder, 1955; Joseph French #30

Murderers make mistakes. UK: Hodder, 1947; Joseph French #27

Mystery in the English Channel. Harper, 1931; UK: Mystery in the Channel. Collins, 1931; Joseph French #7

The mystery of the sleeping car express. UK: Hodder, 1956; Joseph French #31

The pit-prop syndicate. Seltzer, 1925; UK: Collins, 1922; Insp. Willis

The Ponson case. Boni, 1927; UK: Collins, 1921; Insp. Tanner

The purple sickle murders. Harper, 1929; UK: The box office murders. Collins, 1929; Joseph French #5

The sea mystery. Harper, 1928; UK: Collins, 1928; Joseph French #4

Silence for the murderer. Dodd, 1948; UK: Hodder, 1949; Joseph French #28

Sir John Magill's last journey. Harper, 1930; UK: Collins, 1930; Joseph French #6

The Starvel Hollow tragedy. Harper, 1927; UK: Inspector French and the Starvel tragedy. Collins, 1927; Joseph French #3

The strange case of Dr. Earle. Dodd, 1933; UK: The hog's back mystery. Hodder, 1933; Joseph French #10

Sudden death. Harper, 1932; UK: Collins, 1932; Joseph French #8

Tragedy in the Hollow. Dodd, 1939; UK: Fatal venture. Hodder, 1939; Joseph French #19

Willful and premeditated. Dodd, 1934; UK: 12:30 from Croydon. Hodder, 1934; Joseph French #11

CROSS, AMANDA (pseud. of Carolyn Gold Heilbrun, 1926 --)

Death in a tenured position. Dutton, 1981; Kate Fansler #6

In the last analysis. Macmillan, 1964; UK: Gollancz, 1964; Kate Fansler #1

The James Joyce murder. Macmillan, 1967; UK: Gollancz, 1967; Kate Fansler #2

Poetic justice. Knopf, 1970; UK: Gollancz, 1970; Kate Fansler #3; Reed Amhearst

The question of Max. Knopf, 1976; UK: Gollancz, 1976; Kate Fansler #5

Sweet death, kind death. Dutton, 1984; Kate Fansler

The Theban mysteries. Knopf, 1971; UK: Gollancz, 1972; Kate Fansler #4; Reed Amhearst

CROSSEN, KENDELL FOSTER, 1910-1981, see MONIG, CHRISTOPHER (pseud.) or FOSTER, RICHARD (pseud.)

CULLINGFORD, GUY (pseud. of Constance Lindsay Taylor, 1907 --)

Conjurer's coffin. Lippincott, 1954; UK: Hammond, 1954

If wishes were hearses. Lippincott, 1953; UK: Hammond, 1952

Post mortem. Lippincott, 1953; UK: Hammond, 1953

A touch of drama. UK: Hammond, 1960

The whipping boys. UK: Hammond, 1958

CULPAN, MAURICE, 1918 --

The Vasiliko affair. UK: Collins, 1968; Bill Houghton

CUMBERLAND, MARTEN, 1892-1972

And then came fear. Doubleday, 1948; UK: Hurst, 1949; Saturnin Dax #10

Attention! Saturnin Dax! UK: Hutchinson, 1962; Saturnin Dax #30

The charge is murder. UK: Hurst, 1953; Saturnin Dax #20

The dice were loaded. UK: Hutchinson, 1965; Saturnin Dax #33

A dilemma for Dax. Doubleday, 1946; UK: Hearsed in death. Hurst, 1947; Saturnin Dax #7

Etched in violence. UK: Hurst, 1953; Saturnin Dax #18

Fade out the stars. Doubleday, 1952; UK: Hurst, 1952; Saturnin Dax #15

Far better dead! UK: Hutchinson, 1957; Saturnin Dax #24

The frightened brides. UK: Hurst, 1954; Saturnin Dax #21

Grave consequences. Doubleday, 1952; UK: Booked for death. Hurst, 1952; Saturnin Dax #16

Hate finds a way. UK: Hutchinson, 1964; Saturnin Dax #32

Hate for sale. British Book Centre, 1957; UK: Hutchinson, 1957; Saturnin Dax #25

Hate will find a way. Doubleday, 1947; UK: And worms have eaten them. Hurst, 1948; Saturnin Dax #9

The house in the forest. Doubleday, 1950; UK: Confetti can be red. Hurst, 1951; Saturnin Dax #13

The knife will fall. Doubleday, 1944; UK: Hurst, 1943; Saturnin Dax #4

A lovely corpse. UK: Hurst, 1946; Saturnin Dax #8

Lying at death's door. UK: Hurst, 1956; Saturnin Dax #23

The man who covered mirrors. Doubleday, 1949; UK: Hurst, 1951; Saturnin Dax #11

Murmurs in the Rue Morgue. British Book Centre, 1959; UK: Hutchinson, 1959; Saturnin Dax #27

No sentiment in murder. UK: Hutchinson, 1966; Saturnin Dax #34

Nobody is safe. Doubleday, 1953; UK: Which of us is safe? Hurst, 1953; Saturnin Dax #19

Not expected to live. UK: Hurst, 1945; Saturnin Dax #5

On the danger list. UK: Hurst, 1950; Saturnin Dax #14

One foot in the grave. UK: Hurst, 1952; Saturnin Dax #17

Out of this world. British Book Centre, 1959; UK: Hutchinson, 1958; Saturnin Dax #26

Policeman's nightmare. Doubleday, 1949; UK: Hurst, 1950; Saturnin Dax #12

Postscript to a death. UK: Hutchinson, 1963; Saturnin Dax #31

Questionable shape. UK: Hurst, 1941; Saturnin Dax #2

Quislings over Paris. UK: Hurst, 1942; Saturnin Dax #3

Remains to be seen. UK: Hutchinson, 1960; Saturnin Dax #28

Someone must die. UK: Hurst, 1940; Saturnin Dax #1

Steps in the dark. Doubleday,
1945; UK: Hurst, 1945; Saturnin
Dax #6
There must be victims. UK:
Hutchinson, 1961; Saturnin Dax
#29
Unto death utterly. UK: Hurst,
1954; Saturnin Dax #22
CUNNINGHAM, A. B., 1888 --
The affair at the boat landing.
Dutton, 1943; Jess Roden
The cane-patch mystery. Dutton,
1944; UK: Swan, 1953; Jess Roden
Death at "The Bottom." Dutton,
1942; Jess Roden
Death haunts the dark lane. Dutton,
1948; Jess Roden
Death of a bullionaire. Dutton,
1946; Jess Roden
Death of a worldly woman. Dutton,
1948; Jess Roden
Death rides a sorrel horse. Dutton,
1946; Jess Roden
Death visits the apple hole.
Dutton, 1945; Jess Roden
The great Yant mystery. Dutton,
1943; UK: Swan, 1959; Jess Roden
The hunter is hunted. Dutton, 1950;
Jess Roden
The killer watching the manhunt.
Dutton, 1950; UK: Boardman, 1951;
Jess Roden
Murder at Deer Lick. Dutton, 1939;
Jess Roden
Murder at the schoolhouse. Dutton,
1940; Jess Roden
Murder before midnight. Dutton,
1945; Jess Roden
Murder without weapons. Dutton,
1949; UK: Millifont, 1955; Jess
Roden
One man must die. Dutton, 1946;
Jess Roden
Skeleton in the closet. Dutton,
1951; Jess Roden
The strange death of Manny Square.
Dutton, 1941; Jess Roden
Strange return. Dutton, 1952; Jess
Roden
Who killed pretty Becky Low?
Dutton, 1951; Jess Roden
CUNNINGHAM, E. V. (pseud. of Howard
Melvin Fast, 1914 --)
The case of the kidnapped angel.
Delacorte, 1982; Masao Masuto

The case of the murdered Mackenzie.
Delacorte, 1984; Masao Masuto
The case of the one penny orange.
Holt, 1977; UK: Duetsch, 1978;
Masao Masuto #2
The case of the poisoned eclairs.
Holt, 1979; UK: Duetsch, 1980;
Masao Masuto #4
The case of the Russian diplomat;
a Masao Masuto mystery. Holt,
1978; UK: Duetsch, 1979; Masao
Masuto #3
The case of the sliding pool.
Delacorte, 1981; Masao Masuto #5
Cynthia. Morrow, 1968; UK: Duetsch,
1969; Harvey Krim #2
Lydia. Doubleday, 1964; UK:
Duetsch, 1965; Harvey Krim #1
Samantha. Morrow, 1967; UK:
Duetsch, 1968; Masao Masuto #1
CURTIS, PETER (pseud. of Norah
Lofts, 1904 --)
The devil's own. Doubleday, 1960;
UK: Macdonald, 1960
No question of murder. Doubleday,
1959; UK: Dead march in three
keys. Davies, 1940; Emma Plume
CURTISS, URSULA, 1923 --
Danger: hospital zone. Dodd,
1966; UK: Hodder, 1967
The deadly climate. Dodd, 1954;
UK: Eyre, 1955; Caroline Emmet
Death of a crow. Dodd, 1983
Dog in the manger. Dodd, 1982
Don't open the door. Dodd, 1968;
UK: Hodder, 1969
The face of the tiger. Dodd, 1958;
UK: Eyre, 1960; Lou Fabian
The forbidden garden. Dodd, 1962;
UK: Eyre, 1963
Hours to kill. Dodd, 1961; UK:
Eyre, 1962
The house on Plymouth Street and
other stories. Dodd, 1985; Mrs.
Leeds; Mrs. Tyrell
In cold pursuit. Dodd, 1977; UK:
Macmillan, 1978
The menace within. Dodd, 1979; UK:
Macmillan, 1979
The noonday devil. Dodd, 1951; UK:
Eyre, 1953; Andrew Sentry
The poisoned orchard. Dodd, 1980;
UK: Macmillan, 1980
Voice out of darkness. Dodd, 1948;
UK: Evans, 1949; Katy Meredith

CUSSLER, CLIVE
   Pacific vortex! Sphere, 1983; Dirk
   Pitt
CUTTER, LEELA
   Death of the party. St. Martin's,
   1985
   Murder after tea-time. St.
   Martin's, 1981
   Who stole Stonehenge? St. Martin's,
   1983; John David Hilsebeck; Lettie
   Winterbottom

DALE, CELIA, 1912 --
   The deception. Harper, 1980; UK:
   Helping with inquiries. Macmillan,
   1979; Insp. Hogarth
DALE, VIRGINIA
   Nan Thursday. Coward McCann, 1944;
   Nan Thursday
DALMAS, HERBERT
   The Fowler formula. Doubleday,
   1967; UK: Gollancz, 1968; John
   Fowler
D'ALTON, MARTINA
   Fatal finish. Walker, 1982; Harry
   Lansing
DALTON, MORAY
   The body in the road. Harper, 1930;
   UK: Low, 1931; Norman Glade
   The Condamine case. UK: Low, 1947;
   Insp. Collier
   The night of fear. Harper, 1931;
   UK: Low, 1931; Insp. Collier
   The wife of Baal. UK: Low, 1932
DALY, CARROLL JOHN, 1889-1958
   The amateur murderer. Washburn,
   1933; UK: Hutchinson, 1933; Race
   Williams #6
   Better corpses. UK: Hale, 1940;
   Race Williams #8
   Emperor of evil. Stokes, 1937; UK:
   Hutchinson, 1936; Vee Brown #2
   The hidden hand. Clode, 1929; UK:
   Hutchinson, 1930; Race Williams
   #2
   Murder from the East. Stokes, 1935;
   UK: Hutchinson, 1935; Race
   Williams #7
   Murder won't wait. Washburn, 1933;
   UK: Hutchinson, 1934; Vee Brown
   #1
   The mystery of the smoking gun.
   Stokes, 1936; UK: Death's juggler.
   Hutchinson, 1935; Satan Hall #1

Ready to burn. UK: Museum Press,
   1951; Satan Hall #2
The snarl of the beast. Clode,
   1927; UK: Hutchinson, 1928; Race
   Williams #1
The tag murders. Clode, 1930; UK:
   Hutchinson, 1931; Race Williams
   #3
Tainted power. Clode, 1931; UK:
   Hutchinson, 1931; Race Williams
   #4
The third murderer. Farrar, 1931;
   UK: Hutchinson, 1932; Race
   Williams #5
DALY, ELIZABETH, 1878-1967
   And dangerous to know. Rinehart,
   1949; UK: Hammond, 1952; Henry
   Gamadge #13
   Any shape or form. Farrar, 1945;
   UK: Hammond, 1949; Henry Gamadge
   #8
   Arrow pointing nowhere. Farrar,
   1944; UK: Hammond, 1946; Henry
   Gamadge #6
   The book of the crime. Rinehart,
   1951; UK: Hammond, 1954; Henry
   Gamadge #15
   The book of the dead. Farrar,
   1944; UK: Hammond, 1946; Henry
   Gamadge #7
   The book of the lion. Rinehart,
   1948; UK: Hammond, 1951; Henry
   Gamadge #12
   Deadly night shade. Farrar, 1940;
   UK: Hammond, 1948; Henry Gamadge
   #2
   Death and letters. Rinehart, 1950;
   UK: Hammond, 1953; Henry Gamadge
   #14
   Evidence of things seen. Farrar,
   1943; UK: Hammond, 1946; Henry
   Gamadge #5
   The house without the door.
   Farrar, 1942; UK: Hammond, 1945;
   Henry Gamadge #4
   Murders in Volume 2. Farrar, 1941;
   UK: Eyre, 1943; Henry Gamadge #3
   Night walk. Rinehart, 1947; UK:
   Hammond, 1950; Henry Gamadge #11
   Nothing can rescue me. Farrar,
   1943; UK: Hammond, 1945; Henry
   Gamadge #5
   Somewhere in the house. Rinehart,
   1946; UK: Hammond, 1949; Henry
   Gamadge #9

Unexpected night. Farrar, 1940;
    UK: Gollancz, 1940; Henry Gamadge
    #1
The wrong way down. Rinehart,
    1946; UK: Hammond, 1950; Henry
    Gamadge #10
DANE, CLEMENCE (pseud. of Winifred
    Ashton, 1887-1965)
DANE, CLEMENCE and SIMPSON, HELEN
    Author unknown. Cosmopolitan,
    1930; UK: Printer's devil. Hodder,
    1930; John Saumarez #2
    Enter Sir John. Cosmopolitan, 1928;
    UK: Hodder, 1928; John Saumarez #1
    Re-enter Sir John. Farrar, 1932;
    UK: Hodder, 1932; John Saumarez #3
DANE, JOEL (pseud. of Joseph Francis
    Delaney, 1905 --)
    The cabana murders. Doubleday,
    1937; Cass Hartly #2
    The Christmas tree murders.
    Doubleday, 1938; Cass Hartly
    Grasp at straws. Doubleday, 1938;
    Cass Hartly
    Murder cum laude. Smith & Haas,
    1935; UK: Murder in college. Bell,
    1935; Cass Hartly #1
DANIEL, GLYN
    The Cambridge murders. (as Dilwyn
    Rees) UK: Gollancz, 1945; Richard
    Cherrington #1
    Welcome death. Dodd, 1955; UK:
    Gollancz, 1954; Richard
    Cherrington #2
DANIELS, HAROLD R., 1919 --
    The accused. Dell, 1958; UK:
    Duetsch, 1961
    The girl in 304. Dell, 1956
DANNAY, FREDERIC, see QUEEN, ELLERY
    (pseud.) or ROSS, BARNABY (pseud.)
DARNELL, HENRY FAULKNER
    The craze of Christian Englebart.
    Appleton, 1890
DAUKES, SIDNEY HERBERT, see FAIRWAY,
    SIDNEY (pseud.)
DAVEY, JOCELYN (pseud. of Chaim
    Raphael, 1908 --)
    A capitol offense. Knopf, 1956; UK:
    The undoubted deed. Chatto, 1956;
    Ambrose Usher #1
    A killing in hats. UK: Chatto,
    1965; Ambrose Usher #4
    Murder in Paradise. Walker, 1982;
    Ambrose Usher #6

The naked villainy. Knopf, 1958;
    UK: Chatto, 1958; Ambrose Usher
    #2
A touch of stagefright. UK: Chatto,
    1960; Ambrose Usher #3
A treasury alarm. Walker, 1981; UK:
    Chatto, 1976; Ambrose Usher #5
DAVID-NEEL, ALEXANDRA and YONGDEN,
    LAMA
    The power of nothingness.
    Houghton, 1982; Munpa
DAVIDSON, T. L., 1901-1964
    The murder in the laboratory.
    Dutton, 1929; UK: Methuen, 1929;
    Martin Blythe; Insp. Mellison
DAVIES, L. P., 1914 --
    A grave matter. Doubleday, 1967;
    John Morton; Sgt. Derwent
    The Lampton dreamers. Simon &
    Schuster, 1967; UK: Jenkins, 1966
    The land of leys. Doubleday, 1979;
    UK: Hale, 1980
    The reluctant medium. Doubleday,
    1967; David Conway
    What did I do tomorrow? Doubleday,
    1973; UK: Barrie, 1972
DAVIOT, GORDON (pseud.), see TEY,
    JOSEPHINE (pseud.)
DAVIS, DOROTHY SALISBURY, 1916 --
    The clay hand. Scribner's, 1950
    A death in the life. Scribner's,
    1976; UK: Gollancz, 1977; Julie
    Hayes
    Death of an old sinner. Scribner's,
    1957; UK: Secker, 1958; Mrs.
    Norris #1; Jasper Tully #1
    Enemy and brother. Scribner's,
    1966; UK: Hodder, 1967; John
    Eakins
    A gentle murderer. Scribner's,
    1951; Father Duffy; Sgt.
    Goldsmith
    A gentleman called. Scribner's,
    1958; UK: Secker, 1958; Mrs.
    Norris #2; Jasper Tully #2
    The little brothers. Scribner's,
    1973; UK: Barker, 1974
    Lullaby of murder. Scribner's,
    1984; Julie Hayes #3
    Old sinners never die. Scribner's,
    1959; UK: Secker, 1960; Mrs.
    Norris #3
    Scarlet night. Scribner's, 1980;
    UK: Gollancz, 1981; Julie Hayes

Shock wave. Scribner's, 1972; UK:
Barker, 1974; Kate Osborne

A town of masks. Scribner's, 1952;
Hannah Blake

Where the dark streets go.
Scribner's, 1969; UK: Hodder,
1970; Father McMahon

DAVIS, FREDERICK C., 1902-1977. For
other mysteries by this author, see
RANSOME, STEPHEN (pseud.) Another
morgue heard from.
Doubleday, 1954; UK: Deadly
bedfellows. Gollancz, 1955;
Schyler Cole #5; Luke Speare #5

Coffins for three. Doubleday, 1938;
UK: One murder too many.
Heinemann, 1938; Cyrus Hatch #1

The deadly Miss Ashley. Doubleday,
1950; UK: Gollancz, 1950; Schyler
Cole #1; Luke Speare #1

Deep lay the dead. Doubleday, 1942

Detour to oblivion. Doubleday,
1947; Cyrus Hatch #6

Drag the dark. Doubleday, 1953; UK:
Gollancz, 1954; Schyler Cole #4;
Luke Speare #4

Gone tomorrow. Doubleday, 1948;
Cyrus Hatch #8

The graveyard never closes.
Doubleday, 1940; Cyrus Hatch #4

He wouldn't stay dead. Doubleday,
1939; UK: Heinemann, 1938; Cyrus
Hatch #2

Let the skeletons rattle.
Doubleday, 1944; Cyrus Hatch #5

Lillies in her garden grew.
Doubleday, 1951; UK: Gollancz,
1951; Schyler Cole #2; Luke Speare
#2

Night drop. Doubleday, 1955; UK:
Gollancz, 1956; Schyler Cole #6;
Luke Speare #6

Poor, poor Yorick. Doubleday, 1939;
UK: Murder doesn't always out.
Heinemann, 1939; Cyrus Hatch #3

Thursday's blade. Doubleday, 1947;
Cyrus Hatch #7

Tread lightly, angel. Doubleday,
1952; UK: Gollancz, 1952; Schyler
Cole #3; Luke Speare #3

DAVIS, GEORGE
Crime in Threadneedle Street. UK:
Collins, 1968

DAVIS, KEN
Words can kill. Ballantine, 1984;
Garver Bascombe

DAVIS, MARTHA WIRT, see VAN ARSDALE,
WIRT (pseud.)

DAVIS, MILDRED
Scorpion. Random House, 1977; UK:
Hale, 1978

Tell them what's-her-name called.
Random House, 1975; UK: Hale,
1976; Finley Wehrmann

They buried a man. Simon &
Schuster, 1953

DAY-LEWIS, CECIL, see BLAKE, NICHOLAS

DEAN, AMBER, 1902 --
Call me Pandora. Doubleday, 1946;
Albie Harris #3

Chanticleer's muffled crow.
Doubleday, 1945; Albie Harris #2

Dead man's float. Doubleday, 1944;
Albie Harris #1

Deadly contact. Doubleday, 1963;
UK: Hale, 1964

Encounter with evil. Doubleday,
1961

No traveller returns. Doubleday,
1948; Albie Harris #5

Snipe hunt. Doubleday, 1949; Albie
Harris #6

Wrap it up. Doubleday, 1946; Albie
Harris #4

DEAN, S. F. X.
By frequent anguish. Walker, 1982;
Neil Kelly #1

Ceremony of innocence. Walker,
1984; Neil Kelly

Death and the mad heroine. Walker,
1985; Neil Kelly

Such pretty toys. Walker, 1982;
Neil Kelly #2

DEAN, SPENCER (pseud. of Prentice
Winchell, 1895 --)
Credit for a murder. Doubleday,
1961; UK: Boardman, 1962; Don
Cadee #3

DEANDREA, WILLIAM L., 1952 --
Five o'clock lightning. St.
Martin's, 1982; Russ Garrett

Killed on the ice. Doubleday,
1984; Matt Cobb #4

Killed with a passion. Doubleday,
1983; Matt Cobb

DE CAIRE, EDWIN (pseud. of Edwin
Alfred Williams)

Death among the writers. UK:
Hodder, 1952; Insp. Bootle; Sgt.
Swift

DEKKER, CARL (pseud.), see COLLINS,
MICHAEL (pseud.)

DEKOBRA, MAURICE (pseud. of Ernest
Maurice Tessier, 1885-1973)
The Madonna of the sleeping cars.
UK: Laurie, 1927

DELANEY, JOSEPH FRANCIS, see DANE,
JOEL Y. (pseud.)

DE LA TORRE, LILLIAN (pseud. of
Lillian McCue, 1902 --)
The detections of Sam Johnson.
Doubleday, 1960; Samuel Johnson #2
Dr. Samuel Johnson, detective.
Knopf, 1946; UK: Joseph, 1948;
Samuel Johnson #1
Elizabeth is missing. Knopf, 1945;
UK: Joseph, 1947
The heir of Douglas. Knopf, 1952;
UK: Joseph, 1953

DELVING, MICHAEL (pseud. of Jay
Williams, 1914-1978)
Bored to death. Scribner's, 1975;
UK: A wave of fatalities. Collins,
1975; Dave Cannon #4
The devil finds work. Scribner's,
1969; UK: Collins, 1970; Dave
Cannon #2; Bob Eddison #1
Die like a man. Scribner's, 1970;
UK: Collins, 1970; Dave Cannon #3
No sign of life. Strawberry Hill,
1979; UK: Collins, 1978; Dave
Cannon #5
A shadow of himself. Scribner's,
1972; UK: Collins, 1972; Bob
Eddison #2
Smiling, the boy fell dead.
Scribner's, 1967; UK: Macdonald,
1967; Dave Cannon #1

DEMARIS, OVID, 1919 --
Candyleg. Fawcett, 1961; UK:
Muller, 1962
The enforcer. Fawcett, 1960
The extortioners. Fawcett, 1960;
UK: Muller, 1961
The gold-plated sewer. Avon, 1960
The hoods take over. Fawcett, 1957;
Vince Slader #1
The long night. Avon, 1959
The lusting drive. Fawcett, 1958;
UK: Muller, 1961; Vince Slader #3
Ride the gold mare. Fawcett, 1957;
Vince Slader #2

The slasher. Fawcett, 1959

DEMING, RICHARD, 1915 --
Anything but saintly. Permabooks,
1963; Matt Rudd #2
The careful man. UK: Allen, 1962
Death of a pusher. Pocket Books,
1964; Matt Rudd #3
Edge of the law. Berkley, 1960
The gallows in my garden. Rinehart,
1952; UK: Boardman, 1953;
Manville Moon #1
Juvenile delinquent. UK: Boardman,
1958; Manville Moon #4
She'll hate me tomorrow. Monarch,
1963
Tweak the devil's nose. Rinehart,
1953; UK: Boardman, 1953;
Manville Moon #2
Vice cop. Belmont, 1961; Matt Rudd
#1
Whistle past the graveyard.
Rinehart, 1954; UK: Boardman,
1955; Manville Moon #3

DENBIE, ROGER
Death cruises south. Morrow, 1934;
UK: Nicholson, 1934; Quentin Pace
Death on the limited. Morrow,
1933; UK: The timetable murder.
Nicholson, 1934; Quentin Pace

DENKER, HENRY, 1912 --
Outrage. Avon, 1982

DENT, LESTER, 1904-1959
Dead at the take-off. Doubleday,
1946; UK: Cassell, 1948; Chance
Malloy #1
Lady afraid. Doubleday, 1948; UK:
Cassell, 1950
Lady in peril. Ace, 1959
Lady to kill. Doubleday, 1946; UK:
Cassell, 1949; Chance Malloy

DENTINGER, JANE
First hit of the season. Doubleday,
1984; Jocelyn O'Roarke #2;
Phillip Gerrard #2
Murder on cue. Doubleday, 1983;
Jocelyn O'Roarke #1; Phillip
Gerrard #1

DERLETH, AUGUST, 1909-1971
The adventure of the Orient
Express. Candlelight Press, 1965;
Solar Pons #8
The adventures of the unique
Dickensians. Mycroft & Moran,
1968; Solar Pons #11

The casebook of Solar Pons.
Mycroft & Moran, 1965; Solar Pons
#6

The chronicles of Solar Pons.
Mycroft & Moran, 1972; UK: Robson,
1975; Solar Pons #12

Death by design. Arcadia House,
1953

Fell purpose. Arcadia House, 1953;
Ephraim Peck #10

In re: Sherlock Holmes--the
adventures of Solar Pons. Mycroft
& Moran, 1945; UK: The adventures
of Solar Pons. Robson, 1975; Solar
Pons #1

The man on all fours. Loring, 1934;
UK: Newnes, 1936; Ephraim Peck #2

The memoirs of Solar Pons. Mycroft
& Moran, 1951; Solar Pons #2

Mischief in the lane. Scribner's,
1944; UK: Muller, 1948; Ephraim
Peck #8

Mr. Fairlie's final journey. Mycroft
& Moran, 1968; Solar Pons #10

Murder stalks the Wakely family.
Loring, 1934; UK: Death strikes
the Wakely family. Newnes, 1937;
Ephraim Peck #1

The Naracong riddle. Scribner's,
1940; Ephraim Peck #6

No future for Luana. Scribner's,
1945; UK: Muller, 1948; Ephraim
Peck #9

A Praed Street dossier. Mycroft &
Moran, 1968; Solar Pons #9

Praed Street papers. Candlelight
Press, 1965; Solar Pons #7

The reminiscences of Solar Pons.
Mycroft & Moran, 1961; Solar Pons
#5

The return of Solar Pons. Mycroft &
Moran, 1958; Solar Pons #4

Sentence deferred. Scribner's,
1939; UK: Heinemann, 1939; Ephraim
Peck #5

The seven who waited. Scribner's,
1943; UK: Muller, 1945; Ephraim
Peck #7

Sign of fear. Loring, 1935; UK:
Newnes, 1936; Ephraim Peck #4

Three problems for Solar Pons.
Mycroft & Moran, 1952; Solar Pons
#3

Three who died. Loring, 1935;
Ephraim Peck #3

DEVINE, D. M., 1920-1981. For other
mysteries by this author, see
DEVINE, DOMINIC

Death is my bridegroom. Walker,
1969; UK: Collins, 1969

The devil at your elbow. Walker,
1967; UK: Collins, 1966; Insp.
Finney; Arahorn Loudon

Doctors also die. Dodd, 1962; UK:
Collins, 1962

The fifth cord. Walker, 1967; UK:
Collins, 1967

His own appointed day. Walker,
1966; UK: Collins, 1965

My brother's killer. Dodd, 1962;
UK: Collins, 1961

The Royston affair. Dodd, 1964;
UK: Collins, 1964

DEVINE, DOMINIC. For other mysteries
by this author, see DEVINE, D. M.

The sleeping tiger. Walker, 1968;
UK: Collins, 1968; John Prescott

Sunk without a trace. St. Martin's,
1979; UK: Collins, 1978; Judy
Hutchings

This is your death. St. Martin's,
1982

DEWEESE, GENE, see DEWEESE, JEAN
(pseud.)

DEWEESE, JEAN (pseud. of Gene
DeWeese, 1934 --)

Hour of the cat. Doubleday, 1980;
UK: Hale, 1980

DEWETERING, JANWILLEM VAN, see
WETERING, JANWILLEM VAN DE

DEWEY, THOMAS B., 1915 --

And where she stops. Popular
Library, 1957; UK: I. O. U.
murder. Boardman, 1958; Pete
Schofield #1

As good as dead. Jefferson House,
1946; UK: Dakers, 1952; Singer
Batts #2

The brave bad girls. Simon &
Schuster, 1956; UK: Boardman,
1957; Mac #3

The case of the chaste and the
unchaste. Random House, 1959; UK:
Boardman, 1960; Mac #5

Deadline. Simon & Schuster, 1966;
UK: Boardman, 1967; Mac #10

Death and taxes. Putnam, 1967; UK:
Hale, 1969; Mac #11
Don't cry for long. Simon &
Schuster, 1964; UK: Boardman,
1965; Mac #8
Draw the curtain close. Jefferson
House, 1947; UK: Dakers, 1951;
Singer Batts #3
The girl in the punch bowl. Dell,
1964; UK: Boardman, 1965; Pete
Schofield #8
The girl who wasn't there. Simon &
Schuster, 1960; UK: Boardman,
1960; Pete Schofield #3
The girl with the sweet plump
knees. Dell, 1963; UK: Boardman,
1963; Pete Schofield #7
Go, Honeylou. Dell, 1962; UK:
Boardman, 1962; Pete Schofield #6
Go to sleep, Jeannie. Popular
Library, 1959; Pete Schofield #2
The golden hooligan. Dell, 1961;
UK: Boardman, 1961; Pete Schofield
#5
Handle with fear. Mill, 1951; UK:
Dakers, 1955; Singer Batts #5
How hard to kill. Simon & Schuster,
1962; UK: Boardman, 1963; Mac #6
Hue and cry. Jefferson House, 1944;
UK: The murder of Marion Mason.
Dakers, 1951; Singer Batts #1
The king killer. Putnam, 1968; UK:
Death turns right. Hale, 1969; Mac
#12
The love-death thing. Simon &
Schuster, 1969; Mac #13
The mean streets. Simon & Schuster,
1955; UK: Boardman, 1955; Mac #2
Mourning after. Mill, 1950; UK:
Dakers, 1953; Singer Batts #4
Nude in Nevada. Dell, 1965; UK:
Boardman, 1966; Pete Schofield
#10
Only on Tuesdays. Dell, 1964; UK:
Boardman, 1964; Pete Schofield #9
Portrait of a dead heiress. Simon &
Schuster, 1965; UK: Boardman,
1966; Mac #9
Prey for me. Simon & Schuster,
1954; UK: Boardman, 1954; Mac #1
A sad song singing. Simon &
Schuster, 1963; UK: Boardman,
1964; Mac #7

The Taurus trip. Simon & Schuster,
1970; Mac #14
Too hot for Hawaii. Popular
Library, 1960; UK: Boardman,
1963; Pete Schofield #4
You've got him cold. Simon &
Schuster, 1958; UK: Boardman,
1959; Mac #4
DEWHURST, EILEEN
Curtain fall. Doubleday, 1982; UK:
Macmillan, 1977; Joanna Stuart
Drink this. Doubleday, 1981; UK:
Collins, 1980; Neil Carter
The house that Jack built.
Doubleday, 1984; Mrs. Halliday
Trio in three flats. Doubleday,
1981; Neil Carter
DEXTER, COLIN (pseud. of Norman
Colin Dexter, 1930 --)
The dead of Jericho. St. Martin's,
1981; Insp. Morse
Last bus to Woodstock. St.
Martin's, 1975; UK: Macmillan,
1975; Insp. Morse
The riddle of the third mile. St.
Martin's, 1984; Insp. Morse
The silent world of Nicholas
Quinn. St. Martin's, 1977; UK:
Macmillan, 1977; Insp. Morse
DEXTER, NORMAN COLIN, see DEXTER,
COLIN
DEY, FREDERIC MERRIL VAN RENSSELAER,
see VANARDY, VARICK (pseud.)
DICKINSON, PETER, 1927 --
The glass-sided ant's nest.
Harper, 1968; UK: Skin deep.
Hodder, 1968; James Pibble #1
Hindsight. Pantheon, 1983; Paul
Rogers
King + joker. Pantheon, 1976; UK:
Hodder, 1976
The last houseparty. Pantheon, 1982
The lively dead. Pantheon, 1975;
UK: Hodder, 1975
The lizard in the cup. Harper,
1972; UK: Hodder, 1972; James
Pibble #5
The old English peep show. Harper,
1969; UK: A pride of heroes.
Hodder, 1969; James Pibble #2
One foot in the grave. Pantheon,
1980; UK: Hodder, 1979; James
Pibble #6

The poison oracle. Pantheon, 1974;
    UK: Hodder, 1974; Wesley Morris
The sinful stones. Harper, 1970;
    UK: The seals. Hodder, 1970; James
    Pibble #3
Sleep and his brother. Harper,
    1971; UK: Hodder, 1971; James
    Pibble #4
Walking dead. Pantheon, 1978; UK:
    Hodder, 1977

DICKSON, CARTER (pseud. of John
  Dickson Carr). For other mysteries
  by this author, see CARR, JOHN
  DICKSON or RHODE, JOHN
And so to murder. Morrow, 1940;
    UK: Heinemann, 1941; Henry
    Merrivale #10
Behind the crimson blind. Morrow,
    1952; UK: Heinemann, 1952; Henry
    Merrivale #21
The cavalier's cup. Morrow, 1953;
    UK: Heinemann, 1954; Henry
    Merrivale #22
The curse of the bronze lamp.
    Morrow, 1945; UK: Lord of the
    sorcerers. Heinemann, 1946; Henry
    Merrivale #16
Death in five boxes. Morrow, 1938;
    UK: Heinemann, 1938; Henry
    Merrivale #7
The Department of Queer Complaints.
    Morrow, 1940; UK: Heinemann, 1940;
    Col. March
Fear is the same. Morrow, 1956; UK:
    Heinemann, 1956
The gilded man. Morrow, 1942; UK:
    Heinemann, 1942; Henry Merrivale
    #13
A graveyard to let. Morrow, 1949;
    UK: Heinemann, 1950; Henry
    Merrivale #19
He wouldn't kill patience. Morrow,
    1944; UK: Heinemann, 1944; Henry
    Merrivale #15
The Judas window. Morrow, 1938; UK:
    Heinemann, 1938; Henry Merrivale
    #8
My late wives. Morrow, 1946; UK:
    Heinemann, 1947; Henry Merrivale
    #17
Night at the Mocking Widow. Morrow,
    1950; UK: Heinemann, 1951; Henry
    Merrivale #20

Nine and death makes ten. Morrow,
    1940; UK: Murder in the submarine
    zone. Heinemann, 1940; Henry
    Merrivale #11
The peacock feather murders.
    Morrow, 1937; UK: The ten
    teacups. Heinemann, 1937; Henry
    Merrivale #6
The Plague Court murders. Morrow,
    1934; UK: Heinemann, 1935; Henry
    Merrivale #1
The Punch and Judy murders. Morrow,
    1937; UK: The magic lantern
    murders. Heinemann, 1936; Henry
    Merrivale #5
The reader is warned. Morrow, 1939;
    UK: Heinemann, 1939; Henry
    Merrivale #9
The red widow murders. Morrow,
    1935; UK: Heinemann, 1935; Henry
    Merrivale #3
Seeing is believing. Morrow, 1941;
    UK: Heinemann, 1942; Henry
    Merrivale #12
She died a lady. Morrow, 1943; UK:
    Heinemann, 1943; Henry Merrivale
    #14
The skeleton in the clock. Morrow,
    1948; UK: Heinemann, 1949; Henry
    Merrivale #18
The unicorn murders. Morrow, 1936;
    UK: Heinemann, 1936; Henry
    Merrivale #4
The white priory murders. Morrow,
    1934; UK: Heinemann, 1935; Henry
    Merrivale #2

DILLON, EILIS, 1920 --
Death at Crane's court. Walker,
    1963; UK: Faber, 1953; Prof. Daly
    #1
Death in the quadrangle. Walker,
    1968; UK: Faber, 1956; Prof. Daly
    #2
Sent to his account. British Book
    Centre, 1961; UK: Faber, 1954

DI PEGO, GERALD FRANCIS, 1941 --
With a vengeance. McGraw-Hill,
    1977; UK: Macmillan, 1977; Det.
    Dela

DISNEY, DORIS MILES, 1907-1976
Appointment at nine. Doubleday,
    1947; Jim O'Neill #3
Black mail. Doubleday, 1958; UK:
    Foulsham, 1960; David Madden #2

The Chandler policy. Putnam, 1971;
UK: Hale, 1973; Jeff DiMarco #7
A compound for death. Doubleday,
1943; Jim O'Neill #1
Cry for help. Doubleday, 1975; UK:
Hale, 1976; Rachel Carey
Dark Road. Doubleday, 1946; UK:
Nimmo, 1947; Jeff DiMarco #1
The day Miss Bessie Lewis
disappeared. Doubleday, 1972; UK:
Hale, 1973
Did she fall or was she pushed?
Doubleday, 1959; UK: Hale, 1962;
Jeff DiMarco #5
Do not fold, spindle or mutilate.
Doubleday, 1970; UK: Death by
computer. Hale, 1971
Don't go into the woods today.
Doubleday, 1974
Family skeleton. Doubleday, 1949;
Jeff DiMarco #2
Find the woman. Doubleday, 1962;
UK: Hale, 1964; Jeff DiMarco #6
Heavy, heavy hangs. Doubleday,
1952
Here lies. Doubleday, 1963; UK:
Hale, 1964; Griff Hughes
The last straw. Doubleday, 1954;
UK: Driven to kill. Foulsham,
1957; Jim O'Neill #4
Mrs. Meeker's money. Doubleday,
1961; UK: Hale, 1963; David Madden
#3
Murder on a tangent. Doubleday,
1945; Jim O'Neill #2
Room for murder. Doubleday, 1955;
UK: Foulsham, 1957; Aggie Scanlon
Straw man. Doubleday, 1951; UK: The
case of the straw man. Foulsham,
1958; Jeff DiMarco #3
Three's a crowd. Doubleday, 1971;
UK: Hale, 1972
Trick or treat. Doubleday, 1955;
UK: The Hallowe'en murder.
Foulsham, 1957; Jeff DiMarco #4
Unappointed rounds. Doubleday,
1956; UK: The post office case.
Foulsham, 1957; David Madden #1
Voice from the grave. Doubleday,
1968; UK: Hale, 1969
Who rides a tiger. Doubleday, 1946;
UK: Sow the wind. Nimmo, 1948
Winifred. Doubleday, 1976

DOBYNS, STEPHEN, 1941 --
Dancer with one leg. Dutton, 1983;
Det. Lazard
Saratoga headhunter. Viking, 1985;
Charlie Bradshaw #3
Saratoga swimmer. Atheneum, 1981;
Charlie Bradshaw
DODGE, DANIEL, 1910 --
Angel's ransom. Random House, 1956;
UK: Ransom of the angel. Joseph,
1957
Bullets for the bridegroom.
Macmillan, 1944; UK: Joseph,
1944; Whit Whitney #3
Carambola. Little, 1961; UK: High
Corniche. Joseph, 1961
Death and taxes. Macmillan, 1941;
UK: Joseph, 1947; Whit Whitney #1
Hooligan. Macmillan, 1969; UK:
Hatchetman. Joseph, 1970; John
Abraham Lincoln #1
It ain't hay. Simon & Schuster,
1946; UK: A drug on the market.
Joseph, 1949; Whit Whitney #4
The long escape. Random House,
1948; UK: Joseph, 1950; Al Colby
#1
Plunder of the sun. Random House,
1949; UK: Joseph, 1950; Al Colby
#2
The red tassel. Random House,
1950; UK: Joseph, 1951; Al Colby
#3
Shear the black sheep. Macmillan,
1942; UK: Joseph, 1949; Whit
Whitney #2
To catch a thief. Random House,
1952; UK: Joseph, 1953; John
Robie
Troubleshooter. Macmillan, 1971;
UK: Joseph, 1972; John Abraham
Lincoln #2
DOLSON, HILDEGARDE, 1908 --
Beauty sleep. Lippincott, 1977;
UK: Hale, 1979; Lucy Ramsdale #4
A dying fell. Lippincott, 1973;
UK: Curley, 1979; Lucy Ramsdale
#2
Please omit funeral. Lippincott,
1975; Lucy Ramsdale #3
To spite her face. Lippincott,
1971; UK: Curley, 1979; Lucy
Ramsdale #1

DOMINIC, R. B. (pseud. of Mary J. Latis and Martha Hennissart). For other mysteries by these authors, see LATHEN, EMMA (pseud.)

The attending physician. Harper, 1980; UK: Macmillan, 1980; Benton Safford #6

Epitaph for a lobbyist. Doubleday, 1974; UK: Macmillan, 1974; Benton Safford #4

Murder in High Place. Doubleday, 1970; UK: Macmillan, 1969; Benton Safford #2

Murder out of commission. Doubleday, 1976; UK: Macmillan, 1976; Benton Safford #5

Murder sunny side up. Abelard-Schuman, 1968; Benton Safford #1

There is no justice. Doubleday, 1971; UK: Murder out of court. Macmillan, 1971; Benton Safford #3

Unexpected developments. St. Martin's, 1984; Benton Safford #7

DONAVAN, JOHN (pseud. of Nigel Morland, 1905 --). For other mysteries by this author, see FORREST, NORMAN (pseud.)

The case of the beckoning dead. Hillman-Curl, 1938; UK: Hale, 1938; Johnny Lamb #2

The case of the plastic mask. Arcadia House, 1941; UK: The case of the plastic man. Hodder, 1940; Johnny Lamb #5

The case of the rusted room. Hillman-Curl, 1937; UK: Hale, 1937; Johnny Lamb #1

The case of the talking dust. Arcadia House, 1941; UK: Hale, 1938; Johnny Lamb #3

The case of the violet smoke. Arcadia House, 1940; UK: The case of the coloured wind. Hodder, 1939; Johnny Lamb #4

DOODY, MARGARET, 1939 --

Aristotle, detective. Harper, 1980; UK: Bodley Head, 1978; Aristotle; Stephanos

DOUGLASS, DONALD MCNUTT, 1899-1975

Many brave hearts. Harper, 1958; UK: Eyre, 1959; Bolivar Manchenil

Rebecca's pride. Harper, 1956; UK: Eyre, 1956; Bolivar Manchenil

Saba's treasure. Harper, 1961; UK: Eyre, 1963; Bolivar Manchenil

DOWNES, QUENTIN (pseud. of Michael Harrison, 1907 --). For other mysteries by this author, see HARRISON, MICHAEL

Heads I win. Roy, 1955; UK: Wingate, 1953; Abraham Kozminski #2

No smoke, no fire. Roy, 1956; UK: Wingate, 1952; Abraham Kozminski #1

They hadn't a clue. UK: Arco, 1954; Abraham Kozminski #3

DOYLE, ADRIAN CONAN and CARR, JOHN DICKSON

The new exploits of Sherlock Holmes. Random House, 1954; UK: Murray, 1954; Sherlock Holmes

DOYLE, ARTHUR CONAN, 1859-1930

Adventures of Sherlock Holmes. Harper, 1892; UK: Newnes, 1892; Sherlock Holmes #3

The case-book of Sherlock Holmes. Doran, 1927; UK: Murray, 1927; Sherlock Holmes #9

His last bow: some reminiscences of Sherlock Holmes. Doran, 1917; UK: Murray, 1917; Sherlock Holmes #8

The hound of the Baskervilles. McClure, 1902; UK: Newnes, 1902; Sherlock Holmes #4

The memoirs of Sherlock Holmes. Harper, 1894; UK: Newnes, 1894; Sherlock Holmes #5

The return of Sherlock Holmes. McClure, 1905; UK: Newnes, 1905; Sherlock Holmes #6

The sign of the four. Lippincott, 1890; UK: Blackett, 1890; Sherlock Holmes #2

A study in scarlet. Lippincott, 1890; UK: Beeton's Christmas Annual, 1887; Sherlock Holmes #1

The valley of fear. Doran, 1915; UK: Smith-Elder, 1915; Sherlock Holmes #7; James Moriarity

DRUMMOND, CHARLES

Death and the leaping ladies. Walker, 1969; UK: Gollancz, 1968; Sgt. Reed #2

A death at the bar. Walker, 1973; UK: Gollancz, 1972; Sgt. Reed #5

Death at the furlong post. Walker, 1968; UK: Gollancz, 1967; Sgt. Reed #1

The odds on death. Walker, 1970; UK: Gollancz, 1969; Sgt. Reed #3

Stab in the back. Walker, 1970; UK: Gollancz, 1970; Sgt. Reed #4

DRUMMOND, JUNE, 1923 --
Murder on a bad trip. Holt, 1968; UK: The Gantry episode. Gollancz, 1968; David Cope

Slowly the poison. Walker, 1976; UK: Gollancz, 1975

Welcome, proud lady. Holt, 1968; UK: Gollancz, 1964; James Porbeagle

DU MAURIER, DAPHNE, 1907 --
The flight of the falcon. Doubleday, 1965; UK: Gollancz, 1965; Armino Fabbio

DUNCAN, ACTEA CAROLINE, see THOMAS, CAROLYN (pseud.)

DUNLAP, SUSAN
An equal opportunity death. St. Martin's, 1984; Vejay Haskell

As a favor. St. Martin's, 1984; Jill Smith

DUNNE, JOHN GREGORY, 1932 --
True confessions. Dutton, 1977; UK: Weidenfeld, 1978; Tom Spellacy

DUNNETT, ALASTAIR, 1908 --
No thanks to the duke. Doubleday, 1981; UK: Cape, 1978; Barry Raeburn

DUNNETT, DOROTHY, 1923 --
Dolly and the bird of paradise. Knopf, 1984; Johnson Johnson #6

Dolly and nanny bird. Knopf, 1982; UK: Joseph, 1976; Johnson Johnson #5

Match for a murderer. Houghton, 1971; UK: Dolly and the doctor bird. Cassell, 1971; Johnson Johnson #3

Murder in focus. Houghton, 1973; UK: Dolly and the starry bird. Cassell, 1972; Johnson Johnson #4

Murder in the round. Houghton, 1970; UK: Dolly and the cookie bird. Cassell, 1970; Johnson Johnson #2

The photogenic soprano. Houghton, 1968; UK: Dolly and the singing bird. Cassell, 1968; Johnson Johnson #1

DUPUY-MAZUEL, HENRY, see CATALAN, HENRI (pseud.)

DURRANT, DIGBY
With my little eye. St. Martin's, 1978; UK: Gollancz, 1975; Hamish Oath

DURRENMATT, FRIEDRICH
The judge and his hangman. Harper, 1955; UK: Jenkins, 1954; Hans Borlach

DUTTON, CHARLES J., 1888-1964
Black fog. Dodd, 1934; UK: Hurst, 1934; Harley Manners #6

The circle of death. Dodd, 1933; UK: Hurst, 1933; Harley Manners #5

Murder in a library. Dodd, 1931; UK: Hurst, 1931; Harley Manners #3

Poison unknown. Dodd, 1932; UK: The vanishing murderer. Hurst, 1932; Harley Manners #4

The shadow of evil. Stokes, 1930; UK: Hurst, 1930; Harley Manners #2

The shadow on the glass. Dodd, 1923; UK: Jenkins, 1925; John Bartley

Streaked with crimson. Dodd, 1929; Harley Manners #1

DWIGHT, OLIVIA (pseud. of Mary Hazzard, 1928 --)
Close his eyes. Harper, 1961; John Dryden; Gwyneth Jones

DYER, GEORGE, 1903-1978
Adriana. Scribner's, 1939; UK: The mystery at Martha's Vineyard. Heinemann, 1939

The Catalyst Club. Scribner's, 1936; UK: Heinemann, 1937; Catalyst Club

The long death. Scribner's, 1937; UK: Heinemann, 1937; Catalyst Club #4

A storm is rising. Houghton, 1934; UK: Skeffington, 1934

EARLY, JACK
A creative kind of killer. Watts, 1984; Fortune Fanelli

Razzamatazz. Watts, 1985; Colin Maguire

EBERHARD, FREDERICK G., 1889 --
The microbe murders. UK: Macaulay, 1935; Chief Sutherland

EBERHART, MIGNON G., 1899 --
Another man's murder. Random House, 1957; UK: Collins, 1958
The bayou road. Random House, 1979; UK: Collins, 1979
Casa Madrone. Random House, 1980; UK: Collins, 1980; Mallory Bookover
The cases of Susan Dare. Doubleday, 1934; UK: Lane, 1935; Susan Dare
The chiffon scarf. Doubleday, 1939; UK: Collins, 1940
Danger in the dark. Doubleday, 1937; UK: Hand in glove. Collins, 1937
The dark garden. Doubleday, 1933; UK: Death in the fog. Lane, 1934; Det. Crafft
Dead mien's plays. Random House, 1952; UK: Collins, 1953; Sewell Blake
Enemy in the house. Random House, 1962; UK: Collins, 1963
Family affair. Random House, 1981
Family fortune. Random House, 1976; UK: Collins, 1977
Five passengers from Lisbon. Random House, 1946; UK: Collins, 1946
From this dark stairway. Doubleday, 1931; UK: Heinemann, 1932; Sarah Keate #4; Lance O'Leary #4
The glass slipper. Doubleday, 1938; UK: Collins, 1938
The hangman's whip. Doubleday, 1940; UK: Collins, 1941
Hasty wedding. Doubleday, 1938; UK: Collins, 1939
The house on the roof. Doubleday, 1935; UK: Collins, 1935
Hunt with the hounds. Random House, 1950; UK: Collins, 1951
Man missing. Random House, 1954; UK: Collins, 1954; Sarah Keate #7
The man next door. Random House, 1943; UK: Collins, 1944
Melora. Random House, 1959; UK: Collins, 1960
Murder by an aristocrat. Doubleday, 1932; UK: Murder of my patient. Lane, 1934; Sarah Keate #5; Lance O'Leary #5
Murder in waiting. Random House, 1973; UK: Collins, 1974
The mystery of Hunting's End. Doubleday, 1930; UK: Heinemann, 1931; Sarah Keate #2; Lance O'Leary #2
Never look back. Random House, 1951; UK: Collins, 1951
Next of kin. Random House, 1982; Mady Smith
The patient in Cabin C. Random House, 1983
The patient in Room 18. Random House, 1929; UK: Heinemann, 1929; Sarah Keate #1; Lance O'Leary #1
Postmark murder. Random House, 1956; UK: Collins, 1956
El rancho rio. Random House, 1970; UK: Collins, 1971
Unidentified woman. Random House, 1943; UK: Collins, 1945
The unknown quantity. Random House, 1953; UK: Collins, 1953
While the patient slept. Doubleday, 1930; UK: Heinemann, 1930; Sarah Keate #3; Lance O'Leary #3
The white dress. Random House, 1946; UK: Collins, 1947
Wings of fear. Random House, 1945; UK: Collins, 1946
With this ring. Random House, 1941; UK: Collins, 1942
Witness at large. Random House, 1966; UK: Collins, 1967
Wolf in man's clothing. Random House, 1942; UK: Collins, 1943; Sarah Keate #6
Woman on the roof. Random House, 1967; UK: Collins, 1968
EBERSOHN, WESSEL, 1940 --
A lonely place to die. Pantheon, 1979; UK: Gollancz, 1979; Yudel Gordon
EBERT, ARTHUR FRANK, see ARTHUR, FRANK (pseud.)
EDEN, DOROTHY, 1912 --
Waiting for Willa. Coward McCann, 1970; UK: Hodder, 1970; Grace Asherton
EDEN, MATTHEW
The murder of Lawrence of Arabia. Crowell, 1980; UK: New English Library, 1980
EDGLEY, LESLIE, 1912 --
The runaway pigeon. Doubleday, 1953; UK: Diamonds spell death. Barker, 1954
EDMISTON, HELEN JEAN MAY, see ROBERTSON, HELEN (pseud.)

EDWARDS, JAMES G. (pseud. of James
William MacQueen, 1900 --)
But the patient died. Doubleday,
1948; UK: Cherry Tree, 1949;
Victor Bondurant
Death among doctors. Doubleday,
1942; Victor Bondurant
Death elects a major. Doubleday,
1939; Victor Bondurant
F Corridor. Doubleday, 1936;
Victor Bondurant; Paul Ravel
Murder at leisure. Doubleday, 1937
Murder in the surgery. Doubleday,
1935; Victor Bondurant
The odor of bitter almonds.
Doubleday, 1938; Victor Bondurant
The private pavilion. Doubleday,
1935; Paul Ravel; Victor Bondurant
EDWARDS, RUTH DUDLEY
Corridors of death. St. Martin's,
1982; Robert Amiss
The Saint Valentine's Day murders.
St. Martin's, 1985; Robert Amiss
#2
EGAN, LESLEY (pseud. of Elizabeth
Linington, 1921 --). For other
mysteries by this author, see,
LININGTON, ELIZABETH or SHANNON,
DELL (pseud.)
Against the evidence. Harper, 1962;
UK: Gollancz, 1963; Jesse
Falkenstein #2; Vic Varallo #2
The blind search. Doubleday, 1977;
UK: Gollancz, 1977; Jesse
Falkenstein #15; Vic Varallo #15
The borrowed alibi. Harper, 1962;
UK: Gollancz, 1963; Jesse
Falkenstein #3; Vic Varallo #3
A case for appeal. Harper, 1961;
UK: Gollancz, 1962; Jesse
Falkenstein #1; Vic Varallo #1
A choice of crimes. Doubleday,
1980; UK: Gollancz, 1981; Delia
Riordan
Crime for Christmas. Doubleday,
1984
Detective's due. Harper, 1965; UK:
Gollancz, 1966; Jesse Falkenstein
#6; Vic Varallo #6
A dream apart. Doubleday, 1978; UK:
Gollancz, 1978; Jesse Falkenstein
#16; Vic Varallo #16
The hunters and the hunted.
Doubleday, 1979; UK: Gollancz,

1980; Jesse Falkenstein #18; Vic
Varallo #18
In the death of a man. Harper,
1970; UK: Gollancz, 1970; Jesse
Falkenstein #11; Vic Varallo
Little boy lost. Doubleday, 1983;
Jesse Falkenstein; Vic Varallo
Look back on death. Doubleday,
1978; UK: Gollancz, 1979; Jesse
Falkenstein #17; Vic Varallo #17
Malicious mischief. Harper, 1971;
UK: Gollancz, 1972; Jesse
Falkenstein #12; Vic Varallo #12
The miser. Doubleday, 1981; Jesse
Falkenstein; Vic Varallo
My name is Death. Harper, 1964; UK:
Gollancz, 1964; Jesse Falkenstein
#5; Vic Varallo #5
The nameless ones. Harper, 1967;
UK: Gollancz, 1968; Jesse
Falkenstein #8; Vic Varallo #8
Paper chase. Harper, 1972; UK:
Gollancz, 1973; Jesse Falkenstein
#13; Vic Varallo #13
Run to evil. Harper, 1963; UK:
Gollancz, 1964; Jesse Falkenstein
#4; Vic Varallo #4
Scenes of crime. Doubleday, 1976;
UK: Gollancz, 1976; Jesse
Falkenstein #14; Vic Varallo #14
A serious investigation. Harper,
1968; UK: Gollancz, 1969; Jesse
Falkenstein #9; Vic Varallo #9
Some avenger, rise! Harper, 1966;
UK: Gollancz, 1967; Jesse
Falkenstein #7; Vic Varallo #7
The wine of violence. Harper,
1969; UK: Gollancz, 1970; Jesse
Falkenstein #10; Vic Varallo #10
EGGLESTON, EDWARD, 1837-1902
The Graysons. Century, 1887;
Abraham Lincoln
EGLETON, CLIVE, 1927 --
A conflict of interests. Atheneum,
1983; Insp. Coghill
EHRLICH, MAX, 1909 --
Reincarnation in Venice. Simon &
Schuster, 1979; UK: The bond.
Mayflower, 1980
EIKER, MATHILDE, see EVERMAY, MARCH
(pseud.)
EKSTROM, JAN
Deadly reunion. Scribner's, 1982;
Berti Durrell #1

ELKINS, AARON J.
  The dark place. Walker, 1983;
    Gideon Oliver
  Fellowship of fear. Walker, 1982;
    Gideon Oliver
ELLER, JOHN
  Charlie and the ice man. St.
    Martin's, 1981; Charlie Rope
  Rage of heaven. St. Martin's,
    1982; Charlie Rope
ELLES, DORA AMY, see WENTWORTH,
  PATRICIA (pseud.)
ELLIN STANLEY, 1916 --
  The bind. Random House, 1970; UK:
    The man from nowhere. Cape, 1970
  The eighth circle. Random House,
    1958; UK: Boardman, 1959; Murray
    Kirk
  The house of cards. Random House,
    1967; UK: Macdonald, 1967
  The key to Nicholas Street. Simon &
    Schuster, 1952; UK: Boardman,
    1953
  Star light, star bright. Random
    House, 1979; UK: Cape, 1979; John
    Milano
  Stronghold. Random House, 1975; UK:
    Cape, 1975
  The Valentine estate. Random House,
    1968; UK: Macdonald, 1968
ELLROY, JAMES
  Blood on the moon. Mysterious
    Press, 1984; Lloyd Hopkins
  Brown's requiem. Allison & Busby,
    1984; Fritz Brown
ENDORE, GUY, 1900-1970
  Methinks the lady. Duell, 1945; UK:
    Cresset, 1945
  The werewolf of Paris. Farrar,
    1933; UK: Long, 1934
ENGEL, HOWARD
  Murder on location. St. Martin's,
    1985; Benny Cooperman
  Murder sees the light. St.
    Martin's, 1985; Benny Cooperman
    #2
  The ransom game. St. Martin's,
    1984; Benny Cooperman
  The suicide murders. St. Martin's,
    1984; Benny Cooperman #1
ENGLEMAN, PAUL
  Dead in center field. Ballantine,
    1983; Mark Renzler
ERSKINE, MARGARET (pseud. of Margaret
  Wetherby Williams)

Besides, the wench is dead.
  Doubleday, 1973; UK: Hodder,
  1973; Septimus Finch #19
The brood of folly. Doubleday,
  1971; UK: Hodder, 1971; Septimus
  Finch #18
The case of Mary Fielding.
  Doubleday, 1970; UK: Hodder,
  1970; Septimus Finch #17
Case with three husbands.
  Doubleday, 1967; UK: Hodder,
  1967; Septimus Finch #15
Dead by now. Doubleday, 1954;
  UK: Hammond, 1953; Septimus Finch
  #7
The ewe lamb. Doubleday, 1968; UK:
  Hodder, 1968; Septimus Finch #16
The family at Tammerton. Doubleday,
  1966; UK: Take a dark journey.
  Hodder, 1965; Septimus Finch #14
Give up the ghost. Doubleday,
  1949; UK: Hammond, 1949; Septimus
  Finch #4
A graveyard plot. Doubleday, 1959;
  UK: The house of the enchantress.
  Hodder, 1959; Septimus Finch #11
Harriet Farewell. Doubleday, 1975;
  UK: Hodder, 1975; Septimus Finch
  #20
The house in Hook Street.
  Doubleday, 1977; UK: Hale, 1978;
  Septimus Finch #21
I knew MacBean. Doubleday, 1948;
  UK: Hammond, 1948; Septimus Finch
  #3
The limping man. Doubleday, 1939;
  UK: And being dead. Bles, 1938;
  Septimus Finch #1
Look behind you, lady. Doubleday,
  1952; UK: Death of our dear one.
  Hammond, 1952; Septimus Finch #6
No. 9 Belmont Square. Doubleday,
  1963; UK: The house in Belmont
  Square. Hodder, 1963; Septimus
  Finch #13
Old Mrs. Ommanney is dead.
  Doubleday, 1955; UK: Fatal
  relations. Hammond, 1955;
  Septimus Finch #8
The silver ladies. Doubleday,
  1951; UK: The disappearing
  bridegroom. Hammond, 1950;
  Septimus Finch #5
Sleep no more. Ace, 1969; UK:
  Hodder, 1958; Septimus Finch #10

The voice of murder. Doubleday,
1956; UK: Hodder, 1956; Septimus
Finch #9
The voice of the house. Doubleday,
1947; UK: The whispering house.
Hammond, 1947; Septimus Finch #2
The woman at Belguardo. Doubleday,
1961; UK: Hodder, 1961; Septimus
Finch #12
ESCOTT, JONATHAN, 1922 -- , see SCOTT,
JACK S. (pseud.)
ESTEVEN, JOHN (pseud. of Samuel
Shellabarger, 1888-1954)
The door of death. Century, 1928;
UK: Methuen, 1929; Rae Norse
Voodoo. Simon & Schuster, 1930;
UK: Hutchinson, 1930; Rae Norse
ESTLEMAN, LOREN D., 1952 --
Angel eyes. Houghton, 1981; Amos
Walker
Dr. Jekyll and Mr. Holmes.
Doubleday, 1979; UK: Penguin,
1981; Sherlock Holmes; Dr. Jekyll
The glass highway. Houghton, 1983;
Amos Walker
The midnight man. Houghton, 1982;
Amos Walker #3
Motor city blue. Houghton, 1980;
UK: Hale, 1982; Amos Walker
Sherlock Holmes vs. Dracula.
Doubleday, 1978; UK: New English
Library, 1978; Sherlock Holmes;
Count Dracula
The stranglers. Doubleday, 1984;
Page Murdock
Sugartown. Houghton, 1985; Amos
Walker
ESTRIDGE, ROBIN, see LORAINE, PHILIP
(pseud.)
EULO, KEN
Nocturnal. Pocket Books, 1983
EUSTACE, ROBERT, see SAYERS,
DOROTHY L. and EUSTACE, ROBERT
EUSTIS, HELEN, 1916 --
The horizontal man. Harper, 1946;
UK: Hamilton, 1947
EVANS, FALLON, 1925 --
Pistols and pedagogues. Sheed,
1963; Adrian Withers
EVANS, JOHN (pseud.). For other
mysteries by this author, see
BROWNE, HOWARD
Halo for Satan. Bobbs, 1948; UK:
Boardman, 1949; Paul Pine

Halo in blood. Bobbs, 1946; Paul
Pine
Halo in brass. Bobbs, 1949; UK:
Foulsham, 1951; Paul Pine
EVANS, PETER
The Englishman's daughter. Random
House, 1983
EVELYN, JOLIN MICHAEL, see UNDERWOOD,
MICHAEL (pseud.)
EVERMAY, MARCH (pseud. of Mathilde
Eiker, 1893 --)
They talked of poison. Macmillan,
1938; UK: Jarrolds, 1939; Insp.
Glover #1; Harry Curry #1
This death was murder. Macmillan,
1940; UK: Jarrolds, 1940; Harry
Curry #2; Insp. Glover #2

FACKLER, ELIZABETH
Arson. Dodd, 1984; Frank James
FAIR, A. A. (pseud. of Stanley
Gardner). For other mysteries by
this author, see GARDNER, ERLE
STANLEY
All grass isn't green. Morrow,
1970; UK: Heinemann, 1970; Bertha
Cool #29; Donald Lam #28
Bachelors get lonely. Morrow,
1961; UK: Heinemann, 1962; Bertha
Cool #21; Donald Lam #20
Bats fly at dusk. Morrow, 1942;
UK: Hale, 1951; Bertha Cool #7;
Donald Lam #7
Bedrooms have windows. Morrow,
1949; UK: Heinemann, 1956; Bertha
Cool #12; Donald Lam #11
Beware of the curves. Morrow,
1956; UK: Heinemann, 1957; Bertha
Cool #15; Donald Lam #14
The bigger they come. Morrow,
1939; UK: Lam to the slaughter.
Hamilton, 1939; Bertha Cool #1;
Donald Lam #1
Cats prowl at night. Morrow, 1943;
UK: Hale, 1949; Bertha Cool #8
The count of nine. Morrow, 1958;
UK: Heinemann, 1959; Bertha Cool
#18; Donald Lam #17
Crows can't count. Morrow, 1946;
UK: Heinemann, 1953; Bertha Cool
#10; Donald Lam #9
Cut thin to win. Morrow, 1965; UK:
Heinemann, 1966; Bertha Cool #26;
Donald Lam #25

Double or quits. Morrow, 1941; UK: Hale, 1949; Bertha Cool #4; Donald Lam #4

Fish or cut bait. Morrow, 1963; UK: Heinemann, 1964; Bertha Cool #24; Donald Lam #23

Fools die on Friday. Morrow, 1947; UK: Heinemann, 1955; Bertha Cool #11; Donald Lam #10

Give 'em the ax. Morrow, 1944; UK: An axe to grind. Heinemann, 1951; Bertha Cool #9; Donald Lam #8

Gold comes in bricks. Morrow, 1940; UK: Hale, 1942; Bertha Cool #2; Donald Lam #2

Kept women can't quit. Morrow, 1960; UK: Heinemann, 1961; Bertha Cool #20; Donald Lam #19

Owls don't blink. Morrow, 1942; UK: Hale, 1951; Bertha Cool #6; Donald Lam #6

Pass the gravy. Morrow, 1959; UK: Heinemann, 1960; Bertha Cool #19; Donald Lam #18

Shills can't cash chips. Morrow, 1961; UK: Stop at the red light. Heinemann, 1962; Bertha Cool #22; Donald Lam #21

Some slips don't show. Morrow, 1957; UK: Heinemann, 1959; Bertha Cool #17; Donald Lam #16

Some women won't wait. Morrow, 1953; UK: Heinemann, 1958; Bertha Cool #14; Donald Lam #13

Spill the jackpot! Morrow, 1941; UK: Hale, 1948; Bertha Cool #5; Donald Lam #5

Top of the heap. Morrow, 1952; UK: Heinemann, 1957; Bertha Cool #13; Donald Lam #12

Traps need fresh bait. Morrow, 1967; UK: Heinemann, 1968; Bertha Cool #28; Donald Lam #27

Try anything once. Morrow, 1962; UK: Heinemann, 1963; Bertha Cool #23; Donald Lam #22

Turn on the heat. Morrow, 1940; UK: Hamilton, 1940; Bertha Cool #3; Donald Lam #3

Up for grabs. Morrow, 1964; UK: Heinemann, 1965; Bertha Cool #25; Donald Lam #24

Widows wear weeds. Morrow, 1966; UK: Heinemann, 1966; Bertha Cool #27; Donald Lam #26

You can die laughing. Morrow, 1957; UK: Heinemann, 1958; Bertha Cool #16; Donald Lam #15

FAIRWAY, SIDNEY (pseud. of Sidney Herbert Daukes, 1879-)
The long tunnel. Doubleday, 1936; UK: Paul, 1935; Richard Carford

FALKNER, MEADE, 1858-1932
The Nebuly coat. UK: Arnold, 1903

FARJEON, J. JEFFERSON, 1883-1955
The 5:18 mystery. Dial, 1929; UK: Collins, 1929

FARRIS, JOHN
Sharp practice. Simon & Schuster, 1974; UK: Weidenfeld, 1975

When Michael calls. Trident Press, 1967; UK: New English Library, 1970

FAST, HOWARD, see CUNNINGHAM, E. V. (pseud.)

FAUST, FREDERICK, see BRAND, MAX (pseud.)

FEARING, KENNETH, 1902-1961
The big clock. Harcourt, 1946; UK: Bodley Head, 1947; George Stroud

The dagger of the mind. Random House, 1941; UK: Lane, 1941

The loneliest girl in the world. Harcourt, 1951; UK: Bodley Head, 1952

FENISONG, RUTH
Bite the hand. Doubleday, 1956; UK: The blackmailer. Foulsham, 1958; Gridley Nelson #10

But not forgotten. Doubleday, 1960; UK: Sinister assignment. Foulsham, 1960; Gridley Nelson #12

The butler died in Brooklyn. Doubleday, 1943; UK: Aldor, 1946; Gridley Nelson #3

Dead weight. Doubleday, 1962; UK: Hale, 1964; Gridley Nelson #13

Dead yesterday. Doubleday, 1951; Gridley Nelson #6

Deadlock. Doubleday, 1952; Gridley Nelson #7

Death of the party. Doubleday, 1958; Gridley Nelson #11

The drop of a hat. Doubleday, 1970; UK: Hale, 1971; Victoria Tarrant

Grim rehearsal. Doubleday, 1950;
  UK: Foulsham, 1951; Gridley Nelson
  #5
Miscast for murder. Doubleday,
  1954; Gridley Nelson #9
Murder needs a face. Doubleday,
  1942; Gridley Nelson #1
Murder needs a name. Doubleday,
  1942; UK: Swan, 1950; Gridley
  Nelson #2
Murder runs a fever. Doubleday,
  1943; Gridley Nelson #4
The schemers. Doubleday, 1957; UK:
  The case of the gloating landlord.
  Foulsham, 1958
The wench is dead. Doubleday,
  1953; Gridley Nelson #8
Widow's plight. Doubleday, 1955;
  UK: Widow's blackmail. Foulsham,
  1957
FENNELLY, TONY
  The glory hole murders. Carroll &
  Graf, 1985; Matty Sinclair
FENWICK, ELIZABETH, 1920–
  A long way down. Harper, 1959; UK:
  Gollancz, 1959; Matthew Holley
  Poor Harriet. Harper, 1957; UK:
  Gollancz, 1958
FERGUSON, JOHN, 1873 --
  Death comes to Perigord. Dodd,
  1931; UK: Collins, 1931
  The man in the dark. Dodd, 1928;
  UK: Lane, 1928; Francis McNab
  The secret road. Dodd, 1925; UK:
  Bodley Head, 1925
  Stealthy terror. Land, 1918; UK:
  Lane, 1918
  Terror on the island. Vanguard,
  1942; UK: Collins, 1942
FERRARS, E. X. (pseud. of Morna Doris
  Brown, 1907 --)
  Alive and dead. Doubleday, 1975;
  UK: Collins, 1974
  Blood flies upward. Doubleday,
  1977; UK: Collins, 1976
  Death of a minor character.
  Doubleday, 1983; Virginia Freer;
  Felix Freer
  The decayed gentlewoman. Doubleday,
  1963; UK: A legal fiction.
  Collins, 1964
  Depart this life. Doubleday, 1958;
  UK: A tale of two murders.
  Collins, 1959; Insp. Crankshaw

Designs on life. Doubleday, 1980;
  UK: Collins, 1980
Enough to kill a horse. Doubleday,
  1955; UK: Collins, 1955
Experiment with death. Doubleday,
  1981; Emma Ritchie
Foot in the grave. Doubleday, 1972;
  UK: Collins, 1973
Frog in the throat. Doubleday,
  1980; UK: Collins, 1980
Give a corpse a bad name. UK:
  Hodder, 1940; Toby Dyke #1
Hanged man's house. Doubleday,
  1974; UK: Collins, 1974
I, said the fly. Doubleday, 1945;
  UK: Hodder, 1945
In at the kill. Doubleday, 1979;
  UK: Collins, 1978; Charlotte
  Cambry
Last will and testament. Doubleday,
  1978; UK: Collins, 1978; Virginia
  Freer
Murder of a suicide. Doubleday,
  1941; UK: Death in Botanist's
  Bay. Hodder, 1941; Toby Dyke #3
Murderers anonymous. Doubleday,
  1978; UK: Collins, 1977; Matthew
  Tierney
Neck in a noose. Doubleday, 1943;
  UK: Your neck in a noose. Hodder,
  1942; Toby Dyke #5
The pretty pink shroud. Doubleday,
  1977; UK: Collins, 1977; Martin
  Rhymer
Rehearsals for murder. Doubleday,
  1941; UK: Remove the bodies.
  Hodder, 1940; Toby Dyke #2
Root of all evil. Doubleday, 1984;
  Andrew Basnett; Insp. Theobold
The shape of a stain. Doubleday,
  1942; UK: Don't monkey with
  murder. Hodder, 1942; Toby Dyke
  #4
The small world of murder.
  Doubleday, 1973; UK: Collins,
  1973
Something wicked. Doubleday, 1984;
  Andrew Basnett
Thinner than water. Doubleday,
  1982
The wandering widows. Doubleday,
  1962; UK: Collins, 1962
Witness before the fact. Doubleday,
  1980; UK: Collins, 1979; Peter
  Corey

Zero at the bone. Walker, 1968;
UK: Collins, 1967
FERRARS, ELIZABETH see FERRARS, E. X.
FIELD, EVAN
What Nigel knew. Crown, 1981
FIELD, MOIRA
Foreign body. Macmillan, 1951; UK:
Bles, 1950; Insp. Flower
FIELDING, A. (pseud. of Dorothy
Fielding, 1884 --)
Black cats are lucky. Kinsey,
1938; UK: Collins, 1937; Insp.
Pointer #22
The case of the missing diary.
Kinsey, 1936; UK: Collins, 1935;
Insp. Pointer #17
The case of the two pearl
necklaces. Kinsey, 1936; UK:
Collins, 1936; Insp. Pointer
#19
The Cautley mystery. Kinsey, 1934;
UK: The Cautley conundrum.
Collins, 1934; Insp. Pointer #16
The Charteris mystery. Knopf, 1925;
UK: Collins, 1925; Insp. Pointer
#2
The Clifford affair. Knopf, 1927;
UK: Collins, 1927; Insp. Pointer
#4
The Cluny problem. Knopf, 1929; UK:
Collins, 1928; Insp. Pointer #6
The Craig poisoning mystery.
Cosmopolitan, 1930; UK: Collins,
1930; Insp. Pointer #9
Death of John Tait. Kinsey, 1932;
UK: Collins, 1932; Insp. Pointer
#12
The Eames-Erskine case. Knopf,
1925; UK: Collins, 1924; Insp.
Pointer #1
The footsteps that stopped. Knopf,
1926; UK: Collins, 1926; Insp.
Pointer #3
Murder at the nook. Knopf, 1930;
UK: Collins, 1929; Insp. Pointer
#8
The mysterious partner. Knopf,
1929; UK: Collins, 1929; Insp.
Pointer #7
Mystery at the rectory. Kinsey,
1937; UK: Collins, 1936; Insp.
Pointer #20
The net around Joan Ingilby. Knopf,
1928; UK: Collins, 1928; Insp.
Pointer #5

The paper chase mystery. Kinsey,
1935; UK: The paper chase.
Collins, 1934; Insp. Pointer #15
Pointer to a crime. Arcadia House,
1945; UK: Collins, 1944; Insp.
Pointer #23
Scarecrow. Kinsey, 1937; UK:
Collins, 1937; Insp. Pointer #21
The tall house mystery. Kinsey,
1933; UK: Collins, 1933; Insp.
Pointer #14
Tragedy at Beachcroft. Kinsey,
1935; UK: Collins, 1935; Insp.
Pointer #18
The Upfold Farm mystery. Kinsey,
1932; UK: Collins, 1931; Insp.
Pointer #11
The wedding-chest mystery. Kinsey,
1932; UK: Collins, 1930; Insp.
Pointer #10
The Westwood mystery. Kinsey,
1933; UK: Collins, 1932; Insp.
Pointer #13
FINNEGAN, ROBERT (pseud. of Paul
William Ryan, 1906-1947)
The bandaged nude. Simon &
Schuster, 1946; Dan Banion #2
The lying ladies. Simon & Schuster,
1946; UK: Bodley Head, 1949; Dan
Banion #1
Many a monster. Simon & Schuster,
1948; Dan Banion #3
FISCHER, BRUNO, 1908 --
The dead men grin. McKay, 1945;
UK: Quality, 1947; Ben Helm #1
The evil days. Random House, 1974;
UK: Hale, 1976
The hornet's nest. Morrow, 1944;
UK: Quality, 1947; Rick Train #1
Kill to fit. Green, 1946;
Instructive Arts, 1951; Rick
Train #2
More deaths than one. Ziff Davis,
1947; UK: Foulsham, 1950; Ben
Helm #2
The paper circle. Dodd, 1951; UK:
Boardman, 1952; Ben Helm #5
The restless hands. Dodd, 1949;
UK: Foulsham, 1950; Ben Helm #3
The silent dust. Dodd, 1950; UK:
Boardman, 1951; Ben Helm #4
FISH, ROBERT L. 1912 -- . For other
mysteries by this author, see
PIKE, ROBERT L. (pseud.)

Always kill a stranger. Putnam,
1967; Jose da Silva #6

Brazilian sleigh ride. Simon &
Schuster, 1965; UK: Boardman,
1966; Jose da Silva #5

The bridge that went nowhere.
Putnam, 1968; UK: Long, 1970; Jose
da Silva #7

The diamond bubble. Simon &
Schuster, 1965; UK: Boardman,
1967; Jose da Silva #4

The fugitive. Simon & Schuster,
1962; UK: Boardman, 1963; Jose da
Silva #1

The green hell treasure. Putnam,
1971; Jose da Silva #9

A gross carriage of justice.
Doubleday, 1979; Murder League #3

The incredible Schlock Homes. Simon
& Schuster, 1966; Schlock Homes #1

Isle of the snakes. Simon &
Schuster, 1963; UK: Boardman,
1964; Jose da Silva #2

The memoirs of Schlock Homes.
Bobbs, 1974; Schlock Homes #2

The Murder League. Simon & Schuster,
1968; UK: New English Library,
1970; Murder League #1

Rub-a-dub-dub. Simon & Schuster,
1971; Murder League #2

The shrunken head. Simon & Schuster,
1963; UK: Boardman, 1965; Jose da
Silva #3

Trouble in paradise. Doubleday,
1975; Jose da Silva #10

The Xavier affair. Putnam, 1969;
UK: Hale, 1974; Jose da Silva #8

FISHER, DAVID E., 1932 --
Katie's terror. Morrow, 1982; Katie
McGregor Townsend

The last flying tiger. Scribner's,
1976; UK: Allen, 1977

FISHER, DOUGLAS, 1902-1981
What's wrong at Pyford? UK: Hodder,
1950; Jeff Tellford

FISHER, STEPHEN GOULD, 1912-1980, see
GOULD, STEPHEN (pseud.) or FISHER,
STEVE

FISHER, STEVE
I wake up screaming. Dodd, 1941; UK:
Hale, 1943

Murder of the pigboat skipper.
Hillman, 1937

FITZGERALD, NIGEL, 1906 --
Affairs of death. UK: Collins,
1967; Insp. Duffy #9

Black welcome. Macmillan, 1962; UK:
Collins, 1961; Insp. Duffy #7

The candles are all out. Macmillan,
1961; UK: Collins, 1960; Alan
Russell

Echo answers murder. Macmillan,
1965; UK: The day of the adder.
Collins, 1963; Insp. Duffy

Ghost in the making. UK: Collins,
1960; Alan Russell #2

The house is falling. UK: Collins,
1955; Insp. Duffy #3

Imagine a man. UK: Collins, 1956;
Insp. Duffy #4

Midsummer malice. Macmillan, 1959;
UK: Collins, 1953; Insp. Duffy #1

The rosy pastor. UK: Collins,
1954; Insp. Duffy #2

The student body. UK: Collins,
1958; Insp. Duffy #5

Suffer a witch. UK: Collins, 1958;
Insp. Duffy #6

This won't hurt you. Macmillan,
1960; UK: Collins, 1959

FITZGERALD, PENELOPE, 1916 --
The golden child. Scribner's,
1977; UK: Duckworth, 1977;
Heinrich Untermensch; Insp. Mace

FITZSIMMONS, CORTLAND, 1883-1949
The Bainbridge murder. McBride,
1930; UK: Eyre, 1930; Arthur
Martinson

Death rings a bell. Lippincott,
1942; UK: Boardman, 1943; Percy
Peacock #1

70,000 witnesses. McBride, 1931;
Jack Methridge

Tied for murder. Lippincott, 1943;
UK: Boardman, 1945; Percy Peacock
#2

FLEMING, JOAN, 1908-1980
Death of a sardine. Washburn,
1964; UK: Collins, 1963

Every inch a lady. Putnam, 1977;
UK: Collins, 1977

Miss Bones. Washburn, 1960; UK:
Collins, 1959

Nothing is the number when you
die. Washburn, 1965; UK: Collins,
1965; Nuri Iskirlak #2

Screams from a penny dreadful. UK: Hamilton, 1971

Too late! too late! the maiden cried. Putnam, 1975; UK: Hamilton, 1975

When I grow rich. Washburn, 1962; UK: Collins, 1952; Nuri Iskirlak #1

You won't let me Finnish. Putnam, 1974; UK: You won't let me finish. Collins, 1973

FLETCHER, HENRY LANCELOT AUBREY, see WADE, HENRY (pseud.)

FLETCHER, J. S., 1863-1935

The adventures of Archer Dawe, sleuth-hound. UK: The contents of the coffin. Long, 1909; Archer Dawe

Behind the monocle and other stories. UK: Jarrolds, 1928

The case of the artificial eye. Curl, 1939; UK: Paul Campenhaye, specialist in criminology. Ward, 1918; Paul Campenhaye

The Charing Cross mystery. Putnam, 1923; UK: Jenkins, 1923

The copper box. Doran, 1923; UK: Hodder, 1923

The ebony box. Knopf, 1934; UK: Butterworth, 1934; Ronald Camberwell #9

The eleventh hour. Knopf, 1935; UK: Butterworth, 1935; Ronald Camberwell #10

The Herapath property. Knopf, 1921; UK: Ward, 1920

The Middle Temple murder. Knopf, 1919; UK: Ward, 1919; Frank Spargo

The mill house murder. Knopf, 1937; UK: Todmanhowe Grange. Butterworth, 1937; Ronald Camberwell #11

Murder in four degrees. Knopf, 1931; UK: Harrap, 1931; Ronald Camberwell #2

Murder in the squire's pew. Knopf, 1932; UK: Harrap, 1932; Ronald Camberwell #3

Murder in Wrides Park. Knopf, 1931; UK: Harrap, 1931; Ronald Camberwell #1

Murder of a banker. Knopf, 1933; UK: The mystery of a London banker. Harrap, 1933; Ronald Camberwell #6

Murder of the lawyer's clerk. Knopf, 1933; UK: Who killed Alfred Snowe? Harrap, 1933; Ronald Camberwell #7

Murder of the ninth baronet. Knopf, 1932; UK: Harrap, 1932; Ronald Camberwell #4

Murder of the only witness. Knopf, 1933; UK: Harrap, 1933; Ronald Camberwell #5

Murder of the secret agent. Knopf, 1934; UK: Harrap, 1934; Ronald Camberwell #8

The orange-yellow diamond. Knopf, 1921; UK: Newnes, 1920

Scarhaven keep. Knopf, 1922; UK: Ward, 1920

The secret of secrets. Clode, 1929

The secret of the barbican and other stories. Doran, 1925; UK: Hodder, 1924

The Yorkshire Moorland murder. Knopf, 1930; UK: Jenkins, 1930

FLORA, FLETCHER, 1914-1968, see PALMER, STUART and FLORA, FLETCHER

FLOWER, PAT, 1914-1978

Cat's cradle. Stein & Day, 1978; UK: Collins, 1973

Cobweb. Stein & Day, 1978; UK: Collins, 1972

Crisscross. Stein & Day, 1977; UK: Collins, 1976

Odd job. Stein & Day, 1978; UK: Collins, 1974

Shadow show. Stein & Day, 1978; UK: Collins, 1976

Slyboots. Stein & Day, 1978; UK: Collins, 1974

Vanishing point. Stein & Day, 1977; UK: Collins, 1975

FLYNN, CAROL HOULIHAN

Washed in the blood. Seaview, 1983; Able Garret

FLYNN, DON

Murder isn't enough. Walker, 1983; Ed Fitzgerald

Murder on the Hudson. Walker, 1985; Ed Fitzgerald

FOLEY, RAE (pseud. of Elinore Denniston, 1900-1978)

The Barclay place. Dodd, 1975; UK: Hale, 1976

Girl on a high wire. Dodd, 1969; UK: Hale, 1971

Where is Nancy Bostwick? Dodd,
1958; UK: Boardman, 1958; Hiram
Potter

FOOTE-SMITH, ELIZABETH, 1913 --
A gentle albatross. Putnam, 1976;
Will Woodford; Mercy Newcastle
Never say die. Putnam, 1977; Will
Woodfield

FOOTNER, HULBERT (pseud. of William
Hulbert Footner, 1879-1944)
The almost perfect murder: more
Madame Storey mysteries.
Lippincott, 1937; UK: Collins,
1933; Rosika Storey #7
Anybody's pearls. Doubleday, 1930;
UK: Hodder, 1929
The casual murderer. Lippincott,
1937; UK: Collins, 1932; Rosika
Storey #6
Dangerous cargo. Harper, 1934; UK:
Collins, 1934; Rosika Storey #8
The dark ships. Harper, 1937; UK:
Collins, 1937
The death of a celebrity. Harper,
1938; UK: Collins, 1938; Amos Lee
Mappin #2
Death of a saboteur. Harper, 1943;
UK: Collins, 1944; Amos Lee Mappin
#8
The doctor who held hands.
Doubleday, 1929; UK: Collins,
1929; Rosika Storey #4
Easy to kill. Harper, 1931; UK:
Collins, 1931; Rosika Storey #5
The house with the blue door.
Harper, 1942; UK: Collins, 1943;
Amos Lee Mappin #7
The island of fear. Harper, 1936;
UK: Cassell, 1936
Madame Storey. Doran, 1926; UK:
Collins, 1926; Rosika Storey #2
The murder that had everything.
Harper, 1939; UK: Collins, 1939;
Amos Lee Mappin #3
Murderer's vanity. Harper, 1940;
UK: Collins, 1941; Amos Lee Mappin
#5
The mystery of the folded paper.
Harper, 1930; UK: The folded
paper mystery. Collins, 1930;
Amos Lee Mappin #1; Christopher
Morley
The nation's missing guest. Harper,
1939; UK: Collins, 1939; Amos Lee
Mappin #4

The Obeah murders. Harper, 1937;
UK: Murder in the sun. Collins,
1938
Orchids to murder. Harper, 1945;
UK: Collins, 1945; Amos Lee
Mappin #10
Scarred jungle. Harper, 1935; UK:
Cassell, 1935
Tortuous trails. UK: Collins, 1937
Trial by water. Farrar, 1931; UK:
Hodder, 1930
The under dogs. Doran, 1925; UK:
Collins, 1925; Rosika Storey #1
Unneutral murder. Harper, 1944; UK:
Collins, 1944; Amos Lee Mappin #9
The velvet hand: new Madame Storey
mysteries. Doubleday, 1928; UK:
Collins, 1928; Rosika Storey #3
The whip-poor-will mystery.
Harper, 1935; UK: The new made
grave. Collins, 1935
Who killed the husband? Harper,
1941; UK: Collins, 1941; Amos Lee
Mappin #6

FORBES, DANIEL, see KENYON, MICHAEL
FORBES, DELORIS FLORINE STANTON, see
FORBES, STANTON or WELLS, TOBIAS
(pseud.)
FORBES, STANTON
Buried in so sweet a place.
Doubleday, 1977; UK: Hale, 1978
A deadly kind of lonely. Doubleday,
1971; UK: Hale, 1973
Go to thy death bed. Doubleday,
1968; UK: Hale, 1969
Grieve for the past. Doubleday,
1963; UK: Gollancz, 1964
If the two of them are dead.
Doubleday, 1968; UK: Hale, 1968
The last will and testament of
Constance Cobble. Doubleday,
1980; UK: Hale, 1980; Constance
Cobble
The name's Death, remember me?
Doubleday, 1969; UK: Hale, 1970
The sad, sudden death of my fair
lady. Doubleday, 1971; UK: Hale,
1971
She was only the sheriff's
daughter. Doubleday, 1970; UK:
Hale, 1970
Some poisoned by their wives.
Doubleday, 1974; UK: Hale, 1975
Terror touches me. Doubleday,
1966; UK: Hale, 1966

Welcome, my dear, to Belfry House.
Doubleday, 1973; UK: Hale, 1974
FORD, COREY, see RIDDELL, JOHN
(pseud.)
FORD, LESLIE (pseud. of Zenith
Brown, 1898 --). For other
mysteries by this author, see FROME,
DAVID (pseud.)
All for the love of a lady.
Scribner's, 1944; UK: Collins,
1945; Grace Latham #11; Col.
Primrose #11
The Bahamas murder case.
Scribner's, 1952; UK: Collins,
1952
Burn forever. Farrar, 1935; UK:
Mountain madness. Hutchinson,
1935
By the watchman's clock. Farrar,
1932; Col. Primrose #1; Grace
Latham #1
The clue of the Judas tree. Farrar,
1933; Joseph Kelly #2
Date with death. Scribner's, 1949;
UK: Shot in the dark. Collins,
1949
The devil's stronghold. Scribner's,
1948; UK: Collins, 1948; Grace
Latham #15; Col. Primrose #15
False to any man. Scribner's, 1939;
UK: Snow white murder. Collins,
1940; Col. Primrose #6; Grace
Latham #6
The girl from the Mimosa Club.
Scribner's, 1957; UK: Collins,
1957
Honolulu story. Scribner's, 1946;
UK: Honolulu murder story.
Collins, 1947; Grace Latham #13;
Col. Primrose #13
Ill met by midnight. Farrar, 1937;
UK: Collins, 1937; Col. Primrose
#3; Grace Latham #2
Invitation to murder. Scribner's,
1954; UK: Collins, 1955
Murder comes to Eden. Scribner's,
1955; UK: Collins, 1956
Murder in Maryland. Farrar, 1932;
UK: Hutchinson, 1933; Joseph Kelly
#1
Murder in the O. P. M. Scribner's,
1942; UK: The priority murder.
Collins, 1943; Grace Latham #9;
Col. Primrose #9

Murder of the fifth columnist.
Scribner's, 1941; UK: The capitol
crime. Collins, 1941; Grace
Latham #8; Col. Primrose #8
Murder with Southern hospitality.
Scribner's, 1942; UK: Murder down
South. Collins, 1943
Old lover's ghost. Scribner's,
1940; Grace Latham #7; Col.
Primrose #7
The Philadelphia murder story.
Scribner's, 1945; UK: Collins,
1945; Grace Latham #12; Col.
Primrose #12
Reno rendezvous. Farrar, 1939; UK:
Mr. Cromwell is dead. Collins,
1939; Col. Primrose #5; Grace
Latham #5
Road to Folly. Scribner's, 1940;
UK: Collins, 1941
The simple way of poison. Farrar,
1937; UK: Collins, 1938; Col.
Primrose #4; Grace Latham #3
Siren in the night. Scribner's,
1943; UK: Collins, 1944; Grace
Latham #10; Col. Primrose #10
The sound of footsteps. Doubleday,
1931; UK: Footsteps on the
stairs. Gollancz, 1931
The strangled witness. Farrar,
1934; Col. Primrose #2
Three bright pebbles. Farrar,
1938; UK: Collins, 1938; Grace
Latham #4
The town cried murder. Scribner's,
1939; UK: Collins, 1939
Trial by ambush. Scribner's, 1962;
UK: Trial from ambush. Collins,
1962; Col. Primrose #17; Grace
Latham #17
Washington whispers murder.
Scribner's, 1953; UK: The lying
jade. Collins, 1953; Col.
Primrose #16; Grace Latham #16
The woman in black. Scribner's,
1947; UK: Collins, 1948; Grace
Latham #14; Col. Primrose #14
FORD, PAUL LEICESTER, 1865-1902
The great K. & A. train robbery.
Dodd, 1897; UK: Low, 1897
FORESTER, BRUCE M.
In strict confidence. Ashley, 1982
FORESTER, C. S., 1899-1966
Payment deferred. Little, 1942;
UK: Lane, 1926

Plain murder. Dell, 1954; UK: Lane, 1930

FORREST, NORMAN (pseud. of Nigel Morland). For other mysteries by this author, see DONAVAN, JOHN (pseud.)

Death took a Greek god. Hillman, 1938; UK: Harrap, 1937; John Finnegan #2

Death took a publisher. Hillman, 1938; UK: Harrap, 1936; John Finnegan #1

FORREST, RICHARD

The death at Yew Corner. Holt, 1981; Lyon Wentworth; Bea Wentworth

The death in the willows. Holt, 1979; UK: Hale, 1981; Lyon Wentworth

Death under the lilacs. St. Martin's, 1985; Lyon Wentworth

FOSTER, RICHARD (pseud.). For other mysteries by this author, see CHABER, M. E. (pseud.) or MONIG, CHRISTOPHER (pseud.)

Bier for a chaser. Fawcett, 1959; UK: Muller, 1960; Peter Draco #1

Blonde and beautiful. Popular Library, 1955

The invisible man murders. Five Star, 1945; Chin Kwang Kham #2

The laughing Buddha murders. Vulcan, 1944; Chin Kwang Kham #1

Too late for mourning. Fawcett, 1960; UK: Muller, 1961; Peter Draco #2

FOWLER, SYDNEY (pseud. of Sydney Fowler Wright, 1874-1965)

FOX, PETER, 1946 --

Trail of the reaper. St. Martin's, 1983; Jack Lamarre; Alison Prendergast

FOXX, JACK (pseud. of Bill Pronzini). For other mysteries by this author, see PRONZINI, BILL

Dead run. Bobbs, 1975; Dan Connell #2

Freebooty. Bobbs, 1976

The jade figurine. Bobbs, 1972; Dan Connell #1

FRANCIS, DICK, 1920 --

Banker. Putnam, 1983

Blood sport. Harper, 1967; UK: Joseph, 1967; Gene Hawkins; Dave Teller

Bonecrack. Harper, 1972; UK: Joseph, 1971; Neil Griffon

The danger. Putnam, 1984; Andrew Douglas

Dead cert. Harper, 1962; UK: Joseph, 1962; Alan York

Enquiry. Harper, 1969; UK: Joseph, 1969; Kelly Hughes

Flying finish. Harper, 1967; UK: Joseph, 1966

For kicks. Harper, 1965; UK: Joseph, 1965

Forfeit. Harper, 1969; UK: Joseph, 1969; James Tyrone

High stakes. Harper, 1976; UK: Joseph, 1975; Steven Scott

In the frame. Harper, 1977; UK: Joseph, 1976; Charles Todd

Knock down. Harper, 1975; UK: Joseph, 1974; Jonah Dereham

Nerve. Harper, 1964; UK: Joseph, 1964; Rob Finn

Odds against. Harper, 1966; UK: Joseph, 1965; Sid Halley #1

Proof. Putnam, 1985; Tony Beach; Gerard McGregor

Rat race. Harper, 1971; UK: Joseph, 1970; Matt Shore

Reflex. Putnam, 1981; UK: Joseph, 1980; Philip Nore

Risk. Harper, 1978; UK: Joseph, 1977

Slayride. Harper, 1971; UK: Joseph, 1970; David Cleveland

Smokescreen. Harper, 1973; UK: Joseph, 1972

Trial run. Harper, 1979; UK: Joseph, 1978; Randall Drew

Twice shy. Putnam, 1982

Whip hand. Harper, 1980; UK: Joseph, 1979; Sid Halley #2

FRANKAU, PAMELA, 1908-1967

Appointment with death. Dutton, 1940; UK: A democrat dies. Heinemann, 1939

FRASER, ANTONIA, 1932 --

Cool repentence. Norton, 1983; Jemima Shore #4

Oxford blood. Norton, 1985; Jemima Shore #5

Quiet as a nun. Viking, 1977; UK: Weidenfeld, 1977; Jemima Shore #1

A splash of red. Norton, 1982; Jemima Shore #3

The wild island. Norton, 1978; UK:
Weidenfeld, 1978; Jemima Shore #2
FREDERICKS, ERNEST JASON
Shakedown Hotel. Ace, 1958; UK:
Lost Friday. Hale, 1959; Sam
Cates
FREELING, NICOLAS, 1927 --
Aupres de ma blonde. Harper, 1972;
UK: A long silence. Hamilton,
1972; Insp. Van der Valk #11;
Arlette Van der Valk #1
The back of the northwind. Viking,
1983; Henri Castang
Because of the cats. Harper, 1964;
UK: Gollancz, 1963; Insp. Van der
Valk #1
The bugles blowing. Harper, 1976;
UK: What are the bugles blowing
for? Heinemann, 1975; Henri
Castang #2
Castang's city. Pantheon, 1980; UK:
Heinemann, 1980; Henri Castang #5
Criminal conversation. Harper,
1966; UK: Gollancz, 1965; Insp.
Van der Valk #5
Double barrel. Harper, 1965; UK:
Gollancz, 1964; Insp. Van der Valk
#4
The Dresden green. Harper, 1967;
UK: Gollancz, 1966; Insp. Van der
Valk #7
A dressing of diamond. Harper,
1974; UK: Hamilton, 1974; Henri
Castang #1
Gadget. Coward McCann, 1977; UK:
Heinemann, 1977
The king of the rainy country.
Harper, 1966; UK: Gollancz, 1966;
Insp. Van der Valk #6
Love in Amsterdam. Harper, 1963;
UK: Gollancz, 1962; Insp. Van der
Valk #1
The lovely ladies. Harper, 1971;
UK: Over the high side. Hamilton,
1971; Insp. Van der Valk #10
The night lords. Pantheon, 1978;
UK: Heinemann, 1978; Henri Castang
#4
A question of loyalty. Harper,
1964; UK: Guns before butter.
Gollancz, 1963; Insp. Van der Valk
#3
Sabine. Harper, 1978; UK: Lake
Isle. Heinemann, 1976; Henri
Castang #3

Strike out where not applicable.
Harper, 1968; UK: Gollancz, 1967;
Insp. Van der Valk #8
This is the castle. Harper, 1968;
UK: Gollancz, 1968
Tsing-boom! Harper, 1969; UK:
Tsing-boum! Hamilton, 1969; Insp.
Van der Valk #9
The widow. Pantheon, 1979; UK:
Heinemann, 1979; Insp. Van der
Valk #2; Arlette Davidson
FREEMAN, MARTIN J., 1899 --
The case of the blind mouse.
Dutton, 1935; UK: Eldon, 1936;
Jerry Todd
The murder of a midget. Dutton,
1931; UK: Eldon, 1934; Judo
Marriott
The scarf on the scarecrow.
Dutton, 1938; Jerry Todd
FREEMAN, R. AUSTIN, 1862-1943
As a thief in the night. Dodd,
1928; UK: Hodder, 1928; John
Evelyn Thorndyke #5
The blue scarab. Dodd, 1924; UK:
Dr. Thorndyke's case book.
Hodder, 1923; John Evelyn
Thorndyke #8
The cat's eye. Dodd, 1927; UK:
Hodder, 1923; John Evelyn
Thorndyke #9
A certain Dr. Thorndyke. Dodd,
1928; UK: Hodder, 1927; John
Evelyn Thorndyke #14
The D'Arblay mystery. Dodd, 1926;
UK: Hodder, 1926; John Evelyn
Thorndyke #12
Death at the inn. Dodd, 1937; UK:
Felo de se? Hodder, 1937; John
Evelyn Thorndyke #24
Dr. Thorndyke intervenes. Dodd,
1933; UK: Hodder, 1933; John
Evelyn Thorndyke #21
Dr. Thorndyke investigates. UK:
University of London Press, 1930;
John Evelyn Thorndyke #17
Dr. Thorndyke omnibus. Dodd, 1932;
UK: Hodder, 1929; John Evelyn
Thorndyke #16
Dr. Thorndyke's cases. Dodd, 1931;
UK: John Thorndyke's cases.
Chatto, 1909; John Evelyn
Thorndyke #2
Dr. Thorndyke's crime file. Dodd,
1941; John Evelyn Thorndyke #27

Dr. Thorndyke's discovery. Dodd, 1932; UK: When rogues fall out. Hodder, 1932; John Evelyn Thorndyke #20

For the defense: Dr. Thorndyke. Dodd, 1934; UK: For the defence: Dr. Thorndyke. Hodder, 1934; John Evelyn Thorndyke #22

Helen Vardon's confession. UK: Hodder, 1922; John Evelyn Thorndyke #7

The magic casket. Dodd, 1927; UK: Hodder, 1927; John Evelyn Thorndyke #13

Mr. Polton explains. Dodd, 1940; UK: Hodder, 1940; John Evelyn Thorndyke #26

Mr. Pottermack's oversight. Dodd, 1930; UK: Hodder, 1930; John Evelyn Thorndyke #18

The mystery of Angelina Frood. Dodd, 1925; UK: Hodder, 1924; John Evelyn Thorndyke #10

The mystery of 31, New Inn. Winston, 1913; UK: Hodder, 1912; John Evelyn Thorndyke #5

The Penrose mystery. Dodd, 1936; UK: Hodder, 1936; John Evelyn Thorndyke #23

Pontifex, Son and Thorndyke. Dodd, 1931; UK: Hodder, 1931; John Evelyn Thorndyke #19

The red thumb mark. Newton, 1911; UK: Collingwood, 1907; John Evelyn Thorndyke #1

The shadow of the wolf. Dodd, 1925; UK: Hodder, 1925; John Evelyn Thorndyke #11

A silent witness. Winston, 1915; UK: Hodder, 1914; John Evelyn Thorndyke #6

The singing bone. Dodd, 1923; UK: Hodder, 1912; John Evelyn Thorndyke #4

The stoneware monkey. Dodd, 1939; UK: Hodder, 1938; John Evelyn Thorndyke #25

The unconscious witness. Dodd, 1942; UK: Jacob Street mystery. Hodder, 1942; John Evelyn Thorndyke #28

The uttermost farthing. Winston, 1914; UK: A savant's vendetta. Pearson, 1920; Humphrey Challoner

The vanishing man. Dodd, 1929; UK: The eye of Osiris. Hodder, 1911; John Evelyn Thorndyke #3

FREMLIN, CELIA, 1914 --
The parasite person. Doubleday, 1982

The spider-orchid. Doubleday, 1978; UK: Gollancz, 1977

FRIEND, OSCAR JEROME, see JEROME, OWEN FOX (pseud.)

FRIMMER, STEVEN
Dead matter. Holt, 1982

FROME, DAVID (pseud. of Zenith Jones Brown, 1898 --). For other works by this author, see FORD, LESLIE (pseud.)
The black envelope. Farrar, 1937; UK: The guilt is plain. Longman, 1938; Evan Pinkerton #9

The eel pie murders. Farrar, 1933; UK: The eel pie mystery. Longman, 1933; Evan Pinkerton #4

The Hammersmith murders. Doubleday, 1930; UK: Methuen, 1930; Evan Pinkerton #1

Homicide house. Rinehart, 1950; UK: Murder on the square. Hale, 1951; Evan Pinkerton #11

The man from Scotland Yard. Farrar, 1932; UK: Mr. Simpson finds a body. Longman, 1933; Evan Pinkerton #3

Mr. Pinkerton at the Old Angel. Farrar, 1939; UK: Mr. Pinkerton and the Old Angel. Longman, 1939; Evan Pinkerton #10

Mr. Pinkerton finds a body. Farrar, 1934; UK: The body in the Turl. Longman, 1935; Evan Pinkerton #6

Mr. Pinkerton goes to Scotland Yard. Farrar, 1934; UK: Arsenic in Richmond. Longman, 1934; Evan Pinkerton #5

Mr. Pinkerton grows a beard. Farrar, 1935; UK: The body in Bedford Square. Longman, 1935; Evan Pinkerton #7

Mr. Pinkerton has the clue. Farrar, 1936; UK: Longman, 1936; Evan Pinkerton #8

The murder of an old man. UK: Methuen, 1929; Gregory Lewis #1

The strange death of Martin Green.
Doubleday, 1931; UK: The murder on
the sixth hole. Methuen, 1931;
Gregory Lewis #2

Two against Scotland Yard. Farrar,
1931; UK: The by-pass murder.
Longman, 1932; Evan Pinkerton #2

FULLER, DEAN
Passage. Dodd, 1983; Roger Truly

FULLER, ROY, 1912 --
Fantasy and fugue. Macmillan,
1956; UK: Verschoyle, 1954; Harry
Sinton

The father's comedy. UK: Duetsch,
1961

Second curtain. Macmillan, 1956;
UK: Verschoyle, 1956; George
Garner

With my little eye. Macmillan,
1957; UK: Lehmann, 1948

FULLER, SAMUEL, 1911 --
The dark page. Duell, 1944
The naked kiss. Belmont, 1964

FULLER, TIMOTHY, 1914-1971
Harvard has a homicide. Little,
1936; UK: J for Jupiter. Collins,
1937; Edmund Jones #1

Keep cool, Mr. Jones. Little, 1950;
UK: Heinemann, 1951; Edmund Jones
#5

Reunion with murder. Little, 1941;
UK: Heinemann, 1941; Edmund Jones
#2

This is murder, Mr. Jones. Little,
1943; UK: Heinemann, 1944; Edmund
Jones #4

Three thirds of a ghost. Little,
1941; UK: Heinemann, 1947; Edmund
Jones #3

FURST, ALAN, 1941 --
The Caribbean account. Delacorte,
1981; Roger Levin

FUTRELLE, JACQUES, 1875-1912
The chase of the golden plate.
Dodd, 1906; Augustus Van Dusen #1

The diamond master. Bobbs, 1909;
UK: Holden, 1912; Augustus Van
Dusen #4

Great cases of the thinking machine.
UK: Dover, 1977; Augustus Van
Dusen #5

The thinking machine. Dodd, 1907;
UK: Chapman, 1907; Augustus Van
Dusen #2

The thinking machine on the case.
Appleton, 1908; UK: The professor
on the case. Nelson, 1909;
Augustus Van Dusen #3

GADDA, CARLO EMILIO, 1893-1973
That awful mess on Via Merulana.
Braziller, 1965; UK: Secker,
1966; Incra Vallo

GAIR, MALCOLM (pseud. of John Dick
Scott)
Snow job. Doubleday, 1962; UK:
Collins, 1962; Mark Raeburn

GALLAGHER, STEPHEN
Chimera. St. Martin's, 1982; Peter
Carson

GALLICO, PAUL, 1897-1976
Too many ghosts. Doubleday, 1959;
UK: Joseph, 1961; Alexander Hero

GARDINER, DOROTHY, 1894-1979
A drink for Mr. Cherry. Doubleday,
1934; UK: Mr. Watson intervenes.
Hurst, 1935; Mr. Watson #2

Lion in wait. Doubleday, 1963; UK:
Lion? or murder? Hammond, 1964;
Moss Magill #3

The seventh mourner. Doubleday,
1958; UK: Hammond, 1960; Moss
Magill #2

The transatlantic ghost. Doubleday,
1933; UK: Harrap, 1933; Mr.
Watson #1

What crime is it? Doubleday, 1956;
UK: The case of the hula clock.
Hammond, 1957; Moss Magill #1

GARDINER, STEPHEN, 1925 --
Death is an artist. Washburn,
1959; UK: Barker, 1958

GARDNER, ERLE STANLEY, 1889-1970.
For other mysteries by this author,
see FAIR, A. A. (pseud.)
The case of the amorous aunt.
Morrow, 1963; UK: Heinemann,
1969; Perry Mason #70

The case of the angry mourner.
Morrow, 1951; UK: Heinemann,
1958; Perry Mason #38

The case of the backward mule.
Morrow, 1946; UK: Heinemann,
1955; Terry Clane #2

The case of the baited hook.
Morrow, 1940; UK: Cassell, 1940;
Perry Mason #16

The case of the beautiful beggar.
 Morrow, 1965; UK: Heinemann, 1972;
 Perry Mason #76

The case of the bigamous spouse.
 Morrow, 1961; UK: Heinemann, 1967;
 Perry Mason #65

The case of the black-eyed blonde.
 Morrow, 1944; UK: Cassell, 1948;
 Perry Mason #24

The case of the blonde bonanza.
 Morrow, 1962; UK: Heinemann, 1967;
 Perry Mason #67

The case of the borrowed brunette.
 Morrow, 1946; UK: Cassell, 1951;
 Perry Mason #28

The case of the buried clock.
 Morrow, 1943; UK: Cassell, 1945;
 Perry Mason #22

The case of the calendar girl.
 Morrow, 1958; UK: Heinemann, 1964;
 Perry Mason #56

The case of the careless cupid.
 Morrow, 1968; UK: Heinemann, 1973;
 Perry Mason #80

The case of the careless kitten.
 Morrow, 1942; UK: Cassell, 1944;
 Perry Mason #20

The case of the caretaker's cat.
 Morrow, 1935; UK: Cassell, 1936;
 Perry Mason #6

The case of the cautious coquette.
 Morrow, 1949; UK: Heinemann, 1955;
 Perry Mason #33

The case of the counterfeit eye.
 Morrow, 1935; UK: Cassell, 1935;
 Perry Mason #7

The case of the crimson kiss.
 Morrow, 1970; UK: Heinemann, 1975;
 Perry Mason #82

The case of the crooked candle.
 Morrow, 1944; UK: Cassell, 1947;
 Perry Mason #25

The case of the crying swallow.
 Morrow, 1971; UK: Heinemann, 1974;
 Perry Mason #83

The case of the curious bride.
 Morrow, 1934; UK: Cassell, 1935;
 Perry Mason #3

The case of the dangerous dowager.
 Morrow, 1937; UK: Cassell, 1937;
 Perry Mason #10

The case of the daring decoy.
 Morrow, 1957; UK: Heinemann, 1963;
 Perry Mason #53

The case of the daring divorcee.
 Morrow, 1964; UK: Heinemann,
 1969; Perry Mason #73

The case of the deadly toy. Morrow,
 1959; UK: Heinemann, 1964; Perry
 Mason #59

The case of the demure defendent.
 Morrow, 1956; UK: Heinemann,
 1962; Perry Mason #50

The case of the drowning duck.
 Morrow, 1942; UK: Cassell, 1944;
 Perry Mason #21

The case of the drowsy mosquito.
 Morrow, 1943; UK: Cassell, 1946;
 Perry Mason #23

The case of the dubious bridegroom.
 Morrow, 1949; UK: Heinemann,
 1954; Perry Mason #34

The case of the duplicate daughter.
 Morrow, 1960; UK: Heinemann,
 1965; Perry Mason #63

The case of the empty tin. Morrow,
 1941; UK: Cassell, 1943; Perry
 Mason #18

The case of the fabulous fake.
 Morrow, 1969; UK: Heinemann,
 1974; Perry Mason #81

The case of the fan-dancer's
 horse. Morrow, 1947; UK:
 Heinemann, 1952; Perry Mason #29

The case of the fenced-in woman.
 Morrow, 1972; UK: Heinemann,
 1976; Perry Mason #84

The case of the fiery fingers.
 Morrow, 1952; UK: Heinemann,
 1957; Perry Mason #39

The case of the foot-loose doll.
 Morrow, 1958; UK: Heinemann,
 1964; Perry Mason #57

The case of the fugitive nurse.
 Morrow, 1954; UK: Heinemann,
 1959; Perry Mason #44

The case of the gilded lily.
 Morrow, 1956; UK: Heinemann,
 1962; Perry Mason #51

The case of the glamorous ghost.
 Morrow, 1955; UK: Heinemann,
 1960; Perry Mason #47

The case of the gold digger's
 purse. Morrow, 1945; UK: Cassell,
 1948; Perry Mason #26

The case of the green-eyed sister.
 Morrow, 1953; UK: Heinemann,
 1959; Perry Mason #42

The case of the grinning gorilla.
Morrow, 1952; UK: Heinemann, 1958;
Perry Mason #40

The case of the half-awakened
wife. Morrow, 1945; UK: Cassell,
1949; Perry Mason #27

The case of the haunted husband.
Morrow, 1941; UK: Cassell, 1942;
Perry Mason #19

The case of the hesitant hostess.
Morrow, 1953; UK: Heinemann, 1959;
Perry Mason #43

The case of the horrified heirs.
Morrow, 1964; UK: Heinemann, 1971;
Perry Mason #74

The case of the howling dog.
Morrow, 1934; UK: Cassell, 1935;
Perry Mason #4

The case of the ice-cold hands.
Morrow, 1962; UK: Heinemann, 1968;
Perry Mason #68

The case of the irate witness.
Morrow, 1972; UK: Heinemann, 1975;
Perry Mason #85

The case of the lame canary.
Morrow, 1937; UK: Cassell, 1937;
Perry Mason #11

The case of the lazy lover. Morrow,
1947; UK: Heinemann, 1954; Perry
Mason #30

The case of the lonely heiress.
Morrow, 1948; UK: Heinemann, 1952;
Perry Mason #31

The case of the long-legged models.
Morrow, 1958; UK: Heinemann, 1963;
Perry Mason #58

The case of the lucky legs. Morrow,
1934; UK: Harrap, 1934; Perry
Mason #5

The case of the lucky loser.
Morrow, 1957; UK: Heinemann, 1962;
Perry Mason #54

The case of the mischievous doll.
Morrow, 1963; UK: Heinemann, 1968;
Perry Mason #71

The case of the moth-eaten mink.
Morrow, 1952; UK: Heinemann, 1958;
Perry Mason #41

The case of the musical cow.
Morrow, 1950; UK: Heinemann,
1957

The case of the mythical monkeys.
Morrow, 1959; UK: Heinemann, 1965;
Perry Mason #60

The case of the negligent nymph.
Morrow, 1950; UK: Heinemann,
1956; Perry Mason #35

The case of the nervous accomplice.
Morrow, 1955; UK: Heinemann,
1961; Perry Mason #48

The case of the one-eyed witness.
Morrow, 1950; UK: Heinemann,
1956; Perry Mason #37

The case of the perjured parrot.
Morrow, 1939; UK: Cassell, 1939;
Perry Mason #14

The case of the phantom fortune.
Morrow, 1964; UK: Heinemann,
1970; Perry Mason #75

The case of the postponed murder.
Morrow, 1973; UK: Heinemann,
1977; Perry Mason #86

The case of the queenly contestant.
Morrow, 1967; UK: Heinemann,
1973; Perry Mason #79

The case of the reluctant model.
Morrow, 1962; UK: Heinemann,
1967; Perry Mason #69

The case of the restless redhead.
Morrow, 1954; UK: Heinemann,
1960; Perry Mason #45

The case of the rolling bones.
Morrow, 1939; UK: Cassell, 1940;
Perry Mason #15

The case of the runaway corpse.
Morrow, 1954; UK: Heinemann,
1960; Perry Mason #46

The case of the screaming woman.
Morrow, 1957; UK: Heinemann,
1963; Perry Mason #55

The case of the shapely shadow.
Morrow, 1960; UK: Heinemann,
1966; Perry Mason #64

The case of the shoplifter's shoe.
Morrow, 1938; UK: Cassell, 1939;
Perry Mason #12

The case of the silent partner.
Morrow, 1940; UK: Cassell, 1941;
Perry Mason #17

The case of the singing skirt.
Morrow, 1959; UK: Heinemann,
1965; Perry Mason #61

The case of the sleepwalker's
niece. Morrow, 1936; UK: Cassell,
1936; Perry Mason #8

The case of the smoking chimney.
Morrow, 1943; UK: Cassell, 1945;
Gramps Wiggins #2

The case of the spurious spinster.
Morrow, 1961; UK: Heinemann, 1966;
Perry Mason #66

The case of the step-daughter's
secret. Morrow, 1963; UK:
Heinemann, 1968; Perry Mason #72

The case of the stuttering bishop.
Morrow, 1936; UK: Cassell, 1937;
Perry Mason #9

The case of the substitute face.
Morrow, 1938; UK: Cassell, 1938;
Perry Mason #13

The case of the sulky girl.
Morrow, 1933; UK: Harrap, 1934;
Perry Mason #2

The case of the sun bather's
diary. Morrow, 1955; UK:
Heinemann, 1961; Perry Mason #49

The case of the terrified typist.
Morrow, 1956; UK: Heinemann, 1961;
Perry Mason #52

The case of the troubled trustee.
Morrow, 1965; UK: Heinemann, 1971;
Perry Mason #77

The case of the turning tide.
Morrow, 1941; UK: Cassell, 1942;
Gramps Wiggins #1

The case of the vagabond virgin.
Morrow, 1948; UK: Heinemann, 1952;
Perry Mason #32

The case of the velvet claws.
Morrow, 1933; UK: Harrap, 1933;
Perry Mason #1

The case of the waylaid wolf.
Morrow, 1959; UK: Heinemann, 1965;
Perry Mason #62

The case of the worried waitress.
Morrow, 1966; UK: Heinemann, 1972;
Perry Mason #78

The D. A. breaks a seal. Morrow,
1946; UK: Cassell, 1950; Doug
Selby #7

The D. A. breaks an egg. Morrow,
1949; UK: Heinemann, 1957; Doug
Selby #9

The D. A. calls a turn. Morrow,
1944; UK: Cassell, 1947; Doug
Selby #6

The D. A. calls it murder. Morrow,
1937; UK: Cassell, 1937; Doug
Selby #1

The D. A. cooks a goose. Morrow,
1942; UK: Cassell, 1943; Doug
Selby #5

The D. A. draws a circle. Morrow,
1939; UK: Cassell, 1940; Doug
Selby #3

The D. A. goes to trial. Morrow,
1940; UK: Cassell, 1941; Doug
Selby #4

The D. A. holds a candle. Morrow,
1938; UK: Cassell, 1939; Doug
Selby #2

The D. A. takes a chance. Morrow,
1948; UK: Heinemann, 1956; Doug
Selby #8

Murder up my sleeve. Morrow, 1937;
UK: Cassell, 1938; Terry Clane #1

Two clues. Morrow, 1947; UK:
Cassell, 1951; Bill Eldon

GARDNER, JOHN, 1926 --
A complete state of death. Viking,
1969; UK: Cape, 1969; Derek Torry
#1

The corner men. Doubleday, 1976;
UK: Joseph, 1974; Derek Torry #2

The return of Moriarity. Putnam,
1974; UK: Weidenfeld, 1974; James
Moriarity #1; Sherlock Holmes

The revenge of Moriarity. Putnam,
1975; UK: Weidenfeld, 1976;
Sherlock Holmes; James Moriarity
#2

GARFIELD, BRIAN, 1939 --
Death sentence. Evans, 1975; UK:
Macmillan, 1976; Paul Benjamin

The hit. Macmillan, 1970; Simon
Crane

Relentless. World, 1972; UK:
Hodder, 1973; Sam Watchman #1

The threepersons hunt. Evans,
1974; UK: Coronet, 1975; Sam
Watchman #2

GARNET, A. H.
Maze. Ticknor, 1982; Cyrus Wilson
#2

The Santa Claus killer. Ticknor,
1981; Charles Thayer

GARRITY, MARK, see GILL, BARTHOLOMEW
(pseud.)

GARVE, ANDREW, (pseud. of Paul
Winterton, 1908 --). For other
mysteries by this author, see BAX,
ROGER (pseud.) or SOMERS, PAUL
(pseud.)

By-line for murder. Harper, 1951;
UK: A press of suspects. Collins,
1951

The case of Robert Quarry. Harper, 1972; UK: Collins, 1972

The Cuckoo Line affair. Harper, 1953; UK: Collins, 1953

Death and the sky above. Harper, 1954; UK: Collins, 1953

The far sands. Harper, 1960; UK: Collins, 1951

Frame-up. Harper, 1964; UK: Collins, 1964; Insp. Grant

The Galloway case. Harper, 1958; UK: Collins, 1958

Home to roost. Crowell, 1976; UK: Collins, 1976

Murder through the looking glass. Harper, 1952; UK: Murder in Moscow. Collins, 1951

The narrow search. Harper, 1958; UK: Collins, 1957

No tears for Hilda. Harper, 1950; UK: Collins, 1950; Max Easterbrook

Prisoner's friend. Harper, 1962; UK: Collins, 1962

A very quiet place. Harper, 1967; UK: Collins, 1967

GASH, JOE (pseud.). See also GRANGER, BILL

Newspaper murders. Holt, 1985; Terry Flynn; Karen Kovac

Priestly murders. Holt, 1984; Terry Flynn; Karen Kovac

GASH, JONATHAN (pseud. of John Grant, 1933 --)

Gold by Gemini. Harper, 1979; UK: Gold from Gemini. Collins, 1978

The gondola scam. St. Martin's, 1984; Lovejoy

The grail tree. Harper, 1980; UK: Collins, 1979; Lovejoy

Pearlhanger. St. Martin's, 1985; Lovejoy

The sleepers of Erin. Dutton, 1983; Lovejoy

Spend game. Ticknor, 1981; UK: Collins, 1981; Lovejoy

GATENBY, ROSEMARY, 1918 --

The season of danger. Dodd, 1978

The third identity. Dodd, 1979; UK: Hale, 1981; Christie Worthing

Whisper of evil. Dodd, 1978

GAULT, WILLIAM CAMPBELL, 1910 --

The bloody Bokhara. Dutton, 1952; UK: The bloodstained Bokhara. Boardman, 1953

The Cana diversion. Raven House, 1980; Brock Callahan; Joe Puma

The canvas coffin. Dutton, 1953; UK: Boardman, 1953

Come die with me. Random House, 1959; UK: Boardman, 1961; Brock Callahan #4

The convertible hearse. Random House, 1957; UK: Boardman, 1958; Brock Callahan #3

County kill. Simon & Schuster, 1962; UK: Boardman, 1963; Brock Callahan #6

The day of the ram. Random House, 1956; UK: Boardman, 1958; Brock Callahan #2

Dead hero. Dutton, 1963; UK: Boardman, 1964; Brock Callahan #7

The dead seed. Walker, 1985; Brock Callahan

Death in Donegal Bay. Walker, 1984; Brock Callahan

Death out of focus. Random House, 1959; UK: Boardman, 1959

End of a call girl. Fawcett, 1958; UK: Don't call tonight. Boardman, 1960; Joe Puma #1

The hundred-dollar girl. Dutton, 1961; UK: Boardman, 1963; Joe Puma #6

Million dollar tramp. Fawcett, 1960; UK: Boardman, 1962; Joe Puma #5

Night lady. Fawcett, 1958; UK: Boardman, 1960; Joe Puma #2

Ring around Rose. Dutton, 1955; UK: Boardman, 1955; Brock Callahan #1

Sweet wild wench. Fawcett, 1959; UK: Boardman, 1961; Joe Puma #3

Vein of violence. Simon & Schuster, 1961; UK: Boardman, 1962; Brock Callahan #5

The wayward widow. Fawcett, 1959; UK: Boardman, 1960; Joe Puma #4

GEORGE, KARA

Murder at Tomorrow. Walker, 1982; Nick Nicoletti

GEROULD, GORDON HALL, 1877-1953

A midsummer mystery. Appleton, 1925; UK: Appleton, 1925

GETTEL, RONALD E.

Twice burned. Walker, 1983; Chief Hammond; Det. Benedetto

GIELGUD, VAL and MARVELL, HOLT
London calling. Doubleday, 1934;
UK: Death at Broadcasting House.
Rich, 1934; Simon Spears

GILBERT, ANNA (pseud. of MARGUERITE
LAZARUS, 1916 --)
Miss Bede is staying. St. Martin's,
1983; Florence St. Leonard

GILBERT, MICHAEL, 1912 --
The black seraphim. Harper, 1984;
James Scotland
Blood and judgement. Harper, 1959;
UK: Hodder, 1959; Sgt. Petrella
The body of a girl. Harper, 1972;
UK: Hodder, 1972; Insp. Mercer
Close quarters. Walker, 1963; UK:
Hodder, 1947; Insp. Hazelrigg #1
The country-house burglar. Harper,
1955; UK: Sky high. Hodder, 1955;
Mrs. Artside
Danger within. Harper, 1952; UK:
Death in captivity. Hodder, 1952
Death has deep roots. Harper,
1952; UK: Hodder, 1951; Insp.
Hazelrigg #5
The doors open. Walker, 1962; UK:
Hodder, 1949; Insp. Hazelrigg #3
The empty house. Harper, 1979; UK:
Hodder, 1978; Peter Manciple
End-game. Harper, 1982
The family tomb. Harper, 1970; UK:
The Etruscan net. Hodder, 1969
Fear to tread. Harper, 1953; UK:
Hodder, 1953; Insp. Hazelrigg #6
He didn't mind danger. Harper,
1949; UK: They never looked
inside. Hodder, 1948; Insp.
Hazelrigg #2
The killing of Katie Steelstock.
Harper, 1980; UK: Hodder, 1980
Smallbone deceased. Harper, 1950;
UK: Hodder, 1950; Insp. Hazelrigg
#4

GILES, KENNETH, 1922-1972. For other
mysteries by this author, see
DRUMMOND, CHARLES (pseud.)
Death among the stars. Walker,
1968; UK: Gollancz, 1968; Harry
James #5
Death and Mr. Pretty man. Walker,
1969; UK: Gollancz, 1967; Harry
James #3
Death cracks a bottle. Walker,
1970; UK: Gollancz, 1969; Harry
James #6

Death in diamonds. Simon &
Schuster, 1968; UK: Gollancz,
1967; Harry James #4
A death in the church. UK:
Gollancz, 1970; Harry James
A file on death. Walker, 1973; UK:
Gollancz, 1973; Harry James #8
Murder pluperfect. Walker, 1970;
UK: Gollancz, 1970; Harry James
#7
A provenance of death. Simon &
Schuster, 1967; UK: Gollancz,
1966; Harry James #2
Some beasts no more. Walker, 1968;
UK: Gollancz, 1965; Harry James
#1

GILL, B. M.
Death drop. Scribner's, 1980
Suspect. Scribner's, 1981; UK:
Victims. Hodder, 1980
The twelfth juror. Scribner's, 1984

GILL, BARTHOLOMEW (pseud. of Mark
McGarrity, 1943 --)
McGarr and the method of Descartes.
Viking, 1984; Peter McGarr
McGarr and the P. M. of Belgrave
Square. Viking, 1983; Peter
McGarr; Mrs. McGarr
McGarr and the politician's wife.
Scribner's, 1977; UK: Hale, 1978;
Peter McGarr #1
McGarr and the Sienese conspiracy.
Scribner's, 1977; UK: Hale,
1979; Peter McGarr #2
McGarr at the Dublin Horse Show.
Scribner's, 1980; UK: Hale, 1981;
Peter McGarr #4
McGarr on the Cliffs of Moker.
Scribner's, 1978; UK: Hale, 1980;
Peter McGarr #3

GILLESPIE, ROBERT B.
Heads you lose. Dodd, 1985; Ralph
Simmons

GILLIAN, MICHAEL
Warrant for a wanton. Mill, 1952;
Leith Hadley

GILLIS, JACKSON
The killers of starfish.
Lippincott, 1977; UK: Hale, 1979;
Jonas Duncan

GILMAN, DOROTHY, 1923 --
A nun in the closet. Doubleday,
1975; UK: A nun in the cupboard.
Hale, 1976

The tightrope walker. Doubleday,
1979; UK: Hale, 1980; Amelia
Jones

GIROUX, E. X.
A death for a dancer. St. Martin's,
1985; Robert Forsythe
A death for a darling. St.
Martin's, 1985; Robert Forsythe
A death for Adonis. St. Martin's,
1984; Robert Forsythe

GLOAG, JULIAN, 1930 --
Sleeping dogs lie. Dutton, 1980;
UK: Secker, 1980; Hugo Welchman

GODFREY, THOMAS
Murder for Christmas. Mysterious
Press, 1982

GODLEY, ROBERT, see JAMES, FRANKLIN
(pseud.)

GOLDBERG, MARSHALL
The anatomy lesson. Putnam, 1974;
Dan Lassiter

GOLDSMITH, GENE
Murder on his mind. Mill, 1947;
UK: Quality, 1954; Dan Damon

GOLDSTEIN, ARTHUR D., 1937 --
Nobody's sorry he got killed.
Random House, 1976; Max Guttman #3
A person shouldn't die like that.
Random House, 1972; UK: Prior,
1977; Max Guttman #1
You're never too old to die. Random
House, 1974; UK: Prior, 1977; Max
Guttman #2

GOLDTHWAITE, EATON K., 1907 --
First you have to find him.
Doubleday, 1981; Frank Moerson

GOODIS, DAVID, 1917-1967
Of missing persons. Morrow, 1950

GOODMAN, JONATHAN, 1931 --
The last sentence. St. Martin's,
1980; UK: Hutchinson, 1978

GOODRUM, CHARLES A., 1923
Carnage of the realm. Crown, 1979;
UK: Dead for a penny. Gollancz,
1980; Edwin George
Dewey decimated. Crown, 1977; UK:
Curley, 1978; Edwin George

GORDON, GORDON, see THE GORDONS

GORDON, MILDRED, see THE GORDONS

GORDON, NEIL (pseud. of Archibald
Gordon Macdonell, 1895-1941)
The professor's poison. Harcourt,
1928; UK: Longman, 1928; James
Arnold

The silent murders. Doubleday,
1930; UK: Longman, 1929; Insp.
Dewar

GORDON, RICHARD (pseud. of Gordon
Ostlere, 1921 --)
Jack the Ripper. Atheneum, 1980;
UK: The private life of Jack the
Ripper. Collins, 1980; Jack the
Ripper

THE GORDONS, GORDON, GORDON, 1906 --
and GORDON, MILDRED, 1905-1979
Campaign train. Doubleday, 1952;
UK: Wingate, 1952
Captive. Doubleday, 1957; UK:
Macdonald, 1958; John Ripley #3
Case file: FBI. Doubleday, 1953;
UK: Macdonald, 1954; John Ripley
#2
Case of the talking bug. Doubleday,
1955; UK: Playback. Macdonald,
1955
Catnapped. Doubleday, 1974; UK:
Macdonald, 1975; Undercover Cat
#3
FBI story. Doubleday, 1950; UK:
Corgi, 1957; John Ripley #1
The informant. Doubleday, 1973;
UK: Macdonald, 1973; John Ripley
#5
Make haste to live. Doubleday, 1950
The night after the wedding.
Doubleday, 1979; UK: Macdonald,
1980
Operation terror. Doubleday, 1961;
UK: Macdonald, 1961; John Ripley
#4
Ordeal. Doubleday, 1976; UK:
Macdonald, 1977
Power play. Doubleday, 1965; UK:
Macdonald, 1966
Tiger on my back. Doubleday, 1960;
UK: Macdonald, 1960
Undercover Cat. Doubleday, 1963;
UK: Macdonald, 1964; Undercover
Cat #1
Undercover Cat prowls again.
Doubleday, 1966; UK: Macdonald,
1967; Undercover Cat #2

GORE-BROWNE, ROBERT, 1893 --
By way of confession. Doubleday,
1930; UK: Death on delivery.
Collins, 1929; Lucien Clay
In search of a villain. Doubleday,
1928; UK: Murder of an M. P.
Collins, 1927; Lucien Clay

GORES, JOE, 1931 --
Dead skip. Random House, 1972; UK:
Gollancz, 1973; Dan Kearney #1
Final notice. Random House, 1973;
UK: Gollancz, 1974; Dan Kearney #2
Gone, no forwarding. Random House,
1978; UK: Gollancz, 1979; Dan
Kearney #3
Hammett. Putnam, 1975; UK:
Macdonald, 1976; Dashiell Hammett
Interface. Evans, 1974; UK:
Futura, 1977
A time of predators. Random House,
1969; UK: Allen, 1970; Curt
Halstead
GORMAN, EDWARD
New improved murder. St. Martin's,
1985; Jack Dwyer
Roughcut. St. Martin's, 1985
GOSLING, PAULA
Solo blues. Coward McCann, 1981;
UK: Loser's blues. Macmillan,
1980; Johnny Cosatelli
The woman in red. Doubleday, 1984;
Charles Llewellyn
GOULART, RON, 1933 --
A graveyard of my own. Walker,
1985; Burt Kurrie
Odd job no. 101 and other future
crimes. Scribner's, 1975; UK:
Hale, 1976; Jake Pace; Hilda Pace
GOULD, STEPHEN (pseud. of Stephen
Gould Fisher, 1912-1980). For other
mysteries by this author, see
FISHER, STEVE
Murder of the admiral. Macaulay,
1936
GRAAF, PETER (pseud. of Samuel Youd,
1922 --)
The sapphire connection. Washburn,
1959; UK: Joseph, 1959; Joe Dust
GRADY, JAMES
Runner in the street. Macmillan,
1984; John Rankin
GRAE, CAMARIN
The winged dancer. Blazon Books,
1983
GRAEME, BRUCE
Mystery on the Queen Mary.
Lippincott, 1938; UK: Hutchinson,
1937; William Stevens #7; Pierre
Allsin #7

GRAFTON, C. W., 1909-1982
Beyond a reasonable doubt.
Rinehart, 1950; UK: Heinemann,
1951
The rat began to gnaw the rope.
Farrar, 1943; UK: Gollancz, 1944;
Gilmore Henry
The rope began to hang the butcher.
Farrar, 1944; UK: Gollancz, 1945;
Gilmore Henry
GRAFTON, SUE
"A" is for alibi. Holt, 1982;
Kinsey Milhone #1
"B" is for burglar. Holt, 1985;
Kinsey Milhone
GRAHAM, JOHN ALEXANDER, 1941 --
Arthur. Harper, 1969; Arthur
Silverman
The involvement of Arnold Wechsler.
Atlantic Press, 1971; Arnold
Wechsler
GRAHAM, WINSTON, 1909 --
Fortune is a woman. Doubleday,
1953; UK: Hodder, 1952
Take my life. Doubleday, 1967; UK:
Ward, 1947
The wreck of the Grey Cat.
Doubleday, 1958
GRANGER, BILL. See also GASH, JOE
(pseud.)
Public murders. Jove, 1980; UK:
New English Library, 1981; Jack
Donovan; Karen Kovac
GRAYSON, RICHARD (pseud.). See also
GRINDAL, RICHARD
Crime without passion. St.
Martin's, 1984; Insp. Gautier #5
The death of Abbe Didier. St.
Martin's, 1981; Insp. Gautier #3
The Monterant affair. St. Martin's,
1980; UK: Gollancz, 1980; Insp.
Gautier #2
The Montmartre murders. St.
Martin's, 1982; Insp. Gautier #4
The murders at Impasse Louvain.
St. Martin's, 1979; UK: Gollancz,
1978; Insp. Gautier #1
GREELEY, ANDREW M., 1928 --
Death in April. McGraw-Hill, 1980;
Jimmy O'Neill
Happy are the meek. Warner, 1985;
Blackie Ryan
Lord of the dance. Warner, 1984

GREEN, ALAN BAER, see DENBIE, ROGER (pseud.)

GREEN, EDITH PINERO, 1929 --
Rotten apples. Dutton, 1977; UK: Curley, 1980; Dearborn V. Pinch
Sneaks. Dutton, 1979; UK: Curley, 1981; Dearborn V. Pinch

GREEN, THOMAS J.
The flowered box. Beaufort, 1980; Aaron Gates; Caro Bursa

GREENAN, RUSSELL
Keepers. St. Martin's, 1979

GREENBAUM, LEONARD, 1930 --
Out of shape. Harper, 1969; UK: Gollancz, 1970; Paul Gold; Tommy Larkin

GREENLEAF, STEPHEN, 1942 --
Death bed. Dial, 1980; John Marshall Tanner
Grave error. Dial, 1979; UK: New English Library, 1981; John Marshall Tanner
State's evidence. Dial, 1982; John Marshall Tanner

GREENWOOD, JOHN, 1920 -- . For other mysteries by this author, see HILTON, JOHN BUXTON (pseud.)
Mosley by moonlight. Walker, 1985; Insp. Mosley #2
Murder, Mr. Mosley. Walker, 1983; Insp. Mosley

GREGG, CECIL FREEMAN, 1898 --
Murder on the bus. Dial, 1930; UK: Hutchinson, 1930; Cuthbert Higgins
Tragedy at Wembley. Dial, 1936; UK: Methuen, 1936; Cuthbert Higgins

GRIERSON, EDWARD
A crime of one's own. Putnam, 1967; UK: Chatto, 1967
The Massingham affair. Doubleday, 1963; UK: Chatto, 1962
Reputation for a song. Knopf, 1952; UK: Chatto, 1952
The second man. Knopf, 1956; UK: Chatto, 1956; Marion Kerrison

GRIMES, MARTHA
The Anodyne Necklace. Little, 1983; Richard Jury #3
The deer leap. Little, 1985; Richard Jury
The dirty duck. Little, 1984; Richard Jury
Help the poor struggler. Little, 1985; Richard Jury

Jerusalem Inn. Little, 1984; Richard Jury
The man with a load of mischief. Little, 1981; Richard Jury #1
The Old Fox deceiv'd. Little, 1982; Richard Jury #2

GRINDAL, RICHARD. See also GRAYSON, RICHARD (pseud.)
Death stalk. St. Martin's, 1983

GRISMAN, ARNOLD
The winning streak. St. Martin's, 1985; Goldberg

GRUBER, FRANK, 1904-1969. See also VEDDER, JOHN K. (pseud.)
The buffalo box. Farrar, 1942; UK: Nicholson, 1944; Simon Lash #2
The Etruscan bull. Dutton, 1969; UK: Hale, 1970
The French key. Farrar, 1940; UK: Hale, 1941; Johnny Fletcher #1; Sam Cragg #1
The gift horse. Farrar, 1942; UK: Nicholson, 1943; Johnny Fletcher #6; Sam Cragg #6
The gold gap. Dutton, 1968; UK: Hale, 1968
The honest dealer. Rinehart, 1947; Johnny Fletcher #9; Sam Cragg #9
The hungry dog. Farrar, 1941; UK: Nicholson, 1950; Johnny Fletcher #3; Sam Cragg #3
The laughing fox. Farrar, 1940; UK: Nicholson, 1942; Johnny Fletcher #2; Sam Cragg #2
The leather duke. Rinehart, 1949; UK: Pemberton, 1950; Johnny Fletcher #12; Sam Cragg #12
The limping goose. Rinehart, 1954; UK: Barker, 1955; Johnny Fletcher #13; Sam Cragg #13
The lonesome badger. Rinehart, 1954; Otis Beagle #2
The mighty blockhead. Farrar, 1942; UK: Nicholson, 1948; Johnny Fletcher #7; Sam Cragg #7
Murder '97. Rinehart, 1948; UK: Barker, 1956; Simon Lash #3
The navy colt. Farrar, 1941; UK: Nicholson, 1942; Johnny Fletcher #4; Sam Cragg #4
The scarlet feather. Rinehart, 1948; UK: Cherry Tree, 1951; Johnny Fletcher #11; Sam Cragg #11

The silver jackass. Reynal, 1941;
UK: Cherry Tree, 1952; Otis Beagle
#1

The silver tombstone. Farrar,
1945; UK: Nicholson, 1949; Johnny
Fletcher #8; Sam Cragg #8

Simon Lash, private detective.
Farrar, 1941; UK: Simon Lash,
detective. Nicholson, 1943; Simon
Lash #1

Swing low, swing dead. Belmont,
1964; Johnny Fletcher #14; Sam
Cragg #14

The talking clock. Farrar, 1941;
UK: Nicholson, 1942; Johnny
Fletcher #5; Sam Cragg #5

The whispering master. Rinehart,
1947; Johnny Fletcher #10; Sam
Cragg #10

GUILD, NICHOLAS, 1944 --
The favor. St. Martin's, 1981; Ray
Guiness

The lost and found man. Harper's
Magazine Press, 1975; UK: Hale,
1977; William Lukes

Old acquaintance. Seaview, 1979;
Ray Guiness

GULIK, ROBERT VAN
The Chinese bell murders. Harper,
1958; UK: Joseph, 1958; Judge Dee
#3

The Chinese gold murders. Harper,
1961; UK: Joseph, 1959; Judge Dee
#1

The Chinese lake murders. Harper,
1962; UK: Joseph, 1960; Judge Dee
#2

The Chinese maze murders. Gregory
Lounz, 1957; UK: Joseph, 1962;
Judge Dee #4

The Chinese nail murders. Harper,
1962; UK: Joseph, 1961; Judge Dee
#5

The emperor's pearl. Scribner's,
1964; UK: Heinemann, 1963; Judge
Dee

The haunted monastery. Scribner's,
1969; UK: Heinemann, 1963; Judge
Dee

Judge Dee at work. Scribner's,
1973; UK: Heinemann, 1967; Judge
Dee

The lacquer screen. Scribner's,
1970; UK: Heinemann, 1963; Judge
Dee

The monkey and the tiger.
Scribner's, 1966; UK: Heinemann,
1965; Judge Dee

Murder in Canton. Scribner's, 1967;
UK: Heinemann, 1966; Judge Dee

Necklace and calabash. Scribner's,
1971; UK: Heinemann, 1967; Judge
Dee

The phantom of the temple.
Scribner's, 1966; UK: Heinemann,
1966; Judge Dee

Poets and murder. Scribner's, 1972;
UK: Heinemann, 1968; Judge Dee

The red pavilion. Scribner's, 1968;
UK: Heinemann, 1964; Judge Dee

The willow pattern. Scribner's,
1965; UK: Heinemann, 1965; Judge
Dee

GUTHRIE, A. B., JR., 1901 --
The genuine article. Houghton,
1977; Chick Charleston; Jason
Beard

No second wind. Houghton, 1980;
Jason Beard

Wild pitch. Houghton, 1973; Chick
Charleston; Jason Beard

HAGGARD, WILLIAM (pseud. of Richard
Henry Michael Clayton, 1907 --)
A cool day for killing. Walker,
1968; UK: Cassell, 1968; Charles
Russell

HALL, ROBERT LEE, 1941 --
Exit Sherlock Holmes. Scribner's,
1977; UK: Murray, 1977; Sherlock
Holmes

HALLERAN, TUCKER
A cool clear death. St. Martin's,
1985; Cam MacCardle

The King Edward plot. McGraw-Hill,
1980; Frederick Wigmore; King of
England, Edward VII

Sudden death finish. St. Martin's,
1985; Cam MacCardle

HALLIDAY, DOROTHY, see DUNNETT,
DOROTHY

HALLIDAY, MICHAEL (pseud.), see HUNT,
KYLE (pseud.) or YORK, JEREMY
(pseud.)

HALLS, GERALDINE, see JAY, CHARLOTTE
(pseud.)

HAMBLY, BARBARA
The Quirinal Hill affair. St.
Martin's, 1983

HAMILTON, BRUCE, 1900 --
Dead reckoning. Simon & Schuster, 1937; UK: Middle-class murder. Methuen, 1936
Too much of water. Perennial, 1983; UK: Cresset, 1958
HAMILTON, IAN, 1935 --
The creeping vicar. Lippincott, 1967; UK: The man with the brown paper face. Constable, 1967; Pete Heysen
Never die in Honolulu. Lippincott, 1969; UK: Mayflower, 1969; Pete Heysen
The persecutor. Lippincott, 1965; UK: Constable, 1965; Pete Heysen
The thrill machine. UK: Collins, 1972; Pete Heysen
HAMILTON, MOLLIE, see KAYE, M. M.
HAMILTON, NAN
Killer's rights. Walker, 1984; Isamu Ohara
HAMMETT, DASHIELL
The adventures of Sam Spade and other stories. Spivak, 1944; Sam Spade #2
The big knockover: selected stories and short novels. Random House, 1966; UK: The Dashiell Hammett story omnibus. Cassell, 1966; Continental Op #7
The Continental Op. Random House, 1974; UK: Macmillan, 1975; Continental Op #4
The Dain curse. Knopf, 1929; UK: Cassell, 1929; Continental Op #2
The glass key. Knopf, 1931; UK: Cassell, 1931; Ned Beaumont
Hammett homicides. Spivak, 1946; Continental Op #6
The Maltese falcon. Knopf, 1930; UK: Cassell, 1930; Sam Spade #1
$106,000 blood money. Spivak, 1943; UK: The big knock-over. Jonathan, 1948; Continental Op #3
Red harvest. Knopf, 1929; UK: Cassell, 1929; Continental Op #1
The return of the Continental Op. Spivak, 1945; Continental Op #5
The thin man. Knopf, 1934; UK: Barker, 1934; Nick Charles; Nora Charles

HAMMOND, GERALD, 1926 --
Cousin once removed. St. Martin's, 1985; Keith CalderFair game. St. Martin's, 1982; Keith Calder
The game. St. Martin's, 1982; Keith Calder #4
The reward game. St. Martin's, 1980; UK: Macmillan, 1980; Keith Calder
Sauce for the pigeon. St. Martin's, 1985; Keith Calder
HANNAY, JAMES OWEN, see BIRMINGHAM, GEORGE A. (pseud.)
HANSEN, JOSEPH, 1923 --
Backtrack. Countryman Press, 1982; Alan Tarr
Death claims. Harper, 1973; UK: Harrap, 1973; Dave Brandstetter #2
Fadeout. Harper, 1970; UK: Harrap, 1972; Dave Brandstetter #1
Gravedigger. Holt, 1982; Dave Brandstetter #6
The man everybody was afraid of. Holt, 1978; UK: Faber, 1978; Dave Brandstetter #4
Night work. Holt, 1984; Dave Brandstetter #7
Skinflick. Holt, 1979; UK: Faber, 1980; Dave Brandstetter #5
Troublemaker. Harper, 1975; UK: Harrap, 1975; Dave Brandstetter #3
HARBAGE, ALFRED B., see KYD, THOMAS (pseud.)
HARDWICK, ELIZABETH, 1916 --
The simple truth. Harcourt, 1955
HARDWICK, MICHAEL, 1924 --
Prisoner of the devil: Sherlock Holmes and the Dreyfus case. Proteus, 1979; UK: Proteus, 1980; Sherlock Holmes; Capt. Dreyfus
The private life of Dr. Watson. Dutton, 1983; John H. Watson; Sherlock Holmes
Sherlock Holmes: my life and crimes. Doubleday, 1984; Sherlock Holmes; Prof. Moriarity
HARDWICK, MICHAEL and HARDWICK, MOLLIE
The private life of Sherlock Holmes. Bantam, 1971; UK: Mayflower, 1970; Sherlock Holmes

HARDY, WILLIAM M., 1922 --
  Lady killer. Dodd, 1957; UK:
    Hamilton, 1957; Bob Adams; Anne
    Miner
  A little sin. Dodd, 1958; UK:
    Hamilton, 1959; Karen Gordon
HARE, CYRIL (pseud. of Clark, Alfred
  Alexander Gordon, 1900-1958)
  Death is no sportsman. UK: Faber,
    1938; Insp. Mallett #2
  Death walks the woods. Little,
    1954; UK: That yew tree's shade.
    Faber, 1954; Francis Pettigrew #4
  An English murder. Little, 1951;
    UK: Faber, 1951; Wencelaus
    Bottwink; Sgt. Rogers
  Suicide excepted. Macmillan, 1954;
    UK: Faber, 1939; Insp. Mallett #3
  Tenant for death. Dodd, 1977; UK:
    Faber, 1938; Insp. Mallett #1
  Tragedy at law. Harcourt, 1943;
    UK: Faber, 1942; Insp. Mallett #4;
    Francis Pettigrew #1
  Untimely death. Macmillan, 1958;
    UK: He should have died hereafter.
    Faber, 1958; Francis Pettigrew #5;
    Insp. Mallett #6
  The wind blows death. Little, 1950;
    UK: When the wind blows. Faber,
    1949; Francis Pettigrew #3
  With a bare bodkin. UK: Faber,
    1946; Insp. Mallett #5; Francis
    Pettigrew #2
HARLING, ROBERT
  The dark saviour. Harper, 1953; UK:
    Chatto, 1952
  The endless colonnade. Putnam,
    1959; UK: Chatto, 1958
  The enormous shadow. Harper, 1956;
    UK: Chatto, 1955
  The paper palace. Harper, 1951; UK:
    Chatto, 1951
HARRINGTON, JOSEPH, 1903 --
  Blind spot. Lippincott, 1966; UK:
    Hale, 1967; Francis X. Kerrigan #2
  The last doorbell. Lippincott,
    1969; UK: Hale, 1970; Francis X.
    Kerrigan #3; Jane Boardman #2
  The last known address. Lippincott,
    1965; UK: Hale, 1966; Francis X.
    Kerrigan #1; Jane Boardman #1
HARRINGTON, JOYCE
  Family reunion. St. Martin's, 1982;
    Jenny Holland

No one knows my name. St. Martin's,
    1980; UK: Macmillan, 1981
HARRIS, CHARLAINE
  A secret rage. Houghton, 1984;
    Nickief Callahan
  Sweet and deadly. Houghton, 1981;
    Catherine Linton
HARRIS, JOHN, see HEBDEN, MARK
  (pseud.)
HARRIS, LARRY M., 1933 --
  The pickled poodles. Random House,
    1960; UK: Boardman, 1961; John J.
    Malone
HARRIS, TIMOTHY, 1946 --
  Good night and goodbye. Delacorte,
    1979; UK: Pan, 1981; Thomas Kyd
HARRISON, CHIP, see BLOCK, LAWRENCE
HARRISON, MICHAEL, 1907 -- . For
  other mysteries by this author, see
  DOWNES, QUENTIN (pseud.)
  The exploits of Chevalier Dupin.
    Mycroft & Moran, 1968; UK: Murder
    in the Rue Royale. Stacey, 1972;
    C. Auguste Dupin
  I, Sherlock Holmes. Dutton, 1977;
    Sherlock Holmes
HARRISON, RAY
  Why kill Arthur Potter? Scribner's,
    1984; Joseph Bragg; James Morton
HARRISON, WILLIAM, 1933 --
  In a wild sanctuary. Morrow, 1969;
    UK: Gollancz, 1970
HARRISS, WILL
  The Bay Psalm Book murder. Walker,
    1983; Walker, 1983; Clifford
    Dunbar
HART, FRANCES NOYES, 1890-1943
  The Bellamy trial. Doubleday,
    1927; UK: Heinemann, 1927
  The crooked lane. Doubleday, 1934;
    UK: Heinemann, 1934
  Hide in the dark. Doubleday, 1929;
    UK: Heinemann, 1929
HASTINGS, MACDONALD, 1909 --
  Cork and the serpent. UK: Joseph,
    1955; Montague Cork #3
  Cork in bottle. Knopf, 1954; UK:
    Joseph, 1953; Montague Cork #2
  Cork in the doghouse. Knopf, 1958;
    UK: Joseph, 1957; Montague Cork
    #4
  Cork on location. Walker, 1967;
    UK: Cork on the telly. Joseph,
    1966; Montague Cork #5

Cork on the water. Random House, 1951; UK: Joseph, 1951; Montague Cork #1

HASTINGS, W. S. and HOOKER, BRIAN
The professor's mystery. Bobbs, 1911; Prof. Crosby

HAUSER, THOMAS
The Beethoven conspiracy. Macmillan, 1984; Richard Marrett

HAVIGHURST, MARION MARGARET BOYD, see BOYD, MARION (pseud.)

HAYMON, S. T.
Death and the pregnant virgin. St. Martin's, 1980; UK: Constable, 1980; Ben. Jurnet
Ritual murder. St. Martin's, 1982; Ben. Jurnet #2
Stately homicide. St. Martin's, 1984; Ben Jurnet

HAZZARD, MARY, see DWIGHT, OLIVIA

HEAD, MATTHEW (pseud. for John Canaday, 1907 --)
The accomplice. Simon & Schuster, 1947
The Cabinda affair. Simon & Schuster, 1949; UK: Heinemann, 1950; Mary Finney #2
The Congo Venus. Simon & Schuster, 1950; UK: Garland, 1976; Mary Finney #3
The devil in the bush. Simon & Schuster, 1945; Mary Finney #1
Murder at the Flea Club. Simon & Schuster, 1955; UK: Heinemann, 1957; Mary Finney #4
The smell of money. Simon & Schuster, 1943

HEALD, TIM, 1944 --
Blue blood will out. Stein & Day, 1947; UK: Hutchinson, 1974; Simon Bognor #2
Deadline. Stein & Day, 1975; UK: Hutchinson, 1975; Simon Bognor #3
Just desserts. Scribner's, 1979; UK: Hutchinson, 1977; Simon Bognor #5
Let sleeping dogs die. Stein & Day, 1976; UK: Hutchinson, 1976; Simon Bognor #4
Murder at Moose Jaw. Doubleday, 1981; Simon Bognor #6
A small masterpiece. Doubleday, 1982; Simon Bognor #7

Unbecoming habits. Stein & Day, 1973; UK: Hutchinson, 1973; Simon Bognor #1

HEALY, J. F.
Blunt darts. Walker, 1984; John Francis Cuddy

HEARD, H. F., 1889-1971
The notched hairpin. Vanguard, 1949; UK: Cassell, 1951; Mr. Mycroft #3
Reply paid. Vanguard, 1942; Mr. Mycroft #2
A taste for honey. Vanguard, 1941; UK: Cassell, 1942; Mr. Mycroft #1

HEBDEN, MARK (pseud. of John Harris, 1916 --)
The dark side of the island. Harcourt, 1973; UK: Joseph, 1973
Death set to music. Walker, 1983; UK: Hamilton, 1979; Insp. Pel
Pel and the bombers. Walker, 1985; Insp. Pel
Pel and the faceless corpse. Walker, 1982; UK: Hamilton, 1979; Insp. Pel
Pel and the predators. Walker, 1985; Insp. Pel #3
Pel and the staghound. Walker, 1984; Insp. Pel #4

HEBERDEN, M. V. For other mysteries by this author, see LEONARD, CHARLES L. (pseud.)
Drinks on the victim. Doubleday, 1947; Desmond Shannon
Engaged to murder. Doubleday, 1949; Rick Vanning
Murder follows Desmond Shannon. Doubleday, 1942; UK: Hale, 1949; Desmond Shannon
Murder goes astray. Doubleday, 1943; UK: Hale, 1951; Desmond Shannon
They can't all be guilty. Doubleday, 1947; Desmond Shannon
To what dread end? Doubleday, 1944; UK: Hale, 1952

HEBERT, ANNE
In the shadow of the wind. Beaufort, 1984

HECKSTALL-SMITH, ANTHONY, 1904 --
The man with yellow shoes. Roy, 1958; UK: Wingate, 1957
Murder on the brain. Roy, 1958; UK: Wingate, 1958; Insp. Hyde

HEED, RUFUS
Ghosts never die. Vantage, 1954;
Dr. Kent
HEILBRUN, CAROLYN, see CROSS, AMANDA
HELLER, KEITH
Man's illegal life. Scribner's,
1985; George Man
HELWIG, DAVID, 1938 --
The king's evil. Beaufort, 1984
HELY, ELIZABETH
I'll be the judge, I'll be the
jury. Scribner's, 1959; UK:
Dominant third. Heinemann; 1959;
Antoine Cirret
A mark of displeasure. Scribner's,
1960; UK: Heinemann, 1961; Antoine
Cirret
HENEGE, THOMAS
Death of a shipowner. Dodd, 1981;
Henricksen
HENNISSART, MARTHA, see LATHEN, EMMA
(pseud.) and DOMINIC, R. B. (pseud.)
HENSLEY, JOE L.
The color of hate. Ace, 1960
Deliver us to evil. Doubleday,
1971; Donald Robak
Final doors. Doubleday, 1981;
Donald Robak
A killing in gold. Doubleday,
1978; UK: Gollancz, 1979; Donald
Robak
Legislative body. Doubleday,
1972; Donald Robak
Minor murders. Doubleday, 1979;
Donald Robak
The poison summer. Doubleday, 1974;
Donald Robak
Rivertown risk. Doubleday, 1977
Song of corpus juris. Doubleday,
1974; Donald Robak
HENTOFF, NAT
Blues for Charlie Darwin. Morrow,
1982
HERBER, WILLIAM, 1920 --
Death paints a portrait. Lippincott,
1958; UK: Foulsham, 1959
King-sized murder. Lippincott,
1954; UK: Foulsham, 1955; James
Rehm
Live bait for murder. Lippincott,
1955; UK: Foulsham, 1956; James
Rehm
HERVEY, EVELYN
The governess. Doubleday, 1983;
Harriet Unwin

HEXT, HARRINGTON (pseud.). For other
mysteries by this author, see
PHILLPOTTS, EDEN
The thing at their heels.
Macmillan, 1923; UK: Butterworth,
1923; Insp. Midwinter
Who killed Cock Robin? Macmillan,
1924; UK: Butterworth, 1924;
Nicol Hart
HEYER, GEORGETTE, 1902-1974
Behold here's poison! Doubleday,
1936; UK: Hodder, 1936; Insp.
Hannasyde #2
A blunt instrument. Doubleday,
1938; UK: Hodder, 1938; Insp.
Hannasyde #4
Detection unlimited. Dutton, 1969;
UK: Heinemann, 1953; Insp.
Hannasyde #4
Duplicate death. Dutton, 1969; UK:
Heinemann, 1951; Insp. Hemingway
#3
Envious Casca. Doubleday, 1941; UK:
Hodder, 1941; Insp. Hannasyde
#2
Merely murder. Doubleday, 1935; UK:
Death in the stocks. Longman,
1935; Insp. Hannasyde #1
No wind of blame. Doubleday, 1939;
UK: Hodder, 1939; Insp. Hemingway
#1
Penhallow. Dutton, 1943; UK:
Heinemann, 1942
They found him dead. Doubleday,
1937; UK: Hodder, 1937; Insp.
Hannasyde #3
The unfinished clue. Doubleday,
1937; UK: Longman, 1934
Why shoot a bather? Doubleday,
1936; UK: Longman, 1933; Frank
Amberley
HICHENS, ROBERT, 1864-1950
The Paradine case. Doubleday,
1933; UK: Benn, 1933
HIGHSMITH, PATRICIA, 1921 --
The boy who followed Ripley.
Lippincott, 1980; UK: Heinemann,
1980; Tom Ripley
The cry of the owl. Harper, 1962;
UK: Heinemann, 1963
Deep water. Harper, 1957; UK:
Heinemann, 1958
A game for the living. Harper,
1958; UK: Heinemann, 1959

Ripley under ground. Doubleday, 1970; UK: Heinemann, 1971; Tom Ripley #2

Ripley's game. Knopf, 1974; UK: Heinemann, 1974; Tom Ripley #3

The story-teller. Doubleday, 1965; UK: A suspension of mercy. Heinemann, 1965

Strangers on a train. Harper, 1950; UK: Cresset, 1950

The talented Mr. Ripley. Coward McCann, 1955; UK: Cresset, 1957; Tom Ripley #1

Those who walk away. Doubleday, 1967; UK: Heinemann, 1967

The tremor of forgery. Doubleday, 1969; UK: Heinemann, 1969

The two faces of January. Doubleday, 1964; UK: Heinemann, 1964

HILL, REGINALD, 1936 -- . For other mysteries by this author, see RUELL, PATRICK (pseud.)

An advancement of learning. UK: Collins, 1971; Andrew Dalziel #2; Peter Pascoe

An April shroud. UK: Collins, 1975; Andrew Dalziel #4

A clubbable woman. Countryman/Foul Play, 1984; UK: Collins, 1970; Andrew Dalziel; Peter Pascoe

Deadheads. Macmillan, 1984; Andrew Dalziel; Peter Pascoe

Exit lines. Macmillan, 1985; Andrew Dalziel; Peter Pascoe

A killing kindness. Pantheon, 1981; UK: Collins, 1980; Andrew Dalziel

A pinch of snuff. Harper, 1978; UK: Collins, 1978; Andrew Dalziel #5

Ruling passion. Harper, 1977; UK: Collins, 1973; Andrew Dalziel #3

Who guards the prince? Pantheon, 1982; Insp. McHarg

HILLERMAN, TONY, 1925 --

The blessing way. Harper, 1970; UK: Macmillan, 1970; Joe Leaphorn #1

Dance hall of the dead. Harper, 1973; Joe Leaphorn #2

The dark wind. Harper, 1982; Jim Chee

The fly on the wall. Harper, 1971

The ghostway. Harper, 1985; Jim Chee

The listening woman. Harper, 1978; UK: Macmillan, 1979; Joe Leaphorn #3

People of darkness. Harper, 1980; Jim Chee

HILTON, JAMES, see TREVOR, GLEN (pseud.)

HILTON, JOHN BUXTON (pseud.). For other mysteries by this author, see GREENWOOD, JOHN

The anathema stone. St. Martin's, 1980; UK: Collins, 1980; Simon Kenworthy #6

The asking price. St. Martin's, 1983; Simon Kenworthy

Dead-nettle. St. Martin's, 1977; UK: Macmillan, 1977; Thomas Brunt #3

Death in midwinter. Walker, 1969; UK: Cassell, 1969; Simon Kenworthy #2

Death of an alderman. Walker, 1968; UK: Cassell, 1968; Simon Kenworthy #1

Gamekeeper's gallows. St. Martin's, 1977; UK: Macmillan, 1976; Thomas Brunt #2

The green frontier. St. Martin's, 1982; Simon Kenworthy

Hangman's tide. St. Martin's, 1975; UK: Macmillan, 1975; Simon Kenworthy #3

No birds sang. St. Martin's, 1978; UK: Macmillan, 1975; Simon Kenworthy #4

Passion in the peak. St. Martin's, 1985; Simon Kenworthy

The quiet stranger. St. Martin's, 1985; Thomas Brunt #2

Rescue from the rose. St. Martin's, 1976; UK: Macmillan, 1976; Thomas Brunt #1

Some run crooked. St. Martin's, 1978; UK: Macmillan, 1978; Simon Kenworthy #5

The sunset law. St. Martin's, 1982; Simon Kenworthy

HIMES, CHESTER, 1909 --

All shot up. Avon, 1960; UK: Panther, 1969; Coffin Ed Johnson #4; Grave Digger Jones #4

The big gold dream. Avon, 1960; UK: Panther, 1968; Coffin Ed Johnson #5; Grave Digger Jones #5

Blind man with a pistol. Morrow, 1969; UK: Hodder, 1969; Coffin Ed Johnson #8; Grave Digger Jones #8

Cotton comes to Harlem. Putnam, 1965; UK: Muller, 1965; Coffin Ed Johnson #6; Grave Digger Jones #6

The crazy kill. Avon, 1959; UK: Panther, 1968; Coffin Ed Johnson #2; Grave Digger Jones #2

For love of Imabelle. Fawcett, 1959; UK: Panther, 1969; Coffin Ed Johnson #1; Grave Digger Jones #1

The heat's on. Putnam, 1966; UK: Muller, 1966; Coffin Ed Johnson #7; Grave Digger Jones #7

The real cool killers. Avon, 1959; UK: Panther, 1969; Coffin Ed Johnson #3; Grave Digger Jones #3

HINKERMEYER, MICHAEL T.
A time to reap. St. Martin's, 1984; Emil Whippletree

HIRSCHBERG, CORNELIUS, 1901 --
Florentine finish. Harper, 1963; UK: Gollancz, 1964; Saul Handy

HITCHENS, BERT and HITCHENS, DOLORES
End of the line. Doubleday, 1957; UK: Boardman, 1958; John Farrel #1

F. O. B. murder. Doubleday, 1955; UK: Boardman, 1957; Collins #1; McKechnie #1

The grudge. Doubleday, 1963; UK: Boardman, 1964; John Farrel #2

The man who followed women. Doubleday, 1959; UK: Boardman, 1960; Collins #2; McKechnie #2

HITCHENS, DOLORES. For other mysteries by this author, see OLSEN, D. B. (pseud.) or HITCHENS, BERT and HITCHENS, DOLORES
Sleep with slander. Doubleday, 1960; UK: Boardman, 1961; Jim Sader #2

Sleep with strangers. Doubleday, 1955; UK: Macdonald, 1956; Jim Sader #1

HITCHENS, HUBERT, see HITCHENS, BERT and HITCHENS DOLORES

HJORTSBERG, WILLIAM, 1941 --
Falling angel. Harcourt, 1978; UK: Hutchinson, 1979; Harry Angel

HOBSON, FRANCIS
Death on a back bench. Harper, 1959; UK: Eyre, 1959

HOCH, EDWARD D., 1930 --
City of brass and other Simon Ark stories. Leisure Books, 1971; Simon Ark #2

The fellowship of the hand. Walker, 1973; UK: Hale, 1976; Carl Crader #2; Earl Jazine #2

The Frankenstein factory. Warner, 1975; UK: Hale, 1976; Carl Crader #3; Earl Jazine #3

The judges of Hades and other Simon Ark stories. Leisure Books, 1971; Simon Ark #1

The transvection machine. Walker, 1971; UK: Hale, 1974; Carl Crader #1; Earl Jazine #1

HOCH, EDWARD D., ed.
All but impossible! Ticknor & Fields, 1981

HOCKING, ANNE (pseud. of Mona Hocking)
And no one wept. UK: Allen, 1954; William Austen #14

At the cedars. UK: Bles, 1949; William Austen #9

The best laid plans. Doubleday, 1950; UK: Bles, 1952; William Austen #11

Candidates for murder. UK: Long, 1961; William Austen #24

Deadly is the evil tongue. Doubleday, 1940; UK: Old Mrs. Fitzgerald. Bles, 1939; William Austen #1

Death among the tulips. UK: Allen, 1953; William Austen #13

Death at the wedding. UK: Bles, 1946; William Austen #7

Death disturbs Mr. Jefferson. Doubleday, 1950; UK: Bles, 1951; William Austen #10

Death loves a shining mark. Doubleday, 1943; William Austen #4

The finishing touch. Doubleday, 1948; UK: Prussian blue. Bles, 1947; William Austen #8

He had to die. UK: Long, 1962; William Austen #25

Killing kin. Doubleday, 1951; UK: Mediterranean murder. Evans, 1951; William Austen #12

Murder at mid-day. UK: Allen, 1956; William Austen #17

Murder cries out. (completed by Evelyn Healy) UK: Long, 1968; William Austen #26

Nile green. UK: Bles, 1943; William Austen #5

One shall be taken. UK: Bles, 1942; William Austen #3

Poison in paradise. Doubleday, 1955; UK: Allen, 1955; William Austen #15

Poison is a better brew. Doubleday, 1942; UK: Miss Milverton. Bles, 1941; William Austen #2

Poisoned chalice. UK: Long, 1959; William Austen #21

A reason for murder. UK: Allen, 1955; William Austen #16

Relative murder. UK: Allen, 1957; William Austen #18

The simple way of poison. Washburn, 1957; UK: Allen, 1957; William Austen #19

The thin-spun life. UK: Long, 1960; William Austen #23

To cease upon the midnight. UK: Long, 1959; William Austen #22

A victim must be found. Doubleday, 1959; UK: Epitaph for a nurse. Allen, 1958; William Austen #20

The vultures gather. UK: Bles, 1945; William Austen #6

HODGKIN, M. R., 1917 --
Dead indeed. Macmillan, 1956; UK: Gollancz, 1955

Student body. Scribner's, 1949; UK: Gollancz, 1950

HOLDAWAY, NEVILLE ALDRIDGE, 1894 -- , see TEMPLE-ELLIS, N. A. (pseud.)

HOLDEN, GENEVIEVE (pseud. of Genevieve Pou, 1919 --)
Deadlier than the male. Doubleday, 1961; Hank Ferrell

Don't go in alone. Doubleday, 1966; UK: Hale, 1966

Down a dark alley. Doubleday, 1976

HOLDING, ELIZABETH SAXANAY
The blank wall. Simon & Schuster, 1947; Lt. Levy #1

Lady killer. Duell, 1942

Miasma. Dutton, 1929

The old battle axe. Simon & Schuster, 1943

Speak of the devil. Duell, 1941

The strange crime in Bermuda. Dodd, 1937; UK: Lane, 1938

Too many bottles. Simon & Schuster, 1951; UK: Muller, 1953; Lt. Levy #2

Widow's mite. Simon & Schuster, 1953; UK: Muller, 1954; Lt. Levy #3

HOLLAND, ISABELLE, 1920 --
Darcourt. Weybright, 1976; UK: Collins, 1977

A death at St. Anselm's. Doubleday, 1984

Grenelle. Rawson Associates, 1976; UK: Collins, 1978; Susan Grenelle; Mark Czernick

HOLMAN, C. HUGH, 1914-1981
Another man's poison. Mill, 1947; UK: Foulsham, 1950; Sheriff Macready #4

Death like thunder. Phoenix Press, 1942; Norman Travis

Slay the murderer. Mill, 1946; UK: Foulsham, 1950; Sheriff Macready #2

Trout in the milk. Mill, 1945; UK: Boardman, 1951; Sheriff Macready #1

Up this crooked way. Mill, 1946; UK: Foulsham, 1951; Sheriff Macready #3

HOLMAN, HUGH, see HOLMAN, C. HUGH

HOLME, TIMOTHY
A funeral of gondolas. Coward McCann, 1982; Achille Peroni

The Neapolitan streak. Coward McCann, 1980; UK: Macmillan, 1980; Achille Peroni

HOLMES, H. H. (pseud. of William Anthony Parker White, 1911-1968). For other mysteries by this author, see BOUCHER, ANTHONY (pseud.)
Nine times nine. Duell, 1940; Sr. Ursula #1

Rocket to the morgue. Duell, 1942; Sr. Ursula #2

HOLT, HENRY
The midnight mail. Doubleday, 1931; UK: Harrap, 1931

HOLTON, LEONARD (pseud. of Leonard Wibberly, 1915 --)
A corner of paradise. St. Martin's, 1977; Joseph Bredder #11

Deliver us from wolves. Dodd, 1963; Joseph Bredder #4

The devil to play. Dodd, 1974;
  Joseph Bredder #10
Flowers by request. Dodd, 1964;
  Joseph Bredder #5
The mirror of hell. Dodd, 1972;
  Joseph Bredder #9
Out of the depths. Dodd, 1966; UK:
  Hammond, 1967; Joseph Bredder #6
A pact with Satan. Dodd, 1960; UK:
  Hale, 1961; Joseph Bredder #2
A problem in angels. Dodd, 1970;
  Joseph Bredder #8
The saint maker. Dodd, 1959; UK:
  Hale, 1960; Joseph Bredder #1
Secret of the doubting saint.
  Dodd, 1961; Joseph Bredder #3
A touch of Jonah. Dodd, 1968;
  Joseph Bredder #7
HOMES, GEOFFREY (pseud. of David
  Mainwaring, 1902-1978)
Build my gallows high. Morrow, 1946
The doctor died at dusk. Morrow,
  1936; Robin Bishop #1
Finders keepers. Morrow, 1940;
  Humphrey Campbell #3
Forty whacks. Morrow, 1941;
  Humphrey Campbell #4
The kill of the terrified monk.
  Morrow, 1943; Jose Manuel Madero
  #2
The man who didn't exist. Morrow,
  1937; UK: Eyre, 1939; Robin Bishop
  #3
The man who murdered Goliath.
  Morrow, 1938; UK: Eyre, 1940;
  Robin Bishop #4
The man who murdered himself.
  Morrow, 1936; UK: Lane, 1936;
  Robin Bishop #2
No hands on the clock. Morrow,
  1939; Humphrey Campbell #2
Six silver handles. Morrow, 1944;
  UK: Cherry Tree, 1946; Humphrey
  Campbell #5
The street of the crying woman.
  Morrow, 1942; UK: Seven died.
  Cherry Tree, 1943; Jose Manuel
  Madero #1
Then there were three. Morrow,
  1938; UK: Cherry Tree, 1945; Robin
  Bishop #5; Humphrey Campbell #1
HOOD, MARGARET PAGE, 1892 --
The bell on lonely. Coward McCann,
  1959; Gil Donan

Drown the wind. Coward McCann,
  1961; Gil Donan
In the dark night. Coward McCann,
  1957; Gil Donan
The scarlet thread. Coward McCann,
  1956; Gil Donan
The silent women. Coward McCann,
  1953
The sin mark. Coward McCann, 1963
HOOKER, BRIAN, 1880-1946, see
  HASTINGS, W. S. and HOOKER, BRIAN
HOPKINS, A. T. (pseud. of Annette
  Turngren, 1902-1980). For other
  mysteries by this author, see
  TURNGREN, ANNETTE
Have a lovely funeral. Rinehart,
  1954
HOPKINS, HECTOR KENNETH, see HOPKINS,
  KENNETH, 1914 --
HOPKINS, KENNETH 1914 --
Body blow. Holt, 1962; UK:
  Macdonald, 1960; Gideon Manciple
  #3
Dead against my principles. Holt,
  1962; UK: Macdonald, 1960; Gideon
  Manciple #2
She died because. Holt, 1964; UK:
  Macdonald, 1957; Gideon Manciple
  #1
HORNIG, DOUG
Foul shot. Scribner's, 1984; Loren
  Swift
HOUGH, S. B., 1917 --
The bronze Perseus. Walker, 1959;
  UK: Secker, 1959; Insp. Brentford
  #1
Dear daughter dead. Walker, 1966;
  UK: Gollancz, 1975; Insp.
  Brentford #2
Fear fortune, Father. UK: Gollancz,
  1974; Insp. Brentford #4
Sweet sister seduced. Perennial,
  1983; UK: Gollancz, 1968; Insp.
  Brentford #3
HOUSEHOLD, GEOFFREY, 1900 --
Olura. Little, 1965; UK: Joseph,
  1965; Pedro Gonzales
HOVICK, ROSE LOUISE, see LEE, GYPSY
  ROSE (pseud.)
HOWARD, JAMES A., 1922 --
The bullet-proof martyr. Dutton,
  1961; Paul Kenneth Kane
Murder takes a wife. Dutton, 1958
HOYT, RICHARD, 1941 --
Decoys. Evans, 1980; UK: Hale, 1982

Fish story. Viking, 1985; John
Denson

The Siskiyou two-step. Morrow,
1983; John Denson

30 for a Harry. Evans, 1981; John
Denson #2

HUBBARD, MARGARET ANN (pseud. of
Margaret Priley, 1909 --)
Murder at St. Dennis. Bruce, 1952
Murder takes the veil. Bruce,
1950; Mother Theodore

HUBBARD, P. M., 1910-1980
The causeway. Doubleday, 1978;
UK: Macmillan, 1976; Peter
Grant

The country of again. Atheneum,
1969; UK: The custom of the
country. Bles, 1969

The dancing man. Atheneum, 1971;
UK: Macmillan, 1971; Mark
Hawkins

Flush as May. London House, 1963;
UK: Joseph, 1963

The graveyard. Atheneum, 1975; UK:
Macmillan, 1975

High tide. Atheneum, 1970; UK:
Macmillan, 1971

A hive of glass. Atheneum, 1965;
UK: Joseph, 1965

Kill Claudio. Doubleday, 1979; UK:
Macmillan, 1979

Picture of the Millie. Holden,
1964; UK: Joseph, 1964

A thirsty evil. Atheneum, 1974;
UK: Macmillan, 1974

HUGHES, BABETTE PLECHNER, 1906 --
Murder in church. Appleton, 1934;
Ian Craig #2

Murder in the zoo. Appleton, 1932;
UK: Benn, 1932; Ian Craig #1

HUGHES, DOROTHY B., 1904 --
The candy kid. Duell, 1950
The cross-eyed bear. Duell, 1940;
UK: Nicholson, 1943; Insp. Tobin
#2

The expendable man. Random House,
1963; UK: Duetsch, 1964; Hugh
Densmore

The fallen sparrow. Duell, 1942;
UK: Nicholson, 1943; Insp. Tobin
#3

Ride the pink horse. Duell, 1946;
UK: Bantam, 1979

The so blue marble. Duell, 1940;
UK: Bantam, 1979; Insp. Tobin #1

HUGHES, RICHARD
Unholy communion. Doubleday,
1982; Sam McChesney

HUGO, RICHARD
Death and the good life. St.
Martin's, 1981

HULL, RICHARD (pseud. for Richard
Henry Sampson, 1896-1973)
The murderers of Monty. Putnam,
1937; UK: Faber, 1937; Insp.
Fenby

HUME, FERGUS, 1859-1932
The blue talisman. Clode, 1925; UK:
Laurie, 1912

The mystery of a hansom cab. Munro,
1888; UK: Hume, 1886; Samuel
Gorby

HUNT, KYLE (pseud.). For other
mysteries by this author, see
CREASEY, JOHN
Cruel as a cat. Macmillan, 1968;
Emmanuel Cellini

Cunning as a fox. Macmillan, 1965;
Emmanuel Cellini

Sly as a fox. Macmillan, 1967;
Emmanuel Cellini

Wicked as the devil. Macmillan,
1966; Emmanuel Cellini

HUNT, PETER, see YATES, GEORGE
WORTHING (pseud.)

HUNTER, ALAN, 1922 --
Death on the Broadlands. Walker,
1984; George Gently

Death on the heath. Walker, 1982;
George Gently #28

Gently at a gallop. UK: Cassell,
1971; George Gently #18

Gently between tides. Walker,
1982; George Gently

Gently by the shore. Rinehart,
1956; UK: Cassell, 1956; George
Gently #2

Gently coloured. UK: Cassell,
1969; George Gently #16

Gently confidential. UK: Cassell,
1967; George Gently #15

Gently does it. Rinehart, 1955;
UK: Cassell, 1955; George Gently
#1

Gently down the stream. Roy, 1960;
UK: Cassell, 1957; George Gently
#3

Gently floating. Berkley, 1964;
UK: Cassell, 1963; George Gently
#11

Gently French. UK: Cassell, 1973;
George Gently #20

Gently go man. Berkley, 1964; UK:
Cassell, 1961; George Gently #9

Gently in the Highlands. Macmillan,
1975; UK: Gently North-West.
Cassell, 1967; George Gently #14

Gently in the sun. Berkley, 1964;
UK: Cassell, 1959; George Gently
#6

Gently instrumental. UK: Cassell,
1977; George Gently #24

Gently sahib. UK: Cassell, 1964;
George Gently #12

Gently through the mill. UK:
Cassell, 1958; George Gently #5

Gently through the woods.
Macmillan, 1975; UK: Gently in
trees. Cassell, 1974; George
Gently #21

Gently to a sleep. UK: Cassell,
1978; George Gently #25

Gently to the summit. Berkley,
1965; UK: Cassell, 1961; George
Gently #8

Gently where the birds are. UK:
Cassell, 1976; George Gently #23

Gently where the roads go. UK:
Cassell, 1962; George Gently #10

Gently with love. UK: Cassell,
1975; George Gently #22

Gently with the innocents.
Macmillan, 1974; UK: Cassell,
1970; George Gently #17

Gently with the ladies. Macmillan,
1974; UK: Cassell, 1965; George
Gently #13

Gently with the painters. Macmillan,
1976; UK: Cassell, 1960; George
Gently #7

Landed Gently. British Book Centre,
1957; UK: Cassell, 1957; George
Gently #4

Vivienne: Gently where she lay. UK:
Cassell, 1972; George Gently #19

HUNTER, EVAN, see MCBAIN, ED

HUNTINGTON, JOHN (pseud. of Gerald
William Phillips, 1884 --)
The seven black chessmen. Holt,
1928; UK: Howe, 1928; Horton
Forbes

HUTCHINSON, HORACE G.
The mystery of the summer house.
Doran, 1919; UK: Hutchinson,
1925

HUTTON, JOHN, 1929 --
29, Herriott Street. St. Martin's,
1980; UK: Bodley Head, 1979

HUTTON, MALCOLM
Georgina and Georgette. St.
Martin's, 1984

HUTTON, SARA, see WOODS, SARA
(pseud.)

HUXLEY, ELSPETH, 1907 --
The African poison murders. Harper,
1940; UK: Death of an Aryan.
Methuen, 1939; Supt. Vachell #3
The incident at the Merry Hippo.
Morrow, 1964; UK: The Merry
Hippo. Chatto, 1963; Alexander
Barton
Murder at government house. Harper,
1937; UK: Methuen, 1937; Supt.
Vachell #1
Murder on safari. Harper, 1938; UK:
Methuen, 1938; Supt. Vachell #2

HYAMS, JOE
Murder at the Academy Awards. St.
Martin's, 1983; Punch Roberts;
Bonny Cutler

HYLAND, STANLEY, 1914 --
Top bloody secret. Bobbs, 1969; UK:
Gollancz, 1969
Who goes hang? Dodd, 1959; UK:
Gollancz, 1958

IAMS, JACK (pseud. of Samuel H. Iams,
Jr., 1910 --)
The body missed the boat. Morrow,
1947; UK: Rich, 1949
Death draws the line. Morrow,
1949; UK: Rich, 1951
Do not murder before Christmas.
Morrow, 1949; Rocky Rockwell #1
Girl meets body. Morrow, 1947; UK:
Rich, 1950
A shot of murder. Morrow, 1950;
UK: Gollancz, 1952; Rocky
Rockwell #2
What rhymes with murder? Morrow,
1950; UK: Gollancz, 1951; Rocky
Rockwell #3

IBARGUENGOITIA, JORGE
Two crimes. Godine, 1984

ILES, BERT
Murder in mink. Arcadia House, 1966

ILES, FRANCIS. For other mysteries
by this author, see BERKELEY,
ANTHONY (pseud.)

Before the fact. Doubleday, 1932;
UK: Gollancz, 1932

INCHBALD, PETER
Short break in Venice. Doubleday,
1983; Franco Corti
The sweet short grass. Doubleday,
1982; Frank Short

INNES, HAMMOND, 1913 --
The wreck of the Mary Deare.
Knopf, 1956; UK: The Mary Deare.
Collins, 1956; John Sands

INNES, MICHAEL (pseud. of John Innes
Mackintosh Stewart, 1906 --)
The Ampersand papers. Dodd, 1979;
UK: Gollancz, 1978; John Appleby
#32
Appleby and Honeybath. Dodd, 1983;
Charles Honeybath; John Appleby
The Appleby file. Dodd, 1976; UK:
Gollancz, 1975; John Appleby #29
Appleby on Ararat. Dodd, 1941; UK:
Gollancz, 1941; John Appleby #7
Appleby talks again. Dodd, 1957;
UK: Gollancz, 1956; John Appleby
#15
Appleby's answer. Dodd, 1973; UK:
Gollancz, 1973; John Appleby #27
Appleby's end. Dodd, 1945; UK:
Gollancz, 1945; John Appleby #10
Appleby's other story. Dodd, 1974;
UK: Gollancz, 1974; John Appleby
#28
An awkward lie. Dodd, 1971; UK:
Gollancz, 1971; John Appleby #25
The bloody wood. Dodd, 1966; UK:
Gollancz, 1966; John Appleby #21
Carson's conspiracy. Dodd, 1984;
John Appleby
The case of Sonia Wayward. Dodd,
1960; UK: The new Sonia Wayward.
Gollancz, 1960
The case of the journeying boy.
Dodd, 1949; UK: The journeying
boy. Gollancz, 1949; Insp.
Cadogan
A change of heir. Dodd, 1966; UK:
Gollancz, 1966
Christmas at Candleshoe. Dodd,
1953; UK: Gollancz, 1953
Comedy of terrors. Dodd, 1940; UK:
There came both mist and snow.
Gollancz, 1940; John Appleby #5
The crabtree affair. Dodd, 1962;
UK: A connoisseur's case.
Gollancz, 1962; John Appleby #20

The daffodil affair. Dodd, 1942;
UK: Gollancz, 1942; John Appleby
#8
Dead man's shoes. Dodd, 1954; UK:
Appleby talking. Gollancz, 1954;
John Appleby #14
Death at the chase. Dodd, 1970; UK:
Gollancz, 1970; Bobby Appleby #2;
John Appleby #24
Death by water. Dodd, 1968; UK:
Appleby at Alington. Gollancz,
1968; John Appleby #22
Death on a quiet day. Dodd, 1957;
UK: Appleby plays chicken.
Gollancz, 1957; John Appleby #16
The Gay Phoenix. Dodd, 1977; UK:
Gollancz, 1976; John Appleby #30
Going it alone. Dodd, 1980; UK:
Gollancz, 1980
Hamlet, revenge! Dodd, 1937; UK:
Gollancz, 1937; John Appleby #2;
Giles Gott
Hare sitting up. Dodd, 1959; UK:
Gollancz, 1959; John Appleby #18
Honeybath's haven. Dodd, 1978; UK:
Gollancz, 1977; Charles
Honeybath; John Appleby #31
Lament for a maker. Dodd, 1938; UK:
Gollancz, 1938; John Appleby #3
The long farewell. Dodd, 1958; UK:
Gollancz, 1958; John Appleby #17
Lord Mullion's secret. Dodd, 1981;
Charles Honeybath
The man from the sea. Dodd, 1955;
UK: Gollancz, 1955
A night of errors. Dodd, 1947; UK:
Gollancz, 1948; John Appleby #11
One-man show. Dodd, 1952; UK: A
private view. Gollancz, 1952;
John Appleby #13
The open house. Dodd, 1972; UK:
Gollancz, 1972; John Appleby #26
The paper thunderbolt. Dodd, 1951;
UK: Operation Pax. Gollancz,
1951; John Appleby #12
Picture of guilt. Dodd, 1969; UK:
A family affair. Gollancz, 1969;
John Appleby #23; Bobby Appleby
#1
A question of queens. Dodd, 1956;
UK: Old hall, new hall. Gollancz,
1956
The secret vanguard. Dodd, 1941;
UK: Gollancz, 1940; John Appleby
#5

Seven suspects. Dodd, 1937; UK:
Death at the president's lodging.
Gollancz, 1936; Giles Gott; John
Appleby #1

Sheiks and adders. Dodd, 1982;
John Appleby #33

Silence observed. Dodd, 1961; UK:
Gollancz, 1961; John Appleby #19

The spider strikes. Dodd, 1939;
UK: Stop press. Gollancz, 1939;
John Appleby #4

The weight of evidence. Dodd,
1943; UK: Gollancz, 1944; John
Appleby #9

IONS, EDMUND S., see AUBREY, EDMUND
(pseud.)

IRISH, WILLIAM
Deadline at dawn. Lippincott,
1944; UK: Hutchinson, 1947

IRONSIDE, ELIZABETH
A very private enterprise. Hodder,
1985; UK: Hodder, 1985; George
Sinclair

ISAACS, SUSAN, 1943 --
Compromising positions. Times
Books, 1978; UK: Lane, 1978;
Judith Singer; Nelson Sharpe

JACQUEMARD-SENECAL (pseud. of Yves
Jacquemard and Jean-Michel Senecal)
The body vanishes. Dodd, 1980; UK:
Collins, 1980; Supt. Dullac

The eleventh little Indian. Dodd,
1979; UK: The eleventh little
nigger. Collins, 1979

JAHN, MICHAEL, 1943 --
Night rituals. Norton, 1982

JAMES, BRENI
Night of the kill. Simon & Schuster,
1961; UK: Hammond, 1963; Gunnar
Matson

JAMES, FRANKLIN
Killer in the kitchen. Lantern
Press, 1947; Mickey Richards

JAMES, GODFREY WARDEN, see BROOME.
ADAM (pseud.)

JAMES, HENRY, 1843-1916
The other house. Macmillan, 1896;
UK: Heinemann, 1896

JAMES, MARGARET
Footsteps in the fog. St. Martin's,
1980; UK: Hale, 1979

JAMES, P. D., 1920 --
The black tower. Scribner's, 1979;
UK: Faber, 1975; Adam Dagliesh #6

Cover her face. Scribner's, 1966;
UK: Faber, 1962; Adam Dagliesh #1

Death of an expert witness.
Scribner's, 1977; UK: Faber,
1977; Adam Dagliesh #7

A mind to murder. Scribner's, 1967;
UK: Faber, 1963; Adam Dagliesh #2

Shroud for a nightingale.
Scribner's, 1971; UK: Faber,
1971; Adam Dagliesh #4

The skull beneath the skin.
Scribner's, 1982; Cordelia Gray

Unnatural causes. Scribner's, 1967;
UK: Faber, 1967; Adam Dagliesh #3

An unsuitable job for a woman.
Scribner's, 1973; UK: Faber,
1972; Cordelia Gray; Adam
Dagliesh #5

JANIFER, LAURENCE MARK, see HARRIS,
LARRY M. (pseud.)

JAPRISOT, SEBASTIEN
The 10:30 from Marseilles.
Doubleday, 1963; UK: Souvenir,
1964; Insp. Grazzoni

JARRETT, CORA, see KEENE, FARADAY
(pseud.)

JAY, CHARLOTTE (pseud. of Geraldine
Mary Jay, 1919 --)
Arms for Adonis. Harper, 1961; UK:
Collins, 1960

Beat not the bones. Harper, 1953;
UK: Collins, 1952; Emma Warwick

The brink of silence. Harper, 1957;
UK: The feast of the dead. Hale,
1956

The fugitive eye. Harper, 1954;
UK: Collins, 1953

The voice of the crab. Harper,
1974; UK: Constable, 1974

The yellow turban. Harper, 1955;
UK: Collins, 1955; William Brooke

JAY, G. M., see JAY, CHARLOTTE

JAY, GERALDINE MARY, see JAY,
CHARLOTTE (pseud.)

JAY, SIMON (pseud. of Colin James
Alexander, 1920 --)
The adventure of the stalwart.
Harper, 1978; UK: Cassell, 1979;
Theodore Roosevelt; Sherlock
Holmes

Death of a skin diver. Doubleday,
1964; Dr. Much

Sleepers can kill. Doubleday,
1968; UK: Collins, 1968

JEFFERS, H. PAUL
  Murder most irregular. St.
    Martin's, 1983; David Morgan;
    Sherlock Holmes
  Murder on mike. St. Martin's,
    1984; Harry MacNeil
  Rub out at the Onyx. Ticknor &
    Fields, 1981; Harry MacNeil
JEFFREYS, J. G.
  The Pangersbourne murders. Walker,
    1984; Jeremy Sturrock
  Suicide most foul. Walker, 1981;
    Jeremy Sturrock
  A wicked way to die. Walker, 1973;
    UK: Macmillan, 1973; Jeremy
    Sturrock
JEFFRIES, GRAHAM MONTAGUE, see
  GRAEME, BRUCE (pseud.)
JEFFRIES, RODERIC, 1926 -- . For other
  mysteries by this author, see
  ASHFORD, JEFFREY (pseud.) or ALDING,
  PETER (pseud.)
  Dead against the lawyers. Dodd,
    1966; UK: Collins, 1965
  Deadly petard. St. Martin's, 1984;
    Enrique Alvarez #6
  An embarrassing death. Dodd, 1965;
    UK: Collins, 1964; Bill Stemple
  Evidence of the accused. London
    House, 1963; UK: Collins, 1961;
    Supt. Pope
  Layers of deceit. St. Martin's,
    1985; Enrique Alvarez
  Mistakenly in Mallorca. UK:
    Collins, 1974; Enrique Alvarez #1
  Murder begets murder. St. Martin's,
    1979; UK: Collins, 1979; Enrique
    Alvarez #4
  Three and one make five. St.
    Martin's, 1984; Enrique Alvarez
  Troubled deaths. St. Martin's,
    1978; UK: Collins, 1977; Enrique
    Alvarez #3
  Two-faced death. UK: Collins, 1976;
    Enrique Alvarez #2
  Unseemly end. St. Martin's, 1982;
    Enrique Alvarez #5
JENKINS, CECIL, 1927 --
  Message from Sirius. Dodd, 1961;
    UK: Collins, 1961
JENKINS, HERBERT, 1876-1923
  Malcolm Sage, detective. Doran,
    1921; UK: Jenkins, 1921; Malcolm
    Sage

JEPSON, SELWYN, 1899 --
  The death gong. Watts, 1927; UK:
    Harrap, 1927; John Perrin
  Keep murder quiet. Doubleday, 1941;
    UK: Joseph, 1940; Roger Spain
JEROME, OWEN FOX
  The murder at the Avalon Arms.
    Clode, 1931; UK: Hutchinson,
    1930; Philip MacCray
  The red kite clue. Clode, 1928; UK:
    Skeffington, 1929; Artemus Graham
JESSE, F. TENNYSON, 1889-1958
  A pin to see the peepshow.
    Doubleday, 1934; UK: Heinemann,
    1934
  The Solange stories. Macmillan,
    1931; UK: Heinemann, 1931;
    Solange Fontaine
JOHN, ROMILLY and JOHN, KATHERINE
  Death by request. Hogarth Press,
    1984
JOHNSON, E. RICHARD, 1937 --
  Cage five is going to break.
    Harper, 1970; UK: Macmillan, 1971
  The Cardinalli contract. Pyramid
    Books, 1975
  Caseload--maximum. Harper, 1971
  The God keepers. Harper, 1970; UK:
    Macmillan, 1971
  The inside man. Harper, 1969; UK:
    Macmillan, 1970; Tony Lonto
  The Judas. Harper, 1971
  Mongo's back in town. Harper, 1969;
    UK: Macmillan, 1970
  Silver Street. Harper, 1968; UK:
    The Silver Street killer. Hale,
    1969; Tony Lonto
JOHNSON, W. BOLINGBROKE. (pseud. of
  Morris Gilbert Bishop, 1893-1973)
  The widening stain. Knopf, 1942;
    UK: Lane, 1943; Gilda Gorham
JOHNSTON, GEORGE HENRY, see MARTIN,
  SHANE (pseud.)
JOHNSTON, VELDA
  The crystal cat. Dodd, 1985
  The other Karen. Dodd, 1983;
    Catherine Mayhew
  Shadow behind the curtain. Dodd,
    1985; Deborah Channing
JON, MONTAGUE
  A question of law. St. Martin's,
    1982; Stephen Kale
  The Wallington case. St. Martin's,
    1981; Stephen Kale

JONES, CLEO
  Prophet motive. St. Martin's,
    1984; Chris Danville
JONES, JAMES, 1921-1977
  A touch of danger. Doubleday,
    1973; UK: Collins, 1973; Frank
    "Lobo" Jones
JONES, ZENITH, see FORD, LESLIE
  (pseud.) or FROME, DAVID (pseud.)
JORDAN, CATHLEEN
  A carol in the dark. Walker, 1984;
    Will Gray
JORDAN, ROBERT FURNEAUX, see PLAYER,
  ROBERT (pseud.)

KALLEN, LUCILLE
  C. B. Greenfield: no lady in the
    house. Simon & Schuster, 1982; C.
    B. Greenfield #3
  C. B. Greenfield: the piano bird.
    Random House, 1984; C. B.
    Greenfield
  Introducing C. B. Greenfield.
    Crown, 1979; UK: Collins, 1979; C.
    B. Greenfield #1
  The Tanglewood murder. Wyndham,
    1980; UK: Collins, 1980; Maggie
    Rome
KAMARCK, LAWRENCE, 1927 --
  The bell ringer. Random House,
    1969; Charlie Skragg
  Informed sources. Dial, 1979; UK:
    Fontana, 1981
KAMINSKY, STUART
  Black knight in Red Square. Ace,
    1984; Porfiry Rostrikov
  Bullet for a star. St. Martin's,
    1977; UK: Curley, 1978; Toby
    Peters; Errol Flynn
  Catch a falling clown. St. Martin's,
    1982; Toby Peters; Emmett Kelly
  Down for the count. St. Martin's,
    1985; Toby Peters; Joe Louis
  Exercise in terror. St. Martin's,
    1985; Maureen Dietz; Helen Katz
  The Fala factor. St. Martin's,
    1984; Toby Peters; Eleanor
    Roosevelt
  He done her wrong. St. Martin's,
    1983; Toby Peters; Mae West
  High midnight. St. Martin's, 1981;
    Toby Peters; Gary Cooper; Ernest
    Hemingway

The Howard Hughes affair. St.
    Martin's, 1979; UK: Severn, 1980;
    Toby Peters; Basil Rathbone;
    Howard Hughes
Murder on the yellow brick road.
    St. Martin's, 1978; UK: Curley,
    1979; Toby Peters
Never cross a vampire. St.
    Martin's, 1980; Toby Peters; Bela
    Lugosi; William Faulkner
Red chameleon. Scribner's, 1985;
    Porfiry Rostrikov #4
You bet your life. St. Martin's,
    1979; Toby Peters; Marx Brothers;
    Ian Fleming
KAMITSES, ZOE
  Moondreamer. Little, 1983; Courtney
    Brooks
KARK, NINA MARY, see BAWDEN, NINA
  (pseud.)
KATZ, WILLIAM
  Death in December. McGraw-Hill,
    1984; Spencer Cross-Wade
  Surprise party. McGraw-Hill, 1984;
    Spencer Cross-Wade
KATZENBACH, JOHN
  In the heat of the summer.
    Atheneum, 1982; Malcolm Anderson
KAYE, M. M., 1909 --
  Death in Cyprus. St. Martin's,
    1984; UK: Staples, 1956
  Death in Zanzibar. St. Martin's,
    1983; UK: The house of shade.
    Longman, 1959; Dany Ashton; Lash
    Holden
  Death walked in Berlin. UK:
    Staples, 1955
  Later than you think. Coward
    McCann, 1959 (as by Mollie
    Hamilton); UK: Longman, 1958
KAYE, MARVIN, 1938 --
  Bullets for Macbeth. Dutton, 1978;
    UK: Hale, 1978; Hilary Quayle #3
  The Grand Ole Opry murders.
    Dutton, 1974; Hilary Quayle #2
  The Laurel and Hardy murders.
    Dutton, 1977; UK: Curley, 1978;
    Hilary Quayle
  A lively game of death. Dutton,
    1972; UK: Barker, 1974; Hilary
    Quayle #1
  The soap opera slaughter.
    Doubleday, 1982; Hilary Quayle

KEATING, H. R. F., 1926 --
Bats fly up for Inspector Ghote.
Doubleday, 1974; UK: Collins,
1974; Ganesh Ghote #9
Filmi, filmi, Inspector Ghote.
Doubleday, 1977; UK: Collins,
1976; Ganesh Ghote #10
Go West Inspector Ghote. Doubleday,
1981; Ganesh Ghote #12
Inspector Ghote breaks an egg.
Doubleday, 1971; UK: Collins,
1970; Ganesh Ghote #6
Inspector Ghote caught in meshes.
Dutton, 1968; UK: Collins, 1967;
Ganesh Ghote #3
Inspector Ghote draws a line.
Doubleday, 1979; UK: Collins,
1979; Ganesh Ghote #11
Inspector Ghote goes by train.
Doubleday, 1972; UK: Collins,
1971; Ganesh Ghote #7
Inspector Ghote hunts the peacock.
Dutton, 1968; UK: Collins, 1968;
Ganesh Ghote #4
Inspector Ghote plays a joker.
Dutton, 1969; UK: Collins, 1969;
Ganesh Ghote #5
Inspector Ghote trusts the heart.
Doubleday, 1973; UK: Collins,
1972; Ganesh Ghote #8
Inspector Ghote's good crusade.
Dutton, 1966; UK: Collins, 1966;
Ganesh Ghote #2
The murder of the maharajah.
Doubleday, 1980; UK: Collins,
1980; Supt. Howard
The perfect murder. Dutton, 1965;
UK: Collins, 1964; Ganesh Ghote #1
A rush on the ultimate. Doubleday,
1982; UK: Gollancz, 1961
The sheriff of Bombay. Doubleday,
1984; Ganesh Ghote
KEECH, SCOTT (pseud. of John Scott
Keech, 1936 --)
Ciphered. Harper & Row, 1980; Jeff
Adams; Kate Shaw
KEELER, HARRY STEPHEN, 1890-1967
The amazing web. Dutton, 1930; UK:
Ward, 1929; David Crosby
Behind that mask. Dutton, 1938; UK:
Ward, 1933; Terry O'Rourke
The box from Japan. Dutton, 1932;
UK: Ward, 1935

The case of the ivory arrow.
Phoenix Press, 1945; UK: The
search for W-Y-Z. Ward, 1943
The case of the jeweled ragpicker.
Phoenix Press, 1948; UK: The ace
of spades murder. Ward, 1949;
Angus MacWhorten #2
The case of the lavender gripsack.
Phoenix Press, 1944; UK: The
lavender gripsack. Ward, 1941;
Elsa Colby
The case of the mysterious moll.
Phoenix Press, 1945; UK: The iron
ring. Ward, 1944
The chameleon. Dutton, 1939
The face of the man from Saturn.
Dutton, 1933; UK: The Crilly
Court mystery. Ward, 1933; Jimmie
Kentland
Find the clock. Dutton, 1927; UK:
Hutchinson, 1925; Jeff Darrell
Finger! Finger! Dutton, 1938
The five silver Buddhas. Dutton,
1935; UK: Ward, 1935
The fourth king. Dutton, 1930; UK:
Ward, 1929
The green jade hand. Dutton, 1930;
UK: Ward, 1930; Simon Grundt
The man with the crimson box.
Dutton, 1940; The crimson box.
Ward, 1940
The man with wooden spectacles.
Dutton, 1941; UK: The wooden
spectacles. Ward, 1941
The Marceau case. Dutton, 1936; UK:
Ward, 1936
The Matilda Hunter murder. Dutton,
1931; UK: The black satchel.
Ward, 1931
The mysterious Mr. I. Dutton,
1938; UK: Ward, 1937
The mystery of the fiddling
cracksman. Dutton, 1934; UK: The
fiddling cracksman. Ward, 1934;
Billy Hemple
The riddle of the traveling skull.
Dutton, 1934; UK: The traveling
skull. Ward, 1934
The riddle of the yellow Zuri.
Dutton, 1930; UK: The tiger
snake. Ward, 1931
The sharkskin book. Dutton, 1941;
UK: The third degree. Ward, 1948

Sing Sing nights. Dutton, 1928;
UK: Hutchinson, 1927

The skull of the waltzing clown.
Dutton, 1935

The spectacles of Mr. Caligostro.
Dutton, 1929; UK: The blue
spectacles. Hutchinson, 1926

Thieves' nights. Dutton, 1929; UK:
Ward, 1930

The vanishing gold truck. Dutton,
1941; UK: Ward, 1942; Angus
MacWhorten #1

The voice of the seven sparrows.
Dutton, 1928; UK: Hutchinson,
1924

The Washington Square enigma.
Dutton, 1933; UK: Under twelve
stars. Ward, 1933

The wonderful scheme of Mr.
Christopher Thorne. Dutton, 1936;
UK: The wonderful scheme. Ward,
1937

X. Jones of Scotland Yard. Dutton,
1936; UK: X. Jones. Ward, 1936; X.
Jones

Y. Cheung, business detective.
Dutton, 1939; UK: Cheung,
detective. Ward, 1938; Y. Cheung

KEELER, HARRY STEPHEN and GOODWIN,
HAZEL

The case of the barking clock.
Phoenix Press, 1947; UK: The
barking clock. Ward, 1951;
Tuddleton Trotter #2

Stand by--London calling. Ward,
1953; Angus MacWhorton #3

KEENE, FARADAY (pseud. of Cora Hardy
Jarrett, 1877 --)

Pattern in red and black. Houghton,
1934; UK: Barker, 1934; Leonidas
Ames

KEINSLEY, FRANCES, 1922 --

A time to prey. Stein, 1970; UK:
Allen, 1969

KEIRSTEAD, B. S. and CAMPBELL, D.
FREDERICK

The Brownsville murders. Macmillan,
1933

KEITH, DAVID (pseud. of Francis
Steegmuller, 1906 --)

A matter of accent. Dodd, 1943; Ted
S. Weaver

A matter of iodine. Dodd, 1940; UK:
Cassell, 1940; Ted S. Weaver

KELLAND, CLARENCE BUDINGTON,
1881-1964

The case of the nameless corpse.
Harper, 1956; UK: Hale, 1958

Dangerous angel. Harper, 1953; UK:
Hale, 1955

Death keeps a secret. Harper, 1956;
UK: Hale, 1957

The great mail robbery. Harper,
1951; UK: Museum Press, 1954

The key man. Harper, 1952; UK:
Hale, 1954

The lady and the giant. Dodd, 1959;
UK: Hale, 1960

Mark of treachery. Dodd, 1961

The sinister strangers. Dodd, 1961

KELLERMAN, JONATHAN

When the bough breaks. Atheneum,
1985; Alex Davenport

KELLY, MARY, 1927 --

The Christmas egg. Holt, 1966; UK:
Secker, 1958; Brett Nightingale
#3

Cold coming. Walker, 1968; UK:
Secker, 1956; Brett Nightingale
#1

Dead man's riddle. Walker, 1967;
UK: Secker, 1957; Brett
Nightingale #2

The dead of summer. Mill, 1963; UK:
Due to a death. Joseph, 1962;
Nicholson #2

The march to the gallows. Holt,
1965; UK: Joseph, 1964

The spoilt kill. Walker, 1968; UK:
Joseph, 1961; Nicholson #1

The twenty-fifth hour. Walker,
1972; UK: Macmillan, 1971

KELLY, NORA

In the shadow of King's. St.
Martin's, 1985; Gillian Adams;
Det. Gisborne

KELLY, SUSAN

The Gemini man. Walker, 1985; Liz
Connors; Jack Lingemann

KELSEY, VERA

Fear came first. Doubleday, 1945

The owl sang three times.
Doubleday, 1941; Lt. Diego

Satan has six fingers. Doubleday,
1943; Lt. Diego

Whisper murder! Doubleday, 1946

KELTON, ELMER

Stand proud. Doubleday, 1984

KEMELMAN, HARRY, 1908 --
Friday the rabbi slept late.
Crown, 1964; UK: Hutchinson, 1965;
David Small #1
Monday the rabbi took off. Putnam,
1972; UK: Hutchinson, 1972; David
Small #4
The nine mile walk. Putnam, 1967;
UK: Hutchinson, 1968; Nicky Welt
Saturday the rabbi went hungry.
Crown, 1966; UK: Hutchinson, 1967;
David Small #2
Someday the rabbi will leave.
Morrow, 1985; David Small
Sunday the rabbi stayed home.
Putnam, 1969; UK: Hutchinson,
1969; David Small #3
Thursday the rabbi walked out.
Morrow, 1978; UK: Hutchinson,
1979; David Small #7
Tuesday the rabbi saw red. Fields,
1973; UK: Hutchinson, 1974; David
Small #5
Wednesday the rabbi got wet.
Morrow, 1976; UK: Hutchinson,
1976; David Small #6
KEMP, SARAH (pseud. of Michael
Butterworth, 1924 --)
No escape. Doubleday, 1984
Over the edge. Doubleday, 1979;
UK: Goodbye Pussy. Collins, 1979
KENDRICK, BAYNARD H., 1894-1977
The aluminum turtle. Dodd, 1960;
UK: The spear gun murder. Hale,
1961; Duncan Maclain #13
Blind allies. Morrow, 1954; Duncan
Maclain #10
Blind man's bluff. Little, 1943;
UK: Methuen, 1944; Duncan Maclain
#4
Blood on Lake Louisa. Greenberg,
1934; UK: Methuen, 1937
Clear and present danger.
Doubleday, 1958; UK: Hale, 1959;
Duncan Maclain #12
Death beyond the go-thru. Doubleday,
1938; Miles Standish Rice #3
Death knell. Morrow, 1945; UK:
Methuen, 1946; Duncan Maclain #6
The eleven of diamonds. Greenberg,
1936; UK: Methuen, 1937; Miles
Standish Rice #2
Flight from a firing wall. Simon &
Schuster, 1966; UK: Hale, 1968

Frankincense and murder. Dodd,
1961; UK: Hale, 1962; Duncan
Maclain #14
The iron spiders. Greenberg, 1936;
UK: Methuen, 1938; Miles Standish
Rice #1
The last express. Doubleday, 1937;
UK: Methuen, 1938; Duncan Maclain
#1
Make mine Maclain. Morrow, 1947;
Duncan Maclain #7
The murderer who wanted more. Dell,
1951; Duncan Maclain #8
The odor of violets. Little, 1941;
UK: Methuen, 1941; Duncan Maclain
#3
Out of control. Morrow, 1945; UK:
Methuen, 1947; Duncan Maclain #5
Reservations for death. Morrow,
1957; UK: Hale, 1958; Duncan
Maclain #11
The whistling hangman. Doubleday,
1937; UK: Hale, 1959; Duncan
Maclain #2
You die today. Morrow, 1952; UK:
Hale, 1958; Duncan Maclain #9
KENEALLY, THOMAS, 1935 --
The place at Whitten. Walker, 1965;
UK: Cassell, 1964
The survivor. Viking, 1970; UK:
Angus, 1969
A victim of the aurora. Harcourt,
1978; UK: Collins, 1977
KENNEDY, MILWARD (pseud. of Milward
Rodon Kennedy Burge, 1894-1968)
Bull's eye. Kinsey, 1933; UK:
Gollancz, 1933; George Bull #1
Corpse guard parade. Doubleday,
1930; UK: Gollancz, 1929; Insp.
Cornford #2
Corpse in cold storage. Kinsey,
1934; UK: Gollancz, 1934; George
Bull #2
Death in a deck chair. Doubleday,
1931; UK: Gollancz, 1930; H. H.
Huskisson
The man who rang the bell.
Doubleday, 1929; UK: The corpse
on the mat. Gollancz, 1929; Insp.
Cornford #1
The murderer of sleep. Kinsey,
1933; UK: Gollancz, 1932
KENNEDY, ROBERT MILWARD, see KENNEDY,
MILWARD

KENNEY, SUSAN
  Garden of malice. Scribner's,
    1983; Roz Howard
  Graves in academe. Viking, 1985;
    Roz Howard
KENYON, MICHAEL, 1931 --
  A free range wife. Doubleday,
    1983; Harry Peckover
  The man at the wheel. Doubleday,
    1982; Harry Peckover
  May you die in Ireland. Morrow,
    1965; UK: Collins, 1965; Prof.
    Foley
  The 100,000 welcomes. Coward
    McCann, 1970; UK: Collins, 1970;
    Supt. O'Malley #1
  The rapist. Coward McCann, 1977
    (as by Daniel Forbes); UK:
    Collins, 1977; Supt. O'Malley #4
  The shooting of Dan McGrew. McKay,
    1975; UK: Collins, 1972; Supt.
    O'Malley #2
  A sorry state. McKay, 1975; UK:
    Collins, 1974; Supt. O'Malley #3
  The trouble with series three.
    Morrow, 1967; UK: The whole hog.
    Collins, 1967; Arthur Appleyard
KEYES, FRANCES PARKINSON, 1885-1970
  Dinner at Antoine's. Messner,
    1948; UK: Eyre, 1949
  The royal box. Messner, 1954; UK:
    Eyre, 1954
  Station wagon in Spain. Farrar,
    1955; UK: The letter from Spain.
    Eyre, 1959; Allan Lambert
  Victorine. Messner, 1958; UK: The
    gold slippers. Eyre, 1958
KIENZLE, WILLIAM X., 1928 --
  Assault with intent. Andrews,
    1982; Robert Koestler
  Death wears a red hat. Andrews,
    1980; UK: Hodder, 1981; Robert
    Koestler
  Kill and tell. Andrews, 1984;
    Robert Koestler
  The rosary murders. Andrews, 1979;
    UK: Hodder, 1979; Robert Koestler
  Shadow of death. Andrews, 1983;
    Robert Koestler #5
  Sudden death. Andrews, 1985; Robert
    Koestler #7
KINDON, THOMAS
  Murder in the moor. Dutton, 1929;
    UK: Methuen, 1929; Peregrine Smith

KING, C. DALY, 1895-1963
  Arrogant alibi. Appleton, 1939; UK:
    Collins, 1938; Michael Lord #4
  Bermuda burial. Funk, 1941; UK:
    Collins, 1940; Michael Lord #5
  Careless corpse: a thanatophony.
    UK: Collins, 1937; Michael Lord
    #3
  The curious Mr. Tarrant. Dover,
    1977; UK: Collins, 1935; Trevis
    Tarrant
  Obelists at sea. Knopf, 1933; UK:
    Heritage, 1932
  Obelists en route. UK: Collins,
    1934; Michael Lord #1
  Obelists fly high. Smith & Haas,
    1935; UK: Collins, 1935; Michael
    Lord #2
KING, FRANCIS
  Act of darkness. Little, 1983
KING, RUFUS, 1893-1966
  The case of the constant god.
    Doubleday, 1936; UK: Methuen,
    1938; Lt. Valcour #9
  The case of the redoubled cross.
    Doubleday, 1949
  Crime of violence. Doubleday, 1937;
    UK: Methuen, 1938; Lt. Valcour
    #10
  Design in evil. Doubleday, 1942
  Diagnosis: murder. Doubleday, 1941;
    UK: Methuen, 1942
  Duenna to murder. Doubleday, 1951;
    UK: Methuen, 1951
  The faces of danger. Doubleday,
    1964; Stuff Driscoll
  The Lesser Antilles case.
    Doubleday, 1934; Lt. Valcour #7
  Malice in wonderland. Doubleday,
    1958; Stuff Driscoll
  Murder by latitude. Doubleday,
    1930; UK: Heinemann, 1931; Lt.
    Valcour #3
  Murder by the clock. Doubleday,
    1929; UK: Chapman, 1929; Lt.
    Valcour #1
  Murder in the Willett family.
    Doubleday, 1931; Lt. Valcour #4
  Murder masks Miami. Doubleday,
    1939; UK: Methuen, 1939; Lt.
    Valcour #11
  Murder on the yacht. Doubleday,
    1932; UK: Hamilton, 1932; Lt.
    Valcour #5

Mystery deluxe. Doran, 1927; UK:
  Murder DeLuxe. Parsons, 1927
Profile of a murder. Harcourt,
  1935; Lt. Valcour #8
Somewhere in this house. Doubleday,
  1930; UK: A woman is dead.
  Chapman, 1929; Lt. Valcour #2
Valcour meets murder. Doubleday,
  1932; Lt. Valcour #6

KIRK, MICHAEL (pseud.). All Michael
  Kirk titles were published in the
  U.K. as by Robert MacLeod (pseud.).
  For other mysteries by this author,
  see KNOX, BILL; WEBSTER, NOAH
  (pseud.); or MACLEOD, ROBERT
  (pseud.)
All other perils. Doubleday,
  1975; UK: Long, 1974; Andrew Laird
  #1
Cargo risk. Doubleday, 1980; UK:
  Hutchinson, 1980; Andrew Laird #4
Dragonship. Doubleday, 1977; UK:
  Long, 1976; Andrew Laird #2
Mayday from Malaga. Doubleday,
  1983; Andrew Laird #5
Salvage job. Doubleday, 1979; UK:
  Long, 1978; Andrew Laird #3

KIRST, HANS H., 1914 --
Damned to success. Coward McCann,
  1973; UK: A time for scandal.
  Collins, 1973; Det. Keller
Night of the generals. Harper,
  1963; UK: Collins, 1963

KITCHIN, C. H. B., 1895-1967
The Cornish fox. UK: Secker, 1949;
  Malcolm Warren #4
Crime at Christmas. Harcourt,
  1935; UK: Woolf, 1934; Warren
  Malcolm #2
Death of his uncle. UK: Constable,
  1939; Warren Malcolm #3
Death of my aunt. Harcourt, 1930;
  UK: Woolf, 1929; Warren Malcolm #1

KITCHIN, FREDERICK HARCOURT,
  1867-1932, see COPPLESTONE, BENNET
  (pseud.)

KLAWANS, HAROLD L.
Sins of commission. Contemporary
  Books, 1982; Paul Richardson

KLINGER, HENRY, ?-1980
Essence of murder. Permabooks,
  1963; Shomri Shomar #3
Lust for murder. Trident Press,
  1966; Shomri Shomar #4

Murder off Broadway. Permabooks,
  1962; Shomri Shomar #2
Wanton for murder. Permabooks,
  1961; Shomri Shomar #1

KNIGHT, CLIFFORD
The affair at Palm Springs. Dodd,
  1938; Huntoon Rogers #3
The affair in Death Valley. Dodd,
  1940; Huntoon Rogers #7
The affair of the black sombrero.
  Dodd, 1939; Huntoon Rogers #5
The affair of the circus queen.
  Dodd, 1940; Huntoon Rogers #8
The affair of the corpse escort.
  Dodd, 1946; Huntoon Rogers #16
The affair of the dead stranger.
  Dodd, 1944; Huntoon Rogers #15
The affair of the fainting butler.
  Dodd, 1943; Huntoon Rogers #13
The affair of the ginger lei. Dodd,
  1938; Huntoon Rogers #4
The affair of the golden buzzard.
  Dodd, 1946; Huntoon Rogers #17
The affair of the heavenly voice.
  Dodd, 1937; UK: Hale, 1938;
  Huntoon Rogers #2
The affair of the jade monkey.
  Dodd, 1943; Huntoon Rogers #14
The affair of the limping sailor.
  Dodd, 1942; Huntoon Rogers #11
The affair of the painted desert.
  Dodd, 1939; Huntoon Rogers #6
The affair of the scarlet crab.
  Dodd, 1937; Huntoon Rogers #1
The affair of the sixth button.
  McKay, 1947; Huntoon Rogers #18
The affair of the skiing clown.
  Dodd, 1941; Huntoon Rogers #10
The affair of the splintered heart.
  Dodd, 1942; Huntoon Rogers #12
The case of the crimson gull. Dodd,
  1941; Huntoon Rogers #9
Death of a big shot. Dutton, 1951

KNIGHT, DAVID JAMES
Farquhasson's physique and what it
  did to his mind. Stein & Day,
  1971

KNIGHT, KATHLEEN MOORE
Acts of black night. Doubleday,
  1938; Elisha Macomber
Akin to murder. Doubleday, 1953;
  UK: Hammond, 1955; Elisha
  Macomber

Bait for murder. Doubleday, 1948;
   UK: Hammond, 1952; Elisha Macomber
The bass derby murder. Doubleday,
   1949; UK: Hammond, 1953; Elisha
   Macomber
Beauty is a beast. Doubleday,
   1959; UK: Hammond, 1960; Elisha
   Macomber
Bells for the dead. Doubleday,
   1942; UK: Cherry Tree, 1943
Birds of ill omen. Doubleday,
   1948; UK: Hammond, 1951
The clue of the poor man's
   shilling. Doubleday, 1936; UK: The
   poor man's shilling. Hammond,
   1947; Elisha Macomber
Death blew out the match.
   Doubleday, 1935; UK: Heinemann,
   1935; Elisha Macomber
Death came dancing. Doubleday,
   1940; UK: Cherry Tree, 1946;
   Elisha Macomber
Death goes to a reunion. Doubleday,
   1952; UK: Hammond, 1954; Elisha
   Macomber
Design in diamonds. Doubleday,
   1944; UK: Hammond, 1945; Margot
   Blair
Dying echo. Doubleday, 1949; UK:
   Hammond, 1952
Footbridge to death. Doubleday,
   1947; UK: Hammond, 1949; Elisha
   Macomber
Invitation to vengeance. Doubleday,
   1960; UK: Hammond, 1961
The Robineau look. Doubleday,
   1955; UK: The Robineau murders.
   Hammond, 1956
Seven were veiled. Doubleday,
   1937; UK: Seven were suspect.
   Cherry Tree, 1942; Elisha Macomber
The tainted token. Doubleday,
   1938; UK: Cherry Tree, 1942;
   Elisha Macomber
Terror by twilight. Doubleday,
   1942; UK: Cherry Tree, 1943;
   Margot Blair
Three of diamonds. Doubleday, 1953;
   UK: Hammond, 1955; Elisha Macomber
The trouble at Turkey Hill.
   Doubleday, 1946; UK: Hammond,
   1949; Elisha Macomber
Valse macabre. Doubleday, 1952; UK:
   Hammond, 1955; Elisha Macomber

The wheel that turned. Doubleday,
   1936; Elisha Macomber
KNOX, BILL, 1928 -- . For other
   mysteries by this author, see KIRK,
   MICHAEL (pseud.); or WEBSTER, NOAH
   (pseud.); or MACLEOD, ROBERT
   (pseud.)
Blacklight. Doubleday, 1967; UK:
   Long, 1967; Webb Carrick #3
Bloodtide. Doubleday, 1983; Webb
   Carrick #12
Blueback. Doubleday, 1969; UK:
   Long, 1969; Webb Carrick #5
Bombship. Doubleday, 1980; UK:
   Hutchinson, 1980; Webb Carrick
   #11
Death department. UK: Long, 1959;
   Colin Thane #2; Phil Moss #2
Devilweed. Doubleday, 1966; UK:
   Long, 1966; Webb Carrick #2
Draw batons! Doubleday, 1973; UK:
   Long, 1973; Colin Thane #13; Phil
   Moss #13
Figurehead. Doubleday, 1968; UK:
   The Klondyker. Long, 1968; Webb
   Carrick #4
The ghost car. Doubleday, 1966; UK:
   The deep fall. Long, 1966; Colin
   Thane #8; Phil Moss #8
The grey sentinels. Doubleday,
   1963; UK: Sanctuary Isle. Long,
   1962; Colin Thane #5; Phil Moss
   #5
The hanging tree. Doubleday, 1984;
   Colin Thane
Hellspout. Doubleday, 1976; UK:
   Long, 1976; Webb Carrick #9
In at the kill. Doubleday, 1961;
   UK: Deadline for a dream. Long,
   1957; Colin Thane #1; Phil Moss
   #1
Justice on the rocks. Doubleday,
   1967; UK: Long, 1967; Colin Thane
   #9; Phil Moss #9
The killing game. Doubleday, 1963;
   UK: The man in the bottle. Long,
   1963; Colin Thane #6; Phil Moss
   #6
Leave it to the hangman. Doubleday,
   1960; UK: Long, 1960; Colin Thane
   #3; Phil Moss #3
Little drops of blood. Doubleday,
   1962; UK: Long, 1962; Colin Thane
   #4; Phil Moss #4

Live bait. Doubleday, 1979; UK:
Long, 1978; Colin Thane #16; Phil
Moss #16

Pilot error. Doubleday, 1977; UK:
Long, 1977; Colin Thane #15; Phil
Moss #15

Rally to kill. Doubleday, 1975;
UK: Long, 1975; Colin Thane #14;
Phil Moss #14

The scavengers. Doubleday, 1964;
UK: Long, 1964; Webb Carrick #1

Seafire. Doubleday, 1971; UK:
Long, 1970; Webb Carrick #6

Stormtide. Doubleday, 1973; UK:
Long, 1972; Webb Carrick #7

The tallyman. Doubleday, 1969; UK:
Long, 1969; Colin Thane #10; Phil
Moss #10

The taste of proof. Doubleday,
1965; UK: Long, 1965; Colin Thane
#7; Phil Moss #7

To kill a witch. Doubleday, 1972;
UK: Long, 1971; Colin Thane #12;
Phil Moss #12

Whitewater. Doubleday, 1974; UK:
Long, 1974; Webb Carrick #8

Who shot the bull? Doubleday,
1970; UK: Children of the mist.
Long, 1970; Colin Thane #11; Phil
Moss #11

WitchRock. Doubleday, 1978; UK:
Long, 1977; Webb Carrick #10

KNOX, RONALD A., 1888-1957
Double cross purposes. UK: Hodder,
1937; Miles Bredon #5; Angela
Bredon #2

The footsteps at the lock. UK:
Methuen, 1928; Miles Bredon #2

Settled out of court. Dutton,
1934; UK: The body in the silo.
Hodder, 1933; Miles Bredon #3

Still dead. Dutton, 1934; UK:
Hodder, 1934; Miles Bredon #4;
Angela Bredon #1

The three taps. Simon & Schuster,
1927; UK: Methuen, 1927; Miles
Bredon #1

The viaduct murder. Simon &
Schuster, 1926; UK: Methuen, 1925

KOENIG, LAIRD
Rockabye. St. Martin's, 1981;
Susannah Bartok

KOTZWINKLE, WILLIAM, 1938 --
Fata Morgana. Knopf, 1977; UK:
Hutchinson, 1977; Paul Picard

Trouble in bugland: a collection of
Inspector Mantis mysteries.
Godine, 1983; Insp. Mantis

KRASNER, WILLIAM, 1917 --
Death of a minor poet. Scribner's,
1984; Sam Birge #3

North of welfare. Harper, 1956; UK:
Constable, 1955; Sam Birge

The stag party. Harper, 1957; Sam
Birge

Walk the dark streets. Harper,
1949; UK: Corgi, 1952; Sam Birge

KROETSCH, ROBERT
Alibi. Beaufort, 1983

KURNITZ, HARRY, 1907-1968. For other
mysteries by this author, see PAGE,
MARCO (pseud.)
Invasion of privacy. Random House,
1955; UK: Eyre, 1956; Mike Zorn

KUTTNER, HENRY, 1914-1958
Man drowning. Harper, 1952; UK:
Four Square, 1961

KYD, THOMAS (pseud. of Alfred
B[ennett] Harbage, 1901-1976)
Blood is a beggar. Lippincott,
1946; UK: Hammond, 1949; Sam
Phelan #1

Blood of vintage. Lippincott, 1947;
UK: Hammond, 1950; Sam Phelan #2

Blood on the bosom Devine.
Lippincott, 1948; Sam Phelan #3

Cover his face. Lippincott, 1949;
Gilbert E. Weldon

LAFORE, LAURENCE DAVIS, 1917 --
Nine seven Juliet. Doubleday, 1969;
Walter Payne

LAINE, ANNABEL
The melancholy virgin. St.
Martin's, 1982; Charles Domay

LAKE, JOE BARRY, see BARRY, JOE
(pseud.)

LAMB, MARGARET
Chains of gold. St. Martin's, 1985;
Renny Miller

LANDON, CHRISTOPHER
Unseen enemy. Doubleday, 1957; UK:
The shadow of time. Heinemann,
1957; Harry Kent

LANGLEY, LEE (pseud. of Sarah
Langley, 1927 --)
Dead center. Doubleday, 1968;
UK: Dead centre. Hall, 1969;

Christopher Jensen #2; Natalie
Keith #2
Osiris died in autumn. Doubleday,
1964; UK: Twilight of death. Hale,
1965; Natalie Keith #1;
Christopher Jensen #1

LANGLEY, SARAH, see LANGLEY, LEE
(pseud.)

LANGTON, JANE, 1922 --
Dark Nantucket moon. Harper, 1975;
Homer Kelly #1
Emily Dickinson is dead. St.
Martin's, 1984; Homer Kelly
The memorial hall murders. Harper,
1978; Homer Kelly #3
The transcendental murder. Harper,
1964; Homer Kelly

LANKAM, EDWIN, 1904-1979
Death of a Corinthian. Harcourt,
1953; UK: Boardman, 1954; Lt. Gray
Passage to danger. Harcourt, 1962;
UK: Gollancz, 1962

LA ROCHE, K. ALISON
Dear dead professor. Phoenix
Press, 1944; Rufus Jones; Barbara
Crew

LARSON, CHARLES, 1922 --
The Portland murders. Doubleday,
1983; Nils Blixen #3

LATHEN, EMMA (pseud. of Mary J.
Latis and Martha Hennissart). For
other mysteries by this author, see
DOMINIC, R. B. (pseud.)
Accounting for murder. Macmillan,
1964; UK: Gollancz, 1965; John
Putnam Thatcher #3
Ashes to ashes. Simon & Schuster,
1971; UK: Gollancz, 1971; John
Putnam Thatcher #12
Banking on death. Macmillan, 1961;
UK: Gollancz, 1962; John Putnam
Thatcher #1
By hook or by crook. Simon &
Schuster, 1975; UK: Gollancz,
1975; John Putnam Thatcher #16
Come to dust. Simon & Schuster,
1968; UK: Gollancz, 1969; John
Putnam Thatcher #8
Death shall overcome. Macmillan,
1966; UK: Gollancz, 1967; John
Putnam Thatcher #5
Double, double, oil and trouble.
Simon & Schuster, 1978; UK:

Gollancz, 1979; John Putnam
Thatcher #17
Going for the gold. Simon &
Schuster, 1981; John Putnam
Thatcher #18
Green grow the dollars. Simon &
Schuster, 1982; John Putnam
Thatcher #19
The longer the thread. Simon &
Schuster, 1971; UK: Gollancz,
1972; John Putnam Thatcher #13
Murder against the grain.
Macmillan, 1967; UK: Gollancz,
1967; John Putnam Thatcher #6
Murder makes the wheels go 'round.
Macmillan, 1966; UK: Gollancz,
1967; John Putnam Thatcher #4
Murder to go. Simon & Schuster,
1969; UK: Gollancz, 1970; John
Putnam Thatcher #10
Murder without icing. Simon &
Schuster, 1972; UK: Gollancz,
1973; John Putnam Thatcher #14
Pick up sticks. Simon & Schuster,
1970; UK: Gollancz, 1971; John
Putnam Thatcher #11
A place for murder. Macmillan,
1963; UK: Gollancz, 1963; John
Putnam Thatcher #2
A stitch in time. Macmillan, 1968;
UK: Gollancz, 1968; John Putnam
Thatcher #7
Sweet and low. Simon & Schuster,
1974; UK: Gollancz, 1974; John
Putnam Thatcher #15
When in Greece. Simon & Schuster,
1969; UK: Gollancz, 1969; John
Putnam Thatcher #9

LATIMER, JONATHAN, 1906-1983
Black is the fashion for dying.
Random House, 1959; UK: The mink
lined coffin. Methuen, 1960
The dead don't care. Doubleday,
1938; UK: Methuen, 1938; William
Crane #4
Headed for a hearse. Doubleday,
1935; UK: Methuen, 1936; William
Crane #2
The lady in the morgue. Doubleday,
1936; UK: Methuen, 1937; William
Crane #3
Murder in the madhouse. Doubleday,
1935; UK: Hurst, 1935; William
Crane #1

Red gardenias. Doubleday, 1939;
UK: Methuen, 1939; William Crane
#5

Sinners and shrouds. Simon &
Schuster, 1955; UK: Methuen, 1956;
Sam Clay

LATIS, MARY J., see LATHEN, EMMA
(pseud.) or DOMINIC, R. B. (pseud.)

LAUBEN, PHILIP

A nice sound alibi. St. Martin's,
1981; Homer Clay

LAW, JANICE, 1941 --

Death under par. Houghton, 1981;
Anna Peters

The shadow of the palms. Houghton,
1980; UK: Hale, 1981; Anna Peters

LAWRENCE, HILDA (pseud. of
Hildegarde Lawrence, 1906 --)

Blood upon the snow. Simon &
Schuster, 1944; UK: Chapman, 1946;
Mack East #1

Death of a doll. Simon & Schuster,
1947; UK: Chapman, 1948; Mack East
#3

The pavilion. Simon & Schuster,
1946; UK: Chapman, 1948

A time to die. Simon & Schuster,
1945; UK: Chapman, 1947; Mack East
#2

LAWRENCE, HILDEGARDE, see LAWRENCE,
HILDA

LAZARUS, MARGUERITE, see GILBERT,
ANNA (pseud.)

LEATHER, EDWIN, 1919 --

The Duveen letter. Doubleday,
1980; UK: Macmillan, 1980; Rupert
Conway

LEBLANCE, MAURICE

The blonde lady. Doubleday, 1910;
UK: Arsene Lupin vs. Holmloch
Shears. Richards, 1909; Arsene
Lupin; Sherlock Holmes

The confessions of Arsene Lupin.
Doubleday, 1913; UK: Mill, 1912;
Arsene Lupin

The crystal stopper. Doubleday,
1913; UK: Hurst, 1913; Arsene
Lupin

The exploits of Arsene Lupin.
Harper, 1907; UK: Cassell, 1909;
Arsene Lupin

LEE, GYPSY ROSE (pseud. of Rose
Hovick, 1914-1970)

The G-string murders. Simon &
Schuster, 1941; UK: The
strip-tease murders. Lane, 1943;
Gypsy Rose Lee

Mother finds a body. Simon &
Schuster, 1944; UK: Lane, 1944;
Gypsy Rose Lee

LEE, MANFRED, see QUEEN, ELLERY
(pseud.) or ROSS, BARNABY (pseud.)

LEEK, MARGARET (pseud. of Sara Hutton
Bowen-Judd, 1922 --)

The healthy grave. Raven House,
1980; Anne Marryat

LEIGH, ROBERT

First and last murder. St.
Martin's, 1983; Sam Carroll

LEMARCHAND, ELIZABETH

The Affacombe affair. UK: Hart
Davis, 1968; Tom Pollard #2

Alibi for a corpse. UK: Hart Davis,
1969; Tom Pollard #3

Buried in the past. Walker, 1975;
UK: Hart Davis, 1974; Tom Pollard
#7

Change for the worse. Walker, 1981;
UK: Piatkus, 1980; Tom Pollard

Cyanide with compliments. Walker,
1973; UK: MacGibbon, 1972; Tom
Pollard #5

Death of an old girl. Award, 1970;
UK: Hart Davis, 1967; Tom Pollard

Death on doomsday. Walker, 1975;
UK: Hart Davis, 1971; Tom Pollard
#4

No vacation from murder. Walker,
1974; UK: Let or hindrance. Hart
Davis, 1973; Tom Pollard #6

Nothing to do with the case.
Walker, 1981

Step in the dark. Walker, 1977; UK:
Hart Davis, 1976; Tom Pollard #8

Suddenly while gardening. Walker,
1978; UK: Hart Davis, 1978; Tom
Pollard #10

Troubled waters. Walker, 1982

Unhappy returns. Walker, 1978; UK:
Hart Davis, 1977; Tom Pollard #9

The wheel turns. Walker, 1984

LENEHAN, J. C.

The tunnel mystery. Mystery League,
1931; UK: Jenkins, 1929; Insp.
Kilby

LEON, HENRY CECIL, see CECIL, HENRY
(pseud.)

LEONARD, CHARLES L. (pseud.). For other mysteries by this author, see HEBERDEN, M. V.
  The fourth funeral. Doubleday, 1948; UK: Museum Press, 1951; Paul Kilgerrin

LEONARD, ELMORE, 1925 --
  City primeval. Delacorte, 1980; Raymond Cruz
  Fifty-two pickup. Delacorte, 1974; UK: Secker, 1974; Harry Mitchell
  Glitz. Arbor House, 1985; Vincent Mora
  La Brava. Arbor House, 1983; Joe La Brava
  Swag. Delacorte, 1976; Frank Ryan
  Unknown man No. 89. Delacorte, 1977; UK: Secker, 1977; Frank Ryan

LEVI, PETER
  Grave witness. St. Martin's, 1985; Ben Jonson

LEVIN, IRA, 1929 --
  A kiss before dying. Simon & Schuster, 1953; UK: Joseph, 1954

LEVINE, WILLIAM, see LEVINREW, WILL (pseud.)

LEVINREW, WILL (pseud. of William Levine, 1881 --)
  Death points a finger. Mystery League, 1933; Herman Brierly #4
  For sale--murder. Mystery League, 1932
  Murder from the grave. McBride, 1930; UK: Cassell, 1931; Herman Brierly #2
  Murder on the Palisades. McBride, 1930; UK: Gollancz, 1930; Herman Brierly #3
  The poison plague. McBride, 1929; UK: Cassell, 1930; Herman Brierly #1

LEWIN, ELSA
  I, Anna. Penzler Books, 1985; Insp. Bernstein

LEWIN, MICHAEL Z., 1942 --
  Ask the right question. Putnam, 1971; UK: Hamilton, 1972; Albert Samson #1
  The enemies within. Knopf, 1974; UK: Hamilton, 1974; Albert Samson #3
  Hard line. Morrow, 1982; Leroy Powder; Carollee Fleetwood

  Missing woman. Knopf, 1981; Albert Samson #6
  Night cover. Knopf, 1976; UK: Hamilton, 1976; Leroy Powder; Albert Samson #4
  Out of season. Morrow, 1984; Albert Samson
  Outside in. Knopf, 1980; UK: Magnum, 1981
  The silent salesman. Knopf, 1978; UK: Hamilton, 1978; Albert Samson #5
  The way we die now. Putnam, 1973; UK: Hamilton, 1974; Albert Samson #2

LEWIS, ARTHUR H., 1906 --
  Copper beeches. Trident Press, 1971

LEWIS, JOHN ROYSTON, see LEWIS ROY

LEWIS, LANGE (pseud. of Jane Lewis Brandt, 1915 --). For other mysteries by this author, see BEYNON, JANE (pseud.)
  The birthday murder. Bobbs, 1945; UK: Bodley Head, 1951; Richard Tuck
  Juliet dies twice. Bobbs, 1943; UK: Bodley Head, 1948; Richard Tuck
  Murder among friends. Bobbs, 1942; UK: Death among friends. Bodley Head, 1950; Richard Tuck
  The passionate victims. Bobbs, 1952; UK: Bodley Head, 1953; Richard Tuck

LEWIS, MARY CHRISTIANA, see BRAND, CHRISTIANA (pseud.)

LEWIS, ROY (pseud. of John Royston Lewis, 1933 --)
  Blood money. UK: Collins, 1973; Insp. Crow #4
  A distant banner. UK: Collins, 1976
  Dwell in danger. St. Martin's, 1982; Eric Ward
  Error of judgement. UK: Collins, 1971; Insp. Crow #2
  A gathering of ghosts. St. Martin's, 1983; Arnold Landon
  A limited vision. St. Martin's, 1984; Eric Ward #3
  A lover too many. World, 1971; UK: Collins, 1969; Insp. Crow #1
  Most cunning workmen. St. Martin's, 1985; Arnold Landon
  Nothing but foxes. St. Martin's, 1979; UK: Collins, 1977; Insp. Crow #7

A part of virtue. UK: Collins, 1975; Insp. Crow #6

A question of degree. UK: Collins, 1974; Insp. Crow #5

The secret singing. UK: Collins, 1972; Insp. Crow #3

LEWIS, ROY HARLEY

A cracking of spines. St. Martin's, 1982; UK: Hale, 1980; Martin Coll

The manuscript murders. St. Martin's, 1982; Matthew Coll

A pension for death. St. Martin's, 1983; Matthew Coll #3

LEY, ALICE CHETWYND

A reputation dies. St. Martin's, 1985; Anthea Rutherford; Justin Rutherford

LIEBERMAN, HERBERT

City of the dead. Simon & Schuster, 1976; UK: Hutchinson, 1976; Paul Konig

Nightbloom. Putnam, 1984

LILLEY, PETER, see BUCKINGHAM, BRUCE (pseud.)

LILLY, JEAN

False face. Dutton, 1929; William Rutherford Crane; Bruce Perkins #1

LIMNELIUS, GEORGE (pseud. of Lewis Robinson, 1886 --)

The manuscript murder. Doubleday, 1934; Weston Pryme

LINDAP, AUDREY ERSKINE, 1920 --

Journey into stone. Doubleday, 1972; UK: Macmillan, 1973; Det. Grennon

LINDSAY-TAYLOR, CONSTANCE, see CULLINGFORD, GUY

LINDSEY, DAVID L.

Heat from another sun. Harper, 1984; Stuart Haydon

LININGTON, ELIZABETH (pseud. of Barbara Elizabeth Linington, 1921 --). For other mysteries by this author, see EGAN, LESLEY (pseud.) or SHANNON, DELL (pseud.)

Consequence of crime. Doubleday, 1980; UK: Gollancz, 1981; Ivor Maddox; Sue Maddox

Crime by chance. Lippincott, 1973; UK: Gollancz, 1974; Ivor Maddox #7

Date with death. Harper, 1966; UK: Gollancz, 1966; Ivor Maddox #3

Felony report. Doubleday, 1984; Sue Maddox; Ivor Maddox

Greenmask! Harper, 1964; UK: Gollancz, 1965; Ivor Maddox #1

No evil angel. Harper, 1964; UK: Gollancz, 1965; Ivor Maddox #2

No villain need be. Doubleday, 1979; UK: Gollancz, 1979; Ivor Maddox #9; Sue Maddox

Perchance of death. Doubleday, 1977; UK: Gollancz, 1978; Ivor Maddox #8; Sue Maddox

Policeman's late. Harper, 1968; UK: Gollancz, 1969; Ivor Maddox #5

Practice to deceive. Harper, 1971; UK: Gollancz, 1971; Ivor Maddox #6; Sue Carstairs

Skeletons in the closet. Doubleday, 1982; Sue Maddox; Ivor Maddox

Something wrong. Harper, 1967; UK: Gollancz, 1968; Ivor Maddox #4

LINSCOTT, GILLIAN

A healthy body. St. Martin's, 1984; Birdie Linnet

Murder makes tracks. St. Martin's, 1985; Birdie Linnet

LINZEE, DAVID, 1952 --

Belgravia. Seaview, 1980; UK: Hale, 1982; Sarah Saber; Chris Rockwell

LITTLE, CONSTANCE and LITTLE, GWYNETH

The black dream. Doubleday, 1952; UK: Collins, 1953

The black stocking. Doubleday, 1946; UK: Collins, 1947

The black thumb. Doubleday, 1942; UK: Collins, 1943

Great black kanba. Doubleday, 1944; UK: The black express. Collins, 1945

LITTLE, CONYTH (pseud. of Constance and Gwyneth Little)

LITTLE, GWYNETH, see LITTLE, CONSTANCE and LITTLE, GWYNETH

LITTLEFIELD, ANNE

Which Mrs. Bennet? Doubleday, 1959

LITVINOFF, EMANUEL

Falls the shadow. Stein & Day, 1983; Amos Shomron

LITVINOV, IVY, 1889-1977

Moscow mystery. Coward McCann, 1943; UK: His master's voice. Heinemann, 1930; Gollancz, 1973

LIVINGSTON, JACK

Die again, Macready. St. Martin's, 1984; Joe Binney #2

A piece of silence. St. Martin's, 1982; Joe Binney #1

LIVINGSTON, KENNETH (pseud. of Kenneth Livingston Stewart, 1894 --)

The Dodd cases. Doubleday, 1934; UK: Methuen, 1933; Cedric Dodd

LOCHTE, DICK

Sleeping dog. Arbor House, 1985; Leo G. Bloodworth

LOCKRIDGE, FRANCES, see LOCKRIDGE, FRANCES and LOCKRIDGE, RICHARD; LOCKRIDGE, RICHARD and LOCKRIDGE FRANCES; LOCKRIDGE, RICHARD

LOCKRIDGE, FRANCES and LOCKRIDGE, RICHARD

And left for dead. Lippincott, 1962; UK: Hutchinson, 1962; Bernard Simmons #1

Catch as catch can. Lippincott, 1958; UK: Long, 1960; Geoffrey Bowen

Curtain for a jester. Lippincott, 1953; Pam North #18; Jerry North #18

Dead as a dinosaur. Lippincott, 1952; UK: Hutchinson, 1956; Pam North #16; Jerry North #16

Death has a small voice. Lippincott, 1954; UK: Hutchinson, 1954; Pam North #17; Jerry North #17

Death of a tall man. Lippincott, 1946; UK: Hutchinson, 1949; Pam North #9; Jerry North #9

Death of an angel. Lippincott, 1955; UK: Hutchinson, 1957; Pam North #20; Jerry North #20

Death on the aisle. Lippincott, 1942; UK: Hutchinson, 1948; Pam North #4; Jerry North #4

Death takes a bow. Lippincott, 1943; UK: Hutchinson, 1945; Pam North #6; Jerry North #6

The devious ones. Lippincott, 1964; UK: Four hours to fear. Long, 1965; Bernard Simmons #2

The dishonest murderer. Lippincott, 1949; UK: Hutchinson, 1951; Pam North #13; Jerry North #13

The drill is death. Lippincott, 1961; UK: Long, 1963; Nate Shapiro #3; Reginald Grant

The faceless adversary. Lippincott, 1956; Nate Shapiro #1

Hanged for a sheep. Lippincott, 1942; UK: Hutchinson, 1944; Pam North #5; Jerry North #5

The judge is reversed. Lippincott, 1960; UK: Hutchinson, 1961; Pam North #24; Jerry North #24

A key to death. Lippincott, 1954; Pam North #19; Jerry North #19

Killing the goose. Lippincott, 1944; UK: Hutchinson, 1947; Pam North #7; Jerry North #7

The long skeleton. Lippincott, 1958; UK: Hutchinson, 1960; Pam North #22; Jerry North #22

Murder and blueberry pie. Lippincott, 1959; UK: Call it coincidence. Long, 1962; Nate Shapiro #2

Murder by the book. Lippincott, 1963; UK: Hutchinson, 1964; Pam North #26; Jerry North #26

Murder comes first. Lippincott, 1951; Pam North #15; Jerry North #15

Murder has its points. Lippincott, 1961; UK: Hutchinson, 1962; Pam North #25; Jerry North #25

Murder in a hurry. Lippincott, 1950; UK: Hutchinson, 1952; Pam North #14; Jerry North #14

Murder is served. Lippincott, 1948; UK: Hutchinson, 1950; Pam North #12; Jerry North #12

Murder is suggested. Lippincott, 1959; UK: Hutchinson, 1961; Pam North #23; Jerry North #23

Murder out of turn. Stokes, 1941; UK: Joseph, 1941; Pam North #2; Jerry North #2

Murder within murder. Lippincott, 1946; UK: Hutchinson, 1949; Pam North #10; Jerry North #10

Night of shadows. Lippincott, 1962; UK: Long, 1964; Paul Lane #1

The Norths meet murder. Stokes, 1940; UK: Joseph, 1940; Pam North #1; Jerry North #1

Payoff for the banker. Lippincott, 1945; UK: Hutchinson, 1946; Pam North #8; Jerry North #8

A pinch of poison. Stokes, 1941; UK: Hutchinson, 1948; Pam North #3; Jerry North #3

Quest for the bogeyman. Lippincott, 1964; UK: Hutchinson, 1965; Paul Lane #2

The tangled cord. Lippincott, 1957; UK: Hutchinson, 1959; Bill Wiegand

Untidy murder. Lippincott, 1947; Pam North #11; Jerry North #11

Voyage into violence. Lippincott, 1956; UK: Hutchinson, 1959; Pam North #21; Jerry North #21

LOCKRIDGE, RICHARD, 1898 -- . For other mysteries by this author, see LOCKRIDGE, RICHARD and LOCKRIDGE, FRANCES or LOCKRIDGE, FRANCES and LOCKRIDGE, RICHARD

Dead run. Lippincott, 1976; UK: Long, 1977; Merton Heimrich #23

Death in a sunny place. Lippincott, 1972; UK: Long, 1973

Death on the hour. Lippincott, 1974; UK: Long, 1975; Bernard Simmons #7

Die laughing. Lippincott, 1969; UK: Long, 1970; Nate Shapiro #6

Inspector's holiday. Lippincott, 1971; UK: Long, 1972; Merton Heimrich #21

Murder can't wait. Lippincott, 1964; UK: Long, 1965; Merton Heimrich #17; Nate Shapiro #4

Murder for art's sake. Lippincott, 1967; UK: Long, 1968; Nate Shapiro #5

Murder roundabout. Lippincott, 1966; UK: Long, 1967; Merton Heimrich #18

Not I, said the sparrow. Lippincott, 1973; UK: Long, 1974; Merton Heimrich #22

Or was he pushed? Lippincott, 1975; UK: Long, 1976; Nate Shapiro #9

A plate of red herrings. Lippincott, 1968; UK: Long, 1964; Bernard Simmons #4 (as by Frances Richards)

Preach no more. Lippincott, 1971; UK: Long, 1972; Nate Shapiro #7

A risky way to kill. Lippincott, 1969; UK: Long, 1970; Merton Heimrich #20 (as by Frances Richards)

Something up a sleeve. Lippincott, 1972; UK: Long, 1973; Bernard Simmons #6

Squire of death. Lippincott, 1965; UK: Long, 1966; Bernard Simmons #3 (as by Frances Richards)

A streak of light. Lippincott, 1976; UK: Long, 1978; Nate Shapiro #10

The tenth life. Lippincott, 1977; UK: Long, 1979; Merton Heimrich #24

Troubled journey. Lippincott, 1970; UK: Hutchinson, 1971

Twice retired. Lippincott, 1970; UK: Long, 1971; Bernard Simmons #5

With option to die. Lippincott, 1967; UK: Long, 1968; Merton Heimrich #19 (as by Frances Richards)

Write murder down. Lippincott, 1972; UK: Long, 1974; Nate Shapiro #8

LOCKRIDGE, RICHARD and LOCKRIDGE, FRANCES. See also LOCKRIDGE, FRANCES and LOCKRIDGE, RICHARD or LOCKRIDGE, RICHARD

Accent on murder. Lippincott, 1958; UK: Long, 1960; Merton Heimrich #12

Burnt offering. Lippincott, 1955; UK: Hutchinson, 1957; Merton Heimrich #9

A client is cancelled. Lippincott, 1951; UK: Hutchinson, 1955; Merton Heimrich #5

Death and the gentle bull. Lippincott, 1954; UK: Hutchinson, 1956; Merton Heimrich #8

Death by association. Lippincott, 1952; UK: Hutchinson, 1957; Merton Heimrich #6

The distant clue. Lippincott, 1963; UK: Long, 1964; Merton Heimrich #16

First come, first kill. Lippincott, 1962; UK: Long, 1963; Merton Heimrich #15

Foggy, foggy death. Lippincott, 1950; UK: Hutchinson, 1953; Merton Heimrich #4

I want to go home. Lippincott, 1948; Merton Heimrich #2

Let dead enough alone. Lippincott,
1946; UK: Hutchinson, 1948; Merton
Heimrich #10
Practice to deceive. Lippincott,
1955; UK: Hutchinson, 1959; Merton
Heimrich #11
Show red for danger. Lippincott,
1960; UK: Long, 1961; Merton
Heimrich #13
Spin your web, lady! Lippincott,
1949; UK: Hutchinson, 1952; Merton
Heimrich #3
Stand up and die. Lippincott,
1953; UK: Hutchinson, 1953; Merton
Heimrich #7
Think of death. Lippincott, 1947;
Merton Heimrich #5
With one stone. Lippincott, 1961;
UK: No dignity in death. Long,
1962; Merton Heimrich #14
LOFTS, NORAH, see CURTIS, PETER
(pseud.)
LOGUE, JOHN, 1933 --
Follow the leader. Crown, 1949;
John Morris
LONGRIGG, ROGER, see PARRISH, FRANK
(pseud.)
LORAINE, PHILIP
And to my beloved husband. Mill,
1950; UK: White lie the dead.
Hodder, 1950; Insp. Keen
Death wishes. St. Martin's, 1983;
Catherine Walden
A Mafia kiss. Random House, 1969;
UK: Collins, 1968
Nightmare in Dublin. Mill, 1952;
UK: The Dublin nightmare. Hodder,
1952
LORE, PHILLIPS (pseud. of Terrence
Lore Smith)
The looking glass murders. Playboy,
1980; Leo Roi
Murder behind closed doors.
Playboy, 1980; Leo Roi
Who killed the pie man? Saturday
Review Press, 1975; Leo Roi
LOVE, EDMUND G., 1912 --
Set-up. Doubleday, 1980; UK: Set a
trap. Hale, 1981; George Rowe
LOVELL, MARC (pseud.). For other
mysteries by this author, see
MCSHANE, MARK
The blind hypnotist. Doubleday,
1976; Jason Galt #1

Hand over mind. Doubleday, 1979;
UK: Hale, 1980
The second Vanetti affair.
Doubleday, 1977; UK: Hale, 1979;
Jason Galt #2
LOVESEY, PETER, 1936 --
Abracadaver. Dodd, 1972; UK:
Macmillan, 1972; Sgt. Cribb #3;
Constable Thackeray #3
A case of spirits. Dodd, 1975; UK:
Macmillan, 1975; Sgt. Cribb #6;
Constable Thackeray #6
The detective wore silk drawers.
Dodd, 1971; UK: Macmillan, 1971;
Sgt. Cribb #2; Constable
Thackeray #2
The false Inspector Dew. Pantheon,
1982; Walter Baranov
Keystone. Pantheon, 1983; Warwick
Easton
Madhatter's holiday. Dodd, 1973;
UK: Macmillan, 1973; Sgt. Cribb
#4; Constable Thackeray #4
Swing, swing together. Dodd, 1976;
UK: Macmillan, 1976; Sgt. Cribb
#7; Constable Thackeray #7
The tick of death. Dodd, 1974; UK:
Invitation to a dynamite party.
Macmillan, 1974; Sgt. Cribb #5;
Constable Thackeray #5
Waxwork. Pantheon, 1978; UK:
Macmillan, 1978; Sgt. Cribb #8;
Constable Thackeray #8
Wobble to death. Dodd, 1970; UK:
Macmillan, 1970; Sgt. Cribb #1;
Constable Thackeray #1
LOW, IVY, see LITVINOV, IVY
LOWDEN, DESMOND, 1937 --
Sunspot. Holt, 1982; Insp. Gorman;
Constable Hale
LOWNDES, MARIE BELLOC, 1868-1947
The chianti flask. Longman, 1934;
UK: Heinemann, 1935
The end of her honeymoon.
Scribner's, 1913; UK: Methuen,
1914
Letty Lynton. Cape, 1931; UK:
Heinemann, 1931
The lodger. Scribner's, 1913; UK:
Methuen, 1913
The Terriford mystery. Doubleday,
1924; UK: Hutchinson, 1924
Why it happened. Longman, 1938; UK:
Motive. Hutchinson, 1938

LOWNDES, MRS. BELLOC, see LOWNDES, MARIE

LUSTGARDEN, EDGAR, 1907-1978
Game for three losers. Scribner's, 1952; UK: Museum Press, 1952
One more unfortunate. Scribner's, 1947; UK: A case to answer. Eyre, 1947

LUTZ, JOHN
Nightlines. St. Martin's, 1985; Al Nudger

LYNDE, FRANCIS, 1856-1930
Scientific Sprague. Scribner's, 1912; Calvin Sprague

LYONS, ARTHUR, JR., 1946 --
All God's children. Mason/Charter, 1975; UK: Robson, 1977; Jacob Asch #2
At the hands of another. Holt, 1983; Jacob Asch #7
Castles burning. Holt, 1980; Jacob Asch #5
The dead are discreet. Mason/Charter, 1974; UK: Robson, 1977; Jacob Asch #1
Dead ringer. Mason/Charter, 1977; Jacob Asch #4
Hard trade. Holt, 1981; Jacob Asch #6
The killing floor. Mason/Charter, 1976; UK: Houghton, 1979; Jacob Asch #3
Three with a bullet. Holt, 1985; Jacob Asch #8

LYSAGHT, BRIAN
Special circumstances. St. Martin's, 1983; Benjamin O'Malley
Sweet deals. St. Martin's, 1985; Benjamin O'Malley #2

MACCARTHY, JOHN LLOYD, see CORY, DESMOND (pseud.)

MACDONALD, JOHN, see MACDONALD, ROSS

MACDONALD, JOHN D., 1916 --
Bright orange for the shroud. Fawcett, 1965; UK: Hale, 1967; Travis McGee #6
Cinnamon skin. Harper, 1982; Travis McGee #20
The crossroads. Simon & Schuster, 1959
Darker than amber. Lippincott, 1970; UK: Hale, 1968; Travis McGee #7
A deadly shade of gold. Lippincott, 1974; UK: Hale, 1967; Travis McGee #5
The deep blue goodbye. Lippincott, 1975; UK: Hale, 1965; Travis McGee #1
The dreadful lemon sky. Lippincott, 1975; UK: Hale, 1976; Travis McGee #16
Dress her in indigo. Lippincott, 1971; UK: Hale, 1971; Travis McGee #11
The empty copper sea. Lippincott, 1978; UK: Hale, 1979; Travis McGee #17
The flash of green. Simon & Schuster, 1962; UK: Hale, 1971
Free fall in crimson. Harper, 1981; Travis McGee #19
The girl in the plain brown wrapper. Lippincott, 1973; UK: Hale, 1969; Travis McGee #10
The green ripper. Lippincott, 1979; UK: Hale, 1980; Travis McGee #18
The lonely silver rain. Knopf, 1985; Travis McGee #20
The long lavender look. Lippincott, 1972; UK: Fawcett, 1970; Travis McGee #12
Nightmare in pink. Lippincott, 1976; UK: Hale, 1966; Travis McGee #2
One fearful yellow eye. Lippincott, 1978; UK: Hale, 1968; Travis McGee #8
Pale gray for guilt. Lippincott, 1971; UK: Hale, 1969; Travis McGee #9
A purple place for dying. Lippincott, 1976; UK: Hale, 1966; Travis McGee #3
The quick red fox. Lippincott, 1974; UK: Hale, 1966; Travis McGee #4
The scarlet ruse. Lippincott, 1980; UK: Hale, 1975; Travis McGee #14
A tan and sandy silence. Lippincott, 1979; UK: Hale, 1973; Travis McGee #13
The turquoise lament. Lippincott, 1973; UK: Hale, 1975; Travis McGee #15

MACDONALD, JOHN ROSS, see MACDONALD, ROSS

MACDONALD, PHILIP, 1899 --

The crime conductor. Doubleday, 1931; UK: Collins, 1932; Anthony Gethryn #8

Escape. Doubleday, 1932; UK: Mystery in Kensington Gore. Collins, 1932; Dudley Allwright

Guest in the house. Doubleday, 1955; UK: Jenkins, 1956

The link. Doubleday, 1930; UK: Collins, 1930; Anthony Gethryn #3

The list of Adrian Messenger. Doubleday, 1959; UK: Jenkins, 1960; Anthony Gethryn #13

The man out of the rain and other stories. Doubleday, 1955; UK: Jenkins, 1957; Anthony Gethryn #12; Dr. Alcazar #2

Murder gone mad. Doubleday, 1931; UK: Collins, 1931; Arnold Pike

Mystery of the dead police. Doubleday, 1933; UK: X vs. Rex. Collins, 1933

The noose. Dial, 1930; UK: Collins, 1930; Anthony Gethryn #4

Persons unknown. Doubleday, 1931; UK: The maze. Collins, 1932; Anthony Gethryn #6

The Polferry riddle. Doubleday, 1931; UK: The choice. Collins, 1931; Anthony Gethryn #5

The rasp. Doubleday, 1925; UK: Collins, 1924; Anthony Gethryn #1

Rope to spare. Doubleday, 1932; UK: Collins, 1932; Anthony Gethryn #9

Something to hide. Doubleday, 1952; UK: Fingers of fear and other stories. Collins, 1953; Anthony Gethryn #11; Dr. Alcazar #1

Warrant for X. Doubleday, 1938; UK: The nursemaid who disappeared. Collins, 1938; Anthony Gethryn #10

The white crow. Dial, 1928; UK: Collins, 1928; Anthony Gethryn #2

The wraith. Doubleday, 1931; UK: Collins, 1931; Anthony Gethryn #7

MACDONALD, ROSS (pseud. of Kenneth Millar, 1915 --)

The barbarous coast. Knopf, 1956; UK: Cassell, 1957; Lew Archer #7

Black money. Knopf, 1966; UK: Collins, 1966; Lew Archer #13

The blue hammer. Knopf, 1976; UK: Collins, 1976; Lew Archer #18

The chill. Knopf, 1964; UK: Collins, 1964; Lew Archer #11

The doomsters. Knopf, 1958; UK: Collins, 1958; Lew Archer #8

The drowning pool. (originally published as by John Ross Macdonald); Knopf, 1950; UK: Cassell, 1950; Lew Archer #2

The far side of the dollar. Knopf, 1965; UK: Collins, 1965; Lew Archer #12

The Ferguson affair. Knopf, 1960; UK: Collins, 1961; Bill Gunnerson

Find a victim. (originally published as by John Ross Macdonald); Knopf, 1954; UK: Cassell, 1955; Lew Archer #5

The Galton case. Knopf, 1959; UK: Cassell, 1960; Lew Archer #9

The goodbye look. Knopf, 1969; UK: Collins, 1969; Lew Archer #15

The instant enemy. Knopf, 1968; UK: Collins, 1968; Lew Archer #14

The ivory grin. (originally published as by John Ross Macdonald); Knopf, 1952; UK: Cassell, 1953; Lew Archer #4

Lew Archer, private investigator. Mysterious Press, 1977; Lew Archer #19

Meet me at the morgue. (originally published as by John Ross Macdonald); Knopf, 1953; UK: Experience with evil. Cassell, 1954; Howard Cross

The moving target. (originally published as by John Ross Macdonald); Knopf, 1949; UK: Cassell, 1951; Lew Archer #1

The name is Archer. (originally published as by John Ross Macdonald); Bantam, 1955; Lew Archer #6

Sleeping beauty. Knopf, 1973; UK: Collins, 1973; Lew Archer #17

The underground man. Knopf, 1971; UK: Collins, 1971; Lew Archer #16

The way some people die.
(originally published as by John
Ross Macdonald); Knopf, 1951; UK:
Cassell, 1953; Lew Archer #3
The Wycherly woman. Knopf, 1961;
UK: Collins, 1962
The zebra-striped hearse. Knopf,
1962; UK: Collins, 1963; Lew
Archer #10

MACDONALD, WILLIAM COLT, 1891 --
Action at Arcanum. Lippincott,
1961; UK: Hodder, 1961; Gregory
Quist
The gloved Saskia. Avalon, 1964;
UK: Hodder, 1965; Brady Ruskin;
Whit Traxler

MACDONELL, ARCHIBALD GORDON, see
GORDON, NEIL (pseud.)

MACDOUGALL, JAMES K.
Death and the maiden. Bobbs, 1978;
UK: Hale, 1979; David Stuart #2
Weasel hunt. Bobbs, 1977; UK: Hale,
1979; David Stuart

MACHARG, WILLIAM BRIGGS and BALMER,
EDWIN. See also BALMER, EDWIN and
MACHARG, WILLIAM
The blind man's eyes. Little,
1916; UK: Nash, 1916
The Indian drum. Little, 1917; UK:
Paul, 1919
The Surakarta. Small, Maynard, 1913

MACKAY, AMANDA (pseud. of Amanda
MacKay Smith)
Death is academic. McKay, 1976;
UK: Hale, 1980; Hannah Land #1
Death on the Eno. Little, 1981;
Hannah Land #2

MACKENZIE, DONALD, 1908 --
Raven after dark. Houghton, 1979;
UK: Raven feathers his nest.
Macmillan, 1979; John Raven #5
Raven and the kamikaze. Houghton,
1977; UK: Macmillan, 1977; John
Raven #3
Raven and the paperhangers.
Houghton, 1980; UK: Macmillan,
1980; John Raven #6
Raven and the ratcatcher. Houghton,
1977; UK: Macmillan, 1977; John
Raven #2
Raven in flight. Houghton, 1976;
UK: Macmillan, 1976; John Raven
#1

Raven settles a score. Houghton,
1979; UK: Macmillan, 1979; John
Raven #4
Raven's longest night. Doubleday,
1983; John Raven
Raven's revenge. Houghton, 1982;
John Raven

MACKINNON, ALLAN
Cormorant's Isle. Doubleday, 1962;
UK: Long, 1962
House of darkness. Doubleday, 1947;
UK: Collins, 1947; Duncan
MacCallum
Money in the black. Doubleday,
1946; UK: Nine day's murder.
Collins, 1945; Duncan MacCallum
Report from Artyll. Doubleday,
1964; UK: Dead on departure.
Long, 1964; Don Kendrick

MACKINTOSH, ELIZABETH, see TEY,
JOSEPHINE (pseud.)

MACLEOD, ANGUS, 1906 --
Blessed among women. Roy, 1967; UK:
Dobson, 1965; Insp. Gilroy
The tough and the tender. Roy,
1960; UK: Robson, 1960; Insp.
Gillandrew

MACLEOD, CHARLOTTE. See also CRAIG,
ALISA
The Bilbao looking glass.
Doubleday, 1983; Sarah Kelling #4
The convivial codfish. Doubleday,
1984; Max Bittersohn; Sarah
Kelling #5
The curse of the grant hogweed.
Doubleday, 1985; Peter Shandy
The luck runs out. Doubleday, 1979;
UK: Collins, 1981; Peter Shandy
#2
Rest you merry. Doubleday, 1978;
UK: Collins, 1979; Peter Shandy
#1; Helen Marsh
The withdrawing room. Doubleday,
1980; UK: Collins, 1981; Max
Bittersohn
Wrack and rune. Doubleday, 1982;
Peter Shandy #3

MACLEOD, ROBERT (pseud.). For other
mysteries by this author, see KNOX,
BILL; WEBSTER, NOAH (pseud.); KIRK,
MICHAEL (pseud.)
Cave of bats. Holt, 1966; UK: Long,
1964; Talos Cord #1

The iron sanctuary. Holt, 1968; UK:
Lake of fury. Long, 1966; Talos
Cord #2

Isle of dragons. UK: Long, 1967;
Talos Cord #3

Nest of vultures. UK: Long, 1973;
Talos Cord #6

Path of ghosts. McCall, 1971; UK:
Long, 1971; Talos Cord #5

Place of mists. McCall, 1970; UK:
Long, 1970; Talos Cord #4

MACQUEEN, JAMES WILLIAM, see EDWARDS,
JAMES G. (pseud.)

MAGOON, CAREY (pseud. of Elizabeth
Carey and Marian Austin Waite
Magoon)

I smell the devil. Farrar, 1943;
UK: Cassell, 1949; Adelaide Stone

MAGOON, MARIAN AUSTIN WAITE, see
MAGOON, CAREY (pseud.)

MAINWARING, DAVID, see HOMES,
GEOFFREY (pseud.)

MAINWARING, MARION

Murder at midyears. Macmillan,
1953; UK: Gollancz, 1954; Toby
Sampson

Murder in pastiche. Macmillan,
1954; UK: Gollancz, 1955

MALCOLM, JOHN

A back room in Somerstown.
Scribner's, 1985; Tim Simpson

The Godwin sideboard. Scribner's,
1985; Tim Simpson

MALING, ARTHUR, 1923 --

Bent man. Harper, 1975; UK: Prior,
1976; Walter Jackson

Decoy. Harper, 1969; UK: Joseph,
1971

Go-between. Harper, 1970; UK:
Lambert's son. Joseph, 1972

The Hoberg link. Harper, 1979; UK:
Gollancz, 1980; Brockton Potter
#4

Lucky devil. Harper, 1978; UK:
Gollancz, 1979; Brockton Potter
#3

Ripoff. Harper, 1976; UK: Hale,
1977; Brockton Potter #1

Schroeder's game. Harper, 1977;
UK: Gollancz, 1977; Brockton
Potter #2

A taste of treason. Harper, 1983;
Brockton Potter

MALLESON, LUCY BEATRICE, see GILBERT,
MICHAEL (pseud.)

MALONE, MICHAEL

Uncivil seasons. Delacorte, 1983;
Saville Dollard

MANER, WILLIAM

Die of a rose. Doubleday, 1970;
Wilson Harley

The image killer. Doubleday, 1968;
UK: Hale, 1970

MANN, JESSICA

Capture audience. McKay, 1975; UK:
Macmillan, 1975; Theodora Wade
Crawford #2

Charitable end. McKay, 1971; UK:
Collins, 1971

Mrs. Knox's profession. McKay,
1972; UK: Macmillan, 1972

No Man's Island. Doubleday, 1983;
Tamara Hoyland

Troublecross. McKay, 1973; UK: The
only security. Macmillan, 1973;
Theodora Wade Crawford #1

MANN, LEONARD, 1895 --

A murder in Sydney. Doubleday,
1937; UK: Cape, 1937

MANNING, BRUCE, see BRISTOW, GWEN and
MANNING, BRUCE

MANSFIELD, PAUL H., 1922 --

Final exposure. Macmillan, 1958;
UK: Collins, 1957

MANTELL, LAURIE, 1917? --

Murder and chips. Walker, 1982; UK:
Gollancz, 1980; Steven Arrow

Murder in fancy dress. Walker,
1981; UK: Gollancz, 1978; Steven
Arrow

A murder or three. Walker, 1981;
UK: Gollancz, 1980; Steven Arrow

MARDER, IRVING

The Paris bit. Dodd, 1968; UK:
Collins, 1967; Max Moritz

MARKHAM, VIRGIL, 1899 --

The black door. Knopf, 1930; UK:
Shock! Collins, 1930

Death in the dusk. Knopf, 1928; UK:
Knopf, 1928

MARLOWE, DEREK, 1938 --

Nightshade. Viking, 1976; UK: Cape,
1975

Somebody's sister. Viking, 1974;
UK: Cape, 1974; Walter Brackett

MARON, MARGARET

Death of a butterfly. Doubleday,
1984; Sigrid Harold

MARRIC, J. J. (pseud.). For other
mysteries by this author, see

CREASEY, JOHN; MORTON, ANTHONY (pseud.); YORK, JEREMY (pseud.); ASHE, GORDON (pseud.)

Gideon's art. Harper, 1971; UK: Hodder, 1971; George Gideon #17

Gideon's badge. Harper, 1965; UK: Hodder, 1966; George Gideon #12

Gideon's buy. Harper, 1975; George Gideon #21

Gideon's day. Harper, 1955; UK: Hodder, 1955; George Gideon #1

Gideon's drive. Harper, 1976; UK: Hodder, 1976; George Gideon #22

Gideon's fire. Harper, 1961; UK: Hodder, 1961; George Gideon #7

Gideon's fog. Harper, 1974; UK: Hodder, 1975; George Gideon #20

Gideon's force. UK: Ulverscroft, 1978; (Completed by William Butler, posthumously published; this is a large-print edition); George Gideon #23

Gideon's lot. Harper, 1964; UK: Hodder, 1965; George Gideon #11

Gideon's march. Harper, 1962; UK: Hodder, 1962; George Gideon #8

Gideon's men. Harper, 1972; UK: Hodder, 1972; George Gideon #18

Gideon's month. Harper, 1958; UK: Hodder, 1958; George Gideon #4

Gideon's power. Harper, 1969; UK: Hodder, 1969; George Gideon #15

Gideon's press. Harper, 1973; UK: Hodder, 1973; George Gideon #19

Gideon's ride. Harper, 1963; UK: Hodder, 1963; George Gideon #9

Gideon's risk. Harper, 1960; UK: Hodder, 1960; George Gideon #6

Gideon's river. Harper, 1968; UK: Hodder, 1968; George Gideon #14

Gideon's sport. Harper, 1970; UK: Hodder, 1970; George Gideon #16

Gideon's staff. Harper, 1959; UK: Hodder, 1959; George Gideon #5

Gideon's vote. Harper, 1964; UK: Hodder, 1964; George Gideon #10

Gideon's week. Harper, 1956; UK: Hodder, 1956; George Gideon #2

Gideon's wrath. Harper, 1967; UK: Hodder, 1967; George Gideon #13

MARSH, NGAIO (pseud. of Edith Ngaio Marsh, 1899 --)

Artists in crime. Furman, 1938; UK: Bles, 1938; Roderick Alleyn #6

Black as he's painted. Little, 1974; UK: Collins, 1974; Roderick Alleyn #28

Clutch of constables. Little, 1969; UK: Collins, 1968; Roderick Alleyn #25

Colour scheme. Little, 1943; UK: Collins, 1943; Roderick Alleyn #12

Dead water. Little, 1963; UK: Collins, 1964; Roderick Alleyn #23

Death and the dancing footman. Little, 1941; UK: Collins, 1942; Roderick Alleyn #11

Death at the bar. Little, 1940; UK: Collins, 1940; Roderick Alleyn #9

Death in a white tie. Furman, 1938; UK: Bles, 1938; Roderick Alleyn #7

Death in ecstasy. Sheridan, 1941; UK: Bles, 1936; Roderick Alleyn #4

Death of a fool. Little, 1956; UK: Collins, 1957; Roderick Alleyn #19

Death of a peer. Little, 1940; UK: Surfeit of lampreys. Collins, 1941; Roderick Alleyn #10

Died in the wool. Little, 1945; UK: Collins, 1945; Roderick Alleyn #13

Enter a murderer. Pocket Books, 1941; UK: Bles, 1935; Roderick Alleyn #2

False scent. Little, 1959; UK: Collins, 1960; Roderick Alleyn #21

Final curtain. Little, 1947; UK: Collins, 1947; Roderick Alleyn #14

Grave mistake. Little, 1978; UK: Collins, 1978; Roderick Alleyn #30

Hand in glove. Little, 1962; UK: Collins, 1962; Roderick Alleyn #22

Killer dolphin. Little, 1966; UK: Death at the Dolphin. Collins, 1967; Roderick Alleyn #24

Last ditch. Little, 1977; UK: Collins, 1977; Roderick Alleyn #29; Ricky Alleyn

Light thickens. Little, 1982; Roderick Alleyn #32

A man lay dead. Sheridan, 1942; UK:
Bles, 1934; Roderick Alleyn #1

Night at the Vulcan. Little, 1951;
UK: Opening night. Collins, 1951;
Roderick Alleyn #16

Overture to death. Furman, 1939;
UK: Collins, 1939; Roderick Alleyn
#8

Photo finish. Little, 1980; UK:
Collins, 1980; Roderick Alleyn
#31

Scales of justice. Little, 1955;
UK: Collins, 1955; Roderick Alleyn
#18

Singing in the shrouds. Little,
1958; UK: Collins, 1959; Roderick
Alleyn #20

Spinsters in jeopardy. Little,
1953; UK: Collins, 1954; Roderick
Alleyn #17

Tied up in tinsel. Little, 1972;
UK: Collins, 1972; Roderick Alleyn
#27

Vintage murder. Sheridan, 1940;
UK: Bles, 1937; Roderick Alleyn
#5

When in Rome. Little, 1971; UK:
Collins, 1970; Roderick Alleyn
#26

A wreath for Rivera. Little, 1949;
UK: Swing, brother, swing.
Collins, 1949; Roderick Alleyn
#15

MARSH, NGAIO and JELLETT, HENRY
The nursing home murder. Sheridan,
1941; UK: Bles, 1935; Roderick
Alleyn #3

MARSHALL, CHARLES HUNT, see YATES,
GEORGE WORTHING

MARSHALL, SIDNEY
Some like it hot. Morrow, 1941;
Scott Bennet

MARSHALL, WILLIAM, 1944 --
The far away man. Holt, 1984;
Harry Feiffer; Yellowthread Street
Precinct

Perfect end. Holt, 1983; Harry
Feiffer; Yellowthread Street
Precinct

Roadshow. Holt, 1985; Harry
Feiffer; Yellowthread Street
Precinct

Sci-fi. Holt, 1981; Yellowthread
Street Precinct; Harry Feiffer

Skulduggery. Holt, 1980; UK:
Hamilton, 1979; Yellowthread
Street Precinct; Harry Feiffer

Yellowthread Street. Holt, 1976;
UK: Hamilton, 1975; Harry Feiffer
#1; Yellowthread Street Precinct

MARTIN, LEE
Too sane a murder. St. Martin's,
1984; Deb Ralston

MARTIN, ROBERT, 1908-1976
Catch a killer. Dodd, 1956; UK:
Hale, 1958; Jim Bennett

A coffin for two. Curtis, 1972;
UK: Hale, 1962; Jim Bennett

Dark dream. Dodd, 1951; UK: Muller,
1954; Jim Bennett

The echoing shore. Dodd, 1955; UK:
Muller, 1956

Hand-picked for murder. Dodd, 1957;
UK: Hale, 1958; Jim Bennett

A key to the morgue. Dodd, 1958;
UK: Hale, 1960; Jim Bennett

Sleep, my love. Dodd, 1953; UK:
Muller, 1955; Jim Bennett

Tears for the bride. Dodd, 1954;
UK: Muller, 1955; Jim Bennett

To have and to kill. Dodd, 1960;
UK: Hale, 1961; Jim Bennett

MARTIN, ROBERT BERNARD, see BERNARD,
ROBERT (pseud.)

MARTIN, SHANE (pseud. of George Henry
Johnston, 1912-1970)
The man made of tin. UK: Collins,
1958; Ronald Challis #3

Mourner's voyage. Doubleday, 1963;
UK: A wake for mourning. Collins,
1962; Ronald Challis #5

The Saracen shadow. UK: Collins,
1957; Ronald Challis #1

The third statue. Morrow, 1959; UK:
The myth is murder. Collins,
1959; Ronald Challis #4

Twelve girls in the garden. Morrow,
1957; UK: Collins, 1957; Ronald
Challis #2

MARTING, RUTH LENORE, 1907 -- , see
BAILEY, HILEA (pseud.)

MARTYN, WYNDHAM, 1875 --
The murder in Beacon Street.
McBride, 1930; UK: The Bathurst
complex. Jenkins, 1924; John
Southard

Murder Island. McBride, 1929; UK:
Jenkins, 1929; Anthony Trent

MARVELL, HOLT, see GIELGUD, VAL and
MARVELL, HOLT
MASON, A. E. W., 1865-1948
At the Villa Rose. Scribner's,
1910; UK: Hodder, 1910; Insp.
Hanaud #1
The house in Lordship Lane. Dodd,
1946; UK: Hodder, 1946; Insp.
Hanaud #5
The house of the arrow. Doran,
1924; UK: Hodder, 1924; Insp.
Hanaud #2
No other tiger. Doran, 1927; UK:
Hodder, 1927
The prisoner in the opal.
Doubleday, 1928; UK: Hodder, 1928;
Insp. Hanaud #3
The sapphire. Doubleday, 1933; UK:
Hodder, 1933
They wouldn't be chessmen.
Doubleday, 1935; UK: Hodder, 1935;
Insp. Hanaud #4
MASON, F. VANWYCK, see COFFIN,
GEOFFREY (pseud.)
MASON, PHILIP, 1906 -- , see WOODRUFF,
PHILIP (pseud.)
MASON, VAN WYCK, see COFFIN, GEOFFREY
MASTERSON, WHIT (pseud. of Robert
Wade and Bill Miller)
The dark fantastic. Dodd, 1959;
UK: Allen, 1960
The last one kills. Dodd, 1969;
UK: Hale, 1972
The man on a nylon string. Dodd,
1963; UK: Allen, 1963
The slow gallows. Dodd, 1979; UK:
Hale, 1979; John Shu
The undertaker wind. Dodd, 1974;
UK: Hale, 1974
MASUR, HAROLD Q., 1909 --
The big money. Simon & Schuster,
1954; UK: Boardman, 1955; Scott
Jordan #5
The broker. St. Martin's, 1981;
Mike Ryan
Bury me deep. Simon & Schuster,
1947; UK: Boardman, 1961; Scott
Jordan #1
The last gamble. Simon & Schuster,
1958; UK: The last breath.
Boardman, 1958; Scott Jordan #7
The legacy lenders. Random House,
1967; UK: Boardman, 1967; Scott
Jordan #11

Make a killing. Random House,
1964; UK: Boardman, 1964; Scott
Jordan #10
The name is Jordan. Pyramid Books,
1962; Scott Jordan #9
Send another hearse. Simon &
Schuster, 1960; UK: Boardman,
1960; Scott Jordan #8
So rich, so lovely, and so dead.
Simon & Schuster, 1952; UK:
Boardman, 1953; Scott Jordan #4
Suddenly a corpse. Simon &
Schuster, 1949; UK: Boardman,
1950; Scott Jordan #2
Tall, dark, and deadly. Simon &
Schuster, 1956; UK: Boardman,
1957; Scott Jordan #6
You can't live forever. Simon &
Schuster, 1951; UK: Boardman,
1951; Scott Jordan #3
MATHER, FRANK JEWETT, JR.
The collectors. Holt, 1935
MATHIS, EDWARD
From a high place. Scribner's,
1985; Dan Roman #1
MATTHEWS, ANTHONY (pseud.), see
BLACK, LIONEL (pseud.)
MAUGHAM, ROBERT, see MAUGHAM, ROBIN
(pseud.)
MAUGHAM, ROBIN
The link. McGraw-Hill, 1969; UK:
Heinemann, 1969
MCALISTER, ALISTER, see BROCK, LYNN
(pseud.)
MCBAIN, ED (pseud. of Evan Hunter,
1926 --). See also RICE, CRAIG and
MCBAIN, ED
Ax. Simon & Schuster, 1964; UK:
Hamilton, 1964; 87th Precinct #18
Beauty and the beast. Holt,
Rinehart, and Winston, 1983;
Matthew Hope
Blood relatives. Random House,
1975; UK: Hamilton, 1976; Steve
Carella; 87th Precinct #30
Bread. Random House, 1974; UK:
Hamilton, 1974; Steve Carella;
87th Precinct #29
Calypso. Viking, 1979; UK:
Hamilton, 1979; 87th Precinct
#33
The con man. Simon & Schuster,
1957; UK: Boardman, 1960; 87th
Precinct #4

Cop hater. Simon & Schuster, 1956; UK: Boardman, 1958; 87th Precinct #1

Doll. Delacorte, 1965; UK: Hamilton, 1966; 87th Precinct #20

Eight black horses. Arbor House, 1985; The Deaf Man; 87th Precinct; Steve Carella

Eighty million eyes. Delacorte, 1966; UK: Hamilton, 1966; 87th Precinct #21

The empty hours. Simon & Schuster, 1962; UK: Boardman, 1962; 87th Precinct #16

Fuzz. Doubleday, 1968; UK: Hamilton, 1968; Steve Carella; 87th Precinct #22; The Deaf Man

Ghosts. Viking, 1980; UK: Hamilton, 1980; 87th Precinct #34; Steve Carella

Give the boys a great big hand. Simon & Schuster, 1960; UK: Boardman, 1962; 87th Precinct #11

Goldilocks. Arbor House, 1978; UK: Hamilton, 1978; Matt Hope #1

Hail, hail, the gang's all here! Doubleday, 1971; UK: Hamilton, 1971; 87th Precinct #25

Hail to the chief. Random House, 1973; UK: Hamilton, 1973; 87th Precinct #28

He who hesitates. Delacorte, 1965; UK: Hamilton, 1965; 87th Precinct #19

Heat. Viking, 1981; 87th Precinct #35; Steve Carella

The heckler. Simon & Schuster, 1960; UK: Boardman, 1962; 87th Precinct #12; The Deaf Man #1

Ice. Arbor House, 1983; Steve Carella; 87th Precinct

Jack and the beanstalk. Holt, 1984; Matt Hope #4

Jigsaw. Doubleday, 1970; UK: Hamilton, 1970; 87th Precinct #24

Killer's choice. Permabooks, 1958; UK: Boardman, 1960; 87th Precinct #5

Killer's payoff. Permabooks, 1958; UK: Boardman, 1960; 87th Precinct #6

Killer's wedge. Simon & Schuster, 1959; UK: Boardman, 1959; 87th Precinct #8

King's ransom. Simon & Schuster, 1959; UK: Boardman, 1961; 87th Precinct #10

Lady killer. Permabooks, 1958; UK: Boardman, 1961; 87th Precinct #7

Lady, lady, I did it! Simon & Schuster, 1961; UK: Boardman, 1963; 87th Precinct #14

Let's hear it for the Deaf Man. Doubleday, 1973; UK: Hamilton, 1973; Steve Carella; The Deaf Man #3; 87th Precinct #27

Lightning. Arbor House, 1984; 87th Precinct; Steve Carella

Like love. Simon & Schuster, 1962; UK: Hamilton, 1964; 87th Precinct #15

Long time no see. Random House, 1977; UK: Hamilton, 1977; Steve Carella; 87th Precinct #32

The McBain brief. Arbor House, 1983

The mugger. Permabooks, 1956; UK: Boardman, 1959; 87th Precinct #2

The pusher. Permabooks, 1956; UK: Boardman, 1959; 87th Precinct #3

Rumpelstiltskin. Viking, 1981; Matt Hope #2

Sadie when she died. Doubleday, 1972; UK: Hamilton, 1972; Steve Carella; 87th Precinct #26

See them die. Simon & Schuster, 1960; UK: Boardman, 1963; 87th Precinct #13

Shotgun. Doubleday, 1969; UK: Hamilton, 1969; Steve Carella; 87th Precinct #23

Snow White and Rose Red. Holt, 1985; Matt Hope

So long as you both shall live. Random House, 1976; UK: Hamilton, 1976; 87th Precinct #31

Ten plus one. Simon & Schuster, 1963; UK: Hamilton, 1964; 87th Precinct #17

'Til death. Simon & Schuster, 1959; UK: Boardman, 1961; 87th Precinct #9

Where there's Smoke. Random House, 1975; UK: Hamilton, 1975; Benjamin Smoke

MCCABE, CAMERON

The face on the cutting room floor. Gregg, 1981; Gollancz, 1936

MCCLOY, HELEN, 1904 --
Alias Basil Willing. Random House, 1951; UK: Gollancz, 1951; Basil Willing #9
Before I die. Torquil, 1963; UK: Gollancz, 1963
Cue for murder. Morrow, 1942; Basil Willing #5
Dance of death. Morrow, 1938; UK: Design for dying. Heinemann, 1938; Basil Willing #1
The deadly truth. Morrow, 1941; UK: Hamilton, 1942; Basil Willing #3
The goblin market. Morrow, 1943; UK: Hale, 1951; Miguel Urizar; Basil Willing #6
The long body. Random House, 1955; UK: Gollancz, 1955; Basil Willing #10
The man in the moonlight. Morrow, 1941; UK: Hamilton, 1940; Basil Willing #2
Mr. Splitfoot. Dodd, 1968; UK: Gollancz, 1969; Basil Willing #12
The one that got away. Morrow, 1945; UK: Gollancz, 1954; Basil Willing #7
Panic. Morrow, 1944; UK: Gollancz, 1972
She walks alone. Random House, 1948; UK: Coker, 1950; Miguel Urizar
The slayer and the slain. Random House, 1957; UK: Gollancz, 1958
The smoking mirror. Dodd, 1979; UK: Gollancz, 1979
Through a glass darkly. Random House, 1950; UK: Gollancz, 1951; Basil Willing #8
Two-thirds of a ghost. Random House, 1956; UK: Gollancz, 1957; Basil Willing #11
Who's calling. Morrow, 1942; UK: Nicholson, 1948; Basil Willing #4
MCCLURE, JAMES, 1934 --
The artful egg. Pantheon, 1985; Tromp Kramer; Michael Zondi
The blood of an Englishman. Harper, 1981; UK: Macmillan, 1980; Tromp Kramer; Michael Zondi
The caterpillar cop. Harper, 1973; UK: Gollancz, 1972; Tromp Kramer #2; Michael Zondi #2

The gooseberry fool. Harper, 1974; UK: Gollancz, 1974; Tromp Kramer #3; Michael Zondi #3
Rogue eagle. Harper, 1976; UK: Macmillan, 1976
Snake. Harper, 1976; UK: Gollancz, 1975; Tromp Kramer #4; Michael Zondi #4
The steam pig. Harper, 1972; UK: Gollancz, 1971; Tromp Kramer #1; Michael Zondi #1
The Sunday hangman. Harper, 1977; UK: Macmillan, 1977; Tromp Kramer #5; Michael Zondi #5
MCCOLLUM, ROBERT
And then they die. St. Martin's, 1985; Francesca Mills
MCCONNELL, FRANK
Murder among friends. Walker, 1983; Harry Garnish
MCCONNOR, VINCENT
I am Vidocq. Dodd, 1985; Francois Vidocq
The Paris puzzle. Macmillan, 1981; Insp. Damiot
The Provence puzzle. Macmillan, 1980; Insp. Damiot
The Riviera puzzle. Macmillan, 1981; Insp. Damiot
MCCORMICK, CLAIRE
The Club Paradis murders. Walker, 1983; John Waltz
Resume for murder. Walker, 1982; John Waltz
MCCORMICK, JIM, 1920 --
Last seen alive. Doubleday, 1979
MCCUE, LILLIAN, see DE LA TORRE, LILLIAN (pseud.)
MCCUTCHEON, HUGH, 1909 --
And the moon was full. Doubleday, 1967; UK: Killer's moon. Long, 1966
Murder at "The Angel." Dutton, 1952; UK: The angel of light. Rich, 1951; Howard Anthony
Yet she must die. Doubleday, 1962; UK: Long, 1962
MCDONALD, GREGORY, 1937 --
The buck passes Flynn. Ballantine, 1981; Francis X. Flynn #3
Confess, Fletch. Avon, 1976; UK: Gollancz, 1977; Irwin Maurice "Fletch" Fletcher #2; Francis X. Flynn #1

Fletch. Bobbs, 1974; UK: Gollancz, 1976; Irwin Maurice "Fletch" Fletcher #1

Fletch and the man who. Warner, 1983; Irwin Maurice "Fletch" Fletcher

Fletch and the Widow Bradley. Warner, 1981; Irwin Maurice "Fletch" Fletcher

Fletch forever. Doubleday, 1978; Irwin Maurice "Fletch" Fletcher #4

Fletch won. Warner, 1985; Irwin Maurice "Fletch" Fletcher

Fletch's fortune. Avon, 1978; UK: Gollancz, 1979; Irwin Maurice "Fletch" Fletcher #3

Flynn. Avon, 1977; UK: Gollancz, 1978; Francis X. Flynn #2

Flynn's in. Mysterious Press, 1984; Francis X. Flynn

MCDOWELL, MICHAEL, see ALDYNE, NATHAN (pseud.)

MCGARRITY, MARK, see GILL, BARTHOLOMEW (pseud.)

MCGERR, PATRICIA, 1917 --
Catch me if you can. Doubleday, 1948; UK: Collins, 1949

Death in a million living rooms. Doubleday, 1951; UK: Die laughing. Collins, 1952

Fatal in my fashion. Doubleday, 1954; UK: Collins, 1955

...Follow as the night... Doubleday, 1950; UK: Your loving victim. Collins, 1951

Is there a traitor in the house? Doubleday, 1964; UK: Collins, 1965; Selena Mead #1

Legacy for danger. Luce, 1970; Selena Mead #2

Murder is absurd. Doubleday, 1967; UK: Gollancz, 1967

Pick your victim. Doubleday, 1946; UK: Collins, 1947

Save the witness. Doubleday, 1949; UK: Collins, 1950

The seven deadly sisters. Doubleday, 1947; UK: Collins, 1948

MCGINLEY, PATRICK
Bogmail. Ticknor & Fields, 1981; Martin Brian, 1978

MCGIVERN, WILLIAM P., 1927 --
The big heat. Dodd, 1952; UK: Hamilton, 1953; Dave Bannion

But death runs faster. Dodd, 1948; UK: Boardman, 1949

Heaven ran last. Dodd, 1949; UK: Digit, 1958; Insp. Harrigan

Night extra. Dodd, 1957; UK: Collins, 1958; Sam Terrell

Night of the juggler. Putnam, 1975; UK: Collins, 1975; Max Prima; Gypsy Tonnelli

Rogue cop. Dodd, 1954; UK: Collins, 1955

Shield for murder. Dodd, 1951

Very cold for May. Dodd, 1950

MCGOWN, JILL
A perfect match. St. Martin's, 1983; Insp. Lloyd; Judy Hill

MCGUIRE, PAUL (pseud. of Dominic Paul McGuire, 1903 --)
The black rose murder. Brentano's, 1932; UK: Murder in Bostal. Skeffington, 1931; Insp. Cummings #1

Death fugue. UK: Skeffington, 1933; Supt. Fillinger #3

Death tolls the bell. Coward McCann, 1933; UK: The tower mystery. Skeffington, 1932; Supt. Fillinger #1

Enter three witches. Morrow, 1940; UK: The Spanish steps. Heinemann, 1940

A funeral in Eden. Morrow, 1938; UK: Burial service. Heinemann, 1938

Murder at high noon. Doubleday, 1935; UK: Daylight murder. Skeffington, 1934; Insp. Cummings #3; Supt. Fillinger #5

Murder by the law. UK: Skeffington, 1932; Supt. Fillinger #2

Murder in haste. UK: Skeffington, 1934; Insp. Cummings #4; Supt. Fillinger #6

7:30 Victoria. UK: Skeffington, 1935; Insp. Cummings #5

There sits death. UK: Skeffington, 1933; Supt. Fillinger #4

Three dead men. Brentano's, 1932; UK: Skeffington, 1931; Insp. Cummings #2

Threepence to Marble Arch. UK:
Skeffington, 1936; Insp. Wittler

MCILVANNEY, WILLIAM, 1936 --
Laidlaw. Pantheon, 1977; UK:
Hodder, 1977; Jack Laidlaw #1
The papers of Tony Veitch. Pantheon,
1983; Jack Laidlaw #2

MCINERNY, RALPH, see also QUILL,
MONICA (pseud.)
Bishop as pawn. Vanguard, 1978; UK:
Curtis, 1979; Roger Dowling #3
Getting away with murder. Vanguard,
1984; Roger Dowling
The grass widow. Vanguard, 1983;
Roger Dowling #8
Her death of cold. Vanguard, 1977;
UK: Hale, 1979; Roger Dowling #1
A loss of patients. Vanguard, 1982;
Roger Dowling #7
Lying three. Vanguard, 1979; UK:
Hale, 1980; Roger Dowling #4
Rest in pieces. Vanguard, 1985;
Roger Dowling #10
Second vespers. Vanguard, 1980;
UK: Hale, 1981; Roger Dowling #5
The seventh station. Vanguard,
1977; UK: Hale, 1979; Roger
Dowling #2
Thicker than water. Vanguard,
1981; Roger Dowling #6

MCINTOSH, KINN HAMILTON, see AIRD,
CATHERINE

MCINTYRE, JOHN T., 1871-1951
The museum murder. Doubleday,
1929; UK: Bles, 1930; Duddington
Pell Chalmers

MCIVER, N. J.
Come back, Alice Smythereene! St.
Martin's, 1985; Arnold Simon

MCKIMMEY, JAMES, 1923 --
The man with the gloved hand.
Random House, 1972; UK: Hale,
1974
Run if you're guilty. Lippincott,
1963; UK: Boardman, 1964

MCLEAN, ALLAN CAMPBELL, 1922 --
The carpet-slipper murder.
Washburn, 1957; UK: Ward, 1956;
Neil MacLeod
Death on All Hallows. Washburn,
1958; UK: Ward, 1958; Neil
MacLeod

MCLEAVE, HUGH, 1923 --
No face in the mirror. Walker,
1980; Gregor Maclean

MCLIESH, DOUGAL
The valentine victim. Houghton,
1969; Insp. Rodericks

MCMAHON, THOMAS PATRICK
The issue of the bishop's blood.
Doubleday, 1972; UK: Collins,
1973; Dave Peck #1

MCMULLEN, MARY, 1920 --
But Nellie was so nice. Doubleday,
1979; UK: Collins, 1981
A dangerous funeral. Doubleday,
1977; UK: Hale, 1978
Death by bequest. Doubleday, 1977;
UK: Penguin, 1978
Funny Jonas, you don't look dead.
Doubleday, 1976; UK: Hale, 1978
A grave without flowers. Doubleday,
1983
The men with fifty complaints.
Doubleday, 1978; UK: Hale, 1980
My cousin death. Doubleday, 1980;
UK: Collins, 1981
Something of the night. Doubleday,
1980; UK: Collins, 1982; Kells
Cavanaugh
Strangle hold. Harper, 1951; UK:
Death of Miss X. Collins, 1952
Welcome to the grave. Doubleday,
1979; UK: Collins, 1980

MCNEILLE, H. C., 1888-1937
The black gang. Doran, 1922; UK:
Hodder, 1922; Bulldog Drummond #2
Bulldog Drummond. Doran, 1920; UK:
Hodder, 1920; Bulldog Drummond #1
Bulldog Drummond at bay. Doubleday,
1935; UK: Hodder, 1935; Bulldog
Drummond #8
Bulldog Drummond returns.
Doubleday, 1932; UK: The return
of Bulldog Drummond. Hodder,
1932; Bulldog Drummond #7
Bulldog Drummond's third round.
Doran, 1924; UK: The third round.
Hodder, 1924; Bulldog Drummond #3
Challenge. Doubleday, 1937; UK:
Hodder, 1937; Bulldog Drummond #9
The female of the species.
Doubleday, 1928; UK: Hodder,
1928; Bulldog Drummond
The final count. Doran, 1926; UK:
Hodder, 1926; Bulldog Drummond #4
Temple tower. Doubleday, 1929; UK:
Hodder, 1929; Bulldog Drummond
#6

MCSHANE, MARK, 1930 -- . For other
mysteries by this author, see
LOVELL, MARC (pseud.)
The girl nobody knows. Doubleday,
1965; UK: Hale, 1966; Norman Pink
#1
Night's evil. Doubleday, 1966; UK:
Hale, 1966; Norman Pink #2
Seance. Doubleday, 1962; UK: Seance
on a wet afternoon. Cassell, 1961;
Myra Savage #1
Seance for two. Doubleday, 1972;
UK: Hale, 1974; Myra Savage #2
Untimely ripped. Doubleday, 1963;
UK: Cassell, 1962
The way to nowhere. UK: Hale, 1967;
Norman Pink #3
MEANS, MARY, see SCOTT, DENIS (pseud.)
MEGGS, BROWN, 1930 --
The matter of paradise. Random
House, 1975; UK: Collins, 1976
Saturday games. Random House, 1974;
UK: Collins, 1975
MELVILLE, JAMES
The chrysanthemum chain. St.
Martin's, 1982; UK: Secker, 1980;
Tetsuo Otani #2
Death of a daimyo. St. Martin's,
1984; Tetsuo Otani
The ninth netsuke. St. Martin's,
1982; Tetsuo Otani
Sayonara, Sweet Amaryllis. St.
Martin's, 1984; Tetsuo Otani
A sort of samurai. St. Martin's,
1982; Tetsuo Otani
The wages of Zen. Methuen, 1981;
UK: Secker, 1979; Tetsuo Otani #1
MELVILLE, JENNIE (pseud. of
Gwendoline Butler, 1922 --). For
other mysteries by this author, see
BUTLER, GWENDOLINE
Burning is a substitute for
loving. London House, 1964; UK:
Joseph, 1963; Charmian Daniels #2
Come home and be killed. London
House, 1964; UK: Joseph, 1962;
Charmian Daniels #1
Murderer's houses. UK: Joseph,
1965; Charmian Daniels #3
A new kind of killer. McKay, 1971;
UK: A new kind of killer, an old
kind of death. Hodder, 1970;
Charmian Daniels #5
There lies your love. UK: Joseph,
1965; Charmian Daniels #4

MEREDITH, D. R.
The sheriff and the panhandle
murders. Walker, 1984; Charles
Timothy Matthews
MERSEREAU, JOHN, 1898 --
The corpse comes ashore.
Lippincott, 1941
Murder loves company. Lippincott,
1940; James Yates Biddle; Kay
Ritchie
MEYER, LAWRENCE, 1941 --
A capitol crime. Viking, 1977; UK:
Collins, 1977; Tony Jordan
False front. Viking, 1979; UK:
Collins, 1979
MEYER, NICHOLAS, 1945 --
The seven per-cent solution.
Dutton, 1974; UK: Hodder, 1975;
Sherlock Holmes; Sigmund Freud
Target practice. Harcourt, 1974;
UK: Hodder, 1975; Mark Brill
The West End horror. Dutton, 1976;
UK: Hodder, 1976; Sherlock Holmes
MILES, STELLA
Saddled with murder. UK: Jenkins,
1954
MILLAR, KENNETH, 1915-1983. See also
MACDONALD, ROSS (pseud.)
The dark tunnel. Dodd, 1944; Robert
Branch
MILLAR, MARGARET, 1915 --
An air that kills. Random House,
1957; UK: The soft talkers.
Gollancz, 1957
Ask for me tomorrow. Random House,
1976; UK: Gollancz, 1977; Tomas
Aragon
Banshee. Morrow, 1983; Howard
Hyatt; Michael Dunlop
Beast in view. Random House, 1955;
UK: Gollancz, 1955
Beyond this point are monsters.
Random House, 1970; UK: Gollancz,
1971
The devil loves me. Doubleday,
1942; Paul Prye #3; Insp. Sands
The fiend. Random House, 1964; UK:
Gollancz, 1964
Fire will freeze. Random House,
1944
How like an angel. Random House,
1962; UK: Gollancz, 1962; Joe
Quinn

The invisible worm. Doubleday,
1941; UK: Long, 1943; Paul Prye #1

The iron gates. Random House, 1945;
UK: Taste of fears. Hale, 1950;
Insp. Sands #2

The listening walls. Random House,
1959; UK: Gollancz, 1959

Mermaid. Morrow, 1982; Tomas Aragon

The murder of Miranda. Random
House, 1979; UK: Gollancz, 1980;
Tomas Aragon

Rose's last summer. Random House,
1952; UK: Museum Press, 1954

A stranger in my grave. Random
House, 1960; UK: Gollancz, 1960;
Steve Pinata

Vanish in an instant. Random House,
1952; UK: Museum Press, 1953; Eric
Meecham

Wall of eyes. Random House, 1943;
Insp. Sands #1

The weak-eyed bat. Doubleday, 1942;
Paul Prye #2

MILLER, BILL, see MILLER, WADE
(pseud.)

MILLER, JOHN (pseud. of Joseph
Samachson, 1906 --)

Murder of a professor. Putnam,
1937; UK: Hale, 1937; Philip
Waring; Sgt. Fogerty

MILLER, WADE, (pseud. of Robert
Wade, 1920 -- , and Bill Miller,
1920-1961)

Calamity Fair. Farrar, 1950; Max
Thursday #4

Deadly weapon. Farrar, 1946; UK:
Low, 1947; Walter James

Devil on two sticks. Faber, 1949

Fatal step. Farrar, 1948; UK: Low,
1949; Max Thursday #2

Guilty bystander. Farrar, 1947;
UK: Low, 1948; Max Thursday #1

Murder charge. Farrar, 1950; Max
Thursday #5

Shoot to kill. Farrar, 1951; UK:
Allen, 1953; Max Thursday #6

Uneasy Street. Farrar, 1948; UK:
Low, 1949; Max Thursday #3

MILLER, WHIT, see MASTERSON, WHIT
(pseud.)

MILLS, HUGH (pseud.). For other
mysteries by this author, see
TRAVERS, HUGH (pseud.)

In pursuit of evil. Lippincott,
1967; UK: Triton, 1967; Franz
Heppel

MILNE, A. A., 1882-1956

The red house mystery. Dutton,
1928; UK: Methuen, 1922

MINAHAN, JOHN

The great diamond robbery. Norton,
1984; Little John Rawlings

Murder in the English Department.
St. Martin's, 1983

MITCHELL, GLADYS

Adders on the heath. London House,
1963; UK: Joseph, 1963; Beatrice
Bradley #37

Ask a policeman. Morrow, 1933;
Beatrice Bradley #5

Brazen tongue. UK: Joseph, 1940;
Beatrice Bradley #12

Cold, lone and still. UK: Joseph,
1984; Beatrice Bradley

Come away, death. UK: Joseph,
1937; Beatrice Bradley #9

Convent on Styx. UK: Joseph, 1975;
Beatrice Bradley #50

The croaking raven. UK: Joseph,
1966; Beatrice Bradley #40

The crozier pharoahs. UK: Joseph,
1985; Beatrice Lestrange

Dance to your daddy. UK: Joseph,
1969; Beatrice Bradley #43

The dancing druids. UK: Joseph,
1948; Beatrice Bradley #22

Dead men's Morris. UK: Joseph,
1936; Beatrice Bradley #8

Death and the maiden. UK: Joseph,
1947; Beatrice Bradley #21

The death-cap dancers. St.
Martin's, 1981; Beatrice
Bradley

Death in the wet. Macrae Smith,
1934; Grayson, 1934; Beatrice
Bradley #6

Death of a Delft Blue. London
House, 1965; UK: Joseph, 1964;
Beatrice Bradley #38

The devil at Saxon Wall. UK:
Grayson, 1935; Beatrice Bradley
#7

The devil's elbow. UK: Joseph,
1951; Beatrice Bradley #25

The echoing strangers. UK: Joseph,
1952; Beatrice Bradley #26

Faintley speaking. UK: Joseph,
1954; Beatrice Bradley #28

Fault in the structure. UK: Joseph, 1977; Beatrice Bradley #53

Gory dew. UK: Joseph, 1970; Beatrice Bradley #44

Groaning Spinney. UK: Joseph, 1950; Beatrice Bradley #24

Hangman's curfew. UK: Joseph, 1941; Beatrice Bradley #13

A hearse on May-Day. UK: Joseph, 1972; Beatrice Bradley #46

Here comes a chopper. UK: Joseph, 1946; Beatrice Bradley #20

Here lies Gloria Maundy. St. Martin's, 1983; Beatrice Bradley

A javelin for Jonah. UK: Joseph, 1974; Beatrice Bradley #48

Lament for Leto. UK: Joseph, 1971; Beatrice Bradley #45

Late, late in the evening. UK: Joseph, 1976; Beatrice Bradley #51

Laurels are poison. UK: Joseph, 1942; Beatrice Bradley #15

The longer bodies. UK: Gollancz, 1930; Beatrice Bradley #3

The man who grew tomatoes. London House, 1959; UK: Joseph, 1959; Beatrice Bradley #33

Merlin's furlong. UK: Joseph, 1953; Beatrice Bradley #27

Mingled with venom. UK: Joseph, 1978; Beatrice Bradley #55

The mudflats of the dead. UK: Joseph, 1979; Beatrice Bradley #57

The murder of Busy Lizzie. UK: Joseph, 1973; Beatrice Bradley #47

My bones will keep. British Book Centre, 1962; UK: Joseph, 1962; Beatrice Bradley #36

My father sleeps. UK: Joseph, 1944; Beatrice Bradley #18

The mystery of a butcher's shop. Dial, 1930; UK: Gollancz, 1929; Beatrice Bradley #2

Nest of vipers. UK: Joseph, 1979; Beatrice Bradley #56

The nodding canaries. UK: Joseph, 1961; Beatrice Bradley #35

Noonday and night. UK: Joseph, 1977; Beatrice Bradley #52

Pageant of murder. London House, 1965; UK: Joseph, 1965; Beatrice Bradley #39

Printer's error. UK: Joseph, 1939; Beatrice Bradley #11

The rising of the moon. St. Martin's, 1985; UK: Joseph, 1945; Beatrice Bradley

St. Peter's finger. UK: Joseph, 1938; Beatrice Bradley #10

The saltmarsh murders. Macrae Smith, 1933; UK: Gollancz, 1932; Beatrice Bradley #4

Say it with flowers. UK: Joseph, 1960; Beatrice Bradley #34

Skeleton Island. UK: Joseph, 1967; Beatrice Bradley #41

Speedy death. Dial, 1929; UK: Gollancz, 1929; Beatrice Bradley #1

Spotted hemlock. St. Martin's, 1985; UK: Joseph, 1958; Beatrice Bradley #32

Sunset over Soho. UK: Joseph, 1943; Beatrice Bradley #17

Three quick and five dead. UK: Joseph, 1968; Beatrice Bradley #42

Tom Brown's body. UK: Joseph, 1949; Beatrice Bradley #23

Twelve horses and the hangman's noose. UK: Joseph, 1956; Beatrice Bradley #30

The twenty-third man. UK: Joseph, 1957; Beatrice Bradley #31

Uncoffin'd clay. St. Martin's, 1982; UK: Joseph, 1980; Beatrice Bradley

Watson's choice. McKay, 1976; UK: Joseph, 1955; Beatrice Bradley

When last I died. Knopf, 1942; UK: Joseph, 1941; Beatrice Bradley #14

Winking at the brim. McKay, 1977; UK: Joseph, 1974; Beatrice Bradley #49

The worsted viper. UK: Joseph, 1943; Beatrice Bradley #16

Wraiths and changelings. UK: Joseph, 1978; Beatrice Bradley #54

MODELL, MERRIAM, see PIPER, EVELYN (pseud.)

MOFFETT, CLEVELAND, 1863-1926
The Seine mystery. Dodd, 1925; UK: Melrose, 1924; Alan Esterbrooke; Insp. Brousse

Through the wall. Appleton, 1909;
UK: Melrose, 1910; Paul Coquenil

MOFFETT, CLEVELAND and HERFORD OLIVER

The bishop's purse. Appleton, 1913

MONIG, CHRISTOPHER (pseud. of Kendell
Foster Crossen, 1910-1981). For
other mysteries by this author, see
CHABER, M. E. (pseud.); FOSTER,
RICHARD (pseud.)

Abra-cadaver. Dutton, 1958; UK:
Boardman, 1958; Brian Brett #2

The burned man. Dutton, 1956; UK:
Boardman, 1957; Brian Brett #1

The lonely graves. Dutton, 1960;
UK: Boardman, 1961; Brian Brett
#4

Once upon a crime. Dutton, 1959;
UK: Boardman, 1960; Brian Brett
#3

MONTALBAN, MANUEL VAZQUEZ

Murder in the Central Committee.
Academy Chicago, 1985; Pepe
Carvalho

MONTEILHET, HUBERT, 1928 --

Murder at the Frankfurt Book Fair.
Doubleday, 1976; UK: Dead copy.
Macdonald, 1976

The praying mantises. Simon &
Schuster, 1962; UK: Praying
mantis. Hamilton, 1962

Return from the ashes. Simon &
Schuster, 1963; UK: Phoenix from
the ashes. Hamilton, 1963

MONTGOMERY, ROBERT BRUCE, see CRISPIN,
EDMUND

MOORE, BARBARA

The Doberman wore black. St.
Martin's, 1983; Gordon Christy

MORICE, ANNE (pseud. of Felicity
Shaw, 1918 --)

Dead on cue. St. Martin's, 1985;
Tessa Crichton

Death and the dutiful daughter.
St. Martin's, 1974; UK: Macmillan,
1973; Tessa Crichton #5

Death in the Grand Manor. UK:
Macmillan, 1970; Tessa Crichton #1

Death of a gay dog. UK: Macmillan,
1971; Tessa Crichton #3

Death of a heavenly twin. St.
Martin's, 1974; UK: Macmillan,
1973; Tessa Crichton #6

Death of a wedding guest. St.
Martin's, 1976; UK: Macmillan,
1976; Tessa Crichton #9

Getting away with murder? St.
Martin's, 1985; Tessa Crichton

Hollow vengeance. St. Martin's,
1982; Tessa Crichton

Killing with kindness. St.
Martin's, 1975; UK: Macmillan,
1974; Tessa Crichton #7

Murder by proxy. St. Martin's,
1978; UK: Macmillan, 1978; Tessa
Crichton #12

Murder in married life. UK:
Macmillan, 1971; Tessa Crichton
#2

Murder in mimicry. St. Martin's,
1977; UK: Macmillan, 1977; Tessa
Crichton #10

Murder in outline. St. Martin's,
1979; UK: Macmillan, 1979; Tessa
Crichton #13

Murder on French leave. UK:
Macmillan, 1972; Tessa Crichton
#4

Murder postdated. St. Martin's,
1984; Tessa Crichton

Nursery tea and poison. St.
Martin's, 1975; UK: Macmillan,
1975; Tessa Crichton #8

Scared to death. St. Martin's,
1978; UK: Macmillan, 1977; Tessa
Crichton #11

Sleep of death. St. Martin's,
1983; Tessa Crichton

MORISON, B. J.

Beer and skittles. Thorndike, 1985;
Elizabeth Lamb; Worthington

Port and a star boarder. Thorndike,
1984; Elizabeth Lamb; Worthington

MORLEY, CHRISTOPHER, 1890 --

The haunted bookshop. Doubleday,
1919; UK: Chapman, 1920

MORLEY, F. V., 1899-1980

Death in Dwelly Lane. Harper,
1952; UK: Dwelly Lane. Eyre, 1952

MORRAH, DERMOT, 1896-1974

The mummy case mystery. Harper,
1933; UK: The mummy case. Faber,
1933

MORTIMER, JOHN, 1923 --

Rumpole and the golden thread.
Penguin, 1984; Horace Rumpole

Rumpole of the Bailey. Penguin, 1980; UK: Penguin, 1978; Horace Rumpole

Rumpole's return. Penguin, 1982; UK: Penguin, 1980; Horace Rumpole

The trials of Rumpole. Penguin, 1981; UK: Penguin, 1979; Horace Rumpole

MORTON, ANTHONY (pseud. of John Creasey, 1908-1973). For other mysteries by this author, see MARRIC, J. J. (pseud.) or ASHE, GORDON (pseud.) or YORK, JEREMY (pseud.)

Affair for the Baron. Walker, 1968; UK: Hodder, 1967; John Mannering #39

Alias Blue Mask. Lippincott, 1939; UK: Low, 1939; John Mannering; Blue Mask

Attack the Baron. UK: Low, 1951; John Mannering #19

The Baron and the arrogant artist. Walker, 1973; UK: Hodder, 1972; John Mannering #44

The Baron and the beggar. Duell, 1950; UK: Low, 1947; John Mannering #13

The Baron and the Chinese puzzle. Scribner's, 1966; UK: Hodder, 1965; John Mannering #37

The Baron and the missing old masters. Walker, 1969; UK: Hodder, 1968; John Mannering #40

The Baron and the Mogul swords. Scribner's, 1966; UK: A sword for the Baron. Hodder, 1963; John Mannering #35

The Baron and the stolen legacy. Scribner's, 1967; UK: Bad for the Baron. Hodder, 1962; John Mannering #34

The Baron and the unfinished portrait. Walker, 1970; UK: Hodder, 1969; John Mannering #41

The Baron branches out. Scribner's, 1967; UK: A branch for the Baron. Hodder, 1961; John Mannering #33

The Baron comes back. UK: Low, 1943; John Mannering #9

The Baron goes a-buying. Walker, 1972; UK: Hodder, 1971; John Mannering #43

The Baron goes east. UK: Low, 1953; John Mannering #22

The Baron goes fast. Walker, 1972; UK: Hodder, 1954; John Mannering #25

The Baron in France. Walker, 1976; UK: Hodder, 1953; John Mannering #23

The Baron, king-maker. Walker, 1975; UK: Hodder, 1975; John Mannering #46

The Baron on board. Walker, 1968; UK: Hodder, 1964; John Mannering #36

Blame the Baron. Duell, 1951; UK: Low, 1949; John Mannering #14

Blood red. Doubleday, 1960; UK: Red eye for the Baron. Hodder, 1958; John Mannering #30

The Blue Mask at bay. Lippincott, 1938; UK: The Baron at bay. Low, 1938; John Mannering #4; Blue Mask #4

Blue Mask strikes again. Lippincott, 1940; UK: Versus the Baron. Low, 1940; John Mannering #7; Blue Mask #7

Blue Mask victorious. Lippincott, 1940; UK: Call for the Baron. Low, 1940; John Mannering #8; Blue Mask #8

Books for the Baron. Duell, 1952; UK: Low, 1949; John Mannering #16

Burgle the Baron. Walker, 1974; UK: Hodder, 1973; John Mannering #45

Career for the Baron. Duell, 1950; UK: Low, 1946; John Mannering #12

A case for the Baron. Duell, 1949; UK: Low, 1945; John Mannering #10

Challenge Blue Mask! Lippincott, 1939; UK: The Baron at large. Low, 1939; John Mannering #6; Blue Mask #6

Cry for the Baron. Walker, 1970; UK: Low, 1950; John Mannering #17

Danger for the Baron. Walker, 1974; UK: Hodder, 1953; John Mannering #24

Deaf, dumb and blonde. Doubleday, 1961; UK: Nest egg for the Baron. Hodder, 1954; John Mannering #26

The double frame. Doubleday, 1961; UK: Frame the Baron. Hodder, 1957; John Mannering #29

Help from the Baron. Walker, 1977;
UK: Hodder, 1955; John Mannering
#27

Hide the Baron. Walker, 1978; UK:
Hodder, 1956; John Mannering #28

If anything happens to Hester.
Doubleday, 1962; UK: Black for the
Baron. Hodder, 1959; John
Mannering #31

Last laugh for the Baron. Walker,
1971; UK: Hodder, 1970; John
Mannering #42

Love for the Baron. UK: Hodder,
1979; John Mannering #47

The man in the Blue Mask.
Lippincott, 1937; UK: Meet the
Baron. Harrap, 1937; John
Mannering #1; Blue Mask #1

The return of the Blue Mask.
Lippincott, 1937; UK: The Baron
returns. Harrap, 1937; John
Mannering #2; Blue Mask #2

Reward for the Baron. UK: Low,
1945; John Mannering #11

A rope for the Baron. Duell, 1949;
UK: Low, 1948; John Mannering #15

Salute Blue Mask. Lippincott, 1938;
UK: The Baron again. Low, 1938;
John Mannering #3; Blue Mask #3

Salute for the Baron. Walker, 1973;
UK: Salute to the Baron. Hodder,
1960; John Mannering #32

Shadow the Baron. UK: Low, 1951;
John Mannering #20

Sport for the Baron. Walker, 1969;
UK: Hodder, 1966; John Mannering
#38

Trap the Baron. Walker, 1971; UK:
Low, 1950; John Mannering #18

Warn the Baron. UK: Low, 1952;
John Mannering #21

MOYES, PATRICIA, 1923 --

Angel death. Holt, 1981; UK:
Collins, 1980; Henry Tibbett

Black widower. Holt, 1975; UK:
Collins, 1975; Henry Tibbett #12

The coconut killings. Holt, 1977;
UK: To kill a coconut. Collins,
1977; Henry Tibbett #13

The curious affair of the third
dog. Holt, 1973; UK: Collins,
1973; Henry Tibbett #11

Dead men don't ski. Rinehart,
1960; UK: Collins, 1959; Henry
Tibbett #1; Emmy Tibbett

Death and the Dutch uncle. Holt,
1968; UK: Collins, 1968; Henry
Tibbett #8; Emmy Tibbett

Death on the agenda. Holt, 1962;
UK: Collins, 1962; Henry Tibbett
#3; Emmy Tibbett

Down among the dead man. Holt,
1961; UK: The sunken sailor.
Collins, 1961; Henry Tibbett #2;
Emmy Tibbett

Falling star. Holt, 1964; UK:
Collins, 1964; Henry Tibbett #5

Johnny under ground. Holt, 1966;
UK: Collins, 1965; Henry Tibbett
#6; Emmy Tibbett

Many deadly returns. Holt, 1970;
UK: Who saw her die? Collins,
1970; Henry Tibbett #9

Murder a la mode. Holt, 1963; UK:
Collins, 1963; Henry Tibbett #4

Murder fantastical. Holt, 1967;
UK: Collins, 1967; Henry Tibbett
#7; Emmy Tibbett

Season of snows and sins. Holt,
1971; UK: Collins, 1971; Henry
Tibbett #10; Emmy Tibbett

A six-letter word for death. Holt,
1983; Henry Tibbett

Who is Simon Warwick? Holt, 1979;
UK: Collins, 1978; Henry Tibbett
#14

MUIR, AUGUSTUS

The shadow on the left. Bobbs,
1928; UK: Methuen, 1928

MULKEEN, THOMAS, 1923 --

My killer doesn't understand me.
Stein & Day, 1973; Clem Talbot

MULLER, MARCIA, 1944 -- . See also
PRONZINI, BILL and MULLER, MARCIA

Ask the cards a question. St.
Martin's, 1982; Sharon McCone #2

The Cheshire cat's eye. St.
Martin's, 1983; Sharon McCone #3

Edwin of the iron shoes. McKay,
1977; Sharon McCone #1

Gaines to keep the dark away. St.
Martin's, 1984; Sharon McCone #4

Leave a message for Willie. St.
Martin's, 1984; Sharon McCone

The legend of the slain soldiers.
Walker, 1985; Elena Oliverez

There's nothing to be afraid of.
St. Martin's, 1985; Sharon McCone
#6

The tree of death. Walker, 1983;
Elena Oliverez
MULLER, MARCIA and PRONZINI, BILL.
See also PRONZINI, BILL and MULLER,
MARCIA
Chapter and hearse. Morrow, 1985
Child's ploy. Macmillan, 1984
Dark lessons. Macmillan, 1985
MUNDER, LAURA
Therapy for murder. St. Martin's,
1984; Sara Marks
MUNRO, HUGH
The brain robbers. UK: Hale, 1967;
Clutha
Clutha plays a hunch. Washburn,
1959; UK: Macdonald, 1959; Clutha
Who told Clutha? Washburn, 1958;
UK: Macdonald, 1958; Clutha
MURPHY, BRIAN, 1939 --
The Enigma Variations. Scribner's,
1981; Eliot Upton
MURRAY, MAX, 1901-1956
A corpse for breakfast. Washburn,
1957; UK: Breakfast with a corpse.
Joseph, 1956
The doctor and the corpse. Farrar,
1952; UK: Joseph, 1953; Michael
West
The neat little corpse. Farrar,
1950; UK: Joseph, 1951
The Queen and the corpse. Farrar,
1949; UK: No duty on a corpse.
Joseph, 1950
The right honourable corpse.
Farrar, 1951; UK: Joseph, 1952
The voice of the corpse. Farrar,
1947; UK: Joseph, 1948
NABB, MAGDALEN
Death in autumn. Scribner's, 1985;
Salva Guarnaccia
Death in springtime. Scribner's,
1984; Salva Guarnaccia #3
Death of a Dutchman. Scribner's,
1983; Salva Guarnaccia #2
Death of an Englishman. Scribner's,
1982; Salva Guarnaccia #1
NASH, JAY ROBERT
The dark fountain. A & W, 1982
The Mafia diaries. Delacorte,
1984; John Howard Journey
NASH, SIMON (pseud. of Raymond
Chapman, 1924 --)
Dead of a counterplot. UK: Bles,
1962; Adam Ludlow #1

Dead woman's ditch. Roy, 1966; UK:
Bles, 1964; Adam Ludlow #4
Death over deep water. Roy, 1965;
UK: Bles, 1963; Adam Ludlow #3
Killed by scandal. Roy, 1964; UK:
Bles, 1962; Adam Ludlow #2
Unhallowed murder. Roy, 1966; UK:
Bles, 1966; Adam Ludlow #5
NATSUKI, SHIZUKO
Murder at Mt. Fuji. St. Martin's,
1984; Jane Prescott
NEBEL, FREDERICK
Fifty roads to town. Little, 1936;
UK: Cape, 1936
Sleepers east. Little, 1933; UK:
Collins, 1934
NELSON, HUGH LAWRENCE
Dark echo. Rinehart, 1949; UK:
Barker, 1949; Steve Johnson
The fence. Rinehart, 1953; Jim Dunn
Gold in every grave. Rinehart,
1951; Barker, 1953; Jim Dunn
Kill with care. Rinehart, 1953;
Jim Dunn
Murder comes high. Rinehart, 1950;
UK: Barker, 1952; Jim Dunn
Ring the bell at zero. Rinehart,
1949; UK: Barker, 1950; Jim Dunn
The season for murder. Rinehart,
1952; UK: Benn, 1956; Jim Dunn
The sleep is deep. Rinehart, 1952;
UK: Benn, 1955; Jim Dunn
Suspect. Rinehart, 1954; Jim Dunn
The title is murder. Rinehart,
1947; UK: Barker, 1947; Steve
Johnson
NEMEC, DAVID
Mad blood. Dial, 1983; Frank Reppa
NEUMAN, FREDERIC, 1934 --
Manuevers. Dial, 1982; Abe Redden
The seclusion room. Viking, 1978;
UK: Gollancz, 1979
NEUMANN, ROBERT, 1897-1975
The inquest. Dutton, 1945; UK:
Hutchinson, 1944
NEVILLE, BARBARA ALISON, see CANDY,
EDWARD (pseud.)
NEVINS, FRANCIS M., JR., 1943 --
Corrupt and ensnare. Putnam, 1978;
UK: Hale, 1979; Loren Mensing #2
Publish and perish. Putnam, 1975;
UK: Hale, 1977; Loren Mensing #1
NEWMAN, BERNARD, 1897-1968
Death under Gibraltar. UK:
Gollancz, 1938

The Mussolini murder plot.
Hillman-Curl, 1939; UK:
Hutchinson, 1936; Insp. Marshall

Papa Pontivy and the Maginot Line
murder. Holt, 1940; UK: Maginot
Line murder. Gollancz, 1939; Papa
Pontivy

NICHOLS, BEVERLY, 1898 --
Death to slow music. Dutton, 1956;
UK: Hutchinson, 1956; Horatio
Green #3

The moonflower murder. Dutton,
1955; UK: The moonflower.
Hutchinson, 1955; Horatio Green #2

Murder by request. Dutton, 1960;
UK: Hutchinson, 1960; Horatio
Green #5

No man's street. Dutton, 1954; UK:
Hutchinson, 1954; Horatio Green #1

The rich die hard. Dutton, 1958;
UK: Hutchinson, 1957; Horatio
Green #4

NICHOLSON, MARGARET BEDA, see YORKE,
MARGARET (pseud.)

NICOLE, CHRISTOPHER ROBIN, see YORK,
ANDREW (pseud.)

NIELSEN, HELEN, 1918 --
After midnight. Morrow, 1966; UK:
Gollancz, 1967; Simon Drake #2

Borrow the night. Morrow, 1956; UK:
Gollancz, 1956

The brink of murder. UK: Gollancz,
1976; Simon Drake

The crime is murder. Morrow, 1956;
UK: Gollancz, 1957; Lisa Bancroft

The darkest hour. Morrow, 1969; UK:
Gollancz, 1969; Simon Drake

Detour. Washburn, 1953

The fifth caller. Morrow, 1959;
UK: Gollancz, 1959

Gold Coast nocturne. Washburn,
1951; UK: Murder by proxy.
Gollancz, 1952; Simon Drake

A killer in the street. Morrow,
1967; UK: Gollancz, 1967; Simon
Drake

Obit delayed. Washburn, 1952; UK:
Gollancz, 1953

The severed key. UK: Gollancz,
1973; Simon Drake

Sin me a murder. Morrow, 1960; UK:
Gollancz, 1961; Ty Leander

Stranger in the dark. Washburn,
1955; UK: Gollancz, 1956

The woman on the roof. Washburn,
1954; UK: Gollancz, 1955

NOLAN, JEANNETTE, 1897-1974
Sudden squall. Washburn, 1955; UK:
Muller, 1956; Lace White

NOLAN, WILLIAM F.
The Black Mask boys. Morrow, 1984

NORMAN, JAMES (pseud. of James
Norman Schmidt, 1912 --)
An inch of time. Morrow, 1944; UK:
Joseph, 1945; Gimiendo Hernandez
Quinto #2

Murder, chop chop. Morrow, 1942;
UK: Joseph, 1943; Gimiendo
Hernandez Quinto #1

The nightwalkers. Ziff Davis,
1947; UK: Joseph, 1948; Gimiendo
Hernandez Quinto #3

NORTH, SAM
209 Thriller Road. St. Martin's,
1980; UK: New English Library,
1979; Sam North

NOWAK, JACQUELYN
Death at the crossings. Dodd,
1985; Mike Miner

OATES, JOYCE CAROL
Mysteries of Winterthurn. Dutton,
1984; Xavier Kilgarvan

O'CONNOR, RICHARD, 1915-1975, see
WAYLAND, PATRICK (pseud.)

O'CORK, SHANNON
End of the line. St. Martin's,
1981; T. T. Baldwin

Hell bent for heaven. St. Martin's,
1983; T. T. Baldwin

O'DONNELL, LILLIAN, 1926 --
Aftershock. Putnam, 1977; UK:
Hale, 1979; Mici Anhalt #1

Babes in the woods. Abelard 1965;
UK: Abelard 1965

The baby merchants. Putnam, 1975;
UK: Bantam, 1976; Norah
Mulcahaney #4

Children's zoo. Putnam, 1981; Norah
Mulcahaney #7

Cop without a shield. Putnam, 1983;
Norah Mulcahaney

Death Schuss. Abelard 1963; UK:
Abelard 1963

Dial 577-R-A-P-E. Putnam, 1974; UK:
Barker, 1974; Norah Mulcahaney #3

Don't wear your wedding ring.
Putnam, 1973; UK: Barker, 1974;
Norah Mulcahaney #2

Falling star. Putnam, 1979; UK:
Hale, 1981; Mici Anhalt #2
Ladykiller. Putnam, 1984; Norah
Mulcahaney
Leisure dying. Putnam, 1976; Norah
Mulcahaney #5
Murder under the sun. Abelard,
1964; UK: Abelard, 1964
No business being a cop. Putnam,
1979; UK: Hale, 1980; Norah
Mulcahaney #6
The phone calls. Putnam, 1972; UK:
Hodder, 1972; Norah Mulcahaney #1
The Tachi tree. Abelard, 1968; UK:
Abelard, 1968
Wicked designs. Putnam, 1980; Mici
Anhalt #3
OFFORD, LENORE GLEN, 1905 --
Clues to burn. Duell, 1942; UK:
Grayson, 1943; Bill Hastings #2;
Coco Hastings #2
The glass mask. Duell, 1944; UK:
Jarrolds, 1946; Todd McKinnon #2
Murder on Russian Hill. Macrae
Smith, 1938; UK: Murder before
breakfast. Jarrolds, 1938; Bill
Hastings #1; Coco Hastings #1
Skeleton key. Duell, 1943; Todd
McKinnon #1
The smiling tiger. Duell, 1949; UK:
Jarrolds, 1951; Todd McKinnon #3
Walking shadow. Simon & Schuster,
1959; UK: Ward, 1961; Todd
McKinnon #4
OGILVIE, ELISABETH, 1917 --
A dancer in yellow. McGraw-Hill,
1979
The dreaming summer. McGraw, 1976
OGNALL, LEOPOLD HORACE, see
CARMICHAEL, HARRY (pseud.) or
HOWARD, HARTLEY (pseud.)
O'HARA, KENNETH
Nightmare's nest. Doubleday, 1983;
Insp. Hobden; Sgt. Cheal
OLCOTT, ANTHONY
Murder at the Red October. Academy
Chicago, 1981; Det. Duvakin #1
OLESKER, HARRY, 1923?-1969
Exit dying. Random House, 1959;
UK: Boardman, 1961
OLIVER, HERFORD, see MOFFETT,
CLEVELAND
OLMSTED, LORENA ANN, 1890 --
Setup for murder. Avalon, 1962

OLSEN, D. B. (pseud. of Dolores
Hitchens, 1907-1973). For other
mysteries by this author, see
HITCHENS, DELORES or HITCHENS, BERT
and HITCHENS, DOLORES
The alarm of the black cat.
Doubleday, 1942; Rachel Murdock
#2; Jennifer Murdock #2
Bring the bride a shroud.
Doubleday, 1945; UK: Aldor, 1945;
A. Pennyfeather #1
The cat and Capricorn. Doubleday,
1951; Rachel Murdock #11;
Jennifer Murdock #11
The cat saw murder. Doubleday,
1939; UK: Heinemann, 1940;
Jennifer Murdock #1; Stephen
Mayhew #2
The cat walk. Doubleday, 1953;
Rachel Murdock #12; Jennifer
Murdock #12
The cat wears a mask. Doubleday,
1949; Rachel Murdock #9; Jennifer
Murdock #9
The cat wears a noose. Doubleday,
1944; Rachel Murdock #5; Jennifer
Murdock #5; Stephen Mayhew #6
Cat's claw. Doubleday, 1943;
Rachel Murdock #3; Jennifer
Murdock #3; Stephen Mayhew #4
Cats don't need coffins. Doubleday,
1946; UK: Aldor, 1946; Rachel
Murdock #7; Jennifer Murdock #7;
Stephen Mayhew #7
Cats don't smile. Doubleday, 1945;
UK: Aldor, 1948; Rachel Murdock
#6; Jennifer Murdock #6
Cats have tall shadows. Ziff
Davis, 1948; Rachel Murdock #8;
Jennifer Murdock #8
Catspaw for murder. Doubleday,
1943; Rachel Murdock #4; Jennifer
Murdock #4; Stephen Mayhew #5
The clue in the clay. Phoenix
Press, 1938; Stephen Mayhew #1
Death walks on cat's feet.
Doubleday, 1956; Rachel Murdock
#13; Jennifer Murdock #13
Death wears cat's eyes. Doubleday,
1950; Rachel Murdock #10;
Jennifer Murdock #10
Devious design. Doubleday, 1948;
A. Pennyfeather #3
Enrollment cancelled. Doubleday,
1952; A. Pennyfeather #6

Gallows for the groom. Doubleday,
1947; A. Pennyfeather #2
Love me in death. Doubleday, 1951;
A. Pennyfeather #5
Something about midnight. Doubleday,
1950; A. Pennyfeather #4
The ticking heart. Doubleday, 1940;
Stephen Mayhew #3
Widows ought to weep. Ziff Davis,
1947; Mr. Puckett
OLSEN, JACK, 1925 --
Missing persons. Atheneum, 1981;
Severn Gamble; Tally Wickham
OLSON, DONALD
If I don't tell. Putnam, 1976
Sleep before evening. St. Martin's,
1979; Devillo Green
O'MARIE, SR. CAROL ANNE
A novena for murder. Scribner's,
1984; Mary Helen
OPPENHEIM, E. PHILLIPS, 1866-1946
Advice limited. Little, 1936; UK:
Hodder, 1935; Baroness Linz
Curious happenings to the Rookes
legatees. Little, 1938; UK:
Hodder, 1937
The evil shepherd. Little, 1922;
UK: Hodder, 1923
The ex-detective. Little, 1933; UK:
Hodder, 1933; Malcolm Gossett
Floating peril. Little, 1936; UK:
The bird of paradise. Hodder, 1936
General Besserley's puzzle box.
Little, 1935; UK: Hodder, 1935;
Gen. Besserley #1
General Besserley's second puzzle
box. Little, 1940; UK: Hodder,
1939; Gen. Besserley #2
Last train out. Little, 1940; UK:
Hodder, 1941
Milan grill room. Little, 1941;
UK: Hodder, 1940; Charles Lyson
Murder at Monte Carlo. Little,
1933; UK: Hodder, 1933
Nicholas Goade, detective. Little,
1929; UK: Hodder, 1927; Nicholas
Goade
The Ostrikoff jewels. Little,
1932; UK: Hodder, 1932
Peter Ruff. UK: Hodder, 1912;
Peter Ruff #2
Peter Ruff and the double four.
Little, 1912; UK: The double four.
Hodder, 1912; Peter Ruff #1

Prodigals of Monte Carlo. Little,
1926; UK: Hodder, 1926
A pulpit in the grill room.
Little, 1939; UK: Hodder, 1938;
Charles Lyson
Slane's long shots. Little, 1930;
UK: Hodder, 1930; Jasper Slane
ORCZY, BARONESS, 1865-1947
The case of Miss Elliott. UK:
Unwin, 1905; Old man in the
corner #1
Lady Molly of Scotland Yard. Arno,
1976; UK: Cassell, 1910
The man in gray. Doran, 1918; UK:
Cassell, 1918
The man in the corner. Dodd, 1909;
UK: The old man in the corner.
Old man in the corner #2
The old man in the corner unravels
The mystery of the Fulton Gardens
mystery, and the Moorland
tragedy. Doran, 1925; Old man in
the corner #7
The old man in the corner unravels
the mystery of the khaki tunic.
Doran, 1923; Old man in the
corner #3
The old man in the corner unravels
the mystery of the necklace and
the tragedy in the bishop's road.
Doran, 1924; Old man in the
corner #4
The old man in the corner unravels
the mystery of the Russian prince
and of Dog's Tooth Cliff. Doran,
1924; Old man in the corner #5
The old man in the corner unravels
the mystery of the white
carnation, and the Montmorte hat.
Doran, 1925; Old man in the
corner #6
Skin o' my tooth. Doubleday, 1928;
UK: Hodder, 1928; Patrick
Mulligan
Unravelled knots. Doran, 1926; UK:
Hutchinson, 1925; Old man in the
corner #8
ORENSTEIN, FRANK
The man in the gray flannel shroud.
St. Martin's, 1984; Ev Franklin
Murder on Madison Ave. St.
Martin's, 1983; Ev Franklin
ORMEROD, ROGER
Seeing red. Scribner's, 1985; Harry
Kyle; Angela Rollason

ORR, CLIFFORD, 1899-1951
The Dartmouth murders. Farrar,
1929; UK: Hamilton, 1931; Joseph
Harris
The wailing rock murders. Farrar,
1932; UK: Cassell, 1933
OSTER, JERRY
Sweet justice. Harper, 1985; Lt.
Neuman; Sgt. Redfield
OSTLERE, GORDON, 1921 -- , see GORDON,
RICHARD (pseud.)
OSTRANDER, ISABEL, 1883-1924
Island of intrigue. McBride, 1918;
UK: Hurst, 1919
McCarty, Incog. McBride, 1923; UK:
Hurst, 1923; Timothy McCarty
The tattooed arm. McBride, 1922;
UK: Hurst, 1922
The twenty-six clues. Watts, 1919;
UK: Hurst, 1921; Timothy McCarty
OURSLER, FULTON, see ABBOT, ANTHONY
(pseud.)
OVSTEDAL, BARBARA, 1925 -- , see PAUL,
BARBARA (pseud.)
OWEN, PHILIP (pseud. of Judson
Philips). For other mysteries by
this author, see PHILIPS, JUDSON
Mystery at a country inn. Berkshire
Traveller Press, 1979; Don Burton
OWENS, HANS C.
Ways of death. Green Circle Books,
1937; Percival Trout

PAGE, EMMA (pseud. of Honoria Tirbutt)
Add a pinch of cyanide. Walker,
1973; UK: A fortnight by the sea.
Collins, 1973
Last walk home. Walker, 1983;
Insp. Kelsey; Insp. Lambert
PAGE, JAKE (pseud. of James Keena
Page)
Shoot the moon. Bobbs, 1979; UK:
Hale, 1980; Robin Dana
PAGE, JAMES KEENA, see PAGE, JAKE
(pseud.)
PAGE, MARCO (pseud. of Harry Kurnitz,
1909-1968). For other mysteries by
this author, see KURNITZ, HARRY
Fast company. Dodd, 1938; UK:
Heinemann, 1938; Joel Glass
Reclining figure. Random House,
1952; UK: Eyre, 1952; Ellis Blaise

The shadowy third. Dodd, 1946; UK:
Suspects all. Cherry Tree, 1948;
David Calder; Lt. Flummer
PAGE, MARTIN
The man who stole the Mona Lisa.
Pantheon, 1984; Louis Lepine
PALMER, JOHN LESLIE, see BEEDING,
FRANCIS (pseud.)
PALMER, STUART (pseud. of Charles
Stuart Palmer, 1905-1968)
The adventure of the marked man
and one other. Aspen, 1973;
Sherlock Holmes
Cold poison. Mill, 1954; UK: Exit
laughing. Collins, 1954;
Hildegarde Withers #15
Four lost ladies. Mill, 1949;
Hildegarde Withers #11
The green ace. Mill, 1950; UK: At
one fell swoop. Collins, 1951;
Hildegarde Withers #13
Miss Withers regrets. Doubleday,
1947; UK: Collins, 1948;
Hildegarde Withers #10
The monkey murder and other
Hildegarde Withers stories.
Spivak, 1950; Hildegarde Withers
#12
Murder on the blackboard.
Brentano's, 1932; UK: Eldon,
1934; Hildegarde Withers #3
Murder on wheels. Brentano's,
1932; UK: Long, 1932; Hildegarde
Withers #2
Nipped in the bud. Mill, 1951; UK:
Trap for a redhead. Collins,
1952; Hildegarde Withers #14
The penguin pool murders.
Brentano's, 1931; UK: Long, 1932;
Hildegarde Withers
The puzzle of the blue banderilla.
Doubleday, 1937; UK: Collins,
1937; Hildegarde Withers #7
The puzzle of the happy hooligan.
Doubleday, 1941; UK: Collins,
1941; Hildegarde Withers #8
The puzzle of the pepper tree.
Doubleday, 1933; UK: Jarrolds,
1934; Hildegarde Withers #4
The puzzle of the red stallion.
Doubleday, 1936; UK: The puzzle
of the briar pipe. Collins, 1936;
Hildegarde Withers #6

The puzzle of the silver Persian.
Doubleday, 1934; UK: Collins,
1935; Hildegarde Withers #5

The riddles of Hildegarde Withers.
Jonathan, 1947; Hildegarde Withers
#9

Rook takes knight. Random House,
1968; Howie Rook #2

Unhappy hooligan. Harper, 1956; UK:
Death in grease paint. Collins,
1956; Howie Rook #1

PALMER, STUART and FLETCHER, FLORA
Hildegarde Withers makes the scene.
Random House, 1969; Hildegarde
Withers #17

PALMER, STUART and RICE, CRAIG
People vs. Withers and Malone.
Simon & Schuster, 1963; Hildegarde
Withers #16; John J. Malone #13

PAPAZOGLU, ORNIA
Sweet, savage death. Doubleday,
1984; Patience McKenna

PARETSKY, SARA
Deadlock. Dial, 1984; V. I.
Warshawski #2

Indemnity only. Dial, 1982; V. I.
Warshawski #1

Killing orders. Morrow, 1985; V. I.
Warshawski

PARGETER, EDITH, see PETERS, ELLIS
(pseud.)

PARKER, ROBERT B., 1932 --
Ceremony of innocence. Delacorte,
1982; Spenser #9

Early autumn. Delacorte, 1981;
Spenser #7

God save the child. Houghton, 1974;
UK: Duetsch, 1975; Spenser #2

The Godwulf manuscript. Houghton,
1974; UK: Duetsch, 1974; Spenser
#1

Judas goat. Houghton, 1978; UK:
Curley, 1978; Spenser #5

Looking for Rachel Wallace.
Delacorte, 1980; Spenser #6

Mortal stakes. Houghton, 1975; UK:
Duetsch, 1976; Spenser #3

Promised land. Houghton, 1976; UK:
Duetsch, 1977; Spenser #4

A savage place. Delacorte, 1981;
Spenser #8

Valediction. Delacorte, 1984;
Spenser #11

The widening gyre. Delacorte,
1983; Spenser #10

Wilderness. Delacorte, 1979; UK:
Duetsch, 1980

PARKES, ROGER, 1933 --
The guardians. St. Martin's, 1974;
UK: Constable, 1973; Col. Calpin

PARRISH, FRANK (pseud. of Roger
Longrigg, 1929 --)
Bait on the hook. Dodd, 1983; Dan
Mallett

Death in the rain. Dodd, 1984; Dan
Mallett

Fire in the barley. Dodd, 1979;
UK: Constable, 1977; Dan Mallett

Snare in the dark. Dodd, 1981; Dan
Mallett

Sting of the honeybee. Dodd, 1979;
UK: Constable, 1978; Dan Mallett

PARRISH, RANDALL, 1858-1923
The case and the girl. Knopf,
1922; UK: Paul, 1923; Matthew
West

Gordon Craig: soldier of fortune.
McClurg, 1912

The strange case of Cavendish.
Doran, 1918; UK: Hodder, 1919

PATRICK, Q. (pseud. of Richard
Wilson Webb, 1901 -- , and
sometimes jointly with Hugh
Callingham Wheeler, 1913 --). For
other mysteries by this author, see
QUENTIN, PATRICK (pseud.) or
STAGGE, JONATHAN (pseud.)
Cottage sinister. Swain, 1931; UK:
Longman, 1932; Insp. Inge

Death and the maiden. Simon &
Schuster, 1939; UK: Cassell,
1939; Timothy Trant #2

Death for dear Clara. Simon &
Schuster, 1937; UK: Cassell,
1937; Timothy Trant #1

Murder at Cambridge. Farrar, 1933;
UK: Murder at the 'varsity.
Longman, 1933; Insp. Horrocks

Murder at the Women's City Club.
Swain, 1932; UK: Death in the
dovecote. Cassell, 1934

Return to the scene. Simon &
Schuster, 1941; UK: Death in
Bermuda. Cassell, 1941

S. S. Murder. Farrar, 1933; UK:
Cassell, 1933

PATTERSON, RICHARD NORTH, 1947 --
Escape into the night. Random
House, 1983; Peter Carey
The Lasko tangent. Norton, 1979;
UK: Hale, 1980; Christopher Paget
The outside man. Atlantic-Little
Brown, 1981; Adam Shaw
PAUL, BARBARA (pseud. of Barbara
Ovstedal)
A cadenza for Caruso. St. Martin's,
1984; Enrico Caruso
The fourth wall. Doubleday, 1979;
Abby James
Kill fee. Scribner's, 1985; Janus
Murtagh
Prima donna at large. St. Martin's,
1985; Enrico Caruso; Geraldine
Ferrar
The renewable virgin. Scribner's,
1985; Marian Larch
Your eyes are getting heavy.
Doubleday, 1981; Henrietta Snooks;
Gus Bilinski
PAUL, ELLIOT, 1891-1958
The black and the red. Random
House, 1956; Homer Evans #9
The black gardenia. Random House,
1952; Homer Evans #7
Fracas in the foothills. Random
House, 1940; Homer Evans #3
Hugger-mugger in the Louvre. Random
House, 1940; UK: Nicholson, 1949;
Homer Evans
I'll hate myself in the morning,
and Summer in December. Random
House, 1945; UK: Nicholson, 1949;
Homer Evans #5
Mayhem in B-flat. Random House,
1940; UK: Corgi, 1951; Homer Evans
#4
Murder on the left bank. Random
House, 1951; UK: Corgi, 1951;
Homer Evans #6
The mysterious Mickey Finn; or,
murder at the Cafe' du Dome.
Modern Age, 1939; UK: Penguin,
1953; Homer Evans #1
Waylaid in Boston. Random House,
1953; Homer Evans #8
PAUL, RAYMOND
The Thomas Street horror. Viking,
1982; Lon Quinncannon; Davy Cordor
The tragedy at Tiverton. Viking,
1984; Christopher Randolph

PAYNE, LAURENCE
Take the money and run. Doubleday,
1984; Mark Savage
PAYNE, WILL, 1865-1954
The scarred chin. Dodd, 1920
PEDEN, WILLIAM HARWOOD, 1913 --
Twilight at Monticello. Houghton,
1973; Raymond Green; Margaret
Green
PENN, JOHN
An ad for murder. Scribner's, 1982
A deadly sickness. Scribner's,
1985; George Thorne
Mortal term. Scribner's, 1985;
George Thorne
Stag dinner death. Scribner's,
1983; John Breland; Mike Freeman
A will to kill. Scribner's, 1984;
George Thorne
PENTECOST, HUGH (pseud. of Judson
Philips, 1903 --). For other
mysteries by this author, see
PHILIPS, JUDSON
Around dark corners. Dodd, 1970;
George Crowder #1
The assassins. Dodd, 1955
Bargain with death. Dodd, 1974;
UK: Hale, 1974; Pierre Chambrun
The beautiful dead. Dodd, 1973;
UK: Hale, 1975; Julian Quist #3
Beware young lovers. Dodd, 1980;
UK: Hale, 1981; Pierre Chambrun
Birthday, deathday. Dodd, 1972;
UK: Hale, 1975; Pierre Chambrun
The brass chills. Dodd, 1943; UK:
Hale, 1944; Luke Bradley #4
Cancelled in red. Dodd, 1939; UK:
Heinemann, 1939; Luke Bradley #1
The cannibal who over ate. Dodd,
1962; UK: Boardman, 1963; Pierre
Chambrun
The champagne killer. Dodd, 1972;
UK: Hale, 1974; Julian Quist #2
The copycat killers. Dodd, 1983;
George Crowder #2
The creeping hours. Dodd, 1966; UK:
Heinemann, 1967; John Jericho #3
Dead woman of the year. Dodd, 1967;
UK: Macdonald, 1968; John Jericho
#4
The deadly joke. Dodd, 1971; UK:
Boardman, 1962; Pierre Chambrun
Deadly trap. Dodd, 1978; UK: Hale,
1972; Julian Quist #7

Death after breakfast. Dodd, 1978;
UK: Hale, 1979; Pierre Chambrun

Death mask. Dodd, 1980; UK: Hale,
1981; Julian Quist

Don't drop dead tomorrow. Dodd,
1971; UK: Hale, 1973; Julian Quist
#1

The evil that men do. Dodd, 1966;
UK: Boardman, 1966; Pierre
Chambrun

The gilded nightmare. Dodd, 1968;
UK: Gollancz, 1969; Pierre
Chambrun

Girl watcher's funeral. Dodd, 1969;
UK: Gollancz, 1970; Pierre
Chambrun

The girl with six fingers. Dodd,
1969; UK: Gollancz, 1970; John
Jericho #5

The golden trap. Dodd, 1967; UK:
Macdonald, 1968; Pierre Chambrun

Hide her from every eye. Dodd,
1966; UK: Boardman, 1966; John
Jericho #2

The homicidal horse. Dodd, 1979;
UK: Hale, 1980; Julian Quist #8

Honeymoon with death. Dodd, 1975;
UK: Hale, 1976; Julian Quist
#5

I'll sing at your funeral. Dodd,
1942; UK: Hale, 1945; Luke Bradley
#3

The Judas freak. Dodd, 1974; UK:
Hale, 1976; Julian Quist #4

Lieutenant Pascal's tastes in
homicides. Dodd, 1954; UK:
Boardman, 1955; Lt. Pascal

The lonely target. Dodd, 1959; UK:
Boardman, 1960; Grant Simon #2

Memory of murder. Ziff Davis, 1947;
John Smith #1; Luke Bradley

Murder in high places. Dodd, 1983;
Pierre Chambrun

Murder in luxury. Dodd, 1981;
Pierre Chambrun

Murder out of wedlock. Dodd, 1983;
Julian Quist #13

Murder 'round the clock. Dodd,
1985; Pierre Chambrun

Murder sweet and sour. Dodd, 1985;
George Crowder #3

The obituary club. Dodd, 1958; UK:
Boardman, 1959; Grant Simon #1;
Lt. Pascal

Only the rich die young. Dodd,
1964; UK: Boardman, 1964; Lt.
Pascal

Past, present, and murder. Dodd,
1982; Julian Quist

A plague of violence. Dodd, 1970;
UK: Hale, 1972; John Jericho

The price of silence. Dodd, 1984;
George Crowder

Random killer. Dodd, 1979; UK:
Hale, 1980; Pierre Chambrun

Remember to kill me. Dodd, 1984;
Pierre Chambrun

Shadow of madness. Dodd, 1950;
John Smith #3

The shape of fear. Dodd, 1964; UK:
Boardman, 1964; Pierre Chambrun

Sniper. Dodd, 1965; UK: Boardman,
1966; John Jericho #1

Sow death, reap death. Dodd, 1981;
Julian Quist

The Steel Palace. Dodd, 1977; UK:
Hale, 1978; Julian Quist #6

Time of terror. Dodd, 1975; Pierre
Chambrun

The 24th horse. Dodd, 1940; UK:
Hale, 1951; Luke Bradley #2

Walking dead man. Dodd, 1973; UK:
Hale, 1975; Pierre Chambrun

Where the snow was red. Dodd,
1949; UK: Hale, 1951; John Smith
#2

PERDUE, VIRGINIA, 1899-1945
Alarum and excursion. Doubleday,
1944; UK: Jarrolds, 1947

The case of the foster father.
Doubleday, 1942; UK: Jarrolds,
1946

The case of the grieving monkey.
Doubleday, 1941

The singing cloci. Doubleday,
1941; UK: Jarrolds, 1945

PEROWNE, BARRY
All exits blocked. Mystery House,
1942; UK: Gibraltar prisoner.
Cassell, 1942

PERRY, ANNE, 1938 --
Bluegate Fields. St. Martin's,
1984; Thomas Pitt; Charlotte Pitt

Callander Square. St. Martin's,
1980; UK: Hale, 1980; Thomas
Pitt; Charlotte Pitt

The Cater Street hangman. St.
Martin's, 1979; UK: Hale, 1979;
Thomas Pitt

Paragon Walk. St. Martin's, 1981;
Thomas Pitt
Resurrection Row. St. Martin's,
1981; Thomas Pitt
Rutland Place. St. Martin's, 1983;
Charlotte Pitt
PERRY, RITCHIE, 1942 --
Bishop's pawn. Pantheon, 1979; UK:
Collins, 1979; Arthur Philis #9
Dead end. UK: Collins, 1977; Arthur
Philis #7
Dutch courage. Ballantine, 1982;
UK: Collins, 1978; Arthur Philis
#8
The fall guy. Houghton, 1972; UK:
Collins, 1972; Arthur Philis #1
Grand slam. Pantheon, 1980; UK:
Collins, 1980; Arthur Philis
A hard man to kill. Houghton, 1973;
UK: Nowhere man. Collins, 1973;
Arthur Philis #2
Holiday with a vengeance. Houghton,
1975; UK: Collins, 1974; Arthur
Philis #4
MacAllister. Doubleday, 1984; Frank
MacAllister
One good death deserves another.
Houghton, 1977; UK: Collins, 1976;
Arthur Philis #6
Ticket to ride. Houghton, 1974; UK:
Collins, 1973; Arthur Philis #3
Your money and your wife. Houghton,
1976; UK: Collins, 1975; Arthur
Philis #5
PERRY, THOMAS
The butcher's boy. Scribner's,
1982; Elizabeth Waring
PERTWEE, ROLAND, 1885-1963
Interference. Houghton, 1927; UK:
Cassell, 1927
PERUTZ, LEO, 1884-1957
The master of the day of judgement.
Boni, 1930; UK: Mathews, 1929
PETERS, BILL
Blondes die young. Dodd, 1952; UK:
Foulsham, 1956; Bill Canalli
PETERS, ELIZABETH (pseud. of Barbara
Gross Mertz, 1927 --)
Borrower of the night. Dodd, 1973;
UK: Cassell, 1974; Vicky Bliss #1
The Copenhagen connection. Congdon,
1982
The curse of the pharoahs. Dodd,
1981; Amelia Peabody

Die for love. Congdon, 1984;
Jacqueline Kirby
The mummy case. Congdon, 1985;
Amelia Peabody Emerson; Radcliffe
Emerson
The murders of Richard III. Dodd,
1974; Jacqueline Kirby
The seventh sinner. Dodd, 1972;
UK: Coronet, 1975; Jacqueline
Kirby
Street of the five moons. Dodd,
1978; Vicky Bliss #2
PETERS, ELLIS (pseud. of Edith Mary
Pargeter, 1913 --)
Black is the color of my true
love's heart. Morrow, 1967; UK:
Black is the colour of my true
love's heart. Collins, 1967;
Dominic Felse #7; George Felse #6
City of gold and shadows. Morrow,
1974; UK: Macmillan, 1973;
Charlotte Rossignol; George Felse
#9
Dead man's ransom. Morrow, 1985;
Brother Cadfael
Death and the joyful woman.
Doubleday, 1961; UK: Collins,
1961; Dominic Felse #2; George
Felse #3
Death to the landlords! Morrow,
1972; UK: Macmillan, 1972;
Dominic Felse #9
The devil's novice. Morrow, 1984;
Brother Cadfael
Fallen into the pit. UK: Heinemann,
1951; George Felse #1; Dominic
Felse #1
Flight of a witch. Doubleday,
1965; UK: Collins, 1964; George
Felse #4; Dominic Felse #3
The grass-widow's tale. Morrow,
1968; UK: Collins, 1968; Bunty
Felse #2
The house of green turf. Morrow,
1969; UK: Collins, 1969; Bunty
Felse #3; George Felse #7
The knocker on death's door.
Morrow, 1971; UK: Macmillan,
1970; George Felse #8
The leper of St. Giles. Morrow,
1982; Brother Cadfael #5
Monk's-hood. Morrow, 1981; UK:
Macmillan, 1980; Brother Cadfael

A morbid taste for bones. Morrow, 1978; UK: Macmillan, 1977; Brother Cadfael #1

Mourning Raga. Morrow, 1970; UK: Macmillan, 1969; Dominic Felse #8

One corpse too many. Morrow, 1980; UK: Macmillan, 1979; Brother Cadfael #2

The piper on the mountain. Morrow, 1966; UK: Collins, 1966; Tossa Terrell; Dominic Felse #5

Rainbow's end. Morrow, 1979; UK: Macmillan, 1979; George Felse #10

Saint Peter's Fair. Morrow, 1981; Brother Cadfael

The sanctuary sparrow. Morrow, 1983; Brother Cadfael #7

The virgin in ice. Morrow, 1983; Brother Cadfael #6

Where there's a will. Doubleday, 1960; UK: The will and the deed. Collins, 1960; George Felse #2

Who lies here? Morrow, 1965; UK: A nice derangement of epitaphs. Collins, 1965; George Felse #5; Bunty Felse #1; Dominic Felse #4

PETERS, WILLIAM, see PETERS, BILL

PETIEVICH, GERALD

The quality of the informant. Arbor House, 1985; Charles Carr

To die in Beverly Hills. Arbor House, 1983; Charles Carr

PETRIE, RHONA (pseud. of Eileen Marie Duell Buchanan, 1922 --)

Death in Deakins Wood. Dodd, 1964; UK: Gollancz, 1963; Marcus MacLurg #1

MacLurg goes west. UK: Gollancz, 1968; Marcus MacLurg #4

Murder by precedent. UK: Gollancz, 1964; Marcus MacLurg #2

Running deep. UK: Gollancz, 1965; Marcus MacLurg #3

PETTEE, F. M., 1888 --

The Palgrave mummy. Payson and Clarke, 1929; UK: Skeffington, 1929; Digby Gresham

PHILBRICK, W. R.

Shadow kills. Beaufort, 1985

Slow dancer. St. Martin's, 1984; Connie Kale

PHILIP, LORAINE

Death wishes. St. Martin's, 1983

PHILIPS, JUDSON. For other mysteries by this author, see PENTECOST, HUGH (pseud.)

The black glass city. Dodd, 1965; UK: Gollancz, 1965; Peter Styles #2

Death delivers a postcard. Washburn, 1939; UK: Hurst, 1940; Carole Trevor #2; Max Blythe #2

The death syndicate. Washburn, 1938; UK: Hurst, 1939; Carole Trevor #1; Max Blythe #1

Escape a killer. Dodd, 1971; UK: Gollancz, 1972; Peter Styles #8

The fourteenth trump. Dodd, 1942; UK: Hale, 1951; Coyle #2; Donovan #2

Hot summer killing. Dodd, 1968; UK: Gollancz, 1969; Peter Styles #6

The larkspur conspiracy. Dodd, 1973; UK: Gollancz, 1974; Peter Styles #10

The laughter trap. Dodd, 1964; UK: Gollancz, 1965; Peter Styles #1

A murder arranged. Dodd, 1978; UK: Gollancz, 1979; Peter Styles #13

Murder in marble. Dodd, 1940; UK: Hale, 1949

Nightmare at dawn. Dodd, 1970; UK: Gollancz, 1971; Peter Styles #7

Odds on the hot seat. Dodd, 1941; UK: Hale, 1946; Coyle #1; Donovan #1

The power killers. Dodd, 1974; UK: Gollancz, 1975; Peter Styles #11

Target for tragedy. Dodd, 1982; Peter Styles

Thursday's folly. Dodd, 1967; UK: Gollancz, 1968; Peter Styles #5

The twisted people. Dodd, 1965; UK: Gollancz, 1965; Peter Styles #3

The vanishing senator. Dodd, 1972; UK: Gollancz, 1973; Peter Styles #9

Walk a crooked mile. Dodd, 1975; UK: Gollancz, 1976; Peter Styles #12

Why murder? Dodd, 1979; UK: Hale, 1980; Peter Styles #14

The wings of madness. Dodd, 1966; UK: Gollancz, 1967; Peter Styles #4

PHILIPS, MEREDITH
  Death spiral: murder at the Winter
    Olympics. Perseverance Press, 1984
PHILLIPS, DENNIS, see CHAMBERS, PETER
  (pseud.)
PHILLIPS, GERALD WILLIAMS, see
  HUNTINGTON, JOHN (pseud.)
PHILLIPS, STELLA, 1927 --
  Death in sheep's clothing. Walker,
    1983
PHILLPOTTS, EDEN, 1862-1960. For
  other mysteries by this author, see
  HEXT, HARRINGTON (pseud.)
  The anniversary murder. Dutton,
    1936; UK: Physician, heal thyself.
    Hutchinson, 1935
  The book of Avis. UK: Hutchinson,
    1936; Avis Bryden #4
  The Bred in the bone. Macmillan,
    1933; UK: Hutchinson, 1932; Avis
    Bryden #1
  The captain's curio. Macmillan,
    1933; UK: Hutchinson, 1933; Insp.
    Midwinter
  "Found drowned." Macmillan, 1931;
    UK: Hutchinson, 1931
  The grey room. Macmillan, 1921; UK:
    Hurst, 1921; Peter Hardcastle
  Jig-saw. Macmillan, 1926; UK: The
    Marylebone miser. Hutchinson,
    1926; Joseph Ambrose; John
    Ringrose #2
  The jury. Macmillan, 1927; UK:
    Hutchinson, 1927
  Monkshood. Macmillan, 1939; UK:
    Methuen, 1939; Dr. Thorne
  My adventure in the Flying Scotsman.
    Aspen, 1976; UK: Hogg, 1888
  The red Redmaynes. Macmillan, 1922;
    UK: Hutchinson, 1923; Peter
    Ganns
  A shadow passes. Macmillan, 1934;
    UK: Hutchinson, 1933; Avis Bryden
    #2
  They were seven. Macmillan, 1945;
    UK: Hutchinson, 1944
  A voice from the dark. Macmillan,
    1925; UK: Hutchinson, 1925; John
    Ringrose #1
  Witch's cauldron. Macmillan, 1933;
    UK: Hutchinson, 1933; Avis Bryden
    #3

PICANO, FELICE, 1944 --
  The lure. Delacorte, 1979; UK: New
    English Library, 1981; Noel
    Cummings
PIKE, ROBERT L. (pseud.). See also
  FISH, ROBERT L.
  Bank job. Doubleday, 1974; UK:
    Hale, 1975; Jim Reardon #3
  Deadline: 2 AM. Doubleday, 1976;
    UK: Hale, 1977; Jim Reardon #4
  The gremlin's grampa. Doubleday,
    1972; Jim Reardon #2
  Mute witness. Doubleday, 1963; UK:
    Duetsch, 1965; Lt. Clancy #1
  Police blotter. Doubleday, 1965;
    UK: Duetsch, 1966; Lt. Clancy #3
  The quarry. Doubleday, 1964; Lt.
    Clancy #2
  Reardon. Doubleday, 1970; Jim
    Reardon #1
PIKSER, JEREMY
  Junk on the hill. Carroll & Graf,
    1985; Joe Posner #1
PILGRIM, CHAD
  The silent slain. Abelard-Schuman,
    1958; UK: Abelard-Schuman, 1958;
    Matt Ruffins
PINES, PAUL
  The tin angel. Morrow, 1983; Pablo
    Waitz; Maria Ponce
PIPER, EVELYN (pseud. of Merriam
  Modell, 1908 --)
  The naked murderer. Atheneum, 1962
  The plot. Simon & Schuster, 1951;
    UK: Boardman, 1952
  The stand-in. Washburn, 1970
PIPER, PETER
  The corpse that came back. Random
    House, 1954; UK: Death in the
    canongate. Hodder, 1952; Insp.
    Gray
PIPER, THEO (pseud. of Theo Lang)
PLATT, KIN, 1911 --
  Match point for murder. Random
    House, 1975; Max Roper
PLAYER, ROBERT (pseud. of Robert
  Furneaux Jordan, 1905-1978)
  The ingenious Mr. Stone. Rinehart,
    1946; UK: Gollancz, 1945
  Oh! Where are Bloody Mary's
    earrings? Harper, 1973; UK:
    Gollancz, 1972

PLUM, MARY
  Dead man's secret. Harper, 1931;
    UK: Eyre, 1931; John Smith
  The killing of Judge MacFarlane.
    Harper, 1930; UK: Eyre, 1930; John
    Smith
  Murder at the hunting club. Harper,
    1932; UK: Eyre, 1932
  Murder at the World's Fair. Harper,
    1933; UK: The broken vase mystery.
    Eyre, 1933; John Smith
  Murder of a red-haired man. Arcadia
    House, 1952; UK: Eyre, 1951
  State Department cat. Doubleday,
    1945; UK: Eyre, 1946
  Susanna, don't you cry! Doubleday,
    1946
POATE, ERNEST M.
  Behind locked doors. Chelsea, 1923;
    Dr. Bentiron
  Dr. Bentiron, detective. Chelsea,
    1930; Dr. Bentiron
  The trouble at Pinelands. Chelsea,
    1922
POE, EDGAR ALLAN, JR., 1896-
  The house party murders. Lippincott,
    1940
POPKIN, ZELDA, 1898-1983
  Dead man's gift. Lippincott, 1941;
    UK: Hutchinson, 1948; Mary Carner
    #4
  A death of innocence. Lippincott,
    1971; UK: Allen, 1972
  Death wears a white gardenia.
    Lippincott, 1938; UK: Hutchinson,
    1939; Mary Carner #1
  Murder in the mist. Lippincott,
    1940; UK: Hutchinson, 1941; Mary
    Carner #3
  No crime for a lady. Lippincott,
    1942; Mary Carner #5
  Time off for murder. Lippincott,
    1940; UK: Hutchinson, 1940; Mary
    Carner #2
PORLOCK, MARTIN (pseud.), see
  MACDONALD, PHILIP
PORTER, JOYCE, 1924-
  The cart before the crime. UK:
    Weidenfeld, 1979; Constance
    Morrison-Burke #5
  Dead easy for Dover. St. Martin's,
    1979; UK: Weidenfeld, 1978;
    Wilfred Dover #8

  Dover and the claret tappers. UK:
    Weidenfeld, 1977; Wilfred Dover
    #7
  Dover and the unkindest cut of
    all. Scribner's, 1967; UK: Cape,
    1967; Wilfred Dover #4
  Dover beats the band. UK:
    Weidenfeld, 1980; Wilfred Dover
    #9
  Dover goes to Pott. Scribner's,
    1968; UK: Cape, 1968; Wilfred
    Dover #5
  Dover one. Scribner's, 1964; UK:
    Cape, 1964; Wilfred Dover #1
  Dover strikes again. McKay, 1973;
    UK: Weidenfeld, 1970; Wilfred
    Dover #7
  Dover three. Scribner's, 1966; UK:
    Cape, 1965; Wilfred Dover #3
  Dover two. Scribner's, 1965; UK:
    Cape, 1965; Wilfred Dover #2
  It's murder with Dover. McKay,
    1973; UK: Weidenfeld, 1973;
    Wilfred Dover #6
  A meddler and her murder. McKay,
    1973; UK: Weidenfeld, 1972;
    Constance Morrison-Burke #2
  Neither a candle nor a pitchfork.
    McCall, 1970; UK: Weidenfeld,
    1969; Edmund Brown
  The package included murder.
    Bobbs, 1976; UK: Weidenfeld,
    1975; Constance Morrison-Burke #3
  Rather a common sort of crime.
    McCall, 1970; UK: Weidenfeld,
    1970; Constance Morrison-Burke #1
  Sour cream with everything.
    Scribner's, 1966; UK: Cape, 1966;
    Edmund Brown
  Who the heck is Sylvia? UK:
    Weidenfeld, 1977; Constance
    Morrison-Burke #4
POSNER, RICHARD, see CASTOIRE, MARIE
  and POSNER, RICHARD
POST, MELVILLE DAVISSON, 1869-1930
  The Bradmoor murder. Sears, 1929;
    UK: The garden in Asia.
    Brentano's, 1929; Henry Marquis
    #2
  The complete Uncle Abner.
    University of California
    Extension, 1977; Uncle Abner #3
  The corrector of destinies. Clode,
    1908; Randolph Mason #3

The man of last resorts; or, the client of Randolph Mason. Putnam, 1897; Randolph Mason #2

The methods of Uncle Abner. Aspen, 1974; Uncle Abner #2

The silent witness. Farrar, 1930; Col. Braxton

The sleuth of St. James's Square. Appleton, 1920; Henry Marquis #1

The strange schemes of Randolph Mason. Putnam, 1896; Randolph Mason

Uncle Abner, master of mysteries. Appleton, 1918; Uncle Abner #1

POST, MORTIMER (pseud. of Walter Blair, 1900 --)

Candidate for murder. Doubleday, Doran, 1936; Lowell Gaylord

POTTER, GEORGE WILLIAM, JR, 1930 -- , see WITHERS, E. L. (pseud.)

POTTER, JEREMY, 1922-

The dance of death. UK: Constable, 1968; Insp. Hiscock

Death in office. UK: Constable, 1965; Insp. Hiscock

Hazard chase. UK: Constable, 1964

A trail of blood. McCall, 1971; UK: Constable, 1970

POTTS, JEAN, 1910-

An affair of the heart. Scribner's, 1970; UK: Gollancz, 1970

Death of a stray cat. Scribner's, 1955; UK: Gollancz, 1955

The diehard. Scribner's, 1956; UK: Gollancz, 1956

Go lovely rose. Scribner's, 1954; UK: Gollancz, 1955; Sheriff Jeffries; Mr. Pigeon

The troublemaker. Scribner's, 1972; UK: Gollancz, 1973

POU, GENEVIEVE LONG, 1919 -- , see HOLDEN, GENEVIEVE (pseud.)

POWELL, P. H.

Murder premeditated. Roy, 1958; UK: Jenkins, 1951

POWELL, RICHARD, 1908-

False colors. Simon & Schuster, 1955; UK: Hodder, 1956

A shot in the dark. Simon & Schuster, 1952; UK: Leave murder to me. Hodder, 1952

POWERS, ELIZABETH

All that glitters. Doubleday, 1981; Viera Kolarova

POWERS, JAMES

Estate of grace. Harper, 1979; Tom Parcher

PRATT, ELEANOR BLAKE ATKINSON COX, 1899 -- , see BLAKE, ELEANOR A.

PRESCOTT, H. F. M., 1896-

Dead and not buried. Macmillan, 1954; UK: Constable, 1938; Sgt. Tucker

PRICE, ANTHONY, 1928-

Tomorrow's ghost. Doubleday, 1979; UK: Gollancz, 1979; Frances Fitzgibbon

PRIESTLY, J. B., 1894-

Salt is leaving. Harper, 1975; UK: Pan, 1966; Lionel Humphrey Salt; Maggie Culthorpe

Saturn over the water.... Doubleday, 1961; UK: Heinemann, 1961; Tim Bedford

PRILEY, MARGARET, see HUBBARD, MARGARET ANN (pseud.)

PRIOR, ALLAN

The interrogators. Simon & Schuster, 1965; UK: Cassell, 1965; Jack Eaves

PROCTER, MAURICE, 1906-1973

A body to spare. Harper, 1962; UK: Hutchinson, 1962; Harry Martineau #7

The devil was handsome. Harper, 1961; UK: Hutchinson, 1961; Harry Martineau #6

Devil's dues. Harper, 1960; UK: Hutchinson, 1960; Harry Martineau #5

Exercise Hoodwink. Harper, 1967; UK: Hutchinson, 1967; Harry Martineau #13

The graveyard Rolls. Harper, 1964; UK: Moonlight flitting. Hutchinson, 1963; Harry Martineau #8

Hideaway. Harper, 1968; UK: Hutchinson, 1968; Harry Martineau #14

His weight in gold. Harper, 1966; UK: Hutchinson, 1966; Harry Martineau #11

Homicide blonde. Harper, 1965; UK: Death has a shadow. Hutchinson, 1965; Harry Martineau #10

Killer at large. Harper, 1959; UK: Hutchinson, 1959; Harry Martineau #4

Man in ambush. Harper, 1959; UK: Hutchinson, 1958; Harry Martineau #3

The midnight plumber. Harper, 1958; UK: Hutchinson, 1957; Harry Martineau #2

The pennycross murders. Harper, 1953; UK: The Chief Inspector's statement. Hutchinson, 1951; Philip Hunter #1

The pub crawler. Harper, 1957; UK: Hutchinson, 1956; Bill Knight

The ripper. Harper, 1956; UK: I will speak daggers. Hutchinson, 1956; Philip Hunter #2

Rogue running. Harper, 1967; UK: Hutchinson, 1967; Harry Martineau #12

Somewhere in this city. Harper, 1954; UK: Hell is a city. Hutchinson, 1954; Harry Martineau #1

Two men in twenty. Harper, 1964; UK: Hutchinson, 1964; Harry Martineau #9

PRONZINI, BILL, 1943 --. For other mysteries by this author, see FOXX, JACK (pseud.)

Bindlestiff. St. Martin's, 1983; Nameless Detective

Blowback. Random House, 1977; UK: Hale, 1978; Nameless Detective #4

Bones. St. Martin's, 1985; Nameless detective

Case file: the best of the "Nameless detective." St. Martin's, 1983; Nameless Detective

Dragonfire. St. Martin's, 1982; Nameless Detective #9

Games. Putnam, 1976; UK: Hamlyn, 1978

Labyrinth. St. Martin's, 1980; UK: Hale, 1981; Nameless Detective

Masques. Arbor House, 1981; Steven Giroux

Nightshades. St. Martin's, 1984; Nameless Detective

Quicksilver. St. Martin's, 1984; Nameless Detective

Quincannon. Walker, 1985; John Quincannon #2

Scattershot. St. Martin's, 1982; Nameless Detective #8

The snatch. Random House, 1971; UK: Hale, 1974; Nameless Detective #1

Undercurrent. Random House, 1973; UK: Hale, 1975; Nameless Detective #3

The vanished. Random House, 1973; UK: Hale, 1974; Nameless Detective #2

PRONZINI, BILL and LUTZ, JOHN

The eye. Mysterious Press, 1984; E. L. Oxman

PRONZINI, BILL and MULLER, MARCIA. See also MULLER, MARCIA and PRONZINI, BILL

Double. St. Martin's, 1984; Nameless Detective; Sharon McCone

PRONZINI, BILL and WILCOX, COLLIN

Twospot. Putnam, 1978; Nameless Detective #5; Frank Hastings

PROPPER, MILTON, 1906-1962

The blood transfusion murders. Harper, 1943; UK: Murder in sequence. Jenkins, 1947; Tommy Rankin #14

The boudoir murder. Harper, 1931; UK: And then silence. Faber, 1931; Tommy Rankin #3

The case of the cheating bride. Harper, 1938; UK: Harrap, 1939; Tommy Rankin #10

The divorce court murder. Harper, 1934; UK: Faber, 1934; Tommy Rankin #5

The election booth murder. Harper, 1935; UK: Murder at the polls. Harrap, 1936; Tommy Rankin #7

The family burial murders. Harper, 1934; UK: Harrap, 1935; Tommy Rankin #6

The great insurance murders. Harper, 1937; UK: Harrap, 1938; Tommy Rankin #9

The handwriting on the wall. Harper, 1941; UK: You can't gag the dead. Jenkins, 1939; Tommy Rankin #13

Hide the body! Harper, 1939; UK: Harrap, 1940; Tommy Rankin #11

One murdered, two dead. Harper, 1936; UK: Harrap, 1937; Tommy Rankin #8

The station wagon murder. Harrap, 1940; Tommy Rankin #12

The strange disappearance of Mary Young. Harper, 1929; UK: Harrap, 1929; Tommy Rankin #1

The student fraternity murder. Bobbs, 1932; UK: Murder of an initiate. Faber, 1933; Tommy Rankin #4

The ticker-tape murder. Harper, 1930; UK: Faber, 1930; Tommy Rankin #2

PRUITT, ALAN (pseud. of Alvin Emanuel Rose)

The restless corpse. Ziff Davis, 1947; Don Carson

Typed for a corpse. Handi-Books, 1951; Don Carson

PUNNETT, IVAR and PUNNETT, MARGARET, see SIMONS, ROGER (pseud.)

PURTILL, RICHARD L.

Mudercon. Doubleday, 1982; Athena Pierce

PYLE, A. M.

Trouble making toys. Walker, 1985; Cesar Franck

QUEEN, ELLERY (pseud. of Frederic Dannay, 1905 -- and Manfred Bennington Lee, 1905-1971). For other mysteries by this author, see ROSS, BARNABY

The adventures of Ellery Queen. Stokes, 1934; UK: Gollancz, 1935; Ellery Queen #8

American gun mystery. Stokes, 1933; UK: Death at the rodeo. Gollancz, 1933; Ellery Queen #6

And on the eighth day. Random House, 1964; UK: Gollancz, 1964; Ellery Queen #40

Calamity town. Little, 1942; UK: Gollancz, 1942; Ellery Queen #19

Calendar of crime. Little, 1952; UK: Gollancz, 1952; Ellery Queen #29

The case book of Ellery Queen. Spivak, 1945; UK: Gollancz, 1949; Ellery Queen #22

Cat of many tails. Little, 1949; UK: Gollancz, 1949; Ellery Queen #26

Challenge to the reader. Stokes, 1938

The Chinese orange mystery. Stokes, 1934; UK: Gollancz, 1934; Ellery Queen #9

Cop out. World, 1969; UK: Gollancz, 1969; Ellery Queen #49

Death of Don Juan in E. Q. queens full. Random House, 1965; UK: Gollancz, 1966; Ellery Queen #42

The devil to pay. Stokes, 1938; UK: Gollancz, 1938; Ellery Queen #13

The door between. Stokes, 1937; UK: Gollancz, 1937; Ellery Queen #12

Double, double. Little, 1950; UK: Gollancz, 1950; Ellery Queen #27

The dragon's teeth. Stokes, 1939; UK: The virgin heiress. Gollancz, 1939; Ellery Queen #16

The Dutch shoe mystery. Stokes, 1931; UK: Gollancz, 1931; Ellery Queen #4; Richard Queen

Egyptian cross mystery. Stokes, 1932; UK: Gollancz, 1932; Ellery Queen #5

Face to face. New American Library, 1967; UK: Gollancz, 1967; Ellery Queen #46

A fine and private place. World, 1971; UK: Gollancz, 1971; Ellery Queen #51

The finishing stroke. Simon & Schuster, 1958; UK: Gollancz, 1958; Ellery Queen #36

The four of hearts. Stokes, 1938; UK: Gollancz, 1939; Ellery Queen #15

The fourth side of the triangle. Random House, 1965; UK: Gollancz, 1965; Ellery Queen #44

French powder mystery. Stokes, 1930; UK: Gollancz, 1930; Ellery Queen #3

The glass village. Little, 1954; UK: Gollancz, 1954; John Shinn

Greek coffin mystery. Stokes, 1932; UK: Gollancz, 1932; Ellery Queen #1

Halfway house. Stokes, 1936; UK: Gollancz, 1936; Ellery Queen #11

The Hollywood murders. Lippincott, 1957; Ellery Queen #35

The House of Brass. New American Library, 1968; UK: Gollancz, 1968; Richard Queen; Ellery Queen #48

Inspector Queen's own case:
November sony. Simon & Schuster,
1956; UK: Gollancz, 1956; Richard
Queen; Ellery Queen #33

The king is dead. Little, 1952; UK:
Gollancz, 1952; Ellery Queen #30

The last woman in his life. World,
1970; UK: Gollancz, 1970; Ellery
Queen #50

More adventures of Ellery Queen.
Spivak, 1940; Ellery Queen #18

The murderer is a fox. Little,
1945; UK: Gollancz, 1945; Ellery
Queen #23

The new adventures of Ellery Queen.
Stokes, 1940; UK: Gollancz, 1940;
Ellery Queen #17

The origin of evil. Little, 1951;
UK: Gollancz, 1951; Ellery Queen
#28

The player on the other side.
Random House, 1963; UK: Gollancz,
1963; Ellery Queen #39

QBI: Queen's Bureau of
Investigation. Little, 1954; UK:
Gollancz, 1955; Ellery Queen #32

Q.E.D: Queen's experiments in
detection. New American Library,
1968; UK: Gollancz, 1969; Ellery
Queen #47

Queen's full. Random House, 1965;
UK: Gollancz, 1966; Ellery Queen
#41

The Roman hat mystery. Stokes, 1929;
UK: Gollancz, 1929; Richard Queen;
Ellery Queen #2

The scarlet letters. Little, 1953;
UK: Gollancz, 1953; Ellery Queen
#31

Siamese twin mystery. Stokes, 1933;
UK: Gollancz, 1934; Ellery Queen
#7

Spanish cape mystery. Stokes, 1935;
UK: Gollancz, 1935; Ellery Queen
#10

Ten days' wonder. Little, 1948; UK:
Gollancz, 1948; Ellery Queen #24

There was an old woman. Little,
1942; UK: Gollancz, 1944; Ellery
Queen #20

The Wrightsville heirs in E. Q.,
Queen's Full. Random House, 1965;
UK: Gollancz, 1966; Ellery Queen
#43

The Wrightsville murders. Little,
1956; Ellery Queen #34

QUEEN, ELLERY, ed.

The female of the species. Little,
1943; UK: Ladies in crime.

Japanese golden dozen: the
detective story world in Japan.
Charles Tuttle, 1978

The misadventures of Sherlock
Holmes. Little, 1944; Sherlock
Holmes

Sporting blood. Little, 1942

QUENTIN, PATRICK (pseud.). For other
mysteries by this author, see
PATRICK, Q. (pseud.) or STAGGE,
JONATHAN (pseud.)

Black widow. Simon & Schuster,
1952; UK: Fatal woman. Gollancz,
1953; Peter Duluth #8

Family skeletons. Random House,
1965; UK: Gollancz, 1965; Timothy
Trant #4

The follower. Simon & Schuster,
1950; UK: Gollancz, 1950

The man with two wives. Simon &
Schuster, 1955; UK: Gollancz,
1955; Timothy Trant #2

My son, the murderer. Simon &
Schuster, 1954; UK: The wife of
Ronald Sheldon. Gollancz, 1954;
Jake Duluth; Peter Duluth #9

Puzzle for fiends. Simon &
Schuster, 1946; UK: Gollancz,
1947; Peter Duluth #5

A puzzle for fools. Simon &
Schuster, 1936; UK: Gollancz,
1936; Peter Duluth #1

Puzzle for pilgrims. Simon &
Schuster, 1947; UK: Gollancz,
1948; Peter Duluth #6

Puzzle for players. Simon &
Schuster, 1938; UK: Gollancz,
1939; Peter Duluth #2

Puzzle for puppets. Simon &
Schuster, 1944; UK: Gollancz,
1944; Peter Duluth #3

Puzzle for wantons. Simon &
Schuster, 1945; UK: Gollancz,
1946; Peter Duluth #4

Run to death. Simon & Schuster,
1948; UK: Gollancz, 1948; Peter
Duluth #7

Shadow of guilt. Random House,
1959; UK: Gollancz, 1959; Timothy
Trant #3

QUEST, ERICA
The October cabaret. Doubleday,
1979; Tess Pennicott
The silver castle. Doubleday, 1978
QUILL, MONICA (pseud.). See also
MCINERNY, RALPH
And then there was nun. Vanguard,
1984; Mary Teresa
Let us prey. Vanguard, 1982; Mary
Teresa
Nun of the above. Vanguard, 1985;
Mary Teresa
QUIRK, LESLIE, see WINSLOW, HORATIO
and QUIRK, LESLIE W.

RADLEY, SHEILA
The Chief Inspector's daughter.
Scribner's, 1980; Douglas
Quantrill
The Chief Inspector's statement.
Scribner's, 1980; UK: Gollancz,
1981; Douglas Quantrill
Death in the morning. Scribner's,
1979; UK: Death and the maiden.
Hamilton, 1978; Douglas Quantrill
The quiet road to death. Scribner's,
1984; Douglas Quantrill
A talent for destruction.
Scribner's, 1982; Douglas
Quantrill
RAE, HUGH C., 1935 --
The house at Balnesmoor. Coward
McCann, 1969; UK: A few small
bones. Bland, 1968; Insp. McCaig
The marksman. Coward McCann, 1971;
UK: Constable, 1971
The rookery. St. Martin's, 1975;
UK: Constable, 1974
RAMPO, EDOGAWA (pseud. of Taro Hirai,
1894 --)
Japanese tales of mystery and
imagination. Charles Tuttle, 1956
RANDISI, ROBERT J.
Full contact. St. Martin's, 1984;
Miles Jacoby
RANDOLPH, MARION (pseud. of Marie
Fried Rodell, 1912-1975)
Breathe no more. Holt, 1940; UK:
Heinemann, 1940
Grim grow the lilacs. Holt, 1941;
UK: Museum Press, 1943
This'll kill you. Holt, 1940; UK:
Museum Press, 1944

RANSOME, STEPHEN (pseud.). For other
mysteries by this author, see
DAVIS, FREDERICK C.
Alias his wife. Dodd, 1964; UK:
Gollancz, 1965; Lee Barcello #2
Hear no evil. Doubleday, 1953; UK:
Gollancz, 1954; Steve Ransome #1
The hidden hour. Dodd, 1966; UK:
Gollancz, 1966; Lee Barcello #4
One-man jury. Dodd, 1964; UK:
Gollancz, 1965; Lee Barcello #1
The shroud off her back. Doubleday,
1953; UK: Gollancz, 1953; Steve
Ransome #2
The sin file. Dodd, 1965; UK:
Gollancz, 1966; Lee Barcello #3
Trap no. 6. Doubleday, 1971; UK:
Gollancz, 1972; Lee Barcello #5
RAPHAEL, CHAIM, see DAVEY, JOCELYN
(pseud.)
RATHBONE, JULIAN, 1935 --
Watching the detectives. Pantheon,
1984; Jan Aryand #3
RAWSON, CLAYTON, 1906-1971. For
other mysteries by this author, see
TOWNE, STUART (pseud.)
Death from a top hat. Putnam,
1938; UK: Collins, 1938; The
Great Merlini #1
The footprints on the ceiling.
Putnam, 1939; UK: Collins, 1939;
The Great Merlini #2
The Great Merlini. Gregg, 1979;
The Great Merlini #5
The headless lady. Putnam, 1940;
UK: Collins, 1942; The Great
Merlini #3
No coffin for the corpse. Little,
1942; UK: Stacey, 1972; The Great
Merlini #4
RAY, ROBERT J.
Cage of mirrors. Lippincott, 1980;
Yank Taggart
RAYMOND, CLIFFORD S., 1875 --
The men on the dead man's chest.
Bobbs, 1930; John Stanton
REA, M. P.
Compare these dead! Doubleday,
1941; Lt. Powledge
A curtain for crime. Doubleday,
1941; Lt. Powledge
Death of an angel. Doubleday,
1943; Lt. Powledge

Death walks the dry Tortugas.
Doubleday, 1942
REED, ISHMAEL, 1938 --
The last days of Louisiana Red.
Random House, 1974; Papa La Bas #2
Mumbo-jumbo. Doubleday, 1972; Papa
La Bas #1
REES, ARTHUR J.
Mystery at Peak House. Dodd, 1933;
UK: Peak House. Jarrolds, 1933
The shrieking pit. Lane, 1919; UK:
Lane, 1919; David Colwyn
Tragedy at Twelvetrees. Dodd, 1931;
UK: Lane, 1931; Insp. Luckcraft
REES, DILWYN (pseud.), see DANIEL,
GLYN
REEVE, ARTHUR B., 1880-1936
The adventuress. Harper, 1917; UK:
Collins, 1918; Craig Kennedy #8
Atavar. Harper, 1924; Craig Kennedy
#12
The Boy Scouts' Craig Kennedy.
Harper, 1925; Craig Kennedy #15
The clutching hand. Reilly and Lee,
1934; Craig Kennedy #19
Constance Dunlap, woman detective.
Harper, 1913; UK: Hodder, 1916;
Constance Dunlap
Craig Kennedy listens in. Harper,
1923; UK: Hodder, 1924; Craig
Kennedy #11
Craig Kennedy on the farm. Harper,
1925; Craig Kennedy #14
The dream doctor. Hearst's
International Library, 1914; UK:
Hodder, 1916
The ear in the wall. Hearst's
International Library, 1916; UK:
Hodder, 1917; Craig Kennedy #7
Enter Craig Kennedy. Macaulay,
1935; Craig Kennedy #20
The exploits of Elaine. Hearst's
International Library, 1915; UK:
Hodder, 1915; Craig Kennedy #4
The film mystery. Harper, 1921; UK:
Hodder, 1922; Craig Kennedy #10
The fourteen points. Harper, 1925;
Craig Kennedy #13
The gold of the gods. Hearst's
International Library, 1915; UK:
Hodder, 1916; Craig Kennedy #3
The kidnap club. Macaulay, 1932;
Craig Kennedy #18

Pandora. Harper, 1926; Craig
Kennedy #17
The radio detective. Grosset, 1926;
Craig Kennedy #16
The romance of Elaine. Hearst's
International Library, 1916; UK:
Hodder, 1916; Craig Kennedy #5
The silent bullet. Dodd, 1910; UK:
The black hand. Nash, 1912; Craig
Kennedy #1
The soul scar. Harper, 1919; Craig
Kennedy #9
The triumph of Elaine. UK: Hodder,
1916; Craig Kennedy #6
The war terror. Hearst's
International Library, 1915; UK:
Craig Kennedy, detective.
Simpkin, 1916; Craig Kennedy #2
REEVES, JOHN
Murder before matins. Doubleday,
1984; Andrew Coggin; Fred Sump
REEVES, ROBERT
Doubting Thomas. Crown, 1985;
Thomas C. Theron
REILLY, HELEN, 1891-1962
All concerned notified. Doubleday,
1939; UK: Heinemann, 1939;
Christopher McKee #8
The canvas dagger. Random House,
1956; UK: Hale, 1957; Christopher
McKee #27
Certain sleep. Random House, 1961;
UK: Hale, 1962; Christopher McKee
#31
Compartment K. Random House, 1955;
UK: Hale, 1956; Christopher McKee
#26
The day she died. Random House,
1962; UK: Hale, 1963; Christopher
McKee #32
The dead can tell. Random House,
1940; Christopher McKee #10
Dead for a ducat. Doubleday, 1939;
UK: Heinemann, 1939; Christopher
McKee #9
Dead man control. Doubleday, 1936;
UK: Heinemann, 1937; Christopher
McKee #7
Death demands an audience.
Doubleday, 1940; Christopher
McKee #11
The diamond feather. Doubleday,
1930; Christopher McKee #1

Ding, dong bell. Random House, 1958; UK: Hale, 1959; Christopher McKee #28

The doll's trunk murder. Farrar, 1932; UK: Hutchinson, 1933; Christopher McKee #3

The double man. Random House, 1952; UK: Museum Press, 1954; Christopher McKee #23

The farmhouse. Random House, 1947; UK: Hammond, 1950; Christopher McKee #19

Follow me. Random House, 1960; UK: Hale, 1961; Christopher McKee #30

Lament for the bride. Random House, 1951; UK: Museum Press, 1954; Christopher McKee #22

The line-up. Doubleday, 1934; UK: Cassell, 1935; Christopher McKee #4

McKee of Centre Street. Doubleday, 1934; Christopher McKee #5

Mr. Smith's hat. Doubleday, 1936; UK: Cassell, 1936; Christopher McKee #6

Mourned on Sunday. Random House, 1941; Christopher McKee #13

Murder at Arroways. Random House, 1950; UK: Museum Press, 1952; Christopher McKee #21

Murder in shinbone alley. Doubleday, 1940; Christopher McKee #12

Murder in the news. Doubleday, 1931; Christopher McKee #2

Murder on Angler's Island. Random House, 1945; UK: Hammond, 1948; Christopher McKee #17

Name your poison. Random House, 1942; Christopher McKee #15

Not me, Inspector. Random House, 1959; UK: Hale, 1960; Christopher McKee #29

The opening door. Random House, 1944; Christopher McKee #16

The silver leopard. Random House, 1946; UK: Hammond, 1959; Christopher McKee #18

Staircase 4. Random House, 1949; UK: Hammond, 1950; Christopher McKee #20

Tell her it's murder. Random House, 1954; UK: Museum Press, 1955; Christopher McKee #25

Three women in black. Random House, 1941; Christopher McKee #14

The velvet hand. Random House, 1953; UK: Museum Press, 1955; Christopher McKee #24

REILLY, MARY, see MCMULLEN, MARY (pseud.)

RENDELL, RUTH, 1930 --

The best man to die. Doubleday, 1970; UK: Long, 1969; Reginald Wexford #4

Death notes. Pantheon, 1981; Reginald Wexford #13

A demon in my view. Doubleday, 1977; UK: Hutchinson, 1976; Anthony Johnson

The face of trespass. Doubleday, 1974; UK: Hutchinson, 1974

From Doon with death. Doubleday, 1965; UK: Long, 1964; Reginald Wexford #1

A guilty thing surprised. Doubleday, 1970; UK: Hutchinson, 1970; Reginald Wexford #5

A judgement in stone. Doubleday, 1978; UK: Hutchinson, 1977

The killing doll. Pantheon, 1984

The lake of darkness. Doubleday, 1980; UK: Hutchinson, 1980

Make death love me. Doubleday, 1979; UK: Hutchinson, 1979; Reginald Wexford #11

Master of the moor. Pantheon, 1982

Means of evil. Doubleday, 1980; UK: Hutchinson, 1979; Reginald Wexford #12

Murder being once done. Doubleday, 1972; UK: Hutchinson, 1972; Reginald Wexford #7

No more dying then. Doubleday, 1972; UK: Hutchinson, 1971; Reginald Wexford #6

Shake hands for ever. Doubleday, 1975; UK: Hutchinson, 1975; Reginald Wexford #9

Sins of the father. Doubleday, 1967; UK: Long, 1967; Reginald Wexford #2

A sleeping life. Doubleday, 1978; UK: Hutchinson, 1978; Reginald Wexford #10

Some lie and some die. Doubleday, 1973; UK: Hutchinson, 1973; Reginald Wexford #8

Speaker of Mandarin. Pantheon, 1983; Reginald Wexford

Tree of hands. Pantheon, 1985

An unkindness of ravens. Pantheon, 1985; Reginald Wexford #13

Wolf to the slaughter. Doubleday, 1968; UK: Long, 1967; Reginald Wexford #3

RENFROE, MARTHA KAY, 1938 -- , see WREN, M. K. (pseud.)

RENNERT, MAGGIE, 1922 --

Circle of death. Prentice-Hall, 1974; Guy Silvestri #1

Operation Alcestis. Prentice-Hall, 1975; Guy Silvestri #2

RESNICOW, HERBERT

The Gold deadline. St. Martin's, 1984; Alexander Gold #2; Norma Gold #2

The Gold frame. St. Martin's, 1985; Alexander Gold; Norma Gold

The Gold solution. St. Martin's, 1983; Alexander Gold #1; Norma Gold #1

REYNOLDS, WILLIAM J.

The Nebraska quotient. St. Martin's, 1984; Nebraska

RHODE, JOHN (pseud. of Cecil John Charles Street, 1884-1965). For other mysteries by this author, see BURTON, MILES (pseud.)

The affair of the substitute doctor. Dodd, 1951; UK: Dr. Goodwood's locum. Bles, 1951; Lancelot Priestly #53

Blackthorn House. Dodd, 1949; UK: Bles, 1949; Jimmy Waghorn; Lancelot Priestly #48

Body unidentified. Dodd, 1938; UK: Proceed with caution. Collins, 1937; Jimmy Waghorn; Insp. Hanslet; Lancelot Priestly #27

The case of the forty thieves. Dodd, 1954; UK: Death at the inn. Bles, 1953; Lancelot Priestly #57

The Claverton affair. Dodd, 1933; UK: The Claverton mystery. Collins, 1933; Lancelot Priestly #14

The corpse in the car. Dodd, 1935; UK: Bles, 1935; Lancelot Priestly #20

Dead men at the folly. Dodd, 1932; UK: Collins, 1932; Insp. Hanslet; Lancelot Priestly #13

Dead of the night. Dodd, 1942; UK: Night exercise. Collins, 1942

Dead on the track. Dodd, 1943; UK: Collins, 1943; Lancelot Priestly #37

Death at breakfast. Dodd, 1936; UK: Collins, 1936; Jimmy Waghorn; Lancelot Priestly #23

Death at the dance. Dodd, 1952; UK: Bles, 1952; Lancelot Priestly #55

Death at the helm. Dodd, 1941; UK: Collins, 1941; Lancelot Priestly #34

Death in Harley Street. Dodd, 1946; UK: Bles, 1946; Lancelot Priestly #42

Death in Wellington Road. Dodd, 1952; UK: Bles, 1952; Lancelot Priestly #54

Death invades the meeting. Dodd, 1944; UK: Collins, 1944; Lancelot Priestly #39

Death of a bridegroom. Dodd, 1958; UK: Bles, 1957; Lancelot Priestly #64

Death of an artist. Dodd, 1956; UK: An artist dies. Bles, 1956; Jimmy Waghorn; Lancelot Priestly #62

Death of an author. Dodd, 1948; UK: Bles, 1947; Lancelot Priestly #44

Death on the boat-train. Dodd, 1940; UK: Collins, 1940; Lancelot Priestly #32

Death on the lawn. Dodd, 1955; UK: Bles, 1954; Lancelot Priestly #58

Death pays a dividend. Dodd, 1939; UK: Collins, 1939; Insp. Hanslet; Jimmy Waghorn; Lancelot Priestly #31

Death sits on the board. Dodd, 1937; UK: Death on the board. Collins, 1937; Lancelot Priestly #26

Death takes a partner. Dodd, 1959; UK: Bles, 1958; Lancelot Priestly #66

Delayed payment. Dodd, 1956; UK: Death of a godmother. Bles, 1955; Lancelot Priestly #60

Dr. Priestly investigates. Dodd, 1930; UK: Bles, 1930; Lancelot Priestly #9

Dr. Priestly lays a trap. Dodd, 1933; UK: The motor rally mystery. Collins, 1933; Lancelot Priestly #15

Dr. Priestly's quest. UK: Bles, 1926; Lancelot Priestly #2

Double identities. Dodd, 1950; UK: The two graphs. Bles, 1950; Lancelot Priestly #51

The Dovebury murders. Dodd, 1954; UK: Bles, 1954; Lancelot Priestly #59

The Ellerby case. Dodd, 1927; UK: Bles, 1926; Lancelot Priestly #3

The elm-tree murder. Dodd, 1939; UK: Death on Sunday. Collins, 1939; Jimmy Waghorn; Lancelot Priestly #30

Experiment in crime. Dodd, 1947; UK: Nothing but the truth. Bles, 1947; Lancelot Priestly #45; Jimmy Waghorn

The fatal garden. Dodd, 1949; UK: Up the garden path. Bles, 1949; Lancelot Priestly #49

The fatal pool. Dodd, 1961; UK: Bles, 1960; Lancelot Priestly #70

The fire at Greycombe Farm. Dodd, 1932; UK: Mystery at Greycombe Farm. Collins, 1932; Lancelot Priestly #12

The fourth bomb. Dodd, 1942; UK: Collins, 1942; Lancelot Priestly #36; Jimmy Waghorn

Grave matters. Dodd, 1955; UK: The domestic agency. Bles, 1955; Jimmy Waghorn; Lancelot Priestly #61

The hanging woman. Dodd, 1931; UK: Collins, 1931; Lancelot Priestly #10

The harvest murder. Dodd, 1937; UK: Death in the hop fields. Collins, 1937; Lancelot Priestly #25

Hendon's first case. Dodd, 1935; UK: Collins, 1935; Jimmy Waghorn; Insp. Hanslet; Lancelot Priestly #21

The house on Tallard Ridge. Dodd, 1929; UK: Bles, 1929; Lancelot Priestly #6

In the face of the verdict. Dodd, 1936; UK: In face of the verdict. Collins, 1936; Lancelot Priestly #24

Invisible weapons. Dodd, 1938; UK: Collins, 1938; Lancelot Priestly #29

The last suspect. Dodd, 1951; UK: Family affairs. Bles, 1950; Lancelot Priestly #50; Jimmy Waghorn

Licensed for murder. Dodd, 1959; UK: Bles, 1958; Lancelot Priestly #68

The links in the chain. Dodd, 1948; UK: The paper bag. Bles, 1948; Jimmy Waghorn; Lancelot Priestly #46

Men die at Cyprus Lodge. Dodd, 1944; UK: Collins, 1943; Lancelot Priestly #38

Murder at Bratton Grange. Dodd, 1929; UK: The Davidson case. Bles, 1929; Lancelot Priestly #7; Insp. Hanslet

Murder at Derivale. Dodd, 1958; UK: Bles, 1958; Jimmy Waghorn; Lancelot Priestly #67

Murder at Lilac Cottage. Dodd, 1940; UK: Collins, 1940; Lancelot Priestly #33; Harold Merefield

Murder at the motor show. Dodd, 1936; UK: Mystery at Olympia. Collins, 1935; Lancelot Priestly #22

The murders in Praed Street. Dodd, 1928; UK: Bles, 1928; Lancelot Priestly #4

The mysterious suspect. Dodd, 1953; UK: By registered post. Bles, 1953; Lancelot Priestly #56; Harold Merefield

Opening verdict. Dodd, 1957; UK: Bles, 1956; Jimmy Waghorn; Lancelot Priestly #63

The Paddington mystery. UK: Bles, 1925; Lancelot Priestly #1; Harold Merefield

Peril at Cranbury Hall. Dodd, 1930; UK: Bles, 1930; Lancelot Priestly #8; Insp. Hanslet; Harold Merefield

Poison for one. Dodd, 1934; UK: Collins, 1934; Lancelot Priestly #17

Robbing with violence. Dodd, 1957; UK: Bles, 1957; Lancelot Priestly #65

The Rothborne mystery. Dodd, 1934; UK: Collins, 1934; Lancelot Priestly #18

The secret meeting. Dodd, 1952; UK: Bles, 1951; Lancelot Priestly #52

The secret of the lake house. Dodd, 1946; UK: The lake house. Bles, 1946; Lancelot Priestly #43

Shadow of a crime. Dodd, 1945; UK: The bricklayer's arms. Collins, 1945; Lancelot Priestly #40; Jimmy Waghorn

Shadow of an alibi. Dodd, 1949; UK: The telephone call. Bles, 1948; Lancelot Priestly #47

Shot at dawn. Dodd, 1935; UK: Collins, 1934; Lancelot Priestly #19

Signal for death. Dodd, 1941; UK: They watched by night. Collins, 1941; Lancelot Priestly #35

Three cousins die. Dodd, 1960; UK: Bles, 1959; Lancelot Priestly #69; Jimmy Waghorn

Too many suspects. Dodd, 1945; UK: Vegetable duck. Collins, 1944; Jimmy Waghorn; Lancelot Priestly #41

The tower of evil. Dodd, 1938; UK: The bloody tower. Collins, 1938; Lancelot Priestly #28

Tragedy at the Unicorn. Dodd, 1928; UK: Bles, 1928; Lancelot Priestly #5; Harold Merefield

Tragedy on the line. Dodd, 1931; UK: Collins, 1931; Lancelot Priestly #11

Twice dead. Dodd, 1960; UK: Bles, 1960; Lancelot Priestly #71; Jimmy Waghorn

The vanishing diary. Dodd, 1961; UK: Bles, 1961; Lancelot Priestly #72

The Venner crime. Dodd, 1934; UK: Odhams, 1933; Lancelot Priestly #16

The white menace. McBride, 1926; UK: A.S.F.: the story of a great conspiracy. Bles, 1924

RHODE, JOHN and DICKSON, CARTER

Fatal descent. Dodd, 1939; UK: Drop to his death. Heinemann, 1939

RICE, CRAIG (pseud. of Georgianna Ann Randolph, 1908-1957). For other mysteries by this author, see VENNING, MICHAEL (pseud.)

The big midget murders. Simon & Schuster, 1942; John J. Malone #6; Jake Justus #6; Helene Justus #6

But the doctor died. Lancer, 1967; John J. Malone #14; Jake Justus #12; Helene Justus #12

The corpse steps out. Simon & Schuster, 1940; UK: Eyre, 1940; John J. Malone #2; Jake Justus #2; Helene Justus #2

Eight faces at three. Simon & Schuster, 1939; UK: Death at three. Eyre, 1939; John J. Malone #1; Jake Justus #1; Helene Justus #1

The fourth postman. Simon & Schuster, 1948; UK: Hammond, 1951; John J. Malone #9; Jake Justus #9; Helene Justus #9

Having wonderful crime. Simon & Schuster, 1943; UK: Nicholson, 1944; John J. Malone #7; Jake Justus #7; Helene Justus #7

Home sweet homicide. Simon & Schuster, 1944

Knocked for a loop. Simon & Schuster, 1957; UK: The double frame. Hammond, 1958; John J. Malone #10; Jake Justus #10; Helene Justus #10

The lucky stiff. Simon & Schuster, 1945; John J. Malone #8; Jake Justus #8; Helene Justus #8

My kingdom for a hearse. Simon & Schuster, 1957; UK: Hammond, 1959; John J. Malone #11; Jake Justus #11; Helene Justus #11

The name is Malone. Pyramid Books, 1958; UK: Hammond, 1960; John J. Malone #12

The right murder. Simon & Schuster, 1941; UK: Eyre, 1948; John J. Malone #4; Jake Justus #4; Helene Justus #4

The Sunday pigeon murders. Simon & Schuster, 1942; UK: Nicholson, 1948; Bingo Riggs #1; Handsome Kusak #1

Telefair. Bobbs, 1942

The Thursday turkey murders. Simon
& Schuster, 1943; UK: Nicholson,
1946; Bingo Riggs #2; Handsome
Kusak #2

Trial by fury. Simon & Schuster,
1941; UK: Hammond, 1950; John J.
Malone #5; Jake Justus #5; Helene
Justus #5

The wrong murder. Simon & Schuster,
1940; UK: Eyre, 1942; John J.
Malone #3; Jake Justus #3; Helene
Justus #3

RICE, CRAIG and MCBAIN, ED
The April robin murders. Random
House, 1958; UK: Hammond, 1959;
Bingo Riggs #3; Handsome Kusak #3

RICE, CRAIG and PALMER, STUART, see
PALMER, STUART and RICE CRAIG

RICH, VIRGINIA
The baked bean supper murders.
Dutton, 1983; Eugenia Potter #2

The cooking school murders. Dutton,
1982; Eugenia Potter #1

The Nantucket diet murders.
Delacorte, 1985; Eugenia Potter

RICHARDS, FRANCIS (pseud.), see
LOCKRIDGE, FRANCES and LOCKRIDGE
RICHARD or LOCKRIDGE, RICHARD or
LOCKRIDGE, RICHARD and LOCKRIDGE,
FRANCES

RIDDELL, JOHN
The John Riddell murder case.
Scribner's, 1930; Pluto Vance

RIGGS, JOHN
The last laugh. Dembner, 1984;
Garth Ryland

RINEHART, MARY ROBERTS, 1876-1958
The amazing adventures of Letitia
Carberry. Bobbs, 1911; UK: Hodder,
1919; Letitia Carberry

The case of Jennie Brice. Bobbs,
1913; UK: Hodder, 1919; Jennie
Brice

The circular staircase. Bobbs,
1908; UK: Cassell, 1909; Mr.
Jamieson

The door. Farrar, 1930; UK: Hodder,
1930; Insp. Harrison

The frightened wife and other
murder stories. Rinehart, 1953;
UK: Cassell, 1954

Haunted lady. Farrar, 1942; UK:
Cassell, 1942; Miss Pinkerton #3

The man in lower ten. Bobbs, 1909;
UK: Cassell, 1909

Mary Roberts Rinehart's crime book.
Farrar, 1933; Miss Pinkerton #2

Miss Pinkerton. Farrar, 1932; UK:
The double alibi. Cassell, 1932;
Miss Pinkerton #1

The red lamp. Doran, 1925; UK: The
mystery lamp. Hodder, 1925

The swimming pool. Rinehart, 1952;
UK: The pool. Cassell, 1952;
Terrence O'Brien

The yellow room. Farrar, 1945; UK:
Cassell, 1949; Maj. Dane

RIVETT, EDITH CAROLINE, see CARNAC,
CAROL (pseud.)

ROADARMEL, PAUL
The Kaligarh fault. Harper, 1979;
Tommy Berren

ROBERTS, WILLO DAVIS, 1928 --
The sniper. Doubleday, 1984; Jane
Madison

ROBERTSON, HELEN
Swan song. Doubleday, 1960; UK:
The Chinese goose. Macdonald,
1960; Insp. Dynes; Sgt. Benwick

ROBINSON, FRANK M., 1926 --
The power. Lippincott, 1956; UK:
Eyre, 1957

ROBINSON, LEWIS, 1886 -- , see
LIMNELIUS, GEORGE (pseud.)

ROBINSON, ROBERT, 1927 --
Landscape with dead dons. Rinehart,
1956; UK: Gollancz, 1956; Insp.
Autumn

RODELL, MARIE FRIED, see RANDOLPH,
MARION (pseud.)

ROFFMAN, JAN (pseud. of Margaret
Summerton)
A daze of fears. Doubleday, 1968

ROGERS, JOEL TOWNSLEY, 1896 --
The red right hand. Simon &
Schuster, 1960

The stopped clock. Simon &
Schuster, 1958

ROGERS, SAMUEL, 1904 --
Don't look behind you! Harper,
1944; Paul Hatfield #1

You leave me cold! Harper, 1946;
Paul Hatfield #3

You'll be sorry! Harper, 1945; UK:
Murder is grim. Hammond, 1955;
Paul Hatfield #2

ROHMER, SAX (pseud. of Arthur Henry
Sarsfield Ward, 1883-1959)
The bat flies low. Doubleday,
1935; UK: Cassell, 1935

The dream-detective. Doubleday,
1925; UK: Jarrolds, 1920; Moris
Klaw

Hangover House. Random House,
1949; UK: Jenkins, 1950

White velvet. Doubleday, 1936; UK:
Cassell, 1936

ROLLS, ANTHONY (pseud. of C. E.
Vulliamy, 1886-1971)

Clerical error. Little, 1932; UK:
The vicar's experiments. Bles,
1932

ROOF, KATHERINE M.

Murder on the Salem Road. Houghton,
1931

ROOS, AUDREY, see ROOS, KELLEY
(pseud.)

ROOS, KELLEY, (pseud. of Audrey Roos,
1912 -- and William Roos, 1911 --)

Beauty marks the spot. Dell, 1951;
Jeff Troy #9; Haila Troy #9

The blonde died dancing. Dodd,
1956; UK: She died dancing. Eyre,
1947; Connie Barton; Steve Barton

The frightened stiff. Dodd, 1942;
UK: Hale, 1951; Jeff Troy #3;
Haila Troy #3

Ghost of a chance. Wyn, 1947; Jeff
Troy #6; Haila Troy #6

If the shroud fits. Dodd, 1941; UK:
Jonathan, 1951; Jeff Troy #2;
Haila Troy #2

Made up to kill. Dodd, 1940; UK:
Made up for murder. Jarrolds,
1941; Jeff Troy #1; Haila Troy #1

Murder in any language. Wyn, 1948;
Jeff Troy #7; Haila Troy #7

Murder on Martha's Vineyard.
Walker, 1981; Nancy Brewster

One false move. Dodd, 1966; Jeff
Troy #10; Haila Troy #10

Sailor, take warning! Dodd, 1944;
UK: Hale, 1952; Jeff Troy #4;
Haila Troy #4

There was a crooked man. Dodd,
1945; UK: Hale, 1953; Jeff Troy
#5; Haila Troy #5

Triple threats. Wyn, 1949; Jeff
Troy #8; Haila Troy #8

What did Hattie see? Dodd, 1970;
UK: Cassell, 1970

ROOS, WILLIAM, see ROOS, KELLEY
(pseud.)

ROOSEVELT, ELLIOTT

The Hyde Park murder. St. Martin's,
1985; Eleanor Roosevelt #2

Murder and the First Lsdy. St.
Martin's, 1984; Eleanor Roosevelt

ROSCOE, THEODORE

Only in New England. Scribner's,
1959

To live and die in Dixie.
Scribner's, 1961

ROSE, ALVIN EMANUEL, see ALAN,
PRUITT (pseud.)

ROSEN, DOROTHY and ROSEN, SIDNEY

Death and blintzes. Walker, 1985;
Belle Appleman

Strike three you're dead. Walker,
1984; Harvey Blissberg

ROSEN, SIDNEY, see ROSEN, DOROTHY
and ROSEN, SIDNEY

ROSENBLUM, ROBERT, 1938 --

The good thief. Doubleday, 1974;
UK: Hart Davis, 1975

ROSENFELD, LULLA

Death and the I Ching. Potter, 1981

ROSS, BARNABY. For other mysteries
by this author, see QUEEN, ELLERY

Drury Lane's last case. Viking,
1933; UK: Cassell, 1933; Drury
Lane #4

The tragedy of X. Viking, 1932;
UK: Cassell, 1932; Drury Lane #1

The tragedy of Y. Viking, 1932;
UK: Cassell, 1932; Drury Lane #2

The tragedy of Z. Viking, 1933;
UK: Cassell, 1933; Drury Lane #3

ROSS, JONATHON (pseud. of John
Rossiter, 1916). For other
mysteries by this author, see
ROSSITER, JOHN

The blood running cold. UK:
Cassell, 1968; George Rogers #1

The burning of Billy Toober.
Walker, 1976; UK: Constable,
1978; George Rogers #6

Dark blue and dangerous.
Scribner's, 1981; George Rogers
#9

Dead at first hand. UK: Cassell,
1969; George Rogers #3

Dead eye. St. Martin's, 1984;
George Rogers

The deadest thing you ever saw.
McCall, 1970; UK: Cassell, 1967;
George Rogers #4

Death's head. St. Martin's, 1983;
George Rogers
Diminished by death. UK: Cassell,
1968; George Rogers #2
Here lies Nancy Frail. Saturday
Review Press, 1972; UK: Constable,
1972; George Rogers #5
"I know what it's like to die."
Walker, 1978; UK: Constable, 1976;
George Rogers #7
A rattling of old bones. UK:
Constable, 1979; George Rogers #8

ROSS, THOMAS
Missionary stew. Simon & Schuster,
1983; Morgan Citron

ROSS, Z. H., 1912 --
One corpse missing. Bobbs, 1948;
Beau Smith; Pogy Rogers
Overdue for death. Bobbs, 1947
Three down vulnerable. Bobbs, 1946;
Beau Smith; Pogy Rogers

ROSSITER, JOHN, 1916 -- . For other
mysteries by this author, see ROSS,
JONATHON
The deadly gold. Walker, 1975; UK:
The golden virgin. Constable,
1975; Roger Tallis #4
The deadly green. Walker, 1971; UK:
Cassell, 1970; Roger Tallis #2
The murder makers. Walker, 1977;
UK: Cassell, 1970; Roger Tallis #1
A rope for General Dietz. Walker,
1972; UK: Constable, 1972; Roger
Tallis #3

ROSTEN, LEO, 1900 --
King Silky! Harper & Row, 1980;
Sidney Pincus
Silky! Harper, 1979; Sidney Pincus

ROTH, HOLLY, 1916-1964
Button, button. Harcourt, 1966; UK:
Hamilton, 1967; Lt. Kelly
The crimson in the purple. Simon &
Schuster, 1956; UK: Hamilton, 1956
Shadow of a lady. Simon & Schuster,
1957; UK: Hamilton, 1957; Insp.
Medford #1
Too many doctors. Random House,
1963; UK: Operation doctors.
Hamilton, 1962; Insp. Medford #2

ROUDYBUSH, ALEXANDRA, 1911 --
A sybartic death. Doubleday, 1972;
UK: New English Library, 1972

RUBEL, MARC
Flex. St. Martin's, 1983; Rusty
Cutler

RUELL, PATRICK (pseud. of Reginald
Hill, 1936 --). For other
mysteries by this author, see HILL,
REGINALD
Red Christmas. Hawthorn, 1974; UK:
Long, 1972

RUSSELL, CHARLOTTE MURRAY
The case of the topaz flower.
Doubleday, 1939; Wally Kent
Dreadful reckoning. Doubleday, 1941
Hand me a crime. Doubleday, 1949;
UK: Cherry Tree, 1950; Jane
Amanda Edwards
I heard the death bell. Doubleday,
1940; Jane Amanda Edwards
Ill met in Mexico. Doubleday,
1948; Jane Amanda Edwards
The message of the mute dog.
Doubleday, 1942; Jane Amanda
Edwards
Murder steps in. Doubleday, 1942
The tiny diamond. Doubleday, 1937;
UK: World's Work, 1937; Jane
Amanda Edwards

RUSSELL, E. S.
She should have cried on Monday.
Doubleday, 1968; UK: Hale, 1969;
Ben Louis

RUSSELL, MARTIN, 1934 --
Backlash. Walker, 1983; Steven
Cassell
The man without a name. Coward
McCann, 1977; UK: Mr. T. Collins,
1977
The search for Sara. Walker, 1984

RUSSELL, RAY, 1924 --
The case against Satan. Obolensky,
1962; UK: Souvenir, 1963
Incubus. Morrow, 1967

RUTHERFORD, DOUGLAS (pseud. of James
Doublad Rutherford McConnell, 1915
--).
Mystery tour. Walker, 1976; UK:
Collins, 1975
On the track of death.
Abelard-Schuman, 1959; UK: A
shriek of tyres. Collins, 1958
Return load. Walker, 1977; UK:
Collins, 1977
Turbo. St. Martin's, 1980; UK:
Macmillan, 1980; Patrick Malone

RUTTER, AMANDA
Murder at Eastover. Arcadia House,
1958; Irene Tennant

RYAN, PAUL WILLIAM, see FINNEGAN, ROBERT (pseud.)

SADLER, MARK (pseud.). For other mysteries by this author, see ARDEN, WILLIAM (pseud.) or COLLINS, MICHAEL (pseud.)
   Circle of fire. Random House, 1973; Paul Shaw #4
   The falling man. Random House, 1970; Paul Shaw #1
   Here to die. Random House, 1971; Paul Shaw #2
   Mirror image. Random House, 1972; Paul Shaw #3
ST JOHN, DARBY
   The Westgate mystery. Random, 1941
SALE, RICHARD, 1911 --
   Death at sea. Popular Library, 1948; UK: Destination unknown. World's Work, 1943
   Lazarus #7. Simon & Schuster, 1942; UK: Death looks in. Cassell, 1943; Danile Webster
   Passing strange. Simon & Schuster, 1942; Danile Webster
SAMACHSON, JOSEPH, see MILLER, JOHN (pseud.)
SAMPSON, RICHARD HENRY, see HULL, RICHARD (pseud.)
SANCHEZ, THOMAS, 1944 --
   The Zoot-suit murders. Dutton, 1978; UK: Secker, 1980
SANDERS, LAWRENCE, 1920 --
   The first deadly sin. Putnam, 1973; UK: Allen, 1974; Edward X. Delaney #1
   The fourth deadly sin. Putnam, 1985; Edward X. Delaney
   The second deadly sin. Putnam, 1977; UK: Hart Davis, 1978; Edward X. Delaney #3
   The sixth commandment. Putnam, 1979; UK: Granada, 1979
   The third deadly sin. Putnam, 1981; Edward X. Delaney #3
SANTESSON, HANS STEFAN
   The locked room reader. Random House, 1968
SAPPER, see MCNEILE, H. C.
SARIOLA, MAURI
   The Helsinki affair. Walker, 1971; UK: Cassell, 1970; Osmo Kilpi
   The Torvick affair. Walker, 1972

SAUNDERS, HILARY ST. GEORGE, see BEEDING, FRANCIS (pseud.)
SAVAGE, ERNEST
   Two if by sea. Scribner's, 1982
SAYERS, DOROTHY L., 1893-1957
   Busman's honeymoon. Harcourt, 1937; UK: Gollancz, 1937; Peter Wimsey #13
   Clouds of witness. Dial, 1927; UK: Unwin, 1926; Peter Wimsey #2
   The Dawson pedigree. Dial, 1928; UK: Unnatural death. Benn, 1927; Peter Wimsey #3
   Gaudy night. Harcourt, 1936; UK: Gollancz, 1935; Peter Wimsey #12; Harriet Vane
   Hangman's holiday. Harcourt, 1933; UK: Gollancz, 1933; Peter Wimsey #9; Montague Egg
   Have his carcase. Brewer, 1932; UK: Gollancz, 1932; Peter Wimsey #8
   In the teeth of the evidence. Harcourt, 1940; UK: Gollancz, 1939; Peter Wimsey #14; Montague Egg
   Lord Peter: a collection of all the Lord Peter Wimsey stories. Harper, 1972; Peter Wimsey #15
   Lord Peter views the body. Harcourt, 1929; UK: Gollancz, 1928; Peter Wimsey #4
   Murder must advertise. Harcourt, 1933; UK: Gollancz, 1933; Peter Wimsey #10
   The nine tailors. Harcourt, 1934; UK: Gollancz, 1934; Peter Wimsey #11
   Strong poison. Brewer, 1930; UK: Gollancz, 1930; Peter Wimsey #6
   Suspicious characters. Brewer, 1931; UK: The five red herrings. Gollancz, 1931; Peter Wimsey #7
   The unpleasantness at the Bellona Club. Payson and Clarke, 1928; UK: Benn, 1928; Peter Wimsey #4
   Whose body? Boni, 1923; UK: Unwin, 1923; Peter Wimsey #1
SAYERS, DOROTHY and EUSTACE, ROBERT
   The documents in the case. Brewer, 1930; UK: Benn, 1930
SCERBANECO, GIORGIO, 1911-1969
   Duca and the Milan murders. Walker, 1970; UK: Cassell, 1970; Duca Lamberti

SCHERF, MARGARET, 1908-1979
 Always murder a friend. Doubleday,
  1948; UK: Low, 1949; Emily Bryce
  #1; Henry Bryce #1
 The banker's bones. Doubleday,
  1968; Grace Severence #1
 The beaded banana. Doubleday,
  1978; UK: Hale, 1979; Grace
  Severence #4
 The beautiful birthday cake.
  Doubleday, 1971; Grace Severence
  #2
 The cautious overshoes. Doubleday,
  1956; Martin Buell #4
 The corpse in the flannel nightgown.
  Doubleday, 1965; UK: Hale, 1966;
  Martin Buell #6
 The curious custard pie. Doubleday,
  1950; Martin Buell #2
 Dead: Senate Office Building.
  Doubleday, 1953
 The diplomat and the gold piano.
  Doubleday, 1963; UK: Death and the
  diplomat. Hale, 1964; Emily Bryce
  #5; Henry Bryce #5
 Don't wake me up while I'm driving.
  Doubleday, 1977; UK: Hale, 1978;
  Hal Brady
 The elk and the evidence. Doubleday,
  1952; Martin Buell #3
 Gilbert's last toothache. Doubleday,
  1949; Martin Buell #1
 Glass on the stairs. Doubleday,
  1954; UK: Barker, 1955; Emily
  Bryce #4; Henry Bryce #4
 The green plaid pants. Doubleday,
  1951; Emily Bryce #3; Henry Bryce
  #3
 The gun in Daniel Webster's bust.
  Doubleday, 1949; Emily Bryce #2;
  Henry Bryce #2
 If you want murder done. Doubleday,
  1974
 Never turn your back. Doubleday,
  1959; Martin Buell #5
 They came to kill. Putnam, 1942
 To cache a millionaire. Doubleday,
  1972; Grace Severence #3
SCHOLEFIELD, ALAN, 1931 --
 Point of honour. Morrow, 1979; UK:
  Heinemann, 1979
SCHOLEY, JEAN
 The dead past. Macmillan, 1962; UK:
  Heinemann, 1961; Geoffrey Hallden

SCHORR, MARK
 Ace of diamonds. St. Martin's,
  1984; Red Diamond #2
 Bully! St. Martin's, 1985; Theodore
  Roosevelt; Jim White
 Diamond rock. St. Martin's, 1985;
  Red Diamond #3
 Red Diamond: private eye. St.
  Martin's, 1983; Red Diamond #1
SCHUTZ, BENJAMIN M.
 Embrace the wolf. Bluejay, 1985;
  Leo Haggerty
SCHUTZ, DENNIS. See also ALDYNE,
 NATHAN (pseud.)
 The beckoning shadow. Bobbs, 1946;
  UK: Hammond, 1956; Mike James #2
 Murder makes a villain. Bobbs,
  1944; UK: Hammond, 1955; Mike
  James #1
SCOTT, JACK S. (pseud. of Jack
 Escott, 1922 --)
 A clutch of vipers. Harper, 1979;
  UK: Collins, 1979; Stanley Rosher
 Corporal Smithers, deceased. St.
  Martin's, 1983; Sgt. Major
  Ackroyd
 The gospel lamb. Harper, 1980; UK:
  Collins, 1980; Stanley Rosher #6
 The local lads. Dutton, 1983;
  Stanley Rosher
 A time of fine weather. St.
  Martin's, 1985; Charlie Wood
 An uprush of mayhem. Ticknor &
  Fields, 1982; Stanley Rosher #6
 The view from Deacon Hill. Ticknor
  & Fields, 1981; Stanley Rosher #6
SCOTT, JOHN DICK, see GAIR, MALCOLM
 (pseud.)
SCOTT, R. T. M., 1882 --
 The agony column murders. Dutton,
  1946; Aurelius Smith #7
 Ann's crime. Dutton, 1926; UK:
  Heinemann, 1927; Aurelius Smith
  #3
 Aurelius Smith, detective. Dutton,
  1927; UK: Heinemann, 1928;
  Aurelius Smith #4
 The black magician. Dutton, 1925;
  UK: Heinemann, 1926; Aurelius
  Smith #2
 The mad monk. Kendall, 1931; UK:
  Rich, 1935; Aurelius Smith #5
 Murder stalks the mayor. Dutton,
  1936; UK: Rich, 1935; Aurelius
  Smith #6

The nameless ones. Dutton, 1947;
Aurelius Smith #8
Secret Service Smith. Dutton,
1923; UK: Hodder, 1924; Aurelius
Smith #1

SEELEY, MABEL, 1903 --
The beckoning door. Doubleday,
1950; UK: Collins, 1950
The chuckling fingers. Doubleday,
1941; UK: Collins, 1942
The crying sisters. Doubleday,
1939; UK: Collins, 1940
Eleven came back. Doubleday, 1943;
UK: Collins, 1943
The listening house. Doubleday,
1938; UK: Collins, 1939
The whispering cup. Doubleday,
1940; UK: Collins, 1941
The whistling shadow. Doubleday,
1954; UK: Jenkins, 1954

SELLERS, MICHAEL
Cache on the rocks. Doubleday,
1983; Cal Fisher

SELWYN, FRANCIS, 1935 --
Cracksman on velvet. Stein & Day,
1974; UK: Sergeant Verity and the
cracksman. Duetsch, 1974; William
Verity #1
Sergeant Verity and the blood
royal. Stein & Day, 1979; UK:
Duetsch, 1979; William Verity #4
Sergeant Verity and the imperial
diamond. Stein & Day, 1976; UK:
Duetsch, 1975; William Verity #2
Sergeant Verity and the Swell mob.
Stein & Day, 1980; UK: Duetsch,
1980; William Verity #5
Sergeant Verity presents his
compliments. Stein & Day, 1977;
UK: Duetsch, 1977; William Verity
#3

SEMENOV, JULIAN, see SEMYONOV, JULIAN
SEMYONOV, JULIAN, 1931 --
Petrovka 38. Stein & Day, 1966; UK:
MacGibbon, 1965

SERAFIN, DAVID
The body in Cadiz Bay. St. Martin's,
1985; Luis Bernal
Christmas rising. St. Martin's,
1983; Luis Bernal
Madrid underground. St. Martin's,
1984; Luis Bernal

SHANKMAN, SARAH
Impersonal attractions. St.
Martin's, 1985; Annie Tannenbaum

SHANNON, DELL. For other mysteries by
this author, see EGAN, LESLEY
(pseud.) or LIVINGTON, ELIZABETH
The ace of spades. Morrow, 1961;
UK: Oldborne, 1963, as by Barbara
Livington; Luis Mendoza #2
Appearances of death. Morrow, 1977;
UK: Gollancz, 1978; Luis Mendoza
#28
Case pending. Harper, 1960; UK:
Gollancz, 1960; Luis Mendoza #1
Chance to kill. Morrow, 1967; UK:
Gollancz, 1968; Luis Mendoza #13
Coffin corner. Morrow, 1966; UK:
Gollancz, 1967; Luis Mendoza #11
Cold trail. Morrow, 1978; UK:
Gollancz, 1978; Luis Mendoza #29
Crime file. Morrow, 1974; UK:
Gollancz, 1975; Luis Mendoza #25
Crime on their hands. Morrow,
1969; UK: Gollancz, 1970; Luis
Mendoza #17
The death-bringers. Morrow, 1965;
UK: Gollancz, 1966; Luis Mendoza
#9
Death by inches. Morrow, 1965; UK:
Gollancz, 1967; Luis Mendoza #10
Death of a busybody. Morrow, 1963;
UK: Oldborne, 1963, as by
Elizabeth Livington; Luis Mendoza
#5
Destiny of death. Morrow, 1984;
Luis Mendoza #35
Deuces wild. Morrow, 1975; UK:
Gollancz, 1975; Luis Mendoza #26
Double bluff. Morrow, 1963; UK:
Oldborne, 1964, as by Elizabeth
Livington; Luis Mendoza #6
Exploits of death. Morrow, 1983;
Luis Mendoza #34
Extra kill. Morrow, 1962; UK:
Oldborne, 1962, as by Elizabeth
Livington; Luis Mendoza #3
Felony at random. Morrow, 1979;
UK: Gollancz, 1979; Luis Mendoza
#30
Felony file. Morrow, 1980; UK:
Gollancz, 1980; Luis Mendoza #31
Kill with kindness. Morrow, 1968;
UK: Gollancz, 1969; Luis Mendoza
#15
Knave of hearts. Morrow, 1962; UK:
Oldborne, 1963, as by Elizabeth
Livington; Luis Mendoza #4

Mark of murder. Morrow, 1964; UK:
  Gollancz, 1965; Luis Mendoza #7
The motive on record. Morrow,
  1982; Luis Mendoza #33
Murder most strange. Morrow, 1981;
  Luis Mendoza #32
Murder with love. Morrow, 1972;
  UK: Gollancz, 1972; Luis Mendoza
  #21
No holiday for crime. Morrow, 1973;
  UK: Gollancz, 1974; Luis Mendoza
  #23
Rain with violence. Morrow, 1967;
  UK: Gollancz, 1969; Luis Mendoza
  #14
The ringer. Morrow, 1971; UK:
  Gollancz, 1972; Luis Mendoza #20
Root of all evil. Morrow, 1964; UK:
  Gollancz, 1966; Luis Mendoza #8
Schooled to kill. Morrow, 1969; UK:
  Gollancz, 1970; Luis Mendoza #16
Spring of violence. Morrow, 1973;
  UK: Gollancz, 1974; Luis Mendoza
  #24
Streets of death. Morrow, 1976; UK:
  Gollancz, 1977; Luis Mendoza #27
Unexpected death. Morrow, 1970; UK:
  Gollancz, 1971; Luis Mendoza #18
Whim to kill. Morrow, 1971; UK:
  Gollancz, 1971; Luis Mendoza #19
With a vengeance. Morrow, 1966; UK:
  Gollancz, 1968; Luis Mendoza #12
With intent to kill. Morrow, 1972;
  UK: Gollancz, 1973; Luis Mendoza
  #22
SHARP, DAVID
  The code-letter mystery. Houghton,
  1932; UK: None of my business.
  Benn, 1931; Henry Arthur Fielding
  #3
  Disputed quarry. UK: Jenkins, 1939;
  Henry Arthur Fielding #7
  Everybody suspect. UK: Jenkins,
  1939; Henry Arthur Fielding #8
  The frightened sailor. UK: Jenkins,
  1939; Henry Arthur Fielding #9
  I, the criminal. Houghton, 1933;
  UK: Benn, 1932; Henry Arthur
  Fielding #4
  The inconvenient corpse. UK: Benn,
  1933; Henry Arthur Fielding #5
  Marriage and murder. UK: Benn,
  1934; Henry Arthur Fielding #6

My particular murder. Houghton,
  1931; UK: Benn, 1931; Henry
  Arthur Fielding #2
When no man pursueth. UK: Benn,
  1930; Henry Arthur Fielding #1
SHATTUCK, DORA, see SHATTUCK, RICHARD
  (pseud.)
SHATTUCK, RICHARD
  Said the spider to the fly. Simon
  & Schuster, 1944
SHAW, FELICITY, see MORICE, ANNE
  (pseud.)
SHAW, FRANK H., 1878 --
  Atlantic murder. McBride, 1933;
  UK: Mathews, 1932
SHAW, HOWARD, 1934 --
  Death of a don. Scribner's, 1981;
  Insp. Barnaby
  Killing no murder. Scribner's,
  1981; UK: Hale, 1972, as by Colin
  Howard; Insp. Barnaby
SHAW, JOSEPH T.
  The hard-boiled omnibus. Simon &
  Schuster, 1946
SHEARING, JOSEPH (pseud. of Gabrielle
  Margaret Vere Campbell, 1886-1952)
  Airing in a closed carriage.
  Harper, 1943; UK: Hutchinson,
  1943
  Moss Rose. Smith & Haas, 1935; UK:
  Heinemann, 1934
  So evil my love. Harper, 1947; UK:
  For her to see. Hutchinson, 1947
SHELDON, WALTER J.
  The rites of murder. St. Martin's,
  1984; Paul J. Burdock; Joshua
  Prell
SHELLABARGER, SAMUEL, see ESTEVEN,
  JOHN (pseud.)
SHEPHERD, JOHN (pseud.), see BALLARD,
  WILLIS TODHUNTER
SHERBURNE, JAMES
  Death's clenched fist. Houghton,
  1982; Paddy Moretti
  Death's pale horse. Houghton,
  1980; Paddy Moretti
SHERIDAN, JUANITA
  The Kahuna killer. Doubleday,
  1951; UK: Heinemann, 1955; Lily
  Wu; Janice Cameron
  The Mamo murders. Doubleday, 1952;
  UK: While the coffin waited.
  Heinemann, 1953; Lily Wu; Janice
  Cameron

The Waikiki widow. Doubleday, 1953;
Lily Wu; Janice Cameron

SHERWOOD, JOHN, 1913 --

A botanist at bay. Scribner's,
1985; Celia Grant

Death at the BBC. Scribner's, 1983

Green trigger fingers. Scribner's,
1985; Celia Grant

The sleuth and the liar. Doubleday,
1961; UK: The half hunter.
Gollancz, 1961

SHRIBER, IONE SANDBERG, 1911 --

As long as I live. Rinehart, 1947

A body for Bill. Farrar, 1942; UK:
Nicholson, 1946; Bill Grady

Invitation to murder. Farrar, 1943;
UK: Nicholson, 1946; Bill Grady

Murder well done. Farrar, 1941;
Bill Grady

Pattern for murder. Farrar, 1944;
Bill Grady

SIEGEL, DORIS, see WELLS, SUSAN
(pseud.)

SILLER, VAN (pseud. of Hilda van
Siller)

The Biltmore call. UK: Ward, 1967;
Alan Stewart #3

A complete stranger. Doubleday,
1965; UK: Ward, 1966; Alan Stewart
#1

The curtain between. Doubleday,
1947; UK: Jarrolds, 1949; Richard
Massey #2

Echo of a bomb. Doubleday, 1943;
UK: Jarrolds, 1944; Alan Stewart
#1

Good night, ladies. Doubleday, 1943;
UK: Jarrolds, 1945; Pete Rector

The hell with Elaine. Doubleday,
1974; UK: Hale, 1975

The last resort. Lippincott, 1951;
UK: Hammond, 1954

The mood for murder. Doubleday,
1966; UK: Ward, 1967; Alan Stewart
#2

Somber memory. Doubleday, 1945; UK:
Jarrolds, 1946

Under a cloud. Doubleday, 1944; UK:
Jarrolds, 1946; Pete Rector

SIMENON, GEORGES

At the Gai-Moulin, in Maigret
abroad, by Georges Simenon.
Harcourt, 1940; UK: Routledge,
1940; Jules Maigret #5

Battle of nerves, in Patience of
Maigret, by Georges Simenon.
Harcourt, 1940; UK: Routledge,
1939; Jules Maigret #10

The crime at Lock 14, in The shadow
in the courtyard and the crime at
Lock 14, by Georges Simenon.
Covici, 1934; UK: in Triumph of
Inspector Maigret by Georges
Simenon. Hurst, 1934; Jules
Maigret #2

A crime in Holland, in Maigret
abroad, by Georges Simenon.
Harcourt, 1940; UK: Routledge,
1940; Jules Maigret #4

The crime of Inspector Maigret, in
Introducing Inspector Maigret, by
Georges Simenon. Covici, 1932;
UK: Hurst, 1933; Jules Maigret #8

The crossroad murders. Covici,
1933; UK: in Inspector Maigret,
investigator. Hurst, 1933; Jules
Maigret #7

Death of a harbor master, in
Maigret and M. L'Abbe, by Georges
Simenon. Harcourt, 1942; UK:
Death of a harbourmaster.
Routledge, 1941; Jules Maigret
#17

The death of Monsieur Gallet.
Covici, 1932; UK: in Introducing
Monsieur Gallet, by Georges
Simenon. Hurst, 1933; Jules
Maigret #6

A face for a clue, in The patience
of Maigret, by Georges Simenon.
Harcourt, 1940; UK: Routledge,
1939; Jules Maigret #3

The Flemish shop, in Maigret to the
rescue, by Georges Simenon.
Harcourt, 1941; UK: Routledge,
1940; Jules Maigret #12

The Guinguette by the Seine, in
Maigret to the rescue, by Georges
Simenon. Harcourt, 1941; UK:
Routledge, 1940; Jules Maigret
#14

Inspector Maigret and the burglar's
wife. Doubleday, 1956; UK:
Hamilton, 1955; Jules Maigret #38

Inspector Maigret and the dead
girl. Doubleday, 1955; UK:
Maigret and the young girl.
Hamilton, 1955; Jules Maigret #48

Inspector Maigret and the strangled
   stripper. Doubleday, 1954; UK:
   Maigret in Montmarte, in Maigret
   right and wrong, by Georges
   Simenon. Hamilton, 1954; Jules
   Maigret #36
Liberty bar, in Maigret travels
   south, by Georges Simenon.
   Harcourt, 1940; UK: Routledge,
   1940; Jules Maigret #15
The lock at Charenton, in Maigret
   sets it out, by Georges Simenon.
   Harcourt, 1941; UK: Routledge,
   1941; Jules Maigret #18
Madame Maigret's own case.
   Doubleday, 1959; UK: Madame
   Maigret's friend. Hamilton, 1960;
   Jules Maigret #35; Mme. Maigret
The madman of Bergerac, in Maigret
   travels south, by Georges Simenon.
   Harcourt, 1940; UK: Routledge,
   1940; Jules Maigret #13
Maigret afraid. Harcourt, 1983;
   UK: Hamilton, 1961; Jules Maigret
   #43
Maigret and Monsieur Charles. UK:
   Hamilton, 1973; Jules Maigret #76
Maigret and the apparition.
   Harcourt, 1976; UK: Maigret and
   the ghost. Hamilton, 1976; Jules
   Maigret #63
Maigret and the black sheep.
   Harcourt, 1976; UK: Hamilton,
   1976; Jules Maigret #61
Maigret and the bum. Harcourt,
   1974; UK: Maigret and the dosser.
   Hamilton, 1973; Jules Maigret
   #62
Maigret and the Calame report.
   Harcourt, 1969; UK: Hamilton,
   1969; Jules Maigret #47
Maigret and the headless corpse.
   Harcourt, 1968; UK: Hamilton,
   1967; Jules Maigret #49
Maigret and the hotel mystic.
   Harcourt, 1978; UK: Hamilton,
   1977; Jules Maigret #20
Maigret and the informer. Harcourt,
   1973; UK: Hamilton, 1972; Jules
   Maigret #77
Maigret and the killer. Harcourt,
   1971; UK: Hamilton, 1971; Jules
   Maigret #72

Maigret and the killers. Doubleday,
   1954; UK: Hamilton, 1974; Jules
   Maigret #41
Maigret and the lazy burglar, in A
   Maigret trio, by Georges Simenon.
   Harcourt, 1973; UK: Hamilton,
   1963; Jules Maigret #59
Maigret and the loner. Harcourt,
   1975; UK: Hamilton, 1975; Jules
   Maigret #75
Maigret and the madwoman. Harcourt,
   1972; UK: Hamilton, 1972; Jules
   Maigret #73
Maigret and the man on the bench.
   Harcourt, 1975; UK: Maigret and
   the man on the boulevard.
   Hamilton, 1975; Jules Maigret #44
Maigret and the millionaire.
   Harcourt, 1974; UK: Hamilton,
   1974; Jules Maigret #53
Maigret and the Nahour case.
   Harcourt, 1983; UK: Hamilton,
   1967; Jules Maigret #67
Maigret and the old lady, in
   Maigret Cinq., by Georges
   Simenon. Harcourt, 1965; UK:
   Hamilton, 1958; Jules Maigret #27
Maigret and the reluctant witness,
   in Versus Inspector Maigret, by
   Georges Simenon. Doubleday, 1960;
   UK: Hamilton, 1959; Jules Maigret
   #55
Maigret and the Saturday caller.
   White Lion, 1975; UK: Hamilton,
   1964; Jules Maigret #60
Maigret and the spinster. Harcourt,
   1977; UK: Hamilton, 1977; Jules
   Maigret #21
Maigret and the toy village.
   Harcourt, 1979; UK: Hamilton,
   1978; Jules Maigret #23
Maigret and the wine merchant.
   Harcourt, 1971; UK: Hamilton,
   1971; Jules Maigret #74
Maigret at the coroner's. Harcourt,
   1980; UK: Maigret and the
   coroner. Hamilton, 1980; Jules
   Maigret #32
Maigret bides his time. Harcourt,
   1985; Jules Maigret
Maigret goes to school, in Five
   times Maigret, by Georges
   Simenon. Harcourt, 1964; UK:
   Hamilton, 1957; Jules Maigret #46

Maigret has doubts. Harcourt, 1982; UK: Hamilton, 1968; Jules Maigret #56

Maigret has scruples, in Versus Inspector Maigret, by Georges Simenon. Doubleday, 1960; UK: Hamilton, 1959; Jules Maigret #54

Maigret hesitates. Harcourt, 1970; UK: Hamilton, 1970; Jules Maigret #71

Maigret in court. Harcourt, 1983; UK: Hamilton, 1961; Jules Maigret #57

Maigret in exile. Harcourt, 1979; UK: Hamilton, 1978; Jules Maigret #22

Maigret in New York's underworld. Doubleday, 1955; UK: Maigret in New York. Hamilton, 1979; Jules Maigret #28

Maigret in society, in A Maigret trio, by Georges Simenon. Harcourt, 1973; UK: Hamilton, 1962; Jules Maigret #58

Maigret in Vichy. Harcourt, 1969; UK: Maigret takes the waters. Hamilton, 1969; Jules Maigret #70

Maigret loses his temper. Harcourt, 1974; UK: Hamilton, 1965; Jules Maigret #65

Maigret on the defensive. Harcourt, 1981; UK: Hamilton, 1966; Jules Maigret #64

Maigret rents a room. Doubleday, 1961; UK: Maigret takes a room. Hamilton, 1960; Jules Maigret #37

Maigret returns, in Maigret sits it out, by Georges Simenon. Harcourt, 1941; UK: Routledge, 1941; Jules Maigret #19

Maigret sets a trap. Harcourt, 1972; UK: Hamilton, 1965; Jules Maigret #50

Maigret's boyhood friend. Harcourt, 1970; UK: Hamilton, 1970; Jules Maigret #69

Maigret's Christmas: nine stories. Harcourt, 1977; UK: Hamilton, 1976; Jules Maigret #40

Maigret's dead man. Doubleday, 1964; UK: Maigret's special murder. Hamilton, 1964; Jules Maigret #30

Maigret's failure, A Maigret trio by Georges Simenon. Harcourt, 1973; UK: Hamilton, 1962; Jules Maigret #51

Maigret's first case, in Maigret Cinq., by Georges Simenon. Harcourt, 1965; UK: Hamilton, 1958; Jules Maigret #34

Maigret's memoirs. White Lion, 1974; UK: Hamilton, 1963; Jules Maigret #39

Maigret's mistake, Five times Maigret: a Maigret omnibus, by Georges Simenon. Harcourt, 1964; UK: in Maigret right and wrong, by Georges Simenon. Hamilton, 1954; Jules Maigret #45

Maigret's pickpocket. Harcourt, 1968; UK: Hamilton, 1968; Jules Maigret #68

Maigret's pipe. Harcourt, 1978; UK: Hamilton, 1977; Jules Maigret #29

Maigret's revolver. Harcourt, 1984; UK: Hamilton, 1956; Jules Maigret

Maigret's rival. Harcourt, 1979; UK: Hamilton, 1979; Jules Maigret #24

The man who watched the trains go by. Reynal, 1946; UK: Routledge, 1942

The methods of Maigret. Doubleday, 1957; UK: Hamilton, 1966; Jules Maigret #33

No vacation for Maigret. Doubleday, 1953; UK: A summer holiday, in Maigret on holiday, by Georges Simenon. Routledge, 1950; Jules Maigret

None of Maigret's business. Doubleday, 1958; UK: Maigret's little joke. Hamilton, 1957; Jules Maigret #52

The patience of Maigret. UK: Hamilton, 1966; Jules Maigret #66

The sailor's rendezvous, Maigret keeps a rendezvous, by Georges Simenon. Harcourt, 1941; UK: Routledge, 1940; Jules Maigret #1

The Saint-Fiacre affair, in Maigret keeps a rendezvous, by Georges Simenon. Harcourt, 1941; UK: Routledge, 1940; Jules Maigret #11

The shadow in the courtyard, in The shadow in the courtyard and the crime at Lock 14, by Georges Simenon. Covici, 1934; UK: in The triumph of Inspector Maigret, by Georges Simenon. Hurst, 1934; Jules Maigret #16

The short cases of Inspector Maigret. Doubleday, 1959; Jules Maigret #25

The strange case of Peter the Left. Covici, 1933; UK: Maigret and the enigmatic left. Hurst, 1933; Jules Maigret #9

The survivors. Harcourt, 1985; Charles Camet

To any lengths, in Maigret on holiday, by Georges Simenon. UK: Routledge, 1950; Jules Maigret #26

SIMMONS, ADDISON, 1902 --
Death on the campus. Crowell, 1935; Capt. Packer; Kent Bloomingdale

SIMMONS, GEOFFREY, 1943 --
Murdock. Arbor House, 1976; Corey Thatcher

SIMON, ROGER L., 1943 --
The big fix. Simon & Schuster, 1973; UK: Duetsch, 1974; Moses Wine #1

California roll. Villard, 1985; Moses Wine

Peking duck. Simon & Schuster, 1979; UK: Duetsch, 1979; Moses Wine #3

Wild turkey. Simon & Schuster, 1975; UK: Duetsch, 1976; Moses Wine #2

SIMON, S. J., see BRAHMS, CARYE

SIMONS, ROGER (pseud. of Ivar and Margaret Punnett)
Bullet for a beast. Roy, 1964; UK: Bles, 1965; Fadiman Wace

Murder first class. Roy, 1970; UK: Bles, 1969; Fadiman Wace

SIMPSON, DOROTHY
Close her eyes. Scribner's, 1984; Luke Thanet

The night she died. Scribner's, 1981; Luke Thanet #1

Puppet for a corpse. Scribner's, 1983; Luke Thanet #3

Six feet under. Scribner's, 1982; Luke Thanet #2

SIMPSON, HELEN, 1897-1940. For other mysteries by this author, see DANE, CLEMENCE
The prime minister is dead. Doubleday, 1931; UK: Vantage striker. Heinemann, 1931

SIMPSON, HOWARD R.
The jumpmaster. Doubleday, 1984; Roger Bastide

SINCLAIR, MURRAY
Only in L. A. A & W, 1982; Ben Crandel

SINGER, ROCHELLE
Samson's deal. St. Martin's, 1983; Jake Samson

SINGER, SALLY M.
For dying you always have time. Putnam, 1971

SINGER, SHELLY
Free draw. St. Martin's, 1985; Jake Samson; Rosie Vicente

SJOWALL, MAJ and WAHLOO, PER. See also WAHLOO, PER
The abominable man. Pantheon, 1972; Pantheon, 1972; UK: Gollancz, 1973; Martin Beck #7

Cop killer. Pantheon, 1975; UK: Gollancz, 1975; Martin Beck #9

The fire engine that disappeared. Pantheon, 1971; UK: Gollancz, 1972; Martin Beck #5

The laughing policeman. Pantheon, 1970; UK: Gollancz, 1971; Martin Beck #4

The locked room. Pantheon, 1973; UK: Gollancz, 1974; Martin Beck #8

The man on the balcony. Pantheon, 1968; UK: Gollancz, 1969; Martin Beck #2

The man who went up in smoke. Pantheon, 1969; UK: Gollancz, 1970; Martin Beck #3

Murder at the Savoy. Pantheon, 1971; UK: Gollancz, 1972; Martin Beck #6

Roseanna. Pantheon, 1967; UK: Gollancz, 1968; Martin Beck #1

The terrorists. Pantheon, 1976; UK: Gollancz, 1977; Martin Beck #10

SLADEK, JOHN, 1937 --
Black aura. Walker, 1979; UK: Cape, 1974; Thackeray Phin

Invisible green. Walker, 1979; UK:
Gollancz, 1977; Thackeray Phin

SLESAR, HENRY, 1927 --
The gray flannel shroud. Random
House, 1959; UK: Duetsch, 1960;
Dave Robbins
The thing at the door. Random
House, 1974; UK: Hamilton, 1975;
Steve Tyner

SLOANE, WILLIAM, 1906-1974
The edge of running water. Farrar,
1939; UK: Methuen, 1940
To walk the night. Farrar, 1937;
UK: Barker, 1938

SLUNG, MICHELE
Woman's wiles. Harcourt, 1979

SMILEY, JANE
Duplicate keys. Knopf, 1984

SMITH, AMANDA JOAN MCKAY, see MACKAY,
AMANDA

SMITH, CHARLES MERRILL
Rev. Randollph and the avenging
angel. Putnam, 1977; UK: Hale,
1979; Cesare Randollph #2
Reverend Randollph and the fall
from Grace, Inc. Putnam, 1978;
UK: Hale, 1979; Cesare Randollph
#3
Reverend Randollph and the holy
terror. Putnam, 1980; Cesare
Randollph #4
Reverend Randollph and the wages of
sin. UK: Putnam, 1974; UK: Barker,
1975; Cesare Randollph #1

SMITH, FRANK E., 1919 -- , see CRAIG,
JONATHAN (pseud.)

SMITH, H. MAYNARD, 1869-1949
Inspector Frost in the city.
Doubleday, 1930; UK: Benn, 1930;
Insp. Frost

SMITH, J. C. S.
Jacoby's first case. Atheneum,
1980; UK: Hale, 1981; Quentin
Jacoby
Nightcap. Atheneum, 1984; Quentin
Jacoby

SMITH, JULIE
Death turns a trick. Walker, 1982;
Rebecca Schwartz
The sourdough wars. Walker, 1984;
Rebecca Schwartz
True-life adventure. Mysterious
Press, 1985; Paul McDonald

SMITH, KAY NOLTE, 1932 --
Catching fire. Coward McCann, 1981;
Edik Dante

SMITH, MARK, 1935 --
The death of the detective. Knopf,
1974; UK: Secker, 1975; Arned
Magnuson
Toyland. Little, 1965

SMITH, MARTIN CRUZ, 1942 --
Canto for a gypsy. Putnam, 1972;
UK: Barker, 1975; Roman Grey
Gypsy in amber. Putnam, 1971; UK:
Barker, 1975; Roman Grey

SMITH, MICHAEL A., 1942 --
Secrets. St. Martin's, 1981; Frank
Montgomery

SMITH, SHELLEY (pseud. of Nancy
Hermione Bodington, 1912 --)
An afternoon to kill. Harper, 1954;
UK: Collins, 1953
The ballad of the running man.
Harper, 1962; UK: Hamilton, 1961
The cellar at No. 5. Harper, 1954;
UK: The party at No. 5. Collins,
1954
He died of murder! Harper, 1948;
UK: Collins, 1947; Jacob Chaos #2

SMITH, TERRENCE LORE, see LORE,
PHILLIPS (pseud.)

SMITH, WILLARD K.
Bowery murder. Doubleday, 1929; UK:
Collins, 1930; Dan Carr
The sultan's skull. Archer, 1933;
Dan Carr

SMITH, WILLIAM DALE, see ANTHONY
DAVID (pseud.)

SMITHIES, RICHARD H. R., 1936 --
An academic question. Horizon,
1965; Campbell Craig; William
McAlpin
Disposing mind. Horizon, 1966;
William McAlpin

SNELL, DAVID, 1942 --
Lights . . . camera . . . murder.
St. Martin's, 1979; Osgood Bass

SNOW, C. P., 1905-1980
A coat of varnish. Scribner's,
1979; UK: Macmillan, 1979; Frank
Briers
Death under sail. Doubleday, 1932;
UK: Heinemann, 1932

SOMERS, PAUL (pseud. of Paul
Winterton, 1908 --). For other
mysteries by this author, see BAX,

ROGER (pseud.) or GARVE, ANDREW
(pseud.)
Beginner's luck. Harper, 1958; UK:
   Collins, 1958; Hugh Curtis #1
Operation piracy. Harper, 1959;
   UK: Collins, 1958; Hugh Curtis #2
The shivering mountain. Harper,
   1959; UK: Collins, 1959; Hugh
   Curtis #3
SPAIN, JOHN (pseud. of Cleve F.
   Adams). For other mysteries by this
   author, see ADAMS, CLEVE F.
Death is like that. Dutton, 1943;
   Bill Rye #2
Dig me a grave. Dutton, 1942; Bill
   Rye #1
SPENCER, ROSS H., 1942 --
Echoes of zero. St. Martin's, 1981;
   Rip Deston
The missing bishop. Mysterious
   Press, 1985; Buzz Deckard
SPICER, BART, 1918 --
Act of anger. Atheneum, 1962; UK:
   Barker, 1963; Benson Kellogg
Black sheep, run. Dodd, 1951; UK:
   Collins, 1952; Carney Wilde #4
Blues for the prince. Dodd, 1950;
   UK: Collins, 1951; Carney Wilde #2
The dark light. Dodd, 1949; UK:
   Collins, 1950; Carney Wilde #1
Exit running. Dodd, 1959; UK:
   Hodder, 1960; Carney Wilde #7
The golden door. Dodd, 1951; UK:
   Collins, 1951; Carney Wilde #3
Kellogg junction. Atheneum, 1969;
   UK: Hodder, 1970; Benson Kellogg
The long green. Dodd, 1952; UK:
   Shadow of fear. Collins, 1953;
   Carney Wilde #5
The taming of Carney Wilde.
   Constable, 1954; UK: Hodder, 1955;
   Carney Wilde #6
SPILLANE, MICKEY (pseud. of Frank
   Morrison Spillane, 1918 --)
The big kill. Dutton, 1951; UK:
   Barker, 1952; Mike Hammer #4
The body lovers. Dutton, 1967; UK:
   Barker, 1967; Mike Hammer #10
The erection set. Dutton, 1972; UK:
   Allen, 1972; Dogeron Kelly
The girl hunters. Dutton, 1962; UK:
   Barker, 1962; Mike Hammer #7
I, the jury. Dutton, 1947; UK:
   Barker, 1952; Mike Hammer #1

Kiss me, deadly. Dutton, 1952; UK:
   Barker, 1953; Mike Hammer #6
My gun is quick. Dutton, 1950; UK:
   Barker, 1951; Mike Hammer #2
One lonely night. Dutton, 1951; UK:
   Barker, 1952; Mike Hammer #5
The snake. Dutton, 1964; UK:
   Barker, 1964; Mike Hammer #8
Survival . . . zero! Dutton, 1970;
   UK: Corgi, 1970; Mike Hammer #11
The twisted thing. Dutton, 1966;
   UK: Barker, 1966; Mike Hammer #9
Vengeance is mine! Dutton, 1950;
   UK: Barker, 1951; Mike Hammer #8
SPRIGG, CHRISTOPHER ST. JOHN,
   1907-1937
Death of an airman. Doubleday,
   1935; UK: Hutchinson, 1934;
   Bernard Bray
Pass the body. Dial, 1933; UK:
   Crime in Kensington. Eldon, 1933
The perfect alibi. Doubleday, 1934;
   UK: Eldon, 1934; Charles Venables
   #2; Bernard Bray
SPROUL, KATHLEEN
Death and the professors. Dutton,
   1933; UK: Death among the
   professors. Eyre, 1934; Richard
   Van Ryn Wilson
The mystery of a closed car.
   Dutton, 1935; Richard Van Ryn
   Wilson
STAGGE, JONATHAN (pseud.). For other
   mysteries by this author, see
   QUENTIN, PATRICK (pseud.) or
   PATRICK, Q. (pseud.)
Death my darling daughter.
   Doubleday, 1945; UK: Death and
   the dear girls. Joseph, 1946;
   Hugh Westlake #7
Death's old sweet song. Doubleday,
   1946; UK: Joseph, 1947; Hugh
   Westlake #8
The dogs do bark. Doubleday, 1937;
   UK: Murder gone to earth. Joseph,
   1936; Hugh Westlake #1
Murder by prescription. Doubleday,
   1938; UK: Murder or mercy.
   Joseph, 1937; Hugh Westlake #2
The scarlet circle. Doubleday,
   1943; UK: Light from a lantern.
   Joseph, 1943; Hugh Westlake #6
The stars spell death. Doubleday,
   1939; UK: Joseph, 1940; Hugh
   Westlake #3

The three fears. Doubleday, 1949;
UK: Joseph, 1949; Hugh Westlake
#9

Turn of the table. Doubleday,
1940; UK: Funeral for five.
Joseph, 1940; Hugh Westlake #4

The yellow taxi. Doubleday, 1942;
UK: Call a hearse. Joseph, 1942;
Hugh Westlake #5

STANSFELD, ANTHONY, see BUCKINGHAM,
BRUCE (pseud.)

STAPLETON, D.

Corpse and robbers. Arcadia House,
1954

STARRETT, VINCENT (pseud. of Charles
Vincent Emerson Starrett, 1886-1974)

The blue door. Doubleday, 1930;
Jimmie Lavender #1

The case book of Jimmie Lavender.
Gold Label, 1944; Jimmie Lavender
#2

Coffins for two. Covici, 1924

Dead man inside. Doubleday, 1931;
UK: World's Work, 1935; Walter
Ghost #2

The end of Mr. Garment. Doubleday,
1932; Walter Ghost #3

The great hotel murder. Doubleday,
1935; UK: Nicholson, 1935; Riley
Blackwood

Midnight and Percy Jones. Covici,
1936; UK: Nicholson, 1938; Riley
Blackwood

Murder in Peking. Lantern Press,
1946; UK: Edwards, 1947; Riley
Blackwood

Murder on "B" deck. Doubleday,
1929; UK: World's Work, 1936;
Walter Ghost #1

STASHOWER, DAN

The adventures of the ectoplasmic
man. Morrow, 1985; Sherlock
Holmes; Harry Houdini

STEEGMULLER, FRANCIS, 1906 -- , see
KEITH, DAVID (pseud.)

STEEL, KURT (pseud. of Rudolph
Harnaday Kagey, 1904-1946)

Murder goes to college. Bobbs,
1936; Henry Hyer #3

STEIN, AARON MARC, 1906 -- . For other
mysteries by this author, see BAGBY,
GEORGE (pseud.) or STONE, HAMPTON
(pseud.)

Alp murder. Doubleday, 1970; UK:
Hale, 1971; Matt Erridge #9

... and high water. Doubleday,
1946; Tim Mulligan #5; Elsie Mae
Hunt #5

Blood on the stars. Doubleday,
1964; UK: Hale, 1964; Matt
Erridge #4

Body search. Doubleday, 1977; UK:
Hale, 1978; Matt Erridge #13

The bombing run. Doubleday, 1983;
Matt Erridge

The case of the absent-minded
professor. Doubleday, 1943; Tim
Mulligan #4; Elsie Mae Hunt #4

The cheating butcher. Doubleday,
1980; UK: Hale, 1981; Matt
Erridge #18

Chill factor. Doubleday, 1978; UK:
Hale, 1979; Matt Erridge #15

Coffin country. Doubleday, 1976;
UK: Hale, 1976; Matt Erridge #11

The cradle and the grave.
Doubleday, 1948; Tim Mulligan #8;
Elsie Mae Hunt #8

Days of misfortune. Doubleday,
1949; Tim Mulligan #10; Elsie Mae
Hunt #10

The dead thing in the pool.
Doubleday, 1952; Tim Mulligan
#16; Elsie Mae Hunt #16

Deadly delight. Doubleday, 1967;
UK: Hale, 1969; Matt Erridge #6

Death meets 400 rabbits. Doubleday,
1953; Tim Mulligan #17; Elsie Mae
Hunt #17

Death takes a paying guest.
Doubleday, 1947; Tim Mulligan #7;
Elsie Mae Hunt #7

The finger. Doubleday, 1973; UK:
Hale, 1974; Matt Erridge #10

Frightened Amazon. Doubleday, 1950;
Tim Mulligan #12; Elsie Mae Hunt
#12

The garbage collector. Doubleday,
1984; Matt Erridge

Home and murder. Doubleday, 1962;
Matt Erridge #3

I fear the Greeks. Doubleday, 1966;
UK: Executioner's rest. Hale,
1967; Matt Erridge #5

Kill is a four-letter word.
Doubleday, 1968; UK: Hale, 1969;
Matt Erridge #8

Lend me your ears. Doubleday, 1977;
Matt Erridge #12

Mask for murder. Doubleday, 1952;
Tim Mulligan #15; Elsie Mae Hunt
#15

Moonmilk and murder. Doubleday,
1955; UK: Macdonald, 1956; Tim
Mulligan #18; Elsie Mae Hunt #18

Never need an enemy. Doubleday,
1959; UK: Boardman, 1960; Matt
Erridge #2

A nose for it. Doubleday, 1980;
UK: Hale, 1981; Matt Erridge

Nowhere? Doubleday, 1978; UK:
Hale, 1978; Matt Erridge #14

One dip dead. Doubleday, 1979; UK:
Hale, 1980; Matt Erridge #17

Only the guilty. Doubleday, 1942;
Tim Mulligan #3; Elsie Mae Hunt #3

Pistols for two. Doubleday, 1951;
Tim Mulligan #14; Elsie Mae Hunt
#14

The rolling heads. Doubleday, 1979;
UK: Hale, 1979; Matt Erridge #16

The second burial. Doubleday, 1949;
Tim Mulligan #9; Elsie Mae Hunt #9

Shoot me dacent. Doubleday, 1951;
UK: Macdonald, 1957; Tim Mulligan
#13; Elsie Mae Hunt #13

Sitting up dead. Doubleday, 1958;
UK: Macdonald, 1959; Matt Erridge
#1

Snare Andalucian. Doubleday, 1968;
UK: Faces of death. Hale, 1968;
Matt Erridge #7

The sun is a witness. Doubleday,
1940; Tim Mulligan #1; Elsie Mae
Hunt #1

Three--with blood. Doubleday, 1950;
Tim Mulligan #11; Elsie Mae Hunt
#11

Up to no good. Doubleday, 1941; Tim
Mulligan #2; Elsie Mae Hunt #2

We saw him die. Doubleday, 1947;
Tim Mulligan #6; Elsie Mae Hunt #6

STEPHENS, REED
The man who risked his partner.
Ballantine, 1984; Mick Axbrewder;
Ginny Fistoulari

STEPHENSON, H. M., 1882 --
Death on the deep. Doubleday, 1931;
UK: Yo-ho, and a bottle of rum!
Hutchinson, 1930

STERLING, THOMAS, 1921 --
The evil of the day. Simon &
Schuster, 1955; UK: Gollancz,
1955; Capt. Rizzi

The silent siren. Simon & Schuster,
1958; UK: Gollancz, 1958; Capt.
Rizzi

STERN, RICHARD MARTIN, 1915 --
Death in the snow. Scribner's,
1973; UK: Hale, 1974; Johnny
Ortiz #3

The Kessler legacy. Scribner's,
1967; UK: Cassell, 1968; Walter
Spense

Murder in the walls. Scribner's,
1971; UK: Hale, 1973; Johnny
Ortiz #1

You don't need an enemy.
Scribner's, 1971; UK: Hale, 1973;
Johnny Ortiz #2

STEVENSON, RICHARD
On the other hand, death. St.
Martin's, 1984; Donald Strachey

STEWARD, BARBARA and STEWARD, DWIGHT
Evermore. Morrow, 1978; Edgar Allan
Poe

The Lincoln diddle. Morrow, 1979;
Edgar Allan Poe

STEWARD, DWIGHT
The acupuncture murders. Harper,
1973; UK: Barker, 1973

STEWART, GARY
The tenth virgin. St. Martin's,
1983; Gabriel Utley

STEWART, J. I. M., see INNES,
MICHAEL (pseud.)

STEWART, KENNETH LIVINGSTON,
1894 -- , see LIVINGSTON, KENNETH
(pseud.)

STEWART, MARY, 1916 --
Madam, will you talk? Morrow, 1956;
UK: Hodder, 1955; Charity
Selbourne

The moon spinners. Mill, 1963; UK:
Hodder, 1962

My brother Michael. Mill, 1960; UK:
Hodder, 1960; Camilla Haven;
Simon Lester

Thunder on the right. Mill, 1958;
UK: Hodder, 1957; Jennifer Silver

STINSON, JIM
Double exposure. Scribner's, 1985;
Stoney Winston

STOKES, MANNING LEE
The wolf howls "murder." Phoenix
Press, 1945; Barnabas Jones

STONE, HAMPTON (pseud. of Aaron Marc
Stein, 1906 --). For other
mysteries by this author, see

BAGBY, GEORGE (pseud.) or STEIN, AARON MARC

The babe with the twistable arm. Simon & Schuster, 1962; UK: Hale, 1964; Jeremiah X. Gibson #12; Mac #12

The corpse in the corner saloon. Simon & Schuster, 1948; Jeremiah X. Gibson #1; Mac #1

The corpse that refused to stay dead. Simon & Schuster, 1952; UK: Dobson, 1954; Jeremiah X. Gibson #5; Mac #5

The corpse was no bargain at all. Simon & Schuster, 1968; UK: Hale, 1969; Jeremiah X. Gibson #16; Mac #16

The corpse who had too many friends. Simon & Schuster, 1953; UK: Foulsham, 1954; Jeremiah X. Gibson #6; Mac #6

The funniest killer in town. Simon & Schuster, 1967; Jeremiah X. Gibson #15; Mac #15

The girl who kept knocking them dead. Simon & Schuster, 1957; UK: Foulsham, 1957; Jeremiah X. Gibson #9; Mac #9

The girl with the hole in her head. Simon & Schuster, 1949; UK: Boardman, 1958; Jeremiah X. Gibson #2; Mac #2

The kid was last seen hanging ten. Simon & Schuster, 1966; Jeremiah X. Gibson #14; Mac #14

The kid who came with a corpse. Simon & Schuster, 1972; Jeremiah X. Gibson #18; Mac #18

The man who had too much to lose. Simon & Schuster, 1955; UK: Foulsham, 1955; Jeremiah X. Gibson #7; Mac #7

The man who looked death in the eye. Simon & Schuster, 1961; Jeremiah X. Gibson #11; Mac #11

The man who was three jumps ahead. Simon & Schuster, 1959; UK: Boardman, 1960; Jeremiah X. Gibson #10; Mac #10

The murder that wouldn't stay solved. Doubleday, 1951; Jeremiah X. Gibson #4; Mac #4

The needle that wouldn't stay still. Simon & Schuster, 1950; UK: Boardman, 1958; Jeremiah X. Gibson #3; Mac #3

The real serendipitous kill. Simon & Schuster, 1964; Jeremiah X. Gibson #13; Mac #13

The strangler who couldn't let go. Doubleday, 1956; UK: The strangler. Foulsham, 1957; Jeremiah X. Gibson #8; Mac #8

The swinger who swung by the neck. Simon & Schuster, 1970; Jeremiah X. Gibson #17; Mac #17

STORME, PETER (pseud. of Philip Van Doren Stern, 1900 --)

The thing in the brook. Simon & Schuster, 1937; UK: Hale, 1937; Henry Hale

STOUT, REX, 1886-1975

And be a villain. Viking, 1948; UK: More deaths than one. Collins, 1949; Nero Wolfe #13

And four to go. Viking, 1958; UK: Crime and again. Collins, 1959; Nero Wolfe #31

Bad for business, in The second mystery book, by Rex Stout. Farrar, 1940; UK: Collins, 1945; Tecumseh Fox #2

Before I die, in Trouble in triplicate. Viking, 1949; UK: Collins, 1949

Before midnight. Viking, 1955; UK: Collins, 1956; Nero Wolfe #25

The black mountain. Viking, 1954; UK: Collins, 1955; Nero Wolfe #24

Black orchids. Farrar, 1942; UK: Collins, 1945; Nero Wolfe #9

Blood will tell, in Trio for blunt instruments: a Nero Wolfe threesome, by Rex Stout. Viking, 1964; UK: Collins, 1965; Nero Wolfe

Booby trap, in Not quite dead enough, by Rex Stout. Faber, 1944

The broken vase. Farrar, 1941; UK: Collins, 1942; Tecumseh Fox #3

Bullet for one, in Curtains for three, by Rex Stout. Viking, 1951; UK: Collins, 1951

Champagne for one. Viking, 1958; UK: Collins, 1959; Nero Wolfe #30

Christmas party, in And four to go, by Rex Stout. Viking, 1958; UK: Collins, 1959; Nero Wolfe #31

The cop-killer, in Triple jeopardy, by Rex Stout. Viking, 1951; UK: Collins, 1952

Cordially invited to meet death, in Black Orchids, by Rex Stout. Faber, 1942; UK: Collins, 1943

Counterfeit for murder, in Homicide trinity, by Rex Stout. Viking, 1962; UK: Collins, 1963

Curtains for three. Viking, 1950; UK: Collins, 1951; Nero Wolfe #18

Death of a demon, in Homicide Trinity, by Rex Stout. Viking, 1962; UK: Collins, 1963

Death of a doxy. Viking, 1966; UK: Collins, 1967; Nero Wolfe #42

Death of a dude. Viking, 1969; UK: Collins, 1970; Nero Wolfe #44

Die like a dog, in Three witnesses, by Rex Stout. Viking, 1956; UK: Collins, 1956

Disguise for murder, in Curtains for three, by Rex Stout. Viking, 1950; UK: Collins, 1951

Door to death, in Three doors to death, by Rex Stout. Viking, 1950; UK: Collins, 1950

The doorbell rang. Viking, 1965; UK: Collins, 1966; Nero Wolfe #41

Double for death. Farrar, 1939; UK: Collins, 1940; Tecumseh Fox #1

Easter parade, in And four to go, by Rex Stout. Viking, 1958; UK: in Crime and again, by Rex Stout. Collins, 1959

Eeny, meeny murder mo, in Homicide Trinity, by Rex Stout. Viking, 1962; UK: Collins, 1963

A family affair. Viking, 1975; UK: Collins, 1976; Nero Wolfe #46

The father hunt. Viking, 1968; UK: Collins, 1969; Nero Wolfe #43

Fer-de-lance. Farrar, 1934; UK: Cassell, 1935; Nero Wolfe #1

The final deduction. Viking, 1961; UK: Collins, 1962; Nero Wolfe #35

Fourth of July picnic, in And four to go, by Rex Stout. Viking, 1958; UK: in Crime and again, by Rex Stout. Collins, 1959

Gambit. Viking, 1962; UK: Collins, 1963; Nero Wolfe #36

The golden spiders. Viking, 1953; UK: Collins, 1954; Nero Wolfe #22

Help wanted, male, in Trouble in triplicate, by Rex Stout. Viking, 1949; UK: Collins, 1949

Home to roost, in Triple jeopardy. by Rex Stout. Viking, 1951; UK: Collins, 1952

Homicide trinity. Viking, 1962; UK: Collins, 1963; Nero Wolfe #37

If death ever slept. Viking, 1957; UK: Collins, 1958; Nero Wolfe #28

Immune to murder, in Three for the chair, by Rex Stout. Viking, 1957; UK: Collins, 1958; Nero Wolfe #29

In the best families. Viking, 1950; UK: Even in the best of families. Collins, 1951; Nero Wolfe #16

Instead of evidence, in Trouble in triplicate, by Rex Stout. Viking, 1949; UK: Collins, 1949

Invitation to murder. Avon, 1956; UK: Cordially invited to meet death. Jonathan, 1945; also in Three men out, by Rex Stout. Viking, 1954; UK: Collins, 1955

Kill now--pay later, in Trio for blunt instruments, by Rex Stout. Viking, 1964; UK: Collins, 1965

The league of frightened men. Farrar, 1935; UK: Cassell, 1935; Nero Wolfe #2

Man alive, in Three doors to death, by Rex Stout. Viking, 1950; UK: Collins, 1950

Method three for murder, in Three at Wolfe's door, by Rex Stout. Viking, 1960; UK: Collins, 1961

Might as well be dead. Viking, 1956; UK: Collins, 1957; Nero Wolfe #27

The mother hunt. Viking, 1963; UK: Collins, 1964; Nero Wolfe #38

Murder by the book. Viking, 1951; UK: Collins, 1952; Nero Wolfe #19

Murder is corny, in Trio for blunt instruments, by Rex Stout. Viking, 1964; UK: Collins, 1965

Murder is no joke, in And four to go, by Rex Stout. Viking, 1958; UK: in Crime and again, by Rex Stout. Collins, 1959

The next witness, in Three witnesses, by Rex Stout. Viking, 1956; UK: Collins, 1956

Not quite dead enough. Farrar, 1944; Nero Wolfe #10

Omit flowers, in Three doors to death, by Rex Stout. Viking, 1950; UK: Collins, 1950

Over my dead body. Farrar, 1940; UK: Collins, 1940; Nero Wolfe #7

Please pass the guilt. Viking, 1973; UK: Collins, 1974; Nero Wolfe #45

Plot it yourself. Viking, 1959; UK: Murder in style. Collins, 1960; Nero Wolfe

Poison a la carte, in Three at Wolfe's door, by Rex Stout. Viking, 1960; UK: Collins, 1961

Prisoner's base. Viking, 1952; UK: Out goes she. Collins, 1953; Nero Wolfe #21

The red box. Farrar, 1937; UK: Cassell, 1937; Nero Wolfe #4

Red threads, in The mystery book, by Rex Stout. Farrar, 1939; UK: Collins, 1941; Insp. Cramer

A right to die. Viking, 1964; UK: Collins, 1965; Nero Wolfe #39

The rodeo murder, in Three at Wolfe's door, by Rex Stout. Viking, 1960; UK: Collins, 1961

The rubber band. Farrar, 1936; UK: Cassell, 1936; Nero Wolfe #3

The second confession. Viking, 1949; UK: Collins, 1950; Nero Wolfe #14

The silent speaker. Viking, 1946; UK: Collins, 1947; Nero Wolfe #11

Some buried Caesar. Farrar, 1939; UK: Collins, 1939; Nero Wolfe #6

The squirt and the monkey, in Triple jeopardy, by Rex Stout. Viking, 1951; UK: Collins, 1952

This won't kill you, in Three men out, by Rex Stout. Viking, 1954; UK: Collins, 1955

Three at Wolfe's door. Viking, 1960; UK: Collins, 1961; Nero Wolfe #34

Three doors to death. Viking, 1950; UK: Collins, 1950; Nero Wolfe #17

Three for the chair. Viking, 1957; UK: Collins, 1958; Nero Wolfe #29

Three men out. Viking, 1954; UK: Collins, 1955; Nero Wolfe #23

Three witnesses. Viking, 1956; UK: Collins, 1956; Nero Wolfe #26

Too many clients. Viking, 1960; UK: Collins, 1961; Nero Wolfe #33

Too many cooks. Farrar, 1960; UK: Collins, 1961; Nero Wolfe #5

Too many detectives, in Three for the chair, by Rex Stout. Viking, 1957; UK: Collins, 1958

Too many women. Viking, 1947; UK: Collins, 1948; Nero Wolfe #12

Trio for blunt instruments. Viking, 1964; UK: Collins, 1965; Nero Wolfe #40

Triple jeopardy. Viking, 1951; UK: Collins, 1952; Nero Wolfe #20

Trouble in triplicate. Viking, 1949; UK: Collins, 1949; Nero Wolfe #15

Warner & wife, in Justice ends at home, by Rex Stout. Viking, 1977

When a man murders, in Three witnesses, by Rex Stout. Viking, 1956; UK: Collins, 1956

Where there's a will. Farrar, 1940; UK: Collins, 1941; Nero Wolfe #8

A window for death, in Three for the chair, by Rex Stout. Viking, 1957; UK: Collins, 1958

The zero clue, in Three men out, by Rex Stout. Viking, 1954; UK: Collins, 1955

STRAHAN, KAY CLEAVER, 1888-1941

The desert lake mystery. Bobbs, 1936; UK: Methuen, 1937; Lynn MacDonald

The desert moon mystery. Doubleday, 1928; UK: Gollancz, 1928; Lynn MacDonald

Footprints. Doubleday, 1929; UK: Gollancz, 1929; Lynn MacDonald

The Meriweather mystery. Doubleday, 1932; Lynn MacDonald

October house. Doubleday, 1932; UK: Gollancz, 1931; Lynn MacDonald

STRANGE, JOHN STEPHEN (pseud. of Dorothy Stockbridge Tillett, 1896 --)

All men are liars. Doubleday, 1948;
   UK: Come to judgement. Collins,
   1949; George Honegger #2
The bell in the fog. Doubleday,
   1936; UK: Collins, 1937; Barney
   Gantt #1 Black hawthorn.
   Doubleday, 1933;
   UK: The Chinese jar mystery.
   Collins, 1934; Sgt. Potter
Catch the gold ring. Doubleday,
   1955; UK: A handful of silver.
   Collins, 1955; Henri Magritte
The clue of the second murder.
   Doubleday, 1929; UK: Collins,
   1929; Van Dusen Ormsberry #2
Deadly beloved. Doubleday, 1952;
   UK: Collins, 1952; Barney Gantt
   #7; Muriel Gantt
Eye witness. Doubleday, 1961; UK:
   Collins, 1962; George Honegger #3
For the hangman. Doubleday, 1934;
   UK: Collins, 1935
The house on 9th Street. Doubleday,
   1976; Barney Gantt #8
Look your last. Doubleday, 1943;
   UK: Collins, 1944; Barney Gantt #5
Make my bed soon. Doubleday, 1948;
   UK: Collins, 1948; Barney Gantt #6
The man who killed Fortescue.
   Doubleday, 1928; UK: Collins,
   1929; Van Dusen Ormsberry #1
Murder gives a lovely light.
   Doubleday, 1941; UK: Collins,
   1942; George Honegger #1
Murder on the ten-yard line.
   Doubleday, 1931; UK: Murder game.
   Collins, 1942; Van Dusen Ormsberry
   #3
A picture of the victim. Doubleday,
   1940; UK: Collins, 1940; Barney
   Gantt #4
Reasonable doubt. Doubleday, 1951;
   UK: Collins, 1951
Rope enough. Doubleday, 1938; UK:
   Collins, 1939; Barney Gantt #3
Silent witnesses. Doubleday, 1938;
   UK: The corpse and the lady.
   Collins, 1938; Barney Gantt
   #2
STRATTON, ROY, 1909? --
   The decorated corpse. Mill, 1962;
   UK: Boardman, 1963; Scott
   Gregory; Justin Bassett

One among none. Mill, 1965; UK:
   Boardman, 1965; Scott Gregory;
   Justin Bassett
STREET, CECIL JOHN CHARLES, see
   BURTON, MILES (pseud.) or RHODE,
   JOHN (pseud.)
STRIBLING, T. S., 1881-1965
   Best Dr. Poggioli detective
      stories. Dover, 1975; UK: Dover,
      1976; Henry Poggioli
   Clues of the Caribbees. Doubleday,
      1929; UK: Heinemann, 1930; Henry
      Poggioli
STROBEL, MARION, 1895 --
   Ice before killing. Scribner's,
      1943; Lincoln Lacy
STRONG, L. A. G., 1896-1958
   All fall down. Doubleday, 1944; UK:
      Collins, 1944; Ellis McKay
   Murder plays an ugly scene.
      Doubleday, 1945; UK: Othello's
      occupation. Collins, 1945; Ellis
      McKay
   Which I never. Macmillan, 1952; UK:
      Collins, 1950; Ellis McKay
STUART, IAN
   The garb of truth. Doubleday, 1984;
      David Grierson
STUBBS, JEAN, 1926
   The case of Kitty Ogilvie. Walker,
      1971; UK: Macmillan, 1970
   Dear Laura. Stein & Day, 1973; UK:
      Macmillan, 1973; John Joseph
      Lintott #1
   The golden crucible. Stein & Day,
      1976; UK: Macmillan, 1976; John
      Joseph Lintott #3
   My grand enemy. Stein & Day, 1968;
      UK: Macmillan, 1967
   The painted face. Stein & Day,
      1974; UK: Macmillan, 1974; John
      Joseph Lintott #2
STYLES, FRANK SHOWELL, see CARR,
   GLYN (pseud.) or STYLES, SHOWELL
STYLES, SHOWELL
   Hammer Island. UK: Selwyn, 1947;
      Abercrombie Lewker #2
   Kidnap Island. UK: Selwyn, 1947;
      Abercrombie Lewker
SUMMERTON, MARGARET, see ROFFMAN,
   JAN (pseud.)
SUTTON, HENRY (pseud. of David
   Rytman Slavitt, 1935 --)

The sacrifice. Grosset, 1978; UK: Sphere, 1980; Roger Braithwaite

SWARTHOUT, GLENDON, 1918 --
Skeletons. Doubleday, 1979; UK: Secker, 1979; Jimmie Butters

SWINNERTON, FRANK
The woman from Sicily. Doubleday, 1957

SYMONS, JULIAN, 1912 --
The Belting inheritance. Harper, 1965; UK: Collins, 1965

The Blackheath poisonings: a Victorian murder mystery. Harper, 1978; UK: Collins, 1978; Paul Vandervent

Bland beginning. Harper, 1949; UK: Gollancz, 1949; Insp. Bland #3

The color of murder. Harper, 1957; UK: The colour of murder. Collins, 1957

The Detling secret. Viking, 1983

The immaterial murder case. Macmillan, 1957; UK: Gollancz, 1945; Insp. Bland #1

A man called Jones. UK: Gollancz, 1947; Insp. Bland #2

The man who killed himself. Harper, 1967; UK: Collins, 1967

The man who lost his wife. Harper, 1971; UK: Collins, 1970

The name of Annabel Lee. Viking, 1983; Dudley Potter

The narrowing circle. Harper, 1954; UK: Gollancz, 1954

The pipe dream. Harper, 1959; UK: The gigantic shadow. Collins, 1958; Insp. Crambo

The plain man. Harper, 1962; UK: The killing of Francie Lake. Collins, 1962

The players and the game. Harper, 1972; UK: Collins, 1972; Insp. Hazelton

The progress of a crime. Harper, 1960; UK: Collins, 1960; Hugh Bennett

Sweet Adelaide. Harper, 1980; UK: Collins, 1980

A three pipe problem. Harper, 1975; UK: Collins, 1975; Sheridan Haynes

SZANTO, GEORGE
Not working. St. Martin's, 1982; Joe Levy

TAKAGI, AKIMATSU, 1920 --

No patent on murder. Playboy, 1977

TAPPLY, WILLIAM G.
Death at Charity's Point. Scribner's, 1984; Brady Coyne

The Dutch blue error. Scribner's, 1985; Brady Coyne #2

Follow the sharks. Scribner's, 1985; Brady Coyne #3

TARO, HIRAI, 1894 -- , see RAMPO, EDOGAWA (pseud.)

TASCHDJIAN, CLAIRE
The Peking Man is missing. Harper, 1977; UK: New English Library, 1978

TAYLOR, ANDREW
Caroline miniscule. Dodd, 1983; William Dougal

Our father's lies. Dodd, 1985; Ted Dougal; William Dougal

TAYLOR, BERNARD
The kindness of strangers. St. Martin's, 1985

TAYLOR, EDITH, 1913 --
The serpent under it. Norton, 1973; UK: Barker, 1973; Anne Redmond

TAYLOR, ELIZABETH ATWOOD
The cable car murder. St. Martin's, 1981; Maggie Elliott

TAYLOR, L. A.
Deadly objectives. Walker, 1984; Joseph "JJ" Jamison

Footnote to murder. Walker, 1983; Marge Brock

Only half a hoax. Walker, 1983; Joseph "JJ" Jamison

Shed light on death. Walker, 1985; Joseph "JJ" Jamison

TAYLOR, P. WALKER, 1903 --
Murder in the flagship. Mill, 1937; UK: Butterworth, 1936; Commander Wraithlea

Murder in the game reserve. Mill, 1938; UK: Butterworth, 1937; Commander Wraithlea

Murder in the Suez Canal. UK: Butterworth, 1937; Commander Wraithlea

Murder in the Taj Mahal. UK: Butterworth, 1938; Commander Wraithlea

TAYLOR, PHOEBE ATWOOD, 1909-1976.
For other mysteries by this author, see TILTON, ALICE (pseud.)

The Asey Mayo trio. Messner, 1946; UK: Collins, 1946; Asey Mayo #22

Banbury Bog. Norton, 1938; UK: Collins, 1939; Asey Mayo #13

The Cape Cod mystery. Bobbs, 1931; Asey Mayo #1

The criminal C. O. D. Norton, 1940; UK: Collins, 1940; Asey Mayo #15

The Crimson patch. Norton, 1936; UK: Gollancz, 1936; Asey Mayo #8

The deadly sunshade. Norton, 1940; UK: Collins, 1941; Asey Mayo #16

Death lights a candle. Bobbs, 1932; Asey Mayo #2

Deathblow Hill. Hodder, 1935; UK: Gollancz, 1936; Asey Mayo #7

Diplomatic corpse. Little, 1951; UK: Collins, 1951; Asey Mayo #24

Figure away. Norton, 1937; UK: Collins, 1938; Asey Mayo #10

Going, going, gone. Norton, 1943; UK: Collins, 1944; Asey Mayo #20

The headacre plot, in Three plots for Asey Mayo, by Phoebe Atwood Taylor. Norton, 1942

Murder rides the gale, in Asey Mayo trio, by Phoebe Atwood Taylor. Messner, 1946; UK: Collins, 1946

The mystery of the Cape Cod players. Norton, 1933; UK: Eyre, 1934; Asey Mayo #3

Mystery of the Cape Cod tavern. Norton, 1934; UK: Eyre, 1935; Asey Mayo #4

Octagon House. Norton, 1937; UK: Collins, 1938; Asey Mayo #11

Out of order. Norton, 1936; UK: Gollancz, 1937; Asey Mayo #9

The perennial border. Norton, 1941; UK: Collins, 1942; Asey Mayo #17

Proof of the pudding. Norton, 1945; UK: Collins, 1945; Asey Mayo #21

Punch with care. Farrar, 1946; UK: Collins, 1947; Asey Mayo #23

Sandbar sinister. Norton, 1931; UK: Gollancz, 1936; Asey Mayo #5

The six iron spiders. Norton, 1942; UK: Collins, 1943; Asey Mayo #18

Spring harrowing. Norton, 1939; UK: Gollancz, 1939; Asey Mayo #14

The stars spell death, in Asey Mayo trio, by Phoebe Atwood Taylor. Messner, 1946; UK: Collins, 1946

The swan-boat plot, in Three plots for Asey Mayo, by Phoebe Atwood Taylor. Norton, 1942

The third murderer, in Asey Mayo trio, by Phoebe Atwood Taylor. Messner, 1946; UK: Collins, 1946

Three plots for Asey Mayo. Norton, 1942; Asey Mayo #19

Tinkling symbol. Norton, 1935; UK: Gollancz, 1935; Asey Mayo #6

The wander bird plot, in Three plots for Asey Mayo, by Phoebe Atwood Taylor. Norton, 1942

TEDESCHI, FRANK L, see BYFIELD, BARBARA NINDE and TEDESCHI, FRANK L.

TEILHET, DARWIN L., 1904-1964

Death flies high. Morrow, 1931; UK: Long, 1932; Jean Henri St. Amand

The talking sparrow murders. Morrow, 1934; UK: Gollancz, 1934

TEILHET, DARWIN L. with TEILHET, HILDEGARDE

The feather cloak murders. Doubleday, 1936; UK: Gollancz, 1937; Baron Von Kaz

TEMPLE-ELLIS, N. A.

The inconsistent villains. Dutton, 1929; UK: Methuen, 1930; Montrose Arbuthnot; Edmund King

The man who was there. Dutton, 1930; UK: Methuen, 1930; Montrose Arbuthnot; Edmund King

Murder in the ruins. Dial, 1936; UK: Dead in no time. Hodder, 1935; Montrose Arbuthnot

TENNANT, EMMA

The half-mother. Little, 1985

TESSIER, ERNEST MAURICE, 1885-1973, see DEKOBRA, MAURICE (pseud.)

TEY, JOSEPHINE (pseud. of Elizabeth Mackintosh, 1897-1952)

Brat Farrar. Macmillan, 1950; UK: Davies, 1949

The daughter of time. Macmillan, 1952; UK: Davies, 1957; Alan Grant #5

The franchise affair. Macmillan, 1949; UK: Davies, 1948; Alan Grant #3

The man in the queue. Dutton, 1927; UK: Methuen, 1929; Alan Grant #1

Miss Pym disposes. Macmillan, 1948; UK: Davies, 1946; Lucy Pym

A shilling for candles. Macmillan, 1954; UK: Methuen, 1936; Alan Grant #2

The singing sands. Macmillan, 1953; UK: Davies, 1952; Alan Grant #6

To love and be wise. Macmillan,
1951; UK: Davies, 1950; Alan Grant
#4

THAYER, LEE (pseud. of Emma Redington
Thayer, 1874-1973)

Accessory after the fact. Dodd,
1943; UK: Hurst, 1944; Peter
Clancy #35

Accident, manslaughter, or murder?
Dodd, 1945; UK: Hurst, 1946; Peter
Clancy #39

The affair at "The Cedars."
Doubleday, 1921; Peter Clancy #3

Alias Dr. Ely. Doubleday, 1927;
UK: Hurst, 1927; Peter Clancy #8

And one cried murder. Dodd, 1961;
UK: Long, 1962; Peter Clancy #59

Blood on the knight. Dodd, 1952;
UK: Hurst, 1953; Peter Clancy #50

Counterfeit. Sears, 1933; UK: The
counterfeit bill. Hurst, 1934;
Peter Clancy #16

Dark of the moon. Dodd, 1936; UK:
Death in the gorge. Hurst, 1937;
Peter Clancy #21

The darkest spot. Sears, 1928; UK:
Hurst, 1928; Peter Clancy #9

Dead end street, no outlet. Dodd,
1936; UK: Murder in the mirror.
Hurst, 1936; Peter Clancy #22

Dead men's shoes. Sears, 1929; UK:
Hurst, 1929; Peter Clancy #10

Dead on arrival. Dodd, 1960; UK:
Long, 1962; Peter Clancy #58

Dead reckoning. Dodd, 1954; UK:
Murder on the Pacific. Hurst,
1955; Peter Clancy #52

Dead storage. Dodd, 1935; UK: The
death weed. Hurst, 1935; Peter
Clancy #19

Do not disturb. Dodd, 1951; UK:
Clancy's secret mission. Hurst,
1952; Peter Clancy #48

Dusty death. Dodd, 1966; UK: Death
walks in shadow. Long, 1966; Peter
Clancy #60

Evil root. Dodd, 1949; UK: Hurst,
1951; Peter Clancy #45

Five bullets. Dodd, 1944; UK:
Hurst, 1947; Peter Clancy #38

The glass knife. Sears, 1932; UK:
Hurst, 1932; Peter Clancy #14

Guilt edged. Dodd, 1951; UK: Guilt
edged murder. Hurst, 1953; Peter
Clancy #49

Guilt is where you find it. Dodd,
1957; UK: Long, 1958; Peter
Clancy #55

Guilty! Dodd, 1940; UK: Hurst,
1941; Peter Clancy #29

A hair's breadth. Dodd, 1946; UK:
Hurst, 1947; Peter Clancy #40

Hallowe'en homicide. Dodd, 1941;
UK: Hurst, 1942; Peter Clancy
#31

Hanging's too good. Dodd, 1943; UK:
Hurst, 1945; Peter Clancy #36

Hell-gate tides. Sears, 1933; UK:
Hurst, 1933; Peter Clancy #17

The jaws of death. Dodd, 1946; UK:
Hurst, 1948; Peter Clancy #41

The key. Doubleday, 1924; UK:
Hurst, 1924; Peter Clancy #6

The last shot. Sears, 1931; UK:
Hurst, 1931; Peter Clancy #12

Last trump. Dodd, 1937; UK: Hurst,
1937; Peter Clancy #23

Lightning strikes twice. Dodd,
1939; UK: Hurst, 1939; Peter
Clancy #27

A man's enemies. Dodd, 1937; UK:
This man's doom. Hurst, 1938;
Peter Clancy #24

Murder is out. Dodd, 1942; UK:
Hurst, 1943; Peter Clancy #33

Murder on location. Dodd, 1942; UK:
Hurst, 1944; Peter Clancy #34

Murder stalks the circle. Dodd,
1947; UK: Hurst, 1949; Peter
Clancy #42

The mystery of the thirteenth
floor. Century, 1919; Peter
Clancy #1

No holiday for death. Dodd, 1954;
UK: Hurst, 1955; Peter Clancy #53

Out brief candle! Dodd, 1948; UK:
Hurst, 1950; Peter Clancy #43

Persons unknown. Dodd, 1941; UK:
Hurst, 1942; Peter Clancy #32

Pig in a poke. Dodd, 1948; UK: A
clue for Clancy. Hurst, 1950;
Peter Clancy #44

A plain case of murder. Dodd, 1944;
UK: Hurst, 1945; Peter Clancy #37

Poison. Doubleday, 1926; UK:
Heinemann, 1926; Peter Clancy #7

The prisoner pleads "not guilty."
Dodd, 1953; UK: Hurst, 1954;
Peter Clancy #51

Q. E. D. Doubleday, 1921; UK: The puzzle. Hurst, 1923; Peter Clancy #4

Ransom racket. Dodd, 1938; UK: Hurst, 1938; Peter Clancy #25

The scrimshaw millions. Sears, 1932; UK: Hurst, 1933; Peter Clancy #15

The second bullet. Sears, 1934; UK: The second shot. Hurst, 1935; Peter Clancy #18

Set a thief. Sears, 1931; UK: To catch a thief. Hurst, 1932; Peter Clancy #13

The sinister mask. Doubleday, 1923; UK: Hurst, 1923; Peter Clancy #5

Stark murder. Dodd, 1939; UK: Hurst, 1940; Peter Clancy #28

Still no answer. Dodd, 1958; UK: Web of hate. Long, 1959; Peter Clancy #56

Sudden death. Dodd, 1935; UK: Red handed. Hurst, 1936; Peter Clancy #20

That strange Sylvester affair. Dodd, 1938; UK: The strange Sylvester affair. Hurst, 1939; Peter Clancy #26

They tell no tales. Sears, 1930; UK: Hurst, 1930; Peter Clancy #11

Too long endured. Dodd, 1950; UK: Hurst, 1952; Peter Clancy #47

Two ways to die. Dodd, 1959; UK: Long, 1961; Peter Clancy #57

The unlatched door. Century, 1920; Peter Clancy #2

Who benefits? Dodd, 1955; UK: Fatal alibi. Hurst, 1956; Peter Clancy #54

Within the vault. Dodd, 1950; UK: Death within the vault. Hurst, 1951; Peter Clancy #46

X marks the spot. Dodd, 1940; UK: Hurst, 1941; Peter Clancy #30

THAYER, TIFFANY, 1902-1959

One woman. Morrow, 1933; Abe Adams

THOMAS, CAROLYN (pseud. of Actea Caroline Duncan, 1913 --)

The cactus shroud. Lippincott, 1957; UK: Boardman, 1957

The hearse horse snickered. Lippincott, 1954; UK: Boardman, 1955

Narrow gauge to murder. Lippincott, 1953; UK: Boardman, 1956

Prominent among the mourners. Lippincott, 1946; UK: Cherry Tree, 1949; Sheriff Townsend; Susan Eyerly

THOMAS, DONALD

Mad Hatter summer. Viking, 1983; C. L. Dodgson; Alfred Swain

THOMAS, LESLIE

Ormerod's landing. St. Martin's, 1979; UK: Eyre, 1978; George Ormerod

THOMPSON, DAVID LANDSBOROUGH, see DAVIDSON, T. L. (pseud.)

THOMPSON, GENE, 1924 --

Murder mystery. Random House, 1980; UK: Gollancz, 1981; Dade Cooley #1

Nobody cared for Kate. Random House, 1983; Dade Cooley #2

THOMSON, BASIL, 1861-1939

The case of Naomie Clynes. Doubleday, 1934; UK: Inspector Richardson, C. I. D. Eldon, 1934; Insp. Richardson #3

The case of the dead diplomat. Doubleday, 1935; UK: Eldon, 1935; Insp. Richardson #4

The Dartmoor enigma. Doubleday, 1936; UK: Richardson solves a Dartmoor mystery. Eldon, 1935; Insp. Richardson #5

The mystery of the French milliner. Doubleday, 1937; UK: Milliner's hat mystery. Eldon, 1937; Insp. Richardson #7

P. C. Richardson's first case. Doubleday, 1933; UK: Eldon, 1933; Insp. Richardson #1

Richardson's second case. Doubleday, 1934; UK: Richardson scores again. Eldon, 1934; Insp. Richardson #2

When thieves fall out. Doubleday, 1937; UK: A murder arranged. Eldon, 1937; Insp. Richardson #8

Who killed Stella Pomeroy? Doubleday, 1936; UK: Death in the bathroom. Eldon, 1936; Insp. Richardson #6

THOMSON, JUNE, 1930 --

Alibi in time. Doubleday, 1980; UK: Constable, 1980; Insp. Rudd #7

Case closed. Doubleday, 1977; UK:
Constable, 1977; Insp. Rudd #4
Death cap. Doubleday, 1977; UK:
Constable, 1973; Insp. Rudd #2
The habit of loving. Doubleday,
1979; UK: Deadly relations.
Constable, 1979; Insp. Rudd #6
The long revenge. Doubleday, 1975;
UK: Constable, 1974; Insp. Rudd #3
Not one of us. Harper, 1971; UK:
Constable, 1972; Insp. Rudd #1
Portrait of Lillith. Doubleday,
1983; Insp. Rudd #9
A question of identity. Doubleday,
1977; UK: Constable, 1978; Insp.
Rudd #5
Shadow of a doubt. Doubleday,
1982; Insp. Rudd #8
Sound evidence. Doubleday, 1985;
Insp. Rudd #10
THORNE, ANTHONY, 1904 --
So long at the fair. Random House,
1947; UK: Heinemann, 1947
THORNE, PAUL
Murder in the fog. Penn, 1929; Det.
Conroy; Det. McCarthy
Spiderweb clues. Penn, 1928
That evening in Shanghai. Penn, 1931
THORNE, PAUL and THORNE, MABEL
The secret toll. Dodd, 1922; Robert
Forrester
The Sheridan Road mystery. Dodd,
1921; Dave Morgan
TIDYMAN, ERNEST, 1928 --
Goodbye, Mr. Shaft. Dial, 1973; UK:
Weidenfeld, 1974; John Shaft #5
The last Shaft. UK: Weidenfeld,
1975; John Shaft #7
Line of duty. Little, 1974; UK:
Allen, 1974
Shaft. Macmillan, 1970; UK: Joseph,
1971; John Shaft #1
Shaft among the Jews. Dial, 1972;
UK: Weidenfeld, 1973; John Shaft
#2
Shaft has a ball. Bantam, 1973; UK:
Corgi, 1973; John Shaft #4
Shaft's big score. Bantam, 1972;
UK: Corgi, 1972; John Shaft #3
Shaft's carnival of killers.
Bantam, 1974; UK: Bantam, 1974;
John Shaft #6

TILLETT, DOROTHY STOCKBRIDGE, see
STRANGE, JOHN STEPHEN (pseud.)
TILTON, ALICE (pseud.). For other
mysteries by this author, see
TAYLOR, PHOEBE ATWOOD
Beginning with a bash. Norton,
1972; UK: Collins, 1937; Leonidas
Witherall #1
Cold steal. Norton, 1939; UK:
Collins, 1940; Leonidas Witherall
#3
The cut direct. Norton, 1938; UK:
Collins, 1938; Leonidas Witherall
#2
Dead Ernest. Norton, 1944; UK:
Collins, 1945; Leonidas Witherall
#7
File for record. Norton, 1943; UK:
Collins, 1944; Leonidas Witherall
#6
The hollow chest. Norton, 1941; UK:
Collins, 1942; Leonidas Witherall
#5
The iron clew. Farrar, 1947; UK:
The iron hand. Collins, 1947;
Leonidas Witherall #8
The left leg. Norton, 1940; UK:
Collins, 1941; Leonidas Witherall
#4
TINE, ROBERT
Uneasy lies the head. Viking, 1982;
Insp. Smudge; Insp. Pidgeon
TIRBUTT, HONORIA, see PAGE, EMMA
(pseud.)
TODD, RUTHVEN, 1914 -- , see
CAMPBELL, R. T. (pseud.)
TOGAWA, MASAKO
The master key. Dodd, 1985
TOMLINSON, GERALD, 1933 --
On a field of black. Nellin, 1979;
Seth Warriner
TORDAY, URSULA, see BLACKSTOCK,
CHARITY (pseud.)
TOURNEY, LEONARD
Familiar spirits. St. Martin's,
1985; Matthew Stock; Joan Stock
Low treason. Dutton, 1982; Joan
Stock #2; Matthew Stock #2
The player's boy is dead. Harper &
Row, 1980; UK: Hale, 1982;
Matthew Stock

TOWNE, STUART (pseud.). For other
mysteries by this author, see
RAWSON, CLAYTON
Death out of thin air. Coward
McCann, 1941; UK: Cassell, 1947;
Don Diavolo
TRAIN, ARTHUR, 1875-1945
The adventures of Ephraim Tutt.
Scribner's, 1930; Ephraim Tutt #6
The hermit of Turkey Hollow.
Scribner's, 1921; Ephraim Tutt #2
McAllister and his double.
Scribner's, 1905; UK: Newnes,
1905; John Dockbridge
Mr. Tutt at his best. Scribner's,
1961; Ephraim Tutt #14
Mr. Tutt comes home. Scribner's,
1941; Ephraim Tutt #11
Mr. Tutt finds a way. Scribner's,
1945; Ephraim Tutt #13
Mr. Tutt takes the stand.
Scribner's, 1936; Ephraim Tutt #8
Mr. Tutt's case book. Scribner's,
1936; Ephraim Tutt #9
Old man Tutt. Scribner's, 1938;
Ephraim Tutt #10
Page Mr. Tutt. Scribner's, 1926;
Ephraim Tutt #4
Tut, tut! Mr. Tutt. Scribner's,
1923; UK: Nash, 1924; Ephraim Tutt
#3
Tutt and Mr. Tutt. Scribner's,
1920; Ephraim Tutt #1
Tutt for Tutt. Scribner's, 1934;
Ephraim Tutt #7
When Tutt meets Tutt. Scribner's,
1927; Ephraim Tutt #5
Yankee lawyer--Autobiography of
Ephraim Tutt. Scribner's, 1943;
Ephraim Tutt #12
TRAVERS, HUGH (pseud. of Hugh Travers
Mills)
Madame Aubry and the police.
Harper, 1967; UK: Elek, 1966; Mme.
Aubry
Madame Aubry dines with death.
Harper, 1967; UK: Elek, 1967; Mme.
Aubry
TREAT, LAWRENCE (pseud. of Lawrence
Arthur Goldstone, 1903 --)
B as in banshee. Duell, 1940; Carl
Wayward #1
Big shot. Harper, 1951; UK:
Boardman, 1952; Mitch Taylor #3;
Bill Decker #3; Jub Freeman #7

D as in dead. Duell, 1941; Carl
Wayward #2
F as in flight. Morrow, 1948; UK:
Boardman, 1949; Jub Freeman #5;
Bill Decker #1
H as in hangman. Duell, 1942; Carl
Wayward #3
H as in hunted. Duell, 1946; UK:
Boardman, 1950; Jub Freeman #2
Lady drop dead. Abelard-Schuman,
1960; UK: Abelard-Schuman, 1960;
Mitch Taylor #5; Jub Freeman #9
O as in omen. Duell, 1943; Carl
Wayward #4
Over the edge. Morrow, 1948; UK:
Boardman, 1958; Jub Freeman #6;
Bill Decker #2
P as in police. Davies, 1970; Jub
Freeman; Mitch Taylor
Q as in quicksand. Duell, 1947; UK:
Step into quicksand. Boardman,
1959; Jub Freeman #3; Mitch
Taylor #1
T as in trapped. Morrow, 1947;
Mitch Taylor #2; Jub Freeman #4
V as in victim. Duell, 1945; UK:
Rich, 1950; Carl Wayward #5; Jub
Freeman #1
Weep for a wanton. Ace, 1956; UK:
Boardman, 1957; Mitch Taylor #4;
Jub Freeman #8
TRECKER, JANICE LAW, see LAW, JANICE
TREE, GREGORY (pseud. of John
Franklin Barden, 1916-1981)
The case against Butterfly.
Scribner's, 1951; Bill Bradley
#2; Noel Mayberry #2
The case against myself.
Scribner's, 1950; UK: Gollancz,
1951; Bill Bradley #1; Noel
Mayberry #1
TRENCH, JOHN, 1920 --
Beyond the atlas. Macmillan, 1963;
UK: Macdonald, 1963
Dishonored bones. Macmillan, 1955;
UK: Dishonoured bones. Macdonald,
1953; Martin Cotterell #2
Docken dead. Macmillan, 1954; UK:
Macdonald, 1953; Martin Cotterell
#1
What rough beast. Macmillan, 1957;
UK: Macdonald, 1957; Martin
Cotterell #3
TREVOR, GLEN (pseud. of James
Hilton, 1900-1954)

Was it murder? Harper, 1933; UK:
Murder at school. Benn, 1931;
Colin Revell

TRIPP, MILES, 1923 --
Cruel victim. St. Martin's, 1985;
UK: Macmillan, 1979; John Samson
#4

Obsession. UK: Macmillan, 1973;
John Samson #1

The once a year man. UK: Macmillan,
1977; John Samson #2

The wife-smuggler. UK: Macmillan,
1978; John Samson #3

TROLLOPE, ANTHONY, 1815-1882
The Eustace diamonds. Harper,
1872; UK: Chapman, 1876

John Caldigate. UK: Oxford, 1946

TROW, M. J.
The supreme adventure of Inspector
Lestrade. Stein & Day, 1985;
Sholto Lestrade; Sherlock Holmes

TROY, SIMON
Cease upon the midnight. Macmillan,
1965; UK: Gollancz, 1964; Charles
Smith #4

Don't play with the rough boys.
Macmillan, 1964; UK: Gollancz,
1963; Charles Smith #3

No more a-roving. UK: Gollancz,
1965; Charles Smith #5

The road to Rhuine. Dodd, 1952; UK:
Collins, 1952; Charles Smith #1

Second cousin removed. Macmillan,
1962; UK: Gollancz, 1961; Charles
Smith #2

Sup with the devil. UK: Gollancz,
1967; Charles Smith #6

Swift to its close. Stein & Day,
1969; UK: Gollancz, 1969; Charles
Smith #7

Waiting for Oliver. Macmillan,
1963; UK: Gollancz, 1962

TRUAX, RHODA, 1891 --
The accident ward mystery. Little,
1937

TRUMAN, MARGARET
Murder at the FBI. Arbor House,
1985; Ross Lizenby; Chris Saksis

Murder in the Smithsonian. Arbor
House, 1983; Heather McBean; Mac
Hanrahan

Murder in the Supreme Court. Arbor
House, 1982; Martin Teller;
Susanna Pinscher

Murder in the White House. Arbor
House, 1980; UK: Severn, 1981;
Mr. Fairchild

Murder on Capitol Hill. Arbor
House, 1981; Lydia James

Murder on Embassy Row. Arbor House,
1984; Sal Morizio

TRUSS, SELDON, 1892 --
Never fight a lady. Doubleday,
1950; UK: Hodder, 1951; Insp.
Gidleigh

One man's enemies. Doubleday, 1960;
UK: One man's death. Hale, 1960;
Insp. Gidleigh

TUCKER, WILSON, 1914 --
The Chinese doll. Rinehart, 1946;
UK: Cassell, 1948; Charles Horne

The dove. Rinehart, 1948; UK:
Cassell, 1950; Charles Horne

The man in my grave. Rinehart,
1956; UK: Macdonald, 1958

A procession of the damned.
Doubleday, 1965; UK: Hale, 1967

Red herring. Rinehart, 1951;
Charles Horne

The stalking man. Rinehart, 1949;
UK: Cassell, 1950; Charles Horne

Time bomb. Rinehart, 1955; Lt.
Danforth

To keep or kill. Rinehart, 1947;
UK: Cassell, 1950; Charles Horne

TURNBULL, PETER
Big money. St. Martin's, 1984

Dead knock. St. Martin's, 1983;
Insp. Donoghue

Deep and crisp and even. St.
Martin's, 1982; Det. Sussock

Fair Friday. St. Martin's, 1983

TURNGREN, ANNETTE, 1902-1980. For
other mysteries by this author, see
HOPKINS, A. T. (pseud.)
Mystery walks the campus. Funk and
Wagnalls, 1956

TYNAN, KATHLEEN
Agatha. Ballantine, 1978; UK:
Weidenfeld, 1978; Agatha Christie

TYRE, NEDRA, 1921 --
Death of an intruder. Knopf, 1953;
UK: Collins, 1954

Hall of death. Simon & Schuster,
1960

Mouse in eternity. Knopf, 1952;
UK: Macdonald, 1953

UHNAK, DOROTHY, 1933 --
The bait. Simon & Schuster, 1968;
UK: Hodder, 1968; Christie Opara
#1
The investigation. Simon &
Schuster, 1977; UK: Hodder, 1977;
Joe Peters
Law and order. Simon & Schuster,
1973; UK: Hodder, 1973
The ledger. Simon & Schuster,
1970; UK: Hodder, 1971; Christie
Opara #3
The witness. Simon & Schuster,
1969; UK: Hodder, 1970; Christie
Opara #2
ULLMAN, JAMES MICHAEL
Good night, Irene. Simon &
Schuster, 1968; UK: Full coverage.
Cassell, 1966
Lady on fire. Simon & Schuster,
1968; UK: Cassell, 1969; Julian
Forbes
The Venus trap. Simon & Schuster,
1966; UK: House of cards. Cassell,
1967
UNDERWOOD, MICHAEL (pseud. of John
Michael Evelyn, 1916 --)
Adam's case. Doubleday, 1961; UK:
Hammond, 1961; Simon Manton #9
The anxious conspirator. Doubleday,
1965; UK: Macdonald, 1965; Simon
Manton #13
Arm of the law. UK: Hammond, 1959;
Simon Manton #6
The case against Phillip Quest. UK:
Macdonald, 1962; Simon Manton #10
Cause of death. UK: Hammond, 1960;
Simon Manton #7
A clear case of suicide. St.
Martin's, 1980; UK: Macmillan,
1980
The crime of Colin Wise. Doubleday,
1964; UK: Macdonald, 1964; Simon
Manton #12
Crime upon crime. St. Martin's,
1981; UK: Macmillan, 1980; Rosa
Epton
Crooked wood. St. Martin's, 1978;
UK: Macmillan, 1978; Nick Attwell;
Clare Attwell
Death by misadventure. UK: Hammond,
1960; Simon Manton #8
Death in camera. St. Martin's,
1984; Rosa Epton

Death on remand. UK: Hammond, 1956;
Simon Manton #3
Double jeopardy. St. Martin's, 1981
False witness. Walker, 1961; UK:
Hammond, 1957; Simon Manton #4
The fatal trip. St. Martin's, 1977;
UK: Macmillan, 1977; Nick
Attwell; Clare Attwell
Girl found dead. UK: Macdonald,
1963; Simon Manton #11
Hand of fate. St. Martin's, 1982
The hidden man. St. Martin's, 1985;
Rosa Epton
Lawful pursuit. Doubleday, 1958;
UK: Hammond, 1958; Simon Manton
#5
The man who killed too soon. UK:
Macdonald, 1968; Richard Monk
Menaces, menaces. St. Martin's,
1976; UK: Macmillan, 1976
Murder made absolute. Washburn,
1957; UK: Hammond, 1955; Simon
Manton #2
Murder on trial. Washburn, 1958;
UK: Hammond, 1954; Simon Manton
#1
Murder with malice. St. Martin's,
1977; UK: Macmillan, 1977; Nick
Attwell; Clare Attwell
A party to murder. St. Martin's,
1984; Rosa Epton
A pinch of snuff. St. Martin's,
1974; UK: Macmillan, 1974
The silent liars. Doubleday, 1970;
UK: Macmillan, 1970
Smooth justice. St. Martin's,
1979; UK: Macmillan, 1979
Victim of circumstance. St.
Martin's, 1980; UK: Macmillan,
1979
UPFIELD, ARTHUR W., 1888-1964
An author bites the dust.
Doubleday, 1948; UK: Angus, 1948;
Napoleon Bonaparte #11
The bachelors of Broken Hill.
Doubleday, 1950; UK: Heinemann,
1958; Napoleon Bonaparte #14
Battling prophet. UK: Heinemann,
1956; Napoleon Bonaparte #20
The body at Madman's Bend.
Doubleday, 1964; UK: Madmen's
Bend. Heinemann, 1963; Napoleon
Bonaparte #28

The bone is pointed. Doubleday, 1947; UK: Angus, 1938; Napoleon Bonaparte #6

Bony and the black virgin. Collier, 1965; UK: Heinemann, 1959; Napoleon Bonaparte #23

The bushman who came back. Doubleday, 1957; UK: Bony buys a woman. Heinemann, 1957; Napoleon Bonaparte #22

Death of a lake. Doubleday, 1954; UK: Heinemann, 1954; Napoleon Bonaparte #18

Death of a swagman. Doubleday, 1945; UK: Aldor, 1946; Napoleon Bonaparte #9

The devil's steps. Doubleday, 1946; UK: Aldor, 1948; Napoleon Bonaparte #10

Journey to the hangman. Doubleday, 1959; UK: Bony and the mouse. Heinemann, 1959; Napoleon Bonaparte #24

Lake Frome monster. (completed by J. L. Price and Dorothy Strange) UK: Heinemann, 1966; Napoleon Bonaparte #29

The lure of the bush. Doubleday, 1965; UK: The barrakee mystery. Hutchinson, 1929; Napoleon Bonaparte #1

The man of two tribes. Doubleday, 1956; UK: Heinemann, 1956; Napoleon Bonaparte #21

The mountains have a secret. Doubleday, 1948; UK: Heinemann, 1952; Napoleon Bonaparte #12

Murder down under. Doubleday, 1943; UK: Mr. Jelly's business. Angus, 1937; Napoleon Bonaparte #4

Murder must wait. Doubleday, 1953; UK: Heinemann, 1953; Napoleon Bonaparte #17

The mystery of Swordfish Reef. Doubleday, 1943; UK: Angus, 1939; Napoleon Bonaparte #7

The new shoe. Doubleday, 1951; UK: Heinemann, 1952; Napoleon Bonaparte #15

No footprints in the bush. Doubleday, 1944; UK: Bushranger of the skies. Angus, 1940; Napoleon Bonaparte #8

Sands of Windee. UK: Hutchinson, 1931; Napoleon Bonaparte #2

Sinister stones. Doubleday, 1954; UK: Cake in the hatbox. Heinemann, 1955; Napoleon Bonaparte #19

Valley of the smugglers. Doubleday, 1960; UK: Bony and the Kelly gang. Heinemann, 1960; Napoleon Bonaparte #25

Venom House. Doubleday, 1952; UK: Heinemann, 1953; Napoleon Bonaparte #16

The white savage. Doubleday, 1961; UK: Bony and the white savage. Heinemann, 1961; Napoleon Bonaparte #26

The widows of Broome. Doubleday, 1950; UK: Heinemann, 1951; Napoleon Bonaparte #13

The will of the tribe. Doubleday, 1962; UK: Heinemann, 1962; Napoleon Bonaparte #27

Wind of evil. Doubleday, 1944; UK: Angus, 1937; Napoleon Bonaparte #5

Wings above the claypan. Doubleday, 1943; UK: Wings above the Dimantina. Angus, 1936; Napoleon Bonaparte #3

UPTON, ROBERT
Fade out. Viking, 1984; Amos McGriffin

A golden fleecing. St. Martin's, 1979

UTECHIN, NICHOLAS
Sherlock Holmes at Oxford. Dugdale, 1977; Sherlock Holmes

VALIN, JONATHAN, 1948 --
Day of wrath. Congdon, 1982; Harry Stoner

Dead letter. Dodd, 1981; Harry Stoner #3

Final notice. Dodd, 1980; UK: Collins, 1981; Harry Stoner

The lime pit. Dodd, 1980; UK: Collins, 1981; Harry Stoner

Natural causes. Congdon, 1983; Harry Stoner #5

VANARDY, VARICK (pseud. of Frederic Merril Van Reusselaer Day, 1861-1922)
Alias the night wind. Dillingham, 1913; Bingham Harvard #1

The lady of the night wind.
Macaulay, 1919; UK: Skeffington,
1926; Bingham Harvard #4

The night wind's promise.
Dillingham, 1914; Bingham Harvard
#3

The return of the night wind.
Dillingham, 1914; Bingham Harvard
#2

Something doing. Macaulay, 1919;
Crewe #2

The two-faced man. Macaulay, 1918;
UK: Jarrolds, 1920; Crewe #1

Up against it. Macaulay, 1920

VAN ARSDALE, WIRT (pseud. of Martha
Wirt Davis, 1905-1952)
The professor knits a shroud.
Doubleday, 1951; Jose Apodaca

VAN ASH, CAY
Ten years beyond Baker Street.
Harper & Row, 1984; Sherlock
Holmes; Fu Manchu

VAN ATTA, WINFRED, 1910 --
A good place to work and die.
Doubleday, 1970; UK: Hale, 1971;
Jim Ferguson

Hatchet man. Doubleday, 1962; UK:
Boardman, 1964; Ken Mitchell

Shock treatment. Doubleday, 1961;
UK: Boardman, 1964; Dale Nelson

VANCE, JOHN HOLBROOK, 1942 --
The deadly isles. Bobbs, 1969; UK:
Hale, 1970

The Fox Valley murders. Bobbs,
1966; UK: Hale, 1967; Joe Bain #1

The Pleasant Grove murders. Bobbs,
1967; UK: Hale, 1968; Joe Bain #2

VANDERCOOK, JOHN W., 1902-1963
Murder in Fiji. Doubleday, 1936;
UK: Heinemann, 1936; Bertram Lynch
#2; Robert Deane #2

Murder in Haiti. Macmillan, 1956;
UK: Eyre, 1956; Robert Deane #3;
Bertram Lynch #3

Murder in New Guinea. Macmillan,
1959; UK: Allen, 1960; Bertram
Lynch #4; Robert Deane #4

Murder in Trinidad. Doubleday,
1933; UK: Heinemann, 1934; Bertram
Lynch #1; Robert Deane #1

VAN DEVENTER, EMMA MURDOCH, see
LYNCH, LAWRENCE L. (pseud.)

VAN DE WETERING, JANWILLEM, see
WETERING, JANWILLEM VAN DE

VAN DINE, S. S. (pseud. of Willard
Huntington Wright, 1888-1939)
The Benson murder case. Scribner's,
1926; UK: Benn, 1926; Philo Vance
#1

The Bishop murder case. Scribner's,
1929; UK: Cassell, 1929; Philo
Vance #4

The canary murder case. Scribner's,
1927; UK: Benn, 1927; Philo Vance
#2

The casino murder case. Scribner's,
1934; UK: Cassell, 1934; Philo
Vance #8

The dragon murder case. Scribner's,
1933; UK: Cassell, 1934; Philo
Vance #7

The Gorden murder case. Scribner's,
1938; UK: Cassell, 1938; Philo
Vance #10

The Gracie Allen murder case.
Scribner's, 1938; UK: Cassell,
1938; Philo Vance #11; Gracie
Allen

The Greene murder case. Scribner's,
1928; UK: Benn, 1928; Philo Vance
#3

The kennel murder case. Scribner's,
1933; UK: Cassell, 1933; Philo
Vance #6

The kidnap murder case. Scribner's,
1936; UK: Cassell, 1936; Philo
Vance #9

The scarab murder case. Scribner's,
1930; UK: Cassell, 1930; Philo
Vance #5

The winter murder case. Scribner's,
1939; UK: Cassell, 1939; Philo
Vance #12

VAN GULIK, ROBERT, see GULIK, ROBERT
VAN

VAN SILLER, HILDA, see SILLER, VAN
(pseud.)

VEDDER, JOHN K. (pseud. of Frank
Gruber, 1904-1969)
The last doorbell. Holt, 1941;
Frank Sargent

VENABLES, TERRY, see YUILL, P. B.
(pseud.)

VENNING, MICHAEL (pseud. of Georgiana
Ann Randolph, 1908-1957). For other
mysteries by this author, see RICE,
CRAIG (pseud.)

Jethro Hammer. Coward McCann,
1944; UK: Nicholson, 1947;
Melville Fairr #3
The man who slept all day. Coward
McCann, 1942; Melville Fairr #1
Murder through the looking glass.
Coward McCann, 1943; UK:
Nicholson, 1947; Melville Fairr #2
VIDAL, GORE, see BOX, EDGAR

WADE, HENRY (pseud. of Henry Lancelot
Aubrey-Fletcher, 1887-1969)
Bury him darkly. UK: Constable,
1936; Insp. Poole #6
Constable, guard thyself! Houghton,
1935; UK: Constable, 1934; Insp.
Poole #5
The Duke of York's steps. Payson
and Clarke, 1929; UK: Constable,
1929; Insp. Poole #1
A dying fall. Macmillan, 1955; UK:
Constable, 1955; Constable
Netterly
Gold was our grave. Macmillan,
1954; UK: Constable, 1954; Insp.
Poole #9
The hanging captain. Harcourt,
1933; UK: Constable, 1932; Insp.
Poole #3
Heir presumptive. Macmillan, 1953;
UK: Constable, 1935
Lonely Magdalen. UK: Constable,
1940; Insp. Poole #7
The missing partners. Payson and
Clarke, 1928; UK: Constable, 1928;
Insp. Dodd
No friendly drop. Brewer, 1932; UK:
Constable, 1931; Insp. Poole #2
Policeman's lot. UK: Constable,
1933; Insp. Poole #4
Too soon to die. Macmillan, 1954;
UK: Constable, 1953; Insp. Poole
#8
WADE, ROBERT, see MILLER, WADE
(pseud.)
WAGER, WALTER, 1924 --
Blue moon. Arbor House, 1980; UK:
Futura, 1981; Alison Gordon
Blue murder. Arbor House, 1981;
Alison Gordon
WAGONER, DAVID, 1926 --
The man in the middle. Harcourt,
1954; UK: Gollancz, 1955; Charlie
Bell

WAHLOO, PER. For other mysteries by
this author, see SJOWALL, MAJ and
WAHLOO, PER
The steel spring. Delacorte, 1970;
UK: Joseph, 1970; Peter Jensen #2
The thirty-first floor. Knopf,
1966; UK: Murder on the
thirty-first floor. Joseph, 1966;
Peter Jensen #1
WAINWRIGHT, JOHN, 1921 --
Acquittal. St. Martin's, 1976; UK:
Macmillan, 1976
All on a summer's day. St. Martin's
1982
Blayde, R. I. P. St. Martin's, 1982
Brainwash. St. Martin's, 1979; UK:
Macmillan, 1979; David Lyle
Cause for a killing. UK: Macmillan,
1974
The crystallised carbon pig.
Walker, 1967; UK: Collins, 1966;
Supt Gilliant #1
Cul-de-sac. St. Martin's, 1984;
Harry Harker
Death in a sleeping city. UK:
Collins, 1965; Supt. Lewis
Death of a big man. St. Martin's,
1975; UK: Macmillan, 1975; Insp.
Ripley #6
Duty elsewhere. St. Martin's,
1979; UK: Macmillan, 1979; David
Lyle
The evidence I shall give. UK:
Macmillan, 1974; Insp. Lennox #1
Evil intent. UK: Collins, 1966;
Insp. Ripley #1
The eye of the beholder. St.
Martin's, 1980; UK: Macmillan,
1980; Tom Pilter
The forest. St. Martin's, 1984
Freeze thy blood less coldly. UK:
Macmillan, 1970; Insp. Ripley #3
The hard hit. St. Martin's, 1975;
UK: Macmillan, 1974; Insp. Ripley
#5
High-class kill. UK: Macmillan,
1973
Landscape with violence. St.
Martin's, 1976; UK: Macmillan,
1975; Supt. Gilliant #3
The last buccaneer. UK: Macmillan,
1971
Man of law. St. Martin's, 1981;
UK: Macmillan, 1980

Prynter's devil. UK: Macmillan, 1970

Requiem for a loser. UK: Macmillan, 1972; Supt. Gilliant #2

Spiral staircase. St. Martin's, 1983

Square dance. St. Martin's, 1975; UK: Macmillan, 1975; Insp. Lennox #2

Take murder . . . St. Martin's, 1981; UK: Macmillan, 1979; Insp. Caan

Their evil ways. St. Martin's, 1983

Thief of time. St. Martin's, 1978; UK: Macmillan, 1978

A touch of malice. UK: Macmillan, 1973; Insp. Ripley #4

An urge for justice. St. Martin's, 1982

The Venus fly-trap. St. Martin's, 1980; UK: Macmillan, 1980

The worms must wait. UK: Collins, 1967; Insp. Ripley #2

WAKEFIELD, JOHN, 1921 --
Death the sure physician. Dodd, 1966; UK: Constable, 1965; Insp. Speight

WAKEFIELD, R. I. (pseud. of Gertrude Mason White, 1915 --)
You will die today! Dodd, 1953; Lt. Marshall; Judy Meadows

WALKER, WALTER
The two-dude offense. Harper, 1985; Hector Gronig

WALLACE, DAVID RAINS
The turquoise dragon. Sierra Club, 1985; George Kilgore

WALLACE, EDGAR, 1875-1932
Big foot. UK: Long, 1927; Supt. Minter #1

The clue of the new pin. Small, Maynard, 1923; UK: Hodder, 1923

The colossus. Doubleday, 1932; UK: The joker. Hodder, 1926; Insp. Elk #3

The council of justice. UK: Ward, 1908; Four just men #2

The fellowship of the frog. Doubleday, 1928; UK: Ward, 1925; Insp. Elk #2

The four just men. Maynard, 1920; UK: Tallis, 1905; Four just men #1

The gaol breaker. Doubleday, 1930; UK: We shall see! Hodder, 1926

The India-rubber men. Doubleday, 1930; UK: Hodder, 1929; Insp. Elk #5

The just men of Cordova. Doubleday, 1930; UK: Ward, 1917; Four just men #3

Kate plus ten. Small, Maynard, 1917; UK: Ward, 1919; T. B. Smith #2

The law of the three just men. Doubleday, 1931; UK: Again the three just men. Hodder, 1928; Four just men #5

The lone house mystery. UK: Collins, 1929; The Sooper #2

Mr. J. G. Reeder returns. Doubleday, 1932; UK: The guv'nor and other stories. The guv'nor and Mr. Reeder returns. Collins, 1932; J. G. Reeder #5

The murder book of Mr. J. G. Reeder. Doubleday, 1929; UK: The mind of Mr. J. G. Reeder. Hodder, 1925; J. G. Reeder #2

The other man. Dodd, 1911; UK: The nine bears. Ward, 1910; Insp. Elk #1; T. B. Smith #1

Red aces. Doubleday, 1930; UK: Hodder, 1929; J. G. Reeder #4

Room 13. UK: Long, 1924; J. G. Reeder #1

The secret house. Small, Maynard, 1919; UK: Ward, 1917; T. B. Smith #3

Terror keep. Doubleday, 1927; UK: Hodder, 1927; J. G. Reeder #3

The three just men. Doubleday, 1930; UK: Hodder, 1926; Four just men #6

The twister. Doubleday, 1929; UK: Long, 1928; Insp. Elk #4

White face. Doubleday, 1931; UK: Hodder, 1930; Insp. Elk #6

WALLACE, FRANCIS, 1894-1977
Front man. Rinehart, 1952; Johnny Stone; Ruth Dee

WALLING, R. A. J., 1869-1949
The bachelor flat mystery. Morrow, 1934; UK: VIII to IX. Hodder, 1934; Philip Tolefree #5

By hook or crook. Morrow, 1941; UK: By hook or by crook. Hodder, 1941; Philip Tolefree #17

The corpse by any other name. Morrow, 1943; UK: The doodled asterisk. Hodder, 1943; Philip Tolefree #19

The corpse in the coppice. Morrow, 1935; UK: Mr. Tolefree's reluctant witness. Hodder, 1936; Philip Tolefree #7

The corpse in the crimson slippers. Morrow, 1936; UK: Hodder, 1936; Philip Tolefree #9

The corpse in the green pajamas. Morrow, 1935; UK: The cat and the corpse. Hodder, 1935; Philip Tolefree #6

The corpse with the blistered hand. Morrow, 1939; UK: Dust in the vault. Hodder, 1939; Philip Tolefree #14

The corpse with the blue cravat. Morrow, 1938; UK: The coroner doubts. Hodder, 1938; Philip Tolefree #12

The corpse with the dirty face. Morrow, 1936; UK: Hodder, 1936; Philip Tolefree #10

The corpse with the eerie eye. Morrow, 1942; UK: Castle-Dinas. Hodder, 1942; Philip Tolefree #18

The corpse with the floating foot. Morrow, 1936; UK: The mystery of Mr. Mock. Hodder, 1937; Philip Tolefree #8

The corpse with the grimy glove. Morrow, 1938; UK: More than one serpent. Hodder, 1938; Philip Tolefree #13

The corpse with the missing watch. Morrow, 1949; Philip Tolefree #22

The corpse with the red-headed friend. Morrow, 1939; UK: They liked Entwhistle. Hodder, 1939; Philip Tolefree #15

A corpse without a clue. Morrow, 1944; UK: Hodder, 1944; Philip Tolefree #20

The fatal five minutes. Morrow, 1932; UK: Hodder, 1932; Philip Tolefree #1

In time for murder. Morrow, 1933; UK: Follow the blue car. Hodder, 1933; Philip Tolefree #3

The late unlamented. Morrow, 1948; UK: Hodder, 1948; Philip Tolefree #21

Legacy of death. Morrow, 1934; UK: The five suspects. Hodder, 1935; Philip Tolefree #4

Marooned with murder. Morrow, 1937; UK: Bury him deeper. Hodder, 1937; Philip Tolefree #11

Murder at midnight. Morrow, 1932; UK: Behind the yellow blind. Hodder, 1932; Garstang #2

Prove it, Mr. Tolefree. Morrow, 1934; UK: The Tolliver case. Hodder, 1934; Philip Tolefree #2

The spider and the fly. Morrow, 1940; UK: Why did Trethewy die? Hodder, 1940; Philip Tolefree #16

The stroke of one. Morrow, 1931; UK: Methuen, 1931; Garstang #1

That dinner at Bardolph's. Morrow, 1928; UK: The dinner-party at Bardolph's. Jarrolds, 1927

WALLIS, RUTH SATWELL, 1895-1978
Blood from a stone. Dodd, 1945; UK: Hammond, 1955; Susan Kent

Cold bed in the clay. Dodd, 1947; Eric Lund #2

Forget my fate. Dodd, 1950; Eric Lund #3

No bones about it. Dodd, 1944; UK: Hammond, 1950; Eric Lund #1

WALSH, MAURICE, 1879-1964
Danger under the moon. Lippincott, 1957; UK: Chambers, 1956

WALSH, RAY
The Mycroft memoranda. St. Martin's, 1985; Sherlock Holmes; Arthur Conan Doyle; Jack the Ripper

WALSH, THOMAS, 1908 --
Nightmare in Manhattan. Little, 1950; UK: Hamilton, 1951

WALZ, AUDREY BOYER, see BONNAMY, FRANCIS (pseud.)

WARD, ARTHUR HENRY SARSFIELD, see ROHMER, SAX (pseud.)

WARD, COLIN
House party murder. Morrow, 1934; UK: Collins, 1933

WARD, ELIZABETH
Coast Hwy #1. Walker, 1983; Jake Martin

WARNER, MIGNON
Devil's knell. Doubleday, 1983; Edwina Charles

The girl who was clairvoyant.
Doubleday, 1982; Edwina Charles

Illusion. Doubleday, 1984; Edwina
Charles

Speak no evil. Doubleday, 1985;
Edwina Charles

WATSON, CLARISSA

The bishop in the back seat.
Atheneum, 1980; UK: Hale, 1981;
Persis Willum

Runaway. Atheneum, 1985; Persis
Willum

WATSON, COLIN, 1920 --

Blue murder. UK: Eyre, 1979; Insp.
Purbright #10

Bump in the night. Walker, 1962;
UK: Eyre, 1960; Insp. Purbright #2

Charity ends at home. Putnam,
1968; UK: Eyre, 1968; Insp.
Purbright #5

Coffin scarcely used. Putnam,
1967; UK: Eyre, 1958; Insp.
Purbright #1

Hopjoy was here. Walker, 1963; UK:
Eyre, 1962; Insp. Purbright #3

It shouldn't happen to a dog.
Putnam, 1977; UK: One man's meat.
Eyre, 1977; Insp. Purbright #9

Just what the doctor ordered.
Putnam, 1969; UK: The Flaxborough
crab. Eyre, 1969; Insp. Purbright
#6

Kissing covens. Putnam, 1972; UK:
Broomsticks over Flaxborough.
Eyre, 1972; Insp. Purbright #7

Lonelyheart 4122. Putnam, 1967; UK:
Eyre, 1967; Insp. Purbright #4

Six nuns and a shotgun. Putnam,
1975; UK: The naked nuns. Eyre,
1975; Insp. Purbright #8

Whatever's been going on at
Mumblesby? Doubleday, 1983; Insp.
Purbright

WATSON, LAWRENCE

In a dark time. Scribner's, 1980

WAUGH, HILLARY, 1920 --

Born victim. Doubleday, 1962; UK:
Gollancz, 1963; Fred Fellows #4

The con game. Doubleday, 1968; UK:
Gollancz, 1968; Fred Fellows #10

Death and circumstances. Doubleday,
1963; UK: Gollancz, 1963; Fred
Fellows #5

End of a party. Doubleday, 1965;
UK: Gollancz, 1965; Fred Fellows
#8

Finish me off. Doubleday, 1970; UK:
Gollancz, 1971; Frank Sessions
#3

Hope to die. Coward McCann, 1948;
UK: Boardman, 1949; Sheridan
Wesley #2

Last seen wearing . . . Doubleday,
1952; UK: Gollancz, 1953; Chief
Ford

The late Mrs. D. Doubleday, 1962;
UK: Gollancz, 1962; Fred Fellows
#3

Madam will not dine tonight. Coward
McCann, 1947; UK: Boardman, 1949;
Sheridan Wesley #1

The missing man. Doubleday, 1964;
UK: Gollancz, 1964; Fred Fellows
#7

The odds run out. Coward McCann,
1949; UK: Boardman, 1950;
Sheridan Wesley #3

Prisoner's plea. Doubleday, 1963;
UK: Gollancz, 1964; Fred Fellows
#6

Pure poison. Doubleday, 1966; UK:
Gollancz, 1967; Fred Fellows #9

Road block. Doubleday, 1960; UK:
Gollancz, 1961; Fred Fellows #1

Sleep long, my love. Doubleday,
1959; UK: Gollancz, 1960; Fred
Fellows

That night it rained. Doubleday,
1961; UK: Gollancz, 1961; Fred
Fellows #2

30 Manhattan East. Doubleday,
1968; UK: Gollancz, 1968; Frank
Sessions #1

The young prey. Doubleday, 1969;
UK: Gollancz, 1970; Frank
Sessions #2

WAYE, CECIL

The prime minister's pencil.
Kinsey, 1933; UK: Hodder, 1933

WAYLAND, PATRICK (pseud. of Richard
O'Connor, 1915-1975)

The waiting game. Doubleday, 1965;
UK: Hale, 1967; Lloyd Nicolson

WEBB, JACK, 1920 --

The bad blonde. Rinehart, 1956;
UK: Boardman, 1957; Joseph
Shanley #5; Sammy Golden #5

The big sin. Rinehart, 1952; UK:
Boardman, 1953; Joseph Shanley #1;
Sammy Golden #1

The brass halo. Rinehart, 1957;
UK: Boardman, 1958; Joseph Shanley
#6; Sammy Golden #6

The broken doll. Rinehart, 1954;
UK: Boardman, 1956; Joseph Shanley
#4; Sammy Golden #4

The damned lovely. Rinehart, 1954;
UK: Boardman, 1955; Joseph Shanley
#3; Sammy Golden #3

The deadly sex. Rinehart, 1959;
UK: Boardman, 1960; Joseph Shanley
#7; Sammy Golden #7

The delicate darling. Rinehart,
1959; UK: Boardman, 1960; Joseph
Shanley #8; Sammy Golden #8

The gilded witch. Regency, 1963;
UK: Boardman, 1963; Joseph Shanley
#9; Sammy Golden #9

Make my bed soon. Holt, 1963; UK:
Boardman, 1964

The naked angel. Rinehart, 1953;
UK: Such women are dangerous.
Boardman, 1954; Joseph Shanley #2;
Sammy Golden #2

WEBB, MARTHA G.
Darling Corey's head. Walker,
1984; Cheryl Burroughs; Allan
Conyers

A white male running. Walker, 1985;
Tommy Inman

WEBB, RICHARD WILSON, see PATRICK, Q.
(pseud.)

WEBB, VICTORIA
A little lady killing. Dial, 1982;
Stella Pike

WEBER, RUBIN
The grave maker's house. Harper,
1964

WEBSTER, HENRY KITCHELL, 1875-1932
The butterfly. Appleton, 1914;
Brinsley Butler; James Dorgan

The Corbin necklace. Bobbs, 1926;
UK: The mystery of the Corbin
necklace. Hamilton, 1929; Punch
Corbin; Mr. Ethelbert

Who is next? Bobbs, 1931; UK:
Garland, 1976; Pete Murray

WEBSTER, NOAH (pseud.). For other
mysteries by this author, see KIRK,
MICHAEL (pseud.) or KNOX, BILL or
MACLEOD, ROBERT (pseud.)

A burial in Portugal. Doubleday,
1973; UK: Long, 1973; Jonathan
Gaunt #3

Flickering death. Doubleday, 1971;
UK: A property in Cyprus. Long,
1970; Jonathan Gaunt #1

An incident in Iceland. Doubleday,
1979; UK: Long, 1979; Jonathan
Gaunt #6

A killing in Malta. Doubleday,
1972; UK: Long, 1972; Jonathan
Gaunt #2

Legacy from Teneriffe. Doubleday,
1984; Jonathan Gaunt

A pay-off in Switzerland.
Doubleday, 1977; UK: Long, 1977;
Jonathan Gaunt #5

A problem in Prague. Doubleday,
1982; Jonathan Gaunt

A witchdance in Bavaria. Doubleday,
1976; UK: Long, 1975; Jonathan
Gaunt #4

WEES, FRANCES SHELLEY, 1902 --
The maestro murders. Mystery
League, 1931; UK: Detectives,
Ltd. Eyre, 1933; Theresa "Tuck"
Torrie; Bunny Temple; Michael
Forrester

M'Lord, I am not guilty. Doubleday,
1954; UK: Jenkins, 1954

The mystery of the creeping man.
McCrae Smith, 1931; UK: Eyre,
1934; Michael Forrester; Tuck
Forrester

WELCOME, JOHN (pseud. of John
Needham Brennan, 1914 --)
Wanted for killing. Holt, 1967;
UK: Faber, 1965; Simon Harold

WELLS, CAROLYN, 1869-1942
The affair at Flower Acres. Doran,
1923; Pennington Wise #6

All at sea. Lippincott, 1927; UK:
Lippincott, 1927; Fleming Stone
#22

Anybody but Anne. Lippincott,
1914; UK: Lippincott, 1914;
Fleming Stone #5

Anything but the truth. Lippincott,
1925; UK: Lippincott, 1925;
Fleming Stone #18

The beautiful derelict. Lippincott,
1935; UK: Lippincott, 1935;
Fleming Stone #40

The black night murders.
Lippincott, 1941; Fleming Stone
#58

The bride of a moment. Doran,
1916; UK: Hodder, 1920; Alan Ford
#1

The broken O. Lippincott, 1933;
UK: Lippincott, 1933; Fleming
Stone #34

The bronze hand. Lippincott, 1926;
UK: Lippincott, 1926; Fleming
Stone #20

Calling all suspects. Lippincott,
1939; UK: Lippincott, 1939;
Fleming Stone #51

A chain of evidence. Lippincott,
1912; Fleming Stone #3

The clue. Lippincott, 1909; UK:
Lippincott, 1909; Fleming Stone #1

The clue of the eyelash.
Lippincott, 1933; UK: Lippincott,
1933; Fleming Stone #35

The come-back. Doran, 1921; UK:
Hodder, 1921; Pennington Wise #3

The crime in the crypt. Lippincott,
1928; UK: Lippincott, 1928;
Fleming Stone #24

Crime incarnate. Lippincott, 1940;
Fleming Stone #54

Crime tears on. Lippincott, 1939;
Fleming Stone #52

The curved blades. Lippincott,
1916; UK: Lippincott, 1916;
Fleming Stone #7

The daughter of the house.
Lippincott, 1925; UK: Lippincott,
1925; Fleming Stone #19

Deep lake mystery. Doubleday, 1928

Devil's work. Lippincott, 1940;
Fleming Stone #55

The diamond pin. Lippincott, 1919;
UK: Lippincott, 1919; Fleming
Stone #10

The doomed five. Lippincott, 1930;
UK: Lippincott, 1930; Fleming
Stone #28

The doorstep murders. Doubleday,
1930; Kenneth Carlisle #2

Eyes in the wall. Lippincott, 1934;
UK: Lippincott, 1934; Fleming
Stone #37

Face cards. Putnam, 1925; UK:
Putnam, 1925

Faulkner's folly. Doran, 1917; Alan
Ford #2

Feathers left around. Lippincott,
1923; UK: Lippincott, 1923;
Fleming Stone #14

For goodness' sake. Lippincott,
1935; UK: Lippincott, 1935;
Fleming Stone #41

The fourteenth key. Putnam, 1924;
UK: Putnam, 1924; Lorimer Lane #2

Fuller's earth. Lippincott, 1932;
UK: Lippincott, 1932; Fleming
Stone #32

The furthest fury. Lippincott,
1924; UK: Lippincott, 1924;
Fleming Stone #16

The ghost's high noon. Lippincott,
1930; UK: Lippincott, 1930;
Fleming Stone #29

Gilt-edged guilt. Lippincott, 1938;
Fleming Stone #48

The gold bag. Lippincott, 1911; UK:
Lippincott, 1911; Fleming Stone
#2

Horror house. Lippincott, 1931; UK:
Lippincott, 1931; Fleming Stone
#30

The huddle. Lippincott, 1936; UK:
Lippincott, 1936; Fleming Stone
#43

The importance of being murdered.
Lippincott, 1939; Fleming Stone
#53

In the onyx lobby. Doran, 1920;
UK: Hodder, 1920; Pennington Wise
#2

In the tiger's cage. Lippincott,
1934; UK: Lippincott, 1934;
Fleming Stone #38

The killer. Lippincott, 1938;
Fleming Stone #49

The luminous face. Doran, 1921;
Pennington Wise #4

The man who fell through the
earth. Doran, 1919; UK: Harrap,
1924; Pennington Wise #1

The mark of Cain. Lippincott,
1917; UK: Lippincott, 1917;
Fleming Stone #8

The master murderer. Lippincott,
1933; UK: Lippincott, 1933;
Fleming Stone #36

The Maxwell mystery. Lippincott,
1913; UK: Lippincott, 1913;
Fleming Stone #4

The missing link. Lippincott,
1938; Fleming Stone #50
Money musk. Lippincott, 1936; UK:
Lippincott, 1936; Fleming Stone
#44
More lives than one. Boni, 1923;
UK: Hutchinson, 1924; Lorimer Lane
#1
Murder at the casino. Lippincott,
1941; Fleming Stone #59
Murder in the bookshop. Lippincott,
1936; UK: Lippincott, 1936;
Fleming Stone #45
Murder on parade. Lippincott,
1940; Fleming Stone #56
Murder plus. Lippincott, 1940;
Fleming Stone #57
Murder will in. Lippincott, 1942;
Alan Ford #4
The mystery girl. Lippincott,
1922; UK: Lippincott, 1922;
Fleming Stone #13
The mystery of the sycamore.
Lippincott, 1921; UK: Lippincott,
1921; Fleming Stone #12
The mystery of the tarn.
Lippincott, 1937; UK: Lippincott,
1937; Fleming Stone #46
Prilligir. Lippincott, 1924; UK:
Lippincott, 1924; Fleming Stone
#17
The radio studio murder. Lippincott,
1937; UK: Lippincott, 1937;
Fleming Stone #47
Raspberry jam. Lippincott, 1920;
UK: Lippincott, 1920; Fleming
Stone #11
The red-haired girl. Lippincott,
1926; UK: Lippincott, 1926;
Fleming Stone #21
The roll-top desk mystery.
Lippincott, 1932; UK: Lippincott,
1932; Fleming Stone #33
The room with tassels. Doran, 1918;
Alan Ford #3
The skeleton at the feast.
Doubleday, 1931; Kenneth Carlisle
#3
Sleeping dogs. Doubleday, 1929;
Kenneth Carlisle #1
Spooky Hollow. Lippincott, 1923;
UK: Lippincott, 1923; Fleming
Stone #15

The Tannahill tangle. Lippincott,
1928; UK: Lippincott, 1928;
Fleming Stone #25
The tapestry room murder.
Lippincott, 1929; UK: Lippincott,
1929; Fleming Stone #26
Triple murder. Lippincott, 1929;
UK: Lippincott, 1929; Fleming
Stone #27
The umbrella murder. Lippincott,
1931; UK: Lippincott, 1931;
Fleming Stone #31
The vanishing of Betty Varian.
Doran, 1922; UK: Collins, 1924;
Pennington Wise #5
Vicky Van. Lippincott, 1918; UK:
Lippincott, 1918; Fleming Stone
#9
The visiting villain. Lippincott,
1934; UK: Lippincott, 1934;
Fleming Stone #39
Wheels within wheels. Doran, 1923;
Pennington Wise #7
Where's Emily? Lippincott, 1927;
UK: Lippincott, 1927; Fleming
Stone #23
The white alley. Lippincott, 1915;
UK: Lippincott, 1915; Fleming
Stone #6
Who killed Caldwell? Lippincott,
1942; Fleming Stone #60
The wooden Indian. Lippincott,
1935; UK: Lippincott, 1935;
Fleming Stone #42
WELLS, CHARLIE
Let the night cry. Abelard, 1953;
UK: Abelard, 1959
WELLS, SUSAN (pseud. of Doris Siegel)
Death is my name. Scribner's,
1942; UK: Cherry Tree, 1943;
Anthony Ware
Murder is not enough. Simon &
Schuster, 1939; UK: Cassell,
1939; Anthony Ware
WELLS, TOBIAS (pseud. of Deloris
Florine Stanton, 1923 --). For
other mysteries by this author, see
FORBES, STANTON
Brenda's murder. Doubleday, 1973;
UK: Hale, 1974; Knute Severson
#12
A creature was stirring. Doubleday,
1977; UK: Hale, 1978; Knute
Severson #15

Dead by the light of the moon.
Doubleday, 1967; UK: Gollancz,
1968; Knute Severson #3

A die in the country. Doubleday,
1972; UK: Hale, 1974; Knute
Severson #11

Die quickly, dear mother.
Doubleday, 1969; UK: Hale, 1969;
Knute Severson #5

Dinky died. Doubleday, 1970; UK:
Hale, 1970; Knute Severson #7

The Foo dog. Doubleday, 1971; UK:
The lotus affair. Hale, 1973;
Knute Severson #8

Hark, hark, the watchdogs bark.
Doubleday, 1975; UK: Hale, 1976;
Knute Severson #14

Have mercy upon us. Doubleday,
1974; UK: Hale, 1975; Knute
Severson #13

How to kill a man. Doubleday,
1972; UK: Hale, 1973; Knute
Severson #10

A matter of love and death.
Doubleday, 1966; UK: Gollancz,
1966; Knute Severson #1

Murder most fouled up. Doubleday,
1968; UK: Hale, 1969; Knute
Severson #4

What should you know of dying?
Doubleday, 1967; UK: Gollancz,
1967; Knute Severson #2

What to do until the undertaker
comes. Doubleday, 1971; UK: Hale,
1973; Knute Severson #9

The young can die protesting.
Doubleday, 1969; UK: Hale, 1970;
Knute Severson #6

WELTON, ARTHUR D., 1867-1940
The twenty-seventh ride. Sears,
1932

WENTWORTH, PATRICIA (pseud. of Dora
Amy Elles, 1878-1961)
Account rendered. Lippincott, 1940;
UK: Who pays the piper? Hodder,
1940; Ernest Lamb

The Alington inheritance.
Lippincott, 1958; UK: Hodder,
1960; Maud Silver #32

Anna, where are you? Lippincott,
1951; UK: Hodder, 1953; Maud
Silver #20

The Benevent treasure. Lippincott,
1954; UK: Hodder, 1956; Maud
Silver #26

The Brading collection. Lippincott,
1950; UK: Hodder, 1952; Maud
Silver #18

The case is closed. Lippincott,
1937; UK: Hodder, 1937; Maud
Silver #2

The case of William Smith.
Lippincott, 1948; UK: Hodder,
1950; Maud Silver #14

The Catherine wheel. Lippincott,
1949; UK: Hodder, 1951; Maud
Silver #17

The Chinese shawl. Lippincott,
1943; UK: Hodder, 1943; Maud
Silver #6

The clock strikes twelve.
Lippincott, 1944; UK: Hodder,
1945; Maud Silver #9

Eternity ring. Lippincott, 1948;
UK: Hodder, 1950; Maud Silver #15

The fingerprint. Lippincott, 1956;
UK: Hodder, 1959; Maud Silver #31

The gazebo. Lippincott, 1956; UK:
Hodder, 1958; Maud Silver #30

The girl in the cellar. UK: Hodder,
1961; Maud Silver #33

Grey mask. Lippincott, 1929; UK:
Hodder, 1928; Maud Silver #1

In the balance. Lippincott, 1941;
UK: Danger point. Hodder, 1942;
Maud Silver #5

The ivory dagger. Lippincott,
1951; UK: Hodder, 1953; Maud
Silver #21

The key. Lippincott, 1944; UK:
Hodder, 1946; Maud Silver #8

Ladies' bane. Lippincott, 1952;
UK: Hodder, 1954; Maud Silver #23

Latter end. Lippincott, 1947; UK:
Hodder, 1949; Maud Silver #12

Listening eye. Lippincott, 1954;
UK: Hodder, 1957; Maud Silver #29

Lonesome road. Lippincott, 1939;
UK: Hodder, 1939; Maud Silver #3

Miss Silver comes to stay.
Lippincott, 1949; UK: Hodder,
1951; Maud Silver #16

Miss Silver deals with death.
Lippincott, 1943; UK: Miss Silver
intervenes. Hodder, 1944; Maud
Silver #7

Out of the past. Lippincott, 1953;
UK: Hodder, 1955; Maud Silver #25

Pilgrim's rest. Lippincott, 1946;
UK: Hodder, 1948; Maud Silver #11

Poison in the pen. Lippincott,
1955; UK: Hodder, 1957; Maud
Silver #28

Pursuit of a parcel. Lippincott,
1942; UK: Hodder, 1942; Ernest
Lamb

Red Stefan. Lippincott, 1935; UK:
Hodder, 1935

She came back. Lippincott, 1945;
UK: The traveller returns. Hodder,
1948; Maud Silver #10

The silent pool. Lippincott, 1953;
UK: Hodder, 1956; Maud Silver #27

Through the wall. Lippincott,
1950; UK: Hodder, 1952; Maud
Silver #19

Vanishing point. Lippincott, 1953;
UK: Hodder, 1955; Maud Silver #24

The watersplash. Lippincott, 1951;
UK: Hodder, 1953; Maud Silver #22

Wicked uncle. Lippincott, 1947;
UK: Spotlight. Hodder, 1949; Maud
Silver #13

WERRY, RICHARD R.
Casket for a living lady. Dodd,
1985; J. D. Mulroy; Ahmad Dakar

WEST, PAMELA ELIZABETH
Madeline. St. Martin's, 1983; John
Ingles; Madeline Smith

WESTLAKE, DONALD E., see COE, TUCKER

WESTON, CAROLYN, 1921 --
Poor, poor Ophelia. Random House,
1972; UK: Gollancz, 1973; Casey
Kellogg #1; Al Krug #1

Rouse the demon. Random House,
1976; UK: Gollancz, 1977; Casey
Kellogg #3; Al Krug #3

Susannah screaming. Random House,
1975; UK: Gollancz, 1976; Casey
Kellogg #2; Al Krug #2

WESTON, GARNETT
Murder on Shadow Island. Farrar,
1933; UK: Hutchinson, 1933

WETERING, JANWILLEM VAN DE
The blond baboon. Houghton, 1978;
UK: Heinemann, 1978; Det.
Grijpstra; Det. deGier

The corpse on the dike. Houghton,
1976; UK: Heinemann, 1977; Det.
Grijpstra; Det. deGier

Death of a hawker. Houghton, 1977;
UK: Heinemann, 1977; Det.
Grijpstra; Det. deGier

Inspector Sailo's small satori.
Putnam, 1985; Saito Mananobu

The Japanese corpse. Houghton,
1977; UK: Heinemann, 1977; Det.
Grijpstra; Det. deGier

The Maine massacre. Houghton, 1979;
UK: Heinemann, 1979; Det. deGier

The mind-murders. Houghton, 1981;
Det. Grijpstra; Det. deGier

Outsider in Amsterdam. Houghton,
1975; UK: Heinemann, 1976; Det.
Grijpstra; Det. deGier

The street bird. Putnam, 1983; Det.
deGier; Det. Grijpstra

Tumbleweed. Houghton, 1976; UK:
Heinemann, 1976; Det. Grijpstra;
Det. deGier

WHEAT, CAROLYN
Dead man's thoughts. St. Martin's,
1983; Cass Jameson

WHITE, LIONEL, 1905 --
The house next door. Dutton, 1956;
UK: Boardman, 1958

WHILTE, OSMAR, 1909 --
A silent reach. Scribner's, 1980;
UK: Macmillan, 1978; George
Galbraith

WHITE, PHYLLIS DOROTHY, see JAMES,
P. D. (pseud.)

WHITE, R. J., 1905-1971
A second-hand tomb. Harper, 1971;
UK: Macmillan, 1971; Insp.
Badgery

The smartest grave. Harper, 1961;
UK: Collins, 1961; David Brock

The women of Peasenhall. Harper,
1970; UK: Macmillan, 1969; David
Brock

WHITE, TERI
Bleeding hearts. Mysterious Press,
1984; Blue Maguire; Spaceman
Kowalski

WHITE, TERRENCE DE VERE, 1906-1964
My name is Norval. Harper, 1979;
UK: Gollancz, 1978

WHITE, WILLIAM ANTHONY PARKER, see
BOUCHER, ANTHONY (pseud.) or
HOLMES, H. H. (pseud.)

WHITECHURCH, VICTOR L., 1868-1933
The crime at Diana's Pool. Unwin,
1927; Duffield, 1927

Murder at Exbridge. Dodd, 1932;
UK: Murder at the college.
Collins, 1932; Det. Ambrose

The robbery at Rudwick House.
Duffield, 1929

WHITFIELD, RAOUL, 1897-1945
Death in a bowl. Knopf, 1931; Ben
Jardinn
Green ice. Knopf, 1930
The virgin kills. Knopf, 1932; Al
Connors
WHITNEY, PHYLLIS A., 1903 --
Columbella. Doubleday, 1966; UK:
Hale, 1967
Emerald. Doubleday, 1982
Red is for murder. Ziff Davis,
1943; UK: The red carnelian.
Coronet, 1976; Sylvester Hering
Snow fire. Doubleday, 1973; UK:
Heinemann, 1973; Linda Earle
Window on the square. Appleton,
1962; UK: Coronet, 1969
WHITTINGTON, HARRY, 1915 --
The devil wears wings.
Abelard-Schuman, 1960; UK:
Abelard-Schuman, 1960
WIBBERLY, LEONARD, see HOLTON,
LEONARD (pseud.)
WICKWARE, FRANCIS SILL
Dangerous ground. Doubleday, 1945
WIEGAND, WILLIAM, 1928 --
At last, Mr. Tolliver. Rinehart,
1950; UK: Hodder, 1951; Samuel
Tolliver
WILCOX, COLLIN, 1924 -- . For other
mysteries by this author, see
PRONZINI, BILL and WILCOX, COLLIN
Aftershock. Random House, 1975; UK:
Hale, 1976; Frank Hastings #6
The black door. Dodd, 1967; UK:
Cassell, 1968; Stephen Drake #1
Dead aim. Random House, 1971; UK:
Hale, 1973; Frank Hastings #3
The disappearance. Random House,
1970; UK: Hale, 1971; Frank
Hastings #2
Doctor, lawyer.... Random House,
1976; UK: Hale, 1978; Frank
Hastings #8
Hiding place. Random House, 1973;
UK: Hale, 1974; Frank Hastings #4
The lonely hunter. Random House,
1969; UK: Hale, 1971; Frank
Hastings #1
Long way down. Random House, 1974;
UK: Hale, 1975; Frank Hastings #5
Mankiller. Random House, 1980; UK:
Hale, 1981; Frank Hastings
McCloud. Award, 1973; Marshall
McCloud #1

The New Mexico connection. Award,
1974; UK: Tanden, 1974; Frank
Hastings #2
Night games. Random House, 1979;
Frank Hastings #10
Power plays. Random House, 1979;
UK: Hale, 1982; Frank Hastings
#11
Stalking horse. Random House, 1982;
Frank Hastings
The third figure. Dodd, 1968; UK:
Hale, 1969; Stephen Drake #2
The third victim. Dell, 1976; UK:
Hale, 1977; Frank Hastings #7
Victims. Mysterious Press, 1985;
Frank Hastings
The watcher. Random House, 1978;
UK: Hale, 1979; Frank Hastings #9
WILDE, PERCIVAL, 1887-1953
P. Moran, operative. Random House,
1947; UK: Gollancz, 1947; P.
Moran
WILKINSON, SANDRA
Death on call. Dodd, 1984; Rosemary
Cleveland; Pete Tanner
WILLARD, JAMES, 1909 --
The affair in Arcady. Reynal,
1959; Clive Marshall
WILLEFORD, CHARLES
New hope for the dead. St.
Martin's, 1985; Hoke Mosley
WILLIAMS, BEN AMES, 1889-1953
Death on Scurvy Street. Dutton,
1929; UK: The Bellmer mystery.
Paul, 1930; Insp. Tope
WILLIAMS, BRAD, 1918 --
Make a killing. Mill, 1961; UK:
Jenkins, 1962
WILLIAMS, CHARLES, 1909-1975
Aground. Viking, 1960; UK: Cassell,
1961; John Ingram
Dead calm. Viking, 1963; UK:
Cassell, 1964; John Ingram
Man on a leash. Putnam, 1973; UK:
Cassell, 1974
The sailcloth shroud. Viking,
1960; UK: Cassell, 1960
WILLIAMS, DAVID, 1926 --
Advertise for Treasure. St.
Martin's, 1984; Mark Treasure
Copper, gold and Treasure. St.
Martin's, 1982; Mark Treasure
Murder for Treasure. St. Martin's,
1980; UK: Collins, 1980; Mark
Treasure

Treasure by degrees. St. Martin's, 1977; UK: Collins, 1977; Mark Treasure

Treasure preserved. St. Martin's, 1983; Mark Treasure

Treasure up in smoke. St. Martin's, 1978; UK: Collins, 1978; Mark Treasure

Unholy writ. St. Martin's, 1977; UK: Collins, 1976; Mark Treasure

Wedding Treasure. St. Martin's, 1985; Mark Treasure

WILLIAMS, EDWIN ALFRED, see DECAIRE, EDWIN (pseud.)

WILLIAMS, GEORGE VALENTINE, see WILLIAMS, VALENTINE

WILLIAMS, GORDON, see YUILL, P. B. (pseud.)

WILLIAMS, KIRBY

The C. V. C. murders. Doubleday, 1929; UK: Hutchinson, 1929; Thackeray Place

The opera murders. Scribner's, 1933; Thackeray Place

WILLIAMS, MARGARET WETHERBY, see ERSKINE, MARGARET (pseud.)

WILLIAMS, SIDNEY, 1878-1949

The aconite murders. Dodd, 1956; Jabez Twombley

The murder of Miss Betty Sloan. Appleton, 1935; Jabez Twombley

WILLIAMS, TIMOTHY

Red Citroen. St. Martin's, 1983; Commissario Trotti #1

WILLIAMS, VALENTINE (pseud. of George Valentine Williams, 1883-1946)

The clock ticks on. Houghton, 1933; UK: Hodder, 1933; Trevor Dene #3

The clue of the rising moon. Houghton, 1935; UK: Hodder, 1935; Trevor Dene #5

The curiosity of Mr. Treadgold. Houghton, 1937; UK: Mr. Treadgold cuts in. Hodder, 1937; Mr. Treadgold #2

Dead Man Manor. Houghton, 1936; UK: Hodder, 1936; Mr. Treadgold #1

Death answers the bell. Houghton, 1932; UK: Hodder, 1931; Trevor Dene #2

The eye in attendance. Houghton, 1927; UK: Hodder, 1927; Trevor Dene #1

Masks off at midnight. Houghton, 1934; UK: Hodder, 1934; Trevor Dene #4

WILLIAMS, WETHERBY, see ERSKINE, MARGARET (pseud.)

WILLIAMSON, MONCRIEFF

Death in the picture. Beaufort, 1982; Cyrus Finnegan

WILLIS, GEORGE ANTHONY ARMSTRONG, see ARMSTRONG, ANTHONY

WILLOCK, COLIN, 1918 --

Death in covert. UK: Heinemann, 1961; Nathaniel Goss

WILLS, GARRY

At Button's. Sheed, 1979; Gregory Skipwith

WILMOT, J. R.

Death in the theatre. Kendall, 1934; UK: Death in the stalls. Nicholson, 1934

WILSON, BARBARA

Murder in the collective. Seal, 1984

WILSON, COLIN, 1931 --

Necessary doubt. Trident Press, 1964; UK: Barker, 1964; Karl Zweig; Charles Grey

WILSON, P. W.

Black tarn. Farrar, 1945; UK: Boardman, 1948; Julian Morthoe

Bride's castle. Farrar, 1944; UK: Boardman, 1946; Julian Morthoe

The old mill. Rinehart, 1946; UK: Boardman, 1948; Julian Morthoe

WILTZ, CHRIS

The killing circle. Macmillan, 1981; Neal Rafferty

WINCH, ARDEN

Blood royal. Viking, 1982; Supt. Meadows

WINCHELL, PRENTICE, 1895 -- , see DEAN, SPENCER (pseud.)

WINCOR, RICHARD

Sherlock Holmes in Tibet. Weybright, 1968; Sherlock Holmes

WINSLOW, HORATIO and QUIRK, LESLIE W.

Into thin air. Doubleday, 1929; UK: Gollancz, 1928

WINSLOW, PAULINE GLEN

The Rockefeller gift. St. Martin's, 1981; Merle Capricorn

WINSOR, DIANA, 1946

The death convention. Stein & Day, 1978; UK: Macmillan, 1974

WINTERTON, PAUL, see BAX, ROGER
(pseud.) or GARVE, ANDREW (pseud.)
or SOMERS, PAUL (pseud.)

WITHERS, E. L. (pseud. of William
Potter, Jr., 1930 --)
Diminishing returns. Rinehart,
1960; UK: Harrap, 1961

WODEHOUSE, P. G., 1881 --
Wodehouse on crime. Ticknor &
Fields, 1983

WOELFEL, BARRY
Through a glass, darkly. Beaufort,
1984

WOLF, GARY K.
Who censored Roger Rabbit? St.
Martin's, 1981; Eddie Valiant

WOLFE, CARSON
Murder at La Marimba. St. Martin's,
1984; Carlito Rivera

WOOD, CLEMENT, 1888-1950
Death in Ankara. Mystery House,
1944; Lal Reed
Death on the pampas. Mystery
House, 1944; Lal Reed

WOOD, SALLY, 1897 --
Death in Lord Byron's room.
Morrow, 1948

WOOD, TED
Dead in the water. Scribner's,
1983; Reid Bennett #1
Live bait. Scribner's, 1985; Reid
Bennett
Murder on ice. Scribner's, 1984;
Reid Bennett #2

WOODFIN, HENRY
Virginia's thing. Harper, 1968;
John Foley

WOODRUFF, PHILIP (pseud. of Philip
Mason, 1906 --)
Call the next witness. Harcourt,
1946; UK: Cape, 1945

WOODS, KATHERINE, 1886-1968
Murder in a walled town. Houghton,
1934; UK: Eyre, 1936

WOODS, SARA (pseud. of Sara
Bowen-Judd, 1922 --)
And shame the devil. Holt, 1972;
UK: Collins, 1967; Antony Maitland
#13
Away with them to prison. St.
Martin's, 1985; Antony Maitland
#42
The bloody book of law. St.
Martin's, 1984; Antony Maitland

Bloody instructions. Harper, 1962;
UK: Collins, 1962; Antony
Maitland #2

Call back yesterday. St. Martin's,
1983; Antony Maitland

The case is altered. Harper, 1967;
UK: Collins, 1967; Antony
Maitland #12

Cry guilty. St. Martin's, 1981;
Antony Maitland #32

Dearest enemy. St. Martin's, 1981;
Antony Maitland #33

Defy the devil. St. Martin's, 1985;
Antony Maitland

Done to death. Holt, 1975; UK:
Macmillan, 1974; Jenny Maitland;
Antony Maitland #22

Enter a gentlewoman. St. Martin's,
1982; Antony Maitland #34

Enter certain murderers. Harper,
1966; UK: Collins, 1966; Antony
Maitland #10

Enter the corpse. Holt, 1974; UK:
Macmillan, 1973; Antony Maitland
#21

Error of the moon. UK: Collins,
1963; Antony Maitland #5

Exit murderer. St. Martin's, 1978;
UK: Macmillan, 1978; Antony
Maitland #27

The fatal writ. St. Martin's, 1979;
Antony Maitland #28

An improbable fiction. Holt, 1971;
UK: Collins, 1970; Antony
Maitland #17

The knavish crows. Raven House,
1980; UK: Collins, 1971; Antony
Maitland #19; Jenny Maitland

Knives have edges. Holt, 1970; UK:
Collins, 1968; Antony Maitland
#14

The law's delay. St. Martin's,
1977; UK: Macmillan, 1977; Antony
Maitland #25

Let's choose executors. Harper,
1967; UK: Collins, 1966; Antony
Maitland #11

The lie direct. St. Martin's,
1983; Antony Maitland

Malice domestic. UK: Collins,
1962; Antony Maitland #3

Most grievous murder. St. Martin's,
1982; Antony Maitland

My life is done. St. Martin's, 1976; UK: Macmillan, 1976; Antony Maitland #24; Jenny Maitland

An obscure grave. St. Martin's, 1985; Antony Maitland #40

Past praying for. Harper, 1968; UK: Collins, 1968; Antony Maitland #15

Proceed to judgement. St. Martin's, 1980; UK: Macmillan, 1979; Antony Maitland #29

Put out the light. St. Martin's, 1985; Antony Maitland

Serpent's tooth. Holt, 1973; UK: Collins, 1971; Antony Maitland #18

A show of violence. McKay, 1975; UK: Macmillan, 1975; Antony Maitland #23

Tarry and be hanged. Holt, 1971; UK: Collins, 1969; Antony Maitland #16

They love not poison. Holt, 1972; UK: Macmillan, 1972; Antony Maitland #1; Jenny Maitland #1

They stay for death. St. Martin's, 1980; UK: Macmillan, 1980; Antony Maitland #30

A thief or two. St. Martin's, 1977; UK: Macmillan, 1977; Antony Maitland #26

The third encounter. Harper, 1963; UK: The taste of fears. Collins, 1963; Antony Maitland #4

This little measure. UK: Collins, 1964; Antony Maitland #7

Though I know she lies. Holt, 1972; UK: Collins, 1965; Antony Maitland #9

Trusted like the fox. Harper, 1965; UK: Collins, 1964; Antony Maitland #6

Villains by necessity. St. Martin's, 1982; Antony Maitland

Weep for her. St. Martin's, 1980; UK: Macmillan, 1980; Antony Maitland #31

Where should he die? St. Martin's, 1983; Antony Maitland

The windy side of the law. Harper, 1965; UK: Collins, 1965; Antony Maitland #8

Yet she must die. Holt, 1974; UK: Macmillan, 1973; Antony Maitland #20

WOODTHORPE, R. C., 1886 --
Death in a little town. Doubleday, 1935; UK: Nicholson, 1935; Matilda Perks

Rope for a convict. Doubleday, 1940; UK: Nicholson, 1939

The shadow on the downs. Doubleday, 1935; UK: Nicholson, 1935; Matilda Perks

WREN, M. K. (pseud. of Martha Kay Renfroe, 1938 --)
Curiosity didn't kill the cat. Doubleday, 1973; UK: Hale, 1975; Conan Flagg

A multitude of sins. Doubleday, 1975; UK: Hale, 1976; Conan Flagg

Nothing's certain but death. Doubleday, 1978; UK: Hale, 1978; Conan Flagg

Oh bury me not. Doubleday, 1976; UK: Hale, 1978; Conan Flagg

Wake up, Darlin' Corey. Doubleday, 1984; Conan Flagg #6

WRIGHT, ERIC
Death in the old country. Scribner's, 1985; Charlie Salter #3

The night the gods smiled. Scribner's, 1983; Charlie Salter #1

Smoke detector. Scribner's, 1985; Charlie Salter

WRIGHT, L. R.
The suspect. Viking, 1985; Alberg Alberg

WRIGHT, MASON
The army post murders. Farrar, 1931

WRIGHT, RICHARD B., 1937 --
Final things. Dutton, 1980

WRIGHT, WILLARD HUNTINGTON, see VAN DINE, S. S. (pseud.)

WYLIE, JOHN, 1914 --
The butterfly flood. Doubleday, 1975; UK: Barrie, 1977; Dr. Quarshie

Death is a drum . . . beating forever. Doubleday, 1977; UK: Hale, 1979; Dr. Quarshie

The killer breath. Doubleday, 1979; UK: Hale, 1980; Dr. Quarshie

The long, dark night of Baron
Samedi. Doubleday, 1981; Dr.
Quarshie #12
A pocket full of dead. Doubleday,
1978; UK: Hale, 1979; Dr. Quarshie
Skull still bone. Doubleday, 1975;
UK: Barrie, 1975; Dr. Quarshie
A tiger in red weather. Doubleday,
1980; UK: Hale, 1981; Dr. Quarshie
To catch a viper. Doubleday, 1977;
UK: Hale, 1979; Dr. Quarshie
WYLIE, PHILIP, see BALMER, EDWIN and
WYLIE, PHILIP
WYND, GAVIN, 1913 --
Walk softly, men praying. Harcourt,
1967; UK: Cassell, 1967
WYNNE, FRED E., 1870 --
A Mediterranean mystery. Duffield,
1923; UK: Jenkins, 1923

XANTIPPE
Death catches up with Mr. Kluck.
Doubleday, 1935

YARBRO, CHELSEA QUINN, 1942 --
Music when sweet voices die.
Putnam, 1979; Charles Spotted Moon
YATES, BROCK, 1933 --
Dead in the water. Farrar, 1975
YATES, GEORGE WORTHING (pseud. of
Peter Hunt and Charles Hunt
Marshall)
The body that came by post. Morrow,
1937; UK: Dickson, 1937; Hazlitt
Woar
The body that wasn't there. Morrow,
1939; UK: Davies, 1939; Hazlitt
Woar
YATES, MARGARET TAYLER, 1887 --
Death sends a cable. Macmillan,
1939; UK: Davies, 1939; Anne
Davenport McLean
The hush-hush murders. Macmillan,
1937; UK: Dickson, 1938; Anne
Davenport McLean
Midway to murder. Macmillan, 1941;
Anne Davenport McLean
Murder by the yard. Macmillan,
1942; Anne Davenport McLean
YATES, MARGARET and BRAMLETTE, PAULA
The widow's walk. Dutton, 1945
YONGDEN, LAMA, see DAVID-NEEL,
ALEXANDRA

YORK, ANDREW (pseud. of Christopher
Robin Nicole, 1930 --)
Tallant for disaster. Doubleday,
1978; UK: Hutchinson, 1978;
Munroe Tallant #2
Tallant for trouble. Doubleday,
1977; UK: Hutchinson, 1977;
Munroe Tallant #1
YORK, JEREMY (pseud. of John
Creasey). For other mysteries by
this author, see ASHE, GORDON
(pseud.) or CREASEY, JOHN or
MORTON, ANTHONY (pseud.) or MARRIC,
J. J. (pseud.)
Close the door on murder. McKay,
1973; UK: Melrose, 1948; Supt.
Folly #3
Come here and die. Scribner's,
1957
Find the body. Macmillan, 1967; UK:
Melrose, 1945; Supt. Folly #1
Missing. Scribner's, 1959; Insp.
Kennedy
Murder came late. Macmillan, 1969;
UK: Melrose, 1946; Supt. Folly #2
YORKE, MARGARET (pseud. of Margaret
Beda Nicholson, 1924 --)
Cast for death. Walker, 1976; UK:
Hutchinson, 1976; Patrick Grant
#5
Dead in the morning. UK: Bles,
1970; Patrick Grant #1
Find me a villain. St. Martin's,
1983; Nina Crowther
Grave matters. UK: Bles, 1973;
Patrick Grant #3
Intimate kill. St. Martin's, 1985;
Stephen Dawes
Mortal remains. UK: Bles, 1974;
Patrick Grant #4
Silent witness. Walker, 1975;
Patrick Grant #2
YOUD, SAMUEL, see GRAAF, PETER
(pseud.)
YOUNG, EDWARD, 1913 --
The fifth passenger. Harper, 1963;
UK: Cassell, 1963
YOUNGER, ELIZABETH HELY, see HELY,
ELIZABETH
YUILL, P. B. (pseud. of Gordon
Williams and Terry Venables)
Hazell and the menacing jester.
UK: Macmillan, 1976; James Hazell
#3

Hazell and the three card trick.
Walker, 1976; UK: Macmillan, 1975;
James Hazell #2

Hazell plays Solomon. Walker,
1975; UK: Macmillan, 1974; James
Hazell #1

ZACKEL, FRED
Cinderella after midnight. Coward
McCann, 1980; Michael Brennan
Cocaine and blue eyes. Coward
McCann, 1978; Michael Brennan

ZAKE, S. JOSHUA L.
Truckful of gold. Regnery, 1980;
Peter Kayira

ZANGWILL, ISRAEL
The big bow mystery. Rand-McNally,
1895; Insp. Grodman

ZOCHERT, DONALD, 1938 --
Another weeping woman. Holt, 1980;
Nick Caine
Murder in the Hellfire Club. Holt,
1978

Title Index

"A" is for alibi. Grafton, Sue

The ABC murders. Christie, Agatha

A.S.F.: The story of a great conspiracy. Rhode, John

The abominable man. Sjowall, Maj and Wahloo, Per

The abominable snowman. Blake, Nicholas

About the murder of a man afraid of women. Abbot, Anthony

About the murder of a startled lady. Abbot, Anthony

About the murder of Geraldine Foster. Abbot, Anthony

About the murder of the circus queen. Abbot, Anthony

About the murder of the clergyman's mistress. Abbot, Anthony

About the murder of the nightclub lady. Abbot, Anthony

Abracadaver. Lovesey, Peter

Abra-cadaver. Monig, Christopher

An academic question. Smithies, Richard H. R.

Accent on murder. Lockridge, Richard and Lockridge, Frances

Accessory after the fact. Thayer, Lee

Accident for Inspector West. Creasey, John

Accident, manslaughter, or murder? Thayer, Lee

The accident ward mystery. Truax, Rhoda

Accidents do happen. Burton, Miles

The accomplice. Head, Matthew

According to the evidence. Cecil, Henry

Account rendered. Wentworth, Patricia

Accounting for murder. Lathen, Emma

Accuse the Toff. Creasey, John

The accused. Daniels, Harold R.

Ace of diamonds. Schorr, Mark

The ace of spades. Shannon, Dell

The ace of spades murder. Keeler, Harry Stephen

The achievements of Luther Trant. Balmer, Edwin and MacHarg, William

The aconite murders. Williams, Sidney

Acquittal. Wainwright, John

Act of anger. Spicer, Bart

Act of darkness. King, Francis

Act of fear. Collins, Michael

Action at Arcanum. MacDonald, William Colt

Acts of black night. Knight, Kathleen Moore

The acupuncture murders. Steward, Dwight

An ad for murder. Penn, John

Adam's case. Underwood, Michael

Add a pinch of cyanide. Page, Emma

Adders on the heath. Mitchell, Gladys

Adriana. Dyer, George

An advancement of learning. Hill, Reginald

The adventure of the Christmas pudding. Christie, Agatha

The adventure of the marked man and the other. Palmer, Stuart

The adventure of the Orient Express. Derleth, August

The adventure of the stalwart companions. Jeffers, H. Paul

The adventures of Archer Dawe, sleuth-hound. Fletcher, J. S.

The adventures of Dr. Thorndyke. Freeman, R. Austin

The adventures of Ellery Queen. Queen, Ellery

Alibi for a corpse. Lemarchand, Elizabeth

Alibi in time. Thomson, June

The Alington Inheritance. Wentworth, Patricia

Alive and dead. Ferrars, E. X.

All at sea. Wells, Carolyn

All but impossible! Hoch, Edward D., ed.

All concerned notified. Reilly, Helen

All exits blocked. Perowne, Barry

All fall down. Strong, L. A. G.

All for the love of a lady. Ford, Leslie

All God's children. Lyons, Arthur, Jr.

All grass isn't green. Fair, A. A.

All is discovered. Cannan, Joanna

All is vanity. Bell, Josephine

All leads negative. Alding, Peter

All men are liars. Strange, John Stephen

All men are murderers. Blackstock, Charity

All my pretty chickens. Hocking, Anne

All on a summer's day. Wainwright, John

All other perils. Kirk, Michael

All roads to Sospel. Bellairs, George

All shot up. Himes, Chester

All that glitters. Powers, Elizabeth

All the way down. Chaber, M. E.

The Allingham case-book. Allingham, Margery

The Allingham minibus. Allingham, Margery

The almost perfect murder: More Madame Storey mysteries. Footner, Hulbert

Alp murder. Stein, Aaron Marc

The Alpha list. Anderson, James

Alter ego. Arrighi, Mel

The aluminum turtle. Kendrick, Baynard H.

The Alvarez journal. Burns, Rex

Always a body to trade. Constantine, K. C.

Always kill a stranger. Fish, Robert L.

Always murder a friend. Scherf, Margaret

An amateur corpse. Brett, Simon

The amateur murderer. Daly, Carroll John

The amazing adventures of Letitia Carberry. Rinehart, Mary Roberts

The amazing match test crime. Alington, Adrion Richard

The amazing web. Keeler, Harry Stephen

The amber eyes. Crane, Frances

American gun mystery. Queen, Ellery

American quartet. Adler, Warren

American sextet. Adler, Warren

The amethyst spectacles. Crane, Frances

The ampersand papers. Innes, Michael

The anathema stone. Hilton, John Buxton

The anatomy lesson. Goldberg, Marshall

And be a villain. Cannon, Joanna

And be a villain. Stout, Rex

And being dead. Erskine, Margaret

And dangerous to know. Daly, Elizabeth

And four to go. Stout, Rex

. . . and high water. Stein, Aaron Marc

And left for dead. Lockridge, Frances & Richard

And no one wept. Hocking, Anne

And on the eighth day. Queen, Ellery

And one cried murder. Thayer, Lee

And one for the dead. Audemars, Pierre

And shame the devil. Woods, Sara

And so to murder. Dickson, Carter

And sudden death. Adams, Cleve F.

And the moon was full. McCutcheon, Hugh

And then came fear. Cumberland, Marten

And then silence. Propper, Milton

And then there was none. Christie, Agatha

And then there was Nun. Quill, Monica

And then they die. McCollum, Robert

And to my beloved husband. Loraine, Philip

And where she stops. Dewey, Thomas B.

And worms have eaten them. Cumberland, Marten

Andrew's wife. Booton, Kage

Angel death. Moyes, Patricia

Angel eyes. Estleman, Loren D.

The angel of light. McCutcheon, Hugh

Angel without mercy. Cohen, Anthea

Angel's ransom. Dodge, David

The anger of fear. Ashford, Jeffrey

Angle of attack. Burns, Rex

Anna, where are you? Wentworth, Patricia

The anniversary murder. Phillpotts, Eden

Ann's crime. Scott, R. T. M.

The Anodyne Necklace. Grimes, Martha

Another day--another death. Bagby, George

Another man's murder. Eberhart, Mignon G.

Another man's poison. Holman, C. Hugh

Another morgue heard from. Davis, Frederick C.

Another mystery in Suva. Arthur, Frank

Another weeping woman. Zochert, Donald

Antidote to venom. Crofts, Freeman Wills

The anxious conspirator. Underwood, Michael

Any shape or form. Daly, Elizabeth

Anybody but Anne. Wells, Carolyn

Anybody's pearls. Footner, Hulbert

Anything but saintly. Deming, Richard

Anything but the truth. Wells, Carolyn

Anything to declare? Crofts, Freeman Wills

Appearances of death. Shannon, Dell

Appleby and Honeybath. Innes, Michael

Appleby at Arlington. Innes, Michael

The Appleby file. Innes, Michael

Appleby on Ararat. Innes, Michael

Appleby plays chicken. Innes, Michael

Appleby talking. Innes, Michael

Appleby talks again. Innes, Michael

Appleby's answer. Innes, Michael

Appleby's end. Innes, Michael

Appleby's other story. Innes, Michael

The applegreen cat. Crane, Frances

Appointment at nine. Disney, Doris Miles

Appointment in New Orleans. Claymore, Tod

Appointment with death. Christie, Agatha

Appointment with death. Frankau, Pamela

The apprehensive dog. Baley, H. C.

The April robin murders. Rice, Craig and McBain, Ed

An April shroud. Hill, Reginald

The Arabian Nights murder. Carr, John Dickson

The Ariadne clue. Clemeau, Carl

Aristotle, detective. Doody, Margaret

Arlette. Freeling, Nicolas

Arm of the law. Underwood, Michael

Arms for Adonis. Jay, Charlotte

The Army post murders. Wright, Mason.

Around dark corners. Pentecost, Hugh

The arrest of Arsene Lupin. Leblanc, Maurice

Arrogant alibi. King, C. Daly

Arrow pointing nowhere. Daly, Elizabeth

Arsene Lupin vs. Herlock Sholmes. Leblance, Maurice

Arsenic in Richmond. Frome, David

Arson. Fackler, Elizabeth

The artful egg. McClure, James

Arthur. Graham, John Alexander

An artist dies. Rhode, John

Artists in crime. Marsh, Ngaio

As a favor. Dunlap, Susan

As a thief in the night. Freeman, R. Austin

As good as dead. Dewey, Thomas B.

As long as I live. Shriber, Ione Sandberg

As old as Cain. Chaber, M. E.

Asey Mayo trio. Taylor, Phoebe Atwood

Ashes to ashes. Lathan, Emma

Asimov's mysteries. Asimov, Isaac.

Ask a policeman. Mitchell, Gladys

Ask for no tomorrow. Millar, Margaret

Ask the cards a question. Muller, Marcia

Ask the right question. Lewin, Michael Z.

The asking price. Hilton, John Buxton

The assassins. Pentecost, Hugh

Assault with intent. Kienzle, William X.

At Berttram's Hotel. Christie, Agatha

At Button's. Wills, Garry

At death's door. Bruce, Leo

At last, Mr. Tolliver. Wiegand, William

At one fell swoop. Palmer, Stuart

At the cedars. Hocking, Anne

At the Gai-Moulin. Simenon, Georges

At the hands of another. Lyons, Arthur

At the Villa Rose. Mason, A. E. W.

Atavar. Reeve, Arthur B.

Atlantic murder. Shaw, Frank H.

Attack the Baron. Morton, Anthony

The attending physician. Dominic, R. B.

Attention! Saturnin Dax! Cumberland, Marten

The big bow mystery. Zangwill, Israel
Big business murder. Cole, G. D. H.
  and Cole, Margaret
The big call. Ashe, Gordon
The big clock. Fearing, Kenneth
The big fix. Simon, Roger L.
Big foot. Wallace, Edgar
The big four. Christie, Agatha
The big gamble. Coxe, George Harmon
Big game. Brand, Max
The big gold dream. Himes, Chester
A big hand for the corpse. Bagby,
  George
The big heat. McGivern, William P.
The big kill. Spillane, Mickey
The big kiss-off of 1944. Beryman,
  Andrew
The big knockover: Selected stories
  and short novels. Hammett, Dashiell
The big midget murders. Rice, Craig
The big money. Masur, Harold Q.
Big money. Turnbull, Peter
Big shot. Treat, Lawrence
The big sin. Webb, Jack
The big sleep. Chandler, Raymond
The bigger they come. Fair, A. A.
The Bilbao looking glass. MacLeod,
  Charlotte
Billingsgate Shoal. Boyer, Rick
The Biltmore call. Siller, Van
The bind. Ellen, Stanley
Bindlestiff. Pronzini, Bill
Bird walking weather. Bagby, George
Birds of ill omen. Knight, Kathleen
  Moore
Birthday, deathday. Pentecost, Hugh
The birthday murder. Lewis, Lange
Bishop as pawn. McInerny, Ralph
The bishop in the back seat. Watson,
  Clarissa
The Bishop murder case. Van Dine,
  S. S.
The bishop's crime. Bailey, H. C.
Bishop's pawn. Perry, Ritchie
The bishop's purse. Moffett, Cleveland
  and Herford, Oliver
Bite the hand. Fenisong, Ruth
Bitter finish. Barnes, Linda
The black and the red. Paul, Elliot
Black as he's painted. Marsh, Ngaio
Black aura. Sladek, John
The black camel. Biggers, Earl Den
Black cats are lucky. Fielding, A.
The black charade. Burke, John
Black cypress. Crane, Frances

The black door. Adams, Cleve F.
The black door. Markham, Virgil
The black door. Wilcox, Collin
The black dream. Little, Constance
  and Little, Gwyneth
The black Dudley murder. Allingham,
  Margery
The black envelope. Frome, David
The black express. Little, Constance
  and Little, Gwyneth
Black fog. Dutton, Charles J.
Black for the Baron. Morton, Anthony
The black gang. McNeille, H. C.
The black gardenia. Paul, Elliot
The black glass city. Philips, Judson
The black hand. Reeve, Arthur B.
Black hawthorn. Strange, John Stephen
Black is the color of my true love's
  heart. Peters, Ellis
Black is the fashion for dying.
  Latimer, Jonathan
Black knight in Red Square. Kaminsky,
  Stuart M.
Black land, white land. Bailey, H. C.
The black magician. Scott, R. T. M.
Black mail. Disney, Doris Miles
The black mask boys. Nolan,
  William F., ed.
Black money. Macdonald, Ross
The black mountain. Stout, Rex
The black night murders. Wells,
  Carolyn
Black orchids. Stout, Rex
The black rose murder. McGuire, Paul
The black satchel. Keeler, Harry
  Stephen
The black seraphim. Gilbert, Michael
Black sheep, run. Spicer, Bart
The black spectacles. Carr, John
  Dickinson
The black stocking. Little, Constance
  and Little, Gwyneth
Black tarn. Wilson, P. W.
The black thumb. Little, Constance
  and Little, Gwyneth
The black tower. James, P. D.
Black welcome. Fitzgerald, Nigel
Black widow. Quentin, Patrick
Black widower. Moyes, Patricia
The Blackheath poisonings. Symons,
  Julian
Blacklight. Knox, Bill
Blackmail in Blankshire. Alington,
  C. A.
The blackmailer. Fenisong, Ruth

The case of the jeweled ragpicker.
  Keeler, Harry Stephen
The case of the journeying boy.
  Innes, Michael
The case of the jumbo sandwich.
  Bush, Christopher
The case of the kidnapped angel.
  Cunningham, E. V.
The case of the kidnapped colonel.
  Bush, Christopher
The case of the lame canary. Gardner,
  Erle Stanley
The case of the late pig. Allingham,
  Margery
The case of the lavender gripsack.
  Keeler, Harry Stephen
The case of the lazy lover. Gardner,
  Erle Stanley
The case of the leaning man. Bush,
  Christopher
The case of the lonely heiress.
  Gardner, Erle Stanley
The case of the long-legged models.
  Gardner, Erle Stanley
The case of the lucky legs. Gardner,
  Erle Stanley
The case of the lucky loser. Gardner,
  Erle Stanley
The case of the magic mirror. Bush,
  Christopher
The case of the Mexican knife. Homes,
  Geoffrey
The case of the mischievous doll.
  Gardner, Erle Stanley
The case of the missing Bronte.
  Barnard, Robert
The case of the missing coed. Hardy,
  William M.
The case of the missing corpse.
  Lankam, Edwin
The case of the missing diary.
  Fielding, A.
The case of the missing men. Bush,
  Christopher
The case of the missing minutes.
  Bush, Christopher
The case of the missing poison.
  Gardner, Erle Stanley
The case of the Monday murders. Bush,
  Christopher
The case of the moth-eaten mink.
  Gardner, Erle Stanley
The case of the moving finger.
  Christie, Agatha

The case of the murdered Mackenzie.
  Cunningham, E. V.
The case of the murdered major. Bush,
  Christopher
The case of the murdered model.
  Dewey, Thomas B.
The case of the murdered redhead.
  Lockridge, Frances and Lockridge,
  Richard
The case of the musical cow. Gardner,
  Erle Stanley
The case of the mysterious moll.
  Keeler, Harry Stephen
The case of the mythical monkeys.
  Gardner, Erle Stanley
The case of the nameless corpse.
  Kelland, Clarence Budington
The case of the negligent nymph.
  Gardner, Erle Stanley
The case of the nervous accomplice.
  Gardner, Erle Stanley
The case of the one-eyed witness.
  Gardner, Erle Stanley
The case of the 100% alibi. Bush,
  Christopher
The case of the one penny orange.
  Cunningham, E. V.
The case of the perjured parrot.
  Gardner, Erle Stanley
The case of the phantom fortune.
  Gardner, Erle Stanley
The case of the philosopher's ring.
  Collins, Randall
The case of the plastic man. Donavan,
  John
The case of the plastic mask.
  Donavan, John
The case of the platinum blonde.
  Bush, Christopher
The case of the poisoned eclairs.
  Cunningham, E. V.
The case of the postponed murder.
  Gardner, Erle Stanley
The case of the prodigal daughter.
  Bush, Christopher
The case of the purloined picture.
  Bush, Christopher
The case of the queenly contestant.
  Gardner, Erle Stanley
Case of the red box. Stout, Rex
The case of the red brunette. Bush,
  Christopher
The case of the redoubled cross.
  King, Rufus

The frightened woman. Coxe, George
  Harmon
Frog in the throat. Ferrars, E. X.
From a high place. Mathis, Edward
From Doon with death. Rendell, Ruth
From natural causes. Bell, Josephine
From this dark stairway. Eberhart,
  Mignon G.
Front man. Wallace, Francis
The fugitive. Fish, Robert L.
The fugitive eye. Jay, Charlotte
Full contact. Randise, Robert J.
Full coverage. Ullman, James Michael
Fuller's earth. Wells, Carolyn
Funeral for five. Stagge, Jonathan
A funeral in Eden. McGuire, Paul
A funeral of gondolas. Holme, Timothy
Funerals are fatal. Christie, Agatha
The funniest killer in town. Stone,
  Hampton
Funny Jonas, you don't look dead.
  McMullen, Mary
Furious old women. Bruce, Leo
The further adventures of Solar
  Pons. Copper, Basil
The furthest fury. Wells, Carolyn
The fury of Rachel Monette. Abrahams,
  Peter
The futile alibi. Crofts, Freeman
  Wills
Fuzz. McBain, Ed

Gadget. Freeling, Nicolas
The Galloway case. Garve, Andrew
Gallows for the groom. Olsen, D. B.
The gallows garden. Chaber, M. E.
The gallows in my garden. Deming,
  Richard
The Galton case. Macdonald, Ross
Gambit. Stout, Rex
The game. Hammond, Gerald
A game for the living. Highsmith,
  Patricia
Game for three losers. Lustgarten,
  Edgar
A game men play. Bourjaily, Vance
Game, set and danger. Clarke, Anna
The gamecock murders. Gruber, Frank
Gamekeeper's gallows. Hilton, John
  Buxton
Gamemaker. Cohler, David Keith
Games. Pronzini, Bill
Games to keep the dark away. Muller,
  Marcia
Gammon. Bosak, Steven

The Gantry episode. Drummond, June
The gaol breaker. Wallace, Edgar
The garb of truth. Stuart, Ian
The garbage collector. Stein, Aaron
  Marc
The garden in Asia. Post, Melville
  Davisson
The Garden murder case. Van Dine,
  S. S.
Garden of malice. Kenney, Susan
The Garston murder case. Bailey,
  H. C.
Garston's. Bailey, H. C.
A gathering of ghosts. Lewis, Roy
The gathering place. Breen, Jon L.
Gaudy night. Sayers, Dorothy L.
The Gay Head conspiracy. Baker,
  Carlos
The Gay Phoenix. Innes, Michael
The gazebo. Wentworth, Patricia
The G-string murders. Lee, Gypsy Rose
Gelignite gang. Creasey, John
The Gemini man. Kelly, Susan
General Besserley's puzzle box.
  Oppenheim, E. Phillips
General Besserley's second puzzle
  box. Oppenheim, E. Phillips
A gentle albatross. Foote-Smith,
  Elizabeth
A gentle murder. Davis, Dorothy
  Salisbury
A gentleman called. Davis, Dorothy
  Salisbury
Gently at a gallop. Hunter, Alan
Gently between tides. Hunter, Alan
Gently by the shore. Hunter, Alan
Gently coloured. Hunter, Alan
Gently confidential. Hunter, Alan
Gently does it. Hunter, Alan
Gently down the stream. Hunter, Alan
Gently floating. Hunter, Alan
Gently French. Hunter, Alan
Gently go man. Hunter, Alan
Gently in the Highlands. Hunter, Alan
Gently in the sun. Hunter, Alan
Gently in trees. Hunter, Alan
Gently instrumental. Hunter, Alan
Gently north-west. Hunter, Alan
Gently sahib. Hunter, Alan
Gently through the mill. Hunter, Alan
Gently through the woods. Hunter,
  Alan
Gently to a sleep. Hunter, Alan
Gently to the summit. Hunter, Alan

The Guinguette by the Seine. Simenon, Georges

A gun for Inspector West. Creasey, John

The gun in Daniel Webster's bust. Scherf, Margaret

Guns before butter. Freeling, Nicolas

The Guttenberg murders. Bristow, Gwen and Manning, Bruce

The guv'nor and Mr. Reeder. Wallace, Edgar

The guv'nor and other stories. Wallace, Edgar

Gypsy in amber. Smith, Martin Cruz

Gyrth chalice mystery. Allingham, Margery

H as in hangman. Treat, Lawrence

H as in hunted. Treat, Lawrence

The ha-ha case. Connington, J. J.

The habit of loving. Thomson, June

Hag's nook. Carr, John Dickson

Hail, hail, the gang's all here! McBain, Ed

Hail to the chief. McBain, Ed

A hair's breadth. Thayer, Lee

The half hunter. Sherwood, John

Half-mast for the deemster. Bellairs, George

The half-mother. Tennant, Emma

Halfway house. Queen, Ellery

Hall of death. Tyre, Nedra

Hallowe'en homicide. Thayer, Lee

The Hallowe'en murders. Disney, Doris Miles

Hallowe'en party. Christie, Agatha

Halo for Satan. Evans, John

Halo in blood. Evans, John

Halo in brass. Evans, John

Hamlet, revenge! Innes, Michael

Hammer Island. Styles, Showell

Hammer the Toff. Creasey, John

The Hammersmith murders. Frome, David

Hammett. Gores, Joe

Hammett homicides. Hammett, Dashiell

Hand in glove. Eberhart, Mignon G.

Hand in glove. Marsh, Ngaio

Hand me a crime. Russell, Charlotte Murray

Hand of fate. Underwood, Michael

Hand over mind. Lovell, Marc

Hand-picked for murder. Martin, Robert

Handbook for poisoners. Bond, Raymond T., ed.

A handful of silver. Strange, John Stephen

Handle with fear. Dewey, Thomas B.

Hands of death. Colin, Aubrey

The handwriting on the wall. Propper, Milton

Hang the little man. Creasey, John

Hanged for a sheep. Lockridge, Frances and Lockridge, Richard

Hanged man's house. Ferrars, E. X.

The hanging captain. Wade, Henry

The hanging tree. Knox, Bill

The hanging woman. Rhode, John

Hanging's too good. Thayer, Lee

Hangman's curfew. Mitchell, Gladys

Hangman's harvest. Chaber, M. E.

Hangman's holiday. Sayers, Dorothy L.

Hangman's tide. Hilton, John Buxton

The hangman's whip. Eberhart, Mignon G.

Hangover house. Rohmer, Sax

Hapjoy was here. Watson, Colin

Happy are the meek. Greeley, Andrew M.

The hard-boiled omnibus. Shaw, Joseph T., ed.

The hard hit. Wainwright, John

Hard line. Lewin, Michael Z.

A hard man to kill. Perry, Ritchie

Hard trade. Lyons, Arthur

The Hardaway diamonds mystery. Burton, Miles

Hardly a man is now alive. Brean, Herbert

Hare sitting up. Innes, Michael

Hark, hark, the watchdogs bark. Wells, Tobias

The harlot killer. Barnard, Allan, ed.

Harm's way. Aird, Catherine

Harper. Macdonald, Ross

Harriet Farewell. Erskine, Margaret

Harvard has a homicide. Fuller, Timothy

The harvest murder. Rhode, John

Hasty wedding. Eberhart, Mignon G.

Hatchet man. Van Atta, Winfred

Hatchetman. Dodge, David

Hate finds a way. Cumberland, Marten

Hate for sale. Cumberland, Marten

Hate will find a way. Cumberland, Marten

The haunted bookshop. Morley, Christopher

Haunted lady. Rinehart, Mary Roberts

Murder must advertise. Sayers, Dorothy L.

Murder must wait. Upfield, Arthur W

Murder mystery. Thompson, Gene

Murder needs a face. Fenisong, Ruth

Murder needs a name. Fenisong, Ruth

Murder '97. Gruber, Frank

Murder now and then. Brean, Herbert

Murder of a banker. Fletcher, J. S.

Murder of a chemist. Burton, Miles

The murder of a midget. Freeman, Martin J.

Murder of a professor. Miller, John

The murder of a quack. Bellairs, George

Murder of a red haired man. Plum, Mary

The murder of a startled lady. Abbot, Anthony

Murder of a suicide. Ferrars, E. X.

Murder of an initiate. Propper, Milton

Murder of an M. P. Gore-Browne, Robert

The murder of an old man. Frome, David

Murder of an owl. Carr, Glyn

The murder of Busy Lizzie. Mitchell, Gladys

The murder of Geraldine Foster. Abbot, Anthony

The murder of Lawrence of Arabia. Eden, Matthew

The murder of Marion Mason. Dewey, Thomas B.

The murder of Mary Steers. Cooper, Brian

The murder of Miranda. Millar, Margaret

The murder of Miss Betty Sloan. Williams, Sidney

Murder of my patient. Eberhart, Mignon G.

The murder of Roger Ackroyd. Christie, Agatha

Murder of the admiral. Gould, Stephen

The murder of the circus queen. Abbot, Anthony

The murder of the clergyman's mistress. Abbot, Anthony

The murder of the fifth columnist. Ford, Leslie

Murder of the lawyer's clerk. Fletcher, J. S.

The murder of the maharajah. Keating, H. R. F.

The murder of the night club lady. Abbot, Anthony

Murder of the ninth baronet. Fletcher, J. S.

Murder of the only witness. Fletcher, J. S.

Murder out of the past and Under-cover man. Creasey, John

Murder of the pigboat skipper. Fisher, Steve

Murder of the secret agent. Fletcher, J. S.

Murder off Broadway. Klinger, Henry

Murder on a bad trip. Drummond, June

Murder on a tangent. Disney, Doris Miles

Murder on Angler's Island. Reilly, Helen

Murder on "B" deck. Starrett, Vincent

Murder on Broadway. Masur, Harold Q.

Murder on Capitol Hill. Truman, Margaret

Murder on cue. Dentinger, Jane

Murder on duty. Burton, Miles

Murder on Embassy Row. Truman, Margaret

Murder on French leave. Morice, Anne

Murder on his mind. Goldsmith, Gene

Murder on ice. Wood, Ted

Murder on location. Engel, Howard

Murder on location. Thayer, Lee

Murder on Madison Ave. Orenstein, Frank

Murder on Martha's Vineyard. Roos, Kelley

Murder on mike. Jeffers, H. Paul

Murder on Monday. Bush, Christopher

Murder on parade. Wells, Carolyn

Murder on Russian Hill. Offord, Lenore Glen

Murder on safari. Huxley, Elspeth

Murder on Shadow Island. Weston, Garnett

Murder on show. Babson, Marian

Murder on the Appalachian Trail. Carr, Jess

Murder on the blackboard. Palmer, Stuart

Murder on the brain. Heckstall-Smith, Anthony

Murder on the bridge. Brock, Lynn

Murder on the bus. Gregg, Cecil Freeman

Murder on the Calais Coach. Christie, Agatha

Murder on the Costa Brava. Bonett, John and Bonett, Emery

Murder with mushrooms. Ashe, Gordon

Murder with pictures. Coxe, George
Harmon

Murder with southern hospitality.
Ford, Leslie

Murder within murder. Lockridge,
Frances and Lockridge, Richard

Murder without icing. Lathen, Emma

Murder without weapons. Cunningham,
A. B.

Murder won't wait. Daly, Carroll John

Murdercon. Purtill, Richard L.

Murdered: One by one. Beeding, Francis

A murderer in this house. King, Rufus

The murderer of sleep. Kennedy,
Milward

The murderer who wanted more.
Kendrick, Baynard H.

Murderers anonymous. Ferrars, E. X.

The murderer's challenge. Footner,
Hulbert

Murderer's house. Melville, Jennie

Murderers make mistakes. Crofts,
Freeman Wills

The murderers of Monty. Hull, Richard

Murderer's vanity. Footner, Hulbert

The murders at Impasse Louvain.
Grayson, Richard

The murders in Praed Street. Rhode,
John

Murders in Volume 2. Daly, Elizabeth

Murder's little helper. Bagby, George

Murder's nest. Armstrong, Charlotte

The murders of Richard III. Peters,
Elizabeth

The murders on Fox Island. Hood,
Margaret Page

Murdock. Simmons, Geoffrey

Murdock's acid test. Coxe, George
Harmon

Murmurs in the Rue Morgue. Cumberland,
Martin

The museum murder. McIntyre, John T.

Music when sweet voices die. Yarbro,
Chelsea Quinn

The Mussolini murder plot. Newman,
Bernard

Mute witness. Pike, Robert L.

My adventure in the Flying Scotsman.
Phillpotts, Eden

My bones will keep. Mitchell, Gladys

My brother Michael. Stewart, Mary

My brother's killer. Devine, D. M.

My cousin Death. McMullen, Mary

My dead body. Bagby, George

My father sleeps. Mitchell, Gladys

My foe outstretch'd beneath the
tree. Clinton-Baddeley, V. C.

My friend Maigret. Simenon, Georges

My grand enemy. Stubbs, Jean

My gun is quick. Spillane, Mickey

My killer doesn't understand me.
Mulkeen, Thomas

My kingdom for a hearse. Rue, Craig

My late wives. Dickson, Carter

My life is done. Woods, Sara

My name is death. Egan, Lesley

My name is Norval. White, Terrence
de Vere

My particular murder. Sharp, David

My son, the murderer. Quentin,
Patrick

The Mycroft memoranda. Walsh, Ray

Mysteries of Winterthurn. Oates,
Joyce Carol

The mysterious affair at Styles.
Christie, Agatha

The mysterious Mickey Finn; or
Murder at the Cafe' du Dome. Paul,
Elliot

The mysterious Mr. I. Keeler, Harry
Stephen

The mysterious Mr. Quin. Christie,
Agatha

The mysterious partner. Fielding, A.

The mysterious suspect. Rhode, John

Mysteriouser and mysteriouser.
Bagby, George

Mystery at a country inn. Owen,
Philip

Mystery at Greycombe Farm. Rhode,
John

The mystery at Lover's cave.
Berkeley, Anthony

Mystery at Lynden Sands. Connington,
J. J.

The mystery at Martha's Vineyard.
Dyer, George

Mystery at Olympia. Rhode, John

Mystery at Peak House. Rees,
Arthur J.

Mystery at the rectory. Fielding, A.

Mystery deluxe. King, Rufus

The mystery girl. Wells, Carolyn

Mystery in Kensington Gore.
MacDonald, Philip

Mystery in the channel. Crofts,
Freeman Wills

Mystery in the English Channel.
Crofts, Freeman Wills

Not in utter nakedness. Ames, Delano
Not me, Inspector. Reilly, Helen
Not one of us. Thomson, June
Not quite dead enough. Stout, Rex
Not to be taken. Berkely, Anthony
Not working. Szanto, George
Nothing but foxes. Lewis, Roy
Nothing but the truth. Rhode, John
Nothing can rescue me. Daly, Elizabeth
Nothing is the number when you die.
  Fleming, Joan
Nothing like blood. Bruce, Leo
Nothing to do with the case.
  Lemarchand, Elizabeth
Nothing's certain but death. Wren,
  M. K.
North of welfare. Krasner, William
The Norths meet murder. Lockridge,
  Frances and Lockridge, Richard
The Norwich victims. Beeding, Francis
A nose for it. Stein, Aaron Marc
The notched hairpin. Heard, H. F.
The notorious Sophie Lang. Anderson,
  Frederick Irving
A novena for murder. O'Marie, Sr.
  Carol Anne
Now dead is any man. Audemars, Pierre
Now it's my turn. Chaber, M. E.
Nowhere? Stein, Aaron Marc
Nowhere man. Perry, Ritchie
Nude in Nevada. Dewey, Thomas B.
No. 9 Belmont Square. Erskine,
  Margaret
A nun in the closet. Gilman, Dorothy
A nun in the cupboard. Gilman, Dorothy
Nun of the above. Quill, Monica
The nursemaid who disappeared.
  MacDonald, Philip
Nursery tea and poison. Morice, Anne
The nursing home murder. Marsh, Ngaio
  and Jellett, Henry

O as in omen. Treat, Lawrence
The Obeah murders. Footner, Hulbert
Obelists at sea. King, C. Daly
Obelists en route. King, C. Daly
Obelists fly high. King, C. Daley
Obit delayed. Nielsen, Helen
The obituary club. Pentecost, Hugh
The obligations of Hercule. Audemars,
  Pierre
An obscure grave. Woods, Sara
Obsequies at Oxford. Crispin, Edmund
Obsession. Tripp, Miles
Octagon House. Taylor, Phoebe Atwood

The October Cabaret. Quest, Erica
October House. Strahen, Kay Cleaver
The odd flamingo. Bawden, Nina
Odd job. Flower, Pat
Odd job No. 101 and other future
  crimes. Goulart, Ron
Odds against. Francis, Dick
The odds on death. Drummond, Charles
Odds on Miss Seeton. Carvic, Heron
Odds on the hot seat. Philips, Judson
The odds run out. Waugh, Hillary
The odor of bitter almonds. Edwards,
  James G.
The odor of violets. Kendrick,
  Baynard H.
Of missing persons. Goodis, David
Of unsound mind. Carmichael, Harry
Off with her head! Cole, G. D. H.
  and Cole, Margaret
Off with his head. Marsh, Ngaio
Oh bury me not. Wren, M. K.
Oh! Where are Bloody Mary's earrings?
  Player, Robert
Old acquaintance. Guild, Nicholas
The old battle axe. Holding,
  Elizabeth Saxanay
The old English peep show. Dickinson,
  Peter
The Old Fox Deceiv'd. Grimes, Martha
Old hall, new hall. Innes, Michael
Old lover's ghost. Ford, Leslie
The old man in the corner. Orczy,
  Baroness
The old man in the corner unravels
  the mystery of the Fulton Gordens
  mystery, and the Moorland Tragedy.
  Orczy, Baroness
The old man in the corner unravels
  the mystery of the khaki tunic.
  Orczy, Baroness
The old man in the corner unravels
  the mystery of the necklace and the
  tragedy in the bishop's road.
  Orczy, Baroness
The old man in the corner unravels
  the mystery of the Russian prince
  and of Dog's Tooth Cliff. Orczy,
  Baroness
The old man in the corner unravels
  the mystery of the white carnation,
  and the Montmarte hat. Orczy,
  Baroness
Old man Tutt. Train, Arthur
The old mill. Wilson, P. W.

Shaft's carnival of killers. Tidyman,
  Ernest
Shake hands for ever. Rendell, Ruth
Shakedown hotel. Freedericks, Ernest
  Jason
The Shakespeare curse. Boland, John
The shape of a stain. Ferrars, E. X.
The shape of fear. Pentecost, Hugh
The sharkskin book. Keeler, Harry
  Stephen
Sharp practice. Farris, John
A sharp rise in crime. Creasey, John
She asked for it. Berckman, Evelyn
She came back. Wentworth, Patricia
She died a lady. Dickson, Carter
She died because. Hopkins, Kenneth
She died dancing. Roos, Kelley
She shall have murder. Ames, Delano
She should have cried on Monday.
  Russell, E. S.
She walks alone. McCloy, Helen
She was only the sheriff's daughter.
  Forbes, Stanton
She wouldn't say who. Ames, Delano
Shear the black sheep. Dodge, David
Shed light on death. Taylor, L. A.
Sheiks and adders. Innes, Michael
Shelf life. Clark, Douglas
She'll hate me tomorrow. Deming,
  Richard
The Sheridan Road mystery. Thorne,
  Paul and Thorne, Mabel
The sheriff and the panhandle.
  Meredith, D. R.
The sheriff of Bombay. Keating,
  H. R. F.
Sherlock Holmes at Oxford. Utechin,
  Nicholas
Sherlock Holmes in Dallas. Aubrey,
  Edmund
Sherlock Holmes in Tibet. Wincor,
  Richard
Sherlock Holmes: My life and crimes.
  Hardwick, Michael
Sherlock Holmes vs. Arsene Lupin.
  Leblanc, Maurice
Sherlock Holmes vs. Dracula. Estleman,
  Loren D.
Sherlock Holmes vs. Jack the Ripper.
  Queen, Ellery
Shield for murder. McGwein, William P.
The shield of silence. Balmer, Edwin
  and Wylie, Philip
A shilling for candles. Tey,
  Josephine

Shills can't cash chips. Fair, A. A.
The shivering mountain. Somers, Paul
Shock! Markham, Virgil
Shock treatment. Van Atta, Winfred
Shock wave. Davis, Dorothy Salisbury
The shocking pink hat. Crane, Frances
Shoestring. Abelman, Paul
Shoestring's finest hour. Abelman,
  Paul
Shoot me dacent. Stein, Aaron Marc
Shoot the moon. Page, Jake
Shoot to kill. Miller, Wade
The shooting of Dan McGrew. Kenyon,
  Michael
Shooting star. Bloch, Robert
Short break in Venice. Inchbald,
  Peter
The short cases of Inspector Maigret.
  Simenon, Georges
Short stories of today and yesterday.
  Bramah, Ernest
The shortest way to Hades. Caudwell,
  Sarah
Shot at dawn. Rhode, John
Shot in the dark. Ford, Leslie
A shot in the dark. Powell, Richard
A shot of murder. Iams, Jack
Shotgun. McBain, Ed
A show of violence. Woods, Sara
Show red for danger. Lockridge,
  Richard and Lockridge, Frances
A shriek of tyres. Ruthersford,
  Douglas
The shrieking pit. Rees, Arthur J.
Shroud for a lady. Daly, Elizabeth
Shroud for a nightingale. James,
  P. D.
A shroud for Aquarius. Collins, Max
  Allen
The shroud off her back. Ransome,
  Stephen
Shrouded death. Bailey, H. C.
The shrouded way. Caird, Janet
The shrunken head. Fish, Robert L.
The shudders. Abbot, Anthony
Siamese twin mystery. Queen, Ellery
Sign of fear. Derleth, August
The sign of the four. Doyle, Arthur
  Conan
Signal for death. Rhode, John
Silence for the murderer. Crofts,
  Freeman Wills
Silence observed. Innes, Michael
Silenski, master criminal. Wallace,
  Edgar

The taste of ashes. Browne, Howard
Taste of fears. Millar, Margaret
The taste of fears. Woods, Sara
The taste of murder. Cannan, Joanna
A taste of power. Burley, W. J.
The taste of proof. Knox, Bill
A taste of treason. Maling, Arthur
A taste of treasure. Ashe, Gordon
The tattooed arm. Ostrander, Isabel
The tau cross mystery. Connington, J. J.
The Taurus trip. Dewey, Thomas B.
The tea-tray murders. Bush, Christopher
Tears for the bride. Martin, Robert
Telefair. Rice, Craig
The telephone call. Rhode, John
Tell her it's murder. Reilly, Helen
Tell it to the dead. Davies, L. P.
Tell them whats-her-name called. Davis, Mildred
Temple tower. McNeille, H. C.
The temptation of Hercule. Audemars, Pierre
Tend days wonder. Queen, Ellery
Ten little Indians. Christie, Agatha
Ten little niggers. Christie, Agatha
Ten plus one. McBain, Ed
The ten teacups. Dickson, Carter
The 10:30 from Marseilles. Japrisot, Sebastien
Ten were missing. Allingham, Margery
Ten years beyond Baker Street. Van Ash, Cay
Tenant for death. Hare, Cyril
The tender killer. Hough, S. B.
The tender poisoner. Bingham, John
The tenth life. Lockridge, Richard
The tenth virgin. Stewart, Gary
The terrible tide. Craig, Alisa
The Terriford mystery. Lowndes, Marie Belloc
Terror by day. Ashe, Gordon
Terror by twilight. Knight, Kathleen Moore
Terror for the Toff. Creasey, John
Terror keep. Wallace, Edgar
Terror on the island. Ferguson, John
Terror touches me. Forbes, Stanton
The terrorists. Sjowall, Maj and Wahloo, Per
Tether's end. Allingham, Margery
That awful mess on Via Merulana. Gadda, Carlo Emilio
That darn cat. Gordons, The

That dinner at Bardolph's. Walling, R. A. J.
That evening in Shanghai. Thorne, Paul
That night it rained. Waugh, Hillary
That Royle girl. Balmer, Edwin
That yew tree's shade. Hare, Cyril
The Theban mysteries. Cross, Amanda
The theft of Magna Carta. Creasey, John
Their evil ways. Wainwright, John
Their nearest and dearest. Carey, Bernice
Then come violence. Ball, John
Then there were three. Homes, Geoffrey
Therapy for murder. Munder, Laura
There came both mist and snow. Innes, Michael
There goes death. Ashe, Gordon
There is a tide . . . . Christie, Agatha
There is no justice. Dominic, R. B.
There lies your love. Melville, Jennie
There must be victims. Cumberland, Marten
There sits death. McGuire, Paul
There was a crooked man. Roos, Kelley
There was an old woman. Queen, Ellery
There's nothing to be afraid of. Muller, Marcia
There's trouble brewing. Blake, Nicholas
They buried a man. Davis, Mildred
They came to Baghdad. Christie, Agatha
They came to kill. Scherf, Margaret
They can only hang you once. Hammett, Dashiel
They can't all be guilty. Heberden, M. V.
They died in the spring. Cannan, Joanna
They do it with mirrors. Christie, Agatha
They found him dead. Heyer, Georgette
They hadn't a clue. Downes, Quentin
They journey by night. Ames, Delano
They liked Entwhistle. Walling, R. A. J.
They love not poison. Woods, Sara
They never looked inside. Gilbert, Michael
They never say when. Cheyney, Peter

Subject and Setting Index

Kienzle, William X.: Kill and tell.
Knox, Bill: The ghost car.
Lathen, Emma: Murder makes the wheels go 'round.
AUTOMOBILE RACING
Rhode, John: Dr. Priestly lays a trap.
Rutherford, Douglas: On the track of death.
AUTOMOBILE RACING DRIVERS AS DETECTIVES
Ashford, Jeffrey: Guilt with honor.
AUTOMOBILE REPOSSESSORS
Gores, Joe: 3 books
AUTOMOBILES
Gault, William Campbell: The convertible hearse.
Rhode, John: Murder at the motor show.
Rutherford, Douglas: Turbo.

BABIES; see INFANTS
BACHELORS; see SINGLE MEN
BACKGAMMON
Bosak, Steven: Gammon.
BAHAMA ISLANDS
Dunnett, Dorothy: Match for a murderer.
Ford, Leslie: The Bahamas murder case.
Perry, Ritchie: Holiday with a vengeance.
BAKERS; see also COOKERY; COOKS
Taylor, Phoebe Atwood: Banbury boy.
BAKING; see BREAD; COOKERY
BALLET; see also DANCING
Box, Edgar: Death in the fifth position.
Brahms, Caryl and Simon, E. J.: 4 books
Cores, Lucy: Corpse de ballet.
Resnicow, Herbert: The Gold deadline.
Wayland, Patrick: The waiting game.
BANK ROBBERY; see also ROBBERY
Benson, Ben: The silver cobweb.
Gardner, John: A complete state of death.
Pike, Robert L.: Bank job.
BANKERS
Francis, Dick: Banker.
Heberden, M. V.: They can't all be guilty.
Payne, Will: The scarred chin.

Taylor, Phoebe Atwood: Tinkling symbol.
BANKERS AS DETECTIVES
Brown, Robert Carlton: The remarkable adventures of Christopher Poe.
Lathen, Emma: 19 books
Rendell, Ruth: Make death love me.
Welton, Arthur D.: The twenty-seventh side.
Williams, David: 8 books
BANKS AND BANKING
Brown, Robert Carlton: The remarkable adventures of Christopher Poe.
Creasey, John: The trouble at Saxby's.
Gordons, The: Operation Terror.
Masur, Harold Q.: The broker.
Rendell, Ruth: Make death love me.
Rhode, John: Robbery with violence.
Stuart, Ian: The garb of truth.
Thayer, Lee: Within the vault.
Welton, Arthur D.: The twenty-seventh ride.
BARBADOS
Coxe, George Harmon: The man who died twice. Moment of violence. Uninvited guest.
BARS; see TAVERNS, BARS, etc.
BASEBALL
DeAndrea, William L.: Five o'clock lightning.
Engleman, Paul: Dead in center field.
Parker, Robert B.: Mortal stakes.
Rosen, Richard: Strike three you're dead.
Tapply, William G.: Follow the sharks.
BASKETBALL
Drummond, Charles: Death and the leaping ladies.
Hornig, Doug: Foul shot.
Langley, Lee: Dead center.
BEATNIKS
Williams, Brad: Make a killing.
BEAUTY SHOPS
Cores, Lucy: Painted for the kill.
O'Donnell, Lillian: Aftershock.
BEER; see BREWERIES
BEES
Heard, H. F.: A taste for honey.
BEHEADING; see DECAPITATION

BELGIAN CONGO
Head, Matthew: The Congo Venus. The devil in the bush.
BELGIUM
Crofts, Freeman Wills: The Cheyne mystery.
Simenon, Georges: The Flemish shop.
Stein, Aaron Marc: The bombing run.
BELGIUM--BRUSSELS
Jeffreys, J. G.: Suicide most foul.
Simenon, Georges: The crime of Inspector Maigret.
BELIZE
Coxe, George Harmon: The inside man. With intent to kill.
BELLS AND BELL RINGING
Sayers, Dorothy L.: The nine tailors.
BERKSHIRE HILLS; see MASSACHUSETTS--BERKSHIRES
BERMUDA
Burnham, David: Last act in Bermuda.
Denbie, Roger: Death cruises south.
Holding, Elizabeth Saxanay: The strange crime in Bermuda.
King, C. Daly: Bermuda burial.
Patrick, Q.: Return to the scene.
Siller, Van: The last resort.
Thayer, Lee: The prisoner pleads "not guilty."
BETROTHALS; see also HONEYMOONS; WEDDINGS
Fuller, Samuel: The naked kiss.
Penn, John: Stag dinner death.
BIGAMY
Coxe, George Harmon: The man who died twice.
Crofts, Freeman Wills: The Ponson case.
Innes, Michael: The long farewell.
Quentin, Patrick: The man with two wives.
Rendell, Ruth: An unkindness of ravens.
Symons, Julian: The man who killed himself.
Trollope, Anthony: John Caldigate.
BILLIONAIRES
Ellin, Stanley: Star light, star bright.
Pentecost, Hugh: The steel palace.
BIOLOGICAL WARFARE
Bosse, M. J.: The man who loved zoos.

Brean, Herbert: The clock strikes thirteen.
BIRDWATCHING
Borthwick, J. S.: The case of the hook-billed kites.
BIRTHDAYS
Bax, Roger: A grave case of murder.
Moyes, Patricia: Many deadly returns.
BLACK DETECTIVES
Ball, John: 6 books
Baxt, Roger: A queer kind of death. Swing low, sweet Harriet. Topsy and evil.
Bell, Josephine: The Wilberforce legacy.
Burke, J. F.: Kelly among the nightingales.
Cohen, Octavus Roy: 2 books
Douglas, Donald McNutt: 3 books
Green, Thomas J.: The flowered box.
Himes, Chester: 8 books
Hughes, Dorothy B.: The expendable man.
Kamarck, Lawrence: The bell ringer.
McClure, James: 7 books
Reed, Ishmael: 2 books
Tidyman, Ernest: 7 books
Werry, Richard R.: Casket for a living lady.
Wyllie, John: 8 books
Zake, S. Joshua L.: Truckful of gold.
BLACK MAGIC; see WITCHCRAFT
BLACK MARKETEERING
Creasey, John: The Toff goes to market.
MacKinnon, Allan: Money on the black.
Woods, Sara: They love not poison.
BLACKMAIL; see also EXTORTION
Aird, Catherine: Last respects.
Alington, C. A.: Blackmail in Blankshire.
Allingham, Margery: The fashion in shrouds.
Allison, E. M. A.: Through the valley of death.
Ashford, Jeffrey: The double run.
Ashforth, Albert: Murder after the fact.
Bacon, Peggy: Inward eye.
Barnard, Robert: Death in a cold climate.
Barry, Joe: Three for the money.

Blackstock, Lee: Woman in the woods.
Candy, Edward: Which doctor?
Curtiss, Ursula: Death of a crow.
Davis, Dorothy Salisbury: The little brothers.
Heberden, M. V.: They can't all be guilty.
Koenig, Laird: Rockabye.
Macdonald, Ross: The underground man.
MacKinnon, Allan: Cormorant's Isle.
McCloy, Helen: The one that got away.
Parker, Robert B.: God save the child.
Sinclair, Murray: Only in L. A.
Stewart, Mary: Madam, will you talk?
Stout, Rex: The golden spiders.
Uhnak, Dorothy: The investigator.
Winch, Arden: Blood royal.
Woods, Sara: A show of violence.

BRAINWASHING
Wainwright, John: Brainwash.

BRAZIL
Fish, Robert L.: 5 books
Footner, Hulbert: Scarred jungle.
Leonard, Charles L.: The fourth funeral.
Perry, Ritchie: The fall guy. One good death deserves another.

BRAZIL--AMAZON RIVER; see AMAZON RIVER

BRAZIL--ISLANDS
Fish, Robert L.: Isle of snakes.

BRAZIL--RIO DE JANEIRO
Chaber, M. E.: Six who ran.
Fish, Robert L.: 4 books
Kelsey, Vera: 2 books

BRAZIL--SAO PAOLO
Malcolm, John: A back room in Somerstown.

BREAD; see also COOKERY
Smith, Julie: The sourdough wars.

BREWERIES; see also DISTILLERIES; WINES, SPIRITS, etc.
Blake, Nicholas: There's trouble brewing.

BRIBERY
Egan, Lesley: Some avenger, arise!

BRIDGE; see also CARD GAMES
Berckman, Evelyn: A simple case of ill-will.

Christie, Agatha: Cards on the table.
Heyer, Georgette: Duplicate death.

BRITISH BROADCASTING CORPORATION; see also RADIO BROADCASTING; TELEVISION BROADCASTING
Brett, Simon: The dead side of the mike.
Sherwood, John: Death at the B. B. C.

BRITISH IN AFRICA
Anderson, J. R. L.: Death in the greenhouse.
Black, Lionel: Chance to die.
Huxley, Elspeth: 4 books

BRITISH IN ALGERIA
Underwood, Michael: Lawful pursuit.

BRITISH IN ANDORRA
Ames, Delano F.: Murder, maestro please.

BRITISH IN AUSTRALIA
Ashe, Gordon: A taste of treasure.
Barnard, Robert: Death of an old goat.
Creasey, John: The Toff down under.
Morton, Anthony: Sport for the Baron.

BRITISH IN AUSTRIA
Carnac, Carol: Crossed skies.
Carr, Glyn: The corpse in the crevasse. Lewker in Tirol.
Peters, Ellis: The house of green turf. Where there's a will.
Yorke, Margaret: Silent witness.

BRITISH IN BRAZIL
Leonard, Charles L.: The fourth funeral.

BRITISH IN CANADA
Heald, Tim: Murder at Moose Jaw.
Rhode, John: Tragedy on the line.

BRITISH IN CHINA; see also BRITISH IN HONG KONG
Rendell, Ruth: Speaker of Mandarin.

BRITISH IN CYPRUS
Webster, Noah: Flickering death.

BRITISH IN CZECHOSLOVAKIA
Peters, Ellis: The piper on the mountain.
Webster, Noah: A problem in Prague.

BRITISH IN DENMARK
Kirk, Michael: Dragonship.

BRITISH IN EGYPT
Hocking, Anne: Death loves a shining mark. Nile green.

Inchbald, Peter: Short break in Venice.

Mitchell, Gladys: The twenty-third man.

Moyes, Patricia: Dead men don't ski.

Nabb, Magdalen: Death of an Englishman.

Rutherford, Douglas: 3 books

BRITISH IN JAPAN

Melville, James: The chrysanthemum chain. Sayonara, Sweet Amaryllis.

BRITISH IN LEBANON

Jay, Charlotte: Arms for Adonis.

BRITISH IN MALTA

Butler, Gwendoline: Coffin in Malta.

Webster, Noah: A killing in Malta.

BRITISH IN MONACO

Harrison, Ray: Why kill Arthur Potter?

BRITISH IN MOROCCO

Cobb, G. Belton: Corpse at Casablanca.

Dickson, Carter: Behind the crimson blind.

BRITISH IN NEPAL

Carr, Glyn: A corpse at Camp Two.

BRITISH IN NEW GUINEA

Vandercook, John W.: Murder in New Guinea.

BRITISH IN NEW ZEALAND

Marsh, Ngaio: Colour scheme. Died in the wool. Photo finish. Vintage murder.

Sherwood, John: A botanist at bay.

BRITISH IN NIGERIA

Knight, David James: Farquharson's physique and what it did to his mind.

BRITISH IN NORWAY

Barnard, Robert: Death in a cold climate.

Carr, Glyn: Lewker in Norway.

BRITISH IN PAKISTAN

Jay, Charlotte: The yellow turban.

BRITISH IN POLAND

Tripp, Miles: The wife-smuggler.

BRITISH IN PORTUGAL

Kirk, Michael: Salvage job.

MacKenzie, Donald: Raven's longest night.

Perry, Ritchie: MacAllister.

Webster, Noah: A burial in Portugal.

BRITISH IN RUSIA; see BRITISH IN THE U. S. S. R.

BRITISH IN SOUTH AFRICA

Ashe, Gordon: A promise of diamonds.

Creasey, John: Call the Toff.

BRITISH IN SOUTH AMERICA

Rossiter, John: The deadly green.

Taylor, P. Walker: 2 books

BRITISH IN SPAIN

Ames, Delano L.: The man with three chins.

Bonett, John and Emery: 4 books

Bruce, Leo: Death on the black sands.

Carr, Glyn: Holiday with murder.

Dunnett, Dorothy: Murder in the round.

Gosling, Paula: The woman in red.

Household, Geoffrey: Olura.

Jeffries, Roderic: Deadly petard. Murder begets murder. Three and one makes five.

Kirk, Michael: All other perils. Mayday from Malaga.

MacKenzie, Donald: Raven in flight. Raven's longest night.

Rossiter, John: 2 books

Webster, Noah: Legacy from Teneriffe.

BRITISH IN SWITZERLAND

Ames, Delano: Crime out of mind.

Carr, Glyn: Murder on the Matterhorn.

Carr, John Dickson: In spite of thunder.

Carvic, Heron: Miss Seeton sings.

Moyes, Patricia: Death on the agenda. Season of snows and sins.

Webster, Noah: A pay-off in Switzerland.

BRITISH IN THE BAHAMAS

Dunnett, Dorothy: Match for a murderer.

BRITISH IN THE CARIBBEAN; see also BRITISH IN THE WEST INDIES

Davey, Jocelyn: Murder in paradise.

Moyes, Patricia: Angel death. The coconut killings.

BRITISH IN THE FIJI ISLANDS

Vandercook, John W.: Murder in Fiji.

BRITISH IN THE NETHERLANDS

Moyes, Patricia: Death and the Dutch uncle.

BRITISH IN THE U. S. S. R.
  Porter, Joyce: Neither a candle nor a pitchfork. The package included murder. Sour cream with everything.
BRITISH IN THE UNITED STATES
  Ames, Delano L.: Murder begins at home.
  Ashe, Gordon: Drop dead. No need to die. A rabble of rebels.
  Aubrey, Edmund: Sherlock Holmes in Dallas.
  Babson, Marian: A trail of ashes.
  Barnett, James: Marked for destruction.
  Blake, Nicholas: The morning after death.
  Burgess, Gelett: Ladies in boxes.
  Carr, John Dickson: Dark of the moon. The dead man's knock. Panic in Box C.
  Creasey, John: The Toff in New York.
  Davey, Jocelyn: A capitol offense. A touch of stagefright. A treasury alarm.
  Dickson, Carter: A graveyard to let.
  Eberhard, Frederic G.: The microbe murders.
  Garnet, A. H.: Maze.
  Heard, H. F.: Reply paid.
  Hilton, John Buxton: The sunset law.
  Hughes, Babette Plechner: Murder in the zoo.
  Kenyon, Michael: The man at the wheel. The trouble with series three.
  Lewis, Lange: The passionate victims.
  Lockridge, Frances and Richard: The drill is death.
  Lovesey, Peter: Keystone.
  Marlowe, Derek: Somebody's sister.
  Morice, Anne: Murder in mimicry.
  Morton, Anthony: Affair for the Baron. The Baron branches out.
  Plum, Mary: The killing of Judge MacFarlane.
  Rendell, Ruth: Death notes.
  Rossiter, John: The murder makers.
  Selwyn, Francis: Sergeant Verity and the blood royal.

Starrett, Vincent: The end of Mr. Garment.
Thorne, Paul: Spiderweb clues.
Williams, Valentine: 3 books
Winslow, Pauline Glen: The Rockefeller gift.
Woods, Sara: The knavish crows. Most grievous murder.
BRITISH IN THE WEST INDIES; see also BRITISH IN THE CARIBBEAN
  Anderson, J. R. L.: Death in the Caribbean.
  Dunnett, Dorothy: Dolly and the bird of paradise.
  Moyes, Patricia: Black widower.
BRITISH IN TIBET
  Ironside, Elizabeth: A very private enterprise.
  Wincor, Richard: Sherlock Holmes in Tibet.
BRITISH IN TRINIDAD
  Underwood, Michael: Arm of the law.
  Vandercook, John W.: Murder in Trinidad.
BRITISH IN TURKEY
  Fleming, Joan: When I grow rich.
BRITISH IN ZANZIBAR
  Kaye, M. M.: Death in Zanzibar.
BROADCASTING; see RADIO BROADCASTING; TELEVISION BROADCASTING
BROTHERS; see also FRATRICIDE
  Cole, G. D. H. and Margaret: The Brothers Sackville.
  Connington, J. J.: A minor operation. Murder in the maze.
  Davis, Dorothy Salisbury: The little brothers.
  McGivern, William P.: Rogue cop.
  McGuire, Paul: Threepence to Marble Arch.
  Queen, Ellery: The king is dead.
  Rhode, John: Double identities.
  Wainwright, John: The forest.
BROTHERS AND SISTERS
  Boucher, Anthony: The case of the seven sneezes.
  Brand, Christianna: The three-cornered halo.
  Chandler, Raymond: Little sister.
  Ferrars, E. X.: Depart this life.
  Heyer, Georgette: Merely murder.
  Hough, S. B.: Sweet sister seduced.
  Millar, Margaret: Mermaid.
  Simenon, Georges: The crossroad

Masterson, Whit: The slow gallows.

CALIFORNIA--LOS ANGELES

Abercrombie, Barbara: Good riddance.

Adams, Cleve F.: Decoy. What price murder.

Armstrong, Charlotte: Dream of fair woman. The gift shop.

Ballard, Willis Todhunter: Say yes to murder.

Baxt, George: The neon graveyard.

Berckman, Evelyn: She asked for it.

Beynon, Jane: Cypress man.

Boucher, Anthony: The case of the crumpled knave.

Bradbury, Ray: Death is a lonely business.

Brown, Frederic: The wench is dead.

Chaber, M. E.: The day it rained diamonds. The flaming man. Softly in the night.

Chandler, Raymond: Little sister. The long goodbye.

Childs, Timothy: Cold turkey.

Clason, Clyde B.: Green shiver.

Cochran, Alan: Two plus two.

Collins, Michael: The slasher. Woman in marble.

Demaris, Ovid: 5 books

Dewey, Thomas B.: And where she stops. The case of the chaste and the unchaste. Go to sleep, Jeannie. The love-death thing. Only on Tuesdays. The Taurus trip.

Dodge, David: Shear the black sheep.

Dunne, John Gregory: True confessions.

Egan, Lesley: 12 books

Ellroy, James: 2 books

Fair, A. A.: 24 books

Fisher, Steve: I wake up screaming.

Flynn, Carol Houlihan: Washed in the blood.

Ford, Leslie: The devil's stronghold.

Gardner, Erle Stanley: 79 books

Gault, William Campbell: 11 books

Goodis, David: Of missing persons.

Gordons, The: 6 books

Gruber, Frank: The buffalo box. The lonesome badger. Murder '97. Simon Lash, private detective.

Hamilton, Nan: Killer's rights.

Hansen, Joseph: Backtrack. Death claims.

Harris, Timothy: Good night and goodbye.

Hitchens, Bert and Delores: F. O. B. murder.

Hitchens, Delores: Sleep with slander.

Holmes, H. H.: 2 books

Holton, Leonard: 10 books

Hughes, Babette Plechner: Murder in the church.

Johnson, E. Richard: The god keepers.

Kaminsky, Stuart: Bullet for a star. He done her wrong. Murder on the Yellow Brick Road.

Keating, H. R. F.: Go west, Inspector Ghote.

Lewis, Lange: 4 books

Lochte, Dick: Sleeping dog.

Lyons, Arthur: 6 books

Lysaght, Brian: 2 books

Macdonald, Ross: 15 books

Meyer, Nicholas: Target practice.

Millar, Margaret: Beast in view. A stranger in my grave.

Nielsen, Helen: Borrow the night. The woman on the roof.

Olsen, D. B.: 6 books

Page, Marco: Reclining figure.

Palmer, Stuart: The puzzle of the happy hooligan. Rook takes knight.

Paul, Elliot: The black gardenia.

Perdue, Virginia: 2 books

Platt, Kin: Match point for murder.

Rubel, Marc: Flex.

Sadler, Marc: Here to die.

Sale, Richard: Passing strange.

Sanchez, Thomas: The zoot-suit murders.

Shannon, Dell: 35 books

Spain, John: 2 books

Thayer, Lee: Guilty!

Webb, Jack: 9 books

White, Terri: Bleeding hearts.

Williams, Brad: Make a killing.

CALIFORNIA--LOS ANGELES--HOLLYWOOD

Bellem, Robert Leslie: Robert Leslie Bellem's Dan Turner, Hollywood detective.

Bergman, Andrew: Hollywood and LeVine.

Bloch, Robert: Shooting star.

Boucher, Anthony: The case of the Baker Street Irregulars.

Gardner, Erle Stanley: The case of the backward mule. The case of the substitute face. Murder up my sleeve.

Gores, Joe: 6 books

Greenleaf, Stephen: 3 books

Hammett, Dashiell: The adventures of Sam Spade and other stories. The Continental Op. Hammett homicides. The Maltese falcon. The return of the Continental Op.

James, Breni: Night of the kill.

Kelland, Clarence Budington: Dangerous angel.

Marlowe, Derek: Somebody's sister.

Millar, Margaret: The listening walls.

Muller, Marcia: 6 books

Nash, Jay Robert: The dark fountain.

Nelson, Hugh Lawrence: The title is murder.

Offord, Lenore Glen: 2 books

Olsen, D. B.: The clue in the clay.

O'Marie, Carol Anne: A novena for murder.

Palmer, Stuart and Flora, Fletcher: Hildegard Withers makes the scene.

Pike, Robert L.: 4 books

Pronzini, Bill: 8 books

Quentin, Patrick: Puzzle for puppets.

Reed, Ishmael: The last days of Louisiana Red.

Shankman, Sarah: Impersonal attractions.

Singer, Shelley: Free draw.

Smith, Julie: 3 books

Stubbs, Jean: The golden crucible.

Taylor, Elizabeth Atwood: The cable car murder.

Thayer, Lee: And one cried murder. Dead on arrival. A hair's breadth. No holiday for murder. Out brief candle!

Walker, Walter: The two dude offense.

Webb, Victoria: A little lady killing.

Wilcox, Collin: 14 books

Yarbro, Chelsea Quinn: Music when sweet voices die.

Zackel, Fred: 2 books

CALIFORNIA--SAN FRANCISCO--SUBURBS

Ashe, Gordon: A rabble of rebels.

Head, Matthew: The smell of money.

CALIFORNIA--SANTA BARBARA

Muller, Marcia: The legend of the slain soldiers. The tree of death.

CALIFORNIA--SANTA CATALINA

Wells, Susan: Murder is not enough.

CALIFORNIA--SANTA MONICA

Kaminsky, Stuart: Catch a falling clown.

Nielsen, Helen: The fifth caller.

Weston, Carolyn: 3 books

CALIFORNIA--SMALL TOWN LIFE

Cameron, Owen: Catch a tiger.

Gardner, Erle Stanley: The case of the singing skirt.

Hansen, Joseph: The man everybody was afraid of.

MacDonald, John D.: The green ripper.

Vance, John Holbrook: 2 books

CALIFORNIA--SOUTHERN

Breen, Jon L.: Listen for the click.

Carney, William: The rose exterminator.

Chandler, Raymond: Farewell, my lovely. The lady in the lake.

Deming, Richard: Anything but saintly. Death of a pusher. Vice cop.

Gault, William Campbell: The dead seed.

Grafton, Sue: "A" is for alibi.

Hitchens, Bert and Delores: End of the line.

Nielsen, Helen: The darkest hour. Obit delayed. Sing me a murder.

Olsen, D. B.: Enrollment cancelled.

Simon, Roger L.: The big fix.

CAMBRIDGE UNIVERSITY

Broome, Adam: The Cambridge murders.

Clinton-Baddeley, V. C.: Death's bright dart.

Cooper, Brian: Giselle.

Daniel, Glyn: The Cambridge murders.

Patrick, Q.: Murder at Cambridge

CAMELS

Upfield, Arthur W.: The man of two tribes.

CANADA

Bonnamy, Francis: The man in the mist.

Craig, Alisa: A pint of murder.

CHEMISTS AS DETECTIVES
  Asimov, Isaac: A whiff of death.
  Gordon, Neil: The professor's
    poison.
  Lynde, Francis: Scientific Sprague.
  Miller, John: Murder of a professor.
  Rogers, Samuel: 3 books
CHESS
  Stout, Rex: Gambit.
CHILD ABUSE
  Fuller, Samuel: The naked kiss.
  Millar, Margaret: The fiend.
  Parker, Robert B.: Ceremony of
    innocence.
CHILD LABOR
  Hilton, John Buxton: The quiet
    stranger.
CHILDREN; see also ADOPTION; BOYS;
  DAUGHTERS; FOSTER CHILDREN; GIRLS;
  INFANTS; JUVENILE DELINQUENCY;
  ORPHANS; RUNAWAY CHILDREN; RETARDED
  PEOPLE; SONS; STEPDAUGHTERS
  Alding, Peter: Betrayed by death.
  Armstrong, Charlotte: The innocent
    flower.
  Babson, Marian: Murder, murder,
    little star.
  Bailey, H. C.: The bishop's crime.
    The life sentence.
  Carkeet, David: Double negative.
  Chastain, Thomas: Nightscape.
  Christie, Agatha: Hallowe'en party.
  Creasey, John: The Toff and the
    kidnapped child.
  Davies, L. P.: A grave matter.
  Dickinson, Peter: Sleep and his
    brother.
  Freeling, Nicolas: A dressing of
    diamond.
  Grimes, Martha: Help the poor
    struggler.
  Haymon, S. T.: Ritual murder.
  Healy, J. F.: Blunt darts.
  James, Henry: The other house.
  Keating, H. R. F.: Inspector Ghote
    trusts the heart.
  Kellerman, Jonathan: When the
    bough breaks.
  Kemp, Sarah: Over the edge.
  Landon, Christopher: Unseen enemy.
  Marric, J.J.: Gideon's power.
  McMullen, Mary: Something of the
    night.
  Millar, Margaret: The murder of
    Miranda.

  Muller, Marcia and Pronzini, Bill,
    eds.: Child's ploy.
  Prior, Allen: The interrogators.
  Rendell, Ruth: No more dying then.
  Rice, Craig: Knocked for a loop.
  Sjowall, Maj and Wahloo, Per: The
    man on the balcony.
  Tapply, William G.: Follow the
    sharks.
  Tourney, Leonard: The player's boy
    is dead.
  Upfield, Arthur W.: The bushman
    who came back.
CHILDREN AS DETECTIVES; see also BOY
  DETECTIVES; GIRL DETECTIVES
  Bonett, John and Emery: No grave
    for a lady.
  Peters, Elizabeth: The mummy case.
  Rice, Craig: Home sweet homicide.
CHILE
  Dodge, David: The long escape.
    Plunder of the sun.
CHIMPANZEES
  Dickinson, Peter: The poison
    oracle.
CHINA; (for porcelain see POTTERY)
  David-Neal, Alexandra and Yongdin,
    Lama: The power of nothingness.
  Norman, James: 3 books
  Rendell, Ruth: Speaker of Mandarin.
CHINA--7TH CENTURY
  Gulik, Robert van: 16 books
CHINA--CANTON
  Gulik, Robert van: Murder in
Canton.
CHINA--HONG KONG; see HONG KONG
CHINA--ISLANDS
  Gulik, Robert van: The red
pavilion.
CHINA--PEKING
  Simon, Roger L.: Peking duck.
  Starrett, Vincent: Murder in
Peking.
  Taschdjian, Claire: The Peking Man
    is missing.
CHINA--POLITICS
  Gulik, Robert van: Murder in
    Canton.
CHINA--SHANGHAI
  Thorne, Paul: That evening in
    Shanghai.
CHINA--SINGAPORE; see SINGAPORE
CHINESE IN CANADA
  Wood, Ted: Live bait.

Collins, Max Allen: Kill your darlings.

Langton, Jane: Emily Dickinson is dead.

Marshall, William: Sci-Fi.

McDonald, Gregory: Fletch's fortune.

Monteilhet, Hubert: Murder at the Frankfort Book Fair.

Moyes, Patricia: Death on the agenda.

Papazoglu, Ornia: Sweet, savage death.

Peden, William Harwood: Twilight at Monticello.

Peters, Elizabeth: Die for love. The murders of Richard III.

Pronzini, Bill and Muller, Marcia: Double.

Purtill, Richard L.: Murdercon.

Stout, Rex: Too many cooks.

CONNECTICUT

Booton, Kage: Andrew's wife.

Box, Edgar: Death likes it hot.

Bronson, F. W.: The bulldog has the key. The Uncas Island murders.

Collins, Michael: The nightrunners.

Cores, Lucy: Let's kill George.

Coxe, George Harmon: The charred witness. The frightened fiancee. The impetuous mistress.

Curtiss, Ursula: Death of a crow. The face of a tiger. Voice out of darkness.

Disney, Doris Miles: 15 books

Dolson, Hildegard: 4 books

Eberhart, Mignon G.: Murder in waiting.

Fenwick, Elizabeth: Poor Harriet.

Foley, Rae: The Barclay place.

Footner, Hulbert: The whip-poor-will mystery.

Forrest, Richard: 2 books

Goulart, Ron: A graveyard of my own.

Hastings, W. S. and Hooker, Brian: The professor's mystery.

Johnston, Velda: The crystal cat.

Kendrick, Baynard H.: The odor of violets.

King, C. Daly: Arrogant alibi.

Lathen, Emma: A place for murder.

Linzee, David: Belgravia.

Lockridge, Frances and Richard: Catch as catch can. Murder and blueberry pie.

McCloy, Helen: The long body. Two-thirds of a ghost.

McMullen, Mary: Welcome to the grave.

Owen, Philip: Mystery at a country inn.

Pentecost, Hugh: The girl with six fingers. Hide her from every eye. A plague of violence. Sniper.

Philips, Judson: 7 books

Queen, Ellery: Inspector Queen's own case.

Randolph, Marion: Breathe no more.

Reilly, Helen: Certain sleep. Dead for a ducat. Murder at Arroways. Name your poison. Not me, Inspector. The velvet hand.

Rogers, Joel Townsley: The red right hand.

Siller, Van: A complete stranger. The hell with Elaine.

Steward, Dwight: The acupuncture murders.

Strange, John Stephen: Black hawthorn. The clue of the second murder.

Sutton, Henry: The sacrifice.

Thayer, Lee: Dark of the moon. Hanging's too good. Murder stalks the circle. That strange Sylvester affair. Too long endured.

Waugh, Hillary: 11 books

Wells, Carolyn: The black night murders. The doorstep murders. Face cards. The furthest fury. Horror house. Murder plus. Wheels within wheels. The wooden Indian.

Wells, Tobias: How to kill a man.

Wilde, Percival: P. Moran, operative.

CONSERVATION; see also ECOLOGISTS AS DETECTIVES; GAME PRESERVES; NATIONAL PARKS AND RESERVES; RANGERS AS DETECTIVES

Craig, Alisa: The grub and stakers move a mountain.

Wallace, David Rains: The turquoise dragon.

CONSPIRACY

Hull, Richard: The murderers of Monty.

CONTESTS

Stout, Rex: Before midnight.

Allen, Michael: Spence at the blue
  bazaar.
Allingham, Margery: 15 books
Anderson, J. R. L.: A sprig of sea
  lavender.
Anderson, James: The affair of the
  bloodstained egg cosy.
Antony, Peter: How doth the little
  crocodile.
Ashe, Gordon: 39 books
Ashford, Jeffrey: The burden of
  proof. Counsel for the defense.
  The loss of the Culion. A man will
  be kidnapped. The superintendent's
  room.
Babson, Marian: Death swap. A fool
  for murder.
Bailey, H. C.: 33 books
Barnard, Robert: Death and the
  princess. Death of a mystery
  writer. Death on the high C's.
  School for murder.
Barnett, James: The firing squad.
Barry, Charles: The corpse on the
  bridge.
Bawden, Nina: The odd flamingo.
Bax, Roger: A grave case of murder.
Bell, Josephine: Curtain call for a
  corpse. Death in retirement. Death
  of a con man. Death on the Borough
  Council. Murder in hospital. A
  question of inheritance. The
  seeing eye. The summer school
  mystery. The trouble in Hunter
  Ward.
Bellairs, George: 35 books
Benson, E. F.: The blotting book.
Bentley, E. C.: 2 books
Bentley, Nicholas: Inside
  information.
Berckman, Evelyn: The Victorian
  album.
Berkeley, Anthony: 9 books
Bingham, John: Inspector Morgan's
  dilemma.
Birmingham, George A.: The hymn
  tune mystery.
Black, Lionel: 8 books
Blackburn, John: Bound to kill.
Blake, Nicholas: 6 books
Bodkin, M. M'Donnell: 6 books
Bonett, John and Emery: Dead lion.
  No grave for a lady.

Bowers, Dorothy: 3 books
Bramah, Ernest: 7 books
Brand, Christianna: Death of a
  Jezebel.
Bremner, Marjorie: Murder most
  familiar.
Brett, Simon: The dead side of the
  mike. Situation tragedy.
Brock, Lynn: 4 books
Brooks, Edwy Searles: 19 books
Browne, Douglas G.: 4 books
Bruce, Leo: 20 books
Bruton, Eric: Death in ten point
  bold. The wicked saint.
Bullett, Gerald: 2 books
Burke, Thomas: Murder at Elstree.
Burley, W. J.: 9 books
Burton, Miles: 45 books
Bush, Christopher: 53 books
Byrom, James: Take only as
  directed.
Campbell, R. T.: Unholy dying.
Candy, Edward: Which doctor?
Cannan, Joanna: 3 books
Canning, Victor: 2 books
Cargill, Leslie: 2 books
Carmichael, Harry: 31 books
Carnac, Carol: 15 books
Carr, John Dickson: 18 books
Carvic, Heron: Odds on Miss Seeton.
Cecil, Henry: 10 books
Chesterton, G. K.: 8 books
Christie, Agatha: 37 books
Clark, Douglas: Shelf life.
Clarke, Anna: Letter from the dead.
Cleary, John: The high
  commissioner.
Clouston, J. Starer: The lunatic
  at large.
Clutton-Brock, Alan: Liberty Hall.
Cole, G. D. H. and Margaret: 21
  books
Colin, Aubrey: 2 books
Compton, Guy: 2 books
Connington, J. J.: 14 books
Copper, Basil: The secret files of
  Solar Pons. The uncollected cases
  of Solar Pons.
Corbett, James: Murder minus
motive.
Crane, Frances: The applegreen cat.
Creasey, John: 91 books
Crispin, Edmund: 6 books

Giroux, E. X.: 3 books
Grimes, Martha: The deer leap.
   Jerusalem Inn.
Hare, Cyril: An English murder.
Haymon, S. T.: Stately homicide.
Heald, Tim: Blue blood will out.
Heyer, Georgette: Detection
   unlimited. Envious Casca.
Hough, S. B.: Dear daughter dead.
Hubbard, P. M.: A hive of glass.
Hunter, Alan: Landed Gently.
Hutchinson, Horace: The mystery of
   the summer house.
Innes, Michael: 13 books
James, P. D.: Cover her face.
   Unnatural causes.
John, Romilly and Katherine: Death
   by request.
Kennedy, Milward: The murderer of
   sleep.
Kenney, Susan: Garden of malice.
Kitchin, C. H. B.: Death of my aunt.
Lemarchand, Elizabeth: Change for
   the worse. Step in the dark.
Lewis, Roy: Most cunning workmen.
   Nothing but foxes.
MacDonald, Philip: The Polferry
   riddle. The rasp.
Marsh, Ngaio: Death and the dancing
   footman. Grave mistake. Hand in
   glove. A man lay dead. Tied up in
   tinsel.
McMullen, Mary: Something of the
   night.
Milne, A. A.: The red house mystery.
Mitchell, Gladys: The crozier
   pharoahs. Here lies Gloria Maundy.
Moyes, Patricia: Many deadly
   returns.
Nichols, Beverly: The rich die hard.
Perry, Anne: Rutland Place.
Phillpotts, Eden: The grey room.
Porter, Joyce: Dover one.
Powell, P. H.: Murder premeditated.
Rendell, Ruth: A guilty thing
   surprised.
Rhode, John: Dead men at the folly.
Temple-Ellis, N. A.: Murder in the
   ruins.
Tourney, Leonard: The player's boy
   is dead.
Warner, Mignon: Illusion.
Wentworth, Patricia: Ladies' bane.
   The listening eye. Out of the
   past. Silent pool.

Wilson, P. W.: Bride's castle.
Yorke, Margaret: Find me a villain.
ENGLAND--CUMBERLAND
   Gallagher, Stephen: Chimera.
   Phillpotts, Eden: My adventure in
      the Flying Scotsman.
ENGLAND--DERBYSHIRE
   Hilton, John Buxton: The quiet
      stranger.
ENGLAND--DEVONSHIRE
   Blake, Nicholas: The smiler with
      the knife.
   Burley, W. J.: To kill a cat.
   Christie, Agatha: And then there
      were none.
   Clinton-Baddeley, V. C.: No case
      for the police.
   Cobb, G. Belton: Poisoner's base.
   Hubbard, P. M.: High tide.
   Innes, Michael: Death on a quiet
      day.
   Marsh, Ngaio: Death at the bar.
   Oppenheim, E. Philips: Nicholas
      Goade, detective.
   Phillpotts, Eden: The captain's
      curio. Monkshood. The red
      Redmaynes.
   Strong, L. A. G.: 2 books
   Thomson, Basil: The Dartmoor
      enigma.
   Young, Edward: The fifth passenger.
ENGLAND--DORSETSHIRE
   Berkeley, Anthony: A puzzle in
      poison.
   Grimes, Martha: Help the poor
      struggler.
   James, P. D.: The black tower.
   Marsh, Ngaio: Death and the
      dancing footman.
   Phillpotts, Eden: The anniversary
      murder.
   Trench, John: Dishonored bones.
ENGLAND--EAST
   Black, Lionel: Flood.
ENGLAND--EAST ANGLIA
   Curtis, Peter: The devil's own.
   Gash, Jonathan: Pearlhanger.
   Hastings, Macdonald: Cork in
      bottle.
   James, P. D.: Death of an expert
      witness.
   Radley, Sheila: Death in the
      morning.
   Watson, Colin: 11 books

Grierson, Edward: 2 books

Grimes, Martha: The anodyne necklace.

Hare, Cyril: 3 books

Haymon, S. T.: 2 books

Heald, Tim: Unbecoming habits.

Heard, H. F.: A taste for honey.

Hext, Harrington: The thing at their heels.

Heyer, Georgette: Penhallow. Why shoot a butler?

Hilton, John Buxton: Passion in the peak.

Hutton, Malcolm: Georgina and Georgette.

Innes, Michael: Appleby's end. Comedy of terrors. The long farewell. The paper thunderbolt.

Jay, Charlotte: The fugitive eye.

Kennedy, Milward: The murderer of sleep.

Kindon, Thomas: Murder in the moor.

Knox, Ronald A.: Settled out of court. The viaduct murder.

Kyd, Thomas: Cover his face.

Leek, Margaret: The healthy grave.

Lemarchand, Elizabeth: 4 books

Lewis, Roy: A gathering of ghosts.

Lindop, Audrey Erskine: Journey into stone.

MacDonald, Philip: The link.

Marsh, Ngaio: Clutch of constables. The noose. Overture to death. Scales of justice.

McGown, Jill: A perfect match.

McMullen, Mary: A grave without flowers.

Minahan, John: The great diamond robbery.

Mitchell, Gladys: Uncoffin'd clay.

Morice, Anne: Getting away with murder? Hollow vengeance.

Morley, F. V.: Death in Dwelly Lane.

Moyes, Patricia: The curious affair of the third dog.

Nash, Simon: Dead woman's ditch.

O'Hara, Kenneth: Nightmare's nest.

Page, Emma: Last walk home.

Patrick, Q.: Cottage sinister.

Peters, Ellis: Rainbow's end.

Petrie, Rhona: Death in Deakins Wood.

Phillips, Stella: Death in sheep's clothing.

Phillpotts, Eden: "Found drowned." Jig-saw. The jury. They were seven.

Porter, Joyce: Dead easy for Dover. Dover goes to Pott. It's murder with Dover.

Priestly, J. B.: Salt is leaving.

Radley, Sheila: The chief inspector's daughter.

Rendell, Ruth: Master of the moor.

Ruell, Patrick: Red Christmas.

Sayers, Dorothy L.: Busman's honeymoon. The nine tailors.

Scott, Jack S.: The Gospel Lamb. An uprush of mayhem.

Sherwood, John: Green trigger fingers.

Tey, Josephine: The Franchise affair. To love and be wise.

Thomson, June: Shadow of a doubt.

Troy, Simon: The road to Rhuine.

Underwood, Michael: False witness. A party to murder.

Wade, Henry: Bury him darkly.

Warner, Mignon: 2 books

Williams, David: Wedding Treasure.

Woods, Sara: Done to death. Error of the moon. Exit murderer. An obscure grave. They stay for death.

Woodthorpe, R. C.: 2 books

ENGLAND--SCILLY ISLES

Burley, W. J.: Death in a salubrious place.

ENGLAND--SHREWSBURY

Peters, Ellis: 9 books

ENGLAND--SHROPSHIRE

Bawden, Nina: Eyes of green.

ENGLAND--SOCIETY LIFE; for society life in rural areas, see ENGLAND--COUNTRY LIFE

Allan, Stella: A dead giveaway.

Harrison, Ray: Death of an honourable member.

Heyer, Georgette: Duplicate death.

Laine, Annabel: The melancholy virgin.

Ley, Alice Chetwynd: A reputation dies.

Marsh, Ngaio: Death in a white tie.

Penn, John: A deadly sickness.

Perry, Anne: Callander Square. Paragon Walk.

Walling, R. A. J.: That dinner at Bardolph's

Gulik, Robert van: The Willow
pattern.
Lowndes, Marie Belloc: The end of
her honeymoon.
EPISCOPAL CHURCH; see also CHURCH OF
ENGLAND
Holland, Isabel: A death at St.
Anselm's
Murray, Max: The voice of the
corpse.
Smith, Charles Merrill: 3 books
EPISCOPAL PRIESTS; see also ANGLICAN
PRIESTS
Dewhurst, Eileen: Drink this.
Holland, Isabel: 2 books
EPISCOPAL PRIESTS AS DETECTIVES; see
also ANGLICAN PRIESTS AS DETECTIVES
Smith, Charles Merrill: 4 books
ESCAPED CONVICTS; see CONVICTS,
ESCAPED
ESPIONAGE; see also UNITED
KINGDOM--NAVY--INTELLIGENCE; UNITED
STATES--ARMY--INTELLIGENCE; UNITED
STATES--CENTRAL INTELLIGENCE AGENCY;
WIRETAPPING; WORLD WAR,
1939-1945--ESPIONAGE; WORLD WAR,
1939-1945--SECRET SERVICE
Albrand, Martha: A call from
Austria.
Ambler, Eric: A coffin for
Dimitrios. The intercom
conspiracy.
Bingham, John: Brock and the
defector.
Black, Lionel: The lady is a spy.
Blake, Nicholas: The sad variety.
Bonnamy, Francis: The man in the
mist.
Chaber, M. E.: So dead the rose.
Christie, Agatha: They came to
Baghdad.
Crispin, Edmund: Holy disorders.
Eden, Dorothy: Waiting for Willa.
Egleton, Clive: A conflict of
interests.
Elkins, Aaron J.: Fellowship of
fear.
Estleman, Loren D.: Sugartown.
Gordon, Neil: The professor's
poison.
Heald, Tim: A small masterpiece.
Herber, William: Live bait for
murder.
Innes, Michael: Hamlet, revenge!

Keating, H. R. F.: Inspector Ghote
caught in the meshes.
Keech, Scott: Ciphered.
Kenyon, Michael: May you die in
Ireland. The trouble with series
three.
Leather, Edwin: The Duveen letter.
Maling, Arthur: A taste of treason.
Marsh, Ngaio: Colour scheme.
Millar, Kenneth: The dark tunnel.
Moyes, Patricia: Murder
fantastical.
Pentecost, Hugh: The golden trap.
Peters, Ellis: The piper on the
mountain.
Reynolds, William J.: The Nebraska
quotient.
Russell, Charlotte Murray: The
message of the mute dog.
Simenon, Georges: At the
Gai-Moulin.
Stashower, Dan: The adventures of
the ectoplasmic man.
Strong, L. A. G.: Which I never.
Thomson, June: The long revenge.
Wallis, Ruth Satwell: Blood from a
stone.
Winslow, Pauline Glen: The
Rockefeller gift.
ESPIONAGE, INDUSTRIAL
Ashford, Jeffrey: A sense of
loyalty.
Crofts, Freeman Wills: Crime on
the Solent.
Heald, Tim: Unbecoming habits.
Pyle, A. M.: Trouble making toys.
Taylor, L. A.: Deadly objectives.
ETHIOPIA
Trench, John: Beyond the atlas.
EUROPE; see also individual countries
of Europe, such as ENGLAND; FRANCE;
SCOTLAND; etc.
DeKobra, Maurice: The madonna of
the sleeping cars.
Derleth, August: The adventure of
the Orient Express.
Elkins, Aaron J.: Fellowship of
fear.
Kirst, Hans H.: Night of the
generals.
Kotzwinkle, William: Fata Morgana.
Parker, Robert B.: Judas goat.
Rathbone, Julian: Watching the
detectives.

Fisher, Steve: I wake up screaming.
Freeman, R. Austin: For the defense: Dr. Thorndyke.
Gardner, Erle Stanley: The case of the singing skirt.
Garve, Andrew: The Cuckoo Line affair. Death and the sky above. Frame-up.
Gillian, Michael: Warrant for a wanton.
Granger, Bill: Public murders.
Gruber, Frank: The navy colt.
Hammond, Gerald: Sauce for the pigeon.
Hardy, William M.: A little sin.
Heberden, M. V.: They can't all be guilty.
Hill, Reginald: Exit lines.
Hilton, John Buxton: The quiet stranger.
Holman, C. Hugh: Death like thunder.
Inchbald, Peter: The sweet short grass.
Jerome, Owen Fox: The murder at the Avalon Arms.
Johnston, Velda: Shadow behind the curtain.
Jones, Cleo: Prophet motive.
Keeler, Harry Stephen: The fourth king.
Kemelman, Harry: Someday the rabbi will leave.
Latimer, Jonathan: Headed for a hearse.
Lovesey, Peter: Keystone.
Lysaght, Brian: Special circumstances.
MacDonald, Philip: The noose.
Martin, Lee: Too sane a murder.
Masur, Harold Q.: Bury me deep. Tall, dark and deadly.
McCloy, Helen: Before I die.
McGivern, William P.: Night extra.
Moffett, Cleveland: The Seine mystery.
Muller, Marcia: Leave a message for Willie.
Nielsen, Helen: Detour. Sing me a murder.
Popazoglu, Ornia: Sweet, savage death.
Parrish, Frank: Death in the rain.
Pentecost, Hugh: Hide her from every eye.
Queen, Ellery: The glass village.

Randisi, Robert J.: Full contact.
Randolph, Marion: 2 books
Reilly, Helen: Tell her it's murder.
Rendell, Ruth: The face of trespass.
Rhode, John: The Paddington mystery.
Robinson, Frank M.: The power.
Russell, Charlotte Murray: The tiny diamond.
Scherf, Margaret: Don't wake me up while I'm driving.
Shearing, Joseph: Moss rose.
Singer, Shelley: Free draw.
Stout, Rex: Might as well be dead.
Truss, Seldon: Never fight a lady.
Tucker, Wilson: The Chinese doll.
Walker, Walter: The two dude offense.
Webb, Jack: The naked angel.
Weston, Carolyn: Poor, poor Qphelia.
White, Lionel: The house next door.
Woods, Sara: Away with them to prison. Defy the devil.
FALSE IMPRISONMENT
Grierson, Edward: The Massingham affair.
McShane, Mark: Untimely ripped.
Walsh, Maurice: Danger under the moon.
Yorke, Margaret: Intimate kill.
FAMILY LIFE; see also BROTHERS; DAUGHTERS; FATHERS; INCEST; MOTHERS; SISTERS; SONS
Abercrombie, Barbara: Run for your life.
Allingham, Margery: Police at the funeral.
Armstrong, Charlotte: The turret room.
Arnold, Margot: Death of a voodoo doll.
Babson, Marian: Death swap. A fool for murder.
Balmer, Edwin: Resurrection rock.
Barnard, Robert: Corpse in a gilded cage. Death by sheer torture. Death of a perfect mother.
Bax, Roger: A grave case of murder.
Baxt, George: Process of elimination.

Fish, Robert L.: Brazilian sleigh ride.

Innes, Michael: Carson's conspiracy. Picture of guilt. Silence observed.

Irish, William: Deadline at dawn.

Keeler, Harry Stephen: The skull of the waltzing clown.

Kotzwinkle, William: Fata Morgana.

Masur, Harold Q.: Tall, dark and deadly.

Parrish, Randall: The case and the girl.

Roth, Holly: The crimson in the purple.

Smith, Shelley: The ballad of the running man.

Spencer, Ross H.: The missing bishop.

Wade, Henry: Too soon to die.

FREE LOVE

Cochran, Alan T.: Two plus two.

FRENCH EQUATORIAL AFRICA

Head, Matthew: The Congo Venus.

Iams, Jack: The body missed the boat.

FRENCH IN ARGENTINA

Cumberland, Marten: Nobody is safe.

FRENCH IN BELGIUM

Simenon, Georges: The crime of Inspector Maigret.

FRENCH IN ENGLAND; see also FRENCH IN SCOTLAND

Cole, G. D. H. and Margaret: The walking corpse.

Rees, Arthur J.: Tragedy at Twelvetrees.

Simenon, Georges: Maigret's revolver.

Woods, Sara: The case is altered. The third encounter.

FRENCH IN GERMANY

Carr, John Dickson: Castle Skull.

FRENCH IN SCOTLAND

Hely, Elizabeth: A mark of displeasure.

FRENCH IN THE NETHERLANDS

Simenon, Georges: A crime in Holland.

FRENCH IN THE UNITED STATES

Booth, Charles G.: Murder at high tide.

Corbett, Elizabeth Frances: The house across the river.

Roof, Katherine M.: Murder on the Salem road.

Shannon, Dell: Exploits of death.

Simenon, Georges: Maigret at the coroner's. Murder in New York's underworld. The patience of Maigret.

FRENCH IN VIETNAM

Freeling, Nicolas: Tsing boom!

FUND RAISING; see also CHARITIES

Lathen, Emma: Come to dust.

FUNERAL INDUSTRY; see UNDERTAKERS AND UNDERTAKING

FUTURE

Asimov, Isaac: The caves of steel.

Goulart, Ron: Odd job no. 101 and other future crimes.

Hoch, Edward D.: 3 books

Simmons, Geoffrey: Murdock.

Wahloo, Per: The steel spring.

GALAPAGOS ISLANDS; see ECUADOR--GALAPAGOS ISLANDS

GAMBLING

Bentley, John: The Landor case.

Carvic, Heron: Odds on Miss Seeton.

Evans, John: Halo in blood.

Fish, Robert L.: Halo in blood.

Freeman, R. Austin: Death at the inn.

Grisman, Arnold: The winning streak.

Gruber, Frank: The honest dealer.

Leonard, Elmore: Glitz.

MacDonald, Ross: The zebra-striped hearse.

Rosten, Leo: Silky!

Stout, Rex: And be a villain.

Tucker, Wilson: The Chinese doll.

Van Dine, S. S.: The casino murder case. The Garden murder case.

Wallace, Francis: Front man.

GAME PRESERVES; see also CONSERVATION; NATIONAL PARKS AND PRESERVES

Borthwick, J. S.: The case of the hook-billed kites.

GANGS; see JUVENILE DELINQUENCY; ORGANIZED CRIME

GANGSTERS; see ORGANIZED CRIME

GARDENING; see also BOTANY; FLOWERS

Barth, Richard: A ragged plot.

Ford, Leslie: Murder with southern hospitality.

GIBRALTAR
  Perowne, Barry: All exits blocked.
GIRL DETECTIVES
  Lochte, Dick: Sleeping dog.
  Morison, B. J.: 2 books
GIRLS; see also CHILDREN; TEENAGERS
  Armstrong, Charlotte: The gift
    shop.
  Babson, Marian: The lord mayor of
    death.
  Burley, W. J.: Death in willow
    pattern. Wycliffe and the
    schoolgirls.
  Butler, Gwendoline: The dull
    dead.
  Carr, Glynn: The youth hostel
    murders.
  Christie, Agatha: Third girl.
  Egan, Lesley: The blind search.
  Forbes, Stanton: Grieve for the
    past.
  Fremlin, Celia: With no crying.
  Lovesey, Peter: Swing, swing
    together.
  McShane, Mark: The girl nobody
    knows.
  Millar, Margaret: Banshee.
  Procter, Maurice: Killer at large.
  Simpson, Dorothy: Close her eyes.
  Strobel, Marion: Ice before killing.
  Tey, Josephine: Miss Pym disposes.
  Tyre, Nedra: Hall of death.
GOLD
  Bentley, Nicholas: Inside
    information.
  Copper, Basil: Necropolis.
  Jay, Charlotte: Beat not the bones.
  Selwyn, Francis: Cracksman on
    velvet.
  Simpson, Howard R.: The jumpmaster.
  Zake, S. Joshua L.: Truckful of
    gold
GOLF
  Adams, Herbert: The body in the
    bunker.
  Christie, Agatha: Murder on the
    links.
  Ellroy, James: Brown's requiem.
  Knox, Ronald A.: The viaduct
    murder.
  Law, Janice: Death under par.
  Logue, John: Follow the leader.
GOSSIP
  Woods, Sara: They stay for death.

GOVERNESSES
  Butler, Gwendoline: Coffin in
    Oxford.
  Whitney, Phyllis A.: Columbella.
GOVERNESSES AS DETECTIVES
  Babson, Marian: Murder, murder,
    little star.
  Curtis, Peter: No question of
    murder.
  Hervey, Evelyn: The governess.
  Whitney, Phyllis A.: Window on the
    square.
GOVERNMENT EMPLOYEES; see UNITED
  KINGDOM--OFFICIALS AND EMPLOYEES;
  UNITED STATES--OFFICIALS AND
  EMPLOYEES
GRAVE ROBBING; see also
BODYSNATCHING;
  CEMETERIES
  Perry, Anne: Resurrection Row.
GREAT BRITAIN; see ENGLAND; IRELAND;
  SCOTLAND; UNITED KINGDOM; WALES
GREECE
  Bell, Josephine: The catalyst.
  Cole, G. D. H. and Margaret: Greek
    tragedy.
  Davis, Dorothy Salisbury: Enemy and
    brother.
  Lathen, Emma: When in Greece.
  Martin, Shane: The third statue.
  Stewart, Mary: My brother Michael.
  Yorke, Margaret: Grave matter.
GREECE--ATHENS
  Doody, Margaret: Aristotle,
    detective.
  Highsmith, Patricia: The two faces
    of January.
  Stein, Aaron Marc: Body search. I
    fear the Greeks.
GREECE--CRETE
  Highsmith, Patricia: The two faces
    of January.
  Stewart, Mary: The moon spinners.
  Yorke, Margaret: Mortal remains.
GREECE--ISLANDS; see also
GREECE--CRETE; ISLANDS OF THE
MEDITERRANEAN
  Blake, Nicholas: The widow's
    cruise.
  Caudwell, Sarah: The shortest way
    to Hades.
  Dickinson, Peter: The lizard in
    the cup.
  Jones, James: A touch of danger.

HOUSE PARTIES; see also DINNER
  PARTIES; PARTIES
  Abbot, Anthony: The creeps.
  Allen, H. Warner: The uncounted
    hour.
  Allingham, Margery: The Black
    Dudley murder.
  Anderson, James: The affair of the
    bloodstained egg cosy.
  Boucher, Anthony: The case of the
    seven sneezes.
  Burnham, David: Last act in
    Bermuda.
  Christie, Agatha: And then there
    were none. The Hollow. Towards
    zero.
  Connington, J. J.: The Dangerfield
    talisman.
  Dalton, Moray: The night of fear.
Dickinson, Peter: The last
    houseparty.
  Giroux, E. X.: A death for a
    darling.
  Heyer, Georgette: The unfinished
    clue.
  Innes, Michael: Appleby and
    Honeybath. Hamlet, revenge!
  James, P. D.: The skull beneath
    the skin.
  Marsh, Ngaio: Death and the
    dancing footman. A man lay dead.
  McCloy, Helen: The deadly truth.
    Mr. Splitfoot.
  Moyes, Patricia: Many deadly
    returns.
  Plum Mary: Dead man's secret.
  Poe, Edgar Allan, Jr.: The house
    party murders.
  Queen, Ellery: The finishing
    stroke.
  Randolph, Marion: 2 books
  Rohmer, Sax: Hangover house.
  Taylor, Phoebe Atwood: Death
    lights a candle.
  Ward, Colin: House party murder.
  Wentworth, Patricia: Out of the
    past.
HOWARD UNIVERSITY
  Baker, Carlos: The Gay Head
    conspiracy.
HUDSON RIVER; see NEW YORK--HUDSON
  RIVER
HUNGARY
  Sjowall, Maj and Wahloo, Per: The
    man who went up in smoke.

HUNTING; see also FISHING; FOX
  HUNTING; POACHING
  Connington, J. J.: The Brandon
case.
  Hammond, Gerald: Sauce for the
    pigeon.
  Plum, Mary: Murder at the hunting
    club.
HURRICANES; see also TIDAL WAVES;
  TYPHOONS
  Taylor, Phoebe Atwood: Proof of the
    pudding.
HUSBAND AND WIFE DETECTIVES
  Ames, Delano: 11 books
  Bell, Josephine: The seeing eye.
  Blackburn, John: The young man from
    Lima.
  Blake, Nicholas: The smile with the
    knife.
  Bodkin, M. M'Donnell: The capture
    of Paul Beck. Young Beck.
  Brett, Hy and Barbara: Promises to
    keep.
  Christie, Agatha: By the pricking
    of my thumbs. N or M? Partners in
    crime. Postern of fate.
  Coxe, George Harmon: Mrs. Murdock
    takes a case.
  Crane, Frances: 26 books
  Cross, Amanda: The Theban
mysteries.
  Dexter, Colin: Last bus to
    Woodstock.
  Ferrars, E. X.: Death of a minor
    character.
  Forrest, Richard: The death at Yew
    Corner.
  Gill, Bartholomew: McGarr and the
    P. M. of Belgrave Square.
  Goulart, Ron: Odd job no. 101 and
    other future crimes.
  Hammett, Dashiell: The thin man.
  Knox, Ronald A.: Double cross
    purposes. Still dead.
  Linington, Elizabeth: 5 books
  Lockridge, Frances and Richard: 26
    books
  MacLeod, Charlotte: The Convivial
    Codfish.
  Moyes, Patricia: 5 books
  O'Donnell, Lillian: The baby
    merchants. Leisure dying.
  Peden, William Harwood: Twilight
    at Monticello.
  Perry, Anne: 2 books

ILLINOIS--CHICAGO

Ashenhurst, John M.: The World's Fair murders.
Baker, North and Bolton, William: Dead to the world.
Ballinger, Bill S.: 3 books
Balmer, Edwin: 4 books
Balmer, Edwin and MacHarg, William: The achievements of Luther Trant.
Barry, Joe: 4 books
Blake, Eleanor A.: The jade green cats.
Bonnamy, Francis: Death by appointment.
Bradley, Mary Hastings: Nice people poison.
Brown, Frederic: 8 books
Browne, Howard: The taste of ashes.
Carroll, Joy: Babykiller.
Caspary, Vera: Evvie.
Clason, Clyde B.: 4 books
Collins, Max Allen: Kill your darlings. True crime. True detective.
Dale, Virginia: Nan Thursday.
Dewey, Thomas B.: 14 books
Eberhart, Mignon G.: The cases of Susan Dare. The dark garden. Dead men's plans. The glass slipper. The hangman's whip. Hasty wedding. The house on the roof. Postmark murder.
Edgley, Leslie: The runaway pigeon.
Edwards, James G.: 6 books
Evans, John: 3 books
Forbes, Stanton: The sad, sudden death of my fair lady.
Freeman, Martin J.: The case of the blind mouse.
Garfield, Brian: Death sentence.
Gash, Joe: 2 books
Gettel, Ronald E.: Twice burned.
Gillian, Michael: Warrant for a wanton.
Gordons, The: Case file: F. B. I.; F. B. I. story.
Granger, Bill: Public murders.
Greeley, Andrew M.: 3 books
Gruber, Frank: The gold gap. The leather duke. The navy colt. The scarlet letter.
Harris, Larry M.: The pickled poodles.
Harrison, William: In a wild sanctuary.

Heed, Rufus: Ghosts never die.
Herber, William: 3 books
James, Franklin: Killer in the kitchen.
Jerome, Owen Fox: 2 books
Johnson, E. Richard: The Cardinalli contract.
Kaminsky, Stuart: Exercise in terror. You bet your life.
Keeler, Harry Stephen: 26 books
Klawans, Harold L.: Sins of commission.
Latimer, Jonathan: 3 books
Lewin, Michael Z.: The enemies within.
Lore, Phillips: 2 books
MacDonald, John D.: One fearful yellow eye.
MacHarg, William Briggs and Balmer, Edwin: 3 books
Maling, Arthur: 4 books
Marshall, Sidney: Some like it hot.
Masur, Harold Q.: The last gamble.
McGivern, William P.: But death runs faster. Heaven ran last. Very cold for May.
Nash, Jay Robert: The Mafia diaries.
Nielsen, Helen: Gold Coast nocturne.
Paretsky, Sara: 3 books
Parrish, Randall: 2 books
Payne, Will: The scarred chin.
Perdue, Virginia: The singing clock.
Peters, Bill: Blondes die young.
Plum, Mary: 3 books
Pruitt, Alan: 2 books
Quill, Monica: 3 books
Raymond, Clifford S.: The men on the dead man's chest.
Rea, M. P.: 3 books
Rice, Craig: 10 books
Robinson, Frank M.: The power.
Russell, Charlotte Murray: The case of the topaz flower. Dreadful reckoning. The tiny diamond.
Scott, Denis: The beckoning shadow.
Smith, Charles Merrill: 4 books
Smith, Mark: The death of a detective.
Spencer, Ross H.: 2 books
Starrett, Vincent: 7 books
Strobel, Marion: Ice before killing.

Antony, Peter: The woman in the wardrobe.

Asimov, Isaac, et al., eds.: Tantalizing locked room mysteries.

Bentley, John: The Landor case.

Bruce, Leo: A case for three detectives.

Carr, John Dickson: The dead man's knock. The house at Satan's Elbow. The three coffins.

Dickson, Carter: The Judas window. The peacock feather murders.

Ekstrom, Jan: Deadly reunion.

Forrest, Norman: Death took a publisher.

Greeley, Andrew M.: Happy are the meek.

Heyer, Georgette: Envious Casca.

Hoch, Edward D., ed.: All but impossible!

Holmes, H. H.: Nine times nine.

Innes, Michael: Appleby and Honeybath. Seven suspects.

Jeffreys, J. G.: A wicked way to die.

Lore, Phillips: Murder behind closed doors.

MacDonald, Philip: The Polferry riddle.

McBain, Ed: Killer's wedge.

Montalban, Manuel Vazquez: Murder in the Central Committee.

Phillpotts, Eden: Jig-saw.

Pronzini, Bill: Bones. Scattershot.

Queen, Ellery: The Chinese orange mystery. The king is dead.

Resnicow, Herbert: The Gold solution.

Russell, Ray: Incubus.

Santesson, Hans Stefan, ed.: The locked room reader.

Sjowall, Maj and Wahloo, Per: The locked room.

Wainwright, John: High-class kill.

Wallace, Edgar: Big foot. The clue of the new pin. The Four Just Men. The gaol breaker.

Wells, Carolyn: The daughter of the house. Face cards. The mystery girl. Raspberry jam. The Tannahill tangle.

Zangwill, Israel: The big bow mystery.

LONGSHOREMEN; see also SHIPPING

Ard, William: A private party.

LOUISIANA

Crane, Frances: The buttercup case.

Eberhart, Mignon G.: With this ring.

Footner, Hulbert: Trial by water.

Hubbard, Margaret Ann: Murder takes the veil.

Keyes, Frances Parkinson: Victorine.

LOUISIANA--NEW ORLEANS

Arnold, Margot: Death of a voodoo doll.

Bristow, Gwen and Manning, Bruce: 2 books

Carr, John Dickson: The ghosts' high noon. Papa La-bas.

Chaber, M. E.: A hearse of a different color.

Claymore, Tod: 2 books

Coxe, George Harmon: One way out.

Crane, Frances: The indigo necklace.

Eberhart, Mignon G.: The bayou road.

Fair, A. A.: Owls don't blink.

Fennelly, Tony: The glory hole murders.

Herber, William: Live bait for murder.

Holden, Genevieve: Deadlier than the male.

Keeler, Harry Stephen: The voice of the seven sparrows. The wonderful scheme of Mr. Christopher Thorne.

Keys, Frances Parkinson: Dinner at Antoine's.

Pronzini, Bill: Masques.

Thayer, Lee: Guilt edged.

Treat, Lawrence: D as in dead.

Wills, Garry: At Button's.

Wiltz, Chris: The killing circle.

LOVE; see ROMANCE

LOVE TRIANGLES

Bingham, John: Good old Charlie. The tender poisoner.

Branson, H. C.: The fearful passage.

Candy, Edward: Bones of contention.

Christie, Agatha: Sad cypress.

Dickson, Carter: She died a lady.

Eller, John: Rage of heaven.

Garve, Andrew: The case of Robert Quarry. Home to roost. No tears for Hilda.

Hart, Frances Noyes: The Fellamy trial.

Jeffries, Roderic: Evidence of the accused.

Jesse, F. Tennyson: A pin to see the peepshow.

Kelly, Mary: The dead of summer.

Lilly, Jean: False face.

McCloy, Helen: Before I die.

Monteilhet, Hubert: The praying mantises.

Offord, Lenore Glen: Walking shadow.

Queen, Ellery: The fourth side of the triangle.

Stout, Rex: Too many cooks.

Underwood, Michael: False witness.

LYNCHING; see also HANGING

Stout, Rex: The rubber band.

Swarthout, Glendon: Skeletons.

MAFIA; see ORGANIZED CRIME

MAGAZINES; see PERIODICALS

MAGIC; see also SUPERNATURAL PHENOMENA; VOODOOISM; WITCHCRAFT

Stashower, Dan: The adventures of the ectoplasmic man.

MAGICIANS

Cullingford, Guy: Conjurer's coffin.

Taylor, Phoebe Atwood: The mystery of the Cape Cod players.

MAGICIANS AS DETECTIVES

Ballinger, Bill S.: The tooth and the nail.

Rawson, Clayton: 5 books

Towne, Stuart: Death out of thin air.

MAIL ORDER BUSINESS

Lathen, Emma: Green grow the dollars.

MAINE

Bonnamy, Francis: Blood and thirsty.

Bradley, Mary Hastings: Nice people murder.

Daly, Elizabeth: Deadly nightshade.

Disney, Doris Miles: Voice from the grave.

Gilman, Dorothy: The tightrope walker.

Hood, Margaret Page: 3 books

Johnston, Velda: The other Karen.

Kenney, Susan: Graves in academe.

Morison, B. J.: Beer and skittles. Port and a star boarder.

Nebel, Frederick: Fifty roads to town.

Olgivie, Elisabeth: 2 books

Orr, Clifford: The wailing rock murders.

Parker, Robert B.: Early autumn. Wilderness.

Philbrick, W. R.: Slow dancer.

Potts, Jean: The troublemaker.

Pronzini, Bill: Games.

Rich, Virginia: The baked bean supper murders.

Rinehart, Mary Roberts: The yellow room.

Sloane, William: The edge of running water.

Stein, Aaron Marc: Coffin country. A nose for it.

Thayer, Lee: Accident, manslaughter, or murder?

Wells, Carolyn: Murder on parade. The vanishing of Betty Varian.

Wetering, Janwillem van de: The Maine massacre.

MAINE--ISLANDS

Brean, Herbert: The clock strikes thirteen.

Hood, Margaret Page: 3 books

Martyn, Wyndham: Murder Island.

MAJORCA; see SPAIN--MAJORCA

MALAYSIA

Foxx, Jack: Dead run.

MALTA

Butler, Gwendoline: Coffin in Malta.

Webster, Noah: A killing in Malta.

MANUSCRIPTS; see also BOOKS

Anderson, Poul: Murder in black letter.

Barnard, Robert: The case of the missing Bronte.

Berckman, Evelyn: The fourth man on the rope.

Blake, Nicholas: End of a chapter.

Crispin, Edmund: Love lies bleeding.

Daly, Elizabeth: The book of the lion.

Evans, John: Halo for Satan.

Frimmer, Steven: Dead matter.

Holme, Timothy: A funeral for gondolas.

Hoyt, Richard: The Siskiyou two-step.

Limnelius, George: The manuscript murder.

McInerny, Ralph: Second vespers.

Ford, Leslie: By the watchman's clock. The clue and the Judas tree. Date with death. Ill met by moonlight. Murder in Maryland. Three bright pebbles.

Frome, David: The strange death of Martin Green.

Hart, Frances Noyes: Hide in the dark.

McGerr, Patricia: Murder is absurd.

Rice, Craig: Telefair.

MARYLAND--BALTIMORE

Bortner, Norman Stanley: 2 books

Daly, Carroll John: The amateur murderer.

Ford, Leslie: The girl from the Mimosa Club. Trial by ambush.

Strange, John Stephen: For the hangman.

MASS MURDER; see also SERIAL MURDER

Browne, Douglas G.: Plan XVI.

Marshall, William: Perfect end.

Sanders, Lawrence: The third deadly sin.

Sjowall, Maj and Wahloo, Per: The laughing policeman.

Trow, M. J.: The supreme adventure of Inspector Lestrade.

Wilcox, Collin: The lonely hunter.

MASSACHUSETTS

Angus, Douglas Ross: Death on the Jerusalem Road.

Benson, Ben: 17 books

Coxe, George Harmon: 17 books

Curtis, Ursula: The deadly climate. The noonday devil.

Dalmas, Herbert: The Fowler formula.

Daniels, Harold R.: The accused.

Dean, S. F. X.: By frequent anguish.

Eberhart, Mignon G.: Wolf in man's clothing.

Eustis, Helen: The horizontal man.

Forbes, Stanton: Buried in so sweet a place.

Fuller, Timothy: Keep cool, Mr. Jones.

Graham, John Alexander: The involvement of Arnold Wechsler.

Highsmith, Patricia: Deep water.

Kemelman, Harry: 5 books

Langton, Jane: Emily Dickinson is dead.

MacLeod, Charlotte: 4 books

Parker, Robert B.: 7 books

Pentecost, Hugh: Past, present and murder.

Popkin, Zelda: Murder in the mist.

Reeves, John: Doubting Thomas.

Russell, E. S.: She should have cried on Monday.

Stagge, Jonathan: 9 books

Stratton, Roy: One among none.

Tilton, Alice: 8 books

Wallis, Ruth Satwell: No bones about it.

Waugh, Hillary: Last seen wearing . . .

Wells, Carolyn: The beautiful derelict. Fuller's earth. The importance of being murdered. In the tiger's cage. The mystery of the sycamore. The mystery of the Tarn. The roll-top desk mystery.

Wells, Tobias: A creature was stirring.

Wickware, Francis Sill: Dangerous ground.

MASSACHUSETTS--BERKSHIRES

Cross, Amanda: The James Joyce murder.

Daly, Elizabeth: Evidence of things seen.

Kallon, Lucille: The Tanglewood murder.

Pentecost, Hugh: Deadly trap.

Van Dine, S. S.: The winter murder case.

MASSACHUSETTS--BOSTON

Aldyne, Nathan: 3 books

Banks, Oliver: The Rembrandt panel.

Barnes, Linda: Dead heat.

Boyer, Rick: 2 books

Burgess, Gelett: Two o'clock courage.

Carleton, Marjorie: Vanished.

Casey, Robert A.: The Jesus man.

Coxe, George Harmon: 6 books

Davey, Jocelyn: A treasury alarm.

Dobyns, Stephen: Dancer with one leg.

Fuller, Timothy: 2 books

Goldberg, Marshall: The anatomy lesson.

Green, Thomas J.: The flowered box.

Healy, J. F.: Blunt darts.

Kemelman, Harry: Tuesday the rabbi saw red.

MacLeod, Charlotte: The Convivial Codfish. The withdrawing room.

MISTRESSES
  Abbot, Anthony: About the murder of
    the clergyman's mistress.
  Ashford, Jeffrey: The burden of
    proof.
  Boileau, Pierre and Narcejac,
    Thomas: Who was Clare Jallu?
  Ellin, Stanley: The key to Nicholas
    Street.
  Fremlin, Celia: The parasite person.
  Leonard, Elmore: Fifty-two pickup.
  Potts, Jean: An affair of the heart.
  Sarioli, Mauri: The Helsinki affair.
  Uhnak, Dorothy: The ledger.
  West, Pamela Elizabeth: Madeline.
MOBSTERS; see ORGANIZED CRIME
MODELS, FASHION
  Craig, Alisa: The terrible tide.
  Stout, Rex: The red box.
MODERN LANGUAGE ASSOCIATION
  Bernard, Robert: Deadly meeting.
MONACO
  Harrison, Ray: Why kill Arthur
    Potter?
  Mason, A. E. W.: At the Villa Rose.
  Oppenheim, E. Phillips: General
    Besserley's puzzle box. General
    Besserley's second puzzle box.
    Murder at Monte Carlo. Prodigals
    of Monte Carlo.
MONASTICISM AND RELIGIOUS ORDERS
  Allison, E. M. A.: Through the
    valley of death.
  Barry, Charles: The corpse and the
    bridge.
  Carter, Youngman: Mr. Campion's
    farthing.
  David-Neel, Alexandra and Yongden,
    Lama: The power of nothingness.
  Dickinson, Peter: The sinful stones.
  Gulik, Robert van: The haunted
    monastery.
  Heald, Tim: Unbecoming habits.
  Hubbard, P. M.: The dancing man.
  Paretsky, Sara: Killing orders.
  Reeves, John: Murder before matins.
MONKS AS DETECTIVES
  Allison, E. M. A.: Through the
    valley of death.
  Peters, Ellis: 9 books
MONSTERS
  Mitchell, Gladys: Winking at the
    brim.
  Upfield, Arthur W.: Lake Frome
    monster.

Van Dine, S. S.: The Dragon murder
  case.
MONTANA
  Adams, Cleve F.: Shady lady.
  Cameron, Owen: The butcher's wife.
  Cleary, Jon: A sound of lightning.
  Estleman, Loren D.: The stranglers.
  Guthrie, A. B., Jr.: 3 books
  Hugo, Richard: Death and the good
    life.
  Paul, Elliot: Fracas in the
    foothills.
  Scherf, Margaret: 8 books
  Siller, Van: Somber memory. Under
    a cloud.
  Stout, Rex: Death of a dude.
  Zochert, Donald: Another weeping
    woman.
MONUMENTS
  Watson, Colin: Bump in the night.
MORMONS AND MORMONISM
  Burns, Rex: The avenging angel.
  Cook, Thomas: Tabernacle.
  Doyle, Arthur Conan: A study in
    scarlet.
  Jones, Cleo: Prophet motive.
  Stewart, Gary: The tenth virgin.
MOROCCO
  Ames, Delano: Not in utter
    nakedness.
  Byfield, Barbara Ninde: A parcel
    of their fortunes.
  Christie, Agatha: So many steps to
    death.
  Cobb, G. Belton: Corpse at
    Casablanca.
  Crane, Frances: The coral princess
    murders.
  Dickson, Carter: Behind the
    crimson curtain.
  Gordons, The: Tiger on my back.
  McCutcheon, Hugh: Yet she must die.
MOTELS; see HOTELS, MOTELS, ETC.
MOTHERS; see also MATRICIDE;
  STEPMOTHERS; UNWED MOTHERS
  Koenig, Laird: Rockabye.
  Stout, Rex: The mother hunt.
MOTHERS AND DAUGHTERS
  Cannan, Joanna: They rang up the
    police.
  Popkin, Zelda: A death of
    innocence.
  Rendell, Ruth: Tree of hands.
  Stewart, Gary: The tenth virgin.

Tey, Josephine: The Franchise
affair.
MOTHERS AND SONS
Blackburn, John: The broken boy.
Cole, G. D. H. and Margaret: Mrs.
Warrender's profession.
Fenisong, Ruth: Widow's plight.
Woods, Sara: Enter certain
murderers.
MOTHERS AS DETECTIVES
Dewhurst, Eileen: The house that
Jack built.
MOTION PICTURE THEATERS
Field, Moira: Foreign bodies.
MOTION PICTURES; see also ACTORS AND
ACTRESSES
Babson, Marian: Murder, murder
little star.
Bergman, Andrew: Hollywood and
LeVine.
Bonnett, John and Emery: Not in the
script.
Byfield, Barbara Ninde: A parcel of
their fortunes.
Chais, Pamela: Final cut.
Clason, Clyde B.: The whispering
ear.
Cody, Liza: Dupe.
Crispin, Edmund: Sudden vengeance.
Crofts, Freeman Wills: The purple
sickle murders.
Cunningham, E. V.: Samantha.
Dalton, Moray: The Condamine case.
Engel, Howard: Murder on location.
Field, Evan: What Nigel knew.
Gault, William Campbell: Death out
of focus.
Hyams, Joe: Murder at the Academy
Awards.
Kaminsky, Stuart: Black knight in
Red Square. High midnight.
Keating, H. R. F.: Filmi, filmi,
Inspector Ghote.
Kurnitz, Harry: Invasion of privacy.
Latimer, Jonathan: Black is the
fashion for dying.
Lovesey, Peter: Keystone.
MacDonald, John D.: Free fall in
crimson.
Masur, Harold Q.: Make a killing.
McCabe, Cameron: The face on the
cutting room floor.
Moyes, Patricia: Falling star.
Parker, Robert B.: A savage death.

Piper, Peter: The stand-in.
Queen, Ellery: The devil to pay.
The four of hearts.
Rees, Arthur J.: Tragedy at
Twelvetrees.
Sinclair, Murray: Only in L. A.
Snell, David: Lights . . .
camera . . . murder.
Upton, Robert: Fade out.
Woodthorpe, R. C.: Rope for a
convict.
MOUNT SNOWDON; see WALES--MOUNT
SNOWDON
MOUNTAIN LIFE; see also ADIRONDACKS;
ALPS; APPALACHIANS; HIMALAYAS;
WALES--MOUNT SNOWDON
Banks, Carolyn: The darkroom.
Biggers, Earl Derr: Seven keys to
Baldpate.
Keinzley, Frances: A time to prey.
MOUNTAINEERING
Carr, Glyn: 11 books
Hunter, Alan: Gently to the summit.
MOUNTIES AS DETECTIVES
Craig, Alisa: A pint of murder.
Wright, L. R.: The suspect.
MUGGING
O'Donnell, Lillian: Leisure dying.
MULTIPLE PERSONALITY; see also
INSANITY; SCHIZOPHRENICS
Millar, Margaret: Beast in view.
MUMMIES; see also ANTIQUITIES
Pettee, F. M.: The Palgrave
mystery.
MURDER; see the following:
DECAPITATION
DISMEMBERMENT
FRATRICIDE (brother)
INFANTICIDE (infant, child)
LYNCHING
MARITICIDE (husband by wife)
MASS MURDER
MATRICIDE (mother)
PARRICIDE (parent)
PATRICIDE (father)
POISONING
SERIAL MURDER
SUICIDE
UNIDENTIFIED VICTIMS
UXORICIDE (wife by husband)
MUSEUMS; see also ART GALLERIES AND
MUSEUMS; SMITHSONIAN INSTITUTION
Fitzgerald, Penelope: The golden
child.

Guild, Nicholas: The favor.
Wetering, Janwillem van de: 7 books
Winsor, Diana: The death
convention.

NETHERLANDS ANTILLES
Wetering Janwillem van de:
Tumbleweed.

NEVADA
Adams, Cleve F.: The crooking
finger. Sabotage.
Chaber, M. E.: Born to be hanged.
Dewey, Thomas B.: Nude in Nevada.
Dodge, David: Bullets for the
bridegroom.
Eberhart, Mignon G.: El Rancho Rio.
Homes, Geoffrey: Build my gallows
high.
Keeler, Harry Stephen: The case of
the mysterious moll.
McKimmey, James: The man with the
gloved hand.
Queen, Ellery: And on the eighth
day.
Ross, Z. H.: Three down vulnerable.
Strahan, Kay Cleaver: 2 books
Williams, Charles: Man on a leash.

NEVADA--LAKE TAHOE
Biggers, Earl Derr: Keeper of the
keys.

NEVADA--LAS VEGAS
Ballard, Willis Todhunter: 6 books
Fair, A. A.: Spill the jackpot!
Foster, Richard: Blonde and
beautiful.
Gruber, Frank: The honest dealer.
Paul, Elliot: The black and the red.
Perry, Thomas: The butcher's boy.
Scherf, Margaret: If you want
murder well done. To cache a
millionaire.
Schorr, Mark: Ace of diamonds.
Thomas, Carolyn: The cactus shroud.
Tucker, Wilson: A procession of the
damned.
Wager, Walter: Blue moon.

NEVADA--RENO
Fair, A. A.: Spill the jackpot!
Ford, Leslie: Reno rendezvous.
Homes, Geoffrey: No hands on the
clock.
Quentin, Patrick: Puzzle for
wantons.
Ross, Z. H.: One corpse missing.

NEW ENGLAND; see UNITED STATES--NEW
ENGLAND

NEW GUINEA
Jay, Charlotte: Beat not the bones.
The brink of silence.
Vandercook, John W.: Murder in New
Guinea.

NEW GUINEA--PAPUA
Jay, Charlotte: The voice of the
crab.

NEW GUINEANS IN ENGLAND
Dickinson, Peter: The glass-sided
ant's nest.

NEW HAMPSHIRE
Babson, Marian: A trail of ashes.
Borgenicht, Miriam: Extreme
remedies.
Brett, Hy and Barbara: Promises to
keep.
Carleton, Marjorie: Vanished.
Lathen, Emma: Come to dust. Pick
up sticks.
Orr, Clifford: The Dartmouth
murders.

NEW JERSEY
Arden, William: A dark power.
Booton, Kage: Runaway home!
Collins, Michael: Blue death.
Heberden, M. V.: Drinks on the
victim. Murder goes astray.
Iams, Jack: Girl meets body.
Lathen, Emma: Murder to go.
Levinrew, Will: Murder on the
Palisades.
McMullen, Mary: The man with fifty
complaints.
O'Donnell, Lillian: Babes in the
woods.
Pikser, Jeremy: Junk on the hill.
Queen, Ellery: Halfway house.
Rosten, Leo: King Silky!
Sadler, Mark: Mirror image.
Scherf, Margaret: The corpse in
the flannel nightgown.
Thayer, Lee: Dead men's shoes. The
glass knife. The last shot. A
plain case of murder. Poison.
Q. E. D. The second bullet.
Within the vault.
Wells, Carolyn: All at sea. The
clue. The Maxwell mystery. The
umbrella murder.
Yates, George Worthing: The body
that wasn't there.

NEW JERSEY--ATLANTIC CITY
Leonard, Elmore: Glitz
Pentecost, Hugh: The Steel Palace.

NEW YORK--NEW YORK CITY

Abbot, Anthony: 7 books
Anderson, Frederick Irving: 2 books
Ard, William: A private party.
Arden, William: Deadly legacy.
Armstrong, Charlotte: Lay on MacDuff!
Arrighi, Mel: Alter ego.
Asimov, Isaac: The caves of steel. Murder at the A. B. A.
Bacon, Peggy: Inward eye.
Bagby, George: 44 books
Ball, John: The killing in the market.
Ballinger, Bill S.: The tooth and the nail.
Banks, Oliver: The Carravagio obsession.
Barth, Richard: 4 books
Baxt, George: 5 books
Bayer, William: 2 books
Belsky, Dick: One for the money.
Benson, Ben: The running man.
Blochman, Lawrence G.: See you at the morgue.
Block, Lawrence: 7 books
Bourjailly, Vance: A game men play.
Brand, Max: Big game.
Brean, Herbert: The darker the night. A matter of fact. The traces of Brillhart.
Brez, E. M.: Those dark eyes.
Brown, Daniel: Counterweight.
Burgess, Gelett: Ladies in boxes.
Burke, J. F.: Kelly among the nightingales.
Burton, Anthony: Embrace of the butcher.
Byfield, Barbara Ninde and Tedeschi, Frank L.: Solemn high murder.
Caputi, Anthony: Storms and son.
Castoire, Marie and Posner, Richard: Gold shield.
Caunitz, William: One Police Plaza.
Chastain, Thomas: 4 books
Christie, Agatha: The mysterious affair at Styles.
Coe, Tucker: 5 books
Cohler, David Keith: 2 books
Collins, Michael: 9 books
Cores, Lucy: 2 books
Coxe, George Harmon: The fifth key.
Craig, Jonathan: The case of the beautiful body.
Crane, Caroline: Woman vanishes.

Crane, Frances: The cinnamon murder. The pink umbrella.
Creasey, John: The Toff in New York.
Cross, Amanda: 3 books
Cunningham, E. V.: Cynthia. Lydia.
D'Alton, Martina: Fatal finish.
Daly, Carroll John: 7 books
Daly, Elizabeth: 9 books
Dane, Joel Y.: 2 books
Davis, Dorothy Salisbury: 6 books
Davis, Frederick C.: 11 books
Dean, Spencer: Credit for a murder.
DeAndrea, William L.: Killed on the ice.
Dentinger, Jane: 2 books
Early, Jack: A creative kind of killer.
Eberhard, Frederick G.: The microbe hunters.
Eberhart, Mignon G.: Melora. Never look back. Woman on the road.
Eller, John: Rage of heaven.
Ellin, Stanley: The eighth circle.
Esteven, John: 2 books
Fearing, Kenneth: 2 books
Fenisong, Ruth: 13 books
Field, Evan: What Nigel knew.
Fischer, Bruno: The hornet's nest.
Fisher, David E.: Katie's terror.
Flynn, Don: Murder isn't enough.
Foley, Rae: Where is Nancy Bostwick?
Footner, Hulbert: 11 books
Fuller, Samuel: The dark page.
Gardiner, Dorothy: What crime is it?
Goldsmith, Gene: Murder on his mind.
Goldstein, Arthur D.: A person shouldn't be like that.
Gruber, Frank: The French key. The gift horse. The limping goose. The mighty blockhead. Swing low, swing dead.
Hammett, Dashiell: The thin man.
Harrington, Joseph: 3 books
Himes, Chester: 6 books
Hirschberg, Cornelius: Florentine finish.
Hodgkin, M. R.: Dead indeed.
Holland, Isabelle: A death at St. Anselm's.
Hughes, Dorothy B.: 3 books
Iams, Jack: Death draws the line.

Irish, William: Deadline at dawn.
Jahn, Michael: Night rituals.
Kaye, Marvin: 3 books
Keeler, Harry Stephen: The
  wonderful scheme of Mr.
  Christopher Thorne.
Keith, David: A matter of accent.
Kelland, Clarence Budington: The
  great mail robbery.
Kendrick, Baynard H.: 9 books
Klinger, Henry: 3 books
Koenig, Laird: Rockabye.
Kurnitz, Harry: Invasion of privacy.
Lathen, Emma: 10 books
Lawrence, Hilda: Death of a doll.
Lee, Gypsy Rose: The G-string
  murders.
Levinrew, Will: Murder from the
  grave.
Lieberman, Herbert: 2 books
Livingston, Jack: Die again
  Macready.
Lockridge, Frances and Richard: 26
  books
Lockridge, Richard: 10 books
Maling, Arthur: The Koberg link. A
  taste of treason.
Masur, Harold Q.: 12 books
McCloy, Helen: 5 books
McGerr, Patricia: Death in a
  million living rooms.
    . . . follow, as the night. The
  seven deadly sisters.
McIntyre, John T.: The museum
  murder.
McIver, N. J.: Come back, Alice
  Smythereene!
McMullen, Mary: Strangle hold.
Minahan, John: The great diamond
  robbery.
O'Cork, Shannon: Hell bent for
  heaven.
O'Donnell, Lillian: 8 books
Olesker, Harry: Exit dying.
Orenstein, Frank: 2 books
Oster, Jerry: Sweet justice.
Page, Marco: 2 books
Palmer, Stuart: 7 books
Papazoglu, Orria: Sweet, savage
  death.
Patrick, Q.: 3 books
Patterson, Richard North: Escape
  into the night.
Paul, Barbara: 2 books

Pentecost, Hugh: 34 books
Peters, Elizabeth: Die for love.
Philips, Judson: 8 books
Pike, Robert L.: 3 books
Piper, Evelyn: The naked murderer.
Poate, Ernest M.: 2 books
Popkin, Zelda: 4 books
Potts, Jean: An affair of the
  heart.
Powers, Elizabeth: All that
  glitters.
Queen, Ellery: 14 books
Quentin, Patrick: 6 books
Randisi, Robert J.: Full contact.
Randolph, Marion: Grim grow the
  lilacs.
Rawson, Clayton: 3 books
Reeve, Arthur B.: 14 books
Reilly, Helen: 14 books
Resnicow, Herbert: The Gold
  solution.
Rice, Craig: Having wonderful
  crime. The Sunday pigeon murders.
Riddell, John: The John Riddell
  murder case.
Roos, Kelley: 11 books
Roosevelt, Elliott: The Hyde Park
  murder.
Ross, Barnaby: 4 books
Rosten, Leo: Silky!
Roth, Holly: 2 books
Sanders, Lawrence: 4 books
Scherf, Margaret: The diplomat and
  the gold piano. Glass on the
  stairs. The gun in Daniel
  Webster's bust.
Schorr, Mark: Red Diamond: private
  eye.
Scott, R. T. M.: 6 books
Simenon, Georges: Maigret in New
  York's underworld.
Slesar, Henry: 2 books
Smiley, Jane: Duplicate keys.
Smith, J. C. S.: Nightcap.
Smith, Martin Cruz: 2 books
Smithies, Richard H. R.: An
  academic question.
Spillane, Mickey: 11 books
Steel, Kurt: Murder goes to
  college.
Stein, Aaron Marc: Pistols for two.
Stone, Hampton: 14 books
Stout, Rex: 43 books
Strange, John Stephen: 9 books

Ransome, Stephen: Hear no evil. The shroud off her back.

Reilly, Helen: The doll's trunk murder.

Stein, Aaron Marc: Nowhere?

Strange, John Stephen: Make my bed soon.

Tomlinson, Gerald: On a field of black.

PENNSYLVANIA--PHILADELPHIA

Booton, Kage: Who knows Julie Gordon?

Carr, John Dickson: The burning court.

Ford, Leslie: The Philadelphia murder story.

Kyd, Thomas: 2 books

Lewis, Arthur H.: Copper beeches.

McGivern, William P.: The big heat. Shield for murder.

McMullen, Mary: Death by bequest. Funny Jonas, you don't look dead.

Popkin, Zelda: Dead man's gift.

Powell, Richard: False colors.

Propper, Milton: 14 books

Selwyn, Francis: Sergeant Verity and the blood royal.

Spicer, Bart: 5 books

Williams, Sidney: 2 books

PENNSYLVANIA--PITTSBURGH

Rinehart, Mary Roberts: The case of Jennie Brice.

Whitfield, Raoul: Green ice.

PENNSYLVANIA--SMALL TOWN LIFE

Boles, Paul Darcy: The limner.

McCormick, Claire: Resume for murder.

O'Donnell, Lillian: Cop without a shield.

Weber, Rubin: The grave maker's house.

Whitney, Phyllis A.: Snow fire.

PERIODICALS; see also NEWSPAPERS; PUBLISHERS AND PUBLISHING

George, Kara: Murder at "Tomorrow."

Paul, Barbara: Kill fee.

PERU

Stein, Aaron Marc: Up to no good.

Webb, Victoria: A little lady killing.

PETROLEUM INDUSTRY AND TRADE

Crofts, Freeman Wills: Dark journey.

D'Alton, Martina: Fatal finish.

Dickinson, Peter: The poison oracle.

Gill, Bartholomew: McGarr and the Sienese conspiracy.

Hillerman, Tony: People of darknesss.

Lathen, Emma: Double, double, oil and trouble.

Mann, Jessica: No man's island.

Pentecost, Hugh: Deadly trap.

PETS; see also specific animals, such as CATS; DOGS

Lockridge, Richard: The tenth life.

PHARMACISTS

Burton, Miles: Death of a chemist.

PHILANTHROPISTS; see also CHARITIES; ENDOWMENTS

Rendell, Ruth: The lake of darkness.

Stout, Rex: Champagne for one.

Van Dine, S. S. : The scarab murder case.

Williams, David: Treasure by degrees.

PHILATELY; see also POSTAL SERVICE

Cunningham, E. V.: The case of the penny orange.

MacDonald, John D.: The scarlet ruse.

Pentecost, Hugh: Cancelled in red.

Tapply, William G.: The Dutch blue error.

PHILIPPINES

Coxe, George Harmon: Dangerous legacy.

Kenyon, Michael: A sorry state.

Knight, Clifford: The affair of the circus queen.

PHILOSOPHERS AS DETECTIVES

Sladek, John: Black aura.

PHOBIAS; see AGORAPHOBIA

PHOTOGRAPHERS

Garve, Andrew: A very quiet place.

Mansfield, Paul H.: Final exposure.

Marsh, Ngaio: Photo finish.

Pronzini, Bill: Masques.

Tey, Josephine: To love and be wise.

Upfield, Arthur W.: Lake Frome monster.

PHOTOGRAPHERS AS DETECTIVES

Brean, Herbert: The clock strikes thirteen. The darker the night. Hardly a man is now alive. Wilders walk away.

Chaze, Elliott: Little David.

Coxe, George Harmon: 29 books
Francis, Dick: Reflex.
Leonard, Elmore: La Brava.
O'Cork, Shannon: 2 books
Page, Jake: Shoot the moon.
Rice, Craig: The Sunday pigeon
    murders. The Thursday turkey
    murders.
Rice, Craig and McBain, Ed: The
    April robin murders.
Strange, John Stephen: 8 books
PHOTOGRAPHY
Brown, Daniel: The subject of
    Harry Egypt.
PHYSICIANS; see also PATHOLOGISTS;
    PSYCHIATRISTS; PSYCHOLOGISTS
Bell, Josephine: Death of a con
    man.
Blake, Nicholas: The worm of death.
Braddon, George: Judgment deferred.
Burton, Miles: Who killed the
    doctor?
Byrom, James: Take only as
    directed.
Candy, Edward: Bones of contention.
Cannan, Joanna: And be a villain.
Clarke, Anna: Game, set and
    danger. One of us must die.
Corbett, James: Murder minus
    motive.
Crofts, Freeman Wills: Silence for
    the murderer.
Davies, L. P.: The Lampton dreamers.
Dominic, R. B.: The attending
    physician.
Eller, John: Charlie and the ice
    cream man.
Esteven,, John: The door of death.
Freeling, Nicolas: Criminal
    conversation.
Gill, B. M.: Suspect.
Gordon, Richard: Jack the Ripper.
Jon, Montague: A question of law.
Macdonald, Ross: The doomsters.
MacKay, Amanda: Death is academic.
Nielsen, Helen: The fifth caller.
Phillpotts, Eden: The anniversary
    murder.
Rogers, Samuel: You leave me cold!
Roth, Holly: Too many doctors.
Sanders, Lawrence: The sixth
    commandment.
Simpson, Dorothy: Puppet for a
    corpse.
Waugh, Hillary: The late Mrs. D.

Woods, Sara: Tarry and be hanged.
PHYSICIANS AS DETECTIVES
Adams, Herbert: The strange murder
    of Hatton, K. C.
Bailey, H. C.: 24 books
Bell, Josephine: 18 books
Black, Lionel: Outbreak.
Blackwood, Algernon: 2 books
Borthwick, J. S.: The case of the
    hook-billed kites.
Branson, H. C.: 7 books
Disney, Doris Miles: Heavy, heavy
    hangs.
Edwards, James G.: F corridor. The
    private pavilion.
Freeman, R. Austin: 28 books
Head, Matthew: 4 books
Hughes, Dorothy B.: The expendable
    man.
Jay, Simon: Death of a skin diver.
Klawans, Harold L.: Sins of
    commission.
Livingston, Jack: The Dodd cases.
Penn, John: Stag dinner death.
Poate, Ernest M.: 2 books
Priestly, J. B.: Salt is leaving.
Rogers, Joel Townsley: The red
    right hand.
Scerbaneco, Giorgio: Duca and the
    Milan murders.
Scherf, Margaret: The banker's
    bones. The beaded banana. The
    beautiful birthday cake. To cache
    a millionaire.
Stagge, Jonathan: 9 books
Wyllie, John: 8 books
PHYSICISTS
Freeling, Nicolas: Gadget.
PHYSICISTS AS DETECTIVES
Bortner, Norman Stanley: 2 books
PIANISTS AS DETECTIVES
Gosling, Paula: Solo blues.
PIGS; see SWINE
PILOTS; see AIR PILOTS
PIRACY
Browne, Douglas G.: Plan XVI.
PLAGUE; see BIOLOGICAL WARFARE;
    EPIDEMICS
PLAYWRIGHTS; see DRAMATISTS
POACHERS AS DETECTIVES
Parrish, Frank: 5 books
POACHING; see also FISHING; HUNTING
Cody, Liza: Stalker.
Knox, Bill: Whitewater.

Hinkemeyer, Michael T.: A time to reap.
Hough, S. B.: 4 books
Kemp, Sarah: No escape.
Knox, Bill: 17 books
Lemarchand, Elizabeth: Step in the dark.
Lewin, Michael Z.: Hard line.
Lindsey, David L.: Heat from another sun.
Linington, Elizabeth: 12 books
Marric, J. J.: 23 books
Marshall, William: 4 books
McBain, Ed: 38 books
McGivern, William P.: The big heat. Rogue cop.
McIlvanney, William: 2 books
O'Donnell, Lillian: 9 books
Ormerod, Roger: Seeing red.
Petievich, Gerald: The quality of the informant.
Pike, Robert L.: Mute witness. Police blotter. The quarry.
Porter, Joyce: 10 books
Prior, Allan: The interrogators.
Procter, Maurice: 17 books
Propper, Milton: The student fraternity murders.
Pyle, A. M.: Trouble making toys.
Randolph, Marion: This'll kill you.
Rathbone, Julian: Watching the detectives.
Reeves, John: Murder before matins.
Reilly, Helen: 32 books
Rendell, Ruth: Murder being once done.
Ross, Jonathan: 11 books
Sanders, Lawrence: The second deadly sin.
Scott, Jack S.: A time of fine weather.
Semyonov, Julian: Petrovka 38.
Serafin, David: 3 books
Shannon, Dell: 35 books
Sheldon, Walter J.: The rites of murder.
Thomson, Basil: 3 books
Treat, Lawrence: 13 books
Turnbull, Peter: 2 books
Vance, John Holbrook: 2 books
Wade, Henry: Bury him darkly.
Wainwright, John: 11 books
Waugh, Hillary: 15 books
Weston, Carolyn: 3 books

White, Teri: Bleeding hearts.
Wilcox, Collin: 13 books
York, Andrew: 2 books
POLITICS; see FRANCE--POLITICS; SPAIN--POLITICS; UNITED KINGDOM--POLITICS; UNITED STATES--POLITICS; see also ELECTIONS; LOBBYISTS
PORNOGRAPHY
Bagby, George: Innocent bystander.
Early, Jack: A creative kind of killer.
Lindsey, David L.: Heat from another sun.
Parker, Robert B.: Ceremony of innocence.
Randisi, Robert J.: Full contact.
Stinson, Jim: Double exposure.
PORTUGAL
Bosak, Steven: Gammon.
Boyle, Thomas: The cold stove league.
Ferrars, E. X.: Witness before the fact.
Fleming, Joan: Death of a sardine.
Footner, Hulbert: Unneutral murder.
Kirk, Michael: Salvage job.
MacKenzie, Donald: Raven's longest night.
Perry, Ritchie: MacAllister.
Webster, Noah: A burial in Portugal.
PORTUGUESE IN AFRICA
Head, Matthew: The Cabinda affair.
PORTUGUESE IN THE UNITED STATES
O'Marie, Carol Anne: A novena for murder.
POSTAGE STAMPS; see PHILATELY
POSTAL INSPECTORS AS DETECTIVES
Disney, Doris Miles: Black mail. Mrs. Meeker's money. Unappointed rounds.
POSTAL SERVICE
Creasey, John: Death of a postman.
Kelland, Clarence Budington: The great mail.
Rice, Craig: The fourth postman.
Turnbull, Peter: Big money.
Webb, Maurice G.: Darling Corey's dead.
POTTERY
Kelly, Mary: The spoilt kill.
POULTRY
Gruber, Frank: The scarlet feather.

Egan, Lesley: A serious
    investigation.
Lovell, Marc: Hand over mind.
Lovesey, Peter: A case of spirits.
McShane, Mark: 2 books
Woods, Sara: Weep for her.
PSYCHOANALYSIS
Reeve, Arthur B.: The dream doctor.
PSYCHOLOGIST; see also PSYCHIATRISTS
Sanders, Lawrence: The fourth
    deadly sin.
PSYCHOLOGISTS AS DETECTIVES
Angus, Douglas Ross: Death on
    Jerusalem Road.
Balmer, Edwin and MacHarg, William:
    The achievements of Luther Trant.
Dutton, Charles J.: 6 books
Ebersohn, Wessel: A lonely place
    to die.
Fitzsimmons, Cortland: 2 books
Kellerman, Jonathan: When the
    bough breaks.
King, C. Daly: Obelists at sea.
Lewis, Lange: The passionate
    victims.
Owens, Hans C.: Ways of death.
Stribling T. S.: 2 books
Symons, Julian: The color of
    murder.
Tey, Josephine: Miss Pym disposes.
PSYCHOPATHS; see also INSANITY
Barnard, Allan, ed.: The harlot
    killer.
Beynon, Jane: Cypress man.
Blake, Nicholas: The worm of death.
Bloch, Robert: The scarf.
Coughlin, William J.: The stalking
    man.
Early, Jack: Razzmatazz.
Egan, Lesley: The hunters and the
    hunted.
Fox, Peter: Trail of the reaper.
Fremlin, Celia: The parasite person.
Gruber, Frank: The gold gap.
Kelly, Susan: The Gemini man.
Kendrick, Baynard H.: Out of
    control.
Leonard, Elmore: Glitz.
MacDonald, John D.: The deep blue
    goodbye.
McGivern, William P.: Night of the
    juggler.
McKimmey, James: Run if you're
    guilty.

O'Donnell, Lillian: No business
    being a cop.
Rendell, Ruth: A demon in my view.
Sanders, Lawrence: 2 books
Shearing, Joseph: Moss rose.
Siller, Van: Under a cloud.
Simenon, Georges: The madman of
    Bergerac.
Smith, Mark: The death of a
    detective.
Walsh, Ray: The Mycroft memoranda.
Webb, Martha G.: A white male
    running.
Wilcox, Collin: The third victim.
PSYCHOTICS; see INSANITY
PUBLIC RELATIONS
Babson, Marian: Cover up story.
    Murder on show.
Howard, James A.: The bullet-proof
    martyr.
McGivern, William P.: Very cold for
    May.
Pentecost, Hugh: 13 books
PUBLICISTS AS DETECTIVES
Box, Edgar: 3 books
Goodrum, Charles A.: Dewey
    decimated.
Kaye, Marvin: 5 books
PUBLISHERS AND PUBLISHING; see also
    EDITORS; NEWSPAPERS; PERIODICALS
Allingham, Margery: Flowers for the
    judge.
Blake, Nicholas: End of a chapter.
Burke, J. F.: Kelly among the
    nightingales.
Fearing, Kenneth: The big clock.
Forrest, Norman: Death took a
    publisher.
Frimmer, Steven: Dead matter.
George, Kara: Murder at "Tomorrow."
Hodgkin, M. R.: Dead indeed.
Iams, Jack: Death draws the line.
Lockridge, Richard: Write murder
    down.
Muller, Marcia and Pronzini, Bill,
    eds.: Chapter and hearse.
Philbrick, W. R.: Shadow kills.
Rhode, John and Dickson, Carter:
    Fatal descent.
Stout, Rex: Murder by the book.
    Plot it yourself.
Strong, L. A. G.: Which I never.
Symons, Julian: The narrowing
    circle. The plain man.

Wahloo, Per: The thirty-first floor.

PUBLISHERS AS DETECTIVES
Kallen, Lucille: 3 books
McCollum, Robert: And then they die.
Patterson, Richard North: Escape into the night.

PUBS; see TAVERNS, BARS, ETC.

PUERTO RICO
Lathen, Emma: The longer the thread.
Leonard, Elmore: Glitz.
O'Donnell, Lillian: Murder under the sun.

PUZZLES
Moyes, Patricia: A six-letter word for death.

PYRENEES
Wallis, Ruth Satwell: Blood from a stone.

QUAKERS
Ellin, Stanley: Stronghold.

QUEEN MARY (ship)
Graeme, Bruce: Mystery on the Queen Mary.

RABBIS AS DETECTIVES
Kemelman, Harry: 8 books

RACE PROBLEMS
Ball, John: In the heat of the night.
Hansen, Joseph: Night work.
Holton, Leonard: A corner of paradise.
Hornig, Doug: Foul shot.
Hughes Dorothy B.: The expendable man.
Kaminsky, Stuart: Down for the count.
Lathen, Emma: Death shall overcome.
Lockridge, Richard: With option to die.
Marric, J. J.: Gideon's men. Gideon's press.
McClure, James: 5 books
Philips, Judson: Hot summer killing. Nightmare at dawn.
Reed, Ishmael: 2 books
Rennert, Maggie: Circle of death.
Scott, Jack S.: The local lads.
Uhnak, Dorothy: The witness.

Upfield, Arthur W.: The bone is pointed. Journey to the hangman. Sinister stones.

RACING; see AUTOMOBILE RACING

RADIO ANNOUNCERS AS DETECTIVES
Hamilton, Ian: 4 books
Marshall, Sidney: Some like it hot.

RADIO BROADCASTING; see also SOAP OPERAS; TELEVISION BROADCASTING
Abelman, Paul: Shoestring. Shoestring's finest hour.
Barnard, Robert: A little local murder.
Brett, Simon: The dead side of the mike.
Gielgud, Val and Marvell, Holt: London calling.
Jeffers, H. Paul: Murder on mike.
Kamitses, Zoe: Moondreamer.
Keith, David: A matter of accent.
O'Cork, Shannon: Hell bent for heaven.
Sherwood, John: Death at the B. B. C.
Wells, Carolyn: The radio station murder.
Xantippe: Death catches up with Mr. Kluck.

RAILROADS
Brock, Lynn: The slip-carriage mystery.
Burton, Miles: The clue of the silver cellar. Dark is the tunnel.
Carmichael, Harry: Money for murder.
Connington, J. J.: The two-ticket puzzle.
Constantine, K. C.: The Rocksburg Railroad murders.
Creasey, John: Murder on the line.
Crofts, Freeman Wills: Death of a train. Double death. The Groote Park murder.
Ford, Paul Leicester: The great K & A train robbery.
Hitchens, Bert and Delores: End of the line.
Hodgkin, M. R.: Student body.
Holt, Henry: The midnight mail.
Phillpotts, Eden: My adventure in the Flying Scotsman.
Rhode, John: Tragedy on the line.
Tucker, Wilson: The stalking man.

Walsh, Thomas: Nightmare in Manhattan.

RAILROADS--TRAVEL; see also ORIENT EXPRESS

Adler, Warren: Trans-Siberian express.

Armstrong, Anthony: The trail of fear.

Bellairs, George: Death on the last train.

Chalmers, Stephen: The crime in Car 13.

Christie, Agatha: Murder on the Orient Express. The mystery of the blue train. What Mrs. McGillicuddy saw!

Coxe, George Harmon: The groom lay dead.

Crofts, Freeman Wills: Sir John Magill's last journey.

DeKobra, Maurice: The madonna of the sleeping cars.

Denbie, Roger: Death on the limited.

Dent, Lester: Lady to kill.

Derleth, August: The adventure of the Orient Express.

Farjeon, J. Jefferson: The 5:18 mystery.

Gordons, The: Campaign train.

Highsmith, Patricia: Strangers on a train.

Japrisot, Sebastien: The 10:30 from Marseilles.

Keating, H. R. F.: Inspector Ghote goes by train.

King, C. Daly: Obelists en route.

Lenehan, J. C.: The tunnel mystery.

Little, Constance and Gwyneth: Great black Kanba.

MacHarg, William Briggs and Balmer, Edwin: The blind man's eyes.

Nebel, Frederick: Sleepers east.

Reilly, Helen: Compartment K.

Rhode, John: Death on the boat-train.

Simenon, Georges: The strange case of Peter the Lett.

Tey, Josephine: The singing sands.

Tilton, Alice: Cold steal.

RAIN; see DROUGHT

RANCH LIFE

Ames, Delano: Murder begins at home.

Bay, Austin: The coyote cried twice.

Biggers, Earl Derr: The Chinese parrot.

Seeley, Mabel: Eleven came back.

Siller, Van: Under a cloud.

Stout, Rex: Death of a dude.

Upfield, Arthur W.: The mountains have a secret. No footprints in the bush. Sands of Windee. The will of the tribe.

RANGERS AS DETECTIVES; see also CONSERVATION; ECOLOGISTS AS DETECTIVES

Elkins, Aaron J.: The dark place.

RAPE

Angus, Douglas Ross: Death on Jerusalem Road.

Egan, Lesley: Against the evidence.

Ford, Leslie: Trial by ambush.

Hamilton, Nan: Killer's rights.

Harris, Charlaine: A secret rage.

Jon, Montague: A question of law.

Kenyon, Michael: The rapist.

Murphy, Brian: The Enigma Variations.

O'Donnell, Lillian: Dial 577 R-A-P-E.

Penn, John: Mortal term.

Underwood, Michael: Double jeopardy.

Upfield, Arthur W.: The white savage.

RARE BOOKS; see BOOKS--RARITIES

READING; see ILLITERACY

REAL ESTATE DEVELOPMENT

Barth, Richard: The condo kill.

Gardner, Erle Stanley: The case of the fenced-in woman.

Lathen, Emma: Pick up sticks.

Lewis, Roy: A gathering of ghosts.

Livingston, Jack: Die again Macready.

MacDonald, John D.: A flash of green. A tan and sandy silence.

Parker, Robert B.: Promised land.

Pronzini, Bill: Nightshades.

Russell, E. S.: She should have cried on Monday.

Stevenson, Richard: On the other hand, death.

Williams, David: Treasure preserved.

Wren, M. K.: Wake up Darlin' Corey.

REAL PEOPLE

Alexander, Karl: Time after time.

Simenon, Georges: The guinguette
by the Seine.

RESORTS, SUMMER
Blake, Nicholas: The summer camp
mystery.
Brett, Simon: A comedian dies.
Christie, Agatha: A Caribbean
mystery. Evil under the sun.
Lovesey, Peter: Mad hatter's
holiday.
Nielsen, Helen: The darkest hour.
Peters, Ellis: Who lies here?
Siller, Van: The last resort.
Under a cloud.
Tey, Josephine: A shilling for
candles.

RESORTS, WINTER
Carr, Glynn: The corpse in the
crevasse.
Gair, Malcolm: Snow job.
Hughes, Richard: Unholy communion.
Linscott, Gillian: Murder makes
tracks.
Moyes, Patricia: Dead men don't
ski.
Whitney, Phyllis A.: Snowfire.
Yorke, Margaret: Silent witness.

RESTAURANTS, LUNCHROOMS, ETC.; see
also TAVERNS, BARS, ETC.; WAITRESSES
Bond, Michael: Monsieur
Pamplemousse.
Boyle, Thomas: The cold stove
league.
Bruce, Leo: Death with a blue
ribbon.
Keyes, Frances Parkinson: Dinner
at Antoine's.
Lathen Emma: Murder to go.
Oppenheim, E. Phillips: Milan
grill room. A pulpit in the grill
room.
Pentecost, Hugh: Sow death, reap
death.
Simenon, Georges: Battle of
nerves. Maigret's pickpocket.
Smith, J. C. S.: Nightcap.
Wainwright, John: The Venus
Fly-Trap.

RETAIL TRADE; see also BOOKSELLING;
DEPARTMENT STORES
Crispin, Edmund: The moving toyshop.
Davey, Jocelyn: A killing in hats.
Simenon, Georges: The Flemish shop.

RETARDED PEOPLE
Butler, Gwendoline: Coffin in Malta.

Crane, Frances: The amber eyes.
Egan, Lesley: Against the evidence.
Keeler, Harry Stephen: The green
jade hand.
Mantell, Laurie: Murder in fancy
dress.
Millar, Margaret: Mermaid.

REUNIONS
Bronson, F. W.: The bulldog has the
key.
Knight, Kathleen Moore: Death goes
to a reunion.
Lemarchand, Elizabeth: Death of an
old girl.
Meggs, Brown: The matter of
paradise.
Moyes, Patricia: Johnny under
ground.
Sayers, Dorothy L.: Gaudy night.

REVENGE
Ballinger, Bill S.: The tooth and
the nail.
Collins, Michael: Night of the
toads.
Connington, J. J.: Grim vengeance.
Creasey, John: The hounds of
vengeance.
DiPego, Gerald Francis: With a
vengeance.
Gores, Joe: A time of predators.
Jepson, Selwyn: Keep murder quiet.
Knight, Kathleen Moore: Invitation
to vengeance.
Pentecost, Hugh: Past, present, and
murder.
Powell, Richard: A shot in the
dark.
Procter, Maurice: Somewhere in this
city.
Rhode, John: Death in Harley
Street.
Savage, Ernest: Two if by sea.
Spillane, Mickey: Vengeance is
mine!
Wainwright, John: Spiral staircase.
Watson, Colin: Charity ends at
home.

REVOLUTIONS
Harling, Robert: The dark saviour.

RHODE ISLAND
Disney, Doris Miles: Did she fall,
or was she pushed?
Dutton, Charles J.: The shadow on
the glass.
Footner, Hulbert: Easy to kill.

Dillon, Eilis: 2 books
Ferrars, E. X.: Something wicked.
Gault, William Campbell: The Cana
  diversion.
Gillespie, Robert B.: Heads you
  lose.
Goldstein, Arthur D.: 3 books
Goodrum, Charles A.: 2 books
Green, Edith Pinero: 2 books
Hare, Cyril: 5 books
Hilton, John Buxton: The sunset
  law.
Hinkemeyer, Michael T.: A time to
  reap.
Hopkins, Kenneth: 3 books
Innes, Michael: Death by water.
Krasner, William: 4 books
Love, Edmund G.: Set-up
McBain, Ed: Where there's smoke.
Orczy, Baroness: 8 books
Phillpotts, Eden: Monkshood.
Pronzini, Bill: Bones.
Quill, Monica: Nun of the above.
Scherf, Margaret: The banker's
  bones. The beaded banana. The
  beautiful birthday cake. To cache
  a millionaire.
Sherwood, John: A botanist at bay.
Smith, J. C. S.: Jacoby's first
  case.
Smith, Mark: The death of a
  detective.
Thompson, Gene: 2 books
Tilton, Alice: 8 books
Webster, Henry Kitchell: The
  Corbin necklace.
Williamson, Moncrieff: Death in
  the picture.
Zangwill, Israel: The big bow
  mystery.
SERIAL MURDER; see also MASS MURDER
Babson, Marian: Cruise of a
  deathtime.
Beeding, Francis: Murdered: one by
  one.
Belsky, Dick: One for the money.
Block, Lawrence: Make out with
  murder.
Boyle, Thomas: Only the dead know
  Brooklyn.
Burns, Rex: The avenging angel.
Early, Jack: Razzmatazz
Ellroy, James: Blood on the moon.
Fitzsimmons, Cortland: Death rings
  a bell.

Flynn, Carol Houlihan: Washed in
  the blood.
Gore-Browne, Robert: By way of
  confession.
Goulart, Ron: A graveyard of my
  own.
Hill, Reginald: Deadheads.
Jeffries, Roderic: Three and one
  make five.
Lowndes, Marie Belloc: The lodger.
Lutz, John: Nightlines.
MacDonald, Philip: Murder gone mad.
  Mystery of the dead police.
Marshall, William: The far away
  moon.
McCollum, Robert: And then they
  die.
Muller, Marcia: Games to keep the
  dark away.
Nash, Jay Robert: The dark
  fountain.
Olsen, D. B.: Enrollment cancelled.
Oster, Jerry: Sweet justice.
Phillpotts, Eden: The grey room.
Propper, Milton: The blood
  transfusion murders.
Queen, Ellery: Cat of many tails.
Raymond, Clifford S.: The men on
  the dead man's chest.
Roberts, Willo Davis: The sniper.
Serafin, David: Madrid underground.
Simmons, Addison: Death on the
  campus.
Smith, Mark: The death of a
  detective.
Van Dine, S. S.: The Bishop murder
  case.
Withers, E. L.: Diminishing
  returns.
SERVANTS; see also COOKS
Bellairs, George: The four
  unfaithful servants.
Christie, Agatha: Mrs. McGinty's
  dead. A pocket full of rye.
Clarke, T. E. B.: Murder at
  Buckingham Palace.
Cleeve, Brian: Death of a wicked
  servant.
Crofts, Freeman Wills: Sudden
  death.
Ferrars, E. X.: Foot in the grave.
James, P. D.: Cover her face.
Marsh, Ngaio: Death and the dancing
  footman.
Porter, Joyce: Dover one.

Potts, Jean: Go lovely rose.
Tey, Josephine: The Franchise
  affair.
White, R. J.: A second-hand tomb.
SERVANTS AS DETECTIVES
  David-Neel, Alexandra and Yongden,
    Lama: The power of nothingness.
  Davis, Dorothy Salisbury: Death of
    an old sinner. A gentleman called.
    Old sinners never die.
SEX CHANGE; see TRANSSEXUALS
SEXUAL HARASSMENT
  Miner, Valerie: Murder in the
    English Department.
SHAKESPEARE, WILLIAM
  Boland, John: The Shakespeare
    curse.
  Bonney, Joseph L.: Look to the
    lady!
  Kaye, Marvin: Bullets for Macbeth.
  Keating H. R. F.: Filmi, filmi,
    Inspector Ghote.
  Marsh, Ngaio: Light thickens.
SHAW, T. E.
  Eden, Matthew: The murder of
    Lawrence of Arabia.
SHIPPING; see also LONGSHOREMEN
  Anderson, J. R. L.: Death in the
    city.
  Ard, William: A private party.
  Bell, Josephine: The Port of
    London murders.
  Eberhart, Mignon G.: Dead men's
    plans.
  Henege, Thomas: Death of a
    shipowner.
  Kirk, Michael: Mayday from Malaga.
  Paretsky, Sara: Deadlock.
  Rhode, John: Murder at Derivale.
  Thorne, Paul: Murder in the fog.
  Wade, Henry: The missing partners.
SHIPS; see also BOATS AND BOATING;
  OCEAN VOYAGES; SEA STORIES;
  SUBMARINES; YACHTS AND YACHTING
  Adams, Cleve F.: And sudden death.
  Ashford, Jeffrey: The loss of the
    Culion.
  Babson, Marian: Murder sails at
    midnight.
  Barry, Charles: Death of a first
    mate.
  Cameron, Owen: The owl and the
    pussycat.
  Cottrell, Dorothy: Silent reefs.

Coxe, George Harmon: Inland
  passage.
Creasey, John: Murder,
  London--Australia. The Toff on
  board.
Crofts, Freeman Wills: Enemy
  unseen. The loss of the "Jane
  Vosper."
Dodge, David: Angel's ransom.
Eberhart, Mignon G.: Five
  passengers from Lisbon.
Footner, Hulbert: Dangerous cargo.
Forbes, Stanton: The name's Death,
  remember me?
Gould, Stephen: Murder of the
  admiral.
Graham, Winston: The wreck of the
  Grey Cat.
Hocking, Anne: Killing kin.
Holding, Elizabeth Saxanay: Lady
  killer.
Innes, Hammond: The wreck of the
  Mary Deare.
MacHarg, William Briggs and Balmer,
  Edwin: The Indian drum.
Munro, Hugh: Who told Clutha?
Thayer, Lee: Last trump. Lightning
  strikes twice.
Yates, Margaret Tayler: The
  hush-hush murders.
SHOPS; see RETAIL TRADE
SHRINES; see also TEMPLES, BUDDHIST
  Haymon, S. T.: Death and the
    pregnant virgin.
SINGAPORE
  Foxx, Jack: The jade figurine.
  Murray, Max: The doctor and the
    corpse.
SINGERS
  Babson, Marian: Cover up story.
  Biggers, Earl Derr: Keeper of the
    keys.
  Dewey, Thomas B.: A sad song
    singing.
  Dunnett, Dorothy: The photogenic
    soprano.
  Eberhart, Mignon G.: The house on
    the roof.
  Hjortsberg, William: Falling angel.
  McBain, Ed: Rumpelstiltskin.
  Marsh, Ngaio: Photo finish.
  Peters, Ellis: The house of green
    turf.
  Stout, Rex: Death of a doxy.

Sayers, Dorothy L.: Clouds of
 witness. Strong poison.
Simenon, Georges: Maigret in court.
Simon, Roger L.: Peking duck.
Symons, Julian: The color of
 murder.
Tourney, Leonard: Familiar spirits.
Trollope, Anthony: 2 books
Underwood, Michael: 11 books
Wainwright, John: Man of law. An
 urge for justice.
West, Pamela Elizabeth: Madeline.
White, R. J.: The women of
 Peasenhall.
Wickware, Francis Sill: Dangerous
 ground.
Woods, Sara: 20 books
TRINIDAD
 Coxe, George Harmon: One hour to
 kill.
 Underwood, Michael: Arm of the law.
 Vandercook, John W.: Murder in
 Trinidad.
TRIPLETS; see also TWINS
 Innes, Michael: A night of errors.
Keeler, Harry Stephen: Thieves'
 nights.
TRUCKING
 Hansen, Joseph: Night work.
 Rutherford, Douglas: Return load.
TUNISIA
 Jepson, Selwyn: The death gong.
TURKEY
 Arnold, Margot: Exit actors, dying.
 Fleming, Joan: Nothing is the
 number when you die.
 Hyland, Stanley: Top bloody secret.
 Roudybush, Alexandra: A sybartic
 death.
 Wood, Clement: Death in Ankara.
TURKEY--ISTANBUL
 Fleming, Joan: When I grow rich.
 Frimmer, Steven: Dead matter.
 Stein, Aaron Marc: Deadly delight.
TURKS IN ENGLAND
 Christie, Agatha: Cat among
 pigeons.
 Fleming, Joan: Nothing is the
 number when you die.
TURKS IN SCOTLAND
 MacKinnon, Allan: Cormorant's Isle.
TWINS; see also TRIPLETS
 Balmer, Edwin: Keeban.
 Garve, Andrew: The far sands.

Hutton, Malcolm: Georgina and
 Georgette.
Simenon, Georges: The
 survivors.
TYCOONS; see CAPITALISTS AND
FINANCIERS
TYPHOONS; see HURRICANES; TIDAL
WAVES

U. S.; see UNITED STATES
U. S. S. R.; see UNION OF SOVIET
SOCIALIST REPUBLICS
UGANDA
 Zake, S. Joshua L.: Truckful of
 gold.
UNCLES; see also AUNTS; NEPHEWS;
 NIECES
 Ley, Alice Chetwynd: A reputation
 dies.
 Stout, Rex: Bad for business.
 Symons, Julian: The Belting
 inheritance.
 Woods, Sara: Enter the corpse.
 Error of the moon.
UNDERTAKERS AND UNDERTAKING
 Bailey, Hilea: The smiling corpse.
 Lathen, Emma: Ashes to ashes.
UNIDENTIFIED FLYING OBJECTS
 Taylor, L. A.: 2 books
UNIDENTIFIED VICTIMS
 Aird, Catherine: Henrietta who?
 Constantine, K. C.: Always a body
 to trade.
 Gilbert, Michael: The body of a
 girl.
 Hoyt, Richard: The Siskiyou
 two-step.
 Kelland, Clarence Budington: The
 case of the nameless corpse.
 Knight, Clifford: The affair of the
 dead stranger.
 Marshall, William: Skullduggery.
 McShane, Mark: The girl nobody
 knows.
 Rhode, John: Body unidentified.
 Rinehart, Mary Roberts: The yellow
 room.
 Serafin, David: The body in Cadiz
 Bay.
 Simenon, Georges: Maigret and the
 loner.
 Thomson, June: A question of
 identity.

Dunlap, Susan: 2 books
Dwight, Olivia: Close his eyes.
Eberhart, Mignon G.: Casa Madrone. The cases of Susan Dare. Dead men's plans. Next of kin.
Eden, Dorothy: Waiting for Willa.
Egan, Lesley: A choice of crimes.
Elkins, Aaron J.: The dark place.
Eulo, Ken: Nocturnal.
Fair, A. A.: 29 books
Fearing, Kenneth: The loneliest girl in the world.
Ferrars, E. X.: Blood flies upward. Experiment with death. In at the kill. Last will and testament.
Fisher, David E.: Katie's terror.
Foote-Smith, Elizabeth: A gentle albatross.
Footner, Hulbert: The almost perfect murder. The casual murderer. Dangerous cargo. The doctor who held hands. Easy to kill. Madame Storey. The under dogs. The velvet hand.
Ford, Leslie: 16 books
Fox, Peter: Trail of the reaper.
Fraser, Antonia: 5 books
Freeman, Martin J.: The murder of a midget.
Fremlin, Celia: The parasite person.
Garve, Andrew: Death and the sky above.
Gash, Joe: 2 books
Gatenby, Rosemary: The third identity.
Gilbert, Michael: The country-house burglar. Death has deep roots.
Gilman, Dorothy: The tightrope walker.
Goodrum, Charles A.: Dewey decimated.
Grafton, Sue: 2 books
Granger, Bill: Public murders.
Grierson, Edward: The second man.
Hardy, William M.: 2 books
Harrington, Joseph: 2 books
Harrington, Joyce: Family reunion.
Harris, Charlaine: 2 books
Head, Matthew: 4 books
Holland, Isabelle: Grenelle.
Hopkins, Kenneth: Dead against my principles.
Hubbard, P. M.: Flush as May. The graveyard.

Hyams, Joe: Murder at the Academy Awards.
Isaacs, Susan: Compromising positions.
James, P. D.: The skull beneath the skin. An unsuitable job for a woman.
Jay, Charlotte: Beat not the bones.
Jesse, F. Tennyson: The Solange stories.
Johnson, W. Bolingbroke: The widening stain.
Johnston, Velda: 2 books
Kallen, Lucille: The Tanglewood murders.
Kaminsky, Stuart: Exercise in terror.
Kamitses, Zoe: Moondreamer.
Kaye, Marvin: 5 books
Keech, Scott: Ciphered.
Keeler, Harry Stephen: The case of the lavender gripsack.
Kelly, Mary: The march to the gallows.
Kelly, Nora: In the shadow of King's.
Kelly, Susan: The Gemini man.
Kenney, Susan: 2 books
Knight, Kathleen Moore: Design in diamonds.
Koenig, Laird: Rockabye.
Lamb, Margaret: Chains of gold.
Langley, Lee: 2 books
Langton, Jane: The transcendental murder.
LaRoche, K. Alison: Dear dead professor.
Latimer, Jonathan: Red gardenias.
Law, Janice: 2 books
Lawrence, Hilda: Death of a doll.
Lee, Gypsy Rose: 2 books
Leek, Margaret: The healthy grave.
Lewin, Michael Z.: Hard line.
Lewis, Lange: The passionate victims.
Ley, Alice Chetwynd: A reputation dies.
Linington, Elizabeth: Practice to deceive.
Linscott, Gillian: Murder makes tracks.
Linzee, David: Belgravia.
MacKay, Amanda: 2 books
MacLeod, Charlotte: Rest you merry.

Character Index

CHARACTER -- Author: Title(s)
  Titles are listed only if necessary
for location within the Main Entry
Section, which see.
****
ABNER, UNCLE, see UNCLE ABNER
ABBOTT, JEAN appears with ABBOTT,
  PAT, which see
ABBOTT, PAT -- Crane, Frances
ABBOTT, SUPT. -- Ashford, Jeffrey: A
  man will be kidnapped
ACKROYD, SGT. MAJOR -- Scott, Jack
  S.: Corporal Smithers, deceased
ADAMS, ABE -- Thayer, Tiffany
ADAMS, BOB -- Hardy, William M.
ADAMS, CHARLIE -- Boyer, Rick
ADAMS, GILLIAN -- Kelly, Nora
ADAMS, HILDA, see PINKERTON, MISS
ADAMS, JEFF -- Keech, Scott
ALBERG, ALBERG -- Wright, L. R.
ALCAZAR, DR. -- MacDonald, Philip:
  The man out of the rain and other
  stories. Something to hide
ALLAIN, PIERRE -- Graeme, Bruce
ALLEN, GRACIE -- Van Dine, S. S.:
  The Gracie Allen murder case
ALLEN, TOM -- Boyd, Marion
ALLEYN, RICKEY -- Marsh, Ngaio: Last
  ditch
ALLEYN, RODERICK -- Marsh, Ngaio
ALVAREZ, ENRIQUE -- Jeffries, Roderic:
  Deadly petard
ALLWRIGHT, DUDLEY -- MacDonald,
  Philip: Escape
AMATUCCI, AL -- Banks, Carolyn
AMBERLY, FRANK -- Heyer, Georgette:
  Why shoot a butler?
AMBROSE, DET. -- Whitechurch, Victor
  L.

AMBROSE, JOSEPH -- Phillpotts, Eden:
  Jig-saw
AMES, LEONIDAS -- Keene, Faraday
AMHEARST, REED -- Cross, Amanda:
  Poetic justice. The Theban
  mysteries
AMISS, ROBERT -- Edwards, Ruth Dudley
ANDERSON, BEN -- Compton, Guy
ANDERSON, MALCOLM -- Katzenbach, John
ANGEL, HARRY -- Hjortsberg, William
ANGELE, SOEUR -- Catalan, Henri
ANHALT, MICI -- O'Donnell, Lillian:
  Aftershock. Falling star. Wicked
  designs
APODACA, JOSE -- Van Arsdale, Wirt
APPLEBY, BOBBY -- Innes, Michael:
  Death at the chase. Picture of
  guilt
APPLEBY, JOHN -- Innes, Michael
APPLEGATE, LUKE -- Boles, Paul Darcy
APPLEMAN, BELLE -- Rosen, Dorothy
  and Sidney
APPLEYARD, ARTHUR -- Kenyon, Michael:
  The trouble with series three
APRIL, DAN -- Ballinger, Bill S.:
  Portrait in smoke
ARAGON, TOM -- Millar, Margaret: Ask
  for me tomorrow. Mermaid. The
  murder of Miranda
ARBUTHNOT, MONTROSE -- Temple-Ellis,
  N. A.
ARCHER, LEW -- Macdonald, Ross
ARGAND, JAN -- Rathbone, Julian
ARISTOTLE -- Doody, Margaret
ARK, SIMON -- Hoch, Edward D.
ARMISTON, OLIVER -- Anderson,
  Frederick Irving
ARMITAGE, FRANCES -- Babson, Marian:
  Murder, murder little star

463

BENNION, ROGER -- Adams, Herbert

BENT, JOHN -- Branson, H. C.

BENTIRON, DR. -- Poate, Ernest M.

BENWICK, SGT. -- Robertson, Helen

BERESFORD, TOMMY -- Christie, Agatha: By the pricking of my thumbs. N or M? Partners in crime. Postern of fate. The secret adversary

BERESFORD, TUPPENCE -- appears with BERESFORD, TOMMY, which see

BERNAL, LUIS -- Serafin, David

BERNSTEIN, INSP. -- Lewin, Elsa

BERREN, TOMMY -- Roadarmel, Paul

BESSERLEY, GENERAL -- Oppenheim, E. Phillips: General Besserley's puzzle box. General Besserley's second puzzle box

BIDDLE, JAMES YATES -- Mersereau, John

BIGGINS, INSP. -- Boore, W. H.

BILINSKI, GUS -- Paul, Barbara: Your eyes are getting heavy

BINNEY, JOE -- Livingston, Jack

BINTON, MARGARET -- Barth, Richard

BIRGE, SAM -- Krasner, William

BIRUKOV, ANTON -- Chernyonok, Mikhail

BISHOP, ROBIN -- Homes, Geoffrey: The doctor died at dusk. The man who didn't exist. The man who murdered Goliath. The man who murdered himself. Then there were three

BITTERSOHN, MAX -- MacLeod, Charlotte: The Convivial Codfish. The withdrawing room

BLACKIE, BOSTON -- Boyle, Jack

BLACKWOOD, RILEY -- Starrett, Vincent: The great hotel murder. Midnight and Percy Jones. Murder in Peking

BLATCHINGTON, EVERARD -- Coles, G. D. H. and Margaret: The Blatchington tangle. Death in the quarry. The sleeping death

BLAKE, HANNAH -- Davis, Dorothy Salisbury: A town of masks

BLAKE, SEWELL -- Eberhart, Mignon G.: Dead men's plans

BLAIR, INSP. -- Beaton, M. C.

BLAIR, MARGOT -- Knight, Kathleen Moore: Design in diamonds. Terror by twilight

BLAISE, ELLIS -- Page, Marco

BLAIR, PETER -- Anderson, J. R. L.

BLAKE, JIM -- Carr, John Dickson: The ghost's high noon

BLAND. INSP. -- Symons, Julian: Bland beginning. The immaterial murder case. A man called Jones

BLISS, VICKY -- Peters, Elizabeth: Borrower of the night.Street of the Five Moons

BLISSBERG, HARVEY -- Rosen, Richard

BLIXEN, MILS -- Larson, Charles

BLOODWORTH, LEO G. -- Lochte, Dick

BLOOMINGDALE, KENT -- Simmons, Addison

BLOUNT, INSP. -- Blake, Nicholas: The beast must die. Head of a traveler

BLUE, INSP. -- Ashe, Rosalind

BLUE MASK -- Morton, Anthony: early US appellation for "The Baron," or MANNERING, JOHN in the following books: Alias Blue Mask. The Blue Mask at bay. Blue Mask strikes again. Blue Mask victorious. Challenge Blue Mask! The man in the Blue Mask. The return of the Blue Mask. Salute Blue Mask

BLYTHE, MARTIN -- Davidson, T. L.

BLYTHE, MAX -- Philips, Judson: Death delivers a postcard. The death syndicate

BOARDMAN, JANE -- Harrington, Joseph

BOGART, HUMPHREY -- Bergman, Andrew

BOGNOR, SIMON -- Heald, Tim

BONAPARTE, NAPOLEON (Aboriginal detective, not the emperor) -- Upfield, Arthur W.

BONDURANT, VICTOR -- Edwards, James G.

BOOKOVER, MALLORY -- Eberhart, Mignon G.: Casa Madrone

BOOTLE, INSP. -- DeCaire, Edwin

BORGES, INSP. -- Bonett, John and Emery

BORLACH, HANS -- Durrenmatt, Friedrich

BOSTON BLACKIE -- Boyle,Jack

BOTTWINK, WENCELAUS -- Hare, Cyril: An English murder

BOWEN, GEOFFREY -- Lockridge, Frances and Richard: Catch as catch can

BOYDEN, HELEN -- Clarke, Anna

BRACKETT, WALTER -- Marlowe, Derek

BRADBURY, RAY -- Bradbury, Ray

BRADDON, MARK -- Adams, Herbert: The strange case of Hatton, K. C.

BRADE, LOU -- Asimov, Isaac: A whiff of death

CRADER, CARL -- Hoch, Edward D.
CRAFFT, DET. -- Eberhart, Mignon G.:
The dark garden
CRAGG, SAM -- Gruber, Frank
CRAGGS, JOHN -- Alington, C. A.
CRAIG, IAN -- Hughes, Babette
Plechner
CRAIG, MATTHEW -- Campbell, Mary E.
CRAMBO, INSP. -- Symons, Julian: The
pipe dream
CRAMER, INSP. -- Stout, Rex: Red
threads
CRANDEL, BEN -- Sinclair, Murray
CRANE, INSP. -- Ashford, Jeffrey:
Three layers of guilt
CRANE, SIMON -- Garfield, Brian
CRANE, WILLIAM -- Latimer, Jonathan
CRANE, WILLIAM RUTHERFORD -- Lilly,
Jean
CRANKSHAW, INSP. -- Ferrars, E. X.:
Depart this life
CRAWFORD, THEODORA WADE -- Mann,
Jessica
CREWE, BARBARA -- LaRoche, K. Alison
CREWE -- Vanardy, Varick: Something
doing. The two-faced man
CRIBB, SGT. -- Lovesey, Peter
CRICHTON, TESSA -- Morice, Anne
CROFTS, REGGIE -- Broome, Adam
CROMBIE, SAM -- Coxe, George Harmon:
The frightened fiancee. The
impetuous mistress
CROME, DEREK -- Angus, Douglas Ross
CROSBY, DAVID -- Keeler, Harry
Stephen: The amazing web
CROSBY, PROF. -- Hastings, W. S. and
Hooker, Brian
CROSS, HOWARD -- Macdonald, Ross:
Meet me at the morgue
CROSS-WADE, SPENCER -- Katz, William
CROW, INSP. -- Lewis, Roy
CROWDER, GEORGE -- Pentecost, Hugh:
Around dark corners. The copycat
killers. Murder sweet and sour. The
price of silence
CROWTHER, NINA -- Yorker, Margaret:
Find me a villain
CRUZ, RAYMOND -- Leonard, Elmore: City
primeval
CUDDY, JOHN FRANCIS -- Healy, J. F.
CUFF, SGT. -- Collins, Wilkie
CULPEPPER, LUCY -- Aiken, Joan
CULTHORPE, MAGGIE -- Priestly, J. B.

CUMMINGS, INSP. -- McGuire, Paul
CUMMINGS, NOEL -- Picano, Felice
CUNEEN, MATT -- Armstrong, Charlotte:
Dream of fair woman
CUNLIFFE, JEAN -- Armstrong,
Charlotte: The gift shop
CURRAN, VICKIE -- Castoire, Marie and
Posner, Richard
CURRY, HARRY -- Everymay, March
CURTIS, HUGH -- Somers, Paul
CUTLER, BONNY -- Hyams, Joe
CUTLER, RUSTY -- Rubel, Marc
CZERNICK, MARK -- Holland, Isabelle

DAGLIESH, ADAM -- James, P. D.
DAHLQUIST, SERENDIPITY -- Lochte,
Dick
DAKAR, AHMAD -- Werry, Richard R.
DALE, ROGER -- Allen, Steve
DALY, PROF. -- Dillon, Ellis
DALZIEL, ANDREW -- Hill, Reginald
DAMIOT, INSP. -- McConnor, Vincent
DAMON, DAN -- Goldsmith, Gene
DANA, ROBIN -- Page, Jake
DANE, MAJOR -- Rinehart, Mary
Roberts: The yellow room
DANFORTH, L. T. -- Tucker, Wilson:
Time bomb
DANIELS, CHARMIAN -- Melville, Jennie
DANTE, EDIK -- Smith, Kay Nolte
DANVILLE, CHRIS -- Jones, Cleo
DARE, SUSAN -- Eberhart, Mignon G.:
The cases of Susan Dare
DARRELL, JEFF -- Keeler, Harry
Stephen: Find the clock
daSILVA, JOSE -- Fish, Robert L.
DAUNCEY, INSP. -- Browne, Douglas G.:
Death in seven volumes
DAVENPORT, ALEX -- Kellerman,
Jonathan
DAVIDSON, ARLETTE -- Freeling,
Nicolas: The widow. (See also VAN
der VALK, ARLETTE)
DAVIE, R. V. -- Clinton-Baddeley, V.
C.
DAWE, ARCHER -- Fletcher, J. S.: The
adventures of Archer Dawe
DAWES, STEPHEN -- Yorke, Margaret:
Intimate kill
DAWLISH, GORDON -- Ashe, Gordon
DAWSON, WILLIAM -- Copplestone,
Bennet
DAX, SATURNIN -- Cumberland, Marten

Steven Olderr is director of the Riverside (Ill.) Public
Library, which is the regional resource library of the
Suburban Library System for mysteries. Olderr holds an MLS
from Rosary College and a master's in English from DePaul
University. He is the author of Symbolism: A Comprehensive
Dictionary (McFarland, 1986).